ADMINISTRATION REPORT OF TRIPURA STATE SINCE 1902

In 4 Volumes

ADMINISTRATION REPORT OF TRIPURA STATE Since 1902

IN 4 VOLUMES

VOLUME FOUR
1342 T.E. to 1352 T.E.
(1932-33 A.D. to 1942-43 A.D.)

Edited by
Mahadev Chakravarti

GYAN

GYAN PUBLISHING HOUSE
NEW DELHI-110 002

ADMINISTRATION REPORT OF TRIPURA STATE SINCE 1902 IN 4 VOLUMES

(History, Polity, Sociology, Anthropology)

ISBN : 81-212-0468-2 (Set)
ISBN 81-212-0472-0 Vol. 4

Publised 1994 in India by
Gyan Publishing House
5, Ansari Road
New Delhi 110002

Printed at Goyal Offset Works, Delhi

EDITOR'S NOTE

The present Volume contains seven *TAR*s from 1342 T.E.(1932-33 A.D.) to 1352 T.E.(1942-43 A.D.) of which five are Annual Reports and two Consolidated Reports. After the issue of 1346 T.E., the practice of publishing *TAR* annually by the Tripura Government had to be discontinued for the time being for some administrative reasons. Hence, the entire period from 1347 T.E. (1937-38 A.D.) to 1352 T.E. (1942-43 A.D.) is to be found in two Consolidated Reports. The appendices and detailed tables - which are incorporated in each *TAR*-are not be found in the Consolidated Reports, although the table of contents remain the same in all the *TAR*s.

The present Volume deals with the period of Maharaja Bir Bikramkishore Dev Barman, the last eminence of the Manikya Dynasty. Born on 19 August 1908 A.D., the king was only 24 years of age in 1342 T.E., i.e. wherefrom the present Volume begins. The king passed away on 17 May 1947 A.D. , but the last book of the present Volume is of the period 1352 T.E. (1942-43 A.D.).

In a feudal and in some places pre-feudal set up - where modern democratic institutions and political parties are yet to flourish - kingship was the most natural form of rule in Tripura. The British authorities, for their own self-interest, tried to exert pressure through the Political Agent to modernise the system of Tripura administration. At the fag-end of the thirties of the present century, the demand for popular Government under the aegies of the Maharaja was also in the air and it was expressed through newly-borned associations like the Tripura Janamangal Samity and Tripura Rajya Ganaparishad. The enlightened king of Tripura also sometimes wanted to reform the administration by following the model of self-Governemnt in Bengal as much as practicable. From the *TAR*s, listed in the present Volume, one can trace tho course of such developmental process. In book thirty of the present Volume, the idea of a constitution, popularly known as the

Government of Tripura Act or 'Act I of 1351 T.E.', is expressed in detail on the basis of the formation of the (i) *Raj-Sava* or Privy Council as an Advisory Body in respect of executive and judicial matters composed of not less than 5 and not more than 15 notable persons, official and non-official for a term of 5 years; (ii) *Mantri Parishad* or Council of Ministers; (iii) *Vyavasthapak Sava* or Legislative Assembly, with a President and the Ministers as ex-officio members, and 49 other members, of whom 20 to be nominated and 29 to be elected by the following constituencies: (a) Talukdars and Jagirdars 3, (b) Village *Mandalis* 12, (c) Municipality and notified urban areas 3, (d) Tea planting interests 2, (e) Business Communities 3, (f) Lawyers, graduates and under-graduates 2, (g) Backward Communities 3, (h) A special Community of historic importance selected by the Ruler 1, (iv) an improved and re-organised High Court of Judicature; (v) an improved system of financial administration and audit, (vi) constitution of 150 Village *Mandalis*, i.e. rural basic administrative and electoral units etc. It is interesting to read the idea of democracy as conceived by the king because in spirit it was basically an autocracy of the ruler conserving all the powers in him. However, the wish of the king to set up Legislative Assembly, Village *Mandali* did not materialize due to the disturbances caused by the World War II.

In between 1342 T.E. and 1352 T.E., as included in the present Volume, the increase of total population in Tripura was 1,30,560 - from 3,82,450 in 1342 T.E. the figure reached to 5,13,010 in 1352 T.E. The influx of labour from the neighbouring British districts as well as, in the words of the *TAR*, "up-country coolies", is particularly noticeable since 1343 T.E.(1933-34A.D.). In each *TAR* a para is devoted on 'Labour and Wages'. For example, in 1342 T.E. the wages for field labour were 4 to 8 annas per day, in 1352 T.E. it remained the same in the case of female labourers and in the case of male it was from 5 annas to Re. 1-4.The *gharamies* or thatchers earned from 5 to 8 annas per day in 1342 T.E., with the lapse of a decade they could earn from 8 annas to Re. 1-4 per day in 1352 T.E. in the cases of masons, carpenters, blacksmiths, the wages had increased from 8 to12 annas per day in 1342 T.E. to the extent of 12 annas to Rs. 2 per day in 1352 T.E.

We have already seen in the earlier Volumes how the income from the Chakla Roshnabad Estates helped to lay the financial foundation of the Tripura Raj. Although, compared to the income from the State, the income from the zemindaries was less in the present Volume, still, the following table will be no less intersting :

Table No. I

Year	*income from the State the*	*Income from Zemindaries*	*Total income*
1342 T.E.(1932-33)	Rs.13,49,108	Rs. 8,50,918	Rs.22,00,026
1343 T.E.(1933-34)	,, 13,39,810	,, 9,08,361	,, 22,48,171
1344 T.E.(1934-35)	,, 15,79,609	,, 9,87,261	,, 25,66,870
1345 T.E.(1935-36)	,, 16, 96,043	,, 11,07,653	,, 28,03,696
1346 T.E.(1936-37)	,, 18,75,373	,, 12,48,973	,, 31,24,346
1347 T.E.(1937-38)	,, 17,51,623	,, 12,65,702	,, 30,17,325
1348 T.E.(1938-39)	,, 18,15,248	,, 11,79,575	,, 29,94,823
1349 T.E.(1939-40)	,, 19,82,428	,, 13,89,133	,, 33,71,561

1350 T.E.(1940-41)	,, 16,68,357	,, 12,61,887	,, 29,30,244
1351 T.E.(1941-42)	,, 17,98,213	,, 5,65,989	,, 23,64,202
1352 T.E.(1942-43)	,, 22,07,518	,, 11,09,386	,, 33,16,904

The Chakla Roshnabad zemindaries and other estates, consist principally of 23 *Toujis* in the Tippera collectorate, Noakhali collectorate, Maulavi Bazar collectorate, Habiganj collectorate and Karimganj collectorate - i.e. the properties extending over the Tippera, Noakhali and Sylhet Districts comprised an area of 692 square miles approximately. These zemindaries were, in fact, situated in an almost unbroken line contiguous to the western boundary of the Tripura State and having once been comprised in the kingdom of the ancient rulers of Tripura. For administrative purposes, the zemindaries were divided into four units: the Central Division with headquarters at Comilla, the Northern Division with headquarters at Mogra under the Brahmanbaria Subdivision, the Southern Division with headquarters at Feni in the Noakhali District, the Srimangal Division with headqarters at Srimangal in the District of Sylhet. All the above four headquarters are now in Bangladesh.

In almost the entire period (from1342 T.E. to 1351 T.E.), as included in the present Volume, the management and control of the affairs of the zemindaries continued to be entrusted in the hands of J.C.Sen. The *TAR*s would speak why the income from the State and the zemindaries reached the highest point in 1352 T.E. and 1349 T.E. respectively and also at the lowest point in 1343 T.E. and 1351 T.E. respectively in between 1342 T.E. and 1352 T.E.

If the tables under the head 'revenue'of the State - as found in each *TAR* - are closely examined, it is to be found that the Land Revenue, with some little variation, had such an upward swing that the amount virtually became double within a decade, viz. from Rs. 4,18,825 in 1342 T.E. to Rs. 8,44,550 (including the Road Cess) in 1352 T.E. A Road Improvement Fund was opened for the first time in 1347 T.E. and it was shown separately under Land Revenue head. The total collection for Road Improvement Fund since 1347 T.E. was the following :

Table II

Year	*Road Improvement Fund*
1347 T.E.(1937-38)	Rs. 92,182
1348 T.E.(1938-39)	Rs. 1,09,642
1349 T.E.(1939-40)	Rs. 1,03,986
1350 T.E.(1940-41)	Rs. 1,30,235
1351 T.E.(1941-42)	Rs. 1,20,604
1352 T.E.(1942-43)	Rs. 78,714

The sudden decrease of Road Fund in the last year (1352 T.E.) was due to the imposition of restrictions on the export of rice, paddy etc. by road to avert shortage of food in the midst of World War II,

Income from a new item, viz. Money Lenders'License Fees, since 1349 T.E. is recorded in the *TAR*. The '*Ghar Chukti-Kar*' from the tribal *jhumias* - recorded in the *TAR* as 'Family Tax in the hills'- also increased considerably in this period, with some little variations, and in 1349 T.E. it touched the peak. It is interesting to read (*TAR* for 1345 T.E., para 237) that the increased collection under 'Family Tax in the hills' was due to the improved paying capacity of the hill people.

Next to Land Revenue, the second important source of royal income used to come from the toll on forest-produce and in the last year of the present Volume, i.e. in 1352 T.E. (1942-43) it was the maximum. With the exception of a few Mahals, which were let out in *ijara*, all the forests were under *khas* management. Upto 1349 T.E.(1939-40) the total forest area reserved was 530 sq. miles; but in 1351 end 1352 T.E., 630 sq. miles were added and thus the total reserved forest area at the end of 1352 T.E. (1942-43) was about 1160 sq. miles; whereas the total area of princely Tripura was 4,116 sq. miles. Although in the *TAR*s, plantations of Mahogany, Sal (*Shorea robusta*), Sonal(*Cassia fistula*) etc. are mentioned, still, there is no reference anywhere of any extensive afforestation programme and upto 1352 T.E. approximately 148 acres were planted with Gamair (*Gmelina arborea*),Sal (*Shorea robusta*), and Jarul (*Lagerostromia flosreginae*). The main reason for this lack of regeneration, according to the *TAR* (1350-52 T.E., para 181), was due the want of labour (although we have already seen that there was an influx of labour from the other sides of the border).

If the revenue heads, as mentioned in the *TAR*s, are closely scruntinized it is to be found that the increase under the head 'Tax on Cotton and Oil-seeds'- as produced mainly by the hill people - was noticeable in 1345 T.E. This was due to the increased export of cotton to the extent of more than three times of the previous year. The increase under the heads 'Adda Mehal', 'Excise', 'Stamps and Court-Fees' etc. reached the highest point in 1352 T.E., the last year in the present Volume. The implications of such an increase may reveal some interesting points. The marked decrease under the head 'Depreciation Contribution' in 1347 T.E. was due to the discontinuance of the practice of economic cuts and deductions from salary towards the end of that year. The impressive increase in *'Nazar'* in 1348 T.E. was mainly due to the realisation of a very large amount from the Burmah Oil Company Ltd. as premium for prospecting license, as the geologists had discoverd some oil structures in the Baramura, Deotamura and Atharamura ranges of the hills. Some indications of coal, calcareous sandstones were also observed by some geologists in the thirties of the present century. Invertebrate and vertebrate fossils of high scientific value were discovered in Tripura and numerous fossil-woods were noticed. Again, the broad synclinal valleys of Tripura were also studied for indigenous irrigation system and Artesian-well conditions.

The principal export items from Tripura remained more or less the same in the entire decade (1342-52 T.E.) viz.,timber and other forest-produce, such as cotton, oil-seeds (*til* and mustard seeds), paddy, jute, *gur* (molasses) etc. Some home-spun cotton fabrics, manufactured mainly by the hill people and specially by the Manipuris, were also exported. In 1349 T.E. a new Department designated 'Customs Department' was created mainly to deal with the collection of duty on commodities exported from Tripura, and the Customs Department was put under the charge of the Forest Secretary who managed both the Forest and Customs Department together.

In 1342 T.E.(1932-33) there were 50 Forest Stations for collection of duty and prevention of forest offences. From 50 the number increased to 59 in 1347 T.E.(1937-38); but on the establishment of 24 new Customs

Table III

Some important expenditure in Princely Tripura in between 1342 T.E. and 1352 T.E.

Expenditure (in Rs.)	*1342 T.E.*	*1343*	*1344*	*1345*	*1346*	*1347*	*1348*	*1349*	*1350*	*1351*	*1352*
1. General Administration charges:											
(a) State...	5,01,942	5,48,625,	5,42,469	5,44,627	5,76,687	6,36,313	6,31,045	7,09,865	7,18,696	6,85,455	6,45,642
(b) Zemindaries:											
(i) Cost of management...	1,41,279	1,39,358	1,42,745	1,37,956	1,39,290	1,42,174	1,37,557	1,39,873	1,39,292	1,43,057	1,35,430
(ii) Cost of litigation...	1,04,382	1,17,193	1,36,800	1,59,230	1,26,609	1,11,176	1,07,570	1,13,456	1,07,259	92,253	78,788
Total	7,48,[illegible]03	8,05,176	8,22,014	8,41,813	8,42,586	8,89,663	8,76,172	9,63,194	9,65,247	9,20,765	8,59,860
2. Revenue & Taxes paid to the British authorities on account of the Zemindaries...	2,73,821	2,88,830	2,85,540	2,81,546	2,84,317	2,62,041	3,45,211	3,78,969	3,88,609	3,13,768	4,40,377
3. Public Works:											
(a) State...	1,11,079	1,69,413	2,09,062	2,00,017	2,60,797	3,15,871	1,94,253	1,89,101	1,75,026	1,46,915	1,78,046
(b) Zemindaries...	50,491,	60,335	50,996	50,912	76,889	4,42,556	1,60,847	1,00,740	1,33,658	72,489	88,915
4. Municipality:State...	8,000	8,000	9,000	9,000	9,000	12,600	10,000	17,750	23,008	22,423	10,000
5. Education:(a) State...	1,28,441	1,25,021	1,23,867	1,22,027	1,31,956	1,30,817	1,30,783	1,24,215	1,31,773	1,25,399	1,32,920
(b) Zemindaries...	8,086	8,962	9,075	8,557	8,932	9,103	4,130	4,149	6,598	4,156	2,993
6. Medical & Sanitation :											
(a) State ...	94,070	97,829	67,638	66,513	71,950	87,812	76,984	84,791	96,782	83,928	85,534
7. Religious Expenses:											
(a) State...	57,149	62,948	64,971	55,724	55,235	56,592	54,158	56,881	56,335	58,083	58,854
(b) Zemindaries...	6,471	6,339	6,111	6,716	6,565	6,845	6,340	6,779	6,689	6,527	6,897
8. Sultanat- State...	40,125	62,640	52,951	56,962	1,15,859	98,418	69,242	52,816	49,419	41,550	40,649
9. *Sansar* Charges:											
(a) Maharaja's family...	88,672	84,167	85,293	82,291	95,763	1,01,388	72,513	72,273	74,325	71,054	69,368
(b) Other branches of the Raj family...	1,24,202	1,17,830	1,15,454	96,142	88,997	89,229	85,880	85,396	85,947	88,928	79,006

(c) Thakurs...	32,199	31,214	31,675	33,197	30,569	(Transferred to other head)					
(d) *Sansar office*...	13,676	12,875	13,608	12,587	13,099	15,080	13,975	5,440	4,941	3,936	4,211
(e) Miscellaneous...	51,949	97,118	66,670	73,250	94,481	83,825	29,672	21,880	29,950	12,480	14,269
Total	3,10,698	3,43,204	3,12,700	2,97,467	3,22,909	2,89,522	2,02,022	1,84,989	1,95,163	1,76,398	1,66,854
10. Charity & Donation:											
(a) State...	15,636	18,387	13,769	29,007	24,618	17,736	14,142	16,682	12,562	25,011	15,226
(b) Zemindaries...	4,540	6,746	7,046	8,551	9,865	3,026	11,892	14,963	5,917	5,293	1,057
11. Maharaja's *Nij-Tahabil*	1,00,000	1,00,000	1,00,000	1,00,000	1,20,000	1,20,000	1,94,591	1,98,418	2,29,719	2,19,730	2,18,766
12. Maharaja's Tour...	68,000	1,09,495	1,25,000	1,20,500	94,175	1,04,6757	20,000	30,000			

×

Stations and 1 Reserve Forest Office in 1349 T.E.(1939-40), there were altogether 84 Forest and Customs Stations in Princely Tripura upto 1352 T.E.(1942-43).

At the end of 1352 T.E. there were altogether 55 tea gardens in Tripura. The rise and fall of tea industry in Tripura was intertwined with the contemporary world situation. The income fromTea Export Duty touched the peak point in 1352 T.E. when the total area under tea was about 11,366 acres. The *TAR*s would throw ample light why there was no proper growth of infant tea industry in Tripura and why the Tripura Tea Control Amendment order or popularly known as 'Order No. 1 of 1351 T.E.' was passed.

It is interesting to note the trend of the number of defaulting *taluks* brought under the operation of the Sunset Law (including the pending from the previous year) in the period included in the present Volume - viz., 180 in 1342 T.E., 221 in 1343 T.E., 142 in 1344 T.E., 129 in 1345 T.E., 299 in 1346 T.E., 522 in the triennial 1347-49 T.E., and 325 in the last triennial 1350-52 T.E.

From the total number of jail population in different years, one can have an idea of the over-all social situation of the time. The total number of jail population was highest(1393) in 1343 T.E. and lowest (803) in 1350 T.E.The State maintained 8 jails including the Central Jail at Agartala during the years under review. Escapes from the jails were common items in almost all the *TARs*.

Let us now have a look at the expenditure scenario. In Table No. III, only some important items of expenditure are included to show the trend in between 1342 T.E. and 1352 T.E.

A close scrutiny of Table III would show how there was a steady increase in the general administration charges since 1342 T.E. with some minor variations. In the zemindaries, a major amount was spent on litigation and in 1345 T.E. it even crossed the cost of management of the zemindaries. The revenue and taxes paid to the British authorities on account of the Chakla Roshnabad zemindaries etc. remained more or less the same upto 1347 T.E.; but since 1348 T.E. it increased to a considerable extent and the figure touched the peak in the last year (1352 T.E.).This increasw was due to the payment of arrears of previous years and also payment of Education Cess which was imposed in 1348 T.E.

The expenditure on State public works usually had an upward swing upto 1347 T.E. (with the slight exception of 1345 T.E.) ; but since 1348 T.E. the downward trend is noticeable. The abrupt increase of the amount on public works in the zemindaries in 1347 T.E. is very striking, no doubt. The *TAR* would provide some clues in this respect.

The only Municipality at the capital town of Agartala had a population of 9,580 in 1342 T.E.; but within a decade it had increased to 20,000 in 1352. Campared to the increase in population, the grant awarded to the Municipality by the Durbar appeared to be very meagre. Although the grant increased to some extent in between 1348 T.E. and 1351 T.E. it again came down to the original position in 1352 T.E. However, later on, all expenditure under Municipality was shown as expenditure of the State.

In spite of curtailment of expenditure on education in some years, the allocation remained more or less the same in the entire decade as incorporated in the present Volume. The expenditure under this head in the zemindaries was the most minimum. Although Free Compulsory Primary Education was introduced under the State Act 2 of 1342 T.E. in the Agartala Municipal arĉa since 1st Magh 1342 T.E., still, there was virtually no compulsion nor the allocation for Primary Education was very impressive to make it both free and compulsory. A major portion of allocation was reserved for the education of the members of the Raj Family. If we cast a glance at the total expenditure on public instruction of some years, the entire picture will be clear.

Table IV

	1342 T.E.	1343T.E.	1344 T.E.	1345 T.E.
1. Primary Education	27,825	27,686	27,528	27,839
2. SecondaryEducation	49,654	48,458	47,598	46,607
3. Special Training Schools	2,022	2,127	1,859	1,631
4. Compulsory Free Primary Education	276	1,632	1,938	2,217
5. Boarding Institutions for Thakur boys	7,315	6,756	6,870	6,201
6. Education for Kumars and Kumaris	26,159	26,424	21,016	20,682
7. Scholarship & Stipends	6,942	5,611	6,604	5,100.
8. Library	1,744	1,812	2,470	1,855
9. Tripura Boarding..	2,435	3,073	3,432	3,916
10. Miscellaneous	4,069	1,442	4,552	5,979
Total (in Rs.)	1,28,441	1,25,021	1,23,867	1,22,027

In 1342 T.E. four compulsory Primary Schools were started and during the morning hours the U.K. Academy building, Tulsibati Girls' School building, Bejoy Kumar M.E. School house and Thakurpalli L.V.School house provided for their accommodation. The number remained the same upto 1352 T.E. The number of Sanskrit *Tols*, Woodburn Artisan School and Silpasram, Jail Reformatory School remained the same in between 1342 T.E. and 1352 T.E., i.e. 4 *Tols* and the other schools one each. The number of *moktabs* and *Madrassas* decreased from 7 to 4 in between 1342 T.E. and 1352 T.E. The total number of all types of schools (including private schools) in 1342 T.E. was 205; but it was reduced to 150 in 1352 T.E. although there was increase in the case of H.E. School (from 6 in 1342 to 8 in 1352), M.E. School for boys (from 8 to 14), M.E. School for girls (from 1 to 5), L.V. School (from 23 to 29) etc. In fact, the *pathsalas* became the victim.

A comparative statement in Table V will show the number of other than Bengali students receiving education in several schools of Tripura, from 1342 T.E. to 1352 T.E.

Regarding Library, Maharajkumar Narottam Kishore Dev Barman continued to be the Librarian during the entire decade. As usual, the Birchandra

Library at Agartala was maintained in two separate sections : (i) English Section located at the Ujjayanta Palace and (ii) Vernacular Section, open to the public, in a building near the U.K. Academy. From the expenditure under the head 'Library', as shown in Table IV, one can easily guess what type of official patronage was extended for the growth of the Library Movement.

Table V

Year	*1342*	*1343*	*1344*	*1345*	*1346*	*1347*	*1348*	*1349*	*1350*	*1351*	*1352*
Rajkumars	4	5	7	5	2	2	1	6	4	5	5
Thakurs	213	282	290	216	203	320	279	370	303	261	254
Manipuris	634	568	573	704	697	673	825	1220	1095	627	863
Tripuras	1053	977	1007	985	917	983	845	1023	1104	1102	951
Reangs	-	13	18	9	9	20	19	39	45	29	34
Kukis	1	1	-	-	-	-	1	1	17	25	5
Chakmas	2	1	-	1	1	2	1	3	4	3	3
Lushis	1	1	1	-	1	3	6	6	12	2	24
Others	96	44	56	121	112	153	139	231	108	107	69

Although public health turned unsatisfactory throughout the decade (1342-52 T.E.), with malaria, cholera, dysentery and small-pox constantly rampant all round, and the virulence with which cattle diseases raged causing havoc in some places of Tripura in different years; still, the total expenditure on 'Medical and Sanitation' head, as shown in Table III (item 6), is not very impressive and in some years the decrease of expenditure is also noticeable.

The expenditure under the head 'Sultanat', as evident from Table III (item 8), increased abruptly in 1346 T.E. and 1347 T.E. This was, according to the *TAR*, due to the purchase of new motor cars, furniture and other articles for the palace. The decrease of total expenditure under the 'Sansar' head (item 9) since 1347 T.E. was due to the fact that the allowances given to the members of the Thakur families were transferred to 'Pension and Gratuity' head. But the expenditure on 'Miscellaneous'under the 'Sansar' head sometimes equalled the other heads. Another interesting feature to be seen in Table III was that since 1350 T.E. (1940-41) the Maharaja's 'Nij Tahabil' and 'tour' (i.e. items 11 and 12) were clubbed together.

The last two consolidated *TAR*s, as incorporated in the present Volume, are very important for World War II documents. India was dragged into the vortex of the War by a Viceroyal Ordinance the moment Britain declared war against Germany on 3 September 1939. Although princely Tripura had virtually nothing against the Axis Powers, still, it was bound by treaty relations to support the war efforts of the British. However, the vulnerability of Tripura became apparent after the fall of Burma to the Japanese in 1942. During the war period Maharaja Bir Bikramakishore Manikya enforced the Defence of India Ordinance in Tripura and placed the entire resources of the State at the disposal of the British Crown. By royal conscription, tribal youths were recruited in large number for armed forces and sent to British India for training etc. A look at the statement showing the particulars of the Military Force in Tripura, as included in the appendix of each *TAR*, would help one to understand why the number of persons in the infantry of Tripura remained more or less the same (around 400) in between 1342 T.E. and 1350 T.E. and why the figure rose to 732 in 1352 T.E. In the later days, not included in the present Volume, the figure rose very high.

In this connection, let us also take note of some other interesting points of each *TAR* separately from 1342 T.E. to 1352 T.E.

TAR for the year 1342 T.E. (1932-33A.D.)

The all-round economic depression had its adverse effects both on the *Raj* and the people in general. Kashipur Farm was abolished. The infant tea industry was in a deep crisis and two tea estates prayed for relinquishment of portions of their tea settlements with remission of arrear dues. No public funds were available for public works. There was an outbreak of *kala-azar* throughout the State. As a result of the world-wide financial crisis, as mentioned in the *TAR*, retrenchment both in staff and offices was effected throughout Tripura, causing the abolition of the Kulai Tahasil office and the dispensary. R.L. Walker took over charge of the office of the Political Agent on 20 December 1932 after the transfer of Khan Bhadur Abdul Ghaffar. In the Maharaja Match Factory at Agartala, only the match boxes and sticks were made and not the finished matches due to the want of some machineries required. At Agartala a telephone system connecting important public buildings and residences was under construction. In the midst of economic crisis, the Military Forces of Tripura comprising the First and Second Bir Company with State Band, signalling party and other followers marched out an extensive area of the State. A temporary telephone line was constructed from Agartala to Chandra Sadhupara, a village at the foot of the Baramura hills at a distance of 18 miles.

TAR for the year 1343 T.E. (1933-34 A.D.)

Signs of gradual recovery from the effect of world-wide depression and economic slump became, however, perceptible during the year. A slight increase in the land revenue collection is noticeable which was, according to the *TAR*, due more to the better paying capacty of the *Talukdars* than that of the *Jotedars*. But the *TAR* mentions the sufferings of the hill people.

Both the outturn and export of tea increased during 1343 T.E. Even though much hampered by the world-wide depression and even though no new garden was started during the year under report, yet the financial condition of almost all the tea-garden companies in Tripura has appreciably improved as compared to the past years and the tea market was gradually improving on the operations of the International Restriction Scheme.

The birth of a Maharajkumar and heir-apparent to Bikramkishore Manikya was another important event of the year. R.L. Walker continued as Political agent till 19 March 1934, when E.W.Holland took over the charge.

The disputed boundary between the Lushai Hills and Tripura near Phuldengsei village on the Jampui Hills, the watershed line from the Betling to Langterai, the disputed boundary about the source as well as the course the Feni river were jointly inspected by the officers of both Tripura Government and British Government. The construction of the Kamalpur-Ambasa Road upto Salema, the successful diversion work of the course of the Dhalai river to protect the road from rapid erosion in Manik Bhandar were other important events. During the year 1,602 families immigrated into Tripura and particularly at Kulaihaor, families from various directions came to settle down.

As it was found during a survey that a good number of leprosy cases were there in the Sadar Division and in the interior of the hills, chiefly amongest the hill people, two leprosy clinics were opened - one at Agartala and the other at Khowai town. Excessive rains caused flood in the Sabrum, Bilonia and Udaipur Divisions and cholera made its virulent appearance along with small-pox in many Divisions.

The untimely death of Kaliprasanna Sen Gupta, the editor of the *Rajmala* (the official chronicle of the Tripura Raj), hampered the timely publication of the book.

TAR for the year 1344 T.E.(1934-35 A.D.)

During the month of 'Aswin', a terrible flood inundated the whole of Agartala town. The protective embankment could not prevent overfooding of itself against the abnormal rainfall. Flood-affected townsmen took shelter in the palace and public buildings. The *Griha-Prabesh,* i.e. the ceremony of first entrance, into the newly-built Tripura House in Calcutta was performed on 13 August 1934.

By royal proclamations, the names of the following places were changed : from Ompi to Ompinagar, from Natunbazar to Dambarunagar, from Jungthung to Muhuripur. During his visit to various parts of the State, Bir Bikramkishore Manikya laid the foundation-stone of a Siva temple at Tirthamukh. The Military Forces of the king had also traversed a long distance within the state. The king also paid a visit to the massive and extensive ruins at Pilak-Pathar, famous for its impressive archaeological relics of Buddhist influence. The king, Bir Bikramkishore Manikya was accorded a warm welcome both within his own State and the Chakla Roshnabad Zemindary by people belonging to different strata. He also visited Navadwip in Bengal, the headquarter of Vaishnavism, and presided over the opening ceremony of the newly-built magnificent temple at Mayapur, the birth-place of Chaitanya Mahaprabhu. During the year a second Maharajkumar was born. John Anderson, the Governor of Bengal Presidency, paid a visit to Comilla, the headquarters of the British district of Tippera and of Chakla Roshnabad Zemindary of the Maharaja of Tripura. The proposal of the Government of Bengal for revision of the joint management of the Amlighat Toll Station came up for discussion at a conference. The question of renewal of the Excise Agreement between Assam and Tripura (as abruptly terminated some years back), was also considered. The Topographical Survey of Tripura, as it was undertaken by the Eastern Circle, survey of India, was completed.

As 1344 T.E. witnessed an appreciable relaxation in the economic strain - which had been the chronic feature of the last quinquennium - the outturn and export of tea increased rapidly. Regarding reclamation of waste-land, it is found in the *TAR* that a large number of families, like the previous year, came to settle down in Kulaihaor and special mention may be made about the Maghs who came batch by batch from British Bengal, particularly from the Barisal District and Chittagagong Hill Tracts.

As usual, cholera broke out virulently in some parts of the State. The printing and publication of the third part of the *Rajmala*, edited by Kaliprasanna Sen, was completed during the year.

TAR for the year 1345 T.E. (1935-36 A.D.)*

The silver jubilee, i.e. the 25th year reign of Bir Bikramkishore Manikya was celebrated with great eclat throughout Princely Tripura. Bir Bikramkishore Manikya was conferred the Knight Commander of the Most Exalted Order of the Star of India. Party was given at Tripura House, Calcutta, to the Viceroy and the Countess of Willingdon and also to the Governor of Bengal.

With the lifting of the economic strain, a conspicuous advance is noticeable in 1345 T.E. in the outturn of most of the indigenous crops of the State.

A sad event of the year was the premature death of the second Maharajkumar Pradip Bikramkishore Deb Varman.

All offices and institutions of the State remained closed on 26 January 1936 on account of the funeral day of King George V and on receipt of an announcement of the accession of King Edward VIII on the British throne and State. Proclamation was issued through an Extraordinary State Gazette. E.W. Holland continued to be the Political Agent till 9 March 1936, when S.N. Roy took over the charge of the office of the Political Agent.

Other than the Tripura Tea Control Act of 1345 T.E., some other regulations were promulgated during the year (see para 83). Other than small-pox and cholera which prevailed in epidemic from in some parts of the State, there was also an outbreak of rinderpest which swept away a great number of cattle.

TAR for the year 1346 T.E. (1936-37 A.D.)

During his second European tour during the year Maharaja Bir Bikramkishore Manikya, had an audience with the British King Emperor at the Buckingham Palace. He also met Hitler at his residence in Berlin and attended the World Olympic Games in Germany.

The abdication of British throne by Edward VIII in December 1936 and the accession of king George VI were another notable events and a State proclamation was made in an extraordinary issue of the Tripura Gazette.

Two important Durbars were held during the days of the Puja: Tripura-Manipuri Samajik Durbar and the Dusserah Durbar.

John Anderson, the Governor of Bengal, paid a visit to Tripura in March 1937. The political relation of the State with the Bengal Government was transferred to the Agent to the Governor General, Eastern States, with effect from 1 December 1936 - and A.S. Meek, H.W.C. Robson and Murphy succeeded each other as the Agent during the intervening period. S.N. Roy, the District Magistrate of the Tippera District, was the ex-officio Political Agent of Tripura till the transfer of the State to the Eastern States Agency and thereafter G.H. Emerson, Secretary to the Agent to the Governor-

General, was the Political Agent for the Bengal States from 1 December 1936.

The Viceroy and Governor-General of India conferred the title 'Raja', as a personal distinction, upon Rana Bodhjung, Chief Secretary of Tripura, on 1 January 1937.

During 1346 T.E., 1533 persons immigrated into and 1267 persons emigrated out of Tripura. The mags came to settle down in Nalichhera and the Khasias came to Kulaihaor to cultivate *pan* (betel).

Although people in the uplands the growers suffered a lot as the yield of cotton and sesamum was much below the normal, yet in the plains, not only was the outturn of tea, paddy, jute and mustard larger but their prices also maintained a steadily upward tendency.

On 4 July 1934, the Tripura State Bank was formed and it has an interesting history behind it. The total amount of Fixed Deposits received by the bank during 1346 T.E. was more than one lakh.

Consolidated TAR for the Years 1347-49 T.E. (1937-40 A.D.)

The triennium under report records the beginning of the Second World War in 1939 and its adverse effects on the economy of Tripura as prices of some imported necessaries suddenly shot up.

In furtherance of the 'Vidyapattan Scheme' the foundation-stone of the present M.B.B.College, Agartala, was laid by the Maharaja on 24 Baisakh 1347 T.E., corresponding to 7 May 1937 A.D. On 29 Baisakh 1348 T.E. (12 May 1938) the Griha-prabesh cermeony of the newly-built lake view palace 'Nirmahal' on the Rudrasagar in Sonamura Division took place.

In November 1938 Maharaja Bir Bikramkishore Manikya attended a conference of the Chamber of Princes in Bombay and achieved signal success in securing adequate representation of the Eastern Group of States and a revision of the constitution of the Chamber for the purpose. The discussions between the Viceroy and the Rulers of Indian States regarding the establishment of the proposed All India Federation and the accession of the Princely States thereto were nearing completion, when in view of the outbreak of the Second World War the entire matter had to be indefinitely postponed. (See the Appendix). A host of rulers of princely States of India visited Agartala during the triennium.

The most intimate relations that had prevailed between Rabindranath Tagore and four generations of Rulers of Tripura over half century had a been recalled on 22 Poush (7 January 1939) at the time of Bir Bikramkishore Manikya's visit to Santiniketan and Viswa-Bharati on the invitation of the great poet.

Bir Bikramkishore manikya's third European tour which later on developed into a world tour in 1939 took a sensational turn because of the outbreak of the Second World War. His visits to France, England, the United States,Canada,New Zealand, Australia, Java, Bali, Malaya, Singapur, Burma and meetings with world leaders, particularly Franklin Roosevelt, the President of the USA, and his broadcast speech from Los Angeles over the California Radio expatiating on his expectations about the sure victory of Britain and the great part that India was destined to play in the World War

II, and the warm reception to him by the Indian community in the Fiji Islands - these are some of the interesting events recorded in the *TAR*.

On the Coronation of King George VI, Emperor of India, and Queen Elizabeth, in London on 12 May 1937, the Maharaja of Tripura cabled to offer his loyal and respectful congratulations. A proclamation covering the announcement of the Coronation was published in an extraordinary issue of the State Gazette; and with great rejoice, with illumination and attendant festivities, the day was observed as a public holiday throughout Tripura. All offices and institutions were closed again in June 1937 when the Maharaja of Tripura was conferred the honorary rank of Captain.

Lt.Col.W.C. Robson continued as Agent to the Governor-General, Eastern States, upto 11 April 1939 when he was relieved by Lt.Col.L.E. Barton. The designation of the office was changed to 'Resident for the Eastern States' and the headquarters transferred from Ranchi to Calcutta from July 1937. Both Robson and Barton visited Agartala.

During the triennium, we note the following developments: (i) foundation of a Geological Department, (ii) constitution of 'Vidyapattan Governing Committee' with ten members to carry out Vidyapattan Scheme of education, (iii) promulgation of a Charter on the Maharaja Match Factory (see Appendix), (iv) grant of a prospecting license for natural petroleum and natural gas to the Burmah Oil Company for three years, (v) freedom of the excise vendors from paying excise duty to the Government of Bengal for the import of narcotic drugs, (vi) agreement with the Government of India for extradition of persons accused of being concerned in illegal traffic, (vii). implementation of the Tripura Tea Control Act 1348 T.E., (viii) contribution of the State to the King Emperor,s Anti- Tuberculosis Fund for the establishment of a full-fledged Anti-Tuberculosis Hospital, (ix) after the resignation of Justice J.M. Das, Justice K.C. Nag was appointed as the Chief Justice of the State High Court.

A sad event of the period was the accidental and untimely death of Thakur Somendra Chandra Dev Barman on 12 January 1939, a great administrator and author of the famous *Tripura Census Bibarani* (in Bengali).

Towards the end of 1349 T.E. (1939-40) offers were made by the Maharaja of Tripura for an annual contributions of (i) Rs.30,000 from the State to the Viceroy's War Fund, (ii) Rs. 15,000 from the Maharaja,s *Nij Tahabil* (personal funds), to the Red Cross Society and the St. John,s Ambulance Association and (iii) Rs. 5,000 from the same source to the St. Dunstan,s Fund. A War Committee was also formed under the order of the Maharaja dated 19 Magh 1349 T.E. (2 February 1940) in line with the District War Committees in British India. After the constitution of the *Mantri-Parishad*, J.C. Sen was appointed as the Chief Minister.

Special attention was given by the Department of Agriculture to the spread of sericulture and to establish it as a cottage industry in Tripura. To give impetus to plough cultivation among hill people, who were accustomed to the age-old *jhuming* system, an area of eleven thousand *drones* of land was set apart as a Reserve. Many Mag families had already taken to plough cultivation and abandoned *jhuming*.

Consolidated TAR for the year 1350-52 T.E. (1940-43 A.D.)

The *TAR* records the all-pervading repurcussions of the Second World War. But the dangers of the War were accentuated

"by hostile forces of nature at work - with unsettled weather conditions, heavy floods, land-slides and loss of crops, the hill sections in particular being practically in the throes of famine.

2. Prices of rice rose gradually from the second year of the triennium till they reached abnormal proportions towards its end, those of other commodities also evincing a substantial rise, while shortage of stock and high prices in the adjoining British districts had their reaction in the State and gave strong impetus to export and smuggling."

During the triennuim, public health also turned very bad with malaria, cholera, dysentery and small-pox constantly rempant all round. The constitutional reforms, as conceived by the Maharaja, were outlined in detail in the TAR. The retirement and some deaths of some important Ministers of Tripura and the filling up of the resultant vacancies by the appointment of the new are detailed in para 18 of the *TAR*. Raja Rana Bodhjung was appointed as Chief Minister after the retirement of J.C. Sen. A new portfolio of Political Minister was created. In December 1940 the *Tika* or investiture ceremony of the heir-apparent, Maharajkumar Kirit Bikramkishore Dev Barman, was celebrated with great eclat.

In 1941 Tripura came in for a unique experience in the sudden influx of about 15,000 Hindu refugees from Dhaka (Now the capital of Bangladesh) who were victims of serious communal disturbances. John Herbert, Governor of Bengal, expressed his "sincere appreciation of the sympathy shown and the valuable assistance rendered" to the refugees by the Maharaja of Tripura.

On 25 Baisakh 1351 T.E., the eightieth birth-day of Rabindranath Tagore, Bir Bikramkishore Manikya conferred on the poet the title of "Bharat-Bhaskar" (the Sun of India) at a special Darbar at the Ujjayanta Palace. But within three months, on 22 Sravan 1351 T.E. (7 August 1941), the Great Poet left the world. All offices and institutions of Tripura were closed in his honour.

Bir Bikramkishore Manikya was the President of the Council of Rulers, Eastern States. He was promoted to honorary rank of Major in British Army. Lt.Col. L.E. Barton continued as Resident for the Eastern States till he was relieved by Lt. Col. C.P. Hancock in October 1941, the Yearly State contribution of Rs. 30,000 to the Vicerory's War Fund contiued with a total payment of Rs. 90,000 within the triennium, the Maharaja,s Yearly contribution of Rs.20,000 to the Indian Red Cross Society, St. John ambulaence and St. Dunstan's Fund also continued and the total payment during the triennium amounting to Rs. 60,000. The State practically adopted all laws and rules relating to the war as it was in British India. During the month of January 1943 the 1st Tripura Rifles and the Tripura Mahabir Legion (known as Tripforce), took part in the Arakan operations very successfully.

A cattle farm was started at Radhakishorenagar, at a distance of about six miles from Agartala, The "Grow More Food" campaign also started throughout the State. The Tripura State Bank was maintaining its popularity with continued progress and the total amount of deposits in 1352 T.E. stood at more than eight lakh. The Orders, Rules and Regulations promulgated in between 1350 T.E. and 1352 T.E. are listed in para 66.

The Government of Tripura undertook its first Census in collaboration with the Imperial Census of the Indian Empire, which was followed by another in 1881. Since then, in accordance with the British Indian Decennial Census, the operations had been regular. The eighth Census of Tripura was held in 1350 T.E. (1940-41) and a Census Act was passed accordingly to work out the operations.

Department of History
Tripura University
Agartala

Mahadev Chakravarti

CONTENTS

Book Twenty-Five

Report on the Administration of the Tripura State for 1343 T.E. (1933-34)

Book Twenty-Six

Report on the Administration of the Tripura State for 1344 T.E. (1934-35)

Book Twenty-Seven

Report on the Administration of the Tripura State for 1345 T.E. (1935-36)

Book Twenty-Eight

Report on the Adminstration of the Tripura State for 1346 T.E. (1936-37)

Book Twenty-nine

Consolidated Administration Report of the Tripura State for 1347-49 T.E. (1937-40)

Book Thirty

Consolidated Administration Report of the Tripura State for 1350-52 T.E. (1940-43)

APPENDICES

To

His Highness The Bisama-Samara-Bijayee Mahamahodaya
Pancha-Srijukta Maharaja Manikya
BIR BIKRAM KISHORE DEV BARMAN BAHADUR,
Maharaja of Tripura.

Dated, Agartala, the 3rd November, 1933.

YOUR HIGHNESS,

I have the honour to submit the accompanying Report on the General Administration of the State and the attached Zemindaries for the year 1342 T. E., corresponding to the period 14th April, 1932 to the 13th April, 1933.

During the year under report the charge of the Administration as well as of the Zemindaries was with Dewan B. K. Sen Bahadur, M. A., B. L., as Dewan–Shashan and Manager, Chakla Roshnabad Estates, till the 28th August, 1932 and thereafter with Manyabara Rana Bodhjung Bahadur till the forenoon of the 20th November, 1932. On my appointment as Minister, Tripura State and Manager, Chakla Roshnabad Estates I took over charge of my office with effect from the afternoon of that date.

I have tho honour to be,
Your Highness's most obedient servant,
Jyotis Chandra Sen,
MINISTER.

Book Twenty-four
Report on the Administration of the Tripura State for 1342 T. E. (1932-1933 A.D.)

REPORT ON THE ADMINISTRATION

OF

THE TRIPURA STATE

FOR

1342 T. E. (1932-33.)

CHAPTER I—GENERAL AND POLITICAL.

Area of the State—4,116 sq. miles.
Population—3,82,450.
Gross-Revenue (based on the average of the previous five years):—
(*a*) State ... ... Rs. 20,01,308.
(*b*) Zemindaries ... . Rs. 10,41,930.
Tribute—Nil.
Ruler of the State—His Highness The Bisama-Samara-Bijayee Mahamahodaya Pancha-Srijukta Maharaja Manikya Bir Bikramkishore Dev Barman Bahadur. *Age*—24 years. (Born—19th August, 1908). *Caste—Kshatriya* (of the Lunar race).

I.

The year and the people.

1. Economically speaking the year 1342 T. E. was no better for the people of the State and the attached Zemindaries than its predecessor. The world-wide slump was felt in all directions and the tenantry were hard hit by the low prices of jute and paddy. The Durbar realising the difficulties of the situation promptly granted remission of interests all-round and allowed petty demands to be time-barred as in previous years on parol promise of payment. In consequence of similar adverse economic conditions in the adjoining British districts the demand for forest produce was likewise unsatisfactory and this resulted in a drop in the forest revenue. The infant tea industry in the State shared the general depression and the arrear revenue demand increased at the end of the year in comparison with that of the previous year inspite of full remission of interests, payments by easy Instalments allowed and even ungrudging acceptance of the surrender of part of the *Taluqui* land under tea settlement with remission of arrear dues in special cases. Since the close of the year, however, a perceptible rise in prices of tea has brought some relief to the planters.

2. There was no scarcity of food as the harvests of the year were better.

3. The rates of wages of skilled and unskilled labours continued to be low.

4. The year under report opened with a balance of Rs. 10,65,159, against Rs. 9,72,666 in the previous year. The permanent sources of income yielded a revenue of Rs. 22,43,703 against Rs. 20,84,512. Gross receipts including those from deposits, loans as well as law charges recovered stood at Rs. 25,90,046 as against Rs. 25,93,182. The total amount available for expenditure was thus Rs. 36,55,196 as against Rs. 35,65,848. The closing balance of the year stood at Rs. 10,05,281 of which Rs. 2,37,221 was in actual cash in the treasuries and Rs. 7,68,060 under investment in banks and in loans and advances.

Finances of the year.

II.

5. A notable domestic event of the year in the Royal Family was the birth of a Maharajkumari at 3-45 A. M. on the night of the 6th Baisakh, 1342 T. E. (19th April, 1932, early morning), at Mussoorie which gave occasion for rejoicings throughout the State and the attached Zemindaries.

The birth of a Maharajkumari.

6. As mentioned in the previous year's report, His Highness the Maharaja Manikya Bahadur after attending the Annual Session of the Chamber of Princes in Delhi, went to Mussoorie on the 3rd April and joined Their Highnesses the Maharani Saheba and the Dowager Maharani Sahebas who were staying there.

Movement of Their Highnesses.

7. His Highness' stay at Mussoorie was extended till the end of Jaistha, during which time, he went out once on a shooting excursion for a fortnight in the forests of Tehri-Garhwal.

8. On an invitation from His Excellency the Governor of Bengal, to stay with him at Darjeeling as his guest, on the way back to Agartala, His Highness accompanied by the Chief Secretary, Manyabara Rana Bodhjung Bahadur, F. R. G. S., left Mussoorie for Calcutta enroute to Darjeeling on the 16th June and arrived there on the 20th June. His Highness together with Lieut. Col. O. C. Pulley and the Chief Secretary, stayed at the Government House till the 10th Ashar (24th June, 1932) but extended his stay at Darjeeling for some days more and left for Agartala on the 29th June returning there on the night following.

9. The cold weather visit of His Highness the Maharaja Manikya Bahadur to Calcutta lasted from the 20th December, 1932 to 6th January, 1932 during which time, besides attending many functions at the Government House and elsewhere, His Highness had interviews with His Excellency the Viceroy on the 27th December, 1932, and with His Excellency the Governor of Bengal on the 29th December, 1932.

10. This Calcutta visit was followed by the extensive tour of His Highness the Maharaja Manikya Bahadur, accompanied by Her Highness the Maharani Saheba, to the Western and Central India which included Their Highnesses' visits to Bhavnagar, Nawanagar, Dwarka, Baroda, Ujjain, Bhopal, and Panna etc. Their Highnesses reached Bhavnagar on the 11th January, 1933 and were accorded a grand reception by Their Highnesses the Maharaja Saheb and the Maharani Saheba and the general public of Bhavnagar. His Highness enjoyed

the hospitality of the royal hosts for some days after which he went on a short pilgrimage to the sacred shrines of Dwarka.

On the way to Dwarka, His Highness paid a flying visit to Jamnagar where His late Highness Jamsahib Ranjit Singhjee, the then Maharaja of Nawanagar and Chancellor, Chamber of Princes, warmly received His Highness at his capital city.

On their way from Dwarka to Panna, Their Highnesses paid short private visits to Baroda, Ujjain and Bhopal and reached Panna on the 22nd January, 1933. His Highness stayed there till the 2nd February and returned to Calcutta on the following day. After a rest for three or four days in Calcutta, Their Highnesses returned to Agartala on the night of the 25th Magh (7th February, 1933.)

11. At the end of the year under report, His Highness the Maharaja Manikya Bahadur and staff, accompanied by Mahamanyabara Maharajkumar Brajendra Kishore Deb Varma Bahadur, went out on *Shikar* in the Sabroom Division of the State and camped in the Maharajkumar Bahadur's Zemindari at Lilagarh from the 22nd March to the 2nd April, 1933. During this period, His Highness was pleased to pay a short visit to the Divisional head quarters at Sabroom where he was received with great ovation. On His Highness' way up from Feni to Lilagarh and back, huge concourses of people comprising mostly of the subjects of the Zemindaries, Hindus and Mahomedans alike, assembled on the wayside to have *'darsan'* of His Highness and displayed great enthusiasm to greet their beloved Ruler.

III.

Administrative changes.

12. Manyabara Rai J. C. Sen Bahadur, B. A., B. C. S. (retd.), was appointed as Minister of the State and Manager Chakla Roshnabad Estates, on the 20th November, 1932 in succession to Dewan B. K. Sen Bahadur, who retired after a long and meritorious service in the State. The State lost in him a sound adviser and an able administrator who was deservedly popular with the people of the State on account of his sober and sympathetic attitude towards them.

Topographical Survey.

13. No. 12 Party, Survey of India, continued their operations of the Topographical Survey of the State on 1 scale.

14. The previous programme about this survey was to complete the survey of the State during this season (1932–33) but owing to retrenchment, the programme for this year was limited to sheet No. 79M and a part of 79N (State portion only) and only 6 out of 9 sheets of 79M were completed this year and 79N sheet was not taken up at all.

15. During the survey operations the common boundary between the Mayani Reserve Forest in the Chittagong Hill Tracts district and the State was inspected by the Superintendent of Surveys of the State with the Officer-in-charge, No. 12 Party, Survey of India, and a Kanango of the Chittagong Hill Tracts, with the result that the boundary line as shown in the old ¼ survey sheet of 79 M was found to be wrong in that portion.

16. The Survey of the common boundary line has been carried out jointly following the watershed line between the Gumti and Mayani valleys along the Sardeng range in accordance with the arbitration award and shown in the one inch sheet map accordingly.

Political Agent.

17. Khan Bahadur Abdul Ghaffar, B. A., continued as the Political Agent of the State till the forenoon of 9th December, 1932 when, on his transfer, Mr. R. L. Walker, I. C. S., took over charge of the office of the Political Agent from the forenoon of the 20th December, 1932.

CHAPTER II—LAND ADMINISTRATION.

Charge.

18. Mr. S. C. Deb Barman, M. A., (Harvard), Senior Naib Dewan and Thakur K. K. Singh, Naib Dewan, remained in charge of this Department in addition to other duties assigned to them. The former rejoined his duties in the 4th week of April after a sojourn of about 3 months in Switzerland where he went as the guardian of a Maharajkumari.

Area held under Settlement.

19. As shown in the subjoined statement, the total area held under settlement and borne on the *toujis* at the close of the year was 639 sq. miles as against 643 sq. miles in the previous year.

Kinds of settlement.	Area in square miles.		Increase.	Decrease.	REMARKS.
	1342 T.E.	1341 T.E.			
Jotes ...	329	325	4	—	
Taluks ...	310	318	—	8	
Total ...	639	643	4	8	

Tea Settlement.

20. There was no settlement of *Khas* land for tea cultivation during the year under report.

21. The State has always been giving facilities to the infant tea industry during the slump by way of realisation of State dues on easy terms and remission of interests on arrears. In the year under review 2 tea estates prayed for relinquishment of portions of their tea settlements with remission of arrear dues and the Durbar was pleased to grant the same, the area involved being more or less 2250 acres. At the end of the year, 7 petitions for relinquishment of portions of tea grants remained pending.

22. Only 2 tea estates were purchased by the State in auction for arrears of revenue. The quantity of tea exported has decreased by 10,200 lbs. in comparison with the last year.

23. The average of *jama* per *kani* of *jote* lands in *khas mehals* (exclusive of cesses) stood at 15 annas and 4 pies against 15 annas and and 2 pies in the previous year. The maximum rate for *jote* was Rs. 45 per *kani* while the minimum was 4 annas and those for *taluks* Re. 1 and annas 3 respectively. The maximum *jote* rate was a special one in respect of a small piece of bazar land in a very advantageous position.

Rates of *jama.*

24. The different sources of land revenue demand with the collection under each head are detailed below :—

Sources of land Revenue.

Sources.	Current demand.		Arrear demand up to the end of		Realization up to the end of		REMARKS.
	1342 T.E.	1341 T.E.	1341 T.E.	1340 T.E.	1342 T.E.	1341 T.E.	
Taluks ...	1,66,673	1,66,695	3,53,733	2,89,995	1,04,208	1,10,008	
Khas Mehal jotes	5,23,423	5,07,298	13,00,789	10,55,715	2,87,021	2,57,455	
Bazars ...	6,684	7,244	3,790	2,438	6,344	5,742	
Cesses ...	43,548	42,504	1,13,254	92,939	23,406	22,229	
Total ...	7,40,328	7,23,741	17,71,566	14,41,087	4,20,979	3,95,434	

25. The above statement shows that the current demand under all heads was Rs. 7,40,328 and with the arrear demand of Rs. 17,71,566 the total demand of the year was Rs. 25,11,894 against Rs. 21,64,828 in 1341 T. E., Rs. 18,55,696 in 1340 T. E. and Rs. 18,09,495 in 1339 T. E.

Demand.

26. The total collection under all heads during the year amounted to Rs. 4,20,979 being Rs. 1,66,972 under current and Rs. 2,54,007 under arrears, as against Rs. 3,95,434 in the previous year. The percentage of current collection was 22·55 against 24·86 and that of the arrears 14·33 against 14·95. In the *Khas mehal* the percentage of current collection was 11·28 against 12·94 and in *Taluki mehal* the percentage was 62·52 against 60·03 in the previous year.

Collection.

27. Altogether 4,580 certificate cases, covering a demand of Rs. 3,18,472 were instituted during the year. With 4,171 cases valued at Rs. 4,94,340 pending from the previous year, the total number of cases awaiting final orders on disposal of preliminary notices issued on debtors, was 8751 covering a total demand of Rs. 8,12,812. Of these, 19 cases with a demand of Rs. 754 were rejected or struck off and Rs. 18,044 in 495 cases was realised before decree, while 4239 cases with a total value of Rs. 5,86,225 remained pending.

Coercive measure—Certificates

28. Orders under the provisions of the State Certificate Act were passed during the year in 3998 cases with a total value of Rs. 2,07,789 making the demands absolute.

Execution.

29. With 7,504 cases to the value of Rs. 5,38,943 pending in execution from the previous year, the total number of cases, dealt with was 11,502 covering a demand of Rs. 7,46,732. Out of the total demand, Rs. 5526 was remitted or written off and of the remainder, Rs. 90,932 was actually realised leaving a balance of Rs. 6,50,274. Of the amount realised, Rs. 68,256 represents land revenue and Rs. 22,676 miscellaneous demands.

30. The number of defaulting *taluks* brought under the operation of the Sunset law (including 53 pending from the previous year) was 180. Of these, 78 were released on realisation of dues with penalty while 22 were sold in auction and 80 remained undisposed of at the close of the year.

Operation of the Sunset Law.

31. The results of the survey (including resurvey) operations are given in the statement below. It will be seen that an area of 2,609 *drones*, comprising 105 *drones* of *taluk* and 2,504 *drones* of *Khas mehal* was surveyed as against a total of 3,533 *drones* in the previous year. Owing to all-round economic depression affecting the condition of the people, no new programme of survey was sanctioned and the incomplete portion of the previous year's programme was undertaken and finished during the year under review. As regards *Taluki Mehal* the sanctioned programme for survey was for 1,188 *drones*. The total expenditure in the Survey operations in *Khas Mehal* was Rs. 1,316.

Survey.

Names of Divisions.	Quantity of land in *drones* surveyed in 1342 T. E.			Quantity of land in *drones* surveyed in 1341 T. E.			Remarks.
	Taluki land.	*Khas mehal* land.	Total.	*Taluki* land.	*Khas mehal* land.	Total.	
1. Sadar Division ...	74	2,086	2,160	1,305	1,286	2,591	
2. Kailashahar „ ...	—	136	136	62	122	184	
3. Sonamura „ ...	31	—	31	—	—	—	
4. Bilonia „ ...	—	111	111	—	71	71	
5. Khowai „ ...	—	—	—	—	10	10	
6. Dharmanagar „ ...	—	171	171	—	385	385	
7. Udaipur „ ...	—	—	—	—	78	78	
8. Sabroom „ ...	—	—	—	—	201	201	
9. Amarpur Sub „ ...	—	—	—	—	13	13	
TOTAL ...	105	2,504	2,609	1,367	2,166	3,533	

32. This work continued under the direction of Babu Kamini Kumar Kar, Superintendent of Surveys. Compilation of *Mouzmil* maps of the Divisions on a scale of one inch to the mile from the revenue survey maps of villages, *Taluks* and other maps was in progress. 133 maps of villages and *Taluks* were reduced and compiled this year. In addition, 16 maps of villages, reduced last year, were compiled, out of 33 reduced maps remaining uncompiled

Map Compilation.

in the previous years. The divisional *mouzmil* maps also were corrected following above additions.

33. 6 case maps in connection with some disputes about boundary between *Taluks* and *Khash* land within the State and also along the British border line were prepared and three copies of each case map traced.

34. The 1/4″ scale printed State map was reduced to 1/16 scale and 7 copies traced for census work.

35. 8 maps of boundary award, 3 maps of *Taluks* and 5 copies of town map (reduced from scale of 32 inches to 1 mile to a scale of 16 to 1 mile), were traced and the area covered by 2 maps checked with planimeter by the same staff. The total expenditure incurred was Rs. 258-14-3 only.

36. The No. 12 Survey party, Government of India, continued their operations of Topographical survey of the State. Their programme was to complete the survey of the State this year but owing to retrenchment only 6 full sheets were finished. During the survey operations the common boundary between the Mayani Reserve Forest within the district of Chittagong Hill Tracts and this State was inspected by the Superintendent of Surveys of the State with the Officer-in-charge, No. 12 Party, Survey of India, and they found the boundary line shown in the old survey maps, as wrong in places.

Settlement.

37. There was a *Taskhichi taluki* settlement of a plot of *Bazar* land comprising 2 *gandas*. It will be seen from the statement below that settlement operations in respect of 4,379 *drones* of *jote* lands were completed against 4,562 in the previous year.

Nature of Settlement.	1342 T. E.		1341 T. E.		REMARKS.
	Area in *drones*.	*Jama* in whole rupees.	Area in *drones*.	*Jama* in whole rupees.	
1. Permanent *taluki* settlement of cultivated land ...	—	—	—	—	
2. Permanent *taluki* settlement of waste land	—	—	—	—	
3. *Taskhichi taluki* settlement of cultivated land ...	—	5	—	—	
4. *Taskhichi taluki* settlement of waste land	—	—	—	—	
5. *Jotedari* re-settlement of cultivated land	4,289	45,263	4,363	61,891	
6. *Jotedari* settlement of waste land	90	901	199	2,416	
TOTAL. ...	4,379	46,169	4,562	64,307	

Taluki Settlement.

38. One *Taskhichi Taluk* for the site of a *Bazar* shop in Sadar Division comprising 2 *gandas* of land was granted during the year under review. Rs. 71 was fixed as *Nazar*.

Re-settlement of *jote* lands.

39. A net increase of Rs. 10,985 in *jama* was secured by resettlement of *abadi jote* land, the *nazarana* being Rs. 29,666. The average *jama* per *kani* was 10 annas 7 pies against 14 annas 2 pies in the previous year.

***Jotedari* Settlement of waste land.**

40. During the year an area of 90 *drones* of waste land was settled for a prospective rental of Rs. 901, the average *jama* per *kani* obtained being 10 annas against 12 annas 1 pie in the previous year. The maximum and minimum rates were Rs. 4 and annas 4 respectively. The *nazarana* realised was Rs. 1,791, the rent-free period allowed ranging from 1 to 3 years.

Settlement work.

41. No wholetime settlement officer was employed in any Division in the State except in Sadar. Divisional Officers were entrusted with the settlement work in other Divisions within their respective jurisdictions, The total expenditure in the settlement operations was Rs. 3,518.

42. It will be seen that the *nazarana* obtained and obtainable by settlement and re-settlement of *abadi jote* land and settlement of waste land as *jotes* amounted to Rs. 31,456 (Rs. 29,666 + Rs. 1,790).

Private Estates under State Management

43. As detailed below there were altogether 14 private estates under State management during the year under report.

Class.	Name of Estate.	Area.	Revenue.
Encumbered	1. Kakrabon Estate	283 *drones.*	1,871
	2. Jogendranagar Trust Estate	64 ,,	163
	3. Kamalnagar and Mahendranagar Estate	51 ,,	255
	4. Gouranga Tripura's Estate	13 ,,	57
	5. Maharam Ali Chaudhuri Khanje Khan Bahadur's Estate—*Taluk*	236 ,,	450
	Jote	6 ,,	149
	6. Thakur Nalini Mohan Deb Barma's Estate	68 ,,	170
	7. Brajendra Kumar Das's Estate	408 ,,	1,936
	8. Brajapur Estate (Kamala Kanta Deb Barman and others)	246 ,,	982
	9. Kalimulla's Estate	124 ,,	863
	10. Mahammedali Chaudhuri's Estate	21 ,,	76
Unencumbered	11. Prabhu Goswamis' Estate	31 ,,	61
	12. Late Brajakumar Thakur's Estate	47 ,,	297
	13. Naba Kumar Chakrabarty's Estate—*Taluk*	32 ,,	225
	Jote	5 ,,	19
Endowment	14. Taranagar Estate	140 ,,	52

44. The subjoined table shows the demands and collections of the estates during the year under review. Compared with the year previous, collections improved in 5 estates and fell in 6. There was no collection of the estates Nos. 9 and 13. No. 9 came under State management during the later part of the year, so no collection could be made therefrom and No. 13 came under State management in the latter part of the year before last but no realisation could be made during the year under review as the proprietor of the Estate could not furnish

necessary documents. Since the close of the year realisation has commenced to some extent.

Estate No.	Demand			Collection			P. C. of collection
	Current	Arrear	Total	Current	Arrear	Total	
1.	6,531	30,936	37,469	1,082	3,887	4,969	13·22
2.	1,234	6,250	7,484	107	474	581	7·76
3.	1,274	2,324	3,598	143	832	975	27·10
4.	204	183	387	82	152	234	60·47
5.	3,365	14,134	17,499	245	1,353	1,598	9·13
6.	1,163	3,650	4,813	57	570	627	13·03
7.	4,103	4,950	9,053	1,000	1	1,001	11·06
8.	4,218	6,314	10,532	726	2,737	3,463	32·88
9.	—	—	—	—	—	—	—
10.	1,171	834	2,005	33	233	266	13·27
11.	912	3,271	4,183	76	298	374	8·94
12.	1,589	2,902	4,491	161	879	1,040	23·16
13.	—	—	—	—	—	—	—
14.	3,080	10,158	13,238	305	1,694	1,999	15·25

CHAPTER III—PROTECTION.

I. Legislation.

45. There were only two sittings of the Legislative Council both held under the presidency of His Highness the Maharaja Manikya Bahadur himself.

Sittings of the Council.

46. The following bills came up for consideration of the Council and were passed and became law on receipt of His Highness's assent.

Laws enacted

ACT I OF 1342 T. E.—providing for the trial of certain offences by special tribunal.

ACT II OF 1342 T. E.—providing for the introduction of compulsory primary education in any notified area.

II. Military.

47. Major Kumar Dina Mohan Deb Barman Bahadur continued to be in charge of the Military Forces.

Charge.

48. The total strength of the forces at the end of the year was 352 against 412 of the preceding year.

Strength.

49. The approval of the Government of India to the re-organisation of the 2/ Tripura Bikram Company under the Indian Forces scheme was received in September.

Re-organisation.

50. His Highness the Maharaja Manikya Bahadur was pleased to inspect the 1/ Tripura Bir Company in September. Brigadier H. Campbell, D. S. O., M. V. O, Military Adviser-in-Chief, Indian States Forces, made an inspection of the 1st Tripura Bir Company in November and Major Blaxland, Military Adviser, Central India States Forces, also inspected in February, 1933.

Inspection.

51. Armourer Gurudayal Singh was sent to Allahabad Arsenal to qualify himself in a course of instruction to strip, assemble and execute necessary minor repairs to rifles, muskets &c and the result was satisfactory.

Training.

52. Some ordinary improvements and usual petty repairs of the barracks were made during the year. The Military Hospital was removed to a new site in a decent *Katcha* construction near the barracks.

Cantonment.

53. As in the previous year, the health of the forces was generally good. At the end of the year Dr. C. Strickland, M. A., M. D., Professor of Medical Entomology, carried on a careful survey of the locality of the cantonment in connection with a few cases of malaria and submitted a detailed report. It is in contemplation to give effect to his suggestions.

Health.

54. The total expenditure for the year excluding that for the Public works amounted to Rs. 98,016 against Rs. 1,05,730.

Expenditure.

55. During the year the garrisons at Dharmanagar, Kailashahar, Sonamura and Sabroom were abolished.

56. Besides the ordinary sentry and escort duties the force had to do some patrolling work this year also.

Extra Duties.

57. The Military Forces comprising the First Tripura Bir Company and 2nd Tripura Bikram Company with State Band, Signalling party and followers marched out at 6-20 A. M. under their respective Company Commanders from the cantonment on the 22nd November, 1932. His Highness the Maharaja Manikya Bahadur as Commander-in-Chief of the forces accompanied by the Chief Secretary, Military Secretary, Private Secretary and an A. D. C. with the State Engineer headed the party. They reached Chandrasadhu-Para at 2-20 P. M. after marching a distance of 20 miles and camped there for 9 days, during which the force had special trainings and practices. The march was resumed in the early morning of the 1st December. After crossing over the Baramura range, covering a distance of 10 miles, and then continuing the march through 16 miles of marshy land the force reached Kalyanpur in the evening. They stopped there for 4 days and did some practice under Captain Kumar Brajalal Deb Barman Bahadur. On the morning of the 6th December the march was taken up towards Khowai, a distance of 15 miles, reaching the place in the afternoon. There the force halted for 3 days and did parade works. From Khowai the force started in the early morning of 9th December and reached Kalachera Tea Estate at 4 P. M. covering a distance of 20 miles over the hills. Taking rest there for a day only the force commenced march in the early morning of 11th December for 20 miles over rough country and passing through the adjoining ancient village of Dharmagarh, returned to the cantonment in the afternoon, being out for 20 days. During the 5 days of marching the force covered a distance of 101 miles. Considering the nature of the country they had to traverse, the achievement was very satisfactory.

Camping and Tactical Training.

III. Police.

Charge.

58. Honorary Lieutenant J. C. Datta, B. A., continued as Superintendent of Police till 30th Aswin, when he was succeeded by Rai Saheb Akshay Kumar Gupta, late of Bengal Police who held charge for the rest of the year.

59. Babu N. K. Bhattacharjee, B. Sc., continued as Assistant Superintendent of Police during the year.

Strength.

60. The total numerical strength of the police force during the year was 499 against 493 in the previous year.

Rural Police.

61. The total number of village choukidars was 175, as before.

Inspecting staff.

62. There were 4 Inspectors of Police, who were employed mainly to supervise important cases and control the staff, placed under them.

Investigating and prosecuting staff.

63. During the year, there were 24 Sub-Inspectors including one probationary Sub-Inspector and 25 Naib Darogas, as against 25 and 20, respectively, in the previous year.

C. I. D. and Intelligence staff

64. There were 1 Sub-Inspector, 5 Naib Darogas and 5 constables during the year, as against 1 Sub-Inspector, 4 Naib Darogas and 4 constables in the previous year.

Crime.

65. The total number of cases, reported during the year under review, was 1198, as against 1300 in the previous year.

66. The result of the cases is as follows :—

Number of cases reported 1,198

- Enquiry refused 42
- Number investigated 1,094
  - True 760
    - Charge-sheet 432
    - Finally reported 328
  - Intentionally false 88
  - Mistake of law 39
  - Mistake of fact 86
  - Noncognizable 93
  - Doubtful 28
- Number pending 62

Result of prosecution.

67. Altogether, 827 persons were arrested in connection with various offences and 943 persons sent up for trial by police, against 925 and 835, respectively, in the previous year. Of the number sent up, 223 were convicted and 309 acquitted (including 86 on compromise, 43 on withdrawal of cases) while 35 died and 411 awaited trial (including the absconding accused) The percentage of convictions which was 26·96 against 30·97 of the previous year was very poor. Detection of some important cases during the latter part of the year reflects credit on the part of the officers and men concerned.

68. Of the 333 persons awaiting trial at the end of the previous year, 91 were convicted, 125 acquitted (including 25 on compromise and 24 on withdrawal of cases) and 117 were awaiting trial at the end of the year under report.

Bad Livelihood cases

69. Four bad-livelihood cases against 4 persons were instituted during the year, 1 of whom was bound down and the rest were awaiting trial at the close of the year.

Arms Act cases.

70. Eighteen Arms Act cases were instituted against 18 persons, of whom 10 were convicted, 3 discharged and 5 were awaiting trial (including 5 absconding) as the year closed.

Recovery of Stolen Property.

71. Total value of property, stolen during the year, amounted to Rs. 18,282-6-0, against Rs. 20,558-9-9 of the previous year. Of this amount, Rs. 2,692-12-9 was recovered as against Rs. 4,600-6-0 in the previous year. The percentage of recoveries was 14·73, against 22·38 of the previous year.

Dacoity.

72. There were 20 cases of dacoity during the year, against 32 in the previous year. Twentyeight persons were sent up in charge-sheet in connection with 7 cases, of whom 11 were convicted, 9 acquitted and 8 (including 4 absconding) were awaiting trial at the close of the year.

Unnatural death.

73. Eightytwo cases of unnatural deaths were reported during the year. Regular enquiries were held by the Police into all these cases. One transpired to be a case of natural death. No foul play was detected in any of the cases.

Rewards and punishments.

74. Six Sub-Inspectors, 2 Naib Darogas, 1 Havildar and 9 constables received money rewards, while 3 Sub-Inspectors, 2 Naib Darogas, 1 Jamadar (civil), 1 Havildar, 2 Naiks, 7 constables (armed) 21 constables (civil) and 3 choukidars were fined or degraded. None was dismissed.

Tours.

75. The Superintendent of Police was out on tour for 66 days against 57 days in the previos year and the Assistant Superintendent of Police for 50 days, against 30 days in the previous year.

Co-operation.

76. The relation with the neighbouring districts in British India continued to be satisfactory.

Expenditure.

77. The expenditure amounted to Rs. 85,242 against Rs. 83,334 in the previous year.

IV. Justice.

Courts.

78. There were 15 courts of justice in the State during the year under report exercising both civil and criminal jurisdiction, viz :—the Khas Adalat (High Court) with its original and appellate sides and 14 courts of Magistrate-Munsiffs exercising original jurisdiction only.

Khas Adalat (High Court).

79. Babu Jnanendra Mohan Das, B. L., continued as Chief Judge, and Babu Ramani Mohan Goswami, M. A., B. L., as Civil and Sessions Judge in the original side during the year. Uzir B. K. Deb Barman Bahadur continued as Puisne Judge till the middle of Agrahayan when he was succeeded temporarily by Thakur Tarini Charan Deb Barman, a senior retired member of the Tripura Civil Service.

Number of original criminal cases

80. Altogether 2,030 criminal cases were instituted during the year under report as against 1,949 of the previous year. With the balance of 517 pending from the last year, the total number of cases for disposal before the several subordinate original courts was 2,547 as against 2,400 of the previous year as detailed below ; and out of these 2,547 cases, 1,980 were disposed of as against 1,883 of the last year, leaving 567 cases pending at the close of the year. Thus, in the year under report, the number of cases for disposal increased by 147 from that of the previous year, and there was also an increase in disposal by 97.

DESCRIPTION OF OFFENCES.	1341 T. E.	1342 T. E.
Offences against the State and public tranquillity	58	77
Offences against person	631	670
Offences against property	1,206	1,284
Other offences	505	516
TOTAL	2,400	2,547

Extradition from British India.

81. Extradition of 118 persons was asked for during the year. With 108 persons pending surrender at the close of the previous year, the total number of offenders involved in the requisitions was 226, of whom 35 persons were arrested and surrendered by the British Indian Police and 43 persons appeared of their own accord or were subsequently arrested within the State.

Persons brought to trial.

82. The total number of persons awaiting trial in the year under report inclusive of the number pending from the preceding year was 3,503 against 3,056 of the previous year. The number, brought to trial within the year under review was 2,728, of whom 700 persons were arrested by the Police, 575 were produced on warrant, 934 appeared on summons, 509 appeared voluntarily and 10 persons were arrested in the presence of the Magistrates.

Results of cases

83. Out of 3,503 persons before the courts including the Sessions, 1,199 persons were discharged without trial, 854 were acquitted, 633 were convicted, 2 died, 1 person escaped and 814 persons remained under trial at the close of the year. Out of these convicted persons, 191 were sentenced to various terms of imprisonment extending from below 1 month to 5 years and above; 4 persons were imprisoned for life, one person was sentenced to be hanged but the sentence of death was afterwards commuted by the

Appellate Court to one of rigorous imprisonment for life, 389 were sentenced to fine only, 17 were bound down under security and 31 persons were warned for the future. The number of persons actually tried was 1,487 as against 1,345 of the previous year and the percentage of conviction was thus 42·57 against 50·04 of the previous year.

84. Of the 2,547 cases for disposal as stated before, the number of cases in which British subjects were either complainants or defendants was 454 as against 448 of the previous year. Out of these, 362 cases were cognizable and 92 non-cognizable. In 37 cases, British subjects were complainants and in 417 cases they were the accused. In 137 cases both the parties were British subjects. In these cases, 598 persons were actually brought under trial during the year under report, against 606 of the preceding year. Of the persons involved, 271 persons were convicted, 222 aquitted or discharged, 1 escaped and 104 remained under trial at the close of the year.

Cases concerning British subjects.

85. The following statement will show the number of original criminal cases instituted during the last two years.

Comparative Statement.

DESCRIPTION OF OFFENCES.	1341 T.E.	1342 T. E.	Increase.	Decrease.
Offences against the State and public tranquillity ...	46	61	15	0
Offences against person	535	541	6	0
Offences against property	977	1,026	49	0
Other offences	391	402	11	0
TOTAL	1,949	2,030	81	0

Increased by 81.

86. 19 cases were committed to the Sessions during the year under report and 9 cases were pending from the previous year. Out of these 28 cases, 27 were disposed of during the year as detailed in the following table. The number of persons involved in these cases was 77, of whom 20 persons were convicted, 53 were acquitted and 4 remained under trial at the close of the year.

Sessions cases.

Description of cases.	Number of cases	Disposed of.	Pending.	REMARKS.
Murder	6	6	0	
Culpable homicide not amounting to murder	2	2	0	
Attempt to murder	1	1	0	
Grievous hurt and criminal trespass ...	2	2	0	
Wrongful restraint	1	1	0	
Dacoity	2	2	0	
Robbery	9	9	0	
Arson	2	1	1	
Using unlicensed gun	1	1	0	
Using forged documents	1	1	0	
Unnatural offence	1	1	0	
Total	28	27	1	

87. There were altogether 248 criminal appeals as against 308 of the previous year. These appeals were disposed of as shown below :—

Criminal appeals.

Rejected	16
Judgment affirmed	125
Modified	43
Reversed	14
Further enquiry ordered	12
	210
Pending	38
Total	248

88. The percentage of judgments affirmed and modified was 86·60 as against 85·46 of the previous year.

89. The number of original civil suits instituted during the year under report was 2,057 as against 1,919 of the previous year. With the balance of 733 suits from the preceding year, the total number of suits for disposal was 2,790 against 2,707 of the previous year. These were disposed of as shown below :—

Original civil suits.

Exparte	849
Admitted and compromised	308
Dismissed for want of prosecution	244
Disposed of on contest	483
	1,884
Pending	906
Total	2,790

90. The average duration of suits before the civil courts was 2 months and 20 days as against 2 months and 28 days in 1341 T. E.

Duration of suits

91. The total value of civil suits instituted during the year was Rs. 1,72,819-3-10 as against Rs. 2,18,100-15-6 of the previous year, which gives an average of Rs. 84-0-3 per case. Out of 2,057 suits, instituted during the year under review, 359 related to land, 1,328 to money transactions and 370 to other transactions. 1,238 suits were of the value of Rs. 100 and under ; 451 suits were of the value between Rs. 100 and Rs. 500 : 40 suits of value between Rs. 500 and Rs. 1,000 ; 9 suits of value between Rs. 1,000 and Rs. 5,000 ; 1 suit was of value above Rs. 5,000 ; 318 suits were not estimable in money value.

Nature and value of suits.

92. The number of applications for the execution of decrees filed during the year was 922 and there were 612 pending from the previous year. The total number for disposal was thus 1,534 as against 1,457 of the preceding year. The aggregate value of the new applications was Rs. 1,44,567-4-5 and that of the pending applications was Rs. 1,51,444-4-9 ; the value thus amounted to Rs. 2,96011-9-2. The number of applications disposed of was 844, the value of which was Rs. 1,42,752-5-5. The number of execution cases pending at the close of the year was 690, the value thereof being Rs. 1,53,259-3-9.

Execution of decrees.

93. There were 147 civil appeals filed during the year as against 203 of the previous year. With the balance of 167 from the last year, the total number of civil appeals for disposal was 314 against 367 of the preceding year. Out of these cases, 196 were disposed of during the year under report as against 200 of the previous year, leaving a balance of 118 cases at the close of the year.

Civil appeals.

94. The following figures will show the results of appeals in civil suits :—

Results of civil appeals.

Decisions confirmed	...	...	...	86
,, reversed	...	...	...	32
,, modified	...	...	...	15
Remanded ...	...	...	...	30
Compromised and otherwise disposed of			...	33
				196

95. The percentage of judgments wholly or partly upheld, excluding those in the cases compromised, was 61·96 as against 72·61 of the preceding year.

Percentage.

96. The total value of civil appeals filed during the year under review was Rs. 7,894-8-3, and the average duration of each appeal was 3 months and 19 days against 4 months and 5 days of the previous year.

Value and duration of appeals.

97. 15 civil suits were instituted in the original side, Khas Adalat, during the year under report as against 28 of the previous year. With the balance of 64 suits pending from the preceding year, the total for disposal was 79 against 95 of the previous year. Of these, 30 suits were disposed of against 31, leaving 49 suits pending at the close of the year. There were 53 execution cases during the year including 36 cases pending from the previous year. Of these, 19 were disposed of and 34 remained pending at the close of the year. There were 19 applications filed for grant of succession and other certificates during the year under report; with the balance of 16 from the previous year the total number of cases was 35, out of which 15 were disposed of as shown below and 20 remained pending at the close of the year.

Original Side cases.

Description of cases.	Total.	Disposed of.	Pending.
Probate case	2	0	2
Succession certificate	12	4	8
Guardianship	21	11	10
Total	35	15	20

98. The total number of civil and criminal appeals inclusive of the number pending from the last year, was 562 as against 675 of the previous year. Out of these cases, 406 were disposed of as against 446 of the preceding year. The work of the Court had to be suspended for about a fortnight as the Chief Judge had to preside over a Special Tribunal which was constituted to try an armed dacoity case. In comparison with the previous year,

Total number of appeals.

the total number of cases for disposal decreased by 113 and there was a corresponding decrease in disposal by 40.

Description of appeals.	Number of appeals.		Disposed of.	
	Past year.	Present year.	Past year.	Present year.
Civil	367	314	200	196
Criminal	308	248	246	210
Total	675	562	446	406

V. Prisons.

99. The State had one central jail at the capital and 7 sub-jails namely one at each of the Divisions and Sub-Divisions during the year under review. Dr. M. M. Majumdar, Chief Medical Officer, was the Superintendent of the Central Jail as before.

Number of Jails.

100. Prisoners of all classes totalled 1174 during the year as against 1332 in the year before; the daily average being 132·01 against 161·55. Of them, 510 were convicts, 655 undertrials and 9 civil prisoners. 159 prisoners in all remained in the different jails at the end of the year under report as against 162 in the preceding year.

Jail population.

101. Prisoners undergoing imprisonment for more than 2 years were equal in number, viz. 78, in the last two years. The details as to the nature of their offence, period of sentence, number and occupation are shown in the following table.

Long-term prisoners

Class of offence.	Number of prisoners.	Occupation.	REMARKS.
Murder	18	They are employed in brick manufacture, oilmills, *soorki* pounding, *khoa* breaking, bamboo and cane work, gardening, weaving, tailoring, paddy husking, rice manufacturing etc.	51 had sentences of 2 to 5 years, 10 of 5 to 10 years, 2 of 10 to 14 years 15 for life *i. e.* 20 years.
Culpable homicide not amounting to murder... ...	13		
Grievous hurt	6		
Theft	5		
Rape	2		
Unlawful assembly	8		
Robbery	5		
Dacoity	16		
Counterfeiting coin	2		
Section 110 (Security for good behaviour for habitual offenders)	1		
Kidnapping	1		
Forgery	1		
Total	78		

102. Two deaths occurred in the Central Jail during the year under report. One convict died of intestinal tuberculosis and one undertrial of cerebral type of malaria. The health of the Central Jail particularly was not so good as in the previous year.

Jail health.

103. One convict from the Udaipur Jail, 2 undertrials from the Kailashahar Jail, 1 under-trial from the Khowai Jail, 1 undertrial from the Dharmanagar Jail and 1 undertrial from the Sabrum Jail escaped during the year. Of them 2 under-trials were rearrested shortly after escape.

Escape.

104. The Reformatory School attached to the Central Jail, with the help of a paid tutor, trained 21 convicts during the year under report. Of them, 2 appeared at Lower Vernacular and 3 at Pathshala Scholarship Examinations of the State. In the former, one passed in the 3rd division and in the latter 1 in the 1st and 2 in the 3rd. Besides, religious instruction was given as before.

Education.

105. On the occasion of the birth day ceremony of His Highness the Maharaja Manikya Bahadur, 12 convicts, sentenced to imprisonment under one year, were set free.

Special Release.

106. Excepting the sub-jails at Kailashahar and Bilonia, the guarding of all other sub-jails came under the Jail Department with a warder establishment newly created for the purpose. The total number of warders including those of the Central Jail was 57 which included 8 jamadars or senior warders. Of them, one jamadar and 3 warders had to be dismissed.

Warders.

107. The income from all sources in the Central Jail alone totalled Rs. 4107-12-6, out of which Rs. 2.000 had to be spent during the year under report for the purchase of raw materials for jail manufacture.

Income.

108. The total expenditure during the year under review stood at Rs. 21,804 as against Rs. 17,995 in the previous year.

Expenditure.

VI. Registration.

109. The charge of the Department continued with Thakur K. K. Singh, Naib-Dewan.

Charge.

110. The number of Registration offices continued to be 9 as in the previous year there being one at the head quarters Station of each of the Divisions and Sub-Divisions. In the mofussil the Divisional and the Sub-Divisional officers and in certain Divisions the Second Officers acted as Registrars. For the Sadar Division there was a separate Registrar at Agartala.

Registration Offices.

Registration and Disposal.

111. The total number of documents presented for registration during the year including 1,042 documents pending at the end of the previous year was 6,636 against 6302. Of this number 82 deeds were refused registration on different grounds and 96 remained pending at the end of the year against 1042 pending at the end of the previous year.

Value of deeds presented and registered.

112. The total value covered by the documents amounted to Rs. 9,96,275 as compared with Rs. 8,85,085 of the previous year, while the total value covered by the documents actually registered was Rs. 9,63,565 as against Rs. 7,09,868 in the year before.

Suits and appeals.

113. The number of suits filed in Registration Department in respect of documents, the registration of which had been refused in the Registration offices was 24 against 20 suits in the previous year. There were three appeals during the year against none in the year before. There were 31 suits pending from the previous year making a total of 55 suits and 3 appeals during the year under report. Out of these, 11 suits and 1 appeal were disposed of during the year, leaving 44 suits and 2 appeals pending at the close of the year.

Income and expenditure.

114. The total income of the Department from fees and fines amounted to Rs. 6,112 against Rs. 6,897 and the expenditure to Rs. 3,452 against Rs. 3,840 in the previous year. The net income thus amounted to Rs. 2,660 in the year under report against Rs. 3,057 in the previous year. The income of the year was less by Rs. 397 in comparison with that of the previous year, which was mainly due to the continued economic depression during the year under report.

VII. Municipality and Sanitation.

Municipality.

115. During the year under review, the Agartala Municipality was the only institution of its kind in the State with a population of 9,580 as per last census.

Municipal Committee.

116. The Municipal administration was carried on by a committee of nine members, all nominated, including an official Chairman and a non-official Vice-Chairman. Thakur Hridayranjan Deb Barman having resigned the Chairmanship towards the end of the year under report, Babu Jogesh Chandra Dutt, B. A., Personal Assistant to the Minister was appointed Chairman. Babu Haridas Bhattacharjee was the Vice-Chairman.

Income.

117. Apart from the State grant of Rs. 8,000, the total collection from Municipal and latrine taxes including the arrear demand amounted to Rs. 3,594-0-9 as against Rs. 3,509-10-3 of the year before. The total demand under this head was Rs. 12,994-7-9, of which Rs. 1,825-15-3 was irrecoverable. The income under the miscellaneous head came up to Rs. 864-4-0 as against Rs. 908-4-3 in the preceding year. The above figure

includes deposits and advances recovered during the year under report. Thus the income of the Municipality inclusive of State grant totalled Rs. 12,458-4-9.

118. The Municipality spent, in all, Rs. 12,428-12-3 as against Rs. 14,178-9-0 in the previous year. The above figure excludes the sum spent on the Bazar improvement

Expenditure.

119. As before, the Municipal Committee had the control and management of the town municipal market in their hands. The total demand including the arrear demand was Rs. 11.994-11-9 of which Rs. 584-8-6 was irrecoverable and the total receipts amounted to Rs. 6,672 6-6 as against Rs. 6,144-7-6 in the preceding year.

Ishanganja Bazar.

120. The account of income and expenditure is kept separate from that of the general municipal administration. The Bazar fund has been set apart for the improvement of the market only. A sum of Rs. 1,544-13-6 was expended for the above purpose during the year under review leaving a balance of Rs. 38,362-5-3 in the market fund at the end of the year.

121. The health of the town was generally good. There were 22 cases of cholera with 4 deaths and 5 cases of small-pox, all imported—all of which were cured by the State small-pox doctor.

Health.

122. A sum of Rs. 2,396-12-3 was spent on some sanitary works within the town. One new tank was excavated and two old tanks were re-excavated.

Sanitation.

123. As before, Dr. M. M. Majumdar, L. M. S., remained in charge of the Municipal and Sanitation Departments.

Charge.

CHAPTER IV—PRODUCTION AND DISTRIBUTION.

1. Weather and Crops—Agriculture.

124. Manyabara Rana Bodhjung Bahadur, Chief Secretary to His Highness the Maharaja Manikya Bahadur, continued to be in charge of the Agriculture Department being assisted by Mr. J. C. Choudhury, Superintendent of Agriculture.

The Charge of the Department.

125. The average rainfall of the year was 70·56″ against 82·74″ in the previous year. The quinquennial average was 86·37″. Kailashahar Division had the maximum fall of 97·05″ and Amarpur Sub-Division the minimum of 50·84″. The distribution was uneven.

Rainfall.

126. The highest temperature was 96 degree against 97 degree in the previous year and minimum was 45 degree against 52 degree in the previous year.

Temperature.

Tea Industry.

127. The outturn of tea increased a little while export decreased to some extent during the year under review. In spite of slump in the tea market there was some new extension of old plantations and a portion of area abandoned in previous years was replanted. The arrear revenue demand at the end of the year under review was heavier in comparison with the previous year. The State has always been giving facilities to the infant tea industry during the slump by way of remission of interest on arrears and by granting of easy instalments for payment of all State dues and surrender of part of the *taluki* land for tea with remisson of arrear due in special cases. The tea industry was passing through a crisis throughout the year under review but a satisfactory rise in prices since the close of the year has brought some relief to the tea industry.

Condition of the people.

128. The people of the State are mostly cultivators. And the cultivators in general were the worst sufferers through the continued world wide commercial depression. Though the main harvests of the year were considerably better than in the previous year the pecuniary condition of the people did not improve as the prices of the indigeneous commodities continued to be low.

Wages and Labour.

129. Wages for field labour including those for *jooming* were 4 to 8 annas per day, those of masons 8 to 12 annas per day, of carpenters 8 to 12 annas per day, thatchers 5 to 8 annas and of labour for earth work 6 to 8 annas per day.

Activities of the Department

130. One fieldman was placed at Udaipur for the southern Divisions to push Eri-culture and carry on propaganda, and another was placed at Kailashahar for northern Divisions to promote cultivation of various agricultural crops and for pushing improved varieties of crops.

Kashipur Farm.

131. Kashipur Farm was abolished during the year under report.

Cattle.

132. The cultivators could not make up the loss of cattle incurred in the previous year through Rinderpest epidemic. The same disease broke out this year also in Kailashahar.

Veterinary Surgeon

133. Veterinary Surgeon was out on tour for 18 days. He treated 150 cattle at Kailashahar and 1,523 animals at Sadar.

II. Immigration and Emigration.

Charge of the Department.

134. The administration of the Departments of Immigration and Reclamation and of the Reserve area of Kalyanpur, was conducted as in the previous year, direct under the supervision of Manyabara Rana Saheb Bodhjung Bahadur, F. R. G. S., Chief Secretary to His Highness the Maharaja Manikya Bahadur, and Sj. B. C. Dev Varman continued his office as Assistant in these Departments as before.

Increase in number of immigrants in Kulaibaor.

135. The number of immigrants in the immigration area of Kulaibaor increased by 18 Manipuri and 60 Jamatia families who came from the District of Cachar and Chittagong Hill Tracts and are now living there by agriculture in their respective *Jotes*.

136. Most of the immigrants have been reported to have reclaimed the *Jotes* allotted to them, and are thus making those quite fit for agricultural purposes. They have also made their homes in the area.

Health of the immigrants.

137. The health of the immigrants was reported to have been good during the year under report.

Effect of the financial crisis.

138. As a result of the world wide financial crisis retrenchment both in staff and offices was effected through out the State, causing the abolition of the Kulai Tahasil Office and the Dispensary, but the latter was retained at a minimum cost with a new Doctor appointed direct by the Department.

Number of patients treated in the Kulai Dispensary.

139. From the report of the Doctor it appears that 1923 new and 929 old cases making a total of 2852 patients received treatment in the said dispensary; besides these there were 8 minor operations with success. The Doctor possesses qualifications both in Allopathy and Homoeopathy thus affording facilities to the inhabitants to receive treatment equally in both systems.

Scarcity of drinking water.

140. Although certain improvements have by this time been made in the locality scarcity of pure drinking water prevails in the immigration area for the removal of which a proposal is under consideration.

Re-construction of Kamalpur Ambassa Road.

141. Re-construction of the remaining portion of the Kamalpur Ambassa Road was undertaken and completed up to nearly 12 miles from Kamalpur at a cost of nearly Rs. 5000 during the year under report. Further portion including repairs to the whole road where necessary will be taken up during the next season.

Selema Bazar.

142. Selema Bazar made fair progress during the year under review.

Kalyanpur Reserve area.

143. During the year under report 100 *drones* of both *Abadi* and jungle lands in the reserve area of Kalyanpur were settled with hill people, and *Nazar* amounting to Rs. 1127 out of Rs. 2557 was realised.

144. Relinquishment of nearly 133 drones of waste lands was accepted during the year under report.

Staff.

145. 3 Amins (one permanent) were engaged for the survey work and 166 *drones* 3 *Kanis* of lands were surveyed during the year under review. Temporary Amins were discharged at the close of the year.

Improvements under contemplation.

146. Various improvements relating to the construction of new road, excavation of tanks and sinking of tube-wells etc. in the Reserve area are under contemplation.

III. Forests.

147. Babu Jatindra Nath Mitra, Naib Dewan, was in charge of the Department. With the exception of a few *Mahals* which were let out in *Ijara*, all the forests were under *Khas* management as before.

Charge and management.

148. Including the Patrol Staff with one Forester, two Head Guards and fourteen guards, the Department had a staff of 1 Station Officer, 1 Forest Circle Inspector, 14 Foresters, 12 Assistant Foresters, 5 Rangers, 7 Moharers, 22 Head Guards, 11 Literate Guards and 142 guards. The Patrol Staff was out on tour in sections for 9 months and 17 days, namely, twice in the Sabroom Division for a month and twice in the Bilonia Division for 1 month and 24 days, thrice in the Sadar Division for two months and 14 days and twice in the Sonamura Division for four months and 9 days.

Staff.

149. There were 134 Commission Agents for the sale of forest permits for the shoulder-borne export of minor forest produce.

Permit Agents.

150. There were 50 Forest Stations for collection of duty and prevention of forest offences.

Forest Station.

151. The Reserved *Sal* forests of the Sonamura Division continued to be worked under the system of coppice with standards and those of the Udaipur Division under the Improvement Method, while the open unclassed forests were worked under the State Forest Rules of 1323 T. E. But the working rules of the Bengal Forest Department were followed for the Feni River *Mahal* of which a share is held by the Government of Bengal.

Working of the forests.

152. The following table shows the results of the collection of forest revenue :—

Sources of Forest Revenue

Heads of Revenue.	1342 T.E.	1341 T.E.	Increase.	Decrease.	REMARKS.
I. Unclassed open forests :—					
(*a*) Toll on forest produce exported by the river mehals	2,75,001	2,55,805	19,196	—	
(*b*) Toll on forest produce exported by land route under permit	60,191	60,692	—	501	
(*c*) Toll collection (share) of the Feni river mehal ...	28,086	27,850	236	—	
(*d*) Grazing mehal ...	6,003	5,690	313	—	
(*e*) Thatching grass mehal	3,379	4,008	—	629	
II. Reserved Forests :— Sale of *Sal* and *Garjan* trees ...	1,975	1,470	505	—	
III. Elephant Kheddas	1,628	—	1,628	—	
TOTAL ...	3,76,263	3,55,515	21,878	1,130	

153. The total forest revenue of the year under report was Rs. 3,76,263 against Rs. 3,55,515 in the previous year showing an increase of Rs. 20,748.

Receipts.

154. An appreciable increase was noticeable in the river *mahals* which was due to the sudden increase in the demand of forest produce in the later part of the year when there was a rise in the price of jute which mainly controls the demand of forest produce from the State. This was also due to the 25% rebate in duty which was allowed in the year in view of the low prices of all kinds of forest produces. There was a revenue of Rs. 1,628 from the elephant *kheda mahals* in the year under report but there was no revenue in the year before as no *kheda* had been undertaken that year.

155. During the year under report *Kheda* operations were undertaken in the Manoo-Dhalai and the *Deo Doals* in the Kailashahar Division and the *Suknachheri Doal* in the Sonamura Division. The *Kheda* operations in the Manoo-Dhalai and the *Deo Doals* were successful while those in the *Suknachheri Doal* failed. 2 elephants were caught in the *Manoo-Dhalai Doal* and 23 in the *Deo Doal*.

Kheda operations.

156. The joint Toll Station at Amlighat continued to be under the management of the State Forest Department. The total revenue collected at the station in the year under review was Rs. 41,086 against Rs. 39,850 in the previous year. As before, a doctor of the Sub-Assistant Surgeon class was appointed temporarily for four months from December to March last for giving medical relief to the station staff and to the cutters and exporters of forest produce.

Feni River *Mahal*.

157. As in the previous year, the forest produce from the Fee Simple Lots above the Amlighat Toll Station was exported under passes granted by the Collector of Chittagong.

Fee Simple Lots.

158. In the year under review, there were 245 forest cases against 474 persons including 37 cases against 60 persons pending from the previous year. The offences were mainly for illicit export of forest produce without payment of duty.

Forest Offences.

159. Altogether 143 cases against 277 persons were tried, of whom 19 were sentenced to imprisonment only, 221 were punished with fine only and 37 were acquitted. 45 cases against 45 persons were compounded and 57 cases against 145 persons remained pending at the close of the year.

Results

160. One Ranger, two Head Guards and 15 guards were rewarded for intelligent detection of cases of smuggling of forest produce. One Assistant Forester, three Head Guards and three guards were fined for misconduct.

Rewards and punishments.

161. The health of the staff in general was good.

Health of the Staff.

162. In the Match Factory at Agartala, only the match boxes and sticks were made during the year. Finished matches could not be manufactured for want of some of the machineries required.

General.

163. The Naib Dewan could not go out on tour for more than 6 days as he was in charge of the Accounts Department as well.

Tour.

IV. Trade and Manufacture.

164. The principal exports were timber, forest produce of various kinds, cotton, oil-seeds (*til* and mustard seed), paddy, jute, tea, rice and *Gur* (molasses). Some homespun cotton fabrics manufactured by the hillpeople, and especially by the Manipuris were also exported. The principal exports of the year under review and of the previous year are shewn below.

	1340 T. E.	1341 T. E.	1342 T. E.
Cotton ...	54,785 mds.	56,034 mds.	51,918 mds.
Til ...	29,617 ,,	14,761 ,,	36,918 ,,
Mustard seeds	33,270 ,,	25,936 ,,	30,398 ,,
Jute ...	74,512 ,,	30,454 ,,	84,904 ,,
Tea ...	12,18,161 lbs.	15,21,534 lbs.	15,11,334 lbs.

V. Public Works.

165. The Minister was personally in charge of the Public Works Department. Honorary Lieutenant J. N. Bhaduri, B. E., continued as State Engineer during the year.

Charge.

166. The total expenditure on Public Works amounted to Rs. 79,899 as detailed below against Rs. 72,793 in the previous year.

Expenditure.

(1)	Buildings	...	Rs. 46,691
(2)	Roads and Bridges ...	...	,, 13,016
(3)	Tanks and Tube-wells	...	,, 923
(4)	Miscellaneous works ...	...	,, 1,817
(5)	Minor works at the *Rajbari*	...	,, 996
(6)	Establishment charges	...	,, 16,456

167. Besides the above, Rs. 26,499 was spent for improvement works under the following heads :—

Improvement.

(1)	Buildings	...	Rs. 13,973
(2)	Roads and Bridges ...	...	,, 6,125
(3)	Water Supply ...	...	,, 1,924
(4)	Miscellaneous works ...	...	,, 4,477

168. The Minister's Office building could not be completed owing to financial reasons. The following other public buildings were constructed during the year :—

Buildings.

(1) Khowai Thana House with corrugated iron roofing.
(2) Magazine House of the Sadar Police Reserve with corrugated iron roofing.
(3) Sabroom Divisional Office building of steel structure and C. I. roofing.

169. Construction of type quarters for Chief Judge and Military officers proceeded, though slowly.

170. Of the roads and bridges of the year mention may be made of the following :—

Roads and Bridges.

(1). The Palace Avenue Road from the Ujjayanta Palace to Kunjaban. This road was not completed within the year.
(2) Substantial improvement of the Kulai Haor-Ambasha Road in Kailashahar Division.

(3) Reconstruction of a bridge of combined steel structure and cement concrete decking over the Jaji stream on the Agartala-Akhaura Road.

(4) A re-inforced concrete bridge over the Sinai on the Agartala-Bishalgar Road.

Water Supply.

171. A tube-well of 2″ diameter was sunk in Agartala Central Jail compound. Besides, a tank at Amlapara in Agartala was re-excavated and a tank was excavated at Dhaleswar in the suburb of the capital town.

Miscellaneous Works.

172. A compound wall of some height was constructed along the southern bank of the west Palace lake.

173. A temporary telephone line was constructed from Agartala to Chandra Sadhupara, a village at the foot of the Baramura hills at a distance of 18 miles.

174. In the capital a telephone system connecting the important public buildings and residences of important officials with the palace was under construction during the year.

175. The total expenditure in connection with Electric supply was Rs. 17,125.

176. Due to the economic depression no local funds were available for Public Works in the year under report.

CHAPTER V—REVENUE AND FINANCES.

1. Revenue

177. The total collection in the year was Rs. 13,49,108 against Rs. 12,37,252 in the previous year.

178. The details of income under different heads with all variations are given in the statement below :—

Serial number.	Heads of Revenue	1342 T.E.	1341 T.E.	As compared with 1341 T.E.		Remarks.
				Increase.	Decrease.	
1.	Land Revenue	4,18,825	3,97,658	21,167	—	
2.	Rents of markets	6,477	5,485	993	—	
3.	Family Tax in the hills	45,459	42,685	2,774	—	
4.	Toll on forest produce	3,35,192	3,16,497	18,695	—	
5.	Do. Do. on the Feni River	28,086	27,850	236	—	
6.	Elephant & buffalo grazing Mehal	6,003	5,690	313	—	
7.	Thatching grass Mehal	3,379	4,008	—	629	
8.	Reserved *Sal* Forests	1,975	1,470	505	—	
9.	Tax on cotton and oil-seeds ...	1,40,040	1,12,868	27,172	—	
10.	Royalty on elephants caught ...	1,628	—	1,628	—	
11.	Adda Mohal	22,499	23,333	—	834	
12.	Excise	40,279	50,086	—	9,807	
13.	Stamps and Court-fees	66,415	67,070	—	655	
14.	Law and Justice (Fines)... ...	2,274	4,813	—	2,539	
15.	Process fees	11,650	12,563	—	913	
16.	Registration	5,869	6,897	—	1,028	
17.	Jail	2,111	2,254	—	143	
18.	Cattle pounds	4,349	4,566	—	217	
19.	Nazars	25,663	27,390	—	1,727	
20.	Education...	14,086	14,502	—	416	
21.	Tea Export duty	9,318	8,633	685	—	
22.	Jute Export duty	31,388	11,463	19,925	—	
23.	Recovery of personal advances	1,319	3,746	—	2,427	
24.	Depreciation Contribution ...	80,850	42,110	38,740	—	
25.	Interest on bank deposits... ..	—	—	—	—	
26.	Miscellaneous	43,974	43,615	359	—	
	Total	13,49,108	12,37,252	1,33,191	21,335	Net increase—Rs. 1,11,856

179. It will be seen that there was an increase in respect of 13 heads of income. The increase under head Land Revenue does not denote good collection as the percentage of collection has decreased with the increase of current and arrear demand.

180. In 1341 T. E. there was a fall of revenue to the extent of Rs. 10,000 from tea gardens in comparison with the previous year *viz.* 1340 T. E. A further fall of Rs. 9,414 occurred in the year under review. This is attributable to the slump in tea market.

181. The increase under head "Toll on forest produce" has been explained in the Forest Section.

182. The increase under head "Tax on cotton and oil-seeds" in comparison with 1340 and 1341 T. E. was Rs. 32,759 and Rs. 27,172. For the benefit of the hill people a rebate for the last 2 months of the year was granted and good results were achieved in Kailashahar, Khowai and Sonamura Divisions.

183. Jute export duty exceeded the figures of 1339, 1340 and 1341 T. E. by Rs. 265, Rs. 3,410 and Rs. 19,925 respectively, Sonamura Division alone contributing Rs. 20,405 against Rs. 8,046 in the previous year.

184. The increase under head "Depreciation Contribution" is rather illusory as the "Depreciation Contribution" measure was given effect to after 5 months of the year 1341 T. E. was over.

185. The excise revenue already suffered a heavy fall in 1341 T. E. in comparison with the previous year. The year under review witnessed a still heavier fall.

186. The decrease under head "Stamps and court fees" amounted to Rs. 655 in comparison with the previous year and Rs. 16,323 in comparison with 1340 T. E.

187. The income under the head "Registration" decreased in comparison with the previous year and was reduced to half in comparison with 1340 T. E.

II. Finances.

188. A consolidated abstract account of the financial transactions of the State and the attached Zemindaries as compared with those of the previous year is given below :—

Receipts.	1341 T.E.	1342 T.E.
1. Opening balance :—		
(1) State ...	6,01,671	6,51,015
(2) Zemindaries ...	3,70,995	4,14,135
Total ...	9,72,666	10,65,150
2. Income :—		
(1) State ...	12,37,252	13,49,108
(2) Zemindaries ...	7,88,230	8,50,918
Total ...	20,25,482	22,00,026
3. Law charges recovered :—		
(1) Zemindaries ...	52,581	38,414
4. Refunds and compensation for lands acquired :—		
(1) Zemindaries ...	6,449	5,263
5. Deposits :—		
(1) State ...	2,26,312	3,11,572
(2) Zemindaries ...	23,769	34,771
Total ...	2,50,081	3,46,343
6. Loans received :—		
(1) State ...	1,60,222	—
(2) Zemindaries ...	—	—
Total ...	1,60,222	—
7. Provident fund :—		
(1) State ...	21,472	—
(2) Zemindaries ...	1,895	
Total ...	23,367	—
8. Marriage Contribution from Nijtahabil :—		
(1) State ...	75,000	—
Total ...	25,93,182	25,90,046
GRAND TOTAL ...	35,65,848	36,55,196

Expenditure.	1341 T.E.	1342 T.E.
1. General Administration charges :—		
(a) State ...	5,45,910	5,01,942
(b) Zemindaries :—		
1. Cost of management ...	1,55,532	1,41,279
2. Cost of litigation ...	96,967	1,04,882
	2,52,499	2,46,161
Total ...	7,98,409	7,48,103
2. Revenue and Taxes on account of the Zemindaries ...	2,65,974	2,73,821
3. Public Works—(a) State ...	87,231	1,11,079
(b) Zemindaries ...	50,651	50,491
Total ...	1,37,882	1,61,570
4. Electric Light—State ...	17,700	17,125
5. Municipality—State ...	9,000	8,000
6. Education—(a) State ...	1,27,620	1,28,441
(b) Zemindaries ...	13,546	8,086
Total ...	1,41,166	1,36,527
7. Medical and Sanitation :—(a) State ...	65,360	94,070
(b) Zemindaries ...	14,035	11,156
Total ...	79,395	1,05,226
8. Survey and Settlement—(a) State ...	10,237	19,029
(b) Zemindaries ...	440	896
Total ...	10,677	19,925
9. Agriculture, Commerce and Industries—State ...	8,811	7,360
10. Religious Expenses—(a) State ...	45,696	57,149
(b) Zemindaries ...	6,337	6,471
Total ...	52,033	63,620
11. Sultanat—State ...	36,256	40,125
12. Purchase of Land Tenures :—		
(a) State ...	510	711
(b) Zemindaries ...	8,110	3,630
Total ...	8,620	4,341
13. Pension and Gratuity—(a) State ...	41,478	45,145
(b) Zemindaries ...	7,191	7,925
Total ...	48,669	53,070
14. Ordinary *Sansar* charges :—		
(a) His Highness's own and the late Maharaja's family ...	79,995	88,672
(b) Other branches of the Raj family ...	1,31,181	1,24,202
(c) Thakurs ...	33,791	32,199
(d) *Sansar* office establishment ...	11,446	13,676
(e) Miscellaneous ...	39,507	51,949
Total ...	2,95,920	3,10,698
15. Charity and Donation :—(a) State ...	18,950	15,636
(b) Zemindaries ...	5,740	4,540
Total ...	24,690	20,176
16. His Highness's Nij Tahabil :—		
(a) State ...	1,09,000	1,00,000
(b) Zemindaries ...	50,000	—
Total ...	1,59,000	1,00,000
17. His Highness's tour—State ...	19,358	68,000
18. Payment of liabilities and deposits :—		
(a) State ...	57,604	1,90,957
(b) Zemindaries ...	36,598	1,23,626
Total ...	94,202	3,14,583
19. Miscellaneous—(a) State ...	2,440	9,146
(b) Zemindaries ...	6,646	3,703
Total ...	9,086	12,849
20. Advances to employees :—(a) State ...	175	—
(b) Zemindaries ...	995	837
Total ...	1,170	837
21. Expenditure in connection with H. H.'s Marriage, Investiture, Installation etc.—State ...	55,112	—
22 Investment—(a) State ...	—	—
(b) Zemindaries ...	30,000	—
Total ...	30,000	—
23. Write off of irrecoverable advances ...	18,710	10,000
24. Repayment of old debts—State ...	1,78,858	1,33,649
25. Pay of the discharged officers ...	—	40,310
Total Expenditure ...	25,00,698	26,49,915
26 Closing Balance :—		
(a) State		
In Cash ...	93,623	1,39,368
At Bank ...	20,627	5,076
In bonds and advances ...	5,36,765	5,21,639
Total ...	6,51,015	6,66,083
(b) Zemindaries :—		
In Cash ...	92,027	97 853
At Bank ...	1,36,188	49,651
In bonds and advances ...	1,85,920	1,91,694
Total ...	4,14,135	3,39,198
Total of State & Zemindaries' balances ...	10,65,150	10,05,281
Total of State & Zemindaries' expenditure ...	25,00,698	26,49,915
GRAND TOTAL ...	35,65,848	36,55,196

189. The year opened with a balance of Rs. 10,65,150 against Rs. 9,72,666 in the year before. During the year under report, the total receipts from all sources including deposits, loans and law charges recovered, amounted to Rs. 25,90,046 against Rs. 25,93,182 in the previous year. Thus the total sum available for expenditure including the opening balançe was Rs. 36,55,196 against Rs. 35,65,848. The actual income including receipts under debt-heads amounted to Rs. 22,43,703 against Rs. 20,84,512 showing an increase of Rs. 1,59,191.

Receipts.

190. The total expenditure incurred during the year amounted to Rs. 26,49,915 against Rs. 25,00,698 in the year before, showing an increase of Rs. 1,49,217. The year closed with a balance of Rs. 10,05,281 of which Rs. 2,37,221 represented actual cash in the treasuries while the balance of Rs. 7,68,060 was in the banks and in loans and advances.

Expenditure.

191. The noticeable variations in expenditure are explained below :—

i. ADMINISTRATION CHARGES :—

STATE—The actual decrease was Rs. 43,968. The decrease was due to the general curtailment of expenditure under the establishment charges.

ZEMINDARIES—The decrease was Rs. 6,338. The decrease was due to general curtailment of expenditure under the establishment charges.

ii. REVENUE AND TAXES :—

ZEMINDARIES—The increase was Rs. 7,847. This was due to payment of arrears of previous year.

iii. PUBLIC WORKS :—

STATE—The increase was Rs. 23,848. The increase was mainly due to progress of some works which were postponed in previous years for want of funds.

ZEMINDARIES—The decrease is negligible.

iv. ELECTRIC LIGHT :—

The slight decrease was due to general curtailment of expenditure.

v. MUNICIPALITY :—

The slight decrease in expenditure was due to curtailment of some expenditure.

vi. EDUCATION :—

STATE—The increase was mainly due to the travelling expenses of Maharajkumar Durjoy Kishore Deb Burman Bahadur who was prosecuting his studies in the Ajmer Mayo College.

ZEMINDARIES—The decrease was mainly due to curtailment of expenditure.

vii. MEDICAL AND SANITATION :—

STATE—The increase was Rs. 28,710. The increase was mainly due to the treatment of Maharajkumari Basantaprava Debi in Switzerland.

ZEMINDARIES—The slight decrease was due to curtailment of expenditure.

viii. SURVEY AND SETTLEMENT :—

STATE—The increase was Rs. 8,792. This was due to the expenditure incurred in connection with the Topographical survey of the State by the Survey of India authority.

ZEMINDARIES—The slight increase was due to extra provision of pay for the staff.

ix. AGRICULTURE, COMMERCE AND INDUSTRIES :—

STATE—The slight decrease was due to the abolition of the Kashipur Agricultural farm.

x. RELIGIOUS EXPENDITURE :—

STATE—The increase was Rs. 11,453. The provision was almost the same as that of the previous year. But all the expenditure incurred in the previous year could not be paid in that year. This accounts for the comparative increase in the year under report.

xi. SULTANAT :—

The increase was due to extra staff and some miscellaneous expenditure.

xii. PURCHASE OF LAND TENURES .—

STATE—The increase was due to purchase of lands generally under rent-sale.

xiii. PENSION AND GRATUITY :—

The increase was due to retirement of officers both in the State and the Zemindaries.

xiv. ORDINARY SANSAR CHARGES :—

The increase was Rs. 14,778. Additional provision for Her Highness the Maharani Saheba and party and expenditure incurred in connection with the treatment of Her Highness the Sixth Dowager Maharani Saheba account partly for the increase. A considerable amount of expenditure though provided for in the budget, could not be paid in the previous year. This also accounts partly for the increase in the year under report.

xv. CHARITY AND DONATION :—

The slight decrease is negligible.

xvi. HIS HIGHNESS'S TOUR AND NIJTAHABIL :—

STATE—The increase was due to extra provision for tour.

ZEMINDARIES—No provision was made in the year under report.

xvii. PAYMENT OF LIABILITIES AND DEPOSITS :—

STATE—The increase was Rs. 1,33,353. The increase was mainly due to payment of old deposits.

ZEMINDARIES :—The increase was Rs. 87,028. This was due to repayment of the overdraft received from the Imperial Bank of India.

xviii. MISCELLANEOUS :—

The slight increase was in connection with some unforeseen expenditure.

192. Two comparative statements of the receipts and the expenditure of the State and the Zemindaries with the respective revised estimates are given in appendices XXVI and XXVII.

193. In the State the actual receipt shows an increase of Rs. 2,25,680 and Rs. 13,783 the Original and the Revised Budget estimates respectively.

194. In the Zemindaries the actual receipts fell short of the Original Budget estimate by Rs. 634.

195. Babu Jatindra Nath Mitra continued to be in charge of the Accounts and Treasury Departments till the end of the year.

CHAPTER VI—MEDICAL.

196. With the abolition of three and opening of one in the interior, the number of dispensaries stood at 18 including the V. M. Hospital at the capital at the end of the year under review.

New patients.

197. The total number and daily average of new patients treated in all these dispensaries rose by 170 and 151 respectively as shewn in the following comparative statement.

	1341 T. E.			1342 T. E		
	Outdoor.	Indoor.	Total.	Outdoor.	Indoor.	Total.
PATIENTS.	1,27,550	793	1,28,343	1,27,755	758	1,28,513
Daily average	348·49	2·16	350 65	350·01	2·15	352·16

Outdoor attendance.

198. The total number of out-patients (new & old) was 2,14,461 as against 2,30,381 in the preceding year, with a daily average of 644·6 against 629·68.

Indoor patients.

199. With the previous year's balance of 20, the in-patients totalled 758 as against 793 of the year before. Of them 547 were cured, 164 were relieved or otherwise discharged, 27 died and 20 remained under treatment at the end of the year.

Surgical Operations.

200. The total number of surgical operations performed during the year stood at 1,262 including 15 majors, as against 1360 and 8 respectively of the year previous.

Police cases.

201. There were 184 admissions against 162 in the preceding year including 21 *post mortem* cases against 14.

V. M. Hospital.

202. The new out-patients in the V. M. Hospital totalled 18,439 as against 15,888 in the year before, the daily average of new and old patients being 98·28 against 83·65. The in-patients numbered 497 as against 458 with daily average

of 17·58 against 18·60 in the preceding year. Of the total number, 326 were discharged cured, 134 were relieved or otherwise discharged, 24 died and 13 remained under treatment at the close of the year. The total expenditure incurred in the Institution was Rs. 8,472-1-0 against Rs. 9,192-5-3.

Ayurvedic Department.

203. As previously, Kaviraj Surendra Chandra Bhattacharjee, Baidyaratna, alone remained in charge of this Department. He treated 52 patients during the year under report as against 42 of the year before. The total expenditure in this Department on account of his salary and the cost of medicines amounted to Rs. 2,937-11-6 against Rs. 2,404-11-6 in the previous year

Homoeopathic Department.

204. As before, there were two Assistant Homœopaths who treated 16,686 patients against 13,894 in the year before, the daily average, new and old, being 80·87 against 64·26. The total expenditure was Rs. 2,226-15-3 against Rs. 2,226-8-3.

Vaccination.

205. The total number of persons vaccinated throughout the State was 7,257 while the number of successful vaccinations was 5,723 in the year under review as against 5,845 and 4,503 respectively in the preceding year.

206. 32 vaccinators were employed during the year under the supervision of two small-pox doctors and two inspectors. The total expenditure on this account stood at Rs. 1,286 8-6 against Rs. 1,554-6-0 of the year before.

Kala-azar.

207. During the year under review, 269 Kala-azar patients were treated; of them 175 were cured, 72 were relieved or otherwise discharged, 7 died and 15 remained under treatment at the close of the year.

Public Health.

208. Neither cholera nor small-pox broke out in any part of the State in virulent form. 36 deaths from cholera were reported during the year. 6 persons were attacked with small-pox out of which only one died. On the otherhand, chicken-pox broke out in Dharmanagar, Kailashahar and Sadar Divisions.

Staff.

209. Dr. M. M. Majumdar, L. M. S., Chief Medical Officer continued to be in charge of the Medical Department. Dr. S. K. Dutt, L. M. S., Assistant State Physician and Dr. A. Sen Gupta, M. B., Bacteriologist, were his assistants. In addition, there was a staff of medical subordinates in different places and 3 midwives in the capital town.

Inspection.

210. Drs. M. M. Majumdar, S. K. Dutt and A. Sen Gupta inspected Khowai, Radhakishorepur, Sonamura, Dharmanagar, Kailashahar and Kamalpur Dispensaries and were out for 17 days altogether.

Total Expenditure.

211. The total expenditure in the Medical Department in the year under report amounted to Rs. 64,070 against Rs. 65,360.

CHAPTER—VII—PUBLIC INSTRUCTION.

Charge.

212. Mr. S. C. Deb Barman, M. A. (Harvard), Senior Naib Dewan, continued to be in charge of the Education Department.

Number of Schools.

213. The total number of schools (including private schools) during the year under review was 205 against 213 in the previous year, and the total numerical strength 9,623 against 9,230 including 1,823 pupils reading in private institutions numbering 53 as against 34 in the preceding year.

H. E. Schools.

214. There were 5 H. E. Schools as before and one Branch H. E. School in the State, *viz*:—the Umakanta Academy at Agartala, the Radhakishore Institution at Kailashahar, the Brajendrakishore Institution at Bilonia, the Bir Bikram Institution at Dharmanagar, the Navadwip Chandra Institution at Sonamura and the Branch H. E. School at Udaipur. All the H. E. Schools are permanently affiliated to the Calcutta University. Class IX was opened in the year before last provisionally in the Branch H. E. School at Udaipur on condition that the public would bear the additional cost of maintaining extra staff. The total number of pupils in all these institutions was 1,410 as against 1,450 in the previous year, and the average daily attendance

Matriculation Examination.

215. Agartala, the capital of the State, continued to be a centre for the Matriculation Examination. Generally the State H. E. Schools are allowed to send up candidates to this centre. One private student and one candidate from Bramhanbaria Annada H. E. School in Tippera District sat for the Examination in this centre in the year under report in addition to the candidates from the State schools.

216. The Examination was conducted under the direct control and supervision of the Minister of the State. The Department looked after the convenience of the candidates, coming from *Mofussil*, in respect of accommodation and other necessary matters.

Result of the Matriculation Examination.

217. Altogether 74 candidates were sent up for the Matriculation Examination from the State H. E. Schools against 71 in the previous year. The result of the Examination is given below :—

	No. sent up.	Passed.	1st Division.	2nd Division.	3rd Division.
1. U. K. Academy	28	22	3	15	4
2. R. K. Institution	10	7	5	2	0.
3. B. K. Institution	20	10	3	7	0
4. B. B. Institution	10	10	4	6	0
5. N. Ch. Institution	6	5	3	1	1
Total ...	74	54	18	31	5

218. The percentage of successful candidates was 72·97 against 59·6 in the previous year. The percentage of passes in the 1st. Division on the total number of passes was the highest for the R. K. Institution *viz*. 77, and lowest for the U. K. Academy. *viz*. 13. It is noticeable that in this respect the latter Institution has been steadily deteriorating.

219. The three successful candidates topping the list so far as the State was concerned, were awarded scholarships of Rs. 15, Rs. 10 and Rs. 8 per month in order of merit.

M. E. Schools for boys.

220. In the year under review, there were 8 Middle English Schools for boys with 983 pupils on the rolls, against 8 schools with 950 pupils in the previous year. The average daily attendance was 762·22 against 717·34 in the previous year.

M. E. Schools for girls.

221. There was one M. E. School for girls at Agartala, namely, the Maharani Tulsibati Girls' School, the numerical strength of which was 89 as against 85 in the previous year and the average daily attendance was 66·33 against 51·95. By special permission of this Department, some girls were allowed to continue higher studies in this school under the tuition of the Head Mistress. For the conveyance of the girls, motor bus service was continued as before.

H. V. Schools.

222. There was only one Higher Vernacular School for boys as in the previous year, with 77 students on the roll as against 80, the average daily attendance being 62·02 against 58·76 in the year previous.

L. V. Schools

223. The total number of Lower Vernacular Schools for boys was 23 against 25 in the previous year. The total numerical strength was 1,413 against 1,502 and the average daily attendance 1,104·48 against 1,110·30 in the previous year. In some of these schools, boys and girls read together.

Pathshalas for boys.

224. There were 87 *Pathshalas* for boys against 150 in the previous year. The total number of boys was 2,666 against 4,545 and the average daily attendance was 1,957·19 against 2,990·27. In some of these schools, boys and girls read together. Under special orders of the Education Department, some boys of some of these institutions were allowed to read the Lower Vernacular standard.

Pathshalas for girls

225. There were 9 *Pathshalas* for girls in the year under review against 10 in the previous year. The total numerical strength was 273 as against 291 and the average daily attendance was 226·72 against 232·38 in the year preceding. In some of these schools, some girls were allowed, under special orders, to read the Lower Vernacular standard.

Scholarship Examination.

226. Altogether 799 candidates appeared at the different scholarship examinations of this State against 788 in the previous year. Of these, 560 candidates including 59 girls came out successful. The result on the whole, particularly that of the M. E. Scholarship Examination was found to be satisfactory. 51 students passed the M. E. Examination and 2 boys passed the H. V. Examination this year. In the L. V. Examination, the number of successful candidates was 159 including 18 girls, and in the *Pathshala* Examination the number was 348 including 41 girls. Amongst these candidates, 7 appeared from different *Moktabs* and *Madrassas* of the State. On the results of the Examinations, 14 boys and 3 girls were awarded monthly scholarship varying from Rs. 2 to Rs. 5 tenable for two to four years.

227. In the year under review, there were, as before, 12 schools for special training, consisting of 4 Sanskrit *Tols*, 7 *Madrassas* and *Moktabs* and one *Silpasram* (Artisan School.) The Sanskrit *Tols* had 39 students on the rolls against 43 in the previous year and the average daily attendance was 30·01 against 30·25. The *Rajakiya Sanskrit Vidyalaya* at Agartala sent up 5 candidates for the Government Sanskrit Intermediate and Preliminary Examinations against 4 in the preceding year, and one for Preliminary Sanskrit Examination in *Smriti* and one for Title Examination in *Vyakarana* of the *Saraswat Samaj*, in the year under report.

Schools for special training.

228. The result of the examination was satisfactory. 2 passed the Government Intermediate Examination in *Kavya* and one Govt. Preliminary Examination in *Vyakarana*. Both the candidates who appeared at the Examination of the *Saraswat Samaj* came out successful.

229. The *Madrassas* and *Moktabs* had 388 students on the rolls as against 238 in the previous year and the average daily attendance was 300.82 against 160.51.

230. Free Compulsory Primary Education was introduced under the State Act 2 of 1312 T. E. in the Agartala Municipal area since the 1st of Magh under orders of His Highness the Maharaja Manikya Bahadur. Consequently 4 free Primary Schools were started, the U. K. Academy building, Tulsibati Girls' School building, Bejoy Kumar M. E. School house and Thakurpalli L. V. School house providing for their accommodation, each for each, during the morning hours.

Free Compulsory Primary School.

231. The subjoined statement will show the number of students, their communities and their average attendance in the year under review :—

Schools.	No. of Students.		Average daily attendance		Kumars.	Thakurs.	Tripura.	Laskar.	Manipuri.	Bengali Hindu.	Mahommedan
	Boys	Girls.	Boys.	Girls.							
1. No. 1 U. K. Academy	101	83	64·45	50.12	1	2	4	0	0	160	17
2. No. 2 Tulsibati	12	80	5·50	30.45	0	6	6	0	0	80	0
3. No. 3 Bejoy Kumar	12	93	5·50	51.85	0	21	15	0	1	67	1
4. No. 4 Thakur Palli	29	8	20 23	0	0	24	10	0	0	3	0
	154	264	95·64	132·37	1	53	35	0	1	310	18

232. The comparative statement below will show the number of non-Bengalee students receiving education in the several schools of the State :—

Serial number.	Nationality.	Number of students.		Remarks.
		Past year.	Present year.	
1.	Rajkumars	14	4	
2.	Thakurs	163	213	
3.	Manipuris	744	634	
4.	Tripuras	1300	1053	
5.	Reangs	31	0	
6.	Kukis	41	1	
7.	Chakmas	1	2	
8.	Lushais	5	1	
9.	Others...	41	96	
10.	Christians	0	0	
	Total	2,340	2,004	

233. Reward Examination for hill boys was not held during the year.

Reward Examinatin for hill boys.

234. Maharajkumar Durjoy Kishore Deb Barman Bahadur appeared at the Diploma Examination from the Mayo College, Ajmer, and came out successful. He was placed under the special care of Mr. V. A. S. Stow, M. A., I. E. S., V. D., the Principal of the college, and continued his studies under a graduate B. T. teacher as before. The educational progress and health of the Maharajkumar were satisfactory. The Department takes the opportunity to express its appreciation of the kind care taken by the Principal in the general welfare of the Maharajkumar. The Maharajkumar has since joined the Post Diploma Course of the same college.

Education of Princes and Princesses.

235. The Maharajkumaris received their education, as before, under a graduate lady teacher and a Pandit. Special arrangement was made for the education of Maharajkumar Karna Kishore Deb Barman Bahadur as before at Agartala.

236. Kumar Anilendra Chandra Deb Barman Bahadur passed the I. A. Examination this year from the Comilla Victoria College.

Education of other Kumars.

237. The Rajkumar Boarding house at Comilla had 15 inmates of whom 12 were from the different branches of the Ruling family and the remaining 3 were Rana Bahadurs, related to the Raj family. 11 of the inmates were reading in the Comilla Zilla School, one in the Comilla Iswar Pathsala and 3 in the Victoria College, Comilla.

Kumar Boarding House at Comilla.

238. Maharajkumar Hemanta Kishore Deb Barman Bahadur passed the I. Sc. Examination this year. Arrangements are being made for his training in the Roorkee College. The boarders were placed under the charge of a Superintending Tutor, who, in addition to his tutorial work, looked after the management of the boarding house. Three other private tutors including a Pandit, were engaged for coaching the Kumars in the morning and evening.

239. Thakur boys receiving higher education were awarded stipends from the Education Department.

Education of Thakur boys.

240. During the earlier part of the year under report, the number of boarders in the Thakur Boarding House was 28 which came down to 21 in the later part of the year, against 28 in the previous year. The staff consisted of one Guardian Superintendent, one Resident Tutor, one assistant tutor and one Manager Tutor. The average daily attendance of the boarders was 25·2 against 26·11 in the previous year.

Thakur Boarding House at Agartala.

241. There were altogether 18 boarders in the old Tripura Boarding House against 17 in the previous year. All these 18 boarders received free boarding and lodging and were reading in different classes from class IV to Matriculation class. A whole-time Superintending Tutor looked after the boys and managed the affairs of the boarding as before and

Tripura Boarding House at Agartala

another tutor was engaged to coach the boys in the morning. There was a small library in the boarding house and the boys were encouraged in agricultural pursuits within the boarding compound. One Tripura boy belonging to the old Tripura Boarding House was sent up for the Matriculation Examination this year, but he failed to pass the examination. For want of accommodation in the old Tripura Boarding house there was in addition a newly started boarding house with 27 Tripura boys of lower classes in the year. Of these 3 were allowed stipends. A manager tutor was engaged to look after the boarding and to coach the boys both in the morning and evening in addition.

Tripura Boarding House at Khowai.

242. There were 47 boarders in the Tripura Boarding House at Khowai against 41 in the previous year, some receiving free boarding. Two tutors were appointed for coaching the boys both in the morning and the evening and one of the tutors was engaged to look after the boarding.

Ramkumar Boarding School at Kalyanpur.

243. A new L. V. School named Ramkumar Boarding School was started at Kalyanpur during the year on the occasion of His Highness's visit there. There were 32 boarders on the roll and the daily average attendance was 27·98. Two tutors were appointed for coaching them both in the morning and evening.

School for convicts.

244. There were 21 convicts reading in the Primary School in the Central Jail, out of which 5 appeared in the Scholarship Examination in the year under report and 4 came out successful.

Woodburn Artisan School & Silpasram.

245. The Woodburn Artisan School and Silpasram had on the roll 23 students against 26 in the preceding year. In the year under review the average daily attendance was 10·54 against 11·43 in the previous year. There were 12, 5 and 6 students in the Carpentry, Black-smith and Brass-smith Sections respectively. The sub-joined statement will show the number of students, their classes and their average attendance in the year under review. 14 students were awarded monthly stipends varying from Rs. 1-8 to Rs. 8 each.

Name of School	Number of Students	Thakurs	Tripura	Laskar	Manipuri	Bengali Hindu	Mahomedan	Others.	Average attendance
Woodburn Artisan School and Silpasram ...	23	5	—	1	2	11	3	1	11·54

3 boys left the school.

Night School at Agartala.

246. During the year 12 students from the trading and labouring classes received instruction in the Night School at Agartala under the auspices of the local students' association. The monthly grant had to be discontinued due to the financial stringency.

247. 30 students were awarded special stipends in the year under review of whom 17 read in different schools of this State and the remaining 13 prosecuted their studies elsewhere in different schools, colleges and technical institutions.

Special Stipends.

248. The Senior Naib Dewan, inspected some schools and was out on tour for 38 days including his visit on deputation to several states in Orissa in the year under review. There were three Sub-Inspectors of schools as before who inspected all the schools within their respective jurisdictions in Sadar, Khowai, Kailashahar and Dharmanagar Divisions. Their inspection work was satisfactory. Revenue and Forest Inspectors visited and inspected the schools in the remaining Divisions.

Inspection Work.

249. Maharajkumar Narottam Kishore Deb Barman Bahadur continued to be the Librarian of the Bir Chandra Library at Agartala which was maintained in two separate sections as before, *viz* :—(1) the English section, located in the Ujjayanta Palace, and (2) the Vernacular Section in the building, near the local H. E. School. The latter section was open to the public The number of English books (including foreign literature) was 5,025 and that of the Bengali and Sanskrit books was 2,207 as before. In the year under report there were 4 daily newspapers as before and 2 weeklies against 1 and 5 monthlies against 4. The average daily attendance in the Vernacular section of the library was 13·8 against 13 in the previous year and the total number of books issued to the public was 2,658 against 3,765.

Library.

250. The total expenditure on public instruction in the year under report amounted to Rs. 1,28,441 against Rs. 1,27,620. Details of expenditure are noted below :—

Expenditure.

1.	Primary Education	Rs.	27,825
2.	Secondary Education	,,	49,654
3.	Schools for Special Training	,,	2,022
	(a) Compulsory Free Primary Education	,,	276
4.	Boarding Institutions for Thakur boys ...	,,	7,315
5.	Education of Kumars & Kumaris ...	,,	26,159
6.	Scholarships and Stipends	,,	6,942
7.	Library	,,	1,744
8.	Tripura Boarding	,,	2,435
9.	Miscellaneous	,,	4,069
		Rs.	1,28,441

251. The total receipts from the schools amounted to Rs. 14,086 against Rs. 14,502 in the previous year.

Income.

CHAPTER VIII—ZEMINDARIES.

Chakla Roshnabad Estates.

Management.

252. The management of His Highness's Zemindaries in British India continued in the hands of Dewan Bahadur B. K. Sen, M. A., B. L., up to the 11th of Bhadra. Manyabara Rana Bodhjung Bahadur took over charge from him on that date and was in charge of the Zemindaries up to the 4th Agrahayan. He made over charge to Manyabara Rai J. C. Sen Bahadur, B. A., B. C. S. (retired) who was in charge for the rest of the year. The Manager was assisted by a Deputy Manager at Comilla and three Assistant Managers posted at Feni, Mogra and Srimangal.

The year and the tenantry.

253. The all-round economic depression noticed in the previous years continued to have its adverse effects, during the year under review, both on the *Raj* and the tenants—the low prices of jute and paddy being the principal reasons of such depression. Relief was given, as in previous years, to the ***Talukdars*** and other tenants in the shape of general remission of interest etc. during the 2nd and the last ***kists*** of the year, as well as remissions in particular deserving cases occasionally. The policy of allowing petty demands to be time-barred was also continued.

Demand.

254. The gross revenue demand of the year was Rs. 10,22,733 against Rs. 10,22,914 in the previous year.

Receipts.

255. The total receipts amounted to Rs. 9,29,366 (including Rs. 5,432 on account of the Tripura Raj Central Co-operative Bank Ltd. and Rs. 1,802 on account of *Debottar mohals*) against Rs. 8,72,924 in the previous year.

Expenditure.

256. The total expenditure in the year under review was Rs. 10,04,303 including repayment of old debts and deposits to the extent of Rs. 1,23,626 together with a contribution of Rs. 2,50,000 to the State. The total expenditure during the previous year was Rs. 8,29,784. Of the total expenditure during the year under review, Rs. 2,73,821 was on account of Land Revenue, taxes and cesses while the total administration charges of the zemindaries including Public works and Law charges amounted to Rs. 3,09,176 against Rs. 3,17,427 in the previous year, showing a further curtailment of over Rs. 8000.

257. The following other items of expenditure aggregating Rs. 4,21,306 are noticeable :—

1.	Loans and advances	Rs.	837
2.	Donation	,,	4,540
3.	Medical charges	,,	11,156
4.	Education charges	,,	8,086
5.	Religious ceremonies	,,	6,471
6.	Sansar stipends	,,	12,960
7.	Repayment of old deposits	,,	14,123
8.	Contribution to the State	,,	2,50,000
9.	Repayment of old debts	,,	1,69,503
10.	Purchase of property...	,,	3,630
		Rs.	4,21,306

258. The result of the year's settlement operations will appear from the figures noted below :—

Settlement.

	Kinds of settlement.	Addition to rental.	Nazar.
1.	Ry. relinquished land	—	—
2.	*Kaimi* and *Takshishi* settlement in the Comilla Town ...	Rs. 165	Rs. 11,173
3.	Ordinary Town Settlement ...	" 28	" 1,327
4.	*Khas Patit*	" 341	" 3.791
5.	Enhancement of rent	" 1,501	" 5,512
6.	Re-settlement of auction purchased holdings ...	" 46	" 5,474
7.	Settlement of rent free holding	—	—
8.	*Takshishi Taluk* in the *Moffusil*	" 4	" 54
9.	*Ijara* settlement	—	—
		Rs. 2,085	Rs. 27,331

CHAPTER IX—MISCELLANEOUS.

259. The third part of the *Rajmala*, Chronicles of the State, could not be published in the year under report in the absence of necessary maps and sketches printing of which was delayed for financial difficulties. The fourth part was in the press but sufficient progress could not be made with it owing to the increased demand on the press from various quarters. Materials for the compilation of the fifth part were under collection during the year. The total expenditure amounted to Rs. 3,995.

Rajmala.

260. Dewan B. K. Sen Bahadur, Dewan Shashan, was in camp for 30 days during the year under review. Manyabara Rana Bodhjung Bahadur, who was in charge of Dewan Shashan's office for sometime, went out for 3 days ; while Rai J. C. Sen Bahadur, Minister, was in tour for 33 days both in and outside the State.

Tours of High Officials—Dewan-Shashan and Minister.

261. Manyabara Rana Bodhjung Bahadur, F. R. G. S., Chief Secretary, was in Camp with His Highness the Maharaja Manikya Bahadur in all his tours during the year under review.

262. Mr. S. C. Deb Barman, M. A. (Harvard), Senior Naib Dewan, and Thakur K. K. Singh, Naib Dewan were out on tour for 14 days and 15 days respectively.

Tours.

263. The tours of the Divisional Officers and their assistants are noted below :—

State.

1. Sadar—

Sadar Collector	—Thakur Rebati Mohan Deb Barman	...	25 days.
Asst. "	Babu Jogendra Lal Ganguly, B. L.	...	57 "
" "	Kumar Narsingh Chandra Deb Barman Bahadur	...	41 "

2. Kailashahar—
Divisional Officer—Babu Akhil Chandra Majumdar, M. A., B. L. ... 17 days.
Second „ „ Jyotirmay Ghose, M. A. ... 21 „

3. Sonamura—
Divisional Officer—Babu Sasanka Bhusan Ray, M. A. ... 27 „

4. Belonia—
Divisional Officer—Late Babu Kunja Behari Chakravarty, M. A., B. L. ... 18 „
„ „ Babu Surendra Chandra Guha, B. A. ... 10 „
Second „ Kumar Bhupendra Chandra Deb Barman Bahadur, B. A. ... 9 „
„ „ Thakur Kamal Krishna Deb Barman ... 36 „

5. Khowai—
Divisional Officer—Babu Suresh Chandra Chakravarty, B. L. ... 40 „

6. Dharmanagar—
Divisional Officer—Thakur Lalit Mohan Deb Barman, M. A., B. L. ... 33 „

7. Udaipur—
Divisional Officer—Thakur Gokul Chandra Deb Barman ... 8 „
Second „ Thakur Joysing Deb Barman, B. A. ... 73 „

8. Sabroom—
Divisional Officer—Babu Sarada Charan Sarkar, M. A., B. L. ... 31 „

Zemindaries.

1. Babu Pramada Ranjan Bhattacharjee, B. A., Deputy Manager, Chakla Roshnabad Estates, Comilla ... 37 days.
2. Babu Jagadish Chandra Majumdar, M. A., B. L., Assistant Manager, Feni ... 97 „
3. Babu Tarit Mohan Gupta, Assistant Manager, Mogra ... 52 „
4. Babu Surendra Nath Bose, B. L., Assistant Manager, Srimangal ... 14 „
5. Babu Bisweswar Guha, Assistant Manager Srimangal ... 19 „

DATED, AGARTALA,
The 3rd November, 1933.

Jyotis Chandra Sen,
MINISTER.

APPENDIX.

List of the principal Laws and Regulations in force in the Tripura State during 1342 T. E.

Description.	Whether adapted from British Indian Acts.	Whether introduced during the year under report.
CRIMINAL.		
1. Regulation No. III. of 1280 T. E.		
2. Regulation No. I. of 1283 T. E.		
3. Jail Regulation, 1283 T. E.		
4. Regulation No. IV. of 1283 T. E. (Cattle trespass and pound).		
5. Regulation No. III. of 1296 T. E. (Police Regulation).		
6. Act No. IV. of 1321 T. E.--Penal Laws (an amending Act)		
CIVIL.		
1 Civil Law of 1284 T. E.		
2. Rules regarding *chit* suits (small causes) 1287 and 1300 T. E.		
3. Act No. II. of 1313 T. E.—an Act for the regulation of interest on debts.		
4. Act No. II. of 1314 T. E.—Limitation Act	Partly adapted	
5. Succession Act II of 1339 T. E.		
REVENUE.		
1. Act No. I. of 1290 T. E.—Sale Law		
2. Act No. I. of 1296 T. E.—Tenancy Act.		
3. Act No. II. of 1296 T. E.—*Abkari*		
4. Act No. II. of 1297 T. E.—Reserved forests.		
5. Act No. I. of 1304 T. E.—Duties on *til* and cotton.		
6. Act No. I. of 1306 T. E.—Registration	Do.	
7. Survey and Settlement Act, 1309 T.E.	Do.	
8. *Tuccavi* Regulation, 1310 T. E.		
9. Act No. I. of 1313 T. E.—Forests.		
10. Act No. I. of 1314 T. E.—(amending the above)		
11. A Law imposing export duty on jute and mustard-seed, 1317 T. E.		
12. Act No. II. of 1321 T.E. Ghasuri Act		
13. P. W. & Road Cess Act IV of 1339 T. E.		
MISCELLANEOUS.		
1. An Act promulgating certain rules as Law, 1283 T. E.		
2. Regulation for the record of judicial decisions &c., 1284 T. E.		
3 Municipal Regulation, 1284 T. E.		
4. Legal Practitioners' Regulation.		
5. Act No. I. of 1297 T. E.—an Act for the regulation of commissions for the examination of witnesses.		
6. Regulation against cow slaughter		
7. Rules of evidence		
8. Act I. of 1318 T. E.—Constitution of Courts (an amending Act).		
9. Leave and allowance Rules	Do.	
10. Act No. I. of 1321 T. E.—Arms Act	Do.	
11. Act No. III. of 1321 T. E.—Constitution of Courts (an amending Act)		

Description.	Whether adapted from British Indian Acts.	Whether introduced during the year under report.
12. Municipal Act No. I of 1322 T. E.		
13. Revenue Sale Amendment Act—1323 T.E.		
14. An Act for the destruction of old records—1323 T. E.		
15. Act I of 1326 T. E.—Regulation regarding Privy Council Appeals.		
16. Act II of 1326 T. E.—Registration of Births and Deaths		
17. Act III of 1326 T. E.—Vaccination Act	Partly adapted.	
18. Act IV of 1326 T. E.—Public Demands Recovery Act	Do.	
19. Act V of 1326 T. E.—Excise Amendment Act	Do.	
20. Act I of 1327 T. E. Settlement of lands for tea cultivation		
21. Rules of Import and Sale of Opium—1327 T. E.		
22. Regulation No. 1 of 1328 T. E.—regarding Registration of Coolies		
23. Regulation No. 2 of 1328 T. E.—regarding Export of Tea		
24. Act I of 1329 T. E.—(Absconding sepoys Act)		
25. Act II of 1329 T. E.—(Control of prices of food stuff)		
26. Act III of 1329 T. E. (Elephants and buffaloes grazing Act)		
27. Act IV of 1329 T. E. (House tax on Hill tribes)		
28. Act V of 1329 T. E. (Legal practitioners, Act)	Do	
29. Act I of 1332 T. E.—Encumbered Estates Act.		
30. Act III of 1332 T. E.—The Opium and Intoxicating Drugs Act.		
31. Rules and Regulations under the Opium and Intoxicating Drugs Act III of 1332 T. E		
32. Act I of 1336 T. E.—(Hackney Carriages)		
33. Act II of 1336 T. E.—(Amending Act I of 1327)		
34. Act III of 1336 T. E.—(Amending the Survey & Settlement Regulation)		
35. Act IV of 1336 T. E.—(Prevention of gambling)		
36. Act I of 1337 T. E.—(Amending the State Tenancy Act I of 1296 T. E.)		
37. Land Acquisition Rules under Act I of 1337 T. E.		
38. State Motor Vehicles Act I of 1338 T. E.		
39. Act II of 1338 T. E. for prevention of smuggling of elephant tusks.		
40. State Stamp Act III of 1338 T. E.		
41. Tripura State Bank Act I of 1339 T. E.		
42. Census Act III of 1339 T. E.		
43. Act I of 1342 T. E.—providing for trial of certain criminal cases by Special Tribunal.		
44. Compulsory Primary Education Act II of 1342 T. E.		

II

Statement showing the strength, cost and other particulars of the Military Force in Tripura State for 1342 T. E.

Arm of service.	Number of fighting officers and men.					Details of force at the end of the current year.								Total cost on account of pay and allowances of the force, including followers.	Remarks.
			Casualties.						Number of men.						
									Commissioned Officers.						
	At the end of last year	Recruited this year.	Died.	Invalided.	Discharged, deserted, &c.	At the end of the current year.	Number of regiments, battalions, or Batteries.	Number of guns.	European.	Indian.	Non-commissioned officers.	Fighting men.	Buglers.		
1	2	3	4	5	6	7	8	9	10	11	12	13	14	15	16
Infantry ...	391	79	5	—	131	334	—	644	5	16	27	279	7		
Band Party	21	1	—	—	4	18	—	—	—	—	•2	16	—		
Total ...	412	80	5	—	135	352	—	644	5	16	29	295	7	Rs. 98,016	

III.

Statement showing the strength, cost, discipline, and education of the Police for the year 1342 T. E.

Description of office	Number	Grade of pay	Total cost	Punishments. Dismissed.	Punishments. Fined, degraded or suspended departmentally. F.	D.	S.	Punishments. Punished judicially.	Rewards. By promotion.	Rewards. By money.	Education. Number able to read and write.	Education. Number under instruction.	Remarks.
1	2	3	4	5	6			7	8	9	10	11	12
		Rs.			F.	D.	S.						
Superintendent of Police	1	250-0-0	Rs 85,242	—		—		—	—	—	1	—	F. = Fined.
Asst. Superintendent	1	100-5-125		—		—		—	—	—	1	—	D. = Degraded.
Inspectors	4	55-2-65 65 5/2-90		—		—		—	—	—	4	—	S. = Suspended.
Sub-Inspectors	23	25-2-45		—	2	1	0	—	—	6	23	—	
Naib Darogas	20	15-1-25		—	2	0	0	—	—	2	20	—	
Writer Constables	9	15-0-0		—		—		—	—	—	9	—	
Proby. Sub-Inspector	1	15 allowance		—		—		—	—	—	1	—	
Subedar	1	25-2-45		—		—		—	—	—	1	—	
Armed S. I.	1	25-2-45		—		—		—	—	—	1	—	
Jamadars (civil)	6	15-1-25		—	1	0	1	—	—	—	6	—	
Jamadar (Armed)	1	20-1-30		—		—		—	—	—	1	—	
Havildar	1	19-1-25		—	1	0	0	—		1	1	—	
Naiks	4	15-1-20		1	2	0	0	—	—	—	4	—	
Constables (Armed)	25	14-1-15		1	7	0	3	—	—	1	12	—	
Constables (Civil)	218	10 to 13		—	19	2	6	—	—	8	101	—	
Chaukidars	175	5-0-0		—	1	0	2	—	—	—	—	—	
Naib Darogas	5	15 and 5 allowance		—		—		—	—	—	5	—	
Total ..	496			2	35	3	12	—	—	18	183	—	

IV.

Statement showing the working of the Police in the Tripura State during the year 1342 T. E.

State.	Number of offences.		Number of accused arrested.		Number of accused sent up for trial.		Number of accused convicted.		Number of accused acquitted or discharged.		Percentage convicted of accused arrested.		Percentage convicted of accused sent up for trial.		REMARKS.
	Past year.	Present year.	Past year.	Present year.	Past year.	Present year.	Past year.	Present year.	Past year.	Present year.	Past year.	Present year.	Past year.	Present year.	
	2	3	4	5	6	7	8	9	10	11	12	13	14	15	16
Tripura State	1,300	1,198	925	827	835	943	284	223	217	309	30·97	26·96	65·71	* 60·60	* Excluding from col. 7 Pending trial— 411 Withdrawal— 43 Compromise— 86 Dead— 35 575

V.

Statement showing the value of property stolen and amount of recoveries in the Tripura State during the year 1342 T. E.

State.	Amount stolen.		Amount recovered		Percentage of recoveries of property stolen.		REMARKS.
	Past year.	Present year.	Past year.	Present year.	Past year.	Present year.	
1	2	3	4	5	6	7	8
Tripura State ...	Rs 20,558-9-9	Rs 18,282-6-0	Rs 4,600-6-0	Rs 2,692-12-9	22·83	14·73	

VI.

Statement showing the number of crimes committed, number of cases disposed of, and cases awaiting trial in the Tripura State during the year 1342 T. E.

Description of offences.		Number of offences. Balance from past year.	Number of offences. Committed during the present year.	Number of offences. Total.	Number of cases disposed of during the last year.	Number of cases disposed of during the present year.	Number of cases awaiting trial.	Number of persons apprehended.	Number of persons convicted.	Number of persons sentenced. Imprisonment. Simple.	Number of persons sentenced. Imprisonment. Rigorous.	Number of persons sentenced. Imprisonment and fine. Simple.	Number of persons sentenced. Imprisonment and fine. Rigorous.	Fine only.	Whipping.	Capital punishment.	Total.	Number of persons acquitted or discharged.	Number of persons confined being insane.	Number of persons died during or before trial.	Term of imprisonment. Under one month.	From 1 to below 2 months.	From 2 to below 3 months.	From 3 to below 6 months.	From 6 to below 12 months.	From 1 to below 2 years.	From 2 to below 3 years.	From 3 to below 5 years.	5 years and above.	Transportation.	Capital punishment.	Persons awaiting trial.	Remarks.
1		2	3	4	5	6	7	8	9	10	11	12	13	14	15	16	17	18	19	20	21	22	23	24	25	26	27	28	29	30	31	32	33
Class I. Offences against the State, public tranquillity, safety and justice &c.	cognizable ...	4	11	20	9	12	8	65	13	0	0	0	5	8	0		13	28	0	0	1	2	2	0	0	0	0	0	0	0	0	26	*a.* 8 persons were bound down under security.
	non-cognizable	7	50	57	33	51	6	58	a8	0	0	0	0	0	0	0	0	41	0	0	0	0	0	0	0	0	0	0	0	0	0	9	*b.* 2 persons were warned for the future.
Class II. Offences against person.	cognizable ...	88	290	378	250	282	96	572	b87	9	45	0	4	27	0	0	85	331	0	0	10	14	3	10	6	5	1	2	2	5	0	154	*c.* 16 persons were warned for the future and 6 bound down under security.
	non-cognizable	41	251	292	232	253	39	267	30	1	2	0	2	25	0	0	30	211	0	1	3	1	0	1	0	0	0	0	0	0	0	25	
Class III. Offences against property.	cognizable ...	220	811	1031	772	762	269	1760	361	16	54	0	25	244	0	0	339	950	0	2	30	20	8	18	10	4	0	4	1	0	0	447	*d.* 7 persons were warned for the future.
	non-cognizable	38	215	253	176	208	45	351	d36	5	6	0	3	15	0	0	29	263	0	0	4	3	5	2	0	0	0	0	0	0	0	52	*e.* 5 persons were warned for the future.
Class IV. Other offences.	cognizable ...	57	168	225	190	182	43	248	e81	3	7	0	3	63	0	0	76	107	0	0	2	2	3	1	0	1	2	1	1	0	0	60	*f.* One person was warned for the future and 3 persons were bound down under security.
	non-cognizable	57	234	291	201	230	61	182	f17	5	1	0	0	7	0	0	13	124	[illegible]	0	4	0	2	0	[illegible]	0	0	0	0	0	0	41	
Total cognizable ...		374	1280	1654	1221	1238	416	2645	542	28	106	0	37	342	0	0	513	1414	[illegible]	2	43	38	16	29	16	10	3	7	4	5	0	687	
Total non-cognizable ...		143	750	893	662	742	151	858	91	11	9	0	5	47	0	0	72	639	[illegible]	1	11	4	7	3	0	0	0	0	0	0	0	127	
GRAND TOTAL ...		517	2030	2547	1883	1980	567	3503	633	39	115	0	42	389	0	0	585	2053	0	3	54	42	23	32	16	10	3	7	4	5	0	814	

VII.

Statement showing the number of offences reported and dealt with by the various Courts in the Tripura State during the year 1342 T.E.

Name of Court.	Number of offences reported during. Last year.	Number of offences reported during. Present year.	Number of persons dealt with. Remaining at the end of last year.	Brought to trial during present year. Arrested by Police.	Upon warrant.	On summons.	Voluntary.	Arrested in presence of the Magistrate.	Total. Last year.	Total. Present year.	Persons disposed of. Discharged without trial.	Acquitted.	Convicted.	Committed or referred.	Died, escaped, or transferred &c.	Persons remaining at the end of the year.	Remarks.
1	2	3	4	5	6	7	8	9	10	11	12	13	14	15	16	17	18
Sadar Magistracy	538	513	145	211	246	187	20	0	617	809	224	198	186	* 16	2	183	* Of these, 3 persons were committed to the Special Tribunal and all of them were convicted.
Sonamura " ...	231	294	87	79	25	146	63	1	312	401	81	66	113	0	0	138	
Bilonia " ...	243	209	43	98	45	94	71	5	426	356	105	83	110	9	0	49	
Kailashahar " ...	273	262	175	141	64	116	9	0	567	505	211	78	61	5	0	150	
Khowai " ...	113	170	63	11	21	63	3	0	151	161	68	18	42	5	0	28	
Dharmanagar " ...	255	312	187	84	101	165	320	1	605	858	338	290	21	14	0	195	
Udaipur " ...	238	225	33	46	68	158	16	3	283	324	119	52	56	1	0	66	
Sabrum " ...	58	45	12	30	5	5	7	0	76	59	20	16	21	0	1	1	
TOTAL ...	1,949	2,030	745	700	575	934	509	10	3,037	3,173 a	1,199	801	610	50 b	3	810	

a. Excluding 30 persons pending before the Court of Sessions at the close of the previous year.

b. The total number of persons for trial before the Court of Sessions, including 30 persons pending from the last year together with the number before the Special Tribunal was 80, of whom 23 were convicted, 53 acquitted and 4 remained under trial at the close of the year.

VIII.

Statement of Criminal cases in which British Subjects were concerned for 1342 T. E.

Description of Offences.		Cases pending since the previous year.	Cases instituted during the year.	Total number of cases.	Cases in which complainants were British subjects.	Cases in which both parties were British subjects.	Cases in which defendants were British Subjects: Cases pending since the previous year	Cases instituted during the year.	Total number of cases.	Cases disposed of: Rejected, compromised or dismissed without enquiry.	Cases disposed of: Tried.	Cases pending at the close of the year.	Persons under trial at the close of the previous year.	Persons brought to trial during the year.	Total number of persons under trial.	Convicted.	Acquitted or discharged.	Died or escaped &c.	Under trial at the close of the year.
Class I. Offences against the State &c.	cognizable ...	2	2	4	1	1	1	2	3	1	1	1	0	4	4	1	2	1	0
	non-cognizable ...	0	2	2	1	0	0	1	1	1	0	0	0	1	1	0	1	0	0
Class II. Offences against person.	cognizable ...	8	17	25	2	15	8	15	23	10	9	4	15	26	41	13	27	0	1
	non-cognizable ...	4	26	30	4	2	3	23	26	21	2	3	0	28	28	7	21	0	0
Class III. Offences against property.	cognizable ...	45	255	300	19	95	46	235	281	43	147	91	41	403	444	242	111	0	91
	non-cognizable ...	5	36	41	3	13	5	33	38	26	5	7	11	14	25	2	19	0	4
Class IV. Other offences	cognizable ...	14	19	33	2	7	14	17	31	13	8	10	24	15	39	6	27	0	6
	non-cognizable ...	1	18	19	5	4	1	13	14	7	2	5	6	10	16	0	14	0	2
Total cognizable ...		69	293	362	24	118	69	269	338	67	165	106	80	448	528	262	167	1	98
Total non-cognizable ...		10	82	92	13	19	9	70	79	55	9	15	17	53	70	9	55	0	6
GRAND TOTAL ...		79	375	454	37	137	78	339	417	122	174	121	97	501	598*	271	222	1	104

REMARKS.

* Of this number, 85 persons were discharged without trial, the cases being dismissed, compromised or struck off on default. Excluding 1, who escaped and 104 undertrial at the close of the year, the actual number of persons tried was 408, of whom 271 were convicted, the percentage of conviction being 66.42 against 70.07 of the previous year.

IX.

Statement of Extradition Cases for the year 1342 T. E.

Names of Courts.	Nature of cases.	Number Borne on the Register.				Number Brought to Trial.			Result.		Number at large at the close of the year.	Number of persons awaiting trial (after arrest) at the close of the year.	Remarks.
		Number of persons at large at the close of the previous year.	Number of persons awaiting trial at the close of the previous year.	Number of persons against whom warrants were applied for during the year.	Total.	Number of persons arrested and surrendered within the year.	Number of persons who appeared of their own accord or were subsequently arrested in the State within the year.	Total (Columns 4+7+8).	Convicted.	Acquitted or discharged.			
Sadar Magistracy	Criminal breach of trust	0	5	20	25	0	0	5	5	0	20	0	* Committed to Sessions.
	Wrongful confinement	1	0	0	1	0	0	0	0	0	1	0	
	Escape from lawful custody	1	0	2	3	1	0	1	0	0	2	1	
	Theft	0	1	11	12	8	0	9	3	1	3	5	
	Dacoity	0	0	5	5	2	0	2	0	0	3	2	
	Rape	0	0	1	1	0	0	0	0	0	1	0	
	Criminal breach of trust by servant	0	0	1	1	0	1	1	1	0	0	0	
	Grievous hurt	0	0	3	3	0	3	3	0	3	0	0	
	Causing hurt	0	4	1	5	1	0	5	1	4	0	0	
	Desertion from First Tripura Bir Company	0	0	1	1	1	0	1	1	0	0	0	
Bilonia ,, ...	Theft and escape from lawful custody	1	0	0	1	0	0	0	0	0	1	0	
	Theft	13	0	20	33	4	14	18	9	8	15	1	
	Culpable homicide not amounting to murder	1	0	0	1	0	0	0	0	0	1	0	
	Theft and resistance to arrest	0	0	1	1	0	0	0	0	0	1	0	
	Theft and grievous hurt	0	0	19	19	0	16	16	0	0	3	16	
	Theft and causing hurt	0	0	1	1	0	0	0	0	0	1	0	
	Theft, resistance to lawful apprehension and murder ...	8	0	0	8	4	0	4	4	0	4	0	
Sonamura ,, ...	Theft	32	4	13	49	2	9	15	4	1	34	10	
	Theft and escape from lawful custody	0	0	1	1	1	0	1	1	0	0	0	
	Grievous hurt	0	0	1	1	0	0	0	0	0	1	0	
	Dacoity and mischief...	0	2	0	2	0	0	2	0	0	0	2	
	Murder	4	0	0	4	0	0	0	0	0	4	0	
Kailashahar ,, ...	Theft	7	0	8	15	7	0	7	5	1	8	1	
	Criminal breach of trust	0	0	1	1	0	0	0	0	0	1	0	
Dharmanagar ,, ...	Theft	7	1	0	8	0	0	1	1	0	7	0	
	Highway robbery	0	1	0	1	0	0	1	0	0*	0	0	
	Criminal trespass, assault with deadly weapons and theft ...	11	0	0	11	0	0	0	0	0	11	0	
	Theft and wrongful confinement	2	0	0	2	1	0	1	0	0	1	1	
	Arson	9	0	0	9	0	0	0	0	0	9	0	
Khowai ,, ...	Theft	0	0	2	2	0	0	0	0	0	2	0	
	Wrongful confinement	0	1	0	1	0	0	1	1	0	0	0	
Udaipur ,, ...	Theft and receiving stolen property	3	0	0	3	0	0	0	0	0	3	0	
	Murder	1	0	0	1	0	0	0	0	0	1	0	
Sabroom ,, ...	Theft	6	1	4	11	2	0	3	1	2	8	0	
	Escape from lawful custody	1	0	1	2	0	0	0	0	0	2	0	
	Resistance to arrest	0	7	0	7	0	0	7	7	0	0	0	
	Murder	0	0	1	1	0	0	1	0	1	0	0	
	Total ...	108	27	118	253	35	43	105	44	21	148	39	

C

X.

Statement showing the results of appeals against decisions passed by the Criminal Courts in the Tripura State during the year 1342 T. E.

Tribunals.	Number of applications	Number of persons and cases.																Remarks.
		Applications rejected.		Sentences.						Proceedings quashed.		Referred.		Further enquiry &c, ordered.		Pending.		
				Confirmed.		Modified.		Reversed.										
		Persons.	Cases.	Persons.	Cases.	Persons.	Cases.	Persons.	Cases.	Persons.	Cases.	Persons	Cases.	Persons	Cases.	Persons.	Cases.	
Khas Adalat ...	248	16	16	148	125	82	43	17	14	—	—	—	—	19	12	68	38	

XI.

Civil Work—Nature and value of original suits filed and disposed of during the year 1342 T. E.

Tribunal.	Opening balance.		Filed during the year, received by transfer or on remand.		Total.		Disposed of during the year.		Closing balance.	
	Past year.	Present year.	Past year.	Present year.	Past year.	Present year.	Past year.	Present year.	Past year.	Present year.
Khas Adalat Original side	67	64	28	15	95	79	31	30	64	49
Sadar Dewani Adalat	230	182	660	667	890	849	708	587	182	262
Sonamura ,,	56	61	193	208	249	269	188	187	61	82
Bilonia ,,	40	18	98	176	138	194	120	146	18	48
Kailashahar ,,	188	177	280	241	468	418	291	264	177	154
Khowai ,,	47	40	82	117	129	157	89	72	40	85
Dharmanagar ,,	58	77	177	216	235	293	158	218	77	75
Udaipur ,,	90	110	385	400	475	510	365	367	110	143
Sabrum ,,	12	4	16	17	28	21	24	13	4	8
Total ...	788	733	1,919	2,057	2,707	2,790	1,974	1,884	733	906

Tribunal.	Suits filed during present year.									Suits disposed of during present year.						Suits not estimable in money.	Remarks.
	Value.	Suits *re* landed property.	Suits for money transaction.	Suits for other rights.	Number of suits under Rs. 100.	Number of suits above Rs. 100 and under Rs. 500.	Number of suits above Rs. 500 and under Rs. 1,000.	Number of suits above Rs. 1,000 and under Rs. 5,000.	Number of suits above Rs. 5,000.	*Exparte.*	Admitted and compromised.	Struck off the file.	Otherwise disposed of.	Value.	Average duration.		
	Rs. a. p.													*Rs a. p.*	*Y. m. d.*		
Khas Adalat Original side	22,431-14-6	3	7	5	0	0	0	9	1	5	2	7	16	36,957-0-0	0-3-26	5	
Sadar Dewani Adalat	30,406-15-0	223	298	146	400	134	6	0	0	326	106	82	73	52,244-9-6	0-0-23	127	
Sonamura ,,	17,119-1-0	6	182	20	141	47	0	0	0	106	23	17	41	8,572-7-3	0-5-19	20	
Bilonia ,,	10,989-15-9	14	147	15	116	32	1	0	0	86	20	24	16	9,957-11-9	0-3-14	27	
Kailashahar ,,	22,988-6-4	8	178	55	124	66	6	0	0	93	41	8	122	21,335-12-7	0-6-10	45	
Khowai ,,	8,910-5-6	27	75	15	74	29	6	0	0	20	16	16	20	5,340-9-3	0-0-5	8	
Dharmanagar ,,	21,807-15-0	36	101	79	109	70	7	0	0	44	31	29	114	20,750-1-6	0-1-7	30	
Udaipur ,,	35,529-8-9	42	323	35	266	65	13	0	0	167	62	57	81	37,254-7-9	0-1-20	56	
Sabrum ,,	2,635-2-0	0	17	0	8	8	1	0	0	2	7	4	0	1,654-11-0	0-0-28	0	
Total ...	1,72,819-3-10	359	1328	370	1238	451	40	9	1	849	308	244	483	1,94,067-6-7	0-2-20	318	

XII.

Civil Work.—Results of applications for Execution of Decrees, 1342 T.E.

Tribunal.	Opening balance.		Value of opening balance for present year.	Applications brought to the Register.			Total.			Disposed of.			Closing balance.			Nature of applications pending disposal at the close of the year.			Remarks.
	Past year.	Present year.		Past year.	Present year.	Value for present year.	Past year.	Present year.	Value for present year.	Past year.	Present year.	Value for present year.	Past year.	Present year.	Value for present year.	Below 6 months.	Below 12 months.	Above 12 months.	
			Rs. a. p.			Rs. a. p.			Rs. a. p.			Rs. a. p.			Rs. a. p				
Khas Adalat (Original side)	32	36	53,108-9-9	19	17	26,349-15-0	51	53	79,458-8-9	15	19	32,421-5-0	36	34	47,037-3-9	5	9	20	
Sadar Dewani Adalat ...	164	186	33,879-1-6	230	239	28,368-2-9	394	425	62,247-4-3	208	225	25,770-12-6	186	200	36,476-7-9	101	45	54	
Sonamura Ditto ...	21	27	4,676-11-3	67	99	14,980-0-2	88	126	19,656-11-5	61	64	11,636-6-8	27	62	8,020-4-9	45	4	13	
Bilonia Ditto ...	14	24	2,554-6-0	73	67	8,978-12-0	87	91	11,532-12-0	63	72	8,160-11-0	24	19	3,372-1-0	16	1	2	
Kailashahar Ditto ...	37	103	20,517-2-9	111	110	14,544-5-9	198	213	35,061-8-6	95	60	8,278-4-3	103	153	26,783-4-3	70	20	63	
Khowai Ditto ...	30	29	1,898-2-9	44	37	2,127-3-6	94	66	4,025-6-3	65	40	2,724-2-9	29	26	1,301-3-6	17	6	3	
Dharmanagar Ditto ...	22	31	5,584-2-9	59	49	7,841-7-3	81	80	13,425-10-0	50	50	6,826-0-3	31	30	6,599-9-9	22	5	3	
Udaipur Ditto ...	165	166	27,790-1-0	284	299	41,075-10-0	449	465	68,865-11-0	283	303	45,551-4-6	166	162	23,314-6-6	127	23	12	
Sabrum Ditto ...	4	10	1,436-5-0	11	5	301-12-0	15	15	1,738-1-0	5	11	1,383-6-6	10	4	354-10-6	1	1	2	
Total ...	559	612	1,51,444-4-9	898	922	1,44,567-4-5	1,457	1,534	2,96,011-9-2	845	844	1,42,752-5-5	612	690	1,53,259-3-9	404	114	172	

XIII.

Civil Work—Number and results of appeals in civil suits, 1342 T. E.

Tribunal.	Opening balance.		Filed during.		Total.		Disposed of during.		Closing balance.		Value of appeales filed during.		How disposed of.										Average duration.	
													Decisions confirmed.		Decisions reversed.		Decisions amended.		Cases remanded for retrial.		Cases compromised and otherwise disposed of.			
	Past year.	Present year.	Past year.	Present year.	Past year.	Present year.	Past year.	Present year.	Past year.	Present year.	Past year.	Present year.	Past year.	Present year.	Past year.	Present year.	Past year.	Present year.	Past year.	Present year.	Past year.	Present year.	Past year.	Present year.
											Rs. a. p.	Rs. a. p.											Y. m. d.	Y. m. d.
Khas Adalat	164	167	203	147	367	314	200	196	167	118	20,242-2-9	7,894-8-3	85	86	22	32	29	15	21	30	43	33	0-4-5	0-4-10

XIV.

Statement showing the number of persons confined in the jails and lock-ups in the Tripura State during the year 1342 T. E.

Stations.	Number of prisons.	Number of prisoners.				Daily average.		Number of prisoners remaining at the end of the year.	Cost of jails and prisoners.	Average period in days of stay of accused under-trial.	Remarks showing mortality among convicts in jail.
		Remaining from last year.	Admitted during the year.	Total.							
				Past year.	Present year.	Past year.	Present year.				
Agartala	1	125	327	511	452	121·5	10·3	100	Rs. 16,515	39·3	
Sonamura	1	2	107	112	109	·3	·3	3	866	10·22	
Bilonia	1	4	131	181	135	4·17	3·52	16	377	10·68	One convict and one undertrial died in the Central Jail, Agartala. The convict died of Intestinal Tuberculosis and the undertrial of Cerebral type of malaria.
Kailashahar	1	14	160	193	174	13·79	7·82	5	758	16·06	
Dharmanagar	1	11	97	130	108	10·14	9·39	8	1,208	29·3	
Udaipur...	1	2	80	123	82	7·96	4·97	17	767	4·98	
Sabrum	1	2	47	36	49	·09	·13	1	656	32·79	
Khowai	1	2	63	46	65	3·60	2·88	9	657	19·44	
Total ...	8	162	1012	1332	1174	161·55	132·01	159	21,804	20·34	

XV.

Registration of documents in the Tripura State during the year 1342 T.E.

Name of State.	Documents presented for registration including pending from the last year.		Nature of documents presented.										Documents registered.		Value of documents registered.		Documents of which registration has been refused.		Documents remaining unregistered at the end of the year.		Remarks.
			Mortgages.		Sale deeds.		Wills.		Money bonds.		Miscellaneous.										
	Past year.	Present year.	Past year.	Present year.	Past year.	Present year.	Past year.	Present year.	Past year.	Present year.	Past year.	Present year.	Past year.	Present year.	Past year.	Present year.	Past year.	Present year.	Past year.	Present year.	
1	2	3	4	5	6	7	8	9	10	11	12	13	14	15	16	17	18	19	20	21	22
															Rs.	Rs.					
Tripura State	6,302	6,636	1,530	1,252	3,002	3,021	2	4	137	78	1,414	1,239	5,195	6,458	7,09,868	9,63,565	71	82	1,042	96	

XVI.

Statement showing the receipts and expenditure on account of Registration during the year 1342 T.E.

Description.	Past year.			Present year.			Remarks.
	Number of deeds.	Value of property.	Fees realised.	Number of deeds.	Value of property.	Fees realised.	
		Rs.	Rs.		Rs.	Rs.	
Mortgages	1,530	2,31,712	1,572	1,252	3,32,385	1,364	
Sale deeds	3,002	4,38,801	3,326	3,021	4,15,429	2,983	
Wills	2	—	12	4	4,500	34	
Money bonds	137	11,659	126	78	12,394	84	
Miscellaneous	1,414	2,02,913	1,861	1,239	2,31,567	1,647	
Total ...	6,085	8,85,085	6,897	5,594	9,96,275	6,112	
Total Expenditure ...	—	—	38,40	—	—	3,452	
Net Income ...	—	—	3,057	—	—	2,660	

XVII.

Receipts and expenditure of the Municipalities in the Tripura State during the year 1342 T.E.

NAME.	Opening balance.	RECEIPTS DURING THE YEAR.				Total Receipt		EXPENDITURE DURING THE YEAR.		Balance at the close of the year.	REMARKS.
		State grant.	Tax.	Miscellaneous.	Total.	Past year.	Present year	Past.	Present.		
1	2	3	4	5	6	7	8	9	10	11	12
	Rs. A.P.	Rs. A.P.	Rs. A.P.	Rs. A.P.	Rs. A.P.	Rs. A.P.	Rs. A.P.	Rs. A.P.	Rs. A.P.	Rs. A.P.	
Agartala Municipality. ...	33,284-14-3	8,000	3,594-0-9	7,536-10-6 a	19,130-11-3	47,927-14-3	52,415-9-6	14,643-0-0	13,973-9-9 b	38,441-15-9	a. Including Rs. 6,672-6-6 as income from the Bazar and Rs. 40-0-0 as deposits and advances recovered. b. Including Rs. 1,544-13-6 as expenditure on the Bazar improvement. c. Including Rs. 38,362-5-3 of the Bazar improvement fund and Rs. 79-10-6 as income from the Municipality.

XVIII.

Statement of rainfall in the Tripura State during the year 1342 T. E.

STATE.	Baisak.	Jaisth.	Asar.	Sravan.	Bhadra.	Asvin.	Kartik.	Agrahayan.	Pous.	Magh.	Falgoon.	Chait.	Total.	Total of past year.	Average of past 5 years.	REMARKS.
Tripura State ...	9·80	9·92	11·25	14·73	10·36	5·10	6·88	—	·12	·08	·17	2·15	70·56	82·74	86·37	

Maximum in Kailashahar—97·05″ Minimum in Amarpur—50·84″

XIX.

Statement as to the prices of staple food-grains for the year 1342 T. E.

Articles.	Price per maund during Chait, 1341 T. E.			Price per maund during chait, 1342 T. E.			REMARKS.
	Rs.	*a.*	*p.*	*Rs.*	*a.*	*p.*	
(1) RICE							
Maximum	4	0	0	3	2	0	
Minimum	2	0	0	1	6	0	
(2) PADDY							
Maximum	2	0	0	2	0	0	
Minimum	0	12	0	0	10	0	

XX.

Expenditure on Public Works during the year 1342 T.E.

Description of work	State Funds.			Local Funds.			Total.	Remarks.
	Original.	Repairs.	Total.	Original.	Repairs.	Total.		
	Rs.	*Rs.*	*Rs.*	*Rs.*	*Rs.*	*Rs.*	*Rs.*	
Buildings	9,049	37,642	46,691	—	—	—	46,691	
Roads and Bridges ...	309	12,707	13,016	—	—	—	13,016	
Tanks and Tubewells ...	620	303	923	—	—	—	923	
Miscellaneous works ...	990	827	1,817	—	—	—	1,817	* Out of this amount Rs. 26,499 was spent for improvement works under the following heads :— (1) Buildings ... Rs. 13,973 (2) Roads and Bridges ... " 6,125 (3) Water supply ... " 1,924 (4) Miscellaneous ... " 4,477 Total ... Rs. 26,499
Total ...	10,968	51,479	62,447	—	—	—	62,447	
Minor works at the Rajbari (*Karkhana*)	—	996	996	—	—	—	996	
Establishment charges ..	—	—	16,456	—	—	—	16,456	
Grand Total ...	10,968	52,475	79,899*	—	—	—	79,899	

XXI.

Statement showing the number of excise shops and excise revenue of the Tripura State during the year 1342 T. E.

Name of State.	Country spirit.		Country spirit, Opium and Ganja.		Opium and Ganja.		Tari		Total		Remarks.
	Number of shops.	Revenue demand.	Number of shops.	Revenue demand.	Number of shops.	Revenue demand.	Number of shops.	Revenue demand.	Number of shops.	Revenue realised.	
				Rs.						*Rs.*	
Tripura State	—	—	33	48,296	—	—	—	—	33	40,279	

XXII.

Statement of Medical Relief afforded in the Tripura State during the year 1342 T.E.*

Dispensary.	Number of patients treated. (new)		Results of in-door patients. (new)				Expenditure.	Daily average. (old + new)			No. of surgical operations performed.			No. of persons vaccinated during the year.			Remarks.
	Outdoor.	Indoor.	Discharged cured.	Relieved or discharged otherwise.	Died.	Remaining under treatment.		Outdoor.	Indoor.	Total.	Major.	Minor.	Total.	Successfully.	Unsuccessfully.	Total.	
							Rs.										
1. Victoria Memorial Hospital...	18,439	497	326	134	24	13	10,016	98·28	17·38	115·66	10	310	320	735	590	1,325	
2. Palace Dispensary	6.372	0	0	0	0	0	7,878	36·15	0	36·15	0	0	0	0	0	0	
3. Homœopathic	16,686	0	0	0	0	0	2,205	80·87	0	80·87	0	0	0	0	0	0	
4. Dhaleswar	7,247	0	0	0	0	0	1,225	31·01	0	31·01	0	47	47	0	0	0	* This Statement excludes figures regarding Kaviraji treatment.
5. Kunjaban	2,389	230	208	18	0	4	2,001	18·6	4·5	23·1	0	2	2	0	0	0	
6. Old Agartala	5,533	0	0	0	0	0	1,364	37·32	0	37·32	0	34	34	852	228	1,080	† This figure shows the actual number of outdoor patients treated, the total outdoor attendance during the year being 2,14,461 against 2,30,381 in the previous year.
7. Bishalgar	7,854	0	0	0	0	0	1,329	32·87	0	32·87	0	55	55	778	10	788	
8. Mohanpur(*a*)	1,414	0	0	0	0	0	492	13·82	0	13·82	0	26	26	0	0	0	
9. Sonamura	6,295	4	0	3	1	0	1,896	25·28	·19	25·47	1	131	132	347	163	510	
10. Radhakishorpur	9,471	0	0	0	0	0	1,480	38·65	0	38·65	1	66	67	257	93	350	
11. Amarpur	3,471	0	0	0	0	0	1,019	18·75	0	18·75	0	25	25	409	41	450	
12. Sabroom	2,435	2	1	0	1	0	1,322	13·21	·11	13·32	0	63	63	55	20	75	
13. Bilonia	7,254	8	4	4	0	0	1,855	45·81	·02	45·83	0	86	86	426	83	509	These dispensaries (*a*, *b* and *c*) were abolished after 4 months.
14. Loongthung (*b*)	1,283	0	0	0	0	0	431	19·35	0	19·35	0	16	16	0	0	0	
15. Khowai	8,166	0	0	0	0	0	1,599	27·78	0	27·78	0	89	89	214	25	239	
16. Kailashahar	7,737	0	0	0	0	0	1,864	30·6	0	30·6	0	157	157	426	86	512	
17. Fatikroy (*c*)	1,191	0	0	0	0	0	337	13·28	0	13·28	0	10	10	0	0	0	
18. Kamalpur	4,705	0	0	0	0	0	1,513	23·4	0	23·4	3	70	73	543	54	597	
19. Kulai Howar	1,923	0	0	0	0	0	432	7·81	0	7·81	0	8	8	0	0	0	
20. Dharmanagar...	6,517	17	3	5	1	3	1,414	28·44	·57	29·01	0	49	49	438	102	540	
21. Kalyanpur (*d*)	1,073	0	0	0	0	0	619	3·32	0	3·32	0	3	3	243	39	282	(*a*) This dispensary was opened new.
Total	†1,27,755	758	547	164	27	20	42,291	644·6	22·77	667·37	15	1,247	1,262	5,723	1,534	7,257	

XXIII.

Vital statistics of the Tripura State for the year 1342 T.E.

State.	Population.	Births.				Deaths.				Ratio per 1,000 of Population.				Remarks.
										Births.		Deaths.		
		Past year.	Present year.	Increase.	Decrease.	Past year.	Present year.	Increase.	Decrease.	Past year.	Present year.	Past year.	Present year.	
Tripura State ...	3,75,299	2,689	3,136	447	—	2,976	3,091	115	—	7·03	8·21	7·78	8·09	The figures are far from being correct—although attempt was made to collect accurate figures.

XXIV.

Education Return (A)—Particulars as to the schools maintained during the year 1342 T.E.

Number of Schools.		Class of Schools.	Number of Pupils on the Rolls on the Last Day of Chait.		Average Daily Attendance.		Remarks.
Past year.	Present year.		Past year.	Present year.	Past year.	Present year.	
6	6	High English Schools ... ... (including one Branch H. E. School).	1,450	1,410	1,209·25	1,106·55	
8	8	Middle English Schools for boys ...	950	983	717·34	762·22	* In some of these schools boys and girls read together. The fall in the numerical strength is due to the closing of some of the Schools.
1	1	Middle English School for girls ...	85	89	51·95	66·33	
1	1	Higher Vernacular School for boys	80	77	58·76	62·02	
25	23	* Lower Vernacular Schools for boys	1,502	1,413	1,110·30	1,104·48	
150	87	*Pathsalas for boys	4,545	2,666	2,990·27	1,957·19	
10	9	Do for girls	291	273	232·38	226·72	
		Special Schools :—					
—	4	Compulsory Free Primary Schools	—	418	—	242·32	
7	7	Madrassas and Muktabs	238	388	160·51	300·82	
4	4	Sanskrit *Tols*	43	39	30·25	30·01	
1	1	Artisan School & Silpasram ...	26	23	11·43	10·54	
1	1	Jail Reformatory School	20	21	19·45	19·45	
TOTAL 214	152		9,230	7,800	6,591·99	5,888·65	

XXV.

Education Return (B) Race of Students, 1342 T. E.

Names of Divisions.	No. of Schools.				No. of Students.					Race.												Average daily attendance.		REMARKS.
										Hindus.														
	For boys.	For girls.	Total.	Private schools.	Boys.	Girls.	Total.	Students of private schools.	Total	Rajkumars.	Thakurs.	Manipuris.	Tripuras.	Bengalees.	Others.	Reangs.	Chakmas.	Kukis.	Lusais.	Musalmans.	Christians.	Boys.	Girls.	
1. Sadar Division ...	54	2	56	16	3,019	130	3,149	432	3.581	4	198	133	585	13,62	79	0	2	1	0	785	0	2,154·16	104·58	
2. Kailashahar „ ...	23	3	26	9	1,122	180	1,302	264	1,566	0	1	369	27	636	2	0	0	0	0	267	0	866·26	132·3	
3. Sonamura „ ...	20	1	21	4	955	77	1,032	155	1,187	0	10	0	109	219	0	0	0	0	0	694	0	802·68	60·31	
4. Bilonia „ ...	8	1	9	3	621	41	662	387	1,049	0	0	0	31	425	3	0	0	0	0	203	0	475·23	32·	
5. Khowai „ ...	7	1	8	5	313	13	326	167	493	0	0	46	181	85	3	0	0	0	0	11	0	257·46	8·83	
6. Dharmanagar „ ...	14	1	15	8	593	62	655	259	914	0	2	86	0	401	9	0	0	0	1	156	0	436·16	55·61	
7. Udaipur „ ...	9	1	10	1	402	20	422	37	459	0	2	0	66	168	0	0	0	0	0	186	0	308·88	15·11	
8. Sabrum „ ...	6	0	6	1	226	12	238	14	252	0	0	0	53	130	0	0	0	0	0	55	0	159·59	8·25	
9. Amarpur Sub-division ...	1	0	1	6	11	3	14	108	122	0	0	0	1	13	0	0	0	0	0	0	0	9·08	2·16	
TOTAL ...	142	10	152	53	7,262	538	7,800	1,823	9,623	4	213	634	1,053	3.439	96	0	2	1	1	2,357	0	5,469·50	419·15	

N. B.—In the Sub-columns under "Race" the number of students of private schools is not included.

APPENDIX XXVI (A)

Statement of Audited Receipts for the year 1342 T. E.

State.

Heads of Revenue.	1341 T. E. Revised Estimate.	1341 T. E. Actuals.	1342 T. E. Revised Estimate.	1342 T. E. Actuals.	REMARKS.
1. Land Revenue ...	5,10,000	3,97,658	4,15,000	4,18,825	
2. Rents of markets ..	7,000	5,485	6,000	6,477	
3. Family tax in the hills	50,000	42,685	43,000	45,459	
4. Toll on Forest Produce	3,75,000	3,16,497	3,50,000	3,35,192	
5. Do on the Feni River	28,000	27,850	30,000	28,086	
6. Elephant and Buffalo grazing mehals ...	7,000	5,690	6,000	6,003	
7. Thatching grass mehals	5,000	4,008	4,000	3,370	
8. Reserved *Sal* trees ...	3,000	1,470	3,000	1,975	
9. Tax on cotton and Oil seeds ...	1,25,000	1,12,868	1,10,000	1,40,040	
10. Royalty on elephants caught ...	4,000	...	1,000	1,628	
11. *Adda* mehal ...	20,000	23,333	20,000	22,499	
12. Excise ...	75,000	50,086	40,000	40,279	
13. Stamps and Court fees	85,000	67,070	66,000	66,415	
14 Law and Justice (fines)	4,000	4,813	3,000	2,274	
15. Process Fees ...	14,000	12,563	12,000	11,650	
16. Registration ...	12,000	6,897	7,000	5,869	
17. Jail ...	2,000	2,254	2,000	2,111	
18. Cattle pounds ...	5,000	4,566	5,000	4,349	
19. *Nazars* ...	40,000	27,390	27,000	25,663	
20. School Fees ...	17,000	14,502	14,000	14,086	
21. Duty on Tea ...	10,000	8,633	11,000	9,318	
22. Duty on jute ...	15,000	11,463	31,000	31,388	
23. Personal *Howlats* recovered	2,000	3,746	2,000	1,319	
24. Interest on Bank deposit ...		—	—	—	
25. Miscellaneous ...	55,000	43,615	42,000	43,974	
26. Depreciation Contribution ...	50,000	42,110	70,000	80,850	
Total ...	15,20,000	12,37,252	13,20,000	13,49,108	
27. Deposits ...	80,000	2,26,312	3,01,897	3,11,572	
28. Loans from Chakla ...	00,000	30,000	—	..	
29. Contribution from Chakla ...	70,000	70,000	2,75,000	2,50,000	
30. Marriage Contribution	75,000	75,000	—	—	
31. Provident fund ...	20,000	21,472	...	—	
32. Loans from Nijtahabil	2,00,000	1,00,000	..		
33. Other loans ...	--	30,222	—	—	
Total ...	19,95,000	17,90,258	18,96,897	19,10,680	
Opening Balance :-					
Cash ...	1,03,000	1,04,593	1,14,250	1,14,250	
Advances ...	1,98,000	2,02,653	2,61,681	2,61,681	
Loans ...	2,93,000	2,94,425	2,75,084	2,75,084	
Total ...	5,94,000	6,01,671	6,51,015	6,51,015	
Grand Total ...	25,89,000	23,91,929	25,47,912	25,61,695	

APPENDIX XXVI. (B)

Statement of Audited Expenditure for the year 1342 T. E.

State.

Heads of Expenditure.	1341 T. E. Revised estimate.	1341 T. E. Actuals.	1342 T. E. Revised Estimate.	1342 T. E. Actuals.	Remarks.
1. Controlling Charges	82,207	79,157	71,715	69,784	
2. Revenue General ...	88,802	84.853	79,922	75,825	
3. Survey & Settlement	11,930	10,237	19,073	19.029	
4. Tahasil ...	54,033	52,224	44,322	43.071	
5. Registration ...	4,806	3,840	4,119	3.129	
6. Police ...	84.250	83,334	85,739	85,242	
7. Judicial ...	33,142	33,078	38.518	36,060	
8. Jail ...	20,142	17,995	23,018	21,804	
9. Forest ...	55,039	54,009	42,325	41,092	
10. Medical ...	71,566	65,360	64,909	64.070	
11. Municipality and Sanitation ...	9,000	9,000	8,000	8,000	
12. Education General ...	1,32,162	1,27,620	1,28,984	1,28,441	
13. (*a*) Public Works ...	1,46,740	72,793	86,896	79,899	
(*b*) Improvement ...	30,000	8.604	30,000	26,499	
14. Electric Light ...	18.579	17.700	19.398	17,125	
15. Small Donations ...	320	239	300	266	
16. Relief to distressed subjects ...	300	107	300	30	
17. Purchase of Landed Property ...	1.000	510	1,000	711	
18. Repayment of Deposits ...	64,000	49,923	1,91.260	1,90,957	
19. Interest on Deposits	20,000	7.672	—	—	
20. Unforeseen charges ...	2,500	2,136	7,500	4.792	
21. Advances to employees ...	200	175	—	—	
22 Pension ...	37,000	34,646	40,000	38,576	
23. Advisory Council ...	2,280	2.440	1,320	1.320	
24. Chief Secretary's Office & H. H.'s Tour	57.197	53.896	96,360	96,341	
25. Palace Sultanat ...	21,614	16.858	26,171	26,062	
26. Zoo ...	6,135	5,834	5.500	4,681	
27. Agriculture, Commerce and Industries	10,043	8.811	8,211	7,360	
28. Publicity, Reclamation and Immigration	1,379	1.177	1,030	987	
29. H. H.'s Private Secretary's Office ...	8,856	8,372	8,500	8,344	
30. Rajmala Office ...	4.842	2.018	4,000	3,995	
31. Military Secretary's Office ..	2,760	2,750	3.000	2,990	
32. Military ...	1,29.976	1.05,730	1,18,222	98,016	
33. Nijtahabil ...	1,20,000	1.09,000	1,00.000	1.00,000	
34. Expenditure in connection with H. H.'s Installation, Investiture & Marriage etc.	75,000	55,112	—	—	
35. Adjustment of irrecoverable advances ...	10,000	6,865	10.000	10,000	
36. Census ...	2,000	422	500	359	
37. Repayment of old Debts ...	2,00.000	1,78,858	1,34,468	1,33,649	
38. Sansar Charges ...	3,98,200	3,67,559	3,89,882	3,76,796	
39 Salary for the discharged officers...	—	—	40.600	40,310	
40. Expenditure for the treatment of Basnta Kumari...	—	—	30,000	30,000	
Total ...	20,18.000	17,40,914	19,65,090	18,95,612	
Closing balance :—					
Cash ..	1,10,000	1,14,250	56,057	1.44,444	
Advances ...	1,88,000	2,61,681	2,51,681	2.46.408	
Loans issued ...	2,73.000	2.75,084	2,75,084	2,75,231	
Total ...	5,71,000	6.51,015	5.82.822	6.66.083	
Grand Total ...	25,89,000	23.91,929	25,47,912	25,61,695	

APPENDIX XXVII. (A)

Statement of Audited Receipts for the year 1342 T. E.

Chakla Roshnabad Estates.

Heads of Receipts.	1341 T. E.		1342 T. E.		Remarks.
	Revised Estimate.	Actuals.	Revised Estimate.	Actuals.	
1. Rent and Cess ...	7,54,671	7,11,458	8,21,000	8,31,818	
2. Cess for Rent free holdings ...	7,000	8,159	7,000	6,950	
3. Law charges recovered	51,000	52,581	52,000	38,414	
4. Misc. receipts including deposits ...	27,000	98,324	49,000	50,605	
5. Refund of loans and advances ...	3,000	2,402	1,000	1,579	
Total ...	8,42,671	8,72,924	9,30,000	9,29,366	
Opening Balance :—					
Cash ...	76,632	76,632	92,027	92,027	
Advance ...	94,405	94,405	1,12,100	1,12,301	
Loans issued ...	69,831	69,831	73,557	73,619	
Bank deposits ...	1,30,127	1,30,127	1,36,188	1,36,188	
Total ...	3,70,995	3,70,995	4,13,872	4,14,135	
Grand Total ...	12,13,666	12,43,919	13,43,872	13,43,501	

APPENDIX XXVII. (B)

Statement of Audited Expenditure for the year 1342 T. E.

Chakla Roshnabad Estates.

Heads of Expenditure.	1341 T. E. Revised Estimate.	1341 T. E. Actuals.	1342 T. E. Revised Estimate.	1342 T. E. Actuals.	Remarks.
1. Revenue and Cess ...	2,67,033	2,65,974	2,76,000	2,73,821	
2. Establishment ...	1,60,000	1,55,008	1,42,000	1,40,737	
3. Settlement ...	1,000	440	1,300	896	
4. Legal Expenses ...	99,500	96,987	1,08,780	1,04,882	
5. Education ...	13,994	13,546	8,300	8,086	
6. Medical ...	14,300	14,035	11,778	11,156	
7. Public Works ...	68,800	50,651	50,650	50,491	
8. Religious Expenses	6,866	6,337	6,800	6,471	
9. Miscellaneous ...	6,500	5,581	3,000	2,508	
10. Loans and Advances	2,000	995	1,000	837	
11. Pension and Gratuity	7,500	7,191	8,500	7,925	
12. Forest ...	602	524	700	542	
13. Purchase of property	8,150	8,110	3,740	3,630	
14. Unforeseen ...	2,000	1,065	1,200	1,196	
ii. Sansar ...	11,022	11,022	12,960	12,960	
iii. Donation ...	5,800	5,740	4,617	4,540	
iv. Nijtahabil Contribution ...	50,000	50,000	—	—	
v. State Contribution	70,000	70,000	2,75,000	2,50,000	
(*b*) Loans to the State ...	30,000	30,000	—	—	
vi. Repayment of debts	10,700	10,497	1,11,970	1,09,503	
vii. Refund of old deposits ...	26,000	26,101	20,164	14,123	
Total ...	8,61,767	8,29,784	10,48,459	10,04,303	
Closing Balance :— Cash ...	57,536	92,027	81,893	97,853	
Advances ...	88,405	1,12,801	1,05,000	1,11,259	
Loans issued ...	69,770	73,019	73,057	80,435	
Bank deposits ...	1,36,188	1,36,188	35,463	49,651	
Total ...	3,51,899	4,14,135	2,95,413	3,39,198	
Grand Total ...	12,13,666	12,43,919	13,43,872	13,43,501	

MINISTER'S OFFICE,
TRIPURA STATE,
POLITICAL DEPARTMENT.

To

His Highness The Bisama-Samara-Bijayee Mahamahodaya
Pancha-Srijukta Maharaja Manikya
BIR BIKRAM KISHORE DEV BARMAN BAHADUR,
Maharaja of Tripura.

Dated, Agartala, the 10th December, 1934.

MAY IT PLEASE YOUR HIGHNESS,

I have the honour to submit herewith my Report on the General Administration of the State and the attached Zemindaries of which I held charge during the year 1343 T. E., extending from the 14th April, 1933 to the 13th April, 1934.

Reports on the administration of the Military Department as well as of the Departments of Agriculture, Commerce and Industries and Immigration under the control of the Chief Secretary to Your Highness, have also been incorporated in the report.

I have the honour to be
Your Highness's most obedient servant,
Jyotis Chandra Sen,
MINISTER.

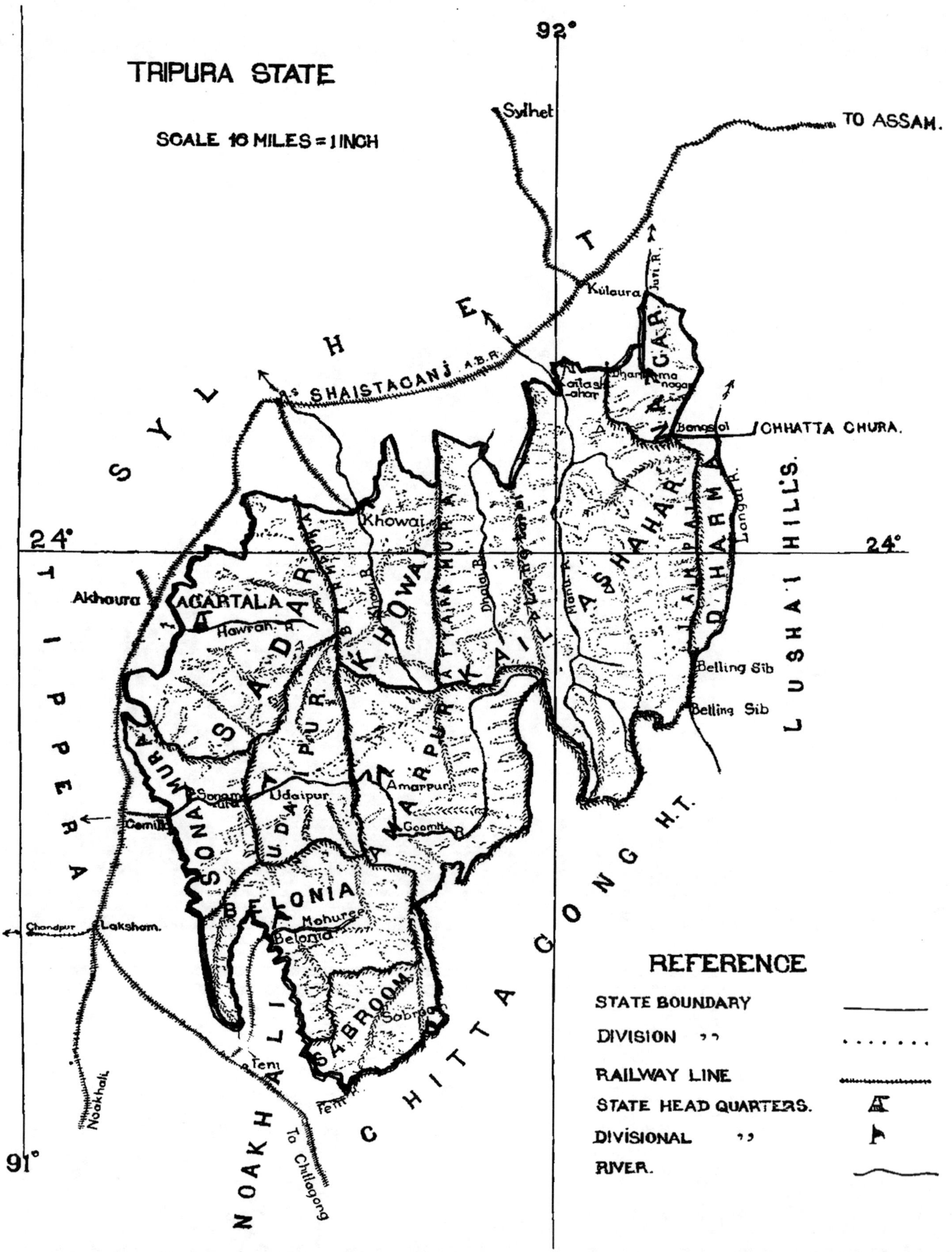
TRIPURA STATE
SCALE 16 MILES = 1 INCH
92°
24°
91°
Sylhet
TO ASSAM.
SYLHET
SHAISTAGANJ A.B.R.
Kulaura
CHHATTA CHURA.
LUSHAI HILLS.
TIPPERA
Akhoura
AGARTALA
Hawrah R.
Khowai
SADAR
KHOWAI
KAILASAHAR
DHARMANAGAR
Belling Sib
Comilla
Sonamura
Udaipur
Amarpur
Gomti R.
SONAMURA
UDAIPUR
AMARPUR
BELONIA
Mohuree
Belonia
SABROOM
Sabroom
Chandpur
Laksham.
Feni
Noakhali
To Chittagong
NOAKHALI
CHITTAGONG H.T.
REFERENCE
STATE BOUNDARY
DIVISION "
RAILWAY LINE
STATE HEAD QUARTERS.
DIVISIONAL "
RIVER.

Book Twenty-five
Report on the Administration of the Tripura State for 1343 T. E. (1933-1934 A.D.)

REPORT ON THE ADMINISTRATION OF THE TRIPURA STATE FOR 1343 T. E. (1933-34.)

CHAPTER I—GENERAL AND POLITICAL.

Area of the State—*4,116 sq. miles.*
Population—*3,82,450.*
Gross Revenue (*based on the average of the previous five years*):—

(*a*) State ... ... Rs. 20,86,795.
(*b*) Zemindaries ... ... Rs. 9,98,727.

Tribute—Nil.
Ruler of the State—His Highness The Bisama-Samara-Bijayee Mahamahodaya Pancha-Srijukta Maharaja Manikya Bir Bikramkishore Dev Barman Bahadur. *Age*—26 years. (Born—19th August, 1908). *Caste*—*Kshatriya* (of the Lunar race).

The year and the people.

During the year under report there was no appreciable improvement in the general economic situation in the State and the attached Zemindaries although hopes were entertained during the earlier part of the year of some improvements here and there. The agricultural people fared no better than in the year preceding. Although the prices of paddy and jute maintained a slightly upward tendency and that of rice remained almost on the same level, that of oilseeds went down to a noticeable extent. The slight increase in the land revenue collection against a heavy accumulation of the demand during these years of economic distress, was due more to the better paying capacity of the Talukdars than that of the Jotedars. The hill people suffered worse. A decrease in the price of cotton and *til* coupled with a heavy fall in the outturn of the latter commodity, affected them and the State alike resulting in a very big fall in the duty on cotton and oilseeds. The demand for forest produce also dwindled comparatively, affecting the forest revenue. As noticed in the previous Report, it was only the tea market that was improving gradually on the operations of the international Restriction Scheme and it is hoped that the progress may not sustain any serious set-back during the period of the international control. Since the close of the year under review, however, the price of tea has not shown signs of improvement. In the Zemindaries, the tenantry did not fare well owing to the low price of paddy and jute although better collection of rent shows some improvement in their economic condition.

2. The rainfall was a little below the average and was unevenly distributed over the various parts of the State territory. Excessive rains in the lower tracts of the Feni valley caused flood in the Sabrum Division where there was scarcity of foodgrains among a section of hill people who received distress loans from the State. The Bilonia Division suffered from the visitation of flood twice in the month of Bhadra. Crops were affected and house property damaged in some parts of the Division. Heavy rainfall in the Gumti valley which has for some years become almost an annual occurrence was responsible for floods in the Udaipur Division affecting crops in the plains in the lower region. The harvests of the year may be said to have been fair on the whole.

3. The condition of the middle classes was not better owing to the slight rise in the prices of some of the foodstuffs and other articles of daily use. The rates of wages of skilled and unskilled labour showed no tendency towards any steady improvement.

Finances of the year.

4. The year opened with a balance of Rs. 10,05,281 against Rs. 10,65,150 in the year before. The total revenue from the permanent sources was Rs. 13,39,810 against Rs. 13,49,108 in the previous year in the State and Rs. 9,08,361 against Rs. 8,50,918 in the Zemindaries. On account of continued financial stringency a loan of nine lacs had to be obtained from the Government of India for liquidation of old liabilities and for stabilization of the finances of the State. With loans and deposits the total receipts from all sources came to Rs. 34,37,193 against Rs. 25,90,046 in the preceding year, the total sum available for expenditure including opening balance being Rs. 44,42,474 against Rs. 36,55,196.

II.

His Highness's movements.

5. The hot weather of the year under review was spent by His Highness the Maharaja Manikya Bahadur at Shillong. Accompanied by Her Highness the Maharani Saheba and the Dowager Maharani Sahebas, His Highness left Agartala for Shillong on the 8th Jaistha and returned to the Capital on the 23rd Sravan.

Calcutta.

6. Just on the eve of the Pujas, His Highness had unfortunately to proceed to Calcutta on expert medical advice, to have anti-rabic treatment as a precautionary measure and to the great relief of the people returned to the Capital in good health after undergoing the full course of it, staying out from the 6th to the 25th Asvin.

Calcutta.

7. His Highness the Maharaja Manikya Bahadur left Agartala for Calcutta on the 11th Agrahayan and joined Her Highness the Maharani Saheba at the latter place where she had been staying for some time. During the stay in Calcutta, His Highness had private interviews, as usual, with His Excellency the Viceroy and His Excellency the Governor of Bengal on the 28th and 7th of December respectively, and besides this, joined

Their Excellencies in various functions at Belvedere and Government House.

8. Amidst the busy programme of His Highness's engagements in Calcutta, the following may be mentioned.

9. On invitation from the Consul-General for Germany, His Highness the Maharaja Manikya Bahadur was present at a reception given in honour of the Captain and Officers of the German Cruiser "Karlsruhe" which called at the Calcutta Port at that time on her way to a cruise round the world. His Highness was also invited by the Consul-General to pay a visit to the "Karlsruhe" and accordingly, he visited the cruiser on the 9th December with his staff. His Highness received the customary salute of 13 guns on his arrival on board and also at the time of his departure and inspected the Guard-of-Honour furnished by her crew. The Consul-General and the Captain accompanied His Highness when he was shown round the cruiser and he was much pleased with what he saw there and thanked them for all the courtesy shown to him.

10. On January 2, 1934, His Highness the Maharaja Manikya Bahadur with staff, joined His Excellency the Naval Commander-in-Chief at a dinner on board the British Cruiser "Enterprise".

11. His Highness visited some of the cultural, religious and educational institutions of the city, e. g. the College of Engineering and Technology, Bengal, Sree Gauriya-Math and the Government Islamia College. At the request of the Hon'ble Alhadj Nawab Bahadur Sir A. K. Ghuznavi, Kt., of Dilduar and the Committee of the Islamia College, His Highness presided over the fifth anniversary of the Student's Duty Fund of the college on the 27th January, 1934. Everywhere His Highness was accorded a most enthusiastic reception and was the recipient of warm addresses eulogistic of his catholic services and those of his illustrious House towards the cause of education and religion. His Highness gave suitable replies to each of them and granted generous donations towards the funds of the above-mentioned institutions.

12. His Highness next availed himself of the kind invitation for shooting offered to him by the Dowager Rani Saheba of Khairagarh and left Calcutta with his staff, on the 21st Pous and stayed there for five days, returning on the 28th idem.

13. A few days after his return from Khairagarh, His Highness, accompanied by Their Highnesses the Dowager Maharani Sahebas paid a short visit to Dehra Dun to see his sister, the Jubrani Saheba of Kotla, who had, after a prolonged stay in Switzerland on medical advice, come back with her health fully recovered.

14. Just before the winter tour came to an end, His Highness the Maharaja Manikya Bahadur went out from Calcutta to the Sunderbans on a shooting excursion for a week. The Hon'ble Alhadj Nawab Bahadur Sir A. K. Ghuznavi, Kt., of Dilduar, the then member of the Executive Council of the Governor of Bengal, was responsible for the excellent arrangements made and facilities extended in connection with this successful and pleasant Shikar cruise.

15. His Highness left Calcutta on the 6th Falgoon and returned to the Capital the following morning.

16. Towards the close of the year under report, His Highness the Maharaja Manikya Bahadur went out to the interior of the State, at Sidhai, on the 16th Chaitra, but after a brief stay there for three days only, had to return to the Capital owing to slight indisposition.

His Highness's Birthday Celebration.

17. The birthday anniversary of His Highness the Maharaja Manikya Bahadur came off on Monday, the 29th Sraban. This auspicious occasion was celebrated with due eclat all over the State and the Zemindaries. At the Capital, as usual, the National Flag of the State was hoisted by His Highness in an open air Durbar, where customary Military Parades were held and some prisoners were released. The poor received charities on this occasion and the whole town was illuminated in the evening.

The Birth of a Maharajkumar.

18. The most outstanding and blissful event of the year was the birth, in Calcutta, of a Maharajkumar and heir-apparent to His Highness the Maharaja Manikya Bahadur—on the night of the 26th Agrahayan corresponding to the early morning of December 13, 1933. The receipt of this auspicious news at the Capital on the following morning was the occasion for highly enthusiastic and loyal demonstrations throughout the length and breadth of the State and the Zemindaries where offices and other institutions were closed for four days on this happy occasion. Hundreds of congratulatory messages from within and outside the State were received by His Highness, amongst which, felicitous messages on the birth of the heir-apparent, from His Majesty the King-Emperor, Their Excellencies the Viceroy, the Governors of Bengal and Assam and their respective Governments and from a number of Ruling Princes were thankfully acknowledged—as also the others.

19. The Surjadarshan ceremony of the newly born Maharajkumar, at the Tripura House in Calcutta, marked by a number of festivities in the State, was heartily enjoyed by the Royal House and the people alike. Deputations representing the Durbars of Panna, Baria, Bhavnagar and Korla were present during the ceremony.

The First Home-coming of the heir-apparent.

20. The first home-coming of the heir-apparent Maharajkumar Bahadur with Their Highnesses the Maharaja Manikya Bahadur and Maharani Saheba on the morning of the 19th February (7th Falgoon) was another occasion of great joy to the people. The arrival was public and attracted, at Akhaura, large crowds of people who longed to have a view of their beloved Maharaja and the heir-apparent. On alighting from the train, His Highness was garlanded and given an ovation after which he, with the Maharani Saheba and the Maharajkumar Bahadur proceeded towards the Capital which was *en fete* to accord a hearty welcome to them. Their Highnesses and the Maharajkumar were lustily cheered by the huge concourse of people as they drove through the important streets to the Palace. En route, at the Installation Pandal,

His Highness was formally received by the public at a mass meeting and was presented with an address of welcome to which he gave a suitable reply.

Death of H. H. the Dowager Maharani Manomanjuri Mahadevi.

21. A very sad event of the year that overtook the Royal Family and the State was the sad demise of Her Highness the Dowager Maharani Manomanjuri Mahadevi, a grand-mother of His Highness, at Agartala, on the 25th Bhadra. Offices and other institutions were closed for three days as a mark of respect to the memory of the late Maharani Mahadevi who passed away at a ripe age of 68.

Death of the Yubaraj Saheb of Baria

22. Yet another very sad event, by the occurrence of which the Royal Family, nay, the whole of the State was cast into gloom was the untimely demise of the Yubaraj Saheb of Baria, after a short illness. This melancholy event took place at the Baria House in Bombay on the 13th Magh and the news was first received in Calcutta. The young Yubaraj Saheb to whom the youngest sister of His Highness was given in marriage only six years ago, had endeared himself to the people of his own land and our State alike, and his premature death was deeply mourned all over the State and the Zemindaries. All offices and other institutions were closed for a week in honour of the departed soul, and a deputation from the Durbar paid a condolence visit to Baria in this connection.

III.

Topographical Survey.

23. The No. 12 Party, Eastern Circle, Survey of India, continued their operations. Their programme was to complete the survey of the State in the previous year but only full 6 sheets could be finished during the year in addition to the 6 sheets finished in the previous year. In all probability, the survey will be finished by the end of 1934. Out of the total contribution of Rs. 45,000 for this purpose, the State paid Rs. 26,000 during the year under review, Rs. 10,000 having been paid in the previous year.

Boundary Disputes.

24. During the topographical survey operations, the village Phuldengsei adjoining the Lushai Hills District, the watershed line from the Betling to Langterai H. S. and the source and course of the Feni river were inspected jointly by the officers of both the Governments.

Political Agent.

25. Mr. R. L. Walker, I. C. S., continued as Political Agent till the afternoon of the 19th March, 1934, when Mr. E. W. Holland, I. C. S., took over charge.

Minister.

26. Rai J. C. Sen Bahadur, B. A., B. C. S. (retired) continued to hold charge of the State and the attached Zemindaries with the exception of the Departments of Agriculture, Commerce & Industry, Immigration and Publicity which were under the control of the Chief Secretary to His Highness.

CHAPMER II—LAND ADMINISTRATION.

Charge.

27. Mr. S. C. Deb Barman, M. A., (Harvard), Senior Naib Dewan and Thakur K. K. Singh, Naib Dewan, remained in charge of this Department in addition to other duties assigned to them upto the 10th Jaistha and thereafter the latter remained in sole charge of the department throughout the year.

Area held under Settlement.

28. As shown in the subjoined statement, the total area held under settlement and borne on the *toujis* at the close of the year was 627 square miles as against 639 square miles in the previous year.

Kinds of settlement.	Area in square miles.		Increase.	Decrease.	REMARKS.
	1343 T.E.	1342 T.E.			
Jotes ...	330	329	1	—	
Taluks ...	297	310	—	13	
Total ...	627	639	1	13	

29. The Decrease was due to the purchase of *Taluk* land by the State in revenue auction sale and relinquishment.

Tea Settlement.

30. Proceedings in 2 cases for re-settlement of portions of tea estates purchased by the State in revenue auction sale were in progress during the year and re-settlement of one of them was concluded.

31. Several petitions for relinquishment of portions of tea garden lands were pending from the year previous. Relinquishment of 1364 acres of land was effected in one case during the year.

Tea Industry.

32. Both the outturn and export of tea increased during the year under review. 26 *drones* of *khas* purchased tea land was re-settled during the year while only one garden was purchased by the State in revenue auction sale during the year under review.

33. The Durbar has always been giving relief to the proprietors of tea gardens by pursuing the policy of granting them temporary suspension and easy instalments for payment of revenue and other State dues. As a consequence of the tea Restriction measures, several gardens have prayed for relinquishment of portions of uncultivated land and the Durbar has not been slow in realising their difficulties and has been taking steps to grant them the relief they deserve giving up a big amount of land revenue for the sake of the welfare of the industry. The arrear revenue at the end of the year amounted to more than 2 lacs having increased in comparison with the previous years with the closing of several tea concerns. Some portion of this demand may have to be written off as irrecoverable.

34. With the rise of price and greater export (2½ lac lbs.) the export duty increased in comparison with the previous 2 years.

35. Following the introduction of the Tea Restriction Scheme and consquent rise in price the industry emerged from slump with prospect

of a more or less bright future. The restriction on extension of cultivation has been hanging heavy on the infant industry in the State. That the gardens of the State do not get enough consideration at the hands of the Indian Tea Licensing Committee has been the general clamour amongst the proprietors. For the fostering of the infant industry in the State, the Durbar started negotiation with the Government of India since the close of the year, and it is expected that it will be possible to get a favourable consideration of the matter.

Rates of *Jama.*

36. The average of *jama* per *kani* of *jote* lands in *khas mehals* (exclusive of cesses) stood at 12 annas and 2 pies against 15 annas and 4 pies in the previous year. The maximum rate for *jote* was Rs. 45 per *kani* while the minimum was 4 annas and that for *taluks* Re. 1 and annas 3 respectively. The maximum *jote* rate was a special one in respect of a small piece of bazar land.

Sources of land Revenue.

37. The different sources of land revenue demand with the collection under each head are detailed below :—

Sources.	Current demand.		Arrear demand up to the end of		Realization up to the end of		REMARKS.
	1343 T.E.	1342 T.E.	1342 T.E.	1341 T.E.	1343 T.E.	1342 T.E.	
Taluks ...	1,59,656	1,66,673	4,03,932	3,53,733	1,28,624	1,04,208	
Khas Mehal jotes	5,34,740	5,23,423	15,37,191	13,00,789	2,94,082	2,87,021	
Bazars ...	6,504	6,684	3,298	3,790	6,019	6,344	
Cesses ...	43,862	43,548	1,32,018	1,13,254	25,829	23,406	
Total ...	7,44,762	7,40,328	20,76,439	17,71,566	4,54,554	4,20,979	

Demand.

38. The above statement shows that the current demand under all heads was Rs. 7,44,762 and with the arrear demand of Rs. 20,76,439 the total demand of the year was Rs. 28,21,201 against Rs. 25,11,894 in the previous year.

Collection.

39. The total collection in round figures under all heads during the year amounted to Rs. 4,54,554 being Rs. 1,62,576 under current and Rs. 2,91,978 under arrears, as against Rs. 4,20,979 in the previous year. The percentage of current collection was 21·82 against 22·55 and that of the arrears 14·06 against 14·33. In the *khas mehal* the percentage of current collection was 8·98 against 11·28 and in *taluki mehal* the percentage was 63·09 against 62·52 in the previous year.

Coercive measure—Certificates.

40. Altogether 4,913 certificate cases covering a demand of Rs. 2,73,042 were instituted during the year. With 4,239 cases valued at Rs. 5,86,225 pending from the previous year, the total number of cases awaiting final orders on disposal of preliminary notices issued on debtors was 9,152

covering a total demand of Rs. 8,59,267. Of these, 37 cases with a demand of Rs. 2,924 were rejected or struck off and Rs. 11,678 in 368 cases was realised before decree, while 4,384 cases with a total value of Rs. 5,57,213 remained pending at the end of the year.

41. Orders under the provisions of the State Certificate Act were passed during the year in 4,363 cases with a total value of Rs. 2,87,452 making the demand absolute.

Execution.

42. With 9,648 cases to the value of Rs. 6,50,274 pending in execution from the previous year, the total number of cases dealt with was 14,011 covering a demand of Rs. 9,37,726. Out of the total demand, Rs. 26,266 was remitted or written off and of the remainder, Rs. 1,43,906, was actually realised leaving a balance of Rs. 7,67,554. Of the amount realised, Rs. 1,33,088 represents land revenue and Rs. 10,818 miscellaneous demands.

43. The number of defaulting *taluks* brought under the operation of the Sunset law (including 80 pending from the previous year) was 221. Of these 135 were released on payment of dues with penalty while 46 were sold in auction and 40 remained undisposed of at the close of the year.

Operation of the Sunset Law.

44. The results of the survey (including resurvey) operations are given in the statement below. It will be seen that an area of 3,486 *drones* comprising 187 *drones* of *taluk* and 3,299 *drones* of *Khas mehal* was surveyed as against a total of 2,609 *drones* in the previous year.

Survey.

Names of Divisions.	Quantity of land in *drones* surveyed in 1343 T. E.			Quantity of land in *drones* surveyed in 1342 T. E.			REMARKS.
	Taluki land.	*Khas mehal* land.	Total.	*Taluki* land.	*Khas mehal* land.	Total.	
1. Sadar Division ...	135	36	171	74	2,086	2,160	
2. Kailashahar ,, ...	29	60	89	—	136	136	
3. Sonamura ,, ...	23	282	305	31	—	31	
4. Bilonia ,, ...	—	1,382	1,382	—	111	111	
5. Khowai ,, ...	—	493	493	—	—	—	
6. Dharmanagar ,, ...	—	470	470	—	171	171	
7. Udaipur ,, ...	—	148	148	—	—	—	
8. Sabroom ,, ...	—	428	428	—	—	—	
9. Amarpur Sub ,, ...	—	—	—	—	—	—	
TOTAL ...	187	3,299	3,486	105	2,504	2,609	

Map Compilation.

45. This work continued under the direction of Babu Kamir Kumar Kar, Superintendent of Surveys. Compilatio of *Mouzmil* maps of the Divisions on a scale of on inch to the mile from the survey maps of villages and *Taluks* was i progress. Maps of 9 villages were reduced to one inch scale an compiled in the *Mouzmil* and 3 maps of villages out of 33 reduced map remaining uncompiled were also compiled this year. The Divisiona *mouzmil* maps were also corrected following the additions. I addition, 6 topographical sheets of the Survey of India were reduce from one mile to the inch to 4 miles to the inch scale and compiled i the State map in order to show correct divisional boundaries in the Stat map, as the old map was found wrong in places.

46. 3 case maps in connection with disputes about boundar between *Taluks* and *Khas* lands within the State and also along th British border line were prepared and 2 copies of one of them were tracec

47. 17 maps of boundary and connected award, 24 maps c villages and *Taluks* and 30 other maps were traced and the area c 3 maps checked with planimeter by the same staff. In addition, som of the line to connect villages for compilation of *mouzmil* maps wer done by some temporary staff. The total expenditure incurred wa Rs. 447-14-3 only.

48. The No. 12 party, E. C. Survey of India, continued thei operations of Topographical survey of the State. Their programm was to complete the survey of the State in the previous year but onl full 6 sheets were finished during the year in addition to the 6 sheet finished in the year previous and the remaining sheets were also unde survey with every probability of completion of the survey of the State b the end of 1934, The State paid Rs. 26,000 in addition to Rs. 10,000 pai in the previous year towards their contribution amounting to Rs. 45,50 and the balance would be paid as arranged in the year following.

49. During the survey operations the disputed boundary betwee the Lushai Hills and this State near Phuldengsei village on the Jampa range in the State was inspected jointly by Major A. G. Mc Call Superintendent, Lushai Hills District as representative of the Assan Government and Babu Sasanka Bhusan Roy, M. A., Divisional Officer Sonamura, as the representative of the State, with Mr. K. L. Dhawan B. A., the survey camp officer of the No. 12 party and the Superintenden of Surveys of the State. The watershed line from the Betling t Langterai H. S. was also inspected jointly by the same representativ of the State and a Kanongo of Chittagong Hill Tracts with the sam Survey camp officer of the Survey of India and the Superintendent o the Surveys of the State and some temporary marks left on the water-shed line. Thakur Joysingh Deb Barman, B. A., S. D. O., Amarpur enquired about the source of the Feni river. The disputed boundar about the source as well as the course of the Feni river was inspected b the Superintendent of Surveys and the disputes were discussed afterward with Lieut. C. A. K. Wilson, O/c., No. 12 party, E. C., Survey of India.

50. The Superintendent of Surveys was out on tour for 104 day in connection with the inspection of the Divisional boundaries an border lines.

Settlement.

51. There was a *Taskhichi taluki* settlement of an area of 26 *drones* comprising 15 *drones* of cultivated land and 11 *drones* of waste land. It will be seen from the statement below that settlement operations in respect of 1,532 *drones* of *jote* lands were completed against 4,379 *drones* in the previous year.

Nature of Settlement.	1343 T. E.		1342 T. E.		REMARKS.
	Area in *drones.*	*Jama* in whole rupees.	Area in *drones.*	*Jama* in whole rupees.	
1. Permanent *taluki* settlement of cultivated land ...	—	—	—	—	
2. Permanent *taluki* settlement of waste land	—	—	—	—	
3. *Taskhichi taluki* settlement of cultivated land ...	15	*258	—	—	
4. *Taskhichi taluki* settlement of waste land	11	—	—	—	
5. *Jotedari* re-settlement of cultivated land	1,392	18,144	4,289	45,263	
6. *Jotedari* settlement of waste land	140	1,302	90	901	
TOTAL ...	1,558	19,704	4,379	46,169	

* 11 *Drones* of waste land together with 15 *drones* of cultivated land was settled at a *jama* of Rs. 258.

Taluki Settlement.

52. Resettlement of a plot of *Khas* purchased tea garden *Taskhichi Taluk* comprising 26 *drones* was granted during the year under review and Rs. 501 was realised as *Nazar*. Another case of resettlement of tea land was in progress at the end of the year.

Resettlement of *jote* lands.

53. A net increase of Rs. 8,839 in *jama* was secured by resettlement of *abadi jote* land, the *Nazarana* being Rs. 14,715. The average *jama* per *kani* was 13 annas against 10 annas and 7 pies in the previous year.

Jotedari Settlement of waste land.

54. During the year, an area of 140 *drones* of waste land was settled for a prospective rental of Rs. 1,302, the average *jama* per *kani* obtained being 9 annas and 4 pies against 10 annas in the previous year. The maximum and minimum rates were Rs. 2/8 and annas 4 respectively. The *Nazarana* realised was Rs. 1,048, the rent-free period allowed ranging from 1 to 3 years.

Settlement work.

55. No wholetime Settlement officer was employed in any Division, but the Divisional officers and the 2nd officers were entrusted with the settlement work within their respective jurisdictions. The total expenditure in the settlement operations was Rs. 967.

56. The *nazarana* obtained and obtainable by settlement and resettlement of *abadi jote* land and settlement of waste land as *jotes* amounted to Rs. 16,671 (Rs. 14,715 + Rs. 1,956).

57. As detailed below there were altogether 15 private estates under State management during the year under report.

Private Estates under State Management.

Class.	Name of Estate.	Area.	Revenue.
Encumbered	1. Kakrabon Estate	283 *drones.*	1,871
	2. Jogendranagar Trust Estate	64 "	163
	3. Kamalnagar and Mahendranagar Estate	51 "	255
	4. Gouranga Tripura's Estate	13 "	57
	5. Maharam Ali Chaudhuri Khanje Khan Bahadur's Estate—*Taluk*	236 "	1230
	Jote	6 "	149
	6. Thakur Nalini Mohan Deb Barma's Estate	68 "	170
	7. Brajendra Kumar Das's Estate	408 "	1,936
	8. Brajapur Estate (Kamala Kanta Deb Barman and others)	246 "	982
	9. Kalimulla's Estate	124 "	863
	10. Mahammedali Chaudhuri's Estate	24 "	76
Unencumbered	11. Girish Chandra Chaudhuri's Estate	36 "	254
	12. Prabhu Goswamis' Estate	31 "	61
	13. Late Brajakumar Thakur's Estate	47 "	297
	14. Naba Kumar Chakrabarty's Estate—*Taluk*	32 "	225
	Jote	5 "	19
Endowment	15. Taranagar Estate	140 "	52

58. The subjoined table shows the demands and collections of the estates during the year under review. Compared with the previous year, collections improved in 8 estates and fell in 4 estates. No. 11 came under State management during the latter part of the year, and hence no collection could be made therein during the year under review. There was no collection of the estates Nos. 9 and 14 in 1342 T. E. as the estates came under State management during the latter part of the year.

Estate No.	DEMAND			COLLECTION			P. C. of collection
	Current	Arrear	Total	Current	Arrear	Total	
1.	6,319	32,500	38,819	525	2,994	3,519	9·07
2.	1,234	6,903	8,137	77	798	875	10·75
3.	1,275	2,623	3,898	103	1,034	1,137	29·17
4.	233	153	386	106	95	201	52·08
5.	3,591	15,901	19,492	205	1,724	1,929	9·89
6.	1,163	4,186	5,349	28	357	385	7·19
7.	3,603	8,052	11,655	24	1,765	1,789	15·35
8.	4,218	7,069	9,287	850	3,041	3,891	41·90
9.	2,425	4,095	6,520	—	92	92	—
10.	1,204	1,739	2,943	—	645	645	21·92
11.	1,149	5,034	6,183	*—	—	—	—
12.	912	3,809	4,721	74	512	586	12·41
13.	1,611	3,451	5,062	56	1,168	1,224	24·38
14.	638	3,555	4,193	25	260	255	6·79
15.	3,080	11,239	14,319	206	1,492	1,698	11·16

*No collection during the year as it came under State management at the latter part of the year.

CHAPTER III—PROTECTION.

I. Legislation.

59. No legislation was undertaken during the year and there was no sitting of the Legislative Council.

II. Military.

Charge.

60. Dewan Sahib Kamala Prasad Dutt, M. A. B. L., F. R. E. S., M. R. A. S. and Major Kumar Dina Mohan Dev Barma Bahadur continued to be in charge of the Military Department and the Military Forces respectively.

Strength.

61. The total strength of the forces at the end of the year was 391 against 352 of the preceding year.

Inspection.

62. His Highness the Maharaja Manikya Bahadur inspected both the 1/ Tripura Bir and 2/ Tripura Bikram Companies on the 19th August 1933.

Training.

63. Capt. Kumar Braja Lal Dev Varma Bahadur, Company Commander, 1/ Tripura Bir Company, attended the Company Commanders' Course at Gwalior with good results. Two Company Officers and ten Platoon Commanders from both Companies and one Jemadar from His Highness' Body Guards were trained in Tactical Exercise Without Troops from the 2nd to the 4th November 1933 under the supervision of Capt. Kumar B. L. Dev Varma Bahadur just after his return from his training course and did satisfactory work. On the 17th February 1934 they were further trained in Compass Bearing, Reading & Writing, Night March with Troops and Night Digging. Besides these, the Companies exercised in Musketry. Armourer Sushil Chandra Dev Varma was sent to Allahabad Arsenal for Preliminary Training in Armoury. The result was satisfactory. One N. C. O. from the 1st Tripura Bir Company attended the Small Arms School, Pachmarhi. His result was very satisfactory.

Cantonment.

64. Some ordinary improvements and petty repairs of the barracks were made during the year.

Health.

65. The health of the forces was generally good as in the previous year.

Expenditure.

66. The total expenditure for the year excluding the Public Works amounted to Rs. 1,06,626 against Rs. 98,016.

Tactical Practice and Camping.

67. On the 29th August 1933, the Police, Jail Warders, Binondias, Body Guards and Palace Volunteers took part in a Town Protection Practice with the Military Forces. His Highness the Maharaja Manikya Bahadur was pleased to watch the forces from the commencement of the practice and inspected the forces in the evening in front of the Durbar Club where all the forces were mobilised. In the month of April the

1/ Tripura Bir and the 2/ Tripura Bikram Companies with Signalling party and followers camped out for about a fortnight and did some Tactical Exercises under Capt. Kumar Brajalal and Capt. Rana Jhapat Jung Bahadur. A platoon from the 1/ Tripura Bir Coy. was sent out for guard and escort duties with His Highness the Maharaja Manikya Bahadur to Sidhai where they encamped for 10 days from 22nd April to 2nd May. On this occassion the troops had some practice in pitching tents and laying out Camp sites.

III. Police.

68. Rai Saheb A. C. Gupta continued as Superintendent of Police during the year.

Charge.

69. Babu N. K. Bhattacharjea, B. SC., continued as Assistant Superintendent of Police during the year but he was on leave from the 13th Sraban to the 8th Agrahayan, the senior Inspector Babu N. N. Bose, B. A., acting for him.

70. The total numerical strength of the Police Force during the year was 512 against 499 in the previous year.

Strength.

71. The total number of village Chaukidars was 175 as before.

Rural Police.

72. There were 4 Inspectors of Police as before, who were employed mainly to supervise important cases and control the staff placed under them.

Inspecting Staff.

73. During the year there were 24 Sub Inspectors including one Probationary Sub-Inspector and 22 Naib Darogas as before, the post of one Naib Daroga having remained vacant during the previous year.

Investigating and Prosecuting staff.

74. Good detective work has been done by some of the Sub Inspectors in tracking and prosecuting several gangs of dacoits and burglars—one in Sabroom where 12 prominent members of Makku Palwan's gang were successfully prosecuted, another in Radhakishorepur P. S. where 14 members of another gang were prosecuted and another in Khowai. In the last case, however, the accused persons were acquitted by the Court of Sessions.

75. Finger print system was introduced during the year under report, resulting in the tracing of 2 old offenders—one with 6 and the other with 15 previous convictions.

76. One of the Sub-Inspectors, 5 of the Naib Darogas and 5 constables were employed in the C. I. D. as in the previous year.

C. I. D. and Intelligence Staff.

77. The total number of cases reported during the year under review was 1,009 as against 1,198 in the previous year.

78. The result of the cases is as follows :—

Number of cases reported
1,009

- Enquiry refused 21
- Number investigated 945
    - True 738
        - Charge-sheet 363
        - Finally reported 375
    - Intentionally false 51
    - Mistake of law 44
    - Mistake of fact 69
    - Noncognizable 43
    - Doubtful 0
- Number pending 43

Result of prosecution

79. Altogether 623 persons were arrested in connection with various offences, and 824 persons sent up for trial by police against 827 and 943 respectively in the previous year. Of the number sent up, 208 were convicted and 178 acquitted (including 59 on compromise and 35 on withdrawal of cases) while 1 died and 437 awaited trial (including the absconding accused). The percentage of convictions was 33·39 against 26·96 of the previous year. This means an improvement over the previous year.

80. Of the 418 persons awaiting trial at the end of the previous year, 111 were convicted, 194 acquitted (including 27 on compromise and 19 on withdrawal of cases) and 113 were awaiting trial at the end of the year under report.

Bad livelihood cases.

81. In the previous year 4 cases of bad livelihood were started against 4 persons, while in the year under report 6 cases were instituted against as many as 33 persons, of whom 28 were bound down, 1 was acquitted and 4 awaited trial.

Arms Act cases.

82. Twenty Arms Act cases were instituted against 21 persons of whom 12 were convicted, 2 discharged and 7 were awaiting trial as the year closed.

83. Five of the stolen guns were recovered by the British Police from the possession of the culprits within their jurisdiction and one by the State Police from within the State.

Recovery of stolen property.

84. Total value of property stolen during the year amounted to Rs. 12,868-9-9 against Rs. 18,282-6-0 of the previous year. Of the amount, Rs. 1,929-7-0 was recovered against Rs. 2,692-12-9 in the previous year. The percentage of recoveries was 14·99 against 14·73 of the previous year.

Dacoity.

85. There were 14 cases of dacoity during the year against 20 in the previous year. 41 persons were sent up in charge sheet in connection with 4 cases, of whom 2 were convicted, 7 acquitted and 32 (including 12 absconding) were awaiting trial at the close of the year.

Unnatural death.

86. Seventyone cases of unnatural deaths were reported during the year. On enquiry, one turned out to be a case of murder. No foul play was detected in any other case.

Rewards and punishments.

87. Two Inspectors, 9 Sub-Inspectors, 9 Naib Darogas, 1 Writer Naib Daroga, 2 Armed constables, 17 constables and one Choukidar received money reward, while 2 Sub-Inspectors, 1 Naib Daroga, 1 Writer Naib Daroga, 3 Jamadars, 1 Havildar, 1 Naik, 8 constables (Armed), and 18 constables (ordinary) were fined or degraded; one Choukidar only was dismissed.

Tour.

88. The Superintendent of Police was out on tour for 61 days against 66 days in the previous year and the Assistant Superintendent of Police for 20 days against 50 days in the previous year.

Co-operation.

89. The relation with the police of the neighbouring districts in British India continued to be satisfactory. The system of co-operation meeting of the Circle Inspectors with their own and British Police Officers concerned of adjoining British Districts was introduced in the year under report.

Town Protection and Musketry Practice.

90. The Superintendent of Police with four Sub-Inspectors, 1 Subadar, 1 armed Sub-Inspetor, 1 Jamadar, 1 Havildar and 35 constables joined the Town Protection Practice.

91. The system of musketry and revolver practice which was introduced in the previous year was continued in the year under review and the result was satisfactory.

Expenditure.

92. The expenditure amounted to Rs. 86,836 against Rs. 85,242 in the previous year.

IV. Justice.

Courts.

93. There were 15 courts of justice in the State during the year under report, exercising both civil and criminal jurisdiction, viz :—the Khas Adalat (High Court) with its original and appellate sides and 14 courts of Magistrate-Munsiffs exercising original jurisdiction only.

Khas Adalat (High Court).

94. Babu Jnanendra Mohan Das, B. L., continued as Chief Judge and Babu Ramani Mohan Goswami, M. A., B. L., as Civil and Sessions Judge in the original side during the year. Thakur Tarini Charan Deb Barman continued as Puisne Judge till the end of the previous year and on his retirement Thakur Hriday Ranjan Deb Barman, a senior member of the Tripura Civil Service, was appointed Puisne Judge and continued as such till the end of the year 1343 T. E.

Number of original criminal cases.

95. Altogether 1966 criminal cases were instituted during the year under report as against 2030 of the previous year. With the balance of 567 pending from the previous year, the total number of cases for disposal before the several subordinate original courts was 2533 as against 2547 of the previous year as detailed below ; and out of these 2533 cases,

1882 were disposed of as against 1980 of the preceding year, leaving 651 cases pending at the close of the year. Thus, in the year under report, the number of cases for disposal decreased by 14 from that of the previous year, and there was also a decrease in disposal by 98.

DESCRIPTION OF OFFENCES.	1342 T. E.	1343 T. E.
Offences against the State and public tranquillity	77	69
Offences against person	670	695
Offences against property	1,284	1,236
Other offences	516	533
TOTAL	2,547	2,533

Extradition from British India.

96. Extradition of 179 persons was asked for during the year. With 153 persons pending surrender at the close of the previous year, the total number of offenders required to be surrendered was 332, of whom 57 persons were arrested and surrendered by the British Indian Police and 106 persons appeared of their own accord or were subsequently arrested within the State.

Persons brought to trial.

97. The total number of persons brought to trial in the year under report inclusive of the number pending from the preceding year was 2953 against 3503 of the previous year. The number brought to trial within the year under review was 2139, of whom 593 persons were arrested by the Police, 503 were produced on warrant, 737 appeared on summons, 294 appeared voluntarily and 11 persons were arrested in the presence of Magistrates.

Result of cases.

98. Out of 2953 persons before the courts including the Sessions Court, 814 persons were discharged without trial, 569 were acquitted, 770 were convicted, 8 died, 2 escaped and 790 persons remained under trial at the close of the year. Out of the convicted persons, 243 were sentenced to various terms of imprisonment extending from below 1 month to 5 years and above, 1 person was imprisoned for life, 488 were sentenced to fines only, 12 were bound down and 26 persons were warned for the future. The number of persons actually tried was 1339 as against 1487 of the previous year and the percentage of conviction was thus 57·50 against 42·57 of the previous year.

Cases concerning British subjects.

99. Of the 2533 cases for disposal as stated above, the number of cases in which British subjects were either complainants or accused was 480 as against 454 of the previous year. Out of these, 399 cases were cognizable and 81 non-cognizable. In 33 cases, British subjects were complainants and in 447 cases they were the accused. In 103 cases both the parties were British subjects. In all, 642 persons were actually brought under trial during the year under report, as against 598 of the preceding year. Out of those 642 persons, 347 persons were convicted, 193 acqitted or discharged 1 escaped and 101 remained under trial at the close of the year.

100. The following statement will show the number of original criminal cases instituted during the last two years.

DESCRIPTION OF OFFENCES.	1342 T.E.	1343 T. E.	Increase.	Decrease.
Offences against the State and public tranquillity ...	61	55	0	6
Offences against person	541	560	19	0
Offences against property	1,026	922	0	104
Other offences	402	429	27	0
TOTAL	2,030	1,966	46	110

Decreased by 64.

101. 27 cases were committed to the Sessions during the year under report and 1 case was pending from the previous year. Out of these 28 cases, 24 were disposed of during the year as detailed in the following table. The number of persons involved in those 28 cases was 70, of whom 30 were convicted, 35 were acquitted, 2 escaped and 3 remained under trial at the close of the year.

Sessions cases.

Description of cases.	Number of cases.	Disposed of.	Pending.	REMARKS.
Culpable homicide	6	5	1	
Lurking house trespass and rape ...	1	1	0	
Murder	1	1	0	
Grievous hurt and culpable homicide ...	1	1	0	
Rape	1	0	1	
Dacoity	7	6	1	
Dacoity and conspiracy	1	1	0	
Arson		3	1	
Assembling for purpose of committing dacoity	1	1	0	
Arson with intent to murder	1	1	0	
False complaint (sec. 211 I. P. C.) ...	1	1	0	
Possessing instruments and materials for counterefiting coins	1	1	0	
Conspiracy and murder with abduction and concealment of dead body ...	1	1	0	
Theft	1	1	0	
Total	28	24	4	

102. There were altogether 236 criminal appeals as against 248 of the previous year. These appeals were disposed of as shown below :—

Criminal appeals.

Rejected	5
Judgment affirmed	107
Modified	42
Reversed	18
Further enquiry ordered	26
	198
Pending	38
Total	236

103. The percentage of judgments affirmed and modified was 77·20 as against 86·60 of the previous year.

104. The number of original civil suits instituted during the year under report was 18,00 as against 2,057 of the previous year. With the balance of 906 suits pending from the preceding year, the total number of suits for disposal

Original Civil suits.

was 2,706 as against 2,790 of the previous year. These were disposed of as shown below :—

Exparte	926
Admitted and compromised	171
Dismissed for want of prosecution ...	167
Disposed of on contest...	593
	1,857
Pending	849
Total	2,706

Duration of suits.

105. The average duration of suits in the civil courts was 2 months and 14 days as against 2 months and 20 days in 1342 T. E.

Nature and value of suits.

106. The total value of civil suits instituted during the year was Rs. 1,53,386-5-9, as against Rs. 1,72,819-3-10 of the previous year, which gives an average of Rs. 85-3-5 per case. Out of 1,800 suits, instituted during the year under review, 342 related to land, 1,085 to money transactions and 373 to other transactions. 1,070 suits were of the value of Rs. 100 and under; 374 suits were of the value between Rs. 100 and Rs. 500; 20 suits of value between Rs. 500 and Rs. 1,000; 16 suits of value between Rs. 1,000 and Rs. 5,000; 1 suit was of value above Rs. 5,000 and 319 suits were not estimable in money value.

Execution of decrees.

107. The number of applications for the execution of decrees filed during the year was 772 and there were 690 pending from the previous years. The total number for disposal was thus 1,462 as against 1,534 of the preceding year. The aggregate value of the new applications was Rs. 1,08,381-0-2 and that of the pending applications Rs. 1,53,259-3-9, the total value thus amounting to Rs. 2,61,640-3-11. The number of applications disposed of was 851, the value of which was Rs. 1,32,754-12-2. The number of execution cases pending at the close of the year was 611, the value thereof being Rs. 1,28,885-7-9.

Civil appeals.

108. There were 147 civil appeals filed during the year as against 174 of the previous year. With the balance of 118 from the previous year, the total number of civil appeals for disposal was 265 against 314 of the preceding year. Out of these cases, 159 were disposed of during the year under report as against 196 of the previous year, leaving a balance of 106 cases at the close of the year.

Results of civil appeals.

109. The following figures will show the results of appeals in civil suits :—

Decisions confirmed	72
,, reversed	31
,, modified	18
Remanded	12
Compromised and otherwise disposed of ...	26
	159

110. The percentage of judgments wholly or partly upheld, excluding those in the cases compromised was 67·66 against 61·96 of the preceding year.

Percentage.

111. The total value of civil appeals filed during the year under review was Rs. 8,627-5-9 and the average duration of each appeal was 4 months and 12 days against 4 months and 10 days of the previous year.

Value and duration of appeals.

112. 26 civil suits were instituted in the original side, Khas Adalat, during the year under report as against 15 of the previous year. With the balance of 49 suits pending from the preceding year, the total for disposal was 75 against 79 of the previous year. Of these, 27 suits were disposed of against 30, leaving 48 suits pending at the close of the year. There were 47 execution cases during the year including 34 cases pending from the previous year. Of these, 10 were disposed of and 37 remained pending at the close of the year. There were 19 applications for succession and other certificates during the year under report; with the balance of 20 from the previous year the total number of cases was 39, out of which 22 were disposed of as shown below and 17 remained pending at the close of the year.

Original Side cases.

Description of cases.	Total.	Disposed of.	Pending.
Probate case	3	0	3
Succession certificate	20	16	4
Guardianship	16	6	10
Total	39	22	17

113. The total number of civil and criminal appeals inclusive of the number pending from the previous year, was 501 as against 562 of the previous year. Out of these cases, 357 were disposed of as against 406 of the preceding year. In comparison with the previous year, total number of cases for disposal decreased by 61 and there was a corresponding decrease in disposal by 49.

Total number of appeals.

Description of appeals.	Number of appeals.		Disposed of.	
	Past year.	Present year.	Past year.	Present year.
Civil	314	265	196	159
Criminal	248	236	210	198
Total	562	501	406	357

V. Prisons.

114. Exclusive of the Central Jail at the Capital, there were 7 sub-jails in the State in the year under report. Dr. M. M. Majumdar, Chief Medical Officer, continued to be the Superintendent of the Central Jail.

Number of Jails.

115. The total jail population during the year numbered 1393 as against 1174 in the previous year—the daily average being 142·82 as against 132·01. Of them, 632 were convicts, 755 undertrials and 6 civil prisoners. Altogether 166 prisoners remained at the close of the year in the jails as against 159 in the year before.

Jail population.

116. Three detenues were admitted into the Central Jail in the course of the year under review.

Detenues

117. 76 prisoners were under more than 2 years' imprisonment as against 78 in the preceding year. Their offence, sentence and occupation are detailed below.

Longterm prisoners.

Class of offence.	Number of prisoners.	Occupation.	REMARKS.
Murder	18	They were employed in brick manufacturing, oilmills, *soorki* pounding, *khoa* breaking, bamboo and cane work, gardening, weaving, tailoring, paddy husking, rice manufacturing etc.	51 had sentences of 2 to 5 years, 10 of 5 to 10 years, 1 of 10 to 14 years and 14 for life *i. e.* 20 years.
Culpable homicide not amounting to murder... ...	12		
Grievous hurt	2		
Robbery	4		
Theft	6		
Dacoity	20		
Counterfeiting coin	1		
Kidnapping	1		
Rape	6		
Unnatural offence	1		
Receiving stolen property ...	2		
Arson	1		
Forgery	1		
Attempt to commit suicide ...	1		
Total	76		

118. 10 undertrials from the Bilonia sub-jail, 1 undertrial from the Kailashahar sub-jail, 4 undertrials from the Sonamura sub-jail and one undertrial from the Dharmanagar sub-jail escaped during the year under report. Excepting 10 undertrials of the Bilonia sub-jail all of them were re-arrested.

Escape.

119. 20 convicts were trained under a paid tutor during the year. Of them, 2 appeared at and passed the Pathshala Scholarship Examination—one in the First Division and the other in the Second Division. Besides, religious instruction was given as before.

Education in the Central Jail Reformatory School

200. With the addition of two sub-jails of Kailashahar and Bilonia during the year the guarding of all sub-jails came under the direct management of the Jail Department. The total number of warders employed in all jails was 69 including 10 Senior Warders or Jamaders. Of them, 2 warders had to be dismissed, 19 warders fined, 13 punished with extra drill and one suspended for offences of sorts.

Warders.

121. Three convicts died in the Central jail during the year under review—one of chronic nephritis, one of bacillary dysentery and the other of chronic diarrhoea. Jail health was generally good.

Jail health

122. The total income from the Central Jail amounted to Rs. 4763-3-3 as against Rs. 4107-12-6 in the preceding year. The subjails fetched no income.

Income.

123. The total expenditure during the year under report stood at Rs. 23,364 as against Rs. 21804 in the year previous.

Expenditure

VI. Registration.

124. Mr. S. C. Deb Barman, M. A. (Harvard), Senior Naib Dewan, remained in charge of the Department.

Charge.

125. The number of Registration offices continued to be 9 as in the previous year—there being one at the headquarters station of each of the Divisions and Sub-divisions. In the moffusil, the Divisional and Sub-divisional Officers and in certain divisions the second officers acted as Registrars. For the Sadar Division there was a separate Registrar at Agartala.

Registration offices.

126. The total number of documents presented for registration during the year including 96 documents pending at the end of the previous year was 6265 against 6636. Of this number, 50 deeds were refused registration on different grounds and 97 remained pending at the end of the year against 96 pending at the end of the previous year.

Registration and Disposal.

127. The total value covered by the documents amounted to Rs. 6,92,895 as against Rs. 9,96,275 of the previous year, while the total value covered by the documents actually registered was Rs. 6,79,981 as against Rs. 9,63,565 in the year before.

Value of deeds presented and registered.

128. The number of suits brought before the Registration Department in respect of documents, the registration of which had been refused in the Registration offices was 17 against 24 suits in the previous year. There was 1 appeal during the year against 3 in the year before. There were 44 suits and 2 appeals pending from the previous year making a total of 61 suits and 3 appeals during the year under report. Out of these, 25 suits and 3 appeals were disposed of during the year, leaving 36 suits pending at the close of the year.

Suits and Appeals.

129. The total income of the Department from fees and fines amounted to Rs. 5,701 against Rs. 6,112 and the expenditure to Rs. 3,574 against Rs. 3,129 in the previous year. The net income thus amounted to Rs. 2,127 in the year

Income and expenditure.

under report against Rs. 2,983 in the previous year. The net income of the year was less by Rs. 856 in comparison with that of the previous year which was mainly due to the world-wide economic depression during the year under review.

VII. Municipality and Sanitation.

130. As before, the capital of Agartala continued to be the only Municipal town in the State with a population of about 10,000 according to the last census.

Municipality.

131. The Municipal Committee consisted of nine members—all nominated, of whom one was official Chairman and another non-official Vice-Chairman who were appointed with the approval of His Highness the Maharaja Manikya Bahadur. Babu Jogesh Chandra Datta, B. A., Personal Assistant to the Minister having resigned the Chairmanship in the month of Baisak, the Vice-Chairman, Babu Haridas Bhattacharjee, officiated till the vacancy was filled in permanently by Mr. S. C. Deb Barma, M. A. (Harvard), Senior Naib Dewan, in the middle of the year under review.

Municipal Committee.

Altogether 6 sittings of the committee were held during the year, the average attendance of members being 5·6 as against 6 of the previous year.

132. The realization on account of Municipal and Latrine taxes showed appreciable improvement, Rs. 4612-11-9 having been collected as against Rs. 3594-0-9 in the preceding year. The total demand inclusive of arrears was Rs. 9048-9-3 of which Rs. 505-1-3 was irrecoverable.

Income.

The income under Miscellaneous head including deposits was Rs. 1061-14-3 as against Rs. 864-4-0 of the year previous. Thus the income of the municipality inclusive of the State grant of Rs. 8000 and an advance of Rs. 2353-14-3 received from the Bazar Improvement fund for the payment of outstanding bills, was Rs. 16028-8-3 as against Rs. 12458-4-9 of the year before.

133. The total expenditure of the Municipality excluding the amount spent on the Bazar improvement amounted to Rs. 16034-0-0 as against Rs. 12428-12-3 in the preceding year.

Expenditure.

134. The control and management of the Bazar at the capital remained, as before, with the Municipal Committee. The total demand including the arrear demand was Rs. 11900-11-9 of which Rs. 584-8-6 was irrecoverable. The total receipts of the year amounted to Rs. 6470-12-3 as against Rs. 6672-6-6 of the previous year.

Ishanganja Bazar.

The Bazar income is set apart for Bazar improvement only. A plot of land had to be acquired at a cost of Rs. 3722-14-0 for the proposed shifting of the Bazar further to the south of the present site. After neccessary expenditure of Rs. 5228-0-9 the Bazar fund stood at Rs. 39605-0-9 as balance at the close of the year.

135. Better arrangement for supply of good drinking water in certain parts of the town appeared necessary and it pleased His Highness the Maharaja Manikya Bahadur to direct excavation of a tank to the north of the Ujjayanta Palace which is likely to remove the want. The Municipality arranged to reserve tanks under proper guard as a safeguard against probable contamination during the cholera epidemic.

Water Supply.

136. The health of the town was on the whole not quite satisfactory. There were 41 cases of cholera with 16 deaths and 4 cases of small-pox which were cured by the local small-pox doctors.

Health.

It may be noted here that malaria prevailed throughout the greater part of the year under report and there was recrudescence of kala-azar also.

137. A sum of Rs. 1305 was spent on some sanitary works within the town. One old tank (Nazir tank) was re-excavated.

Sanitation.

138. As before, Dr. M. M. Majumdar, Chief Medical Officer, remained in charge of the Municipal and Sanitation Departments.

Charge.

139. A very pleasant and notable function of the year under review was the grand civic reception accorded to our beloved newly born Maharaj Kumar Kirit Bikram Deb Barman Bahadur on the occasion of his first entry in the State Capital on the 7th Falgoon. On arrival of H. H. the Maharaja Manikya Bahadur with the beloved prince at the municipal gate erected on the boundary of the town. 101 bombs were fired and they were garlanded and received by the Chairman and the municipal commissioners who then conducted the party to the reception pandel. Agartala, the capital town, was profusely illuminated and the citizens vied with each other in decorating their homesteads.

CHAPTER IV—PRODUCTION AND DISTRIBUTION.

I. Weather and Crops—Agriculture.

140. Manyabara Rana Bodhjung Bahadur F. R. G. S., Chief Secretary to His Highness the Maharaja Manikya Bahadur continued to be in charge of the Department assisted by Mr. J. C. Choudhury, S. E. M. S. A. (Tokio) M. R. A. (Agri) S. (London) as Superintendent of Agriculture.

The charge of the Department.

141. The staff of the Department continued to be the same as it was in the previous year except that one Fieldman U. C. Mazumder died, in the middle of the year, of black-water fever after his return from a long hill tour. This has been detrimental to the progress of sericultural experiments in Udaipur and other southern Divisions of the State.

Staff.

142. Propaganda campaign was continued as before in Khowai, Kailashahar, Dharmanagar, Udaipur and Sonamura Divisions. Special propaganda was carried on towards extension of cultivation of improved variety of sugarcane, cereals, Eri silk and English vegetables. The Propaganda Stand at Agartala Bazar dealt with seed distribution and the use of Niciphos and Sulphate of Ammonia as useful manures for the rainy and winter crops.

Propaganda.

143. The Propaganda Stand at Agartala Bazar served the purpose of demonstration with English vegetable seeds and also rainy season crops. A depot for chemical manures was arranged to be opened at Girish Bank Ltd., supplies being obtained from the Imperial Chemical Industries Ltd. of Calcutta.

144. About 12,000 cuttings of Coimbatore sugarcane were distributed in Kalyanpur and Sadar Division and the result was satisfactory on the whole. Various seeds for horticulture were also distributed among the people.

Seed distribution and demonstration.

145. The highest temperature was 90 degree and the lowest 45 degree in the year under report which was about the same as in the previous year.

Temperature.

146. The average rainfall of the year was 83·02″ against 70·56″ in the previous year. The quinquennial average was 85·44″. Sabroom Division had the maximum fall of 95·41″ and Amarpur Sub-Division the minimum of 65·71″. The rainfall was the heaviest in the month of Bhadra averaging 18·69.″

Rainfall.

147. Due to excessive rains and flood there was scarcity of food grains amongst certain hill people in Sabroom Division and a loan of Rs. 400 was issued. The amount was however realised before the close of the year. Some scarcity was also felt in Amarpur Division but the situatiou did not cause any anxiety.

148. There was flood in Belonia Division twice in Bhadra owing to excessive rain causing damages to crops and house property. For several years Udaipur Division has been subject to flood visitations and the year under review was no exception to the annual inundation. Crops were damaged in the plains of the Division but a good harvest was obtained in the hills.

149. The principal crops were paddy, jute, mustard, *til*, sugarcane and cotton. The cultivation of pineapples increased to a great extent during the year. Potatoes tobacco chillies, and pulses of various types were also grown in some parts of the State.

Crops.

150. Male labourers earned from 4 annas to 8 annas, female labourers from 3 annas to 5 annas a day. Gharamies earned from 4 annas to 8 annas and carpenter and masons from 8 annas to Re. 1 only. Most of the labourers were outsiders from the neighbouring British districts as well as up-country coolies.

Wages and labour.

151. The prices of food-grains were similar to those in the neighbouring British districts. Rice sold from Rs. 2-4 to Rs. 4-8 and paddy sold from Re. 1 to Rs. 2-8 per maund.

Prices.

152. The people of the State are mostly agriculturists. They suffered a great deal owing to financial difficulties, as the price of the indigenous commodities continued to be low. The condition of the hill population was slightly better.

Condition of the people.

153. Even though much hampered by the world-wide depression, Tea Industry undoubtedly made headway towards progress during the year under review. No new garden was started during the year under report, yet the financial condition of almost all the existing Companies within the State has appreciably improved as compared the past two or three years. The export from almost all the companies has increased in comparison with that of the past year and consequently the revenue. As an important factor among the sources of revenue, it is having due attention and backing from the authorities.

Tea Industry.

154. It is now established beyond doubt that the soil, rainfall and climatic condition of this State are quite suitable for tea plantation and this industry, though in its infancy here, shows sure indication of prosperity.

155. No *Taccavi* advances were made during the year under review.

Taccavi.

156. The Superintendent of Agriculture inspected the Kalyanpur Reserve area, Khowai Division and several tea estates on his way to the Kalyanpur Reserve area.

Agricultural Survey of Kalyanpur Reserve.

157. Several private agricultural farms have been started by some enterprising Bhadralok youths and their number is increasing gradually.

Private Farms.

158. Rinderpest, and foot and mouth disease prevailed in various parts of the State. 1401 animals in the Veterinary Dispensary at Agartala and 150 animals at moffusil were treated by the Veterinary Surgeon.

Veterinary.

159. The Superintendent of Agriculture was out on tour for 31 days and the Veterinary Surgeon for 47 days only during the year.

Tour of the Staff.

II. Immigration and Emigration.

160. The charge of the Department was, as before held by Manyabara Rana Saheb Bodhjung Bahadur, F. R. G. S., Chief Secretary to His Highness the Maharaja Manikya Bahadur except during the periods, when he was on duty with His Highness the Maharaja Manikya Bahadur, in mofussil, from 6th Jaistha to 23rd Sravan, 6th Asvin to 25th Asvin and from 11th Agrahayan to 6th Falgoon, when Dewan Saheb K. Dutt, M. A, B. L., F. R. E. S., M. R. A. S., Private Secretary to His Highness the Maharaja Manikya Bahadur remained in charge. The office of the Assistant to the Chief Secretary in this Department, was, as in the previous year, with Mr. B. C. Dev Varman.

Charge of the Department.

161. During the year under review 1,602 families immigrated into the State.

Immigration.

162. Families from various directions came to settle down in Kulaihaor during the year under review and the quantity of land required for them was 464 *drones* 2 *kanis* and 10 *gandas* but proposals in respect of 273 *drones*, 2 *kanis* and 10 *gandas* of land after proper enquiry only for 173 families could be sent up to Kailasahar office for sanction. The total number of 399 families are living in the immigration area and reclaiming lands selected for each of them, thus showing a great deal of progress towards reclamation during the year under report.

Kulaihaor.

163. As settlement could not be made promptly for want of a settlement officer on the spot, arrangements have been made, for the convenience of the applicants to allow them the right of reclaiming lands on payment of a part *Nazar* of Re. 1 out of Rs. 8 per *drone*, pending final settlement. This arrangement has, proved very successful.

164. The health of the immigrants was reported to have been good during the year under review.

Health of the immigrants.

165. The construction of the Kamalpur-Ambassa road up to Salema including temporary bamboo bridges was completed. The entire road is now open to motor traffic, thus rendering facilities to all to travel this distance of 16 miles in a short time. The condition of the road is now very satisfactory.

Condition of the road.

166. The diversion work of the Dhalai course in Manik Bhandar has proved a success. This was imperative to protect the road in that village, from rapid erosion.

Dhalai Diversion Successful in Manik Bhandar.

167. Ranar Bazar at Salema made considerable progress, the number of shops and quantity of sale having increased to some extent, during the year under report.

Ranar Bazar.

168. The natural water flow supplying pure drinking water was a relief in the scarcity of drinking water to some extent.

169. The total number of patients both old and new who received treatment in Kulaihaor Dispensary were new 2796 old 654 = 3450 against 2852 in the previous year.

Kulaihaor Dispensary.

170. During the year under review the Chief Secretary visited the immigration area twice viz.—once in the beginning of the year and again towards the close, when he noted the progress made. In course of the latter journey, the construction of the road with bridges over the cherras and nalas was found to have been completed and the Chief Secretary with his Assistant motored from Srimangal right up to Salema over the new road.

Tour of the Chief Secretary.

171. Jote settlement of 5 *drones* and 8 *Kanis* of lands was granted during the year and a nazar of Rs. 692-8 was realised on this account.

Kalyanpur Reserve area. Jote Settlement.

172. Relinquishment of 62 *drones* of waste lands was accepted and consequently a revenue of Rs. 3893-0-6 has to be remitted.

Relinquishment

173. Namjari Nazar of Rs. 174 was realised during the year against nil in the previous year.

Namjari Nazar.

174. The staff consisted of one permanent and 4 temporary Amins. The Head Amin and the Taujinabis of the Khowai Divisional Office were, in addition to their duties, engaged in the Reserve work till the close of the year when a Moharer for the Reserve work was appointed by this Department.

Staff.

175. During the year under report the total expenditure on account of the Reserve work amounted to Rs. 1343-9-6- against Rs. 1073-12-3 in the previous year.

Expenditure.

III. Forests.

176. Babu Jatindra Nath Mitra, Naib Dewan, was in charge of the Department. With the exception of a few *Mahals* which were let out iu *Ijara*, all the forests were under *Khas* management as before.

Charge & Management.

177. Including the Patrol staff with a Forester, three Head Guards and twenty guards, the Department had a staff of one Station Officer, two Forest Circle Inspectors, fourteen Foresters, fourteen Assistant Foresters, five Rangers, seven Moharers, twentyfour Head guards, eleven Literate Guards and 151 guards.

Staff.

178. During the year under report the Patrol Staff which is in 3 sections was out on tour in the following Divisions :—

179. One Section was on tour in the Sadar Division for 9 months and 22 days, another in Sonamura Division for 7 months only, and the third in Bilonia Division for 4 months and seventeen days and Sabroom Division for 5 days only.

180. There were 134 commissioned agents for the sale of forest permits for the shoulder borne export of minor forest produce.

Permits.

181. There were 51 forest stations for collection of duty and prevention of forest offences. One new Beat Office with a Head Guard and two guards was established during the year under report for the protection of the newly declared Fuel Reserve for supply of fuel in the capital town of Agartala.

Forest Station.

182. The Reserved *Sal* forests of the Sonamura Division continued to be worked under the system of coppice with standards and those of the Udaipur Division under the Improvement Method, while the open unclassed forests were worked under the State Forest Rules of 1323 T. E. but for the Feni river *Mahal* the working rules of the Bengal Forest Department were followed.

Working of the Forests.

183. During the year under report kheda operations were undertaken in 3 places-one in the Kailashahar Division and two in the Sonamura Division. 5 elephants were caught in the Kailasahar Division and 10 in the Sonamura Division.

Kheda operations.

184. The Toll Station at Amlighat continued to be under the management of the State Forest Department. The total revenue collected at the station in the year under review was Rs. 39,073 against Rs. 41,086 in the previous year. As before a Sub-Assistant Surgeon was appointed temporarily for four months from December to March last for giving medical relief to the station staff and to the cutters and exporters of forest produce.

Feni river Mahal.

185. As in the previous year, the forest produce from the Fee Simple Lots above the Amlighat Toll Station was exported under passes granted by the Collector of Chittagong.

Fee Simple Lots.

186. In the year under review there were 238 forest cases against 483 persons including 57 cases against 145 persons pending from the previous year. The offences are mainly for export of forest produce without payment of duty.

Forest Offences.

187. Altogether 174 cases against 358 persons were tried of whom 23 were sentenced to imprisonment only; 266 were punished with fine only; and 20 were both imprisoned and fined; 3 were warned and 46 were acquitted. 11 cases against 15 persons were compounded and 53 cases against 110 persons remained pending at the close of the year.

Results.

188. One Forester, one Assistant Forester, five Head Guards, one Literate Guard and 24 guards were rewarded for intelligent detection of cases of smuggling of forest produce. Two Foresters and one guard were fined for misconduct.

Rewards & Punishment.

189. The health of the staff was generally good.

Health of the Staff.

190. The following table shows the results of the collection of forest revenue :—

Sources of Revenue.

Heads of Revenue.	1343 T.E.	1342 T.E.	Increase.	Decrease.	REMARKS.
I. Unclassed open forests :—					
(a) Toll on forest produce exported by the river mehals	2,59,017	2,75,001	—	15,984	
(b) Toll on forest produce exported by land route under permit	61,835	60,191	1,644	—	
(c) Toll collection (share) of the Feni river mehal ...	27,073	28,086	—	1,013	
(d) Grazing mehal ...	8,041	6,003	2,038	—	
(e) Thatching grass mehal	2,858	3.379	—	521	
II. Reserved Forests :—					
Sale of *Sal* etc	3,894	1,975	1,919	—	
III. Elephant Kheddas	2,616	1 628	988	—	
TOTAL ...	3,65,334	3,76,263	6,589	17,518	

191. Details of collection in the year under report are given below :—

Heads of Revenue.	Quantity of produce exported. Cft.	Duty realised thereon. Rs.	REMARKS.
1. Timber other than Sal...	3,53,563·0	53,350	
2. *Sal*	12,461	2,616	
3. Produce other than timber.			
(*a*) Exported under *bhatials*	—	2,05,667	
(*b*) Exported by land routes under permits ...	—	61,835	
4. Toll collection (State share) of the Feni river			
(*a*) Timber	12,205·2	2,190	
(*b*) Other produce ...	—	24,883	
5. Grazing *Mahal* ...	—	8,041	
6. Thatching grass *Mahal*	—	2,858	
7. Elephant Khedas ...	—	2,616	
Total quantity of timber	3,78,229·2	Total 3,65,334	

Receipts.

192. The total forest revenue of the year under report was Rs. 3,65,334 against Rs. 3,76,263 in the previous year showing a decrease of Rs. 10,929 which is attributable to general trade depression and less export of timber for want of timely flood in the rivers.

Maharaja Match Factory.

193. During the year under report, the Match Factory manufactured 8,360 gross of finished match boxes and paid Rs. 78-6-0 to the State as duty on timber used in making these matches.

General.

194. Plantations of Sal, Mahogany and Sonal were started in His Highness' domain.

Tour.

195. The Naib Dewan was out on tour for 103 days during the year under report.

IV. Trade and Manufacture.

196. The principal exports were timber and other forest produce of various kinds, cotton, oil-seeds (*til* and mustard seed), paddy, jute,

tea, rice and *Gur* (molasses). Some homespun cotton fabrics manufactured by the hill people, especially by the Manipuris were also exported. The principal exports for the year under review and of the Previous years are shown below.

	1341 T. E.	1342 T. E.	1343 T. E.
Cotton ...	56,034 mds.	51,918 mds.	43,290 mds.
Til ...	14,761 „	36,918 „	9,898 „
Mustard seeds	25,936 „	30,398 „	19,704 „
Jute ...	30,454 „	84,904 „	44,162 „
Tea ...	15,21,534 lbs.	15,11,334 lbs.	17,70,097 lbs.

V. Public Works.

197. The Minister himself was in charge of the Public Works Department as before. Honorary Lieutenant J. N. Bhaduri, B. E., continued as State Engineer during the year under report.

Charge.

198. Statement XX in the appendix gives details of the works executed during the year, the total expenditure including Improvement Works being Rs. 1,66,799 as detailed below against Rs. 1,06,398 in the previous year.

Expenditure.

Description of works.	Ordinary Public works.	Improvement works.	TOTAL.
Buildings.	61,873	22,994	84,867
Roads & Bridges.	6,917	34,228	41,145
Tanks & Tube Wells.	1,940	2,180	4,120
Miscellaneous Works.	4,056	13,744	17,800
Minor works at Rajbari.	991	—	991
Establishment charges.	17,876	—	17,876
TOTAL...	93,653	73,146	1,66,799

199. The Minister's Office Building was almost completed during the year under review. The following other works were done during the year :—

Improvement.

1. Manu Teshil Kutchery at Sabroom with C. I. Roof.
2. Bilonia Jail Extension and Lock-up with C. I. Roof.

3. Some additional works on Sabroom Divisional Office building.
4. The earth-work of Prasad Pratuli and Champaknagar Roads.
5. Collection of stone metals for the Akhaura-Agartala. Road.
6. A re-inforced concrete bridge over the Akhaura Khal near the Reserve Police Line.
7. A tank was excavated at Khowai, the cost having been paid from the Local Fund.
8. Rs. 4309 as detailed below, was received from outside for the maintenance of the State roads which was also spent for road improvement.
   (a) Rs. 2809 from the British Government for road development works.
   (b) Rs. 1500 from the District Board of Tippera as their annual contribution for Agartala-Akhaura Road.
9. The total expenditure in connection with Electric Supply was Rs. 15,002 as against Rs. 17,125.

CHAPTER V—REVENUE AND FINANCE.

I. Revenue.

200. The total collection in the year was Rs. 13,39,810 against Rs. 13,49,108 in the previous year.

201. The details of income under different heads with all variations are given in the statement below :—

Serial number.	Heads of Revenue.	1343 T. E.	1342 T. E.	As compared with 1342 T. E.		Remarks.
				Increase.	Decrease.	
1.	Land Revenue	4,50,707	4,18,825	31,882	—	
2.	Rents of markets	6,137	6,477	—	340	
3.	Family Tax in the hills	46,960	45,459	1,501	—	
4.	Toll on forest produce	3,20,852	3,35,192	—	14,340	
5.	Do. Do. on the Feni Rivers	27,073	28,086	—	1,013	
6.	Elephant & buffalo grazing Mehal	8,041	6,003	2,038	—	
7.	Thatching grass Mehal	2,858	3,379	—	521	
8.	Reserved *Sal* Forests	3,894	1,975	1,919	—	
9.	Tax on cotton and oil-seeds ..	1,06,839	1,40,040	—	33,201	
10.	Royalty on elephants caught ...	2,616	1,628	988	—	
11.	Adda Mehal	24,435	22,499	1,936	—	
12.	Excise	41,654	40,279	1,375	—	
13.	Stamps and Court-fees	61,514	66,415	—	4,901	
14.	Law and Justice (Fines)... ...	2,356	2,274	82	—	
15.	Process fees	10,154	11,650	—	1,496	
16.	Registration	6,095	5,869	226	—	
17.	Jail	4,770	2,111	2,659	—	
18.	Cattle pounds	3,747	4,349	—	602	
19.	Nazars	29,620	25,663	3,957	—	
20.	Education...	14,566	14,086	480	—	
21.	Tea Export duty	12,580	9,318	3,262	—	
22.	Jute Export duty	31,964	31,388	576	—	
23.	Depreciation Contribution ...	77,224	80,850	—	3,626	
24.	Recovery of personal advances	—	1,319	—	1,319	
25.	Miscellaneous	43,154	43,974	—	820	
	Total	13,39,810	13,49,108	52,881	62,179	Net increase— Rs. 9,298

202. Income under the head "Recovery of personal advances" has been included into the head "Miscellaneous" during the year under review.

203. There was a decrease in respect of 11 heads of income aggregating Rs. 62,179 against an increase, under 14 heads, amounting to Rs. 52,881 which resulted in a net decrease of Rs. 9,298. It may be noted here that the excise income in the previous year was obtained without incurring any establishment charges while in the year under review several mehals were run under *khas* management and the cost amounted to Rs. 11,992. Adding the same to the net decrease of Rs. 9,298 the real decrease stands at Rs. 21,290.

204. The increase under head Land Revenue should not be taken to denote good collection as the percentage of collection has been on the wane since 1340 T. E.

205. The Tea duty increased in comparison with the previous 2 years which was due to rise in price and larger export.

206. The increase under other heads is not noticeable.

207. The increase under head Excise is not real as the income includes the cost of Khas management of Sadar Excise mehals. With a deduction of the same the income stands at Rs. 29,662 as against Rs. 40,279 in the previous year, which means a net decrease of Rs. 10,617. The fall in Excise income in respect of shops on the Assam border was due to the action of the authorities of the Government of Assam in suddenly reducing the rates of duty on *ganja* from Rs. 69 to Rs. 29 owing to which a number of shops were adversely affected and some surrendered their licences.

208. The income under head "Stamps & Court fees" was Rs. 61,514 as against Rs. 66,415 in the previous year and Rs. 1,06,120 in 1339 T. E. The marked fall under this head as well as under "Process fees" as compared with the previous year does not speak well of the condition of the people.

209. The cause of decrease under head "Toll on Forest produce" has been explained in the Forest section.

210. The decrease under head "Tax on Cotton and Oil-seeds" in comparison with 1342 T. E. was Rs. 33,201 and is attributable to a sudden fall in the price of *til*.

II. Finances.

211. A consolidated abstract account of the financial transactions of the State and the attached Zemindaries as compared with those of the previous year is given below :—

Receipts.	1342 T.E.	1343 T.E.
1. Opening balance :—		
(1) State ...	6,51,015	6,66,083
(2) Zemindaries ...	4,14,135	3,39,198
Total ...	10,65,150	10,05,281
2. Income :—		
(1) State ...	13,49,108	13,39,810
(2) Zemindaries ...	8,50,918	9,08,361
Total ...	22,00,026	22,48,171
3. Law charges recovered :—		
(1) Zemindaries ...	38,414	38,576
4. Refunds and compensation for lands acquired :—		
(1) Zemindaries ...	5,263	2,380
5. Deposits :—		
(1) State ...	3,11,572	2,14,494
(2) Zemindaries ...	34,771	33,572
Total ...	3,46,343	2,48,066
6. Loans received :—		
(1) State ...	—	9,00,000
(2) Zemindaries ...	—	—
Total ...	—	9,00,000
GRAND TOTAL ...	36,55,196	44,42,474

Expenditure.	1342 T.E.	1343 T.E.
1. General Administration charges :—		
(a) State ...	5,01,942	5,48,625
(b) Zemindaries :—		
1. Cost of management ...	1,41,279	1,39,358
2. Cost of litigation ...	1,04,882	1,17,193
	2,46,161	2,56,551
Total ...	7,48,103	8,05,176
2. Revenue and Taxes on account of the Zemindaries ...	2,73,821	2,88,830
3. Public Works—(a) State ...	1,11,079	1,69,413
(b) Zemindaries ...	50,491	60,335
Total ...	1,61,570	2,29,748
4. Electric Light—State ...	17,125	15,002
5. Municipality—State ...	8,000	8,000
6. Education—(a) State ...	1,28,441	1,25,021
(b) Zemindaries ...	8,086	8,962
Total ...	1,36,527	1,33,983
7. Medical and Sanitation :—(a) State ...	94,070	97,829
(b) Zemindaries ...	11,156	11,737
Total ...	1,05,226	1,09,566
8. Survey and Settlement—(a) State ...	19,029	36,545
(b) Zemindaries ...	896	1,188
Total ...	19,925	37,733
9. Agriculture, Commerce and Industries—State ...	7,360	7,929
10. Religious Expenses—(a) State ...	57,149	62,948
(b) Zemindaries ...	6,471	6,339
Total ...	63,620	69,287
11. Sultanat—State ...	40,125	62,640
12. Purchase of Land Tenures :—		
(a) State ...	711	10,021
(b) Zemindaries ...	3,630	1,374
Total ...	4,341	11,395
13. Pension and Gratuity—(a) State ...	45,145	56,312
(b) Zemindaries ...	7,925	9,980
Total ...	53,070	66,292
14. Ordinary *Sansar* charges :—		
(a) His Highness's own and the late Maharaja's family ...	88,672	84,167
(b) Other branches of the Raj family ...	1,24,202	1,17,830
(c) Thakurs ...	32,199	31,214
(d) *Sansar* office establishment ...	13,676	12,875
(e) Miscellaneous ...	51,949	97,118
Total ...	3,10,698	3,43,204
15. Charity and Donation :—(a) State ...	15,636	18,387
(b) Zemindaries ...	4,540	6,746
Total ...	20,176	25,133
16. His Highness's Nij Tahabil :—State ...	1,00,000	1,00,000
17. His Highness's tour—State ...	68,000	1,09,495
18. Payment of liabilities and deposits :—		
(a) State ...	1,90,957	59,311
(b) Zemindaries ...	1,23,626	19,965
Total ...	3,14,583	79,276
19. Miscellaneous—(a) State ...	9,146	12,068
(b) Zemindaries ...	3,703	6,300
Total ...	12,849	18,368
20. Advances to employees :— Zemindaries ...	837	600
21. Write off of irrecoverable advances :— State ...	10,000	924
22. Repayment of old debts—State ...	1,33,649	4,88,611
23. Pay of the discharged officers :— State ...	40,310	—
24. Interest on deposits—State ...	—	28,848
Total ...	26,49,915	30,40,040
25 Closing Balance :—		
(a) State		
In Cash ...	1,39,368	1,85,436
At Bank ...	5,076	2,761
Working balance :—		
In Cash ...	—	20,963
At Bank ...	—	3,94,219
In bonds and advances ...	5,21,639	4,48,835
Total ...	6,66,083	10,52,214
(b) Zemindaries :—		
In Cash ...	97,853	1,04,342
At Bank ...	49,651	51,542
In bonds and advances ...	1,91,694	1,94,336
Total ...	3,39,198	3,50,220
Total of State & Zemindaries' balances ...	10,05,281	14,02,434
Total of State & Zemindaries' expenditure ...	26,49,915	30,40,040
GRAND TOTAL ...	36,55,196	44,42,474

212. The year opened with a balance of Rs. 10,05,281 against Rs. 10,65,150 in the year before. During the year under report, the total receipts from all sources including deposits, loans and law charges recovered, amounted to Rs. 34,37,193 against Rs. 25,90,046 in the previous year. Thus the total sum available for expenditure including the opening balance was Rs. 44,42,474 against Rs. 36,55,196. The actual income including receipts under debt heads amounted to Rs. 22,89,127 against Rs. 22,43,703 showing an increase of Rs. 45,424. During the year under report a loan of Rs. 9,00,000 was taken from the Government of India for liquidation of old debts and stabilisation of the finances of the State.

Receipts.

213. The total Expenditure incurred during the year amounted to Rs. 30,40,040 against Rs. 26,49,915 in the previous year, showing an increase of Rs. 3,90,125. The year closed with a balance of Rs. 14,02,434 of which Rs. 3,10,741 represented actual cash in the Treasuries while the balance of Rs. 10,91,693 was held in banks and in loans and advances.

Expenditure.

214. A quinquennial statement of the Receipts and Expenditure of the State and the attached Zemindaries is given below :—

Serial No.	Year.	State.		Zemindary		Remarks.
		Receipts.	Expenditure.	Receipts,	Expenditure.	
1.	1339 T. E.	22,48,300	23,09,443	11 89,401	11,14,509	The figure for the year 1343 T. E. for the State include on the receipt side the loan of Rs. 9,00,000 (Rupees nine lacs) taken from the Government of India and on the debit side the expenditure incurred for liquidation of old debts.
2.	1340 T. E.	17,50,436	17,44,110	10.19,056	10,27,138	
3.	1341 T. E.	17,90,258	17,40,914	8,72,924	8,29,784	
4.	1342 T. E.	19,10,680	18,95,613	9,29,366	10,04,303	
5.	1343 T. E.	27.34,304	23,48,173	9,82,889	9,71,867	
	Average ...	20,86,795	20,07,650	9,98,727	9,89,520	

The world-wide trade depression which made itself felt in the State in the year 1339 T. E., had its worst effect in the year 1340 T. E. and accounts for the decline in receipts in those years. Signs of gradual recovery from the effect of the economic slump became, however, perceptible in the year 1342 T. E. when the receipts showed appreciable increase in comparison with the previous two years. In view of the fall in receipts a very cautious policy was followed as regards expenditure which had to be cut down to keep it within the receipts.

215. The noticeable variations in expenditure are explained below :—

i. Administration Charges :—

State—The actual increase was Rs. 46,683. The increase was due to the following reasons.

(*a*) Usual time scale increment of pay.

(*b*) Purchase of a motor car for the conveyance of officers.

(*c*) Expenditure in connection with the birthday ceremony of the newly born Maharaj Kumar Bahadur.

(*d*) Departmental management of some excise shops.

(*e*) Appointment of extra staff in Tahasil, Police, Jail, Forest and other Departments.

(*f*) Purchase of an elephant for the Forest Department.

(*g*) Miscellaneous expenditure, specially under the head Military.

ZEMINDARIES—The increase of Rs. 10,390 was due to litigation charges.

ii. REVENUE AND TAXES :—

ZEMINDARIES—The increase of Rs. 15,009 was due to payment of arrears of previous year.

iii. PUBLIC WORKS.

STATE—The increase of Rs. 58,334 was mainly due to progress of Improvement works which were postponed in previous years.

ZEMINDARIES—The increase was Rs. 9,844. This was due to payment of arrear bills.

iv. ELECTRIC LIGHT :—

The decrease was Rs. 2,123. This was due to general curtailment of expenditure.

v. MUNICIPALITY :—

There was no decrease or increase in expenditure.

vi EDUCATION :—

STATE—The decrease was Rs. 3,420. The decrease was due to general curtailment of expenditure.

ZEMINDARIES—The decrease was negligible.

vii. MEDICAL :—

STATE—The increase was Rs. 3,759. This was mainly due to the expenditure incurred in connection with the treatment of Maharajkumari Basantaprava Devi in Switzerland and the usual time scale increment of pay.

ZEMINDARIES :—The increase is negligible.

viii. SURVEY AND SETTLEMENT :—

STATE—The increase was Rs. 17,516. This was due to the expenditure incurred in connection with the Topographical Survey of the State by the Survey of India authority.

ZEMINDARIES—The slight increase was due to extra expenditure on account of pay of the staff.

ix. AGRICULTURE, COMMERCE AND INDUSTRIES :—

STATE—The slight increase was due to the usual time scale increment of pay and miscellaneous expenditure.

x. RELIGIOUS EXPENDITURE :—

STATE—The increase was Rs. 5,799. This was due to some extra expenditure incurred within the year.

ZEMINDARIES—The decrease is negligible.

xi. SULTANAT :—

STATE—The increase was Rs. 22,515. Which was mainly due to the purchase of two motor cycles, four elephants and furniture and pictures for the Palace.

xii. PURCHASE OF LAND TENURES :—

STATE—The increase was Rs. 9,310. This was due to an old account being adjusted within the year under report.

xiii. PENSION AND GRATUITY :—

STATE—The increase was Rs. 11,167. This was due to retirement of officers in the State.

ZEMINDARIES—The slight increase was due to retirement of officers.

xiv. ORDINARY SANSAR CHARGES :—

The increase was Rs. 32,506. This was mainly due to the expenditure incurred in connection with the marriage ceremony of Maharajkumari Jyotsna Devi and Maharajkumari Mallika Devi.

xv. CHARITY AND DONATION :—

The increase was Rs. 4,957. This was due to some special donations to (i) Her Excellency the Countess of Willingdon's Hospital fund. (ii) His Excellency the Viceroy's Earthquake Relief Fund. (iii) The Jadavpur College of Engineering and Technology. (iv) Sree Gouriya Math and (v) Islamia College Duty Fund.

xvi. HIS HIGHNESS'S NIJTAHABIL :—

The expenditure was the same as in the previous year.

xvii. HIS HIGHNESS'S TOUR :—

The increase which was Rs. 41,495 was due mainly to old bills being paid in the year under report.

xviii. PAYMENT OF LIABILITIES AND DEPOSITS :—

STATE—The decrease was Rs. 1,31,646. This was due to some old deposits being repaid from the separate provision for repayment of old debts.

ZEMINDARIES—The decrease was Rs. 1,03,661. In the previous year the excessive expenditure was due to repayment of overdrafts received from the Imperial Bank of India while no such expenditure was necessary in the year under report. This accounts for the decrease.

xix. MISCELLANEOUS :—

The increase was Rs. 5,519. This was due mainly to the expenditure incurred in connection with the Balrampur Succession Certificate case and some unforeseen expenditure.

xxii. REPAYMENT OF OLD DEBTS :—

The increase was Rs. 3,54,962. In the year under report a special provision was made for repayment of old debts. Almost all outstanding debts which could be settled in the year were paid up. This accounts for the increase under this head.

xxiv. PAYMENT OF INTEREST ON DEPOSITS :—

A special provision was made in the year under report for interests on deposits.

216. Two comparative Statements of Receipts and Expenditure of the State and the Zemindaries with the respective Revised Estimates are given in Appendices (XXVI) and (XXVII).

217. In the State, the total Receipts showed an increase of Rs. 8,82,304 and Rs. 17,304 in comparison with the original and revised Budget Estimates respectively. The reason for the appreciable increase in comparison with the original Budget Estimate was that the loan of Rs. 9,00,000 received from the Government of India in September was not included in the original Estimate.

218. In the Zemindaries, the total Receipts fell short of the original Budget Estimate by Rs. 12,111.

219. Babu Jatindra Nath Mitra continued to be in charge of the Accounts and Treasury Department till Thakur Kamini Kumar Singh took charge of the Department on the 18th Jaistha.

CHAPTER VI—MEDICAL.

220. As before, there were, during the year under report, altogether 18 dispensaries in the State—the Victoria Memorial Hospital at the capital included.

New Patients.

221. The total number of new patients treated in the above hospital and dispensaries together with their daily average as compared with the year preceding is shewn in the subjoined statement.

	1342 T. E.			1343 T. E.		
PATIENTS.	Outdoor.	Indoor.	Total.	Outdoor.	Indoor.	Total.
	1,27,755	758	1,28,513	1,30,193	887	1,31,080
Daily average	350·01	2·15	352·16	356 69	2·43	359·12

Outdoor attendance.

222. The out-patients (new+old) tatalled 2,46,246 as against 2,14,461 in the year previous—the daily average being 674·56 against 644·6.

Indoor Patients.

223. Including the previous year's balance of 20, the total number of in-patients was 887 as against 758 in the preceding year. Of these, 707 were cured, 122 were relieved or otherwise discharged, 41 died and 17 remained under treatment at the close of the year. Thus it will be seen that the number of both out-patients and in-patients rose by 2438 and 129 respectively over the previous year's figures.

Surgical Operation.

224. In all, 1230 operations were performed during the year with 20 major cases. The previous year's figures were 1262 and 15 respectively.

Police Cases.

225. Altogether 147 police cases were admitted against 184 cases of the year before, of which post-mortem cases were 15 against 21.

V. M. Hospital.

226. The out-door attendance of new patients in the Victoria Memorial Hospital numbered 21495 as against 18439 in the year preceding—the daily overage of new and old patients being 115·56 against 98·28.

The total admission of in-patients was 518 as against 497 with daily average (new + old) of 16·91 against 17·38. Of the number, 379 were cured, 92 were relieved or discharged otherwise, 39 died and 8 remained under treatment at the end of the year.

Altogether Rs. 9482-13-0 were expended on this institution as against Rs. 8472-1-0 in the year before.

Ayurvedic Department.

227. As before, Kaviraj Surendra Chandra Bhattacharya, Baidyaratna, continued to remain in charge of this Department, during the year under report. 47 patients were treated by him as against 52 in the year preceding.

The expenditure due to his salary and the cost of medicines came upto Rs. 2651-5-0 as against Rs. 2937-11-6 in the previous year,

Homoeopathic Department.

228. Two Assistant Homœopaths under the direct control of Dr. M. M. Majumdar, Chief Medical Officer, performed the work of this Department. 17563 patients were treated during the year under review as against 16686 of the year before—the daily average (new + old) being 91·62 against 80·87.

The total expenditure on this account amounted to Rs. 2324-15-9 as against Rs. 2226-15-3 in the previous year.

Vaccination.

229. 5638 vaccine operations were successful out of 7087 performed as against 5723 and 7257 respectively of the year before.

Vaccinators.

30 Vaccinators worked in the hills and plains. Two Small-pox doctors and two inspectors inspected their works.

The total cost on this account was Rs. 1453-15-6 as against Rs. 1286-8-6.

Kala-azar.

230. In addition to the existing centre at the capital, another centre was opened at Tilabazar in Kailashahar Division in the middle of the year under report. The total number of cases treated in both centres was 263. Of these, 100 were cured, 1 died, 115 were relieved or otherwise discharged and 47 remained under treatment at the end of the year.

The total cost incurred on this account was Rs. 1197 as against Rs. 878 in the year previous.

Leprosy.

231 At the instance of the British Empire Leprosy Association, Bengal Branch, a leprosy survey was carried out in different parts of the State with the result that a good number of cases was found out in the Sadar Division and in the interior of the hills, chiefly amongst the hill people. Two leprosy clinics were opend—one at the Capital town and the other at Khowai town—under the management of Dr. Parbati Charan Sen, M. B., specially appointed for this branch. Dr. B. N. Ghose, Leprosy Propaganda Officer, Bengal, very kindly opened the clinics and inspected them at the end of the year under review. It is in contemplation to open other centres elsewhere in due course. Two cinema shows on all phases of leprosy were arranged in the Capital town which were highly appreciated by all.

Of the total number 145 admitted in both clinics, 9 were cured or made symptom-free, 72 were relieved, 4 remained stationary and 60 left treatment of their own accord—mainly due to the difficulties and inconveniences of having had to walk over long distances crossing hills and streams.

Cholera.

232. Cholera made its appearance in Sadar, Khowai, Kailashahar and Dharmanagar Divisions. In the last named Division it raged in a virulent form. So far as reported, 159 died out of 289 persons attacked. 2742 persons were inoculated. Small-pox appeared sporadically in Sadar Division. 13 persons were attacked but all of them were successfully treated by the Small-pox doctors.

Staff.

233. As before, Dr. M. M. Majumdar, L. M. S., remained in charge of the Medical Department with Dr. S. K. Dutt, L. M. S., Dr. A. Sen Gupta, M. B. and Dr. N. Deb Barma, M. B., as his assistants in the Capital. Besides, a regular staff of Medical subordinates was maintained in different places together with 3 Midwives in the Capital town.

Inspection.

234. Dr. M. M. Majumdar and Dr. A. Sen Gupta were out for 13 days and inspected 3 dispensaries.

Total Expenditure.

235. The total expenditure incurred for the Medical Department in the year under report stood at Rs. 65,329 as against Rs. 64,070 in the preceding year.

CHAPTER VII—PUBLIC INSTRUCTION.

Charge.

236. Mr. S. C. Deb Barman, M. A. (Harvard), Senior Naib Dewan, continued to be in charge of the Education Department.

Number of Schools.

237. The total number of schools (including private schools) during the year under review was 184 against 205 in the previous year, and the total numerical strength 8,342 against 9,623 including 1,093 pupils reading in private institutions numbering 39 as against 53 in the preceding year.

H. E. Schools.

238. There were 5 H. E. Schools as before and one Branch H. E. School in the State. All the H E. Schools are permanently affiliated to the Calcutta University. Class IX was opened provisionally in the Branch H. E. School at Udaipur, on condition that the public would agree to bear the additional cost of maintaining extra staff. The total number of pupils in all these institutions were 1,488 as against 1,410 in the previous year, and the average daily attendance stood at 1,150·15 against 1,106·55.

Matriculation Examination.

239. Agartala, the capital of the State, continued to be a centre for the Matriculation Examination. The State H. E. Schools are allowed to send up candidates to this centre. One female private student and one candidate from Chunta H. E. School in Tipperah district sat for the examination in this centre in the year under report in addition to the candidates from the State schools.

240. The examination was conducted under the direct control and supervision of the Minister. The Department looked after the convenience of the candidates, coming from *Mofussil*, in respect of accommodation and other necessary matters.

Result of the Matriculation Examination.

241. Altogether 60 candidates were sent up for the Matriculation Examination from the State H. E. Schools against 74 in the previous year. The result of the Examination is given below :—

	No. sent up.	Passed.	1st Division.	2nd Division.	3rd Division.
1. U. K. Academy	30	21	6	13	2
2. R. K. Institution	10	9	5	3	1
3. B. K. Institution	10	10	7	3	0
4. B. B. Institution	5	5	3	2	0
5. N. Ch. Institution	5	3	0	2	1
Total ...	60	48	21	23	4

242. The result on the whole was satisfactory, percentage of successful candidates being 80 against 72·97 in the previous year. The percentage of passes in the 1st Division on the total number of passes was the highest for the B. K. Institution *viz.* 70, and lowest for the U. K. Academy *viz.* 28.

243. The three successful candidates topping the list, the first and the second belonging to B. B. Institution and the third belonging to R. K. Institution, were awarded scholarships of Rs. 15, Rs. 10 and Rs. 8 per month in order of merit. The result of the B. B. Institution in the Matriculation Examination is noticeble.

M. E. Schools for boys.

244. In the year under review, there were 9 Middle English Schools for boys with 1,092 pupils on the rolls against 8 schools with 983 pupils in the previous year. The average daily attendance was 883·58 against 762·22 in the previous year.

M. E. Schools for girls.

245. There was one M. E. School for girls at Agartala, namely the Maharani Tulsibati Girls' School, the numerical strength of which was 77 as against 89 in the previous year and the average daily attendance was 62·81 against 66·33. By special permission of this Department, some girls were allowed to continue higher studies in this school under the tuition of the Head Mistress. For conveyance of the girls, motor bus service was continued as before.

H. V. Schools.

246. There was only one Higher Vernacular School for boys as in the previous year, with 77 students on the roll, the average daily attendance being 62·02 but the school was reduced to L. V. School in the year under report.

247. The total number of Lower Vernacular Schools for boys was 26 against 23 in the previous year. The total numerical strength was 1,255 against 1,413 and the average daily attendance was 1,013·7 against 1,104·48 in the previous year. In some of these schools, boys and girls read together.

L. V. Schools.

248. There were 76 *Pathshalas* for boys against 87 in the previous year. The total number of boys was 2,183 against 2,666 and the average daily attendance was 1,733·04 against 1,957·19. In some of these schools boys and girls read together. Under special orders of the Education Department, some boys of some of these institutions were allowed to read the Lower Vernacular standard.

***Pathshalas* for boys.**

249. There were 9 *Pathshalas* for girls in the year under review as in the previous year. The total numerical strength was 319 as against 273 and the average daily attendance was 240·11 against 226·72 in the year preceding. In some of these schools, some girls were allowed, under special orders, to read the Lower Vernacular standard.

***Pathshalas* for girls.**

250. Altogether 784 candidates appeared at the different scholarship examinations of the State against 799 in the previous year. Of these, 662 candidates including 92 girls came out successful. The result on the whole was satisfactory. 61 students including 13 girls passed the M. E. Examination and 2 girls passed the H. V. Examination this year. In the L. V. Examination, the number of successful candidates was 150 including girls, and in the *Pathshala* Examination the number was 448 including 60 girls. Amongst these candidates 9 candidates appeared from different *Moktab* and *Madrassas* of the State. On the results of the examination 13 boys and 6 girls were awarded monthly scholarships varying from Rs. 2 to Rs. 5 tenable for two to four years.

Scholarship Examination.

251. In the year under review, there were 13 schools for special training, consisting of 5 Sanskrit *Tols*, 7 *Madrassas* and *Moktabs* and one *Silpasram* (Artisan School). The Sanskrit *Tols* had 50 students on the rolls against 39 in the previous year and the average daily attendance was 38·27 against 30·01. The *Rajakiya* Sanskrit *Vidyalaya* at Agartala sent up 6 candidates for the Government Sanskrit Title, Intermediate and Preliminary Examinations against 5 in the preceding year and one for Preliminary Sanskrit Examination in *Kavya* and one for Preliminary Sanskrit Examination in *Saraswat Vyakarana* of the Dacca *Saraswat Samaj*, in the year under report,

Schools for special training.

252. The result was satisfactory. All the candidates passed the Government Sanskrit Examinations in different subjects in which they appeared. Amongst the candidates who appeared at the Examination of the *Saraswat Samaj* only one came out successful.

253. The *Madrassas* and *Moktobs* had 235 students on the rolls as against 388 in the previous year and the daily average attendance was 183·6 against 300·82.

254. There were as before 4 Free Primary Schools with 508 pupils including girls against 418 in the previous year. The subjoined statement will show the number of students, their classes and the average daily attendance. The number of Hindu and Mahommedan pupils rose by 91 and 6 respectively but the number from other classes fell by 1.

Free Compulsory Primary Schools.

Schools.		No. of Students. Boys	No. of Students. Girls.	Average daily attendance Boys.	Average daily attendance Girls.	Kumars.	Thakurs.	Tripura.	Laskar.	Manipuri.	Bengali Hindu.	Mahommedan.
1.	No. 1 U. K. Academy	157	125	105.1	95·7	1	6	2	0	0	255	18
2.	No. 2 Tulsibati	16	80	9·4	40·2	0	12	0	0	4	80	0
3.	No. 3 Bejoy Kumar	26	75	10·	59·2	0	22	15	0	0	53	6
.	No. 4 Thakur Palli	29	0	13·01	0	0	12	15	0	0	2	0
		228	280	137·51	195·1	1	52	32	0	4	395	2 4

255. The comparative statement below will show the number of non-Bengalee students receiving education in the several schools of the State, :—

Serial number.	Nationality.	Number of students. Past year.	Number of students. Present year.	Remarks.
1.	Rajkumars	4	5	
2.	Thakurs	213	282	
3.	Manipuris	634	568	
4.	Tripuras	1053	977	
5.	Reangs	0	13	
6.	Kukis		1	
7.	Chakmas	2	1	
8.	Lushais	1	1	
9.	Others...	96	44	
10.	Christians	0	0	
	Total	2,004	1,892	

Education of Princes and Princesses.

256. Maharajkumar Durjoy Kishore Deb Barman Bahadur prosecuted his Post Diploma Course at the Mayo College, Ajmer, up till December and later on joined the Military service of the State and was deputed to Shillong Military Camp for training. He is expected to join the Prince of Wales Military Academy at Dehra Dun.

257. The Maharajkumaries received their education as before under a graduate lady teacher and a Pandit. Special arrangement was made for the education of Maharajkumar Karna Kishore Deb Barman Bahadur as before at Agartala.

Education of other Kumars.

258. Kumar Ramendra Kishore Deb Barman Bahadur passed the Matriculation Examination from the St. Gregory's High School under the Board of Secondary Education, Dacca. Maharajkumar Hemanta Kishore Deb Barman Bahadur after passing the I. Sc. examination of the Calcutta University got himself admitted into Thomason Engineering College at Roorkee but owing to certain reasons, left the college after three months.

Kumar Boarding House at Comilla.

259. The Rajkumar Boarding House at Comilla had 14 inmates of whom 11 were from the different branches of the Ruling family and the remaining 3 were Rana Bahadurs, related to the Raj Family. 11 of the inmates were reading in the Comilla Zilla School, one in the Comilla

Iswar *Pathshala* and 2 in the Victoria College, Comilla. In the year under review 2 Maharajkumars and a Kumar passed the Matriculation Examination and 1 Kumar passed the I. Sc. Examination. The boarders were placed under the charge of a Superintending tutor who in addition to his tutorial works looked after the management of the Boarding House. There was also one assistant graduate resident tutor. Besides the above, one graduate teacher was engaged for coaching some Kumars in the morning.

Education of Thakur boys.

260. 12 Thakur boys receiving higher education in various colleges and technical schools were awarded stipends from the Education Department.

Thakur Boarding House at Agartala.

261. The number of Boarders in the Thakur Boarding House was 32 against 21 in the previous year. The staff consisted of one graduate Guardian Superintendent, one under-graduate Resident Tutor and one Manager Tutor. The average daily attendance of the boarders was 28 against 25·2 in the previous year. 3 Thakur boys appeared at the Matriculation Examination and 2 came out successful.

Tripura Boarding House at Agartala.

262. There were altogether 16 boarders from Class IV to Matriculation Class in the old Tripura Boarding House against 18 in the previous year. All of these 16 boarders received free boarding and lodging. A wholetime graduate Superintending Tutor looked after the boys as well as the boarding management as before. Another tutor was engaged to coach the boys in the morning. There was a small library in the Boarding House and the boys were encouraged in Agricultural pursuits within the Boarding compound. There was a newly started Boarding House with 33 Tripura boys reading in lower classes against 27 in the previous year. Of these 6 were allowed stipends. A manager tutor was engaged to coach the boys both in the morning and evening and was entrusted with the management of the boarding. The boarders were allowed a piece of ground for agricultural pursuits.

Tripura Boarding House at Khowai.

263. There were 61 boarders in the Tripura Boarding House at Khowai against 47 in the previous year, some receiving free boarding. One graduate Superintending Tutor and one assistant tutor were appointed for coaching the boys both in the morning and the evening. The Superintending Tutor looked after the boarding management in addition to his tutorial work. A spacious newly built house was provided at a cost of Rs. 2,000 offering accommodation for 100 hill boys. The number on the roll is gradually increasing, showing an increasing interest of the hill people for education.

Ram Kumar Boarding School at Kalyanpur.

264. There were 33 boarders on the roll in the Ram Kumar Boarding School against 32 in the previous year and the average daily attendance was 28·78 against 27·98 in the preceding year. Two tutors were appointed to coach the boarders and one of them looked after the boarding management in addition.

265. There were 20 convicts reading in the primary school in the Central Jail, out of which 2 appeared in the Scholarship Examination in the year under report and came out successful.

School for convicts.

266. The Woodburn Artisan School and Silpasram continued to be under the control of the Chief Secretary to His Highness the Maharaja Manikya Bahadur. The school had on the roll 22 students against 23 in the preceding year. In the year under review the average daily attendance was 10·25 against 10·54 in the previous year. There were 11, 6 and 5 students in the Carpentry, Black-smith and Brass-smith Sections respectively. The sub-joined statement will show the number of students, their classes (castes) and their average attendance in the year under review. 13 students were awarded monthly stipends varying from Re. 1-8 to Rs. 8 each.

Woodburn Artisan School & Silpasram.

Name of School	Number of Students	Thakurs	Tripura	Laskar	Manipuri	Bengali Hindu	Mahomedan	Others.	Average attendance
Woodburn Artisan School and Silpasram ...	22	4	—	2	2	12	2	—	10·25

267. 3 Lushai boys were awarded Lusai stipends in the year under report of whom one read in one of the H. E. Schools of the State and the other two prosecuted their studies elsewhere in school and college.

Lushai Stipends.

268. 17 students were awarded special stipends in the year under review of whom 10 read in different schools of this State and the remaining 7 prosecuted their studies elsewhere in different schools, colleges, and technical institutions.

Special Stipends.

269. The Senior Naib Dewan was out on tour for 9 days. During the year under review he was away from the station on leave for some months due to illness and was to some extent for that reason unable to go out to some divisions as done in previous years. There were three Sub-Inspectors of schools as before who inspected all the schools other than the H. E. schools, within their respective jurisdictions in Sadar, Khowai, Kailashahar and Dharmanagar Divisions. Revenue and Forest inspectors visited and inspected the schools in the remaining Divisions.

Inspection Work.

270. Maharajkumar Narottam Kishore Deb Barman Bahadur continued to be the Librarian of the Bir Chandra Library at Agartala which was maintained in two separate sections as before, *viz* :—(1) The English section, located in the Ujjayanta Palace, and (2) the Vernacular section in the building, near the local H. E. School. The latter section was open to the public. The number of English books (including foreign literature) and that of the Bengali and Sanskrit books were the same as before. In the year under report there were 4 daily newspapers, 3 weeklies and

Library.

7 monthlies against 4, 2 and 5 respectively in the previous year. The average daily attendance in the vernacular section of the library was 8 against 13·8 in the previous year and the total number of books issued to the public was 3,009 against 2,658.

Expenditure.

271. The total expenditure on public instruction in the year under report amounted to Rs. 1,25,021 against Rs. 1,28,441. Details of expenditure are noted below :—

1.	Primary Education	Rs. 27,686
2.	Secondary Education	,, 48,458
3.	Schools for Special Training	,, 2,127
4.	Compulsory Free Primary Education ...	,, 1,632
5.	Boarding Institutions for Thakur boys ...	,, 6,756
6.	Education of Kumars & Kumaris ...	,, 26,424
7.	Scholarships and Stipends	,, 5,611
8.	Library	,, 1,812
9.	Tripura Boarding	,, 3,073
10.	Miscellaneous...	,, 1,442

Income.

272. The total receipts from the schools amounted to Rs. 14,566 against Rs. 14,086 in the previous year.

CHAPTER VIII—ZEMINDARIES.

Chakla Roshnabad Estates.

Management.

273. The management of His Highness' Zemindaries in British India continued in the hands of Manyabara Rai J. C Sen Bahadur, B. A., B. C. S. (retired) for the whole year. The Manager was assisted by a Deputy Manager at Comilla and three Assistant Managers posted at Feni, Mogra and Srimangal.

The year and the tenantry.

274. The all-round economic depression, noticed in previous years, continued during the whole year owing to low prices of jute and paddy. Relief was given to the Talukdars and the tenants as in the previous years, in the shape of general remission of interest and damages. The policy of allowing petty demands to be time-barred was also continued.

Demand.

275. The gross Revenue demand of the year was Rs. 10,21,376 against Rs. 10,22,733 in the previous year.

Receipts.

276. The total receipts amounted to Rs. 9 82,889 (including Rs. 8,819 of the Tripura Raj Central Co-operative Bank Ltd. and Rs. 2,041 on account of Debotta mahals) against Rs. 9,29,366 in the previous year.

Expenditure.

277. The total expenditure in the year under review was Rs. 9,71,867 including repayment of old debts and refund of deposits to the extent of Rs. 19,965 together with a contribution of Rs. 2,80,000 to the State. The total expenditur

during the previous year was Rs. 10,04.303. Of the total expenditure during the year under review, Rs. 2,88,830 was on account of Land Revenue, taxes and cesses while the total administration charges of the Zemindaries including public works and Law charges amounted to Rs. 3,34.354 against Rs. 3,09,176 in the previous year.

278. The following other items of expenditure aggregating Rs. 3,48,683 are noticeable :—

1.	Loans and advances	Rs.	600
2.	Donations	Rs.	6,746
3.	Medical charges	,,	11,737
4.	Education charges	,,	8,962
5.	Religious ceremonies	,,	6,339
6.	Sansar stipends	,,	12,960
7.	Repayment of old debts and deposits ...	,,	19,965
8.	Contribution to the State	,,	2,80.000
9.	Purchase of property	,,	1.374
			3,48,683

Settlement.

279. The result of the year's settlement operations will appear from the figures noted below :—

	Kinds of settlement.	Addition to rental.	Nazar.
1.	Railway relinquished land	—	—
2.	*Kaimi* and *Takshishi* settlement in the Comilla Town ...	Rs. 4	Rs. 450
3.	Ordinary Town Settlement ...	,, 18	,, 237
4.	*Khas Patit*	,, 295	,, 803
5.	Enhancement of rent	,, 618	,, 4,119
6.	Re-settlement of auction purchased holding ...	,, 78	,, 5,236
7.	Settlement of rent free holding	,, —	—
8.	*Takshishi Taluk* in the *Moffusil*	,, 37	,, 886
9.	*Ijara* settlement	---	—
		Rs. 1,050	Rs. 11,731

280. This year's addition to rent-roll by settlement operations was smaller than that of the previous year. The fall is attributable to the economic depression amongst the tenants in general who were really unable to pay up *Nazarana* and conclude sanctions.

CHAPTER IX—MISCELLANEOUS.

Rajmala.

281. The printing and publication of the *Rajmala* could not make appreciable progress due to the untimely death of its editor Babu Kaliprasanna Sen Gupta, Bidyabhushan, on the 10th Magh of the year under review. The total expenditure amounted to Rs. 4.435.

282. In the death of its editor, the State lost the services of an able and devoted editor who was an authority on the State chronicles. He will not only be remembered as the editor and publisher of several volumes of the *Rajmala*, but also as a devoted servant of this State,

connected for a long time with the administration particularly the Revenue Department. The Darbar takes this opportunity to record its appreciation of his services.

Tours of high officials—Minister.

283. Rai J. C. Sen Bahadur, Minister was in camp for 66 days during the year under review, both in and outside the State

Chief Secretary to His Highness

284. Manyabara Rana Bodhjung Bahadur, F. R. G. S., Chief Secretary to His Highness the Maharaja Manikya Bahadur, was in Camp with His Highness in all his tours during the year. Besides this, he visited the Kalyanpur Reserve Area, Kamalpur and Kulai-Haor on inspection for 13 days, and also went out to Calcutta on two occasions in connection with the construction of His Highness's new residence there and stayed at the latter place for 28 days. His tour during the year under review was for 41 days altogether inclusive of the stay in Camp with His Highness.

285. The tours of the Divisional Officers and their assistants are noted below :—

State.

1.	Sadar—			
	Sadar Collector—Thakur Rebati Mohan Deb Barman	...	70	days.
	Asst. ,, Kumar Narsingh Chandra Deb Barman Bahadur	...	31	,,
	,, ,, Babu Jogendra Lal Ganguly, B. L.	...	44	,,
	,, ,, Kumar Bhupendra Chandra Deb Barman Bahadur, B. A.	...	19	,,
2.	Kailasahar—			
	Divisional Officer—Babu Akhil Chandra Majumdar, M. A., B. L.	...	22	,,
	Second ,, ,, Jyotirmoy Ghose, M. A.	...	31	,,
3.	Sonamura—			
	Divisional Officer—Babu Sasanka Bhusan Roy, M. A.	...	58	,,
	Second ,, ,, Jogendra Lal Ganguly, B. L.	...	6	,,
	Probationer— Sj. Chandrahas Singh, B. L.	...	10	,,
4.	Belonia—			
	Divisional Officer—Thakur Gokul Chandra Deb Barman	...	20	,,
	Second ,, Kamal Krishna Deb Barman	...	37	,,
5.	Khowai—			
	Divisional Officer—Babu Prabha Ranjan Das Gupta, M. A., B. L.	...	26	,,
6.	Dharmanagar—			
	Divisional Officer—Babu Sarada Charan Sarkar, M. A., B. L.	...	7	,,

7. Udaipur—
Divisional Officer—Babu Suresh Chandra
Chakraborty, B. L. ... 31 days.

8. Sabroom—
Divisional Officer—Thakur Jyotilal
Deb Barman, B. L. ... 26 ,,

9. Amarpur—
Sub Divisional Officer—Thakur Joysing
Deb Barman, B. A. ... 51 ,,

Zemindaries.

1. Babu Pramada Ranjan Bhattacharjee, B. A.,
Deputy Manager, Comilla ... 33 days.

2. Babu Tarit Mohan Gupta,
Assistant Manager, Feni ... 30 ,,

3. Babu Bisweswar Guha,
Assistant Manager, Mogra ... 62 ,,

4. Babu Surendra Chandra Guha, B. A.,
Assistant Manager, Srimangal ... 58 ,,

DATED, AGARTALA,
The 10th December, 1934.

Jyotis Chandra Sen,
MINISTER.

APPENDIX.

List of the principal Laws and Regulations in force in the Tripura State during 1343 T.E.

Description.	Whether adapted from British Indian Acts.	Whether introduced during the year under report.
CRIMINAL.		
1. Regulation No. III. of 1280 T. E.		
2. Regulation No. I. of 1283 T. E.		
3. Jail Regulation, 1283 T. E.		
4. Regulation No. IV. of 1283 T. E. (Cattle trespass and pound).		
5. Regulation No. III. of 1296 T. E. (Police Regulation).		
6. Act No. IV. of 1321 T. E.–Penal Laws (an amending Act)		
CIVIL.		
1. Civil Law of 1284 T. E.		
2. Rules regarding *chit* suits (small causes) 1287 and 1300 T. E.		
3. Act No. II. of 1313 T. E.—an Act for the regulation of interest on debts.		
4. Act No. II. of 1314 T. E.—Limitation Act	Partly adapted.	
5. Succession Act II of 1339 T. E.		
REVENUE.		
1. Act No. I. of 1290 T. E.—Sale Law		
2. Act No. I. of 1296 T. E.—Tenancy Act.		
3. Act No. II. of 1296 T. E.—*Abkari*		
4. Act No. II. of 1297 T. E.—Reserved forests.		
5. Act No. I. of 1304 T. E.—Duties on *til* and cotton.		
6. Act No. I. of 1306 T. E.—Registration	Do.	
7. Survey and Settlement Act, 1309 T.E.	Do.	
8. *Tuccavi* Regulation, 1310 T. E.		
9. Act No. I. of 1313 T. E.—Forests.		
10. Act No. I. of 1314 T. E.—(amending the above)		
11. A Law imposing export duty on jute and mustard-seed, 1317 T. E.		
12. Act No. II. of 1321 T.E. Ghasuri Act		
13. P. W. & Road Cess Act IV of 1339 T. E.		
MISCELLANEOUS.		
1. An Act promulgating certain rules as Law, 1283 T. E.		
2. Regulation for the record of judicial decisions &c., 1284 T. E.		
3. Municipal Regulation, 1284 T. E.		
4. Legal Practitioners' Regulation.		
5. Act No. I. of 1297 T. E.—an Act for the regulation of commissions for the examination of witnesses.		
6. Regulation against cow slaughter		
7. Rules of evidence		
8. Act I. of 1318 T. E.—Constitution of Courts—(an amending Act).		
9. Leave and allowance Rules	Do.	
10. Act No. I. of 1321 T. E.—Arms Act	Do.	
11. Act No. III. of 1321 T.E.—Constitution of Courts (an amending Act)		

Description.	Whether adapted from British Indian Acts.	Whether introduced during the year under report.
12. Municipal Act No. I of 1322 T. E.		
13. Revenue Sale Amendment Act—1323 T.E.		
14. An Act for the destruction of old records—1323 T. E.		
15. Act I of 1326 T. E.—Regulation regarding Privy Council Appeals.		
16. Act II of 1326 T. E.—Registration of Births and Deaths		
17. Act III of 1326 T. E.—Vaccination Act	Partly adapted.	
18. Act IV of 1326 T. E.—Public Demands Recovery Act	Do.	
19. Act V of 1326 T. E.—Excise Amendment Act	Do.	
20. Act I of 1327 T. E.—Settlement of lands for tea cultivation		
21. Rules of Import and Sale of Opium—1327 T. E.		
22. Regulation No. 1 of 1328 T. E.—regarding Registration of Coolies		
23. Regulation No. 2 of 1328 T. E.—regarding Export of Tea		
24. Act I of 1329 T. E.—(Absconding sepoys Act)		
25. Act II of 1329 T. E.—(Control of prices of food stuff)		
26. Act III of 1329 T. E. - (Elephants and buffaloes grazing Act)		
27. Act IV of 1329 T. E. - (House tax on Hill tribes)		
28. Act V of 1329 T. E. - (Legal practitioners, Act)	Do	
29. Act I of 1332 T. E.—Encumbered Estates Act.		
30. Act III of 1332 T. E.—The Opium and Intoxicating Drugs Act.		
31. Rules and Regulations under the Opium and Intoxicating Drugs Act III of 1332 T. E.		
32. Act I of 1336 T. E.—(Hackney Carriages)		
33. Act II of 1336 T. E.—(Amending Act I of 1327.)		
34. Act III of 1336 T. E.—(Amending the Survey & Settlement Regulation)		
35. Act IV of 1336 T. E.—(Prevention of gambling)		
36. Act I of 1337 T. E.—(Amending the State Tenancy Act I of 1296 T. E.)		
37. Land Acquisition Rules under Act I of 1337 T. E.		
38. State Motor Vehicles Act I of 1338 T. E.		
39. Act II of 1338 T. E. for prevention of smuggling of elephant tusks.		
40. State Stamp Act III of 1338 T. E.		
41. Tripura State Bank Act I of 1339 T. E.		
42. Census Act III of 1339 T. E.		
43. Act I of 1342 T. E.—providing for trial of certain criminal cases by Special Tribunal.		
44. Compulsory Primary Education Act II of 1342 T. E.		

II

Statement showing the strength, cost and other particulars of the Military Force in Tripura State for 1343 T. E.

Arm of service.	Number of fighting officers and men.						Details of force at the end of the current year.						Buglers.	Total cost on account of pay and allowances of the force, including followers.	Remarks.
	At the end of last year	Recruited this year.	Casualties.			At the end of the current year.	Number of regiments, battalions, or Batteries.	Number of guns.	Number of men.						
									Commisioned Officers.		Non-commissioned officers.	Fighting men.			
			Died.	Invalided.	Discharged, deserted, &c.				European.	Indian.					
1	2	3	4	5	6	7	8	9	10	11	12	13	14	15	16
Infantry ...	334	161	—	122	1	372	1	644	4	15	27	320	6		
Band Party	18	1	—	—	—	19	—	—	—	—	2	17	—		
Total ...	352	162	—	122	1	391	1	644	4	15	29	337	6	Rs. 1,06,626	

III.

Statement showing the strength, cost, discipline, and education of the Police for the year 1343 T. E.

Description of office.	Number.	Grade of pay.	Total cost.	Punishments. Dismissed.	Punishments. Fined, degraded or suspended departmentally.	Punishments. Punished judicially.	Rewards. By promotion.	Rewards. By money.	Education. Number able to read and write.	Education. Number under instruction.	Remarks.
1	2	3	4	5	6	7	8	9	10	11	12
		Rs.			F. D. S.						
Superintendent of Police	1	250-0-0	Rs 86,836	—	—	—	—	—	1	—	F.=Fined. D.=Degraded. S.=Suspended. † Including 5 C. I. D. Naib Darogas and excluding 4 Writer Naib Darogas. (a) Increment of pay stopped temporarily. (b) Promotion stopped for 2 years. (c) Degraded temporarily. (d) Degraded temporarily.
Asst. Superintendent „	1	100-5-125		—	—	—	—	—	1	—	
Inspectors	4	2 65-5/2-90; 2 55-2-65		—	—	—	—	2	4	1	
Sub-Inspectors	23	25-2-45		—	2 (a)	—	—	9	23	—	
Proby. Sub-Inspector	1	15 allowance		—	—	—	—	—	1	—	
Naib Darogas	22 †	15-1-25		—	1 0 0	—	—	9	22	—	
Writer Naib Darogas	5	15-0-0		—	1 (b)	—	—	1	5	—	
Writer Constables	10	15-0-0		—	—	—	—	—	10	—	
Subedar	1	25-2-45		—	—	—	—	—	1	—	
Armed S. I.	1	25-2-45		—	—	—	—	—	1	—	
Jamadars (civil)	6	15-1-25		—	3 0 0	—	—	—	6	—	
Jamadar (Armed)	1	20-1-30		—	—	—	—	—	1	—	
Havildar	1	19-1-25		—	1 0 0	—	—	—	1	—	
Naiks	4	15-1-20		—	1 0 0	—	—	—	4	—	
Constables (Civil)	220	10 to 13		—	14 3 (c) 0	—	—	17	103	—	
Constables (Armed)	33	14-1-15		—	7 1 (d) 0	—	—	2	20	—	
Chaukidars	175	5-0-0		—	—	—	—	1	—	—	
Spies	3	20 and 15		—	—	—	—	—	3	—	
Total ...	512				27 7 0	—	—	41	207	—	

IV.

Statement showing the working of the Police in the Tripura State during the year 1343 T. E.

State.	Number of offences.		Number of accused arrested.		Number of accused sent up for trial.		Number of accused convicted.		Number of accused acquitted or discharged.		Percentage convicted of accused arrested.		Percentage convicted of accused sent up for trial.		REMARKS.
	Past year.	Present year.	Past year.	Present year.	Past year.	Present year.	Past year.	Present year.	Past year.	Present year.	Past year.	Present year.	Past year.	Present year.	
1	2	3	4	5	6	7	8	9	10	11	12	13	14	15	16
Tripura State	1, 98	1,009	827	623	943	824	223	208	309	178	26·96	33·39	60·60	* 70·21	* Excluding from col. 7 Pending trial— 437 Withdrawal— 35 Compromise— 59 Dead— 1 532

V

Statement showing the value of property stolen and amount of recoveries in the Tripura State during the year 1343 T. E.

State.	Amount stolen.		Amount recovered.		Percentage of recoveries of property stolen.		REMARKS.
	Past year.	Present year.	Past year.	Present year.	Past year.	Present year.	
1	2	3	4	5	6	7	8
Tripura State	Rs 18,282-6-0	Rs 12,868-9-9	Rs 2,692-12-9	Rs 1,929-7-0	14·73	14·99	

VI.

Statement showing the number of crimes committed, number of cases disposed of, and cases awaiting trial in the Tripura State during the year 1343 T. E.

Description of offences.		Number of offences.			Number of cases disposed of during the last year.	Number of cases disposed of during the present year.	Number of cases awaiting trial.	Number of persons apprehended.	Number of persons convicted.	Number of persons sentenced.								Number of persons acquitted or discharged.	Number of persons confined being insane.	Number of persons died during or before trial.	Term of imprisonment.											Persons awaiting trial.
		Balance from past year.	Committed during the present year.	Total.						Imprisonment. Simple.	Imprisonment. Rigorous.	Imprisonment and fine. Simple.	Imprisonment and fine. Rigorous.	Fine only.	Whipping.	Capital punishment.	Total.				Under one month.	From 1 to below 2 months.	From 2 to below 3 months.	From 3 to below 6 months.	From 6 to below 12 months.	From 1 to below 2 years.	From 2 to below 3 years.	From 3 to below 5 years.	5 years and above.	Transportation.	Capital punishment.	
1		2	3	4	5	6	7	8	9	10	11	12	13	14	15	16	17	18	19	20	21	22	23	24	25	26	27	28	29	30	31	32
Class I. Offences against the State, public tranquillity, safety and justice &c.	cognizable ...	8	17	25	12	12	13	83	15	0	5	0	5	5	0	0	15	18	0	1	0	7	0	1	1	1	0	0	0	0	0	49
	non-cognizable	6	38	44	51	32	12	24	[a] 5	1	0	0	0	3	0	0	4	15	0	0	0	0	0	0	1	0	0	0	0	0	0	4
Class II. Offences against person.	cognizable ...	96	305	401	282	284	117	538	62	2	38	0	5	16	0	1	62	266	0	2	11	3	1	9	6	3	2	5	5	0	1	208
	non-cognizable	39	255	294	253	243	51	165	32	1	4	0	0	27	0	0	32	115	0	0	5	0	0	0	0	0	0	0	0	0	0	18
Class III. Offences against property.	cognizable ...	269	766	1035	162	763	272	[b] 1451	[c] 501	4	110	0	15	358	0	0	487	574	0	4	21	23	3	53	8	11	9	1	0	0	0	370
	non-cognizable	45	156	201	208	132	69	242	27	0	2	0	0	25	0	0	27	165	0	1	0	2	0	0	0	0	0	0	0	0	0	49
Class IV. Other offences.	cognizable ...	43	137	180	182	134	46	258	[d] 95	4	17	17	2	44	0	0	84	112	0	0	27	0	4	3	3	2	0	1	0	0	0	51
	non-cognizable	61	292	353	230	282	71	192	[e] 33	1	3	6	1	10	0	0	21	118	0	0	6	2	2	0	1	0	0	0	0	0	0	41
Total cognizable		416	1225	1641	238	1193	448	2330	673	10	170	17	27	423	0	1	648	970	0	7	59	33	8	66	18	17	11	7	5	0	1	678
Total non-cognizable		151	741	892	742	689	203	623	97	3	9	6	1	65	0	0	84	413	0	1	11	4	2	0	2	0	0	0	0	0	0	112
Grand Total		567	1966	2533	980	1882	651	2953	770	13	179	23	28	488	0	1	732	1383	0	8	70	37	10	66	20	17	11	7	5	0	1	790

Remarks. (33)

(a) One person was warned for the future.

(b) Two persons escaped.

(c) Fourteen persons were warned for the future.

(d) Eleven persons were warned for the future.

(e) Twelve persons were bound down under security.

VII.

Statement showing the number of offences reported and dealt with by the various Courts in the Tripura State during the year 1343 T.E.

Name of Court.	Number of offences reported during, Last year.	Present year.	Number of persons dealt with. Remaining at the end of last year.	Brought to trial during present year. Arrested by Police.	Upon warrant.	On summons.	Voluntary.	Arrested in presence of the Magistrate.	Total. Last year.	Present year.	Persons disposed of. Discharged without trial.	Acquitted.	Convicted.	Committed or referred.	Died, escaped, or transferred &c.	Persons remaining at the end of the year.	Remarks
1	2	3	4	5	6	7	8	9	10	11	12	13	14	15	16	17	18
Sadar Magistracy	513	602	183	174	127	120	31	—	809	635	170	161	167	12	2	123	
Sonamura „ ...	294	293	138	72	75	171	102	2	401	560	160	93	166	12	1	128	
Bilonia „ ...	209	181	49	109	45	90	60	7	356	360	52	60	219	7	—	22	
Kailashahar „ ...	263	273	150	88	141	88	26	1	505	494	165	83	79	6	1	160	
Khowai „ ...	170	167	28	58	6	52	10	—	161	154	23	52	31	14	—	34	
Dharmanagar „ ...	312	204	195	41	58	106	33	1	858	434	123	41	26	5	4	235	
Udaipur „ ...	235	200	66	32	43	103	9	—	324	253	98	37	35	8	—	75	
Sabrum „ ...	45	43	1	19	8	7	24	—	59	59	23	7	17	2	—	10	
TOTAL ...	2,030	1,966	810	593	503	737	295	11	3,473	2949 *a*	814	534	740	66 *b*	8	787	

a. Excluding 4 persons pending before the Court of Sessions at the close of the previous year.

b. The total number of persons for trial before the Court of Sessions, including 4 persons pending from the last year, was 70, of whom 30 were convicted, 35 acquitted 2 escaped and 3 remained under trial at the close of the year.

VIII.

Statement of Criminal cases in which British Subjects were concerned for 1343 T. E.

DESCRIPTION OF OFFENCES.		Cases pending since the previous year.	Cases instituted during the year.	Total number of cases.	Cases in which complainants were British subjects.	Cases in which both parties were British subjects.	Cases in which defendants were British subjects.														Remarks.
							Cases pending since the previous year	Cases instituted during the year.	Total number of cases.	Cases disposed of.		Cases pending at the close of the year.	Persons under trial at the close of the previous year.	Persons brought to trial during the year.	Total number of persons under trial.	Convicted.	Acquitted or discharged.	Died or escaped &c.	Under trial at the close of the year.	
										Rejected, compromised or dismissed without enquiry.	Tried.									
Class I. Offences against the State &c.	cognizable	1	5	6	0	0	1	5	6	1	1	4	0	5	5	3	1	0	1	
	non-cognizable ...	0	0	0	0	0	0	0	0	0	0	0	0	0	0	0	0	0	0	
Class II. Offences against person.	cognizable	6	38	44	13	10	4	27	31	6	9	16	1	42	43	14	18	0	11	
	non-cognizable ...	3	26	29	4	9	3	22	25	19	3	3	0	22	22	6	10	0	6	
Class III. Offences against property.	cognizable	91	224	315	12	52	91	212	303	70	164	69	91	401	492	290	129	1	72	
	non-cognizable ...	7	21	28	1	14	7	20	27	13	9	5	4	26	30	10	20	0	0	
Class IV. Other offences	cognizable	10	24	34	1	6	10	23	33	12	13	8	6	26	32	21	6	0	5	
	non-cognizable ...	5	19	24	2	12	5	17	22	14	4	4	2	16	18	3	9	0	6	
Total cognizable ...		108	291	399	26	68	106	267	373	89	187	97	98	474	572	328	154	1	89	
Total non-cognizable ...		15	66	81	7	35	15	59	74	46	16	12	6	64	70	19	39	0	12	
GRAND TOTAL ...		123	357	480	33	103	121	326	447	135	203	109	104	538	642	347	193	1	101	

IX.

Statement of Extradition Cases for the year 1343 T. E.

Names of Courts	Nature of cases.	NUMBER BORNE ON THE REGISTER.				NUMBER BROUGHT TO TRIAL.			RESULT.				
		Number of persons at large at the close of the previous year.	Number of persons awaiting trial at the close of the previous year.	Number of persons against whom warrants were applied for during the year.	Total.	Number of persons arrested and surrendered within the year.	Number of persons who appeared of their own accord or were subsequently arrested in the State within the year.	Total (Columns 4+7+8).	Convicted.	Acquitted or discharged.	Number at large at the close of the year.	Number of persons awaiting trial (after arrest) at the close of the year.	REMARKS.
Sadar Magistracy	Criminal breach of trust	10	1	11	22	1	1	3	0	0	19	2 *b*	
	Escape from lawful custody	0	2	1	3	1	0	3	1	1	0	2	
	Theft	8	5	7	20	1	0	6	2	2	14	2	
	Dacoity	0	3	4	7	4	0	7	0	1	0	3 *c*	
	Rape	1	1	0	2	1	0	2	0	1	0	1	*a.* 1 died.
	Desertion from I. S F. Unit	1	0	1	2	0	1	1	0	0	1	1	
	Cheating	0	1	0	1	0	0	1	0	1	0	0	
Bilonia „ ...	Theft and escape from lawful custody	1	0	0	1	1	0	1	1	0	0	0	
	Theft	15	1	21	37	17	15	33	24	5	4	4	
	Culpable homicide not amounting to murder	1	0	0	1	1	0	1	1	0	0	0	
	Theft and resistance to arrest	1	0	0	1	0	1	1	1	0	0	0	
	Theft and Causing grievous hurt	3	16	0	19	0	1	17	17	0	1 *a*	0	
	Theft and causing hurt	1	0	0	1	0	1	1	1	0	0	0	
	Theft, resistance to lawful apprehension and murder ...	4	0	0	4	2	2	4	3	1	0	0	
Sonamura „ ...	Theft	34	10	94	138	11	76	97	47	24	41	26	
	Grievous hurt	1	0	2	3	0	1	1	0	0	2	1	
	Dacoity and mischief...	0	2	0	2	0	0	2	0	2	0	0	
	Murder	4	0	1	5	0	1	1	0	0	4	0 *d*	*c.* 3 Committed to Sessions.
	Escape from lawful custody	0	0	3	3	0	2	2	2	0	1	0	
	Rape	0	0	1	1	0	1	1	0	0	0	0 *e*	
	Voluntarily causing hurt by dangerous weapon &c. ...	0	0	1	1	0	1	1	0	1	0	0	
	Rioting and grievous hurt	0	0	3	3	0	2	2	0	0	1	2	
Kailashahar „ ...	Theft	8	1	3	12	6	0	7	3	2	5	2	
	Criminal breach of trust	1	0	0	1	0	0	0	0	0	1	0	
	Kidnapping	0	0	4	4	3	0	3	0	3	1	0	
	Escape from lawful custody	0	0	1	1	1	0	1	1	0	0	0	
	Causing grievous hurt	0	0	5	5	0	0	0	0	0	5	0	
Dharmanagar „ ...	Theft	7	0	0	7	0	0	0	0	0	7	0	
	Voluntarily causing grievous hurt	0	0	1	1	1	0	1	0	0	0	1	
	Criminal trespass and theft &c.	11	0	0	11	0	0	0	0	0	11	0	
	Theft and wrongful confinement	1	1	0	2	0	0	1	0	1	1	0	
	Arson and unlawful assembly	9	0	0	9	0	0	0	0	0	9	0	
	Escape from lawful custody	0	0	2	2	2	0	2	1	0	0	1	
Khowa „ ...	Theft	2	0	0	2	0	0	0	0	0	2	0	*b, d & e.* One Committed to Sessions.
	Kidnapping	0	0	1	1	0	0	0	0	0	1	1	
Udaipur „ ...	Theft and receiving stolen property	3	0	2	5	2	0	2	2	0	3	0	
	Murder...	1	0	0	1	0	0	0	0	0	1	0	
Sabroom „ ...	Theft	8	0	4	12	2	0	2	1	0	10	1	
	Escape from lawful custody *	2	0	0	2	0	0	0	0	0	2	0	
	Resistance to arrest	0	0	6	6	0	0	0	0	0	6	0	
	Total	138	44	179	361	57	106	207	107	45	153	50	

*The cases have been struck off owing to the persons not being arrested.

X.

Statement showing the results of appeals against decisions passed by the Criminal Courts in the Tripura State during the year 1343 T. E.

Tribunals.	Number of applications.	Number of persons and cases.																Remarks.
		Applications rejected		Sentences.						Proceedings quashed.		Referred.		Further enquiry &c, ordered.		Pending.		
				Confirmed.		Modified.		Reversed.										
		Persons.	Cases.	Persons.	Cases.	Persons.	Cases.	Persons.	Cases.	Persons.	Cases.	Persons	Cases.	Persons	Cases.	Persons.	Cases.	
Khas Adalat ...	236	10	5	141	107	65	42	33	18	—	—	—	—	29	26	86	38	

XI.

Civil Work—Nature and value of original suits filed and disposed of during the year 1343 T. E.

Tribunal.	Opening balance.		Filed during the year, received by transfer or on remand.		Total.		Disposed of during the year.		Closing balance.		Suits filed during present year.									Suits disposed of during present year.						Suits not estimable in money.	Remarks.
	Past year.	Present year.	Past year.	Present year.	Past year.	Present year.	Past year.	Present year.	Past year.	Present year.	Value.	Suits re landed property.	Suits for money transaction.	Suits for other rights.	Number of suits under Rs. 100.	Number of suits above Rs. 100 and under Rs. 500.	Number of suits above Rs. 500 and under Rs. 1,000.	Number of suits above Rs. 1,000 and under Rs. 5,000.	Number of suits above Rs. 5,000.	*Exparte.*	Admitted and compromised.	Struck off the file.	Otherwise disposed of.	Value.	Average duration.		
											Rs. a. p.													*Rs a. p.*	*Y. m. d.*		
Khas Adalat Original side	64	49	15	26	79	75	30	27	49	48	46,977-11-0	7	10	9	0	0	0	16	1	3	3	2	19	43,494-0-0	0-4-14	9	
Sadar Dewani Adalat	182	262	667	728	849	990	587	684	262	306	31,316-14-0	229	301	198	413	173	11	0	0	403	14	40	221	53,245-8-6	0-0-28	131	
Sonamura "	61	82	208	246	269	328	187	277	82	51	20,428-0-6	17	180	49	149	47	5	0	0	128	50	47	52	22,021-15-9	0-3-1	45	
Bilonia "	18	48	176	176	194	224	146	192	48	32	10,150-0-6	40	136	0	112	31	1	0	0	104	13	24	51	9,265-4-9	0-3-15	32	
Kailashahar "	177	154	241	189	418	343	264	168	154	175	12,557-8-6	9	136	44	114	34	1	0	0	78	9	5	76	16,853-12-6	0-5-8	40	
Khowai "	40	85	117	59	157	144	72	109	85	35	5,178-11-0	1	58	0	44	13	1	0	0	41	11	16	41	4,549-10-0	0-0-15	1	
Dharmanagar "	77	75	216	117	293	192	218	112	75	80	10,083-10-0	7	66	44	68	30	0	0	0	18	25	27	42	12,484-11-9	0-2-7	19	
Udaipur "	110	143	400	226	510	369	367	249	143	120	13,384-6-0	32	165	29	149	34	1	0	0	126	41	2	80	17,763-15-3	0-2-0	42	
Sabrum "	4	8	17	33	21	41	13	39	8	2	3,309-8-3	0	33	0	21	12	0	0	0	19	5	4	11	2,909-8-3	0-0-9	0	
Total ...	733	906	2,057	1,800	2,790	2,706	1,884	1,857	906	849	1,53,386-5-9	342	1085	373	1070	374	20	16	1	926	171	167	593	1,82,588-6-9	0-2-14	319	

XII.

Civil Work.—Results of applications for Execution of Decrees, 1343 T.E.

Tribunal.	Opening balance.		Value of opening balance for present year.	Applications brought to the Register.			Total.			Disposed of.			Closing balance.			Nature of applications pending disposal at the close of the year.			Remarks.
	Past year.	Present year.		Past year.	Present year.	Value for present year.	Past year.	Present year.	Value for present year.	Past year.	Present year.	Value for present year.	Past yaer.	Present year.	Value for present year.	Below 6 months.	Below 12 months.	Above 12 months.	
			Rs. a. p.			Rs. a. p.			Rs. a. p.			Rs. a. p.			Rs. a. p				
Khas Adalat (Original side)	36	34	47,057-3-9	17	13	5,928-4-6	53	47	52,765-8-3	19	10	19,304-4-3	34	37	33,461-4-0	3	4	30	
Sadar Dewani Adalat ...	186	200	36,476-7-9	239	252	34,286-12-9	425	452	70,763-4-6	225	252	38,048-8-6	200	200	32,714-12-0	102	34	64	
Sonamura Ditto ...	27	62	8,020-4-9	99	116	16,003-5-2	126	178	24,029-9-11	64	138	16,412-10-11	62	40	7,610-15-0	28	4	8	
Bilonia Ditto ...	24	19	3,372-1-0	67	73	7,230-15-6	91	92	10,603-0-6	72	66	6,997-6-0	19	26	3,605-10-6	21	2	3	
Kailashahar Ditto ...	103	153	26,753-4-3	110	67	7,876-14-0	213	220	34,660-2-3	60	101	13,890-15-6	153	119	20,763-2-9	37	7	75	
Khowai Ditto ...	29	26	1,301-5-6	37	47	7,847-2-3	66	73	9,148-5-9	40	43	2,833-2-9	26	30	6,315-3-0	23	4	3	
Dharmanagar Ditto ...	31	30	6,599-9-0	49	30	4,413-13-0	80	60	11,013-6-9	50	33	6,754-1-3	30	27	4,259-5-6	9	6	12	
Udaipur Ditto ...	166	162	23,314-6-6	299	164	22,991-9-3	465	326	46,305-15-9	303	196	26,526-6-0	162	130	19,779-9-9	76	31	23	
Sabrum Ditto ...	10	4	354-10-6	5	10	2,002-3-9	15	14	2,350-14-3	11	12	1,981-5-0	4	2	375-9-3	2	0	0	
Total ...	612	690	1,53,259-3-9	922	772	1,08,381-0-2	1,534	1,462	2,61,640-3-11	844	851	1,32,754-12-2	690	611	1,28,885-7-9	301	92	218	

XIII.

Civil Work—Number and results of appeals in civil suits, 1343 T. E.

Tribunal.	Opening balance.		Filed during.		Total.		Disposed of during.		Closing balance.		Value of appeales filed during.		How disposed of.										Average duration.	
													Decisions confirmed.		Decisions reversed.		Decisions amended.		Cases remanded for retrial.		Cases compromised and otherwise disposed of.			
	Past year.	Present year.	Past year.	Present year.	Past year.	Present year.	Past year.	Present year.	Past year.	Present year.	Past year.	Present year.	Past year.	Present year.	Past year.	Present year.	Past year.	Present year.	Past year.	Present year.	Past year.	Present year.	Past year.	Present year.
											Rs. a. p.	*Rs. a. p.*											*Y.m.d.*	*Y.m.d.*
Khas Adalat	167	118	147	147	314	265	196	159	118	106	7,894-8-3	8,627-5-9	86	72	32	31	15	18	30	12	33	26	0-4-10	0-4-12

XIV.

Statement showing the number of persons confined in the jails and lock-ups in the Tripura State during the year 1343 T. E.

Stations.	Number of prisons.	Number of prisoners.				Daily average.		Number of prisoners remaining at the end of the year.	Cost of jails and prisoners.	Average period in days of stay of accused under-trial.	Remarks showing mortality among convicts in jail.
		Remaining from last year.	Admitted during the year.	Total.							
				Past year.	Present year.	Past year.	Present year.		Rs.		
Agartala	1	100	338	452	438	103	103'7	108	14,007	33'5	Three convicts died in the Central Jail during the year 1343 T. E. :—One of chronic nephritis, one of bacillary dysentery, and one of chronic diarrhoea.
Sonamura	1	3	265	109	268	'3	'74	24	1,469	14'62	
Bilonia	1	16	231	135	247	3'52	14'36	7	1,277	33'68	
Kailashahar	1	5	126	174	131	7'82	4'56	7	749	11'92	
Dharmanagar	1	8	64	108	72	9'39	3'49	2	1,098	14'23	
Udaipur...	1	17	90	82	107	4'97	11'36	8	1,317	11'35	
Sabrum	1	1	50	49	51	'13	'13	6	763	17'71	
Khowai	1	9	70	65	79	2'88	4'48	4	955	24'96	
TOTAL. ...	8	159	1234	1174	1393	132'01	142'82	166	21,635	20'24	

XV.

Registration of documents in the Tripura State during the year 1343 T.E.

Name of State.	Documents presented for registration including pending from the last year.		Nature of documents presented.										Documents registered.		Value of documents registered.		Documents of which registration has been refused.		Documents remaining unregistered at the end of the year.		Remarks.
			Mortgages.		Sale deeds.		Wills.		Money bonds.		Miscellaneous.										
	Past year.	Present year.	Past year.	Present year.	Past year.	Present year.	Past year.	Present year.	Past year.	Present year.	Past year.	Present year.	Past year.	Present year.	Past year.	Present year.	Past year.	Present year.	Past year.	Present year.	
1	2	3	4	5	6	7	8	9	10	11	12	13	14	15	16	17	18	19	20	21	22
															Rs.	Rs.					
Tripura State	6,636	6,265	1,252	1,202	3,021	3,513	4	1	78	47	1,239	1,406	6,458	6,118	9,63,565	6,79,981	82	50	96	97	

XVI.

Statement showing the receipts and expenditure on account of Registration during the year 1343 T.E.

Description.	Past Year.			Present Year.			Remarks.
	Number of deeds.	Value of property.	Fees realised.	Number of deeds.	Value of property.	Fees realised.	
		Rs.	Rs.		Rs.	Rs.	
Mortgages	1,252	3,32,385	1,364	1,202	1,43,948	961	
Sale deeds	3,021	4,15,429	2,983	·3,513	3,72,998	3,008	
Wills	4	4,500	34	1	—	5	
Money bonds	78	12,394	84	47	8,710	82	
Miscellaneous	[illegible],239	2,31,567	1,647	1,406	1,67,239	1,645	
Total ...	5,594	9,96,275	6,112	6,169	6,92,895	5,701	
Total Expenditure ...	—	—	3,452	—	—	3,574	
Net Income ...	—	—	2,660	—	—	2,127	

XVII.

Receipts and expenditure of the Municipalities in the Tripura State during the year 1343 T.E.

NAME.	Opening balance.	RECEIPTS DURING THE YEAR.				Total Receipt		EXPENDITURE DURING THE YEAR.		Balance at the close of the year.	REMARKS.
		State grant.	Tax.	Miscellaneous.	Total.	Past year.	Present year	Past.	Present.		
1	2	3	4	5	6	7	8	9	10	11	12
	Rs. A.P.	Rs. A.P.	Rs. A.P.	Rs. A.P.	Rs. A.P.	Rs. A.P.	Rs. A.P.	Rs. A.P.	Rs. A.P.	Rs. A.P.	
Agartala Municipality. ...	38,391-13-9 a	8,000	4,612-11-9	9,886-8-9 b	22,499-4-6	52,415-9-6	60,891-2-3	13,973-9-9	21,262-0-9 c	39,629-1-6 d	a. Includes Rs. 38,362-5-3 of the Bazar Improvement fund. b. Including Rs. 6,470-12-3 as income from the Bazar and Rs. 2,353-14-3 as advance from the Bazar Improvement fund. c. Including Rs. 5,228-0-9 as expenditure on the Bazar improvement. d. Including Rs. 39,605-0-9 of the Bazar Improvement fund.

XVIII.

Statement of rainfall in the Tripura State during the year 1343 T. E.

STATE.	Baisak.	Jaisth.	Asar.	Sravan.	Bhadra.	Asvin.	Kartik.	Agrahayan.	Pous.	Magh.	Falgoon.	Chait.	Total.	Total of past year.	Average of past 5 years.	REMARKS.
Tripura State ...	6·36	14·72	14·51	16·43	18·69	4·30	·76	—	·11	·09	5·51	1·54	83·02	70·56	85·44	

Maximum in Sabroom—95·41″ Minimum in Amarpur—65·71″

XIX.

Statement as to the prices of staple food-grains for the year 1343 T. E.

Articles.	Price per maund during Chait, 1342 T. E.			Price per maund during chait, 1343 T. E.			REMARKS.
	Rs.	*a.*	*p.*	*Rs.*	*a.*	*p.*	
(1) RICE							
Maximum	3	2	0	4	8	0	
Minimum	1	6	0	2	4	0	
(2) PADDY							
Maximum	2	0	0	2	8	0	
Minimum	0	10	0	1	0	0	

XX.

Expenditure on Public Works during the year 1343 T.E.

Description of work.	State funds.			Local funds.			Total.	Remarks.
	Original.	Repairs.	Total.	Original.	Repairs.	Total.		
	Rs.	*Rs.*	*Rs.*	*Rs.*	*Rs.*	*Rs.*	*Rs.*	
Buildings—								
Ordinary Budget ...	15,724	46,149	61,873	—	—	—	61,873	
Improvement „ ...	22,994	—	22,994	—	—	—	22,994	
Roads and Bridges—								
Ordinary Budget ...	445	6,472	6,917	—	—	—	6,917	
Improvement „ ...	34,228	—	34,228	—	—	—	34,228	
Tanks and Tubewells—								
Ordinary Budget ...	350	435	785	1,155	—	1,155	1,940	*Out of the total expenditure Rs. 93653 was spent for ordinary public works and Rs. 71,841 for improvement works and Rs. 1,305 on sanitation works
Improvement „ ...	2,180	—	2,180	—	—	—	2,180	
Miscellaneous works—								
Ordinary Budget ...	2,656	1,400	4,056	—	—	—	4,056	
Improvement „ ...	13,744	—	13,744	—	—	—	13,744	
Total ...	92,321	54,456	1,46,777	1,155	—	1,155	1,47,932	
Minor works at the Rajbari (*Karkhana*)	—	991	991	—	—	—	991	
Establishment charges ..	—	—	17,876	—	—	—	17,876	
Grand Total ...	92,321	55,447	1,65,644	1,155	—	1,155	1,66,799*	

XXI.

Statement showing the number of excise shops and excise revenue of the Tripura State during the year 1343 T. E.

Name of State.	Country spirit.		Country spirit, Opium and Ganja.		Opium and Ganja.		Tari		Total		Remarks.
	Number of shops.	Revenue demand.	Number of shops.	Revenue demand.	Number of shops.	Revenue demand.	Number of shops.	Revenue. demand.	Number of shops.	Revenue realised.	
				Rs.						*Rs.*	
Tripura State	—	—	33	34,932	—	—	—	—	33	41,654	

Note:—Cost of Departmental management of some shops amounted to Rs. 11,992.

XXII.

Statement of Medical Relief afforded in the Tripura State during the year 1343 T.E.*

Dispensary.	Number of patients treated. (new) Outdoor.	Indoor.	Results of in-door patients. (new) Discharged cured.	Relieved or discharged otherwise.	Died.	Remaining under treatment.	Expenditure.	Daily average. (old + new) Outdoor.	Indoor.	Total.	No. of surgical operations performed. Major.	Minor.	Total.	No. of persons vaccinated during the year. Successfully.	Unsuccessfully.	Total.	Remarks.
							Rs.										
1. Victoria Memorial Hospital ...	21,495	518	379	92	39	8	9,943	115·56	16·91	132·47	2	347	349	843	410	1,258	* This Statement excludes figures regarding Kaviraji treatment.
2. Palace Dispensary	3,498	0	0	0	0	0	5,736	39·43	0	39·43	0	0	0	0	0	0	† This figure shows the actual number of outdoor patients treated, the total outdoor attendance during the year being 2,46,246 against 2,14,461 in the year before.
3. Homoeopathic	17,563	0	0	0	0	0	2,253	91·62	0	91·62	0	0	0	0	0	0	
4. Dhaleswar	3,401	0	0	0	0	0	1,357	53·51	0	53·51	0	38	38	0	0	0	
5. Kunjaban	2,116	314	293	13	0	8	2,023	16·75	6·12	22·87	0	11	11	101	176	277	
6. Old Agartala	5,742	0	0	0	0	0	1,531	41·22	0	41·22	0	44	44	597	152	749	
7. Bishalgar	7,861	0	0	0	0	0	1,408	33·22	0	33·22	0	46	46	616	81	697	
8. Sonamura	3,251	6	4	2	0	0	1,939	34·18	·14	34·32	5	149	154	428	46	474	
9. Radhakishorpur	11,609	0	0	0	0	0	1,513	44·85	0	44·85	5	125	130	764	153	917	
10. Amarpur	3,063	0	0	0	0	0	1,014	16·76	0	16·76	0	21	21	266	38	304	
11. Sabroom	3,026	3	2	1	0	0	1,463	17·19	·13	17·32	0	53	53	244	31	275	
12. Bilonia	6,473	3	3	0	0	0	1,909	36·49	·24	36·73	0	74	74	508	58	566	
13. Khowai	7,019	0	0	0	0	0	1,623	24·94	0	24·94	0	92	92	82	53	135	
14. Kailashahar	7,046	13	11	2	1	0	1,919	39·91	·63	40·54	5	58	63	332	74	406	
15. Kamalpur	3,922	0	0	0	0	0	1,236	23·18	0	23·18	1	51	52	373	112	485	
16. Kulai Howar	2,796	0	0	0	0	0	367	9·45	0	9·45	0	16	16	0	0	0	
17. Kalyanpur	1,430	0	0	0	0	0	616	4·20	0	4·20	0	0	0	211	20	231	
18. Dharmanagar	5,882	30	16	12	1	1	1,284	32·10	1·21	33·31	2	85	87	268	45	313	
Total	*1,30,193	887	707	122	41	17	39,164	674·56	25·38	699·94	20	1,210	1,230	5,638	1,449	7,087	

XXIII.

Vital statistics of the Tripura State for the year 1343 T. E. *

STATE.	Population.	BIRTHS.				DEATHS.				RATIO PER 1,000 OF POPULATION.				REMARKS.
										BIRTHS.		DEATHS.		
		Past year.	Present year.	Increase.	Decrease.	Past year.	Present year.	Increase.	Decrease.	Past year.	Present year.	Past year.	Present year.	
Tripura State ...	3,81,861	3,136	3,406	270	—	3,091	3,753	662	—	8·21	8·91	8·09	9·81	

* This shows the number of births and deaths so far as registered.

XXIV.

Education Return (A)—Particulars as to the schools maintained during the year 1343 T.E.

Number of Schools. Past year	Number of Schools. Present year.	Class of Schools.	Number of Pupils on the rolls on the last day of Chait. Past year.	Number of Pupils on the rolls on the last day of Chait. Present year.	Average Daily Attendance. Past year.	Average Daily Attendance. Present year.	Remarks.
6	6	High English Schools ... ... (including one Branch H. E. School).	1,410	1,488	1,106·55	1,150·15	
8	9	Middle English Schools for boys ...	983	1,092	762·22	883·58	* In some of these schools boys and girls read together. The fall in the numerical strength was due to the closing of some of the Schools.
1	1	Middle English School for girls ...	89	77	66·33	62·81	
1	—	Higher Vernacular School for boys	77	—	62·02	—	
23	26	* Lower Vernacular Schools for boys	1,413	1,255	1,104·48	1,013·7	
87	76	*Pathsalas for boys	2,666	2,183	1,957·19	1,733·04	
9	9	Do for girls	273	319	226·72	240·11	
		Special Schools :—					
4	4	Compulsory Free Primary Schools	418	508	242·32	282·61	
7	7	Madrassas and Muktabs	388	235	300·82	183·60	
4	5	Sanskrit *Tols*	39	50	30·01	38·27	† Excluding students of private Schools.
1	1	Artisan School & Silpasram ...	23	22	10·54	10·25	
1	1	Jail Reformatory School	21	20	19·45	19·45	
TOTAL 152	145		7,800	7,249†	5,888·65	5,617·57	

XXV.

Education Return (B) Race of Students, 1343 T. E.

Names of Divisions.	No. of Schools.				No. of Students.					Race.												Average daily attendance.		REMARKS.
										Hindus,														
	For boys.	For girls.	Total.	Private schools.	Boys.	Girls.	Total.	Students of private schools.	Total.	Rajkumars.	Thakurs.	Manipuris.	Tripuras.	Bengalees.	Others.	Reangs.	Chakmas.	Kukis.	Lusais.	Musalmans.	Christians.	Boys.	Girls.	
1. Sadar Division ...	51	2	53	9	2,366	396	2,762	250	3,012	5	269	130	590	1,161	18	1	1	1	0	586	0	1,834·83	278·21	
2. Kailashahar „	22	3	25	10	1,047	184	1,231	275	1,506	0	1	330	5	641	0	0	0	0	0	254	0	821·64	133·98	
3. Sonamura „	19	1	20	3	913	95	1,008	112	1,120	0	8	1	55	220	0	0	0	0	0	724	0	737·49	72·88	
4. Bilonia „	8	1	9	2	576	45	621	62	683	0	0	0	29	391	3	0	0	0	0	198	0	459·87	34·9	
5. Khowai „	6	1	7	2	301	17	318	69	387	0	0	33	184	73	9	0	0	0	0	19	0	230·15	12·13	
6. Dharmanagar „	13	1	14	7	583	77	660	182	842	0	0	74	3	437	12	0	0	0	1	133	0	434·3	64·69	
7. Udaipur „	9	1	10	3	380	18	398	77	475	0	3	0	62	153	0	0	0	0	0	180	0	306·61	14·63	
8. Sabrum „	6	0	6	1	202	12	214	31	245	0	0	0	44	124	2	0	0	0	0	44	0	152·95	8·97	
9. Amarpur Sub-division ...	1	0	1	2	31	6	37	35	72	0	1	0	5	16	0	12	0	0	0	3	0	15·53	3·81	
TOTAL ...	135	10	145	39	6,399	850	7,249	1,093	8,342	5	282	568	977	3,216	44	13	1	1	1	2,141	0	4,993·37	624·20	

N. B.—In the Sub-columns under "Race" the number of students of private schools is not included.

APPENDIX XXVI. (A)

Statement of Audited Receipts for the year 1343 T. E.

State.

Heads of Revenue.	1342 T. E.		1343 T. E.		REMARKS.
	Revised Estimate.	Actuals.	Revised Estimate.	Actuals.	
1. Land Revenue ...	4,15,000	4,18,825	4,38,000	4,50,707	
2. Rents of markets ..	6,000	6,477	6,000	6,137	
3. Family tax in the hills	43,000	45,459	45,000	46,960	
4. Toll on Forest Produce	3,50,000	3,35,192	3,28,000	3,20,852	
5. Do on the Feni River	30,000	28,086	28,000	27,073	
6. Elephant and Buffalo grazing mehals ...	6,000	6,003	6,000	8,041	
7. Thatching grass mehals	4,000	3,379	3,300	2,856	
8. Reserved *Sal* trees ...	3,000	1,975	3,500	3,894	
9. Tax on cotton and Oil seeds ...	1,10,000	1,40,040	1,17,000	1,06,839	
10. Royalty on elephants caught ...	1,000	1,628	3,000	2,616	
11. *Adda* mehal ...	20,000	22,499	23,000	24,435	
12. Excise ...	40,000	40,279	48,000	41,654	
13. Stamps and Court fees	66,000	66,415	64,000	61,514	
14. Law and Justice (fines)	3,000	2,274	2,200	2,356	
15. Process Fees ...	12,000	11,650	10,500	10,154	
16. Registration ...	7,000	5,869	5,500	6,095	
17. Jail ...	2,000	2,111	5,000	4,770	
18. Cattle pounds ...	5,000	4,349	4,000	3,747	
19. *Nazars* ...	27,000	25,663	28,000	29,620	
20. School Fees ...	14,000	14,086	14,000	14,566	
21. Duty on Tea ...	11,000	9,318	11,000	12,580	
22. Duty on jute ...	31,000	31,388	31,000	31,964	
23. Personal *Howlats* recovered	2,000	1,319	—	—	
24. Miscellaneous ...	42,000	43,974	45,000	43,154	
25. Depreciation Contribution ...	70,000	80,850	81,000	77,224	
Toatl ...	13,20,000	13,49,108	13,50,000	13,39,810	
26. Deposits ...	3,01,897	3,11,572	1,87,000	2,14,494	
27. Contribution from Chakla ...	2,75,000	2,50,000	2,80,000	2,80,000	
28. Loan from Government	—	—	9,00,000	9,00,000	
Total ...	18,96,897	19,10,680	27,17,000	27,34,304	
Opening Balance :— Cash ...	1,14,250	1,14,250	1,56,879	1,44,444	
Advances ...	2,61,681	2,61,681	2,45,632	2,46,408	
Loans ...	2,75,084	2,75,084	2,74,982	2,75,231	
Total ...	6,51,015	6,51,015	6,77,493	6,66,083	
Grand Total ...	25,47,912	25,61,695	33,94,493	34,00,387	

APPENDIX XXVI. (B)

Statement of Audited Expenditure for the year 1343 T. E.

State.

Heads of Expenditure.	1342 T. E.		1343 T. E.		REMARKS.
	Revised estimate.	Actuals.	Revised Estimate.	Actuals.	
1. Controlling Charges	71,715	69,784	86,196	84,862	
2. Revenue General ...	79,922	75,825	99,750	88,886	
3. Survey & Settlement	19,073	19,029	37,315	36,545	
4. Tahasil ...	44,322	43,071	47,650	46,007	
5. Registration ...	4,119	3,129	3,832	3,574	
6. Police ...	85,739	85,242	87,690	86,836	
7. Judicial ...	38,518	36,060	33,335	32,056	
8. Jail ...	23,048	21,804	23,733	23,364	
9. Forest ...	42,325	41,092	47,973	46,159	
10. Medical ...	64,909	64,070	65,899	65,329	
11. Municipality ...	8,000	8,000	8,000	8,000	
12. Education General ...	1,28,984	1,28,441	1,30,798	1,25,021	
13. (*a*) Public Works ...	86,896	79,899	93,454	92,498	
(*b*) Improvement ...	30,000	26,499	72,250	71,841	
14. Electric Light ...	19,396	17,125	16,332	15,002	
15. Small Donations ...	300	266	325	318	
16. Relief to distressed subjects ...	300	30	300	282	
17. Purchase of Landed Property ...	1,000	711	10,260	10,021	
18. Repayment of Deposits ...	1,91,260	1,90,957	60,000	59,311	
19. Interest on Deposits	—	—	30,000	28,848	
20. Unforeseen charges...	7,500	4,792	7,500	7,263	
21. Pension ...	40,000	38,576	49,500	49,465	
22. Advisory Council ...	1,320	1,320	—	—	
23. Chief Secretary's Office & H. H.'s Tour	96,360	96,341	1,42,724	1,41,747	
24. Palace Sultanat ...	26,171	26,062	45,813	45,714	
25. Zoo ...	5,500	4,681	3,769	3,769	
26. Agriculture, Commerce and Industries	8,211	7,360	8,165	7,929	
27. Publicity, Reclamation & Immigration ...	1,030	987	3,030	2,843	
28. H. H.'s Private Secretary's Office ...	8,500	8,344	8,900	8,866	
29. Rajmala Office ...	4,000	3,995	5,200	4,435	
30. Military Secretary's Office ...	3,000	2,990	3,240	3,220	
31. Military ...	1,18,222	98,016	1,18,222	1,06,626	
32. Nijtahabil ...	1,00,000	1,00,000	1,00,000	1,00,000	
33. Adjustment of irrecoverable advances...	10,000	10,000	940	924	
34. Census ...	500	359	500	370	
35. Repayment of old Debts ...	1,34,468	1,33,649	5,50,000	4,84,818	
36. Sansar Charges ...	3,89,882	3,76,796	4,18,849	4,16,619	
37. Salary for the discharged officers ...	40,600	40,310	—	—	
38. Expenditure for the treatment of Maharaj Kumari Basanta Prava...	30,000	30,000	32,919	32,500	
39. H. H.'s special donation ..	—	—	5,000	5,000	
40. Sanitation ...	—	—	1,400	1,305	
Total ...	19,65,090	18,95,612	24,60,763	23,48,173	
Closing balance :—					
Cash ...	56,057	1,44,441	1,05,000	1,88,197	
Advances ...	2,51,681	2,46,408	2,03,061	1.73,407	
Loans issued ...	2,75,084	2,75,231	2,75,669	2,75,428	
Working balance ...	—	—	3,50,000	4,15,182	
Total ...	5,82,822	6,66,083	9.33.730	10,52,214	
Grand Total ...	25,47,912	25,61,695	33,94,493	34,00,387	

APPENDIX XXVII. (A)

Statement of Audited Receipts for the year 1343 T. E.

Chakla Roshnabad Estates.

Heads of Receipts.	1342 T. E. Revised Estimate.	1342 T. E. Actuals.	1343 T. E. Revised Estimate.	1343 T. E. Actuals.	Remarks.
1. Rent and Cess ...	8,21,000	8,31,818	8,38,000	8,88,198	
2. Cess for Rent free holdings ...	7,000	6,950	8,000	8,217	
3. Law charges recovered	52,000	38,414	54,000	38,576	
4. Misc. receipts including deposits ...	49,000	50,605	94,000	46,911	
5. Refund of loans and advances ...	1,000	1,579	1,000	987	
Total ...	9,30,000	9,29,366	9,95,000	9,82,889	
Opening Balance :—					
Cash ...	92,027	92,027	98,936	97,853	
Advance ...	1,12,100	1,12,301	1,05,000	1,11,259	
Loans issued ...	73,557	73,619	73,057	80,435	
Bank deposits ...	1,36,188	1,36,188	31,331	49,651	
Total ...	4,13,872	4,14,135	3,08,324	3,39,198	
Grand Total ...	13,43,872	13,43,501	13,03,324	13,22,087	

APPENDIX XXVII. (B)

Statement of Audited Expenditure for the year 1343 T. E.

Chakla Roshnabad Estates.

Heads of Expenditure.	1342 T. E. Revised Estimate.	1342 T. E. Actuals	1343 T. E. Revised Estimate.	1343 T. E. Actuals.	REMARKS.
i. 1. Revenue and Cess ...	2,76,000	2,73,821	2,95,835	2,88,830	
2. Establishment ...	1,42,000	1,40,737	1,44,523	1,38,759	
3. Settlement ...	1,300	896	1,440	1,188	
4. Legal Expenses ...	1,08,780	1,04,882	1,17,899	1,17,193	
5. Education ...	8,300	8,086	9,354	8,962	
6. Medical ...	11,778	11,156	12,864	11,737	
7. Public Works ...	50,650	50,491	61,200	60,335	
8. Religious Expenses	6,800	6,471	6,800	6,339	
9. Miscellaneous ...	3,000	2,508	6,000	5,629	
10. Loans and Advances	1,000	837	1,000	600	
11. Pension and Gratuity	8,500	7,925	10,500	9,980	
12. Forest ...	700	542	700	599	
13. Purchase of property	3,740	3,630	2,000	1,374	
14. Unforeseen ...	1,200	1,195	1,000	671	
ii. Sansar ...	12,960	12,960	12,960	12,960	
iii. Donation ...	4,617	4,540	6,750	6,746	
v. State Contribution	2,75,000	2,50,000	2,80,000	2,80,000	
v. Repayment of debts	1,11,970	1,09,503	20,000	19,965	
vi. Refund of old deposits ...	20,164	14,123			
Total ...	10,48,459	10,04,303	9,90,825	9,71,867	
Closing Balance :—					
Cash ...	81,893	97,853	1,02,719	1,04,342	
Advances ...	1,05,000	1,11,259	1,04,780	1,15,477	
Loans issued ...	73,057	80,435	73,000	78,859	
Bank deposits ...	35,463	49,651	32,000	51,542	
Total ...	2,95,413	3,39,198	3,12,499	3,50,220	
Grand Total ...	13,43,872	13,43,501	13,03,324	13,22,087	

MINISTER'S OFFICE,
TRIPURA STATE,
POLITICAL DEPARTMENT.

To

His Highness The Bisama-Samara-Bijayee Mahamahodaya
Pancha-Srijukta Maharaja Manikya
SIR BIR BIKRAM KISHORE
DEV BARMAN BAHADUR, K. C. S. I.,
Maharaja of Tripura.

Dated, Agartala, the 20th December, 1935.

MAY IT PLEASE YOUR HIGHNESS,

I have the honour to submit the accompanying Report on the General Administration of the State and the attached Zemindaries for the year 1344 T. E., extending from the 14th April, 1934 to the 13th April, 1935.

The reports on the administration of the Military Department as well as of the Departments of Agriculture, Commerce and Industries and Immigration under the control of the Chief Secretary to Your Highness, have been incorporated in the Report.

I have the honour to be
Your Highness's most obedient servant,
Jyotis Chandra Sen,
MINISTER.

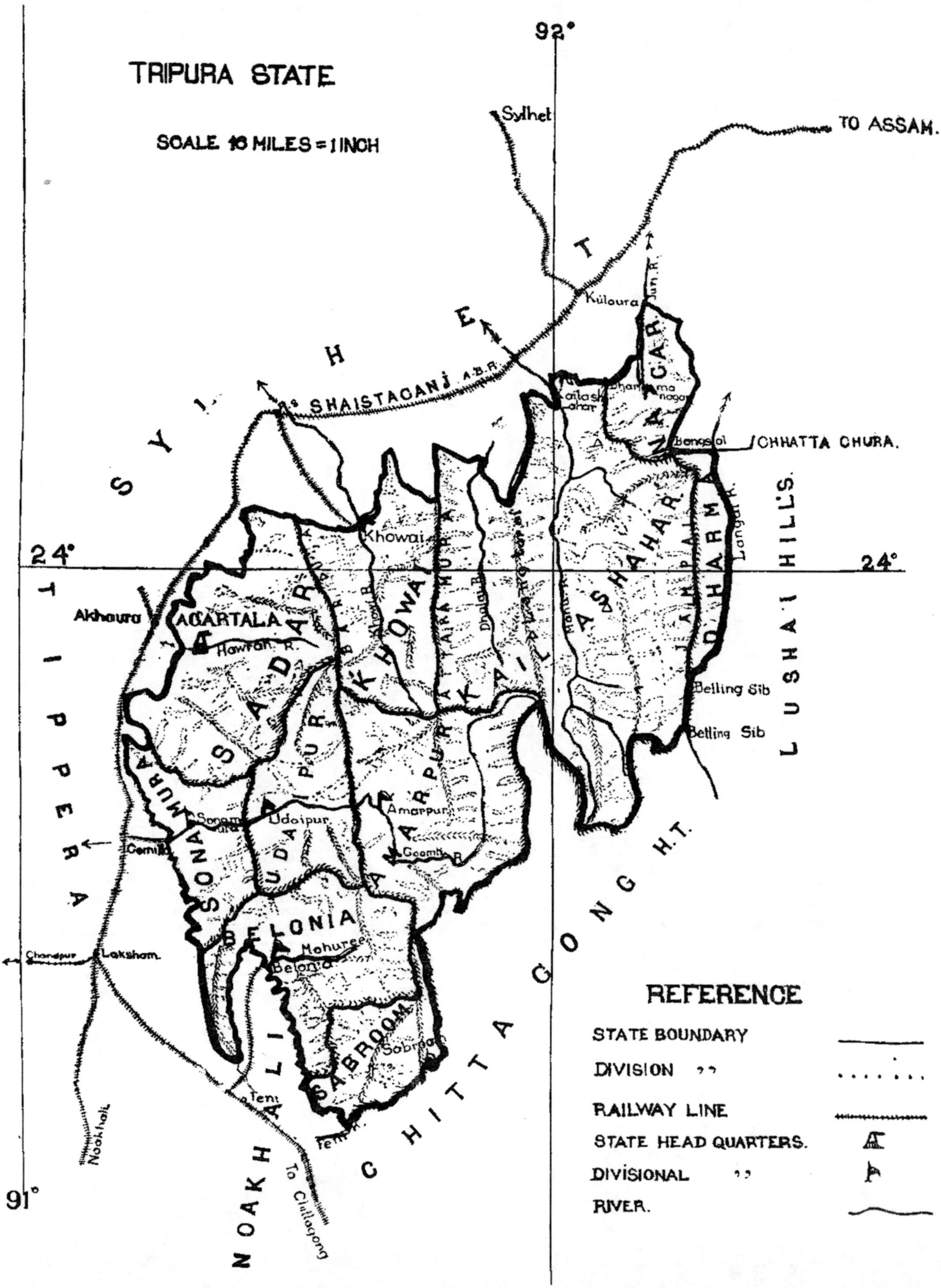
TRIPURA STATE
SCALE 16 MILES = 1 INCH
92°
24°
24°
91°
Sylhet
TO ASSAM.
SYLHET
SHAISTAGANJ A.B.R.
Kuloura
Kailashahar
Dharmanagar
Bengsol
CHHATTA CHURA.
LUSHAI HILLS.
Langai R.
Khowai
Akhaura
AGARTALA
Howrah R.
SADAR
KHOWAI
KAILASHAHAR
DHARMANAGAR
Belling Sib
Belling Sib
TIPPERA
SONAMURA
Sonamura
Udaipur
UDAIPUR
AMARPUR
Amarpur
Goomti R.
Comilla
BELONIA
Mohuree
Belonia
Chandpur
Laksham.
SABROOM
Sabroom
Feni
Feni R.
Noakhali
NOAKHALI
To Chittagong
CHITTAGONG H.T.
REFERENCE
STATE BOUNDARY
DIVISION ,,
RAILWAY LINE
STATE HEAD QUARTERS.
DIVISIONAL ,,
RIVER.

Book Twenty-six

Report on the Administration of the Tripura State for 1344 T. E. (1934-1935 A.D.)

REPORT ON THE ADMINISTRATION

OF

THE TRIPURA STATE

FOR

1344 T. E. (1934-35.)

CHAPTER I—GENERAL AND POLITICAL.

Area of the State—4,116 sq. miles.
Population—3,82,450.
Gross Revenue (based on the average of five years):—

(*a*) State ... ... Rs. 20,32,806.
(*b*) Zemindaries ... ... Rs. 9,76,490.

Tribute—Nil.

Ruler of the State—His Highness The Bisama-Samara-Bijayee Mahamahodaya Pancha-Srijukta Maharaja Manikya Sir Bir Bikramkishore Dev Barman Bahadur, K. C. S. I. *Age*—27 years. (Born—19th August, 1908). *Caste*—*Kshatriya* (of the Lunar race).

The year and the people.

The year under review witnessed an appreciable relaxation in the economic strain which has been the distressing feature of the last quinquennium since its commencement, and it may not perhaps be too optimistic a view to take that the tide of depression has at last reached its lowest limit. The perceptibly steady and at times comparatively high level of prices of some of the indigenous commodities combined with the increased outturn of most of the money crops contributed towards alleviation of the economic condition of the people in the plains and hills to an appreciable extent. Although the average price of paddy and jute remained at practically the same level as in the previous year, that of rice, cotton and *til* (sesame) maintained a steady, though not very substantial, rise throughout the year.

2. Weather conditions were generally favourable with satisfactory effect on crops in the hills and plains alike, and there was increased outturn of paddy, cotton and oilseeds, although some damage to paddy crops over small areas was caused by floods in Sonamura and Sadar Divisions. The output of tea went up by 27 per cent., but the yield of jute dropped to a noticeable extent which can only be ascribed to the intensive propaganda carried out in connection with the jute restriction scheme inaugurated in Bengal.

3. The economic life of the middle-class people was not better than in the year preceding. There was no material change in the rates of wages of skilled and unskilled labour.

4. In the Zemindaries the general conditions of the tenantry showed some improvement.

Floods in Agartala.

5. A natural calamity overtook the people of the capital by surprise on the morning of the 17th Aswin. On account of incessant and heavy rainfall of over nine inches on the previous night, there was a tremendous rush of water in the river Howrah. At places the embankment was submerged, while several breaches occurred in the embankment over the heart of the town and the whole town was entirely submerged. Most of the townsmen took shelter in the Palace and the public buildings, thrown open for the purpose, and they had to be supplied with provisions by the State. Boats had to be obtained from Mogra and Akhaura and some provisions from Brahmanbaria. His Highness himself moved about by boat over the flooded roads and wading through water and mud at places, seeing for himself the state of things and giving directions wherever necessary. Prompt and adequate measures were taken to give relief to the flood-stricken people. There was fortunately no loss of life but considerable damage was caused to homesteads. Relief and sanitary measures after the floods were organised by a Committee. It took 36 hours for the flood-water to subside completely.

The finances of the year.

6. The year opened with a balance of Rs. 14,02,434 against Rs. 10,05,281 in the year before. The total revenue from permanent sources was Rs. 15,79,609 against Rs. 13,39,810 in the preceding year in the State and Rs. 9,87,261 against Rs. 9,08,361 in the Zemindaries. With deposits, the total receipts from all sources came to Rs. 29,21,572 against Rs. 34,37,193, the total sum available for expenditure being Rs. 43,24,006 as against Rs. 44,42,474 which includes a loan of Rs. 9 lacs from the Government of India. The collection of land revenue was encouraging and the increase in the duty on cotton and oilseeds as well as tea was also satisfactory, but there was a drop of Rs. 20,303 in the forest revenue.

II

Visit to Mussoorie.

7. Their Highnesses the Maharaja Manikya Bahadur and the Maharani Saheba spent the summer of the year under report at Mussoorie. Their Highnesses left the Capital on the night of May 1, 1934 (18th Baisakh) for Calcutta, *en route* to Mussoorie. Her Highness the Dowager Madhyam Maharani Saheba went to Shillong for a short stay and joined His Highness in Calcutta on his way back from Mussoorie.

8. While at Mussoorie, a Tea and two Dinner parties were given by His Highness at the Trocadero on the 20th June, and 4th and 17th July respectively. At the former, besides others, Their Highnesses the Maharani Saheba and the Dowager Maharani Saheba of Rajpipla, Their Highnesses the Raja Saheb and Rani Saheba of Kalsia, Raja Sahebs of Sarila, Bansi and Chingera were present, and at the latter

functions besides the guests whose names are mentioned above, those present, included the Raja Saheb of Nanpara and the Tica Rani Saheba of Kapurthala.

9. On the 30th June, His Highness, with staff, dined with His Highness the Maharaja Saheb of Alwar at the Charleville Hotel, and on the 19th of July he had tea with the Tica Rani Saheba of Kapurthala at the Chateau.

10. On the 11th of June, His Highness was pleased to extend his kind patronage to a Charity Show arranged at the Palladium, for the benefit of the Anjuman-Islamia H. E. School at Mussoorie. Besides this, on the 2nd July, another grand-variety Charity Show at the Hackman's Hotel was held at the instance and under the patronage of His Highness in aid of the Bihar Earthquake Relief. His Highness evinced keen interest in making the function a success. A substantial amount was collected and sent to the Viceroy's Bihar Earthquake Relief Fund

Dholpur Visit.

11. Towards the end of their stay at Mussoorie, Their Highnesses, on being invited by His Highness the Maharana Saheb of Dholpur, went to Dholpur and stayed there for a few days. His Highness and the party were very cordially received by the Maharaj-Rana Saheb and elaborate arrangements were made for Their Highnesses' stay there as well as for some enjoyable excursions.

"*Griha-Prabesh*" to Tripura House.

12. On their way back to Agartala, the *Griha-Prabesh* ceremony of the newly-built Tripura House in Calcutta was duly performed by Their Highnesses on the 28th Sravan, corresponding to the 13th August, 1934.

13. Their Highnesses and party returned to Agartala on the 18th August.

His Highness's Birthday Celebrations.

14. The 16th of Bhadra, corresponding to the 2nd September, 1934, was eventful on account of the usual felicitations and celebrations in connection with His Highness's auspicious birthday anniversary. A big Durbar was held at the U. K. Academy grounds at Agartala where the customary National Flag hoisting ceremony was performed by His Highness; Military parade was held and a number of prisoners were released to mark the happy occasion.

H. H. Dowager Madhyam Maharani Saheba's Visit to Calcutta.

15. Her Highness the Dowager Madhyam Maharani Saheba proceeded to Calcutta on the 30th Asvin, for treatment and stayed there for about a month. She progressed there satisfactorily but had to hurry back to the Capital where His Highness was ailing. To the great relief of Her Highness and the public in general, His Highness recovered soon from his indisposition and his health was restored to its normal condition in a few days' time.

Cold weather Visit to Calcutta.

16. The cold weather visit of His Highness the Maharaja Manikya Bahadur to Calcutta, extended from the 5th December, 1934 to the 8th January following, during which besides the usual engagements, the following important functions were carried out.

17. Their Excellencies the Viceroy and the Countess of Willingdon honoured His Highness by lunching with him at Tripura House on the 18th December, 1934. Their Highnesses the Maharaja and Dowager Maharani of Cooch Behar, Nawab Bahadur of Murshidabad, Raja Saheb of Khairagarh, Consuls-General for Germany, Italy, France, Japan and U. S. A. and many leading gentlemen of the City also joined in the function.

Luncheon to Viceroy.

18. Another Luncheon Party was given to meet His Excellency the Right Hon'ble Sir John Anderson, P. C., G. C. B., G. C. I. E., Governor of Bengal, at Tripura House on the 20th December, 1934. Most of the higher officials of the Government of Bengal were invited to the same.

Luncheon to Governor.

19. In a few more functions at the same house, many important visitors of the season including Their Highnesses of Jaipur, Kapurthala, Travancore, Bhutan, Indore, Cooch Behar, Mayurbhanj and others were entertained by His Highness.

20. His Highness the Maharaja Manikya Bahadur had a private interview with His Excellency the Viceroy at the Viceroy's House, on the 22nd December, and also had two such interviews with H. E. the Governor on the 24th of the same month and 5th January, 1935.

21. His Highness attended functions both at the Viceroy's and Government Houses as usual. Besides these, a few engagements elsewhere may also be noted. On the 27th of December, His Highness presided over the opening ceremony of the All Bengal Music Competition at the Senate House. He accepted invitations of Their Highnesses of Travancore and Cooch Behar and also the Hon'ble President of the Bengal Legislative Council to parties.

22. Their Highnesses the Maharaj-Rana Saheb and Maharani Saheba of Dholpur, with party returned His Highness's visit and stayed with him as his guests in Calcutta from the 25th December to 5th January, 1935.

23. His Highness the Mahendra Maharaja Saheb of Panna and staff arrived at Tripura House on the 21st December as His Highness's guest and left on the 5th January.

24. The Raja Saheb of Khairagarh came to stay with His Highness on the 14th December and left Tripura House on the 31st idem.

25. His Highness the Maharaja Manikya Bahadur returned to Agartala on the 8th January. Her Highness the Maharani Saheba went to Panna from Calcutta on the 5th January and after a month's stay there came back to Calcutta.

26. His Highness's cold weather camping-out within the State began from the 1st of February, 1935.

27. With the State Military Forces and a few hundreds of Tripur-Kshatriya-Mandali Sardars, its Sampadaka (Secretary), Tripur Volunteers and other followers, His Highness the Maharaja Manikya Bahadur left the capital for the interior, stopping *en route* at Ompinagar, Amarpur, Dambarunagar, Muhuripur and Bilonia. The tour lasted 13 days providing sufficient time for His Highness to proceed by stages and gather local experience and hear direct from the hill populace.

Cold weather tour within the State.

28. The first stop after leaving the Capital was made at Ompi, where His Highness reached late in the evening and was received by some thousands of people amidst cheers.

Ompinagar.

29. A Durbar was held the next day at which by a proclamation, His Highness was pleased to change the name of the place from Ompi to Ompinagar.

Amarpur.

30. The next Camp was at Amarpur where also a similar Durbar was held. It was during his stay here that His Highness ordered the construction of some roads, the Amarpur–Radhakishorpur road being the most important among them.

Dambarunagar and visit to Dambur falls.

31. At Natunbazar, which name was changed to Dambarunagar by His Highness at a largely attended Durbar held there, the party made a halt for three days. From this place His Highness paid a visit to the famous and picturesque Dambur Falls down which the river Gumti becomes navigable. At Tirthamukh His Highness was pleased to lay the foundation stone of a Siva temple.

Muhuripur and visit to Pilak Pathar.

32. Leaving Dambarunagar, His Highness stayed the night at Kalsicherra and then arrived at Lungthung where also scenes of intense enthusiasm and loyal fervour were witnessed. His Highness was accorded an ovation by thousands of his loyal subjects most of whom were Maghs and Chakmas. Yet another very big Durbar was held here at which a proclamation was made by His Highness changing the name of the place from Lungthung to Muhuripur. A rest house was ordered to be built there and the charitable dispensary which had been closed a few years back was ordered to be reopened.

33. While at Muhuripur, His Highness went to visit the massive and extensive ruins of Pilak Pathar, famous for its impressive and archæological relics.

34. The extensive tour through the hills ended with His Highness's arrival at Belonia on the 13th February. This tour, which was undertaken with a good amount of physical strain and was borne by His Highness admirably, contributed valuable experience of the land and the people, to his zealous and inquisitive mind The entire amount of *Nazar* received at the Durbars at these place was given to the respective local committees for improvement works in respect of the construction of roads and excavation of tanks.

Belonia.

35. A befitting reception was given to His Highness on his arrival at Belonia from Muhuripura. A Durbar was held the next morning at which His Highness was the recipient of several addresses of welcome from the public as well as some local institutions to which he gave a joint reply. At the close of the Durbar, His Highness was pleased to direct the formation of the Belonia Improvement Committee and it was also announced that the entire amount of *Nazar* collected at the Durbar would be handed over to that Committee for improvement works in that locality.

36. His Highness and party left Belonia by Special train on the morning of the 16th February (4th Falgoon) for Agartala. This journey through the Zemindaries up to Feni was also eventful and unique in character. The train had to be pulled up at certain places besides the scheduled stoppages at Parasuram, Fulgazi Pirbuxhat and Bandhua-Daulatpur to allow the monster crowds to have a *Dursan* of His Highness. During those brief stoppages even, His Highness was presented with addresses and *Dalis*.

Departure from Belonia.

37. The train arrived at Feni, the South-Divisional headquarters of Chakla Roshnabad Estates, at 11-30 A. M. and stopped there for the whole day. His Highness's visit was an official one, and the befitting reception that His Highness received there from all classes of people, official and non-official, was indeed, unprecedented in the annals of the town.

Official visit to Feni.

38. His Highness the Maharaja Manikya Bahadur was received at the Station by Mr. A. Whittaker, I. C. S., District Magistrate, Noakhali and the members of the Reception Committee representative of all classes and creeds which was constituted for the occasion. As soon as His Highness alighted from the train, a Guard of Honour of 50 rank and file of the Bengal Armed Police presented arms, a salute of 13 guns was fired and the State Band played the State National Anthem. His Highness then inspected the Guard-of-Honour and retired to his saloon.

Reception at the station.

39. A deputation from the Reception Committee then waited on His Highness and escorted him to the Feni College where arrangements for a public reception had been made. The routes from the Railway Station to the Feni College presented the spectacle of a veritable sea of human heads and it was with much difficulty that His Highness's car could proceed through the struggling crowd rushing enthusiastically to come near the car.

40. At the Feni College Hall, His Highness received addresses of welcome from the Reception Committee, the Governing Body of the Feni College, Feni Union Board and other local bodies to which he gave a very appreciative joint reply followed by an announcement, by the Minister, of His Highness's donations to various institutions as detailed below :—

Public reception at Feni College.

1.	Feni College	...	...	Rs. 5,000
2.	G. A. Academy	...	...	„ 500
3.	Pagla Mia's Takia	.	...	„ 500
4.	Kalibari	...	...	„ 500
5.	Madrassa	...	...	„ 250
6.	Girls' School	...	...	„ 250
7.	Sarbananda Chatuspathi	...	...	„ 100
8.	Ukilpara Jagannathbari	...	...	„ 100
				Rs. 7,200
9.	Sweets for boys and girls	...	...	„ 500
		TOTAL ...		Rs. 7,700

41. On arrival at and departure from the College. the State troops presented arms to His Highness and the State Band played the State National Anthem.

Visit to Divisional Office.

42. At 3-30 in the afternoon, His Highness paid a visit to the Divisional Office at Feni where also he was the recipient of addresses from the Raj Officers of the Southern Division, Chakla Roshnabad Estates and from the merchants of the Birendraganj (Feni) bazar. His Highness in a neat little reply, appreciated the sentiments expressed therein and extended his kind assurance to all concerned.

Inter-District Schools sports.

43. The Inter-district Schools sports were arranged at the College grounds and His Highness was pleased to preside over the function and distribute prizes.

Afternoon Party.

44. After a drive through the Feni Bazar which was equally crowded and decorated with arches, flags and festoons, His Highness went to attend an Afternoon Party which was arranged in his honour and at which, all sections of the public were widely represented.

45. The numerous engagements of His Highness were not yet finished and in the evening, he attended a theatrical performance in the College building.

46. A Dinner Party was given at Feni by His Highness to which the heads of the district Executive and Judiciary and also some leading gentlemen were invited.

Return to Agartala.

47. His Highness the Maharaja Manikya Bahadur left Feni by Special train the same night and returned to Agartala on the following morning (17th February) after successful completion of the hill tour and Feni visit.

H. H.'s Calcutta visit at the end of the year.

48. On the 19th Falgoon, His Highness with the party accompanying left Agartala again for Calcutta where Her Highness was staying.

Sreedham Mayapur and Navadwip visit.

49. The foremost public engagement during this stay was the visit to Sreedham Mayapur (Navadwip) on invitation by the Calcutta *Gaudiya Math*, to preside over the opening ceremony of the newly-built magnificient temple on the birth site of Sri Chaitanya Mahaprabhu.

50. His Higness with his staff left Calcutta in the morning and arrived at Mayapur where he was accorded a right royal reception. In the afternoon, before a huge congregation assembled in a beautifully decorated quadrangle, His Highness received several addresses from Sree Navadwipdham Pracharini Sabha and other sister institutions of Sreedham Mayapur, to which, he gave a joint reply. His Highness then proceeded towards the temple and declared it open. He then visited some places of interest in and around Mayapur and also paid a fiying visit to Navadwip and returned to Calcutta the same night.

Birth of second Maharajkumar.

51. On the 12th Chaitra (early morning of 27th March) a second Maharajkumar Bahadur was born to Her Highness the Maharani Saheba at Tripura House in Calcutta which was an occasion for great rejoicings there and also all over the State and the Zemindaries.

52. During His Highness's stay in Calcutta, Maharājkumari Srila Srimati Jati Devi, one of his half-sisters was given in marriage to Manyabara Rana Bodh Jung Bahadur, F. R. G. S., of Phapamow Castle, Allahabad. The ceremony was celebrated at Tripura House on the 27th Falgoon with due pomp and rejoicings.

Marriage of Maharaj-kumari Jati Devi.

53. On the 17th March, His Highness was the host at a Dinner party given at Tripura House in which H. H. The Maharaja Saheb of Mayurbhanj, the Rulers and Chiefs of Khairagarh, Bamra, Talchar, Kharswan, Kawardha, Dhankanel, Daspalla, Khandpara, Nilgiri and other States participated.

54. His Highness remained in Calcutta at the close of the year and was due to return to Agartala by the middle of Baisakh of the following year.

III

55. A notable event of the year was the visit on 23rd July, 1934, of His Excellency the Right Hon'ble Sir John Anderson, P. C., G. C. B., G. C. I. E., Governor of the Presidency of Bengal, to Comilla, the headquarters station of the British district of Tippera and of His Highness's Chakla Roshnabad Estates. His Excellency was pleased to stay at His Highness's Dharmasagar residence. His Highness being away at Mussourie was unfortunately unable to join. A dinner on His Highness's behalf was given in honour of His Excellency in which the Hon'ble Nawab K. G. M. Faroqui of Ratanpur, high Government officials present at Comilla on the occasion and some distinguished gentlemen of the town as well as high District officials and State officials from Agartala joined. The State band was in attendance. After dinner, Prof. Gupto of Calcutta entertained the guests with his conjuring performances, followed by a display of fireworks.

His Excellency the Governor's visit to Comilla.

56. Mr. E. W. Holland, I. C. S., District Magistrate of Tippera, continued to be Political Agent *ex officio*.

Political Agent.

57. Rai J. C. Sen Bahadur, B. A., B. C. S. (retired) continued as Minister who was also the Manager of the Chakla Roshnabad Estates. He was out on tour for 82 days.

Minister.

58. One outstanding point in the Government of Bengal's proposals for revision of the joint management of the Toll Station came up for discussion at a conference in the Chief Secretary's Office at the Bengal Secretariat at which the State's view point received support from the Chief Secretary as well as the Political Agent and it was agreed that the question might be reconsidered by Government.

Amlighat Toll Station.

59. The Excise Agreement between Assam and this State which had worked quite satisfactorily for over two decades, terminated abruptly some years back. Since then the matter has been under correspondence. At a conference with the Excise Commissioner of Bengal at his office, the State's view point was fully and frankly explained, and the question of renewal of the agreement is under correspondence with the Assam Goverment.

Excise Agreements with Assam.

Topographical Survey.

60. The last instalment of Rs. 9,500 towards the State's contribution amounting to Rs. 45,000 was paid to the Tippera Treasury during the year. The survey which was undertaken by the Eastern Circle, Survey of India, was completed. Printed copies of several sheets were received. The administration records its thankfulness for the ardous task shouldered and completed by the Survey Department of the Government of India.

Tea Restriction Scheme.

61. There was a considerable amount of demurring by the planters in the State at the discrimination of the Tea Licensing Committee in regard to the allotment of extension quota which was withheld from them and the matter was taken up with the Government of India since the close of the year.

State's share in all-India duty on petrol.

62. No communication from Government has as yet been received regarding the State's share of provisional allotment from the Road Development Account for the year 1934-35.

State's share in excise duty on matches.

63. In accordance with the Agreement, entered into, the State shared in the proceeds of the pool of Excise Duty on Matches levied by the Government of India. A sum Rs. 15,676 was annouced to be the allotment for the year 1934–35.

Re-payment of loan from Government.

64. The first instalment of Rs. 92,666 due on 21st September, 1934, towards the re-payment of the loan of Rs. 9 lacs, was duly paid to the Accountant General, Bengal, through the Lloyds Bank, Calcutta.

CHAPTER II—LAND ADMINISTRATION.

Charge.

65. Thakur K. K. Singh, Naib Dewan, remained in charge of this Department in addition to other duties.

Area held under Settlement.

66. As shown in the subjoined statement, the total area under settlement and borne on the *toujis* at the close of the year was 630 sq. miles as against 627 sq. miles in the previous year.

Kinds of settlement.	Area in square miles.		Increase.	Decrease.	REMARKS.
	1344 T.E.	1343 T.E.			
Jotes ...	328	330	—	2	
Taluks ...	302	297	5	—	
Total ...	630	627	5	2	

Tea Settlement.

67. Resettlement of a portion of a tea estate in Kailashahar Division purchased by the State was concluded during the year.

68. Several petitions for relinquishment of portions of tea garden lands were enquired into during the year and relinquishment of 1357 acres of land was accepted in one case during the year.

Tea Industry.

69. Both the outturn and export of tea increased during the year under review. 90 *drones* of *khas* purchased tea land was resettled during the year while 2 gardens were

purchased by the State in revenue auction sale during the year under review.

70. The Durbar has been continuing the policy of giving facilities to the tea estates by way of granting easy instalments of payment of arrear dues and remission of interests and acceptance of surrender of part of the *taluki* land belonging to tea plantations. While general petitions for relinquishment were awaiting final orders at the close of the year, relinquishment involving 1357 acres out of a tea grant of 2000 acres was finally accepted. The State has thus been foregoing some amount of permanent revenue in the interest of the industry. The gardens in the State have not been allotted any extension quota since the inauguration of the Restriction Scheme to which the State is a participant. As the tea industry in the State is still in its early stage, the pioneer plantations being now in the middle of the second decade of their existence and the youngest group barely a couple of years old, there can be no denying the necessity for extension of plantation which is but natural. The matter has been taken up with the Government of India but no reply has hitherto been received from them.

71. The arrear demand upto the end of 1344 T. E. still amounted to more than 2 *lacs*, of which a portion may have to be written off as irrecoverable.

72. The current demand from tea grants amounted to about Rs. 62,000. The total realisation from them was Rs. 85,415, including Rs. 39,810 on account of current demand.

Rates of *Jama*.

73. The average of *jama* per *kani* of *jote* lands in *khas mahals* (exclusive of cesses) stood at 1 Rupee, 1 anna and 3 pies against 12 annas and 2 pies in the previous year. The maximum rate for *jote* was Rs. 25 per *kani* while the minimum was 4 annas and those for *taluks* Re. 1 and annas 3 respectively.

Sources of Land Revenue.

74. The different sources of land revenue demand with the collection under each head are detailed below :—

Sources.	Current demand.		Arrear demand up to the end of		Realization up to the end of		REMARKS.
	1344 T.E.	1343 T.E.	1343 T.E.	1342 T.E.	1344 T.E.	1343 T.E.	
Taluks ...	1,62,675	1,59,656	4,52,368	4,03,932	1,97,877	1,28,624	
Khas Mehal jotes	5,36,255	5,34,740	17,72,543	15,37,191	4,02,891	2,94,082	
Bazars ...	6,414	6,504	3,781	3,298	6,052	6,019	
Cesses ...	43,896	43,862	1,50,011	1,32,018	36,771	25,829	
Total ...	7,49,240	7,44,762	23,78,703	20,76,439	6,43,591	4,54,554	

Demand.

75. The above statement shows that the current demand under all heads was Rs. 7,49,240 and with the arrear demand of Rs. 23,78,703 the total demand of the year was Rs. 31,27,943 against Rs. 28,21,201 in the previous year.

Collection.

76. The total collection in round figures under all heads during the year amounted to Rs. 6,43,591 being Rs. 2,01,038 under current and Rs. 4,42,553 under arrear, as against Rs. 4,54,554 in the previous year. The percentage of current

collection was 26·83 against 21·82 and that of the arrears 18·6 against 14·06. In the khas mehal, the percentage of current collecton was 11·08 against 8·98 and in taluki mehal the percentage was 77·24 against 63·09 in the previous year. The percentage of collection on the whole was not satisfactory.

Coercive measures—Certificates.

77. Altogether 6,572 certificate cases covering a demand of Rs. 3,70,154 were instituted during the year. With 4,384 cases valued at Rs. 5,57,213 pending from the previous year, the total number of cases awaiting final orders on disposal of preliminary notices issued on debtors was 10,956 covering a total demand of Rs. 9,27,385. Of these, 15 cases with a demand of Rs. 746 were rejected or struck off and Rs. 7,243 in 356 cases was realised before decree, while 5,672 cases with a total value of Rs. 6,82,643 remained pending at the end of the year.

Execution.

78. Orders under the provisions of the State Certificate Act were passed during the year in 4,913 cases with a total value of Rs. 2,86,753 making the demand absolute.

79. With 8,723 cases to the value of Rs. 7,67,554 pending in execution from the previous year, the total number of cases dealt with was 13,636 covering a demand of Rs. 10,04,307. Out of the total demand, Rs. 10,400 was remitted or written off and of the remainder, Rs. 1,54,306 was actually realised leaving a balance of Rs. 8,39,601. Of the amount realised, Rs. 1,30,656 represents land revenue and Rs. 23,650 miscellaneous demands. In view of the heavy accumulation of the arrear demand strict measures appear to be called for.

Operation of the Sunset Law.

80. The number of defaulting *taluks* brought under the operation of the sunset law (including 40 pending from the previous year) was 142. Of these 76 were released on payment of dues with penalty while 26 were sold by auction and 40 remained undisposed of at the close of the year.

Survey.

81. The results of the survey (including resurvey) operations are given in the statement below. It will be seen that an area of 3,987 *drones* comprising 32 *drones* of *taluk* and 3,955 *drones* of *khas mehal* was surveyed as against a total of 3,486 *drones* in the previous year.

Names of Divisions.	Quantity of land in *drones* surveyed in 1344 T. E.			Quantity of land in *drones* surveyed in 1343 T. E.			REMARKS.
	Taluki land.	*Khas mehal* land.	Total.	*Taluki* land.	*Khas mehal* land.	Total.	
1. Sadar Division ...	—	236	236	135	36	171	
2. Kailashahar " ...	—	25	25	29	60	89	
3. Sonamura " ...	32	86	118	23	282	305	
4. Bilonia " ...	—	1,259	1,259	—	1,382	1,382	
5. Khowai " ...	—	721	721	—	493	493	
6. Dharmanagar " ...	—	867	867	—	470	470	
7. Udaipur " ...	—	195	195	—	148	148	
8. Sabroom " ...	—	566	566	—	428	428	
9. Amarpur Sub " ...	—	—	—	—	—	—	
TOTAL ...	32	3,955	3,987	187	3,299	3,486	

82. This work continued under the direction of Babu Kamini Kumar Kar, Superintendent of Surveys. Compilation of the *Mouzmil* maps of the Divisions on a scale of one inch to the mile from the survey maps of villages and *Taluks* was in progress.

Map Compilation

83. 36 maps of 24 villages and 49 tie lines of villages were reduced to one inch scale and maps of 19 villages were compiled in the *mouzmil* and 10 maps out of 30 reduced maps remaining uncompiled were also compiled this year. In all, maps of 25 villages reduced to one inch, remained uncompiled.

84. 3 case maps in connection with the disputes along the British border were prepared and 3 copies of each of them were traced.

85. 10 maps of boundary and connected award, 15 maps of villages and *taluks* and 20 other maps were traced and the area of 3 maps were checked with planimeter by the same staff. In addition, 49 tie lines to connect villages for compilation of *mouzmil* maps were surveyed by a temporary staff. The total expenditure incurred was Rs. 341-15-9.

86. The No. 12 party, E. C., Survey of India, continued their operation of the Topographical survey and completed the survey of the State and several sheet maps were also published by them during the year. The State paid the balance of Rs. 9,500 in addition to Rs. 36,000 paid in the previous years towards their contribution amounting to Rs 45,500.

87. During the recess time of the Survey of India, the Minister assisted by the Superintendent of Surveys of the State, discussed with the Officer-in-charge, No. 12 party and the then officer in charge of the Director's Office, Eastern Circle at Shillong, some boundary disputes.

88. The Superintendent of Surveys again went to Shillong and joined discussion with the Political Agent of the State and the Chief Secretary to the Government of Assam about the trijunction point of the Sylhet and the Lushai Hills District and this State on the Langai river.

89. The Superintendent of Surveys was out on tour for 52 days in connection with the inspection of survey of the border line and to attend discussion in various places about boundary disputes.

90. There was *Taskhichi taluki* settlement of an area of 90 *drones* of waste land. It will be seen that settlement operations in respect of 1,156 *drones* of *jote* lands were completed against 1,532 *drones* in the previous year.

Settlement.

Nature of Settlement.	1344 T. E.		1343 T. E.		Remarks.
	Area in *drones.*	*Jama* in whole rupees.	Area in *drones.*	*Jama* in whole rupees.	
1. Permanent *taluki* settlement of cultivated land ...	—	—	—	—	
2. Permanent *taluki* settlement of waste land ...	—	—	—	—	
3. *Taskhichi taluki* settlement of cultivated land ...	—	—	15	258	
4. *Taskhichi taluki* settlement of waste land ...	90	722	11	—	
5. *Jotedari* re-settlement of cultivated land	1,093	13,506	1,392	18,144	
6. *Jotedari* settlement of waste land	63	1,167	140	1,302	
Total ...	1,246	15,395	1,558	19,704	

Taluki Settlement.

91. Resettlement of a plot of *khas* purchased *takshichi taluk* for tea plantation comprising 80 *drones* was granted during the year under review and Rs. 2425 was realised as *Nazar*. There was a *Tashkkhichi* settlement of about 10 *drones* of waste land in Udaypur Division and a *Selami* of Rs. 98 was realised. *Tashkkhichi* settlement of 4½ *kanis* of Bazar land in the capital with the original owners was concluded during the year but no *Selami* was realised for the same.

Resettlement of *Jote* lands.

92. A net increase of Rs. 3697 in *jama* was secured by resettlement of *abadi jote* land, the *Nazarana* being Rs. 8940. The average *jama* per *kani* was 12 annas 9 pies against 13 annas in the previous year.

Jotedari settlement of waste land.

93. During the year, an area of 63 *drones* of waste land was settled for a prospective rental of Rs. 1,167, the average *jama* per *kani* obtained being Rs. 1-2-6 pies against 9 annas 4 pies in the previous year. The maximum and minimum rates were Rs. 2-10 and five annas respectively. The *Nazarana* realised was Rs. 1,913, the rent-free period allowed, ranging from 1 to 3 years.

Settlement work.

94. No wholetime settlement officer was employed in any Division but the Divisional Officers and the Second officers were entrusted with the settlement work within their respective jurisdictions. The total expenditure in the settlement operations was Rs. 1,132.

95. It will be seen that the *Nazarana* obtained and obtainable by settlement of *abadi jote* land and settlement of waste land as *jotes* amounted to Rs. 10,048 (Rs. 8,135 + Rs. 1,913).

Private Estates under State Management

96. As detailed below, there were altogether 17 private Estates under State management during the year under report.

Class.	Name of Estate.	Area.	Revenue.
ncumbered	1. Kakrabon Estate	283 *drones.*	1,871
	2. Jogendranagar Trust Estate	64 ,,	163
	3. Kamalnagar and Mahendranagar Estate	51 ,,	255
	4. Gouranga Tripura's Estate	13 ,,	57
	5. Maharam Ali Chaudhuri Khanje Khan Bahadur's Estate—*Taluk*	236 ,,	1230
	Jote	6 ,,	149
	6. Thakur Nalini Mohan Deb Barma's Estate	68 ,,	170
	7. Brajendra Kumar Das's Estate	408 ,,	1,936
	8. Brajapur Estate (Kamala Kanta Deb Barman and others)	246 ,,	982
	9. Kalimulla's Estate	124 ,,	863
	10. Mahammadali Chaudhuri's Estate	24 ,,	76
Unencumbered	11. Prabhu Goswamis' Estate	31 ,,	61
	12. Dowager Maharanee's Estate	169	766
	13. Late Girish Chandra Chaudhuri's Estate	36 ,,	254
	14. Late Brajakumar Thakur's Estate	47 ,,	297
	15. Naba Kumar Chakrabarty's Estate—*Taluk*	32 ,,	225
	Jote	5 ,,	19
	16. Nilkantha Sen's Estate	75 ,,	374
Endowment	17. Taranagar Estate	140 ,,	52

97. The subjoined table shows the demands and collections of the estates during the year under review. Compared with the previous year, collections improved in 11 estates and fell in 4 estates. No. 12 and 16 came under State management during the latter part of the year, and hence no collection could be made therein during the year under review. There was no collection of the Estate No. 13 (last year's No. 11) in 1343 T. E. as the Estate came under State management during the latter part of the year.

Estate No.	Demand			Collection			P. C. of collection
	Current	Arrear	Total	Current	Arrear	Total	
1.	5,991	35,249	41,240	280	4,277	4,557	11·04
2.	1,234	7,305	8,539	59	337	396	4·63
3.	1,297	2,883	4,180	130	1,105	1,235	29·54
4.	204	186	390	93	140	233	59·74
5.	3,710	18,864	22,574	286	1,885	2,171	9·61
6.	1,163	4,970	6,133	62	694	756	12·32
7.	3,603	11,015	14,618	1,523	1,996	3,519	24·07
8.	3,004	5,430	8,434	417	2,195	2,612	31·08
9.	2,425	4,095	6,520	223	16	239	3·66
10.	1,204	2,354	3,558	4	528	532	14·94
11.	912	4,189	5,101	45	185	230	4·70
12.	—	—	—	—	—	—	—
13.	1,149	5,034	6,183	212	513	725	11·72
14.	1,613	4,010	5,623	85	1,319	1,403	24·94
15.	646	3,915	4,561	26	371	397	8·70
16	—	—	—	—	—	—	—
17	3,082	12,917	15,999	364	2,231	2,595	16·21

CHAPTER III—PROTECTION.

I. Legislation.

98. No legislation was undertaken during the year and there was no sitting of the Legislative Council.

II. Military.

99. Dewan Sahib Kamala Prasad Dutt, M. A., B. L., F. R. E. S., M. R. A. S. and Major Kumar Dina Mohan Deb Varman Bahadur continued to be in charge of the Military Department and the Military Forces respectively.

Charge.

100. The total strength of the Forces at the end of the year was 368 against 391 of the preceding year.

Strength.

101. Major J. A. Blood, Military Adviser, Central India States Forces, inspected both the 1st Tripura Bir and 2nd Tripura Bikram Companies in August 1934. During his inspection he delivered a lecture on Field Works, Battle Formations and other subjects.

Inspector.

102. Captain Rana Jhapatjung Bahadur, Company Commander-in-charge, 2nd Tripura Bikram Company, attended the Company Commanders' Course at Gwalior. The result of his work was satisfactory. Two N. C. O's. from both the 1st Tripura Bir and 2nd Tripura Bikram Companies attended the S. A. S., Gwalior and the result was very satisfactory. In this year the Companies did Musketry Work.

Training.

103. Some ordinary improvements and petty repairs of the barracks were made during the year.

Cantonment.

104. The health of the Forces was generally good as in the previous year.

Health.

105. The total expenditure for the year excluding the Public Works amounted to Rs. 1,01,039 against Rs. 1,06,626.

Expenditure.

106. The Military Forces consisting of the 1st Tripura Bir Company and the 2nd Tripura Bikram Company with State Band, Signalling Party, Binondias, Body Guards and Followers numbering 395 marched out in the early morning of the 31st January 1935 under their respective Company Commanders from the Cantonment and after traversing a distance of about 20 miles reached Champaknagar in the afternoon where they camped for the night. Early in the next morning His Highness the Maharaja Manikya Bahadur accompanied by the Chief Secretary, Commandant of the Military Forces, the State Engineer, Naib Dewan, Forest Department, two State Medical Officers and with some hundred followers joined the Forces at Champaknagar. The Sampadak, Tripura Kshatriya Kendriya Sabha, with 250 Tripura Mandali Sardars and Volunteers also joined the Forces at Champaknagar. The combined Forces marched out at about 7 A. M. under the personal command of His Highness the Maharaja Manikya Bahadur. After crossing the Baramura range over a rough and undulatory tract of land about 15 miles long during which the troops had to do some stiff climbing and negotiate 13 miles of low land mostly covered with forests—the party reached Ompi, a Tahasil Station, at 8–30 P. M., where the party stopped for the night. On the day following, His Highness held a Durbar attended by the Military Forces. Here the party was joined by some 100 more Sardars and Volunteers. Arrangement for the supply of rations to all was done by the Military Forces during the march. On the morning of the 3rd February the march was resumed and the Forces had to pass through a dense forest and hilly country and paddy fields before they reached Amarpur in the afternoon, after covering a distance of about 15 miles. At Amarpur, the party encamped for two days. Here His Highness held a Najar Darbar during which the Forces gave Royal Salute and the Military Band played National Anthem. After this, His Highness reviewed the Forces and Volunteers. Early in the morning of the 6th February the party again started for Nutan Bazar and after marching a distance of 20 miles over a hilly country reached its destination at 6–50 P. M. The Forces halted there for three days. At this place a Robakari Durbar was held in which the name of the locality was changed into Dumbaranagar. The

Camping and Tactical Practice by the Military Forces during the year, 1935 (1344 T. E.)

Military Forces attended the Durbar and gave a Royal Salute. Here some parades were held. On the 10th February the party left Dumbaranagar and after marching a distance of about 15 miles over rough hilly bamboo-clad country, reached Kulsi Chhara the midway between Dumbaranagar and Lungthung and passed the night there. Next morning *i. e.*, on the 11th February the Forces started for Lungthung and after marching a distance of 15 miles reached their destination at 5-30 P. M. On their way the Forces had to negotiate some very difficult country and also had to pass a considerable distance through the Kulsi stream. At Lungthung (subsequently changed into Muhuripur) the Forces camped for the night and the following day. Here also the Forces did some parade work. The march was again taken up on the 13th February and the Companies, after marching over a distance of 12 miles reached Belonia in the evening where they camped for two days. At Belonia, His Highness the Maharaja Manikya Bahadur held a big Najar Durbar. The Military Forces with the State Band furnished a Guard of Honour to His Highness during the Durbar. On the 16th February morning the Party left by a Special Train and arrived at Feni Station at 10–30 A. M. As soon as the train halted at the Station, the State Military Band took up their position on the platform. As His Highness the Maharaja Manikya Bahadur alighted from the Special Train a Guard of Honour was drawn up and a salute of 13 guns was fired by the British Armed Forces. The State Military Band played the State National Anthem. On His Highness's return to his saloon the State troops with Band proceeded to the College Ground and furnished a Guard of Honour to His Highness where a big public reception was given to him. After this, the State troops returned to the Railway Station. At 10 P. M. the party left for Agartala by a Special train and reached Akhaura at 3 A. M. on the 17th February and marched back to their Cantonment. Considering the distance and difficult nature of the country the troops had to traverse, their enthusiasm and endurance were very satisfactory.

III. Police.

107. Rai Saheb A. C. Gupta continued to be the Superintendent of Police during the whole year.

Charge.

108. Babu Naresh Kumar Bhattacherjee, B. SC., also continued as Assistant Superintendent of Police during the whole year.

A. S. P

109. The total numerical strength of the Police force during the year was 515 against 512 in the previous year. As the sanctioned strength of the Armed constables could not cope with the work, 5 new hands were sanctioned temporarily in the middle of the year.

Strength.

110. The total number of village choukidars was 176 against 175 in the previous year.

Rural Police

Inspecting Staff.

111. There were 4 Inspectors of Police, as before, who were employed mainly to supervise important cases and to control the staff placed under them and for maintenance of discipline amongst their subordinates.

Investigating and Prosecuting staff.

112. During the year, there were 24 Sub-Inspectors including 1 Probationary Sub-Inspector and 22 Naib Darogas, as before.

113. The officers continued to show their detective ability in the investigation of cases. A formidable gang of dacoits residing within the jurisdiction of the Brahmanbaria Police station in the Tippera district was traced as being responsible for a number of dacoities committed in the jurisdictions of the Kotwali and the Sidhai Police stations of the State. Closer vigilance was maintained on smuggling of liquor and ganja and the officers deserving were properly rewarded. Credit is also due to several officers for detection of burglary cases. Both the Inspectors and Sub-Inspectors discharged their duties with a keener sense of responsibility in the matter of prevention and detection of crime as well as in their dealings with the public.

C. I. D. and Intelligence Staff.

114. One of the Sub-Inspectors, 5 of the Naib Darogas and 5 constables were employed in the C. I. D. as in the previous year.

Crime.

115. The total number of cases reported during the year under review was 894, as against 1,009 in the previous year.

116. The result of the cases is as follows :—

Number of cases reported 894

- Enquiry refused 6
- Number investigated 845
    - True 703
        - Charge-sheet 404
        - Finally reported 299
    - Intentionally false 50
    - Mistake of law 21
    - Mistake of fact 36
    - Noncognizable 35
    - Doubtful 0
- Number pending 43

Result of prosecution.

117. Altogether 675 persons were arrested in connection with various offences and 819 persons were sent up for trial by police, as against 623 and 824 respectively in the previous year.

Of the number sent up, 209 were convicted and 137 acquitted (including 48 on compromise and 17 on withdrawal of cases), while 1 died and 472 (including the absconding accused) awaited trial. The percentage of conviction was 30·96 as against 33·39 of the previous year and 26·96 of the year before last.

118. Of 437 accused awaiting trial at the end of the previous year, 102 were convicted, 135 acquitted (including 20 on compromise

and 14 on withdrawal of cases) and 200 were pending trial at the end of the year under report.

119. In the previous year, 6 cases of bad-livelihood were started against 33 persons, of whom 28 were bound down, 1 acquitted and 4 awaited trial, while in the year under report 5 cases were started against 9 persons, of whom 1 was convicted, 1 acquitted and 7 were awaiting trial at the close of the year.

Bad livelihood cases.

120. Nine Arms Act cases were instituted against 10 persons, of whom 3 were convicted, 2 discharged and 5 were awaiting trial as the year closed. In one of them 1 revolver and 1 pistol were seized from the house of a young man of the town, and in another 1 revolver was recovered from the possession of a school boy.

Arms Act cases.

2 of the stolen guns and a barrel of a gun were recovered in the British territory by the British police.

121. Total value of property stolen during the year, amounted to Rs. 14,675-4-9 against Rs. 12,868-9-9 of the previous year and Rs. 18,282-6-0 of the year before last. Of this amount, Rs. 1,721-11-6 was recovered against Rs. 1,929-7-0 in the previous year. The percentage of recoveries was 11·73 against 14·99 of the previous year.

Recovery of stolen property.

122. There were 28 cases of dacoity during the year, against 14 in the previous year and 20 in the year before last. Twentyfive persons were sent up in charge sheet in connection with 7 cases, of whom 5 were convicted, 4 acquitted and 16 (including the absconding accused) were awaiting trial at the close of the year. The increase of this crime is engaging anxious attention of the Department.

Dacoity.

123. Seventythree cases of unnatural deaths were reported during the year. Regular enquiries were held by the police into all these cases. On enquiry, Final Report as mistake of fact was submitted in 1 case. No foul play was detected in any case.

Unnatural deaths.

124. Two Inspectors, 8 Sub-Inspectors, 3 Naib Darogas, 1 Writer Naib Daroga, 1 Jamadar, 1 Armed constable, 5 constables (civil) received money rewards, while 1 Jamadar, 1 Naik, 16 Armed constables, 22 constables (civil) and 1 choukidar were fined or degraded and 1 Writer Naib Daroga, 1 Naik, 6 constables (civil) and 4 choukidars were dismissed.

Rewards and punishment.

125. The Superintendent of Police was out on tour for 53 days against 61 days in the previous year and the Assistant Superintendent for 26 days against 20 days in the year before.

Tour.

126. The relation with the Police of the neighbouring districts in British India continued to be satisfactory. The system of co-operation meeting of the Circle Inspectors with their own and British Police officers of the adjoining jurisdictions was continued this year also.

Co-operation.

127. The local police officers and men as well as the staff deputed from the headquarters worked satisfactorily in connection with His Highness the Maharaja Manikya Bahadur's camping march with the military through the Sadar, Udaipur and Belonia Divisions.

Police duty during His Highness's tour.

128. The system of musketry and revolver practice was continued in the year under review and the result was satisfactory.

Musketry practice.

129. The expenditure amounted to Rs. 87,340 against Rs. 86,836 in the previous year.

Expenditure.

IV. Justice.

130. There were 17 courts of justice in the State during the year under report, exercising both civil and criminal jurisdictions *viz.* :—Khas Adalat (High Court) with its original and appellate sides, and 16 courts of Magistrate-Munsiffs exercising original jurisdictions only.

Courts.

131. Babu Jnanendra Mohan Das, B. L., continued as Chief Judge, Thakur Hriday Ranjan Deb Barma as Puisne Judge (appellate side) and Babu Ramani Mohan Goswami, M. A., B. L. as Civil and Sessions Judge (Original Side) during the year.

Khas Adalat (High Court).

132. Altogether 2,023 criminal cases were instituted during the year under report as against 1,966 of the previous year. With the balance of 651 pending from the previous year, the total number of cases for disposal before the several subordinate courts was 2,674 as against 2,533 of the previous year as detailed below ; and out of these 2,674 cases, 1,886 were disposed of as against 1,882 of the preceding year, leaving 788 cases pending at the close of the year. Thus in the year under report, the number of cases for disposal increased from that of the previous year by 141 cases and there was also an increase in disposal by 4.

Number of original criminal cases.

DESCRIPTION OF OFFENCES.	1343 T.E.	1344 T.E.
Offences against the State and public tranquillity	69	92
Offences against person	695	676
Offences against property	1,236	1,304
Other offences	533	602
TOTAL	2,533	2,674

133. Altogether extradition of 105 persons was asked for during the year under report, of whom 39 persons were arrested by the British Indian Police and surrendered to the State and 39 persons appeared of their own accord or were subsequently arrested within the State territory.

Extradition from British India.

134. The number of persons brought to trial within the year under report was 2,316; the number awaiting trial from the preceding year was 790; the total number of persons thus brought to trial in the year under report was 3,106 as against 2,953 of the previous year. Out of the aforesaid 2,316 persons, 725 were arrested by the police, 443 were produced on warrant, 923 appeared on summons, 218 appeared voluntarily and 7 persons were arrested in the presence of Magistrates.

Persons brought to trial.

135. Out of the aforesaid 3,106 persons brought to trial before the several courts including the Sessions Court, 864 persons were discharged, 583 were acquitted, 680 were convicted, 15 died and 1 escaped, while 963 persons were awaiting trial at the close of the year. Out of the convicted persons, 241 were sentenced to various terms of imprisonment extending from less than one month to 5 years and above, 318 were sentenced to fine only, 12 were bound down and 109 persons were warned for the future. The number of persons actually tried was 1,263 (excluding those discharged) as against 1,339 of the previous year and the percentage of conviction was thus 53·84 against 57·50 of the previous year.

Result of cases.

136. Out of 2,674 cases for disposal as stated above, the number of cases in which British subjects were concerned either as complainants or accused, was 439 as against 480 of the previous year. Out of these, 348 cases were cognizable and 91 non-cognizable. In 67 cases, British subjects were complainants and in 372 cases they were the accused. In 90 cases both the parties were British subjects. In all, 527 persons were actually brought under trial in those cases during the year under report as against 642 of the previous year. Out of these 527 persons, 219 persons were convicted, 182 acquitted or discharged, 2 died and 124 remained under trial at the close of the year.

Cases concerning British subjects.

137. The following statement will show the number of original criminal cases instituted during the last two years.

DESCRIPTION OF OFFENCES.	1343 T.E.	1344 T.E.	Increase.	Decrease.
Offences against the State and public tranquillity ...	55	67	12	0
Offences against person	560	508	0	52
Offences against property	922	963	41	0
Other offences	430	485	56	0
TOTAL	1,966	2,023	109	52

Increased by 57.

138. 19 cases were committed to the Sessions during the year under report and 4 cases were pending from the previous year. Out of these 23 cases, 19 were disposed of during the year as detailed below. The number of persons involved in those 23 cases was 50, of whom 24 were convicted, 12 were

Sessions cases.

acquitted, 1 was discharged—the case against him being withdrawn, 1 escaped and 12 remained under trial at the close of the year.

Description of cases.	Number of cases.	Disposed of.	Pending.	REMARKS.
Murder	3	3	0	
Culpable homicide not amounting to murder	5	3	2	
Rape	1	1	0	
Grievous hurt	2	2	0	
Dacoity	2	2*	0	* 1 case was withdrawn.
Attempt to commit dacoity	1	1	0	
Arson	1	1	0	
Perjury	1	1	0	
Receiving stolen property and using unlicensed gun	1	1	0	
Moving with fire-arms	1	1	0	
Keeping gun-powder in possession without license	2	1	1	
Forgery	1	0	1	
Keeping coining tools in possession for the purpose of counterfeiting coins ...	2	2	0	
Total	23	19	4	

139. There were altogether 236 criminal appeals as against the same number of the previous year. These appeals were disposed of as shown below :—

Criminal appeals.

Rejected	6
Judgment affirmed	115
Modified	40
Reversed	24
Further enquiry ordered	23
	208
Pending	28
Total	236

140. The percentage of the judgments affirmed and modified was 76·35 as against 77·20 of the previous year.

141. The number of original civil suits instituted during the year under report was 1,631 as against 1,800 of the previous year. With the balance of 849 suits pending from the preceding year, the total number of suits for disposal was 2,480 as against 2,706 of the previous year. These suits were disposed of as shown below :—

Original civil suits.

Exparte	827
Admitted and compromised	153
Dismissed for want of prosecution ...	281
Disposed of on contest	440
	1,701
Pending	779
Total	2,480

142. The average duration of suits in the civil courts was 4 months as against 2 months and 14 days in 1343 T. E.

Duration of suits.

Nature and value of suits

143. The total value of civil suits instituted during the year, was Rs. 1,37,388-0-8 as against Rs. 1,53,386-5-9 of the previous year, which gives an average of Rs. 84-3-9 per case. Out of 1,631 suits, instituted during the year under review, 402 related to land, 959 to money transactions and 270 suits were of other classes. 964 suits were of the value of Rs. 100 and under; 343 suits were of the value between Rs. 100 and Rs. 500; 24 suits of value between Rs. 500 and Rs. 1,000; 13 suits of value between Rs. 1,000 and Rs. 5,000 and 287 suits were not estimable in money value.

Execution of decrees.

144. The number of applications for the execution of decrees filed during the year was 838 and there were 611 pending from the previous year. The total number for disposal was thus 1,449 as against 1,462 of the preceding year. The aggregate value of the new applications was Rs. 1,37,067-15-5 and that of the pending applications was Rs. 1,28,885-7-9; the total value thus amounting to Rs. 2,65,953-7-2. The number of applications disposed of was 804, the value of which was Rs. 1,50,448-13-2. The number of execution cases pending at the close of the year was 645, the value thereof being Rs. 1,15,504-10-0.

Civil appeals.

145. There were 108 civil appeals filed during the year, as against 147 of the previous year. With the balance of 106 from the previous year, the total number of civil appeals for disposal was 214 as against 265 of the preceding year. Out of these cases, 142 were disposed of during the year under report as against 159 of the previous year, leaving a balance of 72 cases at the close of the year.

Result of civil appeals.

146. The following figures will show the result of appeals in civil suits :—

Decisions confirmed	62
Decisions reversed	31
Decisions modified	12
Remanded	8
Compromised or otherwise disposed of ...	29
	142

Percentage.

147. The percentage of judgments wholly or partly upheld, excluding those in the cases compromised, was 65·49 against 67·66 of the preceding year.

Value and duration of appeals.

148. The total value of civil appeals filed during the year under review was Rs. 10,571-7-6 and the average duration of each appeal was 5 months and 3 days as against 4 months and 12 days in the previous year.

Original Side cases.

149. 17 civil suits were instituted in the original side, Khas Adalat, during the year under report as against 26 of the previous year. With the balance of 48 suits pending from the preceding year, the total number for disposal was 65 as against 75 of the previous year. Of these, 14 suits were disposed

of against 27, leaving 51 suits pending at the close of the year. There were 52 execution cases during the year, including 37 cases pending from the previous year. Of these, 22 were disposed of and 30 remained pending at the close of the year. There were 18 applications for succession and other certificates during the year under report ; with the balance of 17 of the previous year, the total number of such applications was 35, out of which 21 were disposed of as shown below and 14 remained pending at the close of the year :—

Description of cases.	Total.	Disposed of.	Pending.
Probate case	3	0	3
Succession certificate	15	12	3
Guardianship	17	9	8
Total	35	21	14

150. The total number of civil and criminal appeals including the number of cases pending from the previous year, was 450 as against 501 of the preceding year. Out of these appeals, 350 were disposed of as against 357 of the previous year.

Total number of appeals.

151. In comparison with the preceding year, the total number of appeals for disposal decreased by 51 and there was a decrease in disposal by 7 only.

Description of appeals.	Number of appeals.		Disposed of.	
	Past year.	Present year.	Past year.	Present year.
Civil	265	214	159	142
Criminal	236	236	198	208
Total	501	450	357	350

V. Prisons.

152. Apart from the Central Jail at the capital, there were 7 Divisional Jails in the State during the year under review. Dr. M. M. Majumdar, Chief Medical Officer, was the Superintendent of the jails as in the previous year.

Number of Jails.

153. The total number of prisoners of all classes was 1192 as against 1393 in the preceding year-the daily average being 176·16 against 142·82. Of them, 544 were convicts, 632 undertrials, 8 civil prisoners, 5 lunatics and 3 detenus. 198 prisoners in all remained in the jails at the end of the year against 166 in the year before.

Jail population.

154. The number of prisoners undergoing imprisonment for more than 2 years along with the nature of their offence. period of sentence and occupation are shewn

Long-term prisoners.

in the subjoined table... The number totalled 90 against 76 of the year preceding.

Class of offence.	Number of prisoners.	Occupation.	REMARKS.
Murder	15	They were employed in brick manufacturing, oilmills, *soorki* pounding, *khoa* breaking, bamboo and cane work, gardening, weaving, tailoring, paddy husking, rice manufacturing etc.	66 had sentences of 2 to 5 years, 7 of 5 to 10 years, 4 of 10 to 14 years and 13 for life *i. e.* 20 years.
Culpable homicide not amounting to murder... ...	19		
Robbery	3		
Theft	9		
Dacoity	14		
Counterfeiting coin	5		
Kidnapping	2		
Rape	3		
Unnatural offence	1		
Receiving stolen property ...	2		
Arson	1		
Forgery	1		
Attempt to commit suicide ...	1		
Keeping Revolver in possession without license ...	2		
Section 110 (security for good behaviour for habitual offenders) ...	12		
Total	90		

155. Only one convict died of typhoid and pneumonia at the Central Jail during the year. On the whole the health of the Central Jail and the Divisional Jails was good.

Health.

156. Two undertrials from the Belonia Jail, 1 undertrial from the Kailashahar Jail, 1 undertrial from the Sonamura Jail and 4 undertrials from the Sabroom Jail made good their escape during the year under review. Of them, one of the Kailashahar Jail surrendered himself to the court after a few days and one of the Sonamura Jail was re-arrested on the very day of escape.

Escape.

157. The Reformatory school in the Central Jail in which convicts are trained and reformed by way of education, had under training, 22 convicts under a paid tutor. Of them, 2 appeared at the Lower Vernacular and 2 at the Pathshala Scholarship examinations of the State. One of the former and 2 of the latter passed in the 3rd Division. In addition to this, religious instruction was given as before.

Education.

158. On the auspicious occasion of His Highness the Maharaja Manikya Bahadur's birthday ceremony, 6 convicts were set at liberty shortly before the expiry of the term of their sentence during the year under report.

Special release.

159. Inclusive of those of the Central Jail, the Jamadars and Warders numbered 10 and 57 respectively. Of them, 3 Jamadars and 15 Warders were fined and 2 Warders were discharged from service.

Jail staff.

160. The income of the Central Jail from the different sources came up to Rs. 2,237 as against Rs. 4,770 of the year previous. The heavy fall in income noticed in the year under review was due to the increase in the preceding year

Income

from the adjustment of the account carried over from the year previous as also to the loss of income from the garden caused by the serious flood of the year.

161. The total expenses during the year amounted to Rs. 26,321 as against Rs. 23,364 of the previous year.

Expenditure.

VI. Registration.

162. Mr. S. C. Deb Barman, M. A. (Harvard), Senior Naib Dewan, remained in charge of the Department.

Charge.

163. The number of offices continued to be 9 as in the previous year—there being one at the headquarters station of each of the Divisions and Sub-divisions. There was a Registrar for the Sadar Division stationed at Agartala but in the mofussil the Divisional and Sub-divisional Officers and in certain divisions the Second Officers acted as Registrars.

Registration Offices.

164. The total number of documents presented for registration during the year including 97 pending at the end of the previous year was 6,615 against 6,265. Of this number, 60 deeds were refused registration on various grounds and 131 remained pending at the end of the year against 97 pending at the end of the previous year.

Registration and Disposal.

165. The total value covered by the documents amounted to Rs. 8,33,344 as against Rs. 6,92,895 in the previous year, while the total value covered by the documents actually registered was Rs. 8,32,679 as against Rs. 6,79,981 in the year before.

Value of deeds presented and registered.

166. The number of suits brought before the Registration Department in respect of the documents, registration of which had been refused in the Registration offices was 12 against 17 in the previous year. There were 5 appeals during the year against 1 in the year before. There were 36 suits but no appeal pending from the previous year making a total of 48 suits and 5 appeals during the year under report. Out of these, 42 suits and 5 appeals were disposed of during the year, leaving 6 suits pending at the close of the year.

Suits and Appeals.

167. The total income of the Department from fees and fines amounted to Rs. 6,030 against Rs. 5,701 and the expenditure to Rs. 3,555 against Rs. 3,574 in the previous year. The net income thus amounted to Rs. 2,475 in the year under report against Rs. 2,127 in the previous year.

Income and Expenditure.

VII. Municipality and Sanitation.

168. As before, the State had the only Municipal institution in the Capital town of Agartala during the year under report, with a population of about 10,000 according to the last census.

Municipality.

169. On the expiry of the term of the previous committee, a new committee with 9 members—all nominated—including an official Chairman and a non-official Vice-Chairman was formed towards the end of the year. Mr. S. C. Deb Barman, M. A. (Harvard), Senior Naib Dewan, Minister's Office, was nominated Chairman of the new committee and Babu Haridas Bhattacharjee was elected Vice-Chairman by the unanimous vote of the committee. Altogether five sittings of the committee were held during the year, the average attendance of members being about 6·1 as against 5·6 of the previous year.

Committee

170. The realization on account of Municipal and Latrine taxes showed appreciable improvement. Rs. 5,376-15-0 was collected as against Rs. 4,612-11-9 of the previous year. The total demand inclusive of arrears was Rs. 9,592-13-9 of which Rs. 469-14-0 was irrecoverable.

Income.

The miscellaneous income from all sources including deposits and advances recovered amounted to Rs. 991-5-6 as against Rs. 1,061-14-3 of the previous year. The State grant for the year was Rs. 9,000. Thus the total income of the Municipality came up to Rs. 15,368-4-6 as against Rs. 16,028-8-3 of the previous year (the latter figure includes Rs. 2,353-14-3 received from the Bazar fund as advance to pay outstanding bills of the Municipality).

171. The total expenditure of the Municipality amounted to Rs. 15,181-8-0 as against Rs. 16,034 in the previous year.

Expenditure.

172. The control and management of the local Bazar continued to be in the hands of the Municipal Committee. The total collection including Rs. 553-14-3 as advance recovered from the Municipatity came up to Rs. 6827 as against 6470-12-3 in the preceding year. The total demand including arrears was Rs. 12,088-11-9 of which Rs. 612-10-0 was irrecoverable. After necessary expenditure of Rs. 2264-14-6 the Bazar improvement fund stood at Rs. 44,167-2-3 at the close of the year.

Ishanganja Bazar.

173. The public health of the town was on the whole good. There were 25 cases of cholera with 9 deaths and 3 cases of small-pox with one death.

Public Health.

174. A sum of Rs. 721-12-0 was spent on some sanitary works within the town under the direct supervision of the Officer-in-charge of the Sanitation Department.

Sanitation.

175. As before, the charge of the Municipal and Sanitation Departments remained with Dr. M. M. Majumdar, Chief Medical Officer of the State.

Charge.

176. During the year under report, a terrible flood inundated practically the whole Agartala town on the 17th Aswin. The town remained under water for about 36 hours. Had it not been for the immediate relief given to the people by His Highness the Maharaja Manikya Bahadur, the sufferings of the people would have known no bounds. People, in order to save

Flood.

their lives took shelter in the local school, Minister's Office, Khash Adalat, Thakur Boarding house and other places and even the doors of the Ujjayanta Palace were thrown open to the public for shelter, where thousands of people rushed in and stayed with a relief of sigh.

177. Relief centres were opened and His Highness personally visited the different centres and graciously ordered arrangements to be made for giving immediate relief to the distressed people by free distribution of food. water and medical aid.

178. In this connection Municipality had also taken active measures to relieve the distressed people as far as practicable. Municipality was entrusted with the charge of distributing food to every centres according to their requisition. The local school volunteers worked bravely for supplying food-stuffs from the relief centres and for transportation of the people to relief centres from flooded homes.

179. Rescue parties with volunteers did splendid services in this connection outside the town areas in distributing food, medicine etc. Thanks to the Almighty, no death took place except that of some goats and other cattle.

180. The flood having subsided, in order to avert any outbreak of epidemic in the town, His Highness promulgated prompt measures to remove all accumulated filth, debris and water hyacinth from the town. Municipality too had taken necessary steps to clear the town and disinfected the tanks reserved for drinking water and repaired the roads and drains.

181. A relief committee was constituted to assist the flood-stricken people with money to re-construct their houses and Thakur Lalit Mohan Deb Barman, M. A., B. L, Sadar Magistrate was appointed Secretary of the committee.

182. Our sincere and grateful thanks are due to His Highness whose timely help and action saved the town from impending danger and sufferings of the people at that time.

183. The teachers and students of the U. K. Academy deserves our thanks for all they did in helping the Municipality in this connection.

184. During the year under report a suitable plot of land was acquired for the Municipal Mali-Basti in Dhaleswar Mouza and a tank was excavated there. Two more small tanks were partly excavated at a cost of Rs. 450 in the plot acquired for the removal of the Ishanganja Bazar.

CHAPTER IV—PRODUCTION AND DISTRIBUTION.

I. Weather and Crops—Agriculture.

Charge of the Department.

185. Manyabara Rana Bodhjung Bahadur, F. R. G. S., Chief Secretary to His Highness the Maharaja Manikya Bahadur of Tripura continued to be in charge of the Department assisted by Mr. J. C. Choudhury, S. E., M. S. A. (Tokio), M. R. Agri. S. (Lond.) as Superintendent of Agriculture.

186. The Staff of the Department continued to be the same as it was in the previous year. The vacant post of one Fieldman was abolished in the year.

Staff.

187. The propaganda work—though carried on as far as practicable—was much hampered for want of staff—the post of late U. C. Majumdar being abolished. Improved sugarcane, cereals and English vegetables were specially dealt with in this connection.

Propaganda.

188. Usefulness of chemical manures was explained and demonstrated with various vegetables at the Propaganda Stand at the local market at Agartala.

189. Arrangements were made from the department to distribute Coimbatore sugarcane seed cuttings through the farmers to whom these were originally distributed from the department. This improved variety of sugarcane was fairly spread over Sadar and Kalyanpur Divisions. 20,000 Coimbatore No. 213 seed cuttings were distributed from the Department in Kailashahar Division and 75,000 in Sadar *Elaka*.

Seed Distribution.

190. The highest temperature was 95 degree and the lowest 47 in the year under report—which was higher than that of the previous year.

Temperature.

191. The average rainfall of the year was 91·3 inches against 83·02 inches in the previous year. The quinquennial average was 84·04″. Kailashahar Division had the maximum fall of 113·66″ and Amarpur Sub-Division the minimum of 70·72″. Heaviest rainfall averaging 22·22″ was registered in the month of Jaistha.

Rainfall.

192. The principal crops in the State were paddy, jute, mustard, *til* (sesame), sugarcane and cotton. In the near future, pine-apple is going to be one of the principal crops. It grows splendidly on hills and its plantation both on high and low lands is being taken up by the people right earnestly. Potatoes, tobacco, chillies and pulses of various types were also grown in some parts of the State.

Crops.

193. Male labourers earned from 3 to 8 annas, female labourers from 2 to 5 annas a day. Gharamies earned from 5 to 8 annas and carpenters and masons from annas 6 to rupee one only. Most of the labourers were outsiders from the neighbouring British Districts as well as up-country coolies.

Labour and Wages.

194. Prices of food-grains varied very little from that in the neighbouring British Districts. Rice sold from Rs. 2 to Rs. 4-8 and paddy sold from Rs. 1 to Rs. 2-4 per maund.

Prices.

195. The outturn of tea increased by 27% and the export by 36% in comparison with the previous year and tea export duty has doubled. A portion of the duty realised was however on account of arrear dues.

Tea Industry.

196. From the above it is clear that the tea industry has a bright future in this State if the market continues as heretofore. The

Durbar has been continuing the policy of helping the infant tea industry by way of remission and acceptance of relinquishment of portions of tea grants.

Taccavi.

197. No taccavi advances were made during the year.

All India Conference for the protection of wild life.

198. The Superintendent of Agriculture was deputed to attend the All India Conference for the protection of wild life held at Delhi and after that he was engaged in an investigation regarding the possibilities of fruit preservation (preservation of pine-apples) and this kept him engaged in Calcutta for two weeks.

Veterinary.

199. No disease in epidemic form was reported during the year. 1572 animals in the Veterinary Dispensary and 103 animals at *mofussil* were treated by the Veterinary Surgeon.

Tour of the Staff.

200. The Superintendent of Agriculture was out on tour for 35 days and the Veterinary Surgeon for 15 days.

II. Immigration and Emigration.

Charge of the Departments.

201. The charge of these Departments was, as in the previous year, in the hands of Manyabara Rana Saheb Bodhjung Bahadur, F. R. G. S., Chief Secretary to His Highness the Maharaja Manikya Bahadur, who was assisted by Sj. B. C. Dev Varman, Assistant, in these Departments.

Immigration & Emigration.

202. During the year under review, 1,727 families immigrated into the State.

Kulaihaor.

203. Many families of different classes from various directions came to settle down in Kulaihaor and special mention may be made here about the Maghs who came batch by batch from Barisal District and Chittagong Hill Tracts. Some of these Mags were allowed lands in Bhatkhawri and in Abhanga *Moujas.* The reclamation by the Mags was very satisfactory, as a result of which the major portion of Bhatkhawri it has now turned into a small decent village.

204. It is most gratifying to note that during the year, the Nath settlers of Nalicherra *Mouja* managed to worship the Goddess Durga according to Hindu rites in such a dense forest, a part of which now looks like a small decent village.

205. The reclamation work in Abhanga and Singhinala *Moujas* was also very satisfactory. In both these *Moujas*, small villages have now grown up, the inhabitants being mostly Manipuris, Naths and Coolies.

206. To remove the scarcity of drinking water, the excavation of a tank, measuring 100 cubits by 75 cubits, was undertaken and completed during the year. Moreover the natural water-flow continued to supply drinking water.

Salema Bazar.

207. The Bazar at Salema remained the same as it was in the previous year.

208. The road from Kurmaghat to Salema was thoroughly repaired during the year and the temporary bridges were reconstructed.

Repair of Roads.

209. The total number of patients receiving treatment in Salema Dispensary was 3799, both old and new, against 3,450 in the previous year.

Salema Dispensary.

210. *Jote* settlement of 27 *Drones* 8 *Kanis* 5 *Gandas* 1 *Kara* and 15 *Dhurs* of cultivated land was granted during the year under review and a nazar of Rs. 186 was realised on this account, while a *jote* of 38 *Drones*, 7 *Kanis*, 3 *Karas* and 17½ *Dhurs* of waste land was also granted and a *nazar* of Rs. 72 was realised. Thus the total amount of *nazar* amounted to Rs. 258 against Rs. 692-8 in the previous year. Since the close of the year arrangements have been made to realise the *nazar* through the Tahasil Office where a *Touji* roll has been opened for this purpose.

Kalyanpur Reserve Settlement.

211. Relinquishment of 13 *Drones*, 8 *Kanis* and 11 *Gandas* of waste lands was accepted from different classes of tenants and consequently a revenue of Rs. 1005-9-9 had to be remitted.

Relinquishment.

212. No *namjari* was effected during the year and consequently no *nazar* was realised against Rs. 174 in the previous year.

Namjari.

213. The staff of the Kalyanpur Reserve office consisted of a Moharer, a permanant Amin with a Moharer and a Nali. Besides these, in the winter season some temporary Amins were taken for Survey works. Moreover, to help the settlement works, Sjt. Ramkumar Thakur and Sjt. Nabin Chandra Thakur were engaged with fixed allowance.

Staff.

214. During the year under report, the total expenditure on account of the Reserve amounted to Rs. 1,343-12 against Rs. 1343-4-6 in the previous year.

Expenditure.

215. On the 12th Baisakh, the Chief Secretary went out to visit Kalyanpur, but unfortunately he had to return on the next evening due to sudden indisposition.

III. Forests.

216. Babu Jatindra Nath Mitra, Naib Dewan, was in charge of the Department. With the exception of a few mahals which were let out in *Ijara*, all the forests were under khas management as before.

Charge & Management

217. Including the Patrol staff with a Forester, three Head Guards and twenty guards, the Department had a staff of one Station Officer, three Forest Circle Inspectors, fourteen Forsters, seventeen Assistant Foresters, three

Staff.

Rangers, six Moharers, twentyfour head guards, twelve literate guards, one hundred and fortynine guards, three peons, one orderly and six boatmen.

218. During the year under report the patrol staff was sent out in three sections. They worked in Sadar Division for 9 months and 12 days, in Belonia Division for 6 months and 19 days and in Sabroom Division for 3 days. One section patrolled in the Sonamura Division throughout the year under review.

Permits

219. There were 156 commissioned agents for the sale of the forest permits for the shoulder-borne export of minor forest produce by land routes.

Forest stations

220. There were 51 forest stations for collection of duty and prevention of forest offences.

Working of the Forests.

221. The Reserved Sal forests of the Sonamura Division continued to be worked under the system of coppice with standards and those of the Udaipur Division under Improvement Method, while the open unclassed forests were worked under the State Forest Rules of 1323 T. E. ; but for the Feni River Mahal, the working rules of the Bengal Forest Department were followed.

***Kheda* Operations.**

222. During the year under report, 3 ***khedas*** were undertaken—two in the Kailashahar and one in the Sonamura–Udaipur tracts. 9 elephants were caught in the former and 15 in the latter.

Feni river mahal.

223. The Toll Station at Amlighat continued to be under the management of the State Forest Department. The total revenue collected at the Station in the year under review was Rs. 39,655 against Rs. 39,073 in the previous year. As before, a doctor of the Sub-Assistant Surgeon class was appointed temporarily for four months from December to March for giving medical relief to the Station staff and to the cutters and exporters of forest produce.

Fee Simple Lots.

224. As in the previous years, the forest produce from the Fee simple lots above the Amlighat toll Station was exported under passes granted by the Collecter of Chittagong.

Forest Offences.

225. In the year under review, there were 196 forest cases against 422 persons, including 53 cases against 110 persons pending from the previous year. The offences were mainly export of forest produce without payment of duty.

Results.

226. Altogether 112 cases against 215 persons were tried, of whom 25 persons were sentenced to imprisonment only ; 153 were punished with fine only ; one was imprisoned and fined ; 19 were warned and 16 acquitted while one died during the course of the trial. 7 cases against 18 persons were compounded. 77 cases against 189 persons remained pending at the close of the year. The number of pending cases appears to be more than what might be expected.

227. One Moharer, two Head Guards, 11 guards and one boatman were rewarded for intelligent detection of cases of smuggling of forest produce. One Forester and two guards were fined for misconduct.

Rewards & punishment.

228. The health of the staff was generally good. One Ranger, however, died of dysentery during the year.

Health of the staff.

229. The following table shows the results of the collection of forest revenue.

Sources of income.

Heads of Revenue.	1344 T.E.	1343 T.E.	Increase.	Decrease.	REMARKS.
	Rs.	Rs.			
Unclassed open forests :—					
(a) Toll on forest produce exported by the river mehals	2,39,056	2,59,017	—	19,961	
(b) Toll on forest produce exported by land route under permit	63,851	61,835	2,016	—	
(c) Toll collection (share) of the Feni river mehal ...	27,155	27,073	82	—	
(d) Grazing mehal ...	6,678	8,041	—	1,363	
(e) Thatching grass mehal	2,906	2,858	48	—	
II. Reserved Forests :—					
Sale of *Sal* etc	3,070	3,894	—	824	
III. Elephant Kheddas	2,315	2,616	—	301	
TOTAL ...	3,45 031	3,65,334	2,146	22,449	

230. Details of collection in the year under report are given below :—

	Heads of Revenue.	Quantity of produce exported.	Duty realised thereon.	REMARKS.
		Cft.	Rs. as. p.	
1.	Timber other than Sal...	5,12,867·0	83,969-2-3	
2.	*Sal*	6,592·9	2,754-11-6	
3.	Produce other than timber.			
	(a) Exported by *bhatials*	—	1 55,402-2-3	
	(b) Exported by land routes under permits	—	63,851	
4.	Toll collection (State share) of the Feni river			
	(a) Timber	10,056·5	1,665-11-6	
	(b) Other produce ...	—	25,489-3-6	
5.	Grazing *Mahal* ...	—	6,678	
6.	Thatching grass *Mahal*	—	2 906	
7.	Elephant Khedas ...	—	2,315	
	Total quantity of timber in Cft.	5,29,516·4	3,45,031	

231. The total forest revenue of the year under report was
Receipts. Rs. 3,45,031 against Rs. 3,65,334 in the previous year, showing a falling-off of Rs. 20,303. This was due to the general trade depression and want of sufficient demand for forest produce.

232. During the year under report the Maharaja Match Factory manufactured 8896½ gross of finished matches and paid Rs. 65-9-6 as duty on the timber used in making these matches.

233. Rs. 1,327-1-4 was realised as Excise duty on 1,400 gross of matches.

234. Plantation of *Sal, Sonal* and *Mahogany* were continued
Plantation. during the year under report.

235. The Naib Dewan was out on tour for 82 days during the
Tour. year against 103 days in the previous year.

IV. Trade and Manufacture.

236. The principal export were timber and other forest produce of various kinds, cotton, oil-seeds (*til* and mustard seed), paddy, jute, tea, rice and *Gur* (molasses). Some homespun cotton fabrics manufactured by the hill people, and specially by the Manipuries were also exported. The principal exports for the year under review and of the previous two years are shown below.

	1342 T. E.	1343 T. E.	1344 T. E.
Coton	51,918 mds.	43,290 mds.	30,837 mds.
Til	36,918 ,,	9,898 ,,	54,640 ,,
Mustard seeds	30,398 ,,	19,704 ,,	34,986 ,,
Jute	84,904 ,,	88,324 ,,	72,274 ,,
Tea	15,11,334 lb.	17 70,097 lb.	24,66,331 lb.

V. Public Works.

237. The Minister himself was in charge of the Public Works
Charge. Department as before. Honorary Lieutenant J. N. Bhaduri, B. E., continued as State Engineer during the year.

238. The Statement XX in the appendix gives details of the works executed during the year, the total expenditure including improvement works being Rs. 2,14,552 as detailed below against Rs. 1,66,799 in the previous year.

Expenditure.

Description of works.	Ordinary Public works.	Improvement works.	TOTAL.
Buildings...	64,329	61,277	1,25,606
Roads & Bridges	15,936	39,611	55,547
Tanks & Tube Wells ...	1,366	250	1,616
Miscellaneous Works ...	9,093	3,381	12,474
Minor works at Rajbari (*Karkhana*) ...	999	—	999
Establishment charges ...	18,310	—	18,310
TOTAL ...	1,10,033	1,04,519	2,14,552

239. The following major works were done during the year :—

1. Office Building as per sanctioned estimate. Additional work is being done now.
2. Type quarters at Kunjaban.
3. Improvement of Thakur Boarding.
4. Construction of roof of the Pandal.
5. Palace Avenue Road (*Prasad Protoli*).
6. Improvement of Akhaura Road (District Board portion.)
7. Chandra Sadhu Para Road.
8. Billiards room at the Palace.
9. Pavillion on the north bank of the Palace east *Dighi*.
10. Extension of Lakshmi Narayan Road from Thana Road to Jail.
11. Drainage for anti-malarial works round the cantonment area, Kunjaban.
12. Constructing 2 buildings at Andar.
13. Considerable progress of His Highness's *Baitakkhana*.
14. Excavation of a lake in the town.
15. Metalling a portion of Prasad Protoli and Radhanagar Roads.
16. Constructing a garage at Minister's House.
17. Constructing a *Pucca* bridge over a breach on the Akhaura Road (District Board portion.)
18. Excavating Krishnanagar Road Canal.
19. Bitumening Central Road (portion between the main gate and the Jackson Gate).
20. Masonry railings from *Singhadwar* to Jackson Gate.
21. Lowering and widening the Akhaura Road between Jagannathbari Road and Ronaldshay Road.
22. Improvement of Ronaldshay Road.
23. Constructing a new road from Sadar to Sonamura Division.
24. Re-excavating Akhaura *Khal* between the Central Road and the Ronaldshay Road.
25. Protective works at Sonamura *Gangail*.
26. Constructing Sabharmura Forest Office.
27. Improvement of bridges on the Sabharmura–Bibirbazar Road.
28. Siddhinagar Beat Office at Belonia (Tin shed).
29. Improvement of the Belonia Dak Bungalow.
30. Constructing Kali Temple at Kailashahar.
31. Constructing Kurti *Tehsil Katchari* at Dharmanagar (Tin shed).
32. Constructing 2 wooden bridges at Dharmanagar on the Juri River.

240. The total expenditure in connection with electric supply

Power House. was Rs. 16,299 against Rs. 15,002 during the year.

241. Out of the total expenditure for Public Works, Rs. 3.978

Flood. was spent for relief works in connection with the flood which took place at Agartala on the 17th Aswin. A full description of the flood is noted below :—

(i) Excessive rainfall on the night of the 16th Aswin had the natural effect of inundating the whole town. the natural drainage being unable to cope with the situation. The protective embankment, though sufficiently high, could not prevent overflooding of itself against the abnormal rain-fall of 12" in twelve hours without intermission. The fall of the country being from east to west, the eastern embankment over-flowed during the early hours of the 17th Aswin and by day-break, the southern embankment had but the barest margin left above the high water of the Howra River when fortunately there occurred three breaches on its western third end which had the effect of spreading the water out of the bounds of the town proper.

(ii) Though the water of the Howra River was brought down by the above breaches, the eastern embankment was over-flowing till past 1 P. M. and the water level over the town rose till just 3 P. M., so much so that in pleaces the level of water rose to above 7' deep, the Palace proper and a patch of land on the eastern portion of the town only keeping above the flood level.

(iii) It was due to the very kind personal interest taken by His Highness the Maharaja Manikya Bahadur and His personal staff aided by the Administration officers that no loss of life was reported. The Palace and the Guest Houses, the High School and Administration Buildings and the High Court were thrown open to the public. It was indeed a gratifying relief to the sufferers to see His Highness all wet yet plodding his way with them through the rising waters from one end of the town to the other and personally looking after the comforts of those accommodating themselves in the public Buildings. Credit is also due to the School Volunteers for looking after the comforts and conveyance of many sufferers by rafts to places of shelters.

(iv) There being no rainfall during the major portion of the day, the water level did not rise further than 3" below the Administration Building, and fell substantially by the morning of the 18th Aswin. By afternoon of this day the greater portion of the Building was vacated, but the High Court and the School Buildings were kept in occupation by the worst sufferers for about a week.

CHAPTER V—REVENUE AND FINANCES.

I. Revenue.

242. The total collection in the year was Rs. 15,79,609 against Rs. 13,39,810 in the previous year.

243. The details of income under different heads with all variations are given in the statement below :—

Serial number.	Heads of Revenue.	1344 T.E.	1343 T.E.	As compared with 1342 T.E.		Remarks.
				Increase.	Decrease.	
1.	Land Revenue	6,44,452	4,50,707	1,93,745	—	
2.	Rents of markets	6,180	6,137	43	—	
3.	Family Tax in the hills	52,593	46,960	5,633	—	
4.	Toll on forest produce	3,02,907	3,20,852	—	17,945	
5.	Do. Do. on the Feni Rivers	27,155	27,073	82	—	
6.	Elephant & buffalo grazing Mehal	6,678	8,041	—	1,363	
7.	Thatching grass Mehal	2,906	2,858	48	—	
8.	Reserved *Sal* Forests	3,070	3,894	—	824	
9.	Tax on cotton and oil-seeds ..	1,35,224	1,06,839	28,385	—	
10.	Royalty on elephants caught ...	2,315	2,616	—	301	
11.	Adda Mehal	25,533	24,435	1,098	—	
12.	Excise	42,901	41,654	1,247	—	
13.	Stamps and Court-fees	64,240	61,514	2,726	—	
14.	Law and Justice (Fines)... ..	2,172	2,356	—	184	
15.	Process fees	10,396	10,154	242	—	
16.	Registration	5,555	6,095	—	540	
17.	Jail	2,237	4,770	—	2,533	
18.	Cattle pounds	3,826	3,747	79	—	
19.	Nazars	31,918	29,620	2,298	—	
20.	Education...	15,034	14,566	468	—	
21.	Tea Export duty	27,723	12,580	15,143	—	
22.	Jute Export duty	27,112	31,964	—	4,852	
23.	Depreciation Contribution ...	78,071	77,224	847	—	
24.	Miscellaneous	59,411	43,154	16,257	—	
	Total	15,79,609	13,39,810	2,68,341	28,542	Net increase—Rs. 2,39,799

244. It will be seen that there was an increase in respect of 16 heads of income aggregating Rs. 2,68,341 against a decrease under 8 heads amounting to Rs. 28,542 which resulted in a net increase of Rs. 2,39,799

245. The decrease under head Toll on forest produce, Elephant and buffalo grazing *mehal*, Reserved Sal trees and Royalty on elephants caught, will be explained in the section relating to the Forest Department.

246. The income under the head Land Revenue exceeded the figures of 1339, 1340, 1341, 1342 and 1343 T. E. by Rs. 1,137 ; Rs. 2,04,272 ; Rs. 2,46,794 ; Rs. 2,25,627 and Rs. 1,93,745 respectively. Tea Garden land revenue contributed Rs. 85,415 against Rs. 46,173 in the previous year.

247. On the whole the percentage of collection is a little more than 20·5 as against 16·03 of the previous year, but it does not denote satisfactory collection in view of the large demand of Rs. 29,23,841.

248. The increase under the head Family Tax in the hills may be attributed to the improved paying capacity of the hill people and that under Tax on cotton and oil-seeds was due to the increased export of oil-seeds which more than counter-balanced the decrease in the export of cotton.

249. The slight decrease under head Jute export duty was due to the slump in the trade.

II. Finances.

250. A consolidated abstract account of the financial transactions of the State and the attached Zemindaries as compared with those of the previous year is given below :—

Receipts.	1343 T. E.	1344 T. R.
1 Opening balance :—		
(1) State ...	6,66,083	10,52,214
(2) Zemindaries ...	3,39,198	3,50,220
Total ...	10,05,281	14,02,434
2 Income :—		
(1) State ...	13,39,810	15,79,609
(2) Zemindaries ...	9,08,361	9,87,261
Total ...	22,48,171	25,66,870
3. Law charges recovered :—		
(1) Zemindaries ...	38,576	46,963
4. Refunds and compensation for lands acquired :—		
(1) Zemindaries ...	2,380	4,417
5 Deposits :—		
(1) State ...	2,14,494	2,63,746
(2) Zemindaries ...	33,572	39,576
Total ...	2,48,066	3,03,322
6 Loans received :—		
(1) State ...	9,00,000	—
(2) Zemindaries ...	—	—
Total ...	9,00,000	—
GRAND TOTAL ...	44,42,474	43,24,006

Expenditure.	1343 T. E.	1344 T. R.
1. General Administration charges :—		
(a) State	5,48,625	5,42,469
(b) Zemindaries :—		
1. Cost of management	1,39,358	1,42,745
2. Cost of litigation	1,17,193	1,36,800
	2,56,551	2,79,545
Total ...	8,05,176	8,22,014
2. Revenue and Taxes on account of the Zemindaries	2,88,830	2,85,540
3. Public Works—(a) State	1,69,413	2,09,062
(b) Zemindaries ...	60,335	50,996
Total ...	2,29,748	2,60,058
4. Electric Light—State	15,002	16,299
5. Municipality—State	8,000	9,000
6. Education—(a) State	1,25,021	1,23,867
(b) Zemindaries	8,962	9,075
Total ...	1,33,983	1,32,942
7. Medical and Sanitation :—(a) State ...	97,829	67,638
(b) Zemindaries ...	11,737	11,469
Total ...	1,09,566	79,107
8. Survey and Settlement—(a) State ...	36,545	20,119
(b) Zemindaries ...	1,188	916
Total ...	37,733	21,035
9. Agriculture, Commerce and Industries—State	7,929	7,859
10. Religious Expenses—(a) State ...	62,948	64,971
(b) Zemindaries ...	6,339	6,111
Total ...	69,287	71,082
11. Sultanat—State	62,640	52,951
12. Purchase of Land Tenures :—		
(a) State	10,021	6,845
(b) Zemindaries	1,374	6,573
Total ...	11,395	13,418
13. Pension and Gratuity—(a) State ...	56,312	59,268
(b) Zemindaries ...	9,980	10,915
Total ...	66,292	70,183
14. Ordinary *Sansar* charges :—		
(a) His Highness's own and the late Maharaja's family	84,167	85,293
(b) Other branches of the Raj family...	1,17,830	1,15,454
(c) Thakurs	31,214	31,675
(d) *Sansar* office establishment ...	12,875	13,608
(e) Miscellaneous	97,118	66,670
Total ...	3,43,204	3,12,700
15. Charity and Donation :—(a) State ...	18,387	18,769
(b) Zemindaries ...	6,746	7,046
Total ...	25,133	20,815
16. His Highness's Nij Tahabil :—State ...	1,00,000	1,00,000
17. His Highness's tour—State	1,09,495	1,25,000
18. Payment of liabilities and deposits :—		
(a) State	59,311	77,171
(b) Zemindaries	19,965	30,066
Total ...	79,276	1,07,237
19. Miscellaneous—(a) State	12,068	10,164
(b) Zemindaries ...	6,300	11,723
Total ...	18,368	21,887
20 Advances to employees :— Zemindaries ...	600	—
21. Write off of irrecoverable advances :— State ...	924	5,577
22. Repayment of old debts—State ...	4,88,611	96,502
23. Interest on deposits—State	28,848	29,339
24. Advance to *Nijtahabil*—Zemindaries ...	—	1,87,000
Total ...	30,40,040	28,47,545
25 Closing Balance :—		
(a) State		
In Cash	1,85,436	1,85,411
At Bank	2,761	3,468
Working balance :—		
In Cash	20,963	12,299
At Bank	3,94,219	2,12,701
In advances	—	1,90,182
In bonds and advances	4,48,835	4,88,898
Total ...	10,52,214	10,92,959
(b) Zemindaries :—		
In Cash	1,04,342	1,11 086
At Bank	51,542	71,050
In bonds and advances	1,94,336	2,01,366
Total ...	3,50,220	3,83,502
Total of State & Zemindaries' balances ...	14,02,434	14,76,461
otal of State & Zemindaries' expenditure ...	30,40,040	28,47,545
GRAND TOTAL ...	44,42,474	43,24,006

251. The year opened with a balance of Rs. 14,02,434 against Rs. 10,05,281 in the year before. During the year under report, the total receipts from all sources including deposits, loans and law charges recovered amounted to Rs. 29,21,572 against Rs. 34,37,193 in the previous year. Thus the total sum available for expenditure was Rs. 43,24,006 against Rs. 44,42,474. The actual income excluding receipts under debt heads amounted to Rs. 26,18,250 against Rs. 22,89,127 showing an increase of Rs. 3,29,123. Out of the loan of Rs. 9,00,000 taken from the Government, Rs. 4,84,818 was spent in the previous year for repayment of old debts and the balance of Rs. 4,15,182 was brought forward as working fund for the year under review.

Receipts.

252. Total expenditure incurred during the year amounted to Rs. 28,47,545 against Rs. 30,40,040 in the previous year, showing a decrease of Rs. 1,92,495.

Expenditure.

253. The year closed with a balance of Rs. 14,76,461 of which Rs. 3,08,796 represented cash in the treasuries, Rs. 2,87,219 was held in Banks while the balance of Rs. 8,80,446 was held in loans and advances.

Closing balance.

254. A quinquennial statement of the Receipts and Expenditure of the State and the attached Zemindaries is given below :—

Quinquennial Review of Receipts and Expenditure.

Serial No.	Year.	State.		Zemindary		Remarks.
		Receipts.	Expenditure.	Receipts.	Expenditure.	
1.	1340 T. E.	17,50,436	17,44,110	10,19,056	10,27,138	The figures for the year 1343 T. E. for the State include on the receipt side the loan of Rs. 9,00,000 (Rupees nine lacs) taken from the Government of India and on the debit side the expenditure incurred for liquidation of old debts.
2.	1341 T. E.	17,90,258	17,40,914	8,72,924	8,29,784	
3.	1342 T. E.	19,10,680	18,95,612	9,29,366	10,04,303	
4.	1343 T. E.	27,34,304	23,48,173	9,82,889	9,71,867	
5.	1344 T. E.	19,78,355	19,37,610	10,78,217	10,44,935	
Average ...		20,32,806	19,33,284	9,76,490	9,75,605	

255. The world-wide trade depression which made itself felt in the State had its worst effect in the years 1340 and 1341 T. E. and accounts for the decline in receipts in those years. Signs of gradual recovery from the economic slump became, however, perceptible in the year 1342 T. E. and the year under report shows a marked improvement of the situation. A very cautious policy was, however, followed as regards expenditure which had to be cut down to keep it within the receipts.

256. The noticeable variations in expenditure are explained below :—

i. Administration Charges :—

State—The decrease was Rs. 6,156. Some special kind of expenditure which was incurred in the previous year was not required in the year under report. The Departmental management of excise shops was discontinued in the year. This accounts for the decrease.

ZEMINDARIES—The increase was Rs. 22,994. This was due to time-scale increment of pay and increased litigation charges.

ii. REVENUE AND TAXES :—

The decrease of Rs. 3,290 was due to the rebate received on account of timely payment of road cess.

iii. PUBLIC WORKS :—

STATE—The increase of Rs. 39,649 was due to progress of Improvement works.

ZEMINDARIES—The decrease of Rs. 9,339 was due to curtailment of expenditure.

iv. ELECTRIC LIGHT :—

The increase of Rs. 1,297 was due to the appointment of a probationer and owing to some miscellaneous expenditure.

v. MUNICIPALITY :—

The increase of Rs. 1,000 was due to the enhancement of the grant.

vi. EDUCATION :—

STATE—The decrease of Rs. 1,154 was due to general curtailment of expenditure.

ZEMINDARIES—The increase was Rs. 113.

vii. MEDICAL :—

STATE—The decrease was Rs. 30,191. In the previous year some extra expenditure was incurred in connection with the treatment of Maharaj Kumari Basantaprava Debi in Switzerland. This was not necessary in the year under report and accounts for the decrease.

ZEMINDARIES—The decrease was Rs. 268.

viii. SURVEY AND SETTLEMENT :—

STATE—The decrease was Rs. 16,426. The expenditure incurred in connection with the Topographical Survey of the State in the year under report was less than that in the previous year. This accounts for the decrease.

ZEMINDARIES—The decrease was Rs. 272.

ix. AGRICULTURE, COMMERCE AND INDUSTRIES :—

The decrease was Rs. 70 only.

x. RELIGIOUS EXPENDITURE :—

STATE—The increase was Rs. 2,023. This was due to some extra ceremonies necessary in the year under report.

ZEMINDARIES :—The decrease was Rs. 228.

xi. SULTANAT :—

STATE—The decrease was Rs. 9,689. Some extra expenditure was incurred in the previous year which was not necessary in the year under report. This accounts for the decrease.

xii. PURCHASE OF LAND TENURES :—

STATE—The decrease was Rs. 3,176.

ZEMINDARIES—The increase was Rs. 5,199. This was due to purchase of some new properties.

xiii. PENSION AND GRATUITY :—

STATE—The increase was 2,956. This was due to retirement of officers in the State.

ZEMINDARIES—The increase was Rs. 935.

xiv. ORDINARY SANSAR CHARGES :—

The decrease was Rs. 30,504. In the previous year some

extra expenditure was incurred in connection with the marriage ceremony of Maharajkumari Jyotsna Debi and Maharajkumari Mallika Debi. This was not necessary in the year under report. This accounts for the decrease.

xv. CHARITY AND DONATION :—

STATE—The decrease was Rs. 4,618. Some special donations were made in the previous year while no such donation was made in the year under report. This accounts for the decrease,

ZEMINDARIES—The increase was Rs. 300.

xvi. HIS HIGHNESS'S NIJTAHABIL.

The expenditure was the same as in the previous year.

xvii. HIS HIGHNESS'S TOUR :—

The increase was Rs. 15,505.

xviii. PAYMENT OF LIABILITIES AND DEPOSITS.

STATE—The increase was Rs. 17,860. Some old accounts were adjusted against this head in the year under report and some providend fund deposits were also refunded. This accounts for the increase.

ZEMINDARIES—The increase was Rs. 10,101. This was due to refund of a considerable amount of deposits to the Tripura Raj Central Co-operative Bank.

xix. MISCELLANEOUS :—

STATE—The decrease was Rs. 1904.

ZEMINDARIES—The increase of Rs. 5423 was due to some unforeseen expenditure on some special occasions.

xxi. WRITING OFF IRRECOVERABLE ADVANCES :—

STATE—The increase of Rs. 4,653 was due to adjustment of some old accounts.

xxii. REPAYMENT OF OLD DEBTS.

STATE—The decrease was Rs 3,92,109. In the previous year a special provision was made for repayment of all outstanding debts. No such provision was necessary in the year under report. This accounts for the decrease.

xxiii. PAYMENT OF INTERESTS ON DEPOSITS :—

The increase was Rs. 491.

xxiv. ADVANCE TO HIS HIGHNESS'S NIJTAHABIL :—

This special provision was made on account of the construction of the new Palace at Ballygunj in Calcutta.

257. Two comparative statements of Receipts and Expenditure of the State and the Zamindaries with the respective Revised Estimates are given in appendices (XXVI) and (XXVII).

258. In the State, the total receipts showed an increase of Rs. 1,53,355 and Rs. 34,173 in comparison with the original and the revised Budget estimates respectively.

259. In the Zamindaries the total receipts showed an increase of Rs. 60,010 and Rs. 75,010 in comparison with the original and the revised Budget estimates respectively.

260. Thakur Kamini Kumar Singh continued to be in charge of the Department.

CHAPTER VI—MEDICAL.

261. The State had, during the year under review, the Victoria Memorial Hospital at the capital and 17 other dispensaries for medical relief as in the past year.

New patients.

262. The following comparative statement for the two consecutive years shows the total number of new patients treated in them all as also their daily average.

	1343 T. E.			1344 T. E		
	Outdoor.	Indoor.	Total.	Outdoor.	Indoor.	Total.
PATIENTS.	1,30,193	887	1,31,080	1,32,243	906	1,33,149
Daily average	356·69	2·43	359·12	362·3	2·48	364·78

Outdoor attendance.

263. The outdoor patients (old+new) numbered 2,55,303 as against 2,46,246 in the year before, the daily average being 699·42 against 674·56.

Indoor attendance.

264. With the balance of 17 remaining from the previous year, 906 patients were admitted for indoor treatment as against 887 of the year previous. Of them, 692 were discharged cured, 27 died, 165 were relieved or left of their own accord and 22 remained over for treatment at the beginning of the following year.

265. The increase in both outdoor and indoor attendance was thus 9057 and 19 respectively over that of the preceding year.

Surgical Operation.

266. Altogether 1289 cases were surgically treated during the year under report as against 1230 of the year previous, the major cases numbering 25 against 20.

Police Case.

267. In all, 162 police cases were attended to as against 147 in the preceding year including 13 post-mortem cases against 15.

V. M. Hospital

268. The total number of new out-patients in the Victoria Memorial Hospital was 24805 as against 21495 in the year previous with the daily average of 67·95 against 58·89 while the daily average of new and old out-patients was 131·08 against 115·56. The new in-patients totalled 579 as against 518, the daily average of new and old being 20·61 against 16·91. Of these, 408 were discharged cured, 122 were relieved or otherwise discharged, 27 died and 22 remained under treatment.

The total expenditure on this institution was Rs. 10,110-9-9 against Rs. 9482-13-0 of the year before.

Anti-rabic treatment Centre.

269. A centre was opened for Anti-rabic treatment in the V. M. Hospital in the middle of the year under review. Dr. N. Deb Barman, M. B., who had received special training in this subject, was in charge of this centre. 29 human cases and 3 dogs were treated. Rs. 317-4-6 was spent towards the cost of Anti-rabic vaccine and other necessary articles.

270. Dr. A. Sen Gupta, M. B., State Bacteriologist, was in charge of the laboratory. 504 clinical samples were examined during the year under report as against 301 of the previous year.

Clinical Laboratory

271. Kaviraj Surendra Chandra Bhattacharjee, Baidyaratna, continued to be in charge of this Department as before. He treated 32 patients during the year against 47 in preceding year.

Ayurvedic Department.

The total expenditure incurred on account of the salary and cost of medicines was Rs. 2392-3-0 against Rs. 2651-5-0

272. As before, there were two assistant homœopaths under the control of Dr. M. M. Majumdar, Chief Medical Officer. They treated 18,966 patients as against 17,563 in the preceding year—the daily average of new and old patients being 96·06 against 91·62.

Homœopathic Department.

Rs. 2280-12-9 was spent on this account as against Rs. 2324-15-9 of the year before.

273. The total number of persons vaccinated during the year under review was 8137 against 7087. 6952 cases were successful against 5638 of the previous year. 30 vaccinators were employed under two Small-pox doctors and two Inspectors.

Vaccination.

The total cost on this acccount stood at Rs. 1543-10-3 as against Rs. 1453 15-6.

274. The two Kala-azar centres—one at the capital and the other at Tillabazar in Kailashahar Division were regularly worked during the year under report. 300 patients were treated in all, of whom 170 were cured, 89 left treatment and 41 remained over.

Kala-azar.

275. The total expenditure on this account amounted to Rs. 1280 as against Rs. 1197 of the preceding year.

276. Dr. Parbati Charan Sen, M. B., was in charge of the two Leprosy Clinics—one at the Capital and the other at Khowai—the total number of new patients treated was 54 as against 145. Rs. 1859-7-3 was expended on these Clinics as against Rs. 1467-5-9 of the year previous.

Leprosy.

277. Cholera broke out more or less virulently in some parts of the State specially in Sadar, Khowai, Dharmanagar, Udaipur and Kailashahar Divisions. 289 seizures with 82 deaths were reported during the year as against 289 and 159 respectively in the preceding year. 3723 persons were inoculated against 2742 in the year before. Small-pox visited the Sadar Division only. 23 persons were attacked of whom 4 died and 19 were cured.

Public Health.

278. Dr. M. M. Majumdar, L. M. S. Chief Medical Officer, continued to be in charge of the Medical Department. Dr. S. K. Dutt, L. M. S. Assistant State Physician, Dr. A. Sen Gupta, M. B., State Bacteriologist, Dr. N. Deb Barman, M B., Anti-rabic Physician and Dr. P. C. Sen, M. B, Leprosy Officer were his

Staff.

assistants. In addition, a staff of medical subordinates in different dispensaries and three midwives at the Capital was kept regularly employed.

279. Dr. M. M. Majumdar and Dr. A. Sen Gupta were out for 18 and 11 days respectively and inspected Sonamura, Belonia, Kailashahar, Kamalpur and Dharmanagar dispensaries.

Tour.

280. The total expenditure in the Medical Department in the year under review amounted to Rs. 67,638 as against Rs. 65,329 of the preceding year.

Total Expenditure.

CHAPTER VII—PUBLIC INSTRUCTION.

281. Mr. S. C. Deb Barman, M. A. (Harvard), Senior Naib Dewan, continued to be in charge of the Education Department.

Charge.

282. The total number of schools (including private schools) during the year under review was 193 against 184 in the previous year, and the total numerical strength 9,106 against 8,342 including 1,360 pupils reading in private institutions numbering 50 as against 39 in the preceding year.

Number of Schools.

283. There were 5 H. E. Schools as before and one Branch H. E. School in the State. All the H. E. Schools are permanently affiliated to the Calcutta University. Class IX was opened provisionally in the Branch H. E. School at Udaipur, on condition that the public would agree to bear the additional cost of maintaining extra staff. The total number of pupils in all these institutions were 1,597 as against 1,488 in the previous year, and the average daily attendance stood at 1,186·46 against 1,150·15.

H. E. Schools.

284. Agartala, the capital of the State, continued to be a centre for the Matriculation Examination. The State H. E. Schools are allowed to send up candidates to this centre. One female private student and two candidates from Devagram H. E. School in Tipperah district sat for the examination in this centre in the year under report in addition to the candidates from the State schools.

Matriculation Examination.

285. The examination was conducted under the direct control and supervision of the Minister with the assistance of the Senior Naib Dewan, in charge of the Education Department. The Department looked after the convenience of the candidates coming from *Mofussil*, in respect of accommodation and other necessary matters.

286. Altogether 64 candidates were sent up for the Matriculation Examination from the State H. E. Schools against 60 in the previous year. The result of the Examination is given below :—

Result of the Matriculation Examination.

	No. sent up.	passed.	1st Division.	2nd Division.	3rd Division.
1. U. K. Academy	23	20	7	13	0
2. R. K. Institution	12	11	3	7	1
3. B. K. Institution	14	14	6	7	1
4. B. B. Institution	6	6	4	2	0
5. N. Ch. Institution	9	6	1	4	1
Total ...	64	57	21	33	3

287. The result on the whole was satisfactory, percentage of successful candidates being 89·06 against 80 in the previous year. The percentage of passes in the 1st Division on the total number of passes was the highest for the B. B. Institution, *viz.*, 66·66 and the lowest for the N. Ch. Institution, *viz.*, 16·66.

288. The three successful candidates topping the list, the first and the third belonging to U. K. Academy and the second belonging to B. B. Institution, were awarded scholarships of Rs. 10, Rs. 8, and Rs. 8 per month in order of merit.

289. In the year under review, there were 9 Middle English Schools for boys with 1,132 pupils on the rolls against the same number of schools with 1,092 pupils in the previous year. The average daily attendance was 847·06 against 883·58 in the previous year.

M. E Schools for boys.

290. There was one M. E. School for girls at Agartala, namely the Maharani Tulsibati Girls' School, the numerical strength of which was 68 against 77 in the previous year and the average daily attendance was 59·16 against 62·81. By special permission of this Department, some girls were allowed to continue higher studies in this school under the tuition of the head mistress. For conveyance of the girls, motor bus service was continued as before.

M. E. Schools for girls.

291. The total number of Lower Vernacular Schools for boys was 26 against the same number in the previous year. The total numerical strength was 1,243 against 1,255 and the average daily attendance was 1010·11 against 1013·7 in the previous year. In some of these schools, boys and girls read together.

L. V. Schools.

292. There were 76 *Pathshalas* for boys against the same number in the previous year. The total number of boys was 2,519 against 2,183 and the average daily attendance was 1918·18 against 1733·04. In some of these schools boys and girls read together. Under special orders of the Education Department, some boys of some of these institutions were allowed to read the Lower Vernacular standard.

Pathshalas for boys

Pathshalas for girls.

293. There were 9 ***Pathshalas*** for girls in the year under review as in the previous year. The total numerical strength was 329 as against 319 and the average daily attendance was 248·70 against 240·11 in the year preceding. In some of these schools, some girls were allowed, under special orders, to read the Lower Vernacular standard.

Scholarship Examination.

294. Altogether 803 candidates appeared at the different scholarship examinations of the State against 784 in the previous year. Of these, 676 candidates including 93 girls came out successful. The result on the whole was satisfactory. 51 students including 6 girls passed the M. E. Examination and 2 girls passed the H. V. Examination. In the L. V. Examination, the number of successful candidates was 189 including 25 girls, and in the ***Pathshala*** Examination the number was 433 including 60 girls. Amongst these candidates 14 candidates appeared from different ***Maktabs*** and ***Madrassas*** of the State. On the results of the examination 12 boys and 4 girls were awarded monthly scholarships varying from Rs. 2 to Rs. 5 tenable for two to four years.

Schools for special training.

295. In the year under review, there were 11 schools for special training, consisting of 5 Sanskrit ***Tols***, 5 ***Madrassas*** and ***Maktabs*** and one ***Silpasram*** (Artisan School). The Sanskrit ***Tols*** had 47 students on the rolls against 50 in the previous year and the average daily attendance was 34·18 against 38·27. The ***Rajakiya*** Sanskrit ***Vidyalaya*** at Agartala sent up 6 candidates for the Government Sanskrit Title, Intermediate and Preliminary Examinations against the same number in the preceding year.

296. The result was satisfactory. All the candidates passed the Government Sanskrit Examinations in different subjects in which they appeared.

297. The ***Madrassas*** and ***Moktabs*** had 178 students on the rolls as against 235 in the previous year and the average daily attendance was 135·88 against 183·60.

Free Compulsory Primary Schools.

298. There were, as before, 4 Free Primary Schools with 585 pupils including girls against 508 in the previous year. The subjoined statement will show the number of students, their classes and the average daily attendance.

Compulsory Free Primary Schools.	No. of Students.		Average daily attendance.		Kumars.	Thakurs.	Tripura.	Laskar.	Manipuri	Bengali Hindu.	Mahommedans.	Others
	Boys.	Girls.	Boys.	Girls.								
1. No. 1 U. K. Academy ...	182	143	133·69	89·99	1	10	5	0	0	280	21	8
2. No. 2 Tulsibati	29	82	10·4	57·3	0	6	0	0	10	93	2	0
3. No. 3 Bejoy Kumar ...	35	84	24·8	48·25	0	26	13	0	0	76	4	0
4. No. 4 Thakur Paily ..	30	0	14·51	0	0	14	16	0	0	0	0	0
	276	309	183·40	205·54	1	56	34	0	10	449	27	8

299. The comparative statement below will show the number of non-Bengalee students receiving education in the several schools of the State :—

Serial number.	Nationality.	Number of students.		Remarks.
		Past year.	Present year.	
1.	Rajkumars...	5	7	
2.	Thakurs	282	290	
3.	Manipuris	568	573	
4.	Tripuras	977	1,007	
5.	Reangs	13	18	
6.	Kukis...	1	0	
7.	Chakmas	1	0	
8.	Lushais	1	1	
9.	Others	44	56	
10.	Christians	0	0	
	Total	1,892	1,952	

Education of Princes and Princesses.

300. The Maharajkumaris received their education as before under a graduate lady teacher and a Pandit.

Education of other Kumars.

301. Maharajkumar Hemanta Kishore Dev Barman Bahadur got himself admitted into Bengal Engineering College, Sibpur, after leaving Thomason Engineering College, Roorkee. Maharajkumars Aditya Kishore and Mohan Kishore Dev Barman Bahadurs after passing the Matriculation Examination in the 2nd Division, got themselves admitted into the Agricultural College, Nagpur and College of Engineering and Technology, Jadavpur respectively. The young Maharajkumars received their education under a tutor.

Kumar Boarding House at Comilla.

302. The Rajkumar Boarding House at Comilla had 11 inmates of whom 8 were from the different branches of the Ruling family and the remaining 3 were Rana Bahadurs, related to the Raj family. Nine of the inmates were reading in the Comilla Zilla School and two in the Comilla Victoria College. In the year under review one Kumar passed the Matriculation Examination. The boarders were placed under the charge of a Superintending tutor who in addition to his tutorial works looked after the management of the Boarding House. There was also one Graduate Assistant Resident Tutor. Besides the above, one graduate teacher was engaged for coaching some of the boarders both in the morning and evening.

Education of Thakur boys.

303. Nine Thakur boys and one girl named Miss Bina Deb Barman receiving higher education in various colleges and technical schools were awarded stipends.

Thakur Boarding House at Agartala.

304. The number of boarders in the Thakur Boarding House was 32 against the same number in the preceding year. The staff consisted of one graduate Guardian Superintendent, one under-graduate Resident Tutor and one Manager-tutor. The average daily attendance of the boarders was 26·2 against 28 in the previous year. Two Thakur boys appeared at the Matriculation Examination and both of them came out successful in the second division.

Tripura Boarding House at Agartala.

305. There were altogether 16 boarders from Class IV to Matriculation Class in the old Tripura Boarding House against 16 in the previous year. Out of these, 15 boarders received free boarding and lodging. A wholetime graduate Superintending Tutor looked after the boys as well as the boarding management as before. Another tutor was engaged to coach the boys in the morning. There was a small library in the Boarding House and the boys were encouraged in agricultural pursuits within the Boarding compound. One Tripura boy was sent up for Matriculation Examination and came out successful in the second division. There was also a newly-started Boarding House with 35 Tripura boys reading in lower classes against 33 in the previous year. A tutor was engaged to coach the boys both in the morning and evening and was entrusted with the management of the boarding. The boarders were allowed a piece of ground in front of the Boarding House for agricultural pursuits.

Tripura Boarding House at Khowai.

306. There were 60 boarders in the Tripura Boarding House at Khowai against 61 in the previous year. One graduate Superintending Tutor and one Assistant Tutor were engaged as before for coaching the boys both in the morning and evening. The Superintending Tutor looked after the boarding management in addition to his tutorial work.

Ramkumar Boarding School at Kalyanpur.

307. There were 40 boarders on the roll in the Ramkumar Boarding School against 33 in the previous year and the average daily attendance was 23·42 against 28·78 in the preceding year. Two tutors were engaged as before to coach the boarders and one of them looked after the boarding management in addition.

School for convicts.

308. There were 20 convicts reading in the Primary School in the Central Jail, out of whom 4 appeared in the Scholarship Examination in the year under report and 3 came out successful.

Woodburn Artisan School & Silpasram.

309. The Woodburn Artisan School and Silpasram continued to be under the direct control of Manyabara Rana Bodhjung Bahadur, F. R. G. S., Chief Secretary to His Highness the Maharaja Manikya Bahadur. The School had on the roll 28 students against 22 in the preceding year. In the year under review the average daily attendance was 11·75 against 10·25 in the previous year. 14 students were awarded monthly stipends varying from Re. 1-8 to Rs. 8 each. There were 17, 6 and 5 students in the Carpentry, Black-smith and Brass-smith sections respectively. The sub-joined statement will show the number of students, their classes (castes) and their average attendance in the year under review.

Name of School.	Number of Students.	Thakurs.	Tripura.	Laskar.	Manipuri.	Bengali Hindu.	Mahomedan.	Others.	Averags attendance.
Woodburn Artisan School and Silpasram	28	6	1	2	1	15	3	—	11·75

310. 3 Lushai boys were awarded Lushai stipends in the year under report of whom one read in the Bengal Survey School at Mainamati and the other two prosecuted their studies in M. C. College, Sylhet.

Lushai Stipends.

311. 19 students were awarded special stipends in the year under review of whom 10 read in different schools of this State and the remaining 9 prosecuted their studies elsewhere in different schools, colleges and technical institutions.

Special Stipends.

312. The Senior Naib Dewan was out on tour for 9 days during the year under review.

Inspection Work.

There were three Sub-Inspectors of Schools as before who inspected all the schools other than the H. E. Schools within their respective jurisdictions in Sadar, Khowai, Kailashahar and Dharmanagar Divisions. Revenue Inspectors of Sonamura and Belonia inspected some schools in their respective Divisions.

313. Maharajkumar Narottam Kishore Deb Barman Bahadur continued to be the Librarian of the Bir Chandra Library at Agartala which was maintained in two separate sections as before, *viz* :—(1) The English section, located in the Ujjayanta Palace, and (2) the Vernacular section in a building, near the local H. E. School. The latter section was open to the public. The number of English books (including foreign literature) were the same as before. The number of Bengali and Sanskrit books were 2,249 against 2,207 in the previous year. There were 4 daily newspapers, 2 weeklies and 7 monthlies against 4, 3 and 7 respectively in the preceding year. The average daily attendance in the vernacular section of the library was 7 against 8 in the previous year and the total number of books issued to the public was 2,076 against 3,009.

Library

314. The total expenditure on public instruction in the year under report amounted to Rs. 1,23,867 against Rs. 1,25,021. Details of expenditure are noted below :—

Expenditure.

1.	Primary Education	Rs. 27,528
2.	Secondary Education	„ 47,598
3.	Schools for special Training	„ 1,859
4.	Compulsory Free Primary Education ...	„ 1,938
5.	Boarding Institutions for Thakur boys ...	„ 6,870
6.	Education of Kumars and Kumaris ...	„ 21,016
7.	Scholarships and stipends	„ 6,604
8.	Library	„ 2,470
9.	Tripura Boarding	„ 3,432
10.	Miscellaneous	„ 4,552

315. The total receipts from the schools amounted to Rs. 15,034 against Rs. 14,566 in the previous year.

Income.

CHAPTER VIII—ZEMINDARIES.

Chakla Roshnabad Estates.

Management.

316. The management of His Highness's Zemindaries in British India continued in the hands of Manyabara Rai J. C. Sen Bahadur, B. A., B. C. S. (retired) for the whole year. He was assisted by a Deputy Manager posted at Comilla and three Assistant Managers posted at Feni, Mogra and Srimangal.

The year and the tenantry.

317. The all-round economic depression, noticed in previous years, continued during the year under review also. Relief was given to the Talukdars and the tenants this year too, as in previous years, in the shape of general remission of interest and damages almost throughout the whole year and the policy of allowing petty demands to be time-barred was also continued.

Demand.

318. The gross Revenue demand of the year was Rs. 10,21,090 against Rs. 10,21,376 in the previous year.

Receipt.

319. Total receipts amounted to Rs. 10,78,217 (including Rs. 585 of the Tripura Raj Central Co-operative Bank Ltd. and Rs. 1,892 on account of Debottar Mahal) against Rs. 9,82,889 in the previous year.

Expenditure.

320. The total expenditure in the year under review was Rs. 10,44,935 including repayment of old debts and refund of deposits to the extent of Rs. 30,066 together with a contribution of Rs. 1,35,000 to the State and advances amounting to Rs. 1,87,000 to Nij Tahabil. The total expenditure during the previous year was Rs. 9,71,867.

321. Of the total expenditure during the year under review, Rs. 2,85,540 was on account of Land Revenue, taxes and cesses while the total administration charges of the Zemindaries including the expenditure on Public Works and the Law Charges amounted to Rs. 3,53,096 against Rs. 3,34,354 in the previous year.

322. The following other items of expenditure aggregating Rs. 4,06,299 are noticeable :—

1.	Education...	Rs.	9,075
2.	Medical charges	„	11,469
3.	Religious ceremonies	„	6,111
4.	Purchase of property	„	6,573
5.	Loan and advance	„	999
6.	Samsar stipends	„	12,960
7.	Donations	„	7,046
8.	Repayment of old debts and deposits ...	„	30,066
9.	Advance to His Highness's Nij Tahabil	„	1,87,000
10.	Contribution to the State	„	1,35,000
		Rs.	4,06,299

323. The result of the year's settlement operations will appear from the figures noted below :—

Settlement.

	Kinds of settlement.		Addition to rental.	Nazar.
1.	*Kaimi* and *Takshishi Taluki* in the Comilla Town	...	Rs. 97	Rs. 5,280
2.	Ordinary Town Settlement	.	,, 112	,, 1,640
3.	*Khas Patit* land	.	,, 347	,, 1,084
4.	Enhancement of rent ...	...	,, 787	,, 1,548
5.	Re-settlement of auction purchased holdings	...	,, 157	,, 10,792
6.	*Takshishi Taluki* in the *Moffusil*		,, 32	,, 862
7.	*Ijara*		—	—
			Rs. 1,532	Rs. 21,206

324. The corresponding figures for the previous year were Rs. 1,050 and Rs. 11,731 respectively.

325. Considering the all-round economic depression, the settlement operations may be considered satisfactory in comparison with those of the previous year.

CHAPTER IX—MISCELLANEOUS.

326. The printing of the third part of the Rajmala, the State chronicles, was completed and duly published during the year under report. The distribution of the same are also going on. The late editor, Kaliprasanna Sen, Vidyabhusan, in his life time, completed the manuscript of the fourth part. The printing of the same was taken up by the State Press. More than twenty forms have already been printed, *i. e.* about the half has been done. In the absence of a permanent editor the work is almost suspended.

Rajmala.

327. The total expenditure incurred during the year under review was Rs. 3,520.

328. Manyabara Rana Bodhjung Bahadur, F. R. G. S., Chief Secretary was in camp with His Highness the Maharaja Manikya Bahadur during all his tours in the year under review. He went to visit the Kalyanpur Reserve area for 2 days in connection with settlement schemes. From Mussoorie, he was sent by His Highness to Agartala and was deputed in connection with H. E. the Governor's visit to Comilla in July. He rejoined His Highness at Dholpur, staying out for 18 days.

329. Thakur K. K. Singh, Naib Dewan was out on tour for 19 days.

330. The tours of the Divisional Officers and their assistants are noted below :—

State.

1.	Sadar—			
	Sadar Collector—Babu Shashanka Bhusan Roy, M. A., B. L.		....	26 days.
	Asst. ,,	Kumar Narshing Chandra Deb Barman Bahadur	...	0

2. Kailashahar—
Divisional Officer—Babu Akhil Chandra Majumdar, M. A., B. L. ... 16 days.
Second Officer—Jyotirmay Ghose, M. A. ... 24 ,,

3. Sonamura—
Divisional Officer—Thakur Revati Mohan Deb Barman ... 3 ,,
Second Officer—Thakur Jyotilal Deb Barman, B. L. ... 10 ,,

4. Belonia—
Divisional Officer—Thakur Gokul Chandra Deb Barman ... 17 ,,
Second Officer—Thakur Kamal Krishna Deb Barman ... 48 ,,

5. Khowai—
Divisional Officer—Babu Prava Ranjan Das Gupta, M. A., B. L. ... 44 ,,
Probationer—Thakur Hiran Kumar Deb Barman, B. A. ... 7 ,,
,, Babu Narendra Narayan Chaudhuri, B. L. ... 1 ,,

6. Dharmanagar—
Divisional Officer—Babu Sarada Charan Sarkar, M. A. B. L. ... 24 ,,
Probationer—Sj. Chandrahas Singh, B. L. ... ... 18 ,,

7. Udaipur—
Divisional Officer—Babu Suresh Chandra Chakravarty, B. L. ... 46 ,,
Probationer—Babu Mahendra Kumar Ray, B. L. ... 38 ,,

8. Sabroom—
Divisional Officer—Babu Jogendra Lal Ganguly, B. L. ... 73 ,,

9. Amarpur—
Sub-Divisional Officer—Thakur Joysing Deb Barman, B. A. ... 90 ,,

Zemindaries.

1. Babu Pramada Ranjan Bhattacharjee, B. A., Deputy Manager, Comilla ... 41 days.
2. Babu Jagadish Chandra Majumdar, M. A., B. L., Assistant Manager, Feni ... 7 ,,
   Babu Tarit Mohan Gupta, Assistant Manager, Feni ... 15 ,,
3. Babu Bisweswar Guha, B. A., Assistant Manager, Mogra ... 72 ,,
4. Babu Surendra Chandra Guha, B. A., Assistant Manager, Srimangal ... 64 ,,

DATED, AGARTALA,
The 20th December, 1935.

Jyotis Chandra Sen,
MINISTER.

APPENDIX.

List of the principal Laws and Regulations in force in the Tripura State during 1344 T. E.

Description.	Whether adapted from British Indian Acts.	Whether introduced during the year under report.
CRIMINAL.		
1. Regulation No. III. of 1280 T. E.		
2. Regulation No. I. of 1283 T. E.		
3. Jail Regulation, 1283 T. E.		
4. Regulation No. IV. of 1283 T. E. (Cattle trespass and pound).		
5. Regulation No. III. of 1296 T. E. (Police Regulation).		
6. Act No. IV. of 1321 T. E.–Penal Laws (an amending Act)		
CIVIL.		
1. Civil Law of 1284 T. E.		
2. Rules regarding *chit* suits (small causes) 1287 and 1300 T. E.		
3. Act No. II. of 1313 T. E.—an Act for the regulation of interest on debts.		
4. Act No. II. of 1314 T. E.—Limitation Act	Partly adapted.	
5. Succession Act II of 1339 T. E.		
REVENUE.		
1. Act No. I. of 1290 T. E.—Sale Law		
2. Act No. I. of 1296 T. E.—Tenancy Act.		
3. Act No. II. of 1296 T. E.—*Abkari*		
4. Act No. II. of 1297 T. E.—Reserved forests.		
5. Act No. I. of 1304 T. E.—Duties on *til* and cotton.		
6. Act No. I. of 1306 T. E.—Registration	Do.	
7. Survey and Settlement Act, 1309 T.E.	Do.	
8. *Tuccavi* Regulation, 1310 T. E.		
9. Act No. I. of 1313 T. E.—Forests.		
10. Act No. I. of 1314 T. E.—(amending the above)		
11. A Law imposing export duty on jute and mustard-seed, 1317 T. E.		
12. Act No. II. of 1321 T.E.—Ghasuri Act		
13. P. W. & Road Cess Act IV of 1339 T. E.		
MISCELLANEOUS.		
1. An Act promulgating certain rules as Law, 1283 T. E.		
2. Regulation for the record of judicial decisions &c., 1284 T. E.		
3 Municipal Regulation, 1284 T. E.		
4. Legal Practitioners' Regulation.		
5. Act No. I. of 1297 T. E.—an Act for the regulation of commissions for the examination of witnesses.		
6. Regulation against cow slaughter		
7. Rules of evidence		
8. Act I. of 1318 T. E.—Constitution of Courts—(an amending Act).		
9. Leave and allowance Rules	Do.	
10. Act No. I. of 1321 T. E.—Arms Act	Do.	
11. Act No. III. of 1321 T. E.—Constitution of Courts (an amending Act)		

Description.	Whether adapted from British Indian Acts.	Whether introduced during the year under report.
12. Municipal Act No. I of 1322 T. E.		
13. Revenue Sale Amendment Act—1323 T.E.		
14. An Act for the destruction of old records—1323 T. E.		
15. Act I of 1326 T. E.—Regulation regarding Privy Council Appeals.		
16. Act II of 1326 T. E.—Registration of Births and Deaths		
17. Act III of 1326 T. E.—Vaccination Act	Partly adapted.	
18. Act IV of 1326 T. E.—Public Demands Recovery Act	Do.	
19. Act V of 1326 T. E.—Excise Amendment Act	Do.	
20. Act I of 1327 T. E.—Settlement of lands for tea cultivation		
21. Rules of Import and Sale of Opium—1327 T. E.		
22. Regulation No. 1 of 1328 T. E.—regarding Registration of Coolies		
23. Regulation No. 2 of 1328 T. E.—regarding Export of Tea		
24. Act I of 1329 T. E.—(Absconding sepoys Act)		
25. Act II of 1329 T. E.—(Control of prices of food stuff)		
26. Act III of 1329 T. E. (Elephants and buffaloes grazing Act)		
27. Act IV of 1329 T. E. (House tax on Hill tribes)		
28. Act V of 1329 T. E. (Legal practitioners, Act)	Do	
29. Act I of 1332 T. E.—Encumbered Estates Act.		
30. Act III of 1332 T. E.—The Opium and Intoxicating Drugs Act.		
31. Rules and Regulations under the Opium and Intoxicating Drugs Act III of 1332 T. E.		
32. Act I of 1336 T. E.—(Hackney Carriages)		
33. Act II of 1336 T. E.—(Amending Act I of 1327.)		
34. Act III of 1336 T. E.—(Amending the Survey & Settlement Regulation)		
35. Act IV of 1336 T. E.—(Prevention of gambling)		
36. Act I of 1337 T. E.—(Amending the State Tenancy Act I of 1296 T. E.)		
37. Land Acquisition Rules under Act I of 1337 T. E.		
38. State Motor Vehicles Act I of 1338 T. E.		
39. Act II of 1338 T. E. for prevention of smuggling of elephant tusks.		
40. State Stamp Act III of 1338 T. E.		
41. Tripura State Bank Act I of 1339 T. E.		
42. Census Act III of 1339 T. E.		
43. Act I of 1342 T. E.—providing for trial of certain criminal cases by Special Tribunal.		
44. Compulsory Primary Education Act II of 1342 T. E.		

II

Statement showing the strength, cost and other particulars of the Military Force in Tripura State for 1344 T. E.

Arm of service.	Number of fighting officers and men.						Details of force at the end of the current year.						Buglers.	Total cost on account of pay and allowances of the force, including followers.	Remarks.
	At the end of last year	Recruited this year.	Casualties.			At the end of the current year.	Number of regiments, battalions, or Batteries.	Number of guns.	Number of men.						
			Died.	Invalided.	Discharged, deserted, &c.				Commisioned Officers. European.	Commisioned Officers. Indian.	Non-commissioned officers.	Fighting men.			
1	2	3	4	5	6	7	8	9	10	11	12	13	14	15	16
Infantry ...	372	86	1	—	108	349	1	540	4	16	33	289	7		
Band Party	19	1	—	—	1	19	—	—	—	—	2	17 Bandman	—		
Total ...	391	87	1	—	109	368	1	540	4	16	35	306	7	Rs. 1,01,039	

III.

Statement showing the strength, cost, discipline, and education of the Police for the year 1344 T. E.

Description of office.	Number.	Grade of pay.	Total cost.	PUNISHMENTS. Dismissed.	Fined, degraded or suspended departmentally. F.	D.	S.	Punished judicially.	REWARDS. By promotion.	By money.	EDUCATION. Number able to read and write.	Number under instruction.	REMARKS.
1	2	3	4	5	6			7	8	9	10	11	12
		Rs.											
Superintendent of Police	1	250-0-0	Rs 87,340	—		—		—	—	—	1	—	F. = Fined. D. = Degraded. S. = Suspended.
Asst. Superintendent "	1	100-5-125		—		—		—	—	—	1	—	
Inspectors	4	265-5/2-90 255-2-65		—		—		—	—	2	4	—	
Sub-Inspectors	23	25-2-45		—		—		—	—	8	23	—	
Proby. Sub-Inspector	1	15 allowance		—		—		—	—	—	1	—	
Naib Darogas	22	15-1-25		—		—		—	—	3	22	—	
Writer Naib Darogas	17	15-0-0		1		—		—	—	1	17	—	
Subedar	1	25-2-45		—		—		—	—	—	1	—	
Armed S. I.	1	25-2-45		—		—		—	—	—	1	—	
Jamadars (civil)	6	15-1-25		—		—		—	—	1	6	—	
Jamadar (Armed)	1	20-1-30		—	1	0	0	—	—	—	1	—	
Havildar	1	19-1-25		—		—		—		—	1	—	
Naiks	4	15-1-20		1	1	0	0	—	—	—	4	—	
Constables (Armed)	38	14-1-15		—	15	1	0	—	—	1	22	—	
Constables (Civil)	220	10 to 13		6	17	5	0	—	—	5	115	—	
Chaukidars	176	5-0-0		4	1	0	0	—	—	—	5	—	
Spies	3	20 and 15		—		—		—	—	—	3	—	
Total ...	520			12	35	6	0		—	21	228	—	

IV.

Statement showing the working of the Police in the Tripura State during the year 1344 T. E.

State.	Number of offences.		Number of accused arrested.		Number of accused sent up for trial.		Number of accused convicted.		Number of accused acquitted or discharged.		Percentage convicted of accused arrested.		Percentage convicted of accused sent up for trial.		REMARKS.
	Past year.	Present year.	Pas year.	Present year.	Past year.	Present year.	Past year.	Present year.	Past year.	Present year.	Past year.	Present year.	Past year.	Present year.	
1	2	3	4	5	6	7	8	9	10	11	12	13	14	15	16
Tripura State	1,009	894	623	675	824	819	208	209	178	137	33'39	30'96	70'21	* 74'38	* Excluding:— Pending trial— 472 Withdrawal— 17 Compromise— 48 Dead— 1 538

V

Statement showing the value of property stolen and amount of recoveries in the Tripura State during the year 1344 T. E.

State.	Amount stolen.		Amount recovered.		Percentage of recoveries of property stolen.		REMARKS.
	Past year.	Present year.	Past year.	Present year.	Past year.	Present year.	
1	2	3	4	5	6	7	8
Tripura State	Rs 12,868-9-9	Rs 14,675-4-9	Rs 1,929-7-0	Rs 1,721-11-6	14'99	11'73	

VI.

Statement showing the number of crimes committed, number of cases disposed of, and cases awaiting trial in the Tripura State during the year 1344 T. E.

Description of offences.		Number of offences: Balance from past year.	Number of offences: Committed during the present year.	Number of offences: Total.	Number of cases disposed of during the past year.	Number of cases disposed of during the present year.	Number of cases awaiting trial.	Number of persons apprehended.	Number of persons convicted.	Number of persons sentenced: Imprisonment: Simple.	Number of persons sentenced: Imprisonment: Rigorous.	Number of persons sentenced: Imprisonment and fine: Simple.	Number of persons sentenced: Imprisonment and fine: Rigorous.	Fine only.	Whipping.	Capital punishment.	Total.	Number of persons acquitted or discharged.	Number of persons confined being insane.	Number of persons died during or before trial.	Term of imprisonment: Under one month.	From 1 to below 2 months.	From 2 to below 3 months.	From 3 to below 6 months.	From 6 to below 12 months.	From 1 to below 2 years.	From 2 to below 3 years.	From 3 to below 5 years.	5 years and above.	Imprisonment for life.	Capital punishment.	Persons awaiting trial.	Remarks.
1		2	3	4	5	6	7	8	9	10	11	12	13	14	15	16	17	18	19	20	21	22	23	24	25	26	27	28	29	30	31	32	33
Class I. Offences against the State, public tranquillity, safety and justice &c.	cognizable ...	13	13	26	12	17	9	89	a44	0	29	0	0	5	0	0	34	23	0	2	0	0	2	12	13	2	0	0	0	0	0	20	(a) 10 persons were warned for the future.
	non-cognizable	12	54	66	32	52	14	33	b6	0	0	0	0	0	0	0	0	20	0	0	0	0	0	0	0	0	0	0	0	0	0	7	(b) 6 persons were bound down under security.
Class II. Offences against person.	cognizable ..	117	307	424	284	282	142	663	c91	5	44	0	2	19	0	0	70	317	0	4	8	4	4	10	9	6	1	1	8	0	0	251	(c) 21 persons were warned for the future.
	non-cognizable	51	201	252	243	197	55	210	24	0	3	1	1	19	0	0	24	128	0	0	2	2	1	0	0	0	0	0	0	0	0	58	
Class III. Offences against property.	cognizable ...	272	721	993	763	672	321	1417	d337	8	80	0	36	201	0	0	325	635	0	10	40	20	21	26	7	4	6	0	0	0	0	435	(d) 7 persons were warned for the future and 5 persons bound down under security
	non-cognizable	69	242	311	132	191	120	250	20	2	0	0	0	18	0	0	20	124	0	0	1	1	0	0	0	0	0	0	0	0	0	106	
Class IV. Other offences.	cognizable ...	46	269	315	134	251	64	268	e137	1	8	13	3	46	0	0	71	75	0	0	8	5	0	3	3	0	2	4	0	0	0	56	(e) 66 persons were warned for the future.
	non-cognizable	71	216	287	282	224	63	176	f21	3	2	0	0	10	0	0	15	125	0	0	1	3	0	1	0	0	0	0	0	0	0	30	
Total cognizable ...		448	1310	1758	1193	1222	536	2437	609	14	161	13	41	271	0	0	500	1050	0	16	56	29	27	51	32	12	9	5	8	0	0	762	(f) 5 persons were warned for the future and 1 person was bound down under security.
Total non-cognizable ...		203	713	916	589	664	252	669	71	5	5	1	1	47	0	0	59	397	0	0	4	6	1	1	0	0	0	0	0	0	0	201	
GRAND TOTAL ...		651	2023	2674	1382	1886	788	3106	680	19	116	14	42	318	0	0	559	1447	0	16	60	35	28	52	32	12	9	5	8	0	0	963	

VII.

Statement showing the number of offences reported and dealt with by the various Courts in the Tripura State during the year 1344 T.E.

Name of Court.	Number of offences reported during.		Number of persons dealt with.								Persons disposed of.					Persons remaining at the end of the year.	Remarks
			Remaining at the end of last year.	Brought to trial during present year.				Total.									
	Last year.	Present year.		Arrested by Police.	Upon warrant.	On summons.	Voluntary.	Arrested in presence of the Magistrate.	Last year.	Present year.	Discharged without trial.	Acquitted.	Convicted.	Committed or referred.	Died, escaped, or transferred &c.		
1	2	3	4	5	6	7	8	9	10	11	12	13	14	15	16	17	18
Sadar Magistracy	602	607	123	167	159	207	24	—	635	680	193	173	110	21	5	178	
Sonamura " ...	293	219	128	65	59	101	71	1	560	425	115	86	100	14	2	108	
Bilonia " ...	184	219	22	101	42	90	47	4	360	306	100	32	107	3	—	64	
Kailashahar " ...	273	307	160	143	37	99	17	1	491	457	100	67	170	—	4	116	
Khowai " ...	167	204	34	48	22	77	28		154	209	36	60	58	1	1	53	
Dharmanagar " ...	204	248	235	125	80	108	21	—	434	569	180	84	51	1	3	250	
Udaipur " ...	200	176	75	45	41	200	5	—	253	366	99	58	30	7	—	172	
Sabrum " ...	43	43	10	31	3	41	5	1	59	91	41	10	30	—	—	10	
TOTAL ...	1,966	2,023	787	725	443	923	218	7	2,949	3,103 *a*	864	570	656	47 *b*	15 *c*	951	

a. Excluding 3 persons pending before the Court of Sessions at the close of the previous year.

b. The total number of persons for trial before the Court of Sessions, (including 3 persons pending from the last year) was 50, of whom 24 persons were convicted, 12 acquitted, 1 set free—the case being withdrawn, 1 person absconded and 12 remained under trial at the close of the year.

c. Excluding 1 person absconding before the trial of sessions case.

VIII.

Statement of Criminal cases in which British Subjects were concerned for 1344 T. E.

Description of Offences.		Cases pending since the previous year.	Cases instituted during the year.	Total number of cases.	Cases in which complainants were British subjects.	Cases in which both parties were British subjects.	Cases in which defendants were British Subjects.															Remarks.
							Cases pending since the previous year.	Cases instituted during the year.	Total number of cases.	Cases disposed of.		Cases pending at the close of the year.	Persons under trial at the close of the previous year.	Persons brought to trial during the year.	Total number of persons under trial.	Convicted.	Acquitted or discharged.	Died or escaped &c.	Under trial at the close of the year.	
										Rejected, compromised without enquiry.	Tried.									
Class I. Offences against the State &c.	cognizable ...	4	3	7	0	0	4	3	7	1	3	3	1	16	17	14	0	0	3	*Of this number, 58 persons were discharged without trial the cases being dismissed etc. excluding 2 persons dead and 124 remaining under trial at the close of the year; the actual number of persons tried was 343, of whom 219 persons were convicted; the percentage of conviction was thus 63·85 during the year under report.
	non-cognizable ...	0	0	0	0	0	0	0	0	0	0	0	0	0	0	0	0	0	0	
Class II. Offences against person.	cognizable ...	17	30	47	10	10	16	21	37	14	11	12	11	64	75	28	24	1	22	
	non-cognizable ...	2	23	25	5	8	3	17	20	10	2	8	6	28	29	8	11	0	10	
Class III. Offences against property.	cognizable ...	69	178	247	22	35	69	156	225	62	104	59	72	234	306	134	99	1	72	
	non-cognizable ...	5	25	30	10	14	5	15	20	28	2	10	0	23	23	2	13	0	8	
Class IV. Other offences	cognizable ...	8	39	47	2	11	8	37	45	21	11	13	5	50	55	28	19	0	8	
	non-cognizable ...	3	33	36	18	12	4	14	18	15	2	1	6	16	22	5	16	0	1	
Total cognizable ...		98	250	348	34	56	97	217	314	98	129	87	89	364	453	204	142	2	105	
Total non-cognizable ...		10	81	91	33	34	12	49	58	33	6	19	12	62	74	15	40	0	19	
Grand Total ...		108	331	439	67	90	109	263	372	131	135	106	101	426	*527	219	182	2	124	

IX.

Statement of Extradition Cases for the year 1344 T. E.

Names of Courts.	Nature of cases	Number Borne on the Register.				Number Brought to Trial.			Result.		Number at large at the close of the year.	Number of persons awaiting trial (after arrest) at the close of the year.	Remarks.
		Number of persons at large at the close of the previous year.	Number of persons awaiting trial at the close of the previous year.	Number of persons against whom warrants were applied for during the year.	Total.	Number of persons arrested and surrendered within the year.	Number of persons who appeared of their own accord or were subsequently arrested in the State within the year.	Total (Columns 4+7+8).	Convicted.	Acquitted or discharged.			
Sadar Magistracy	Theft	0	0	10	10	6	1	7	0	2	3	5	
	Criminal breach of trust	0	0	12	12	3	1	4	0	3	8	1	
	Escape from lawful custody	0	0	1	1	1	0	1	0	1	0	0	
	Kidnapping	0	0	2	2	0	0	0	0	0	2	0	
	Mischief	0	0	1	1	0	0	0	0	0	1	0	
	Dacoity	0	0	5	5	4	1	5	0	0	0	5	
	Forgery	0	0	1	1	1	0	1	0	1	0	0	
Kailashahar " ...	Theft	7	0	1	8	2	0	2	2	0	6	0	
	Kidnapping	1	0	1	2	1	0	1	0	1	1	0	
	Criminal breach of trust	1	0	0	1	0	0	0	0	0	1	0	
	Theft by servant	1	0	0	1	1	0	1	0	1	0	0	
Sonamura " ...	Theft	41	26	40	107	3	27	56	35	9	51	12	
	Murder	4	0	0	4	0	4	4	4	0	0	0	
	Escape from lawful custody	1	0	0	1	0	1	1	1	0	0	0	
	Causing grievous hurt	2	1	0	3	0	2	3	1	2	0	0	
	Rioting and causing grievous hurt...	1	2	0	3	0	0	2	2	0	1	0	
Dharmanagar " ...	Causing grievous hurt	0	1	0	1	0	0	1	1	0	0	0	
	Abduction	0	0	6	6	0	0	0	0	0	6	0	
	Escape from lawful custody	0	1	0	1	0	0	1	1	0	0	0	
Bilonia " ...	Theft	0	4	16	20	8	0	12	3	1	8	8	
Khowai " ...	Theft	2	0	1	3	1	1	2	0	0	1	2	
	Kidnapping	1	0	1	2	1	0	1	1	0	1	0	
	Abduction	2	0	0	2	2	0	2	0	2	0	0	
	Causing hurt	1	0	0	1	1	0	1	1	0	0	0	
	Cheating	0	0	2	2	0	1	1	0	0	1	1	
Udaipur " ...	Theft and receiving stolen property	1	0	0	1	0	0	0	0	0	1	0	
	Murder...	1	0	0	1	0	0	0	0	0	1	0	
Sabroom " ...	Theft	10	1	2	13	1	0	2	2	0	11	0	
	Resistence to arrest	6	0	0	6	2	0	2	2	0	4	0	
	Dacoity	0	0	3	3	1	0	1	1	0	2	0	
	Total	83	36	105	224	39	39	114	57	23	110	34	

X.

Statement showing the result of appeals against decisions passed by the Criminal Courts in the Tripura State during the year 1344 T. E.

Tribunal.	Number of applications	Number of persons and cases.																Remarks.
		Applications rejected.		Sentences.						Proceedings quashed.		Referred.		Further enquiry &c, ordered.		Pending		
				Confirmed.		Modified.		Reversed.										
		Persons.	Cases.	Persons.	Cases.	Persons.	Cases.	Persons.	Cases.	Persons.	Cases.	Persons.	Cases.	Persons.	Cases.	Persons.	Cases.	
Khas Adalat ...	236	9	6	125	115	89	40	45	24	—	—	—	—	34	23	55	28	

XI.

Civil Work—Nature and value of original suits filed and disposed of during the year 1344 T. E.

Tribunal.	Opening balance. Past year.	Opening balance. Present year.	Filed during the year, received by transfer or on remand. Past year.	Filed during the year, received by transfer or on remand. Present year.	Total. Past year.	Total. Present year.	Disposed of during the year. Past year.	Disposed of during the year. Present year.	Closing balance. Past year.	Closing balance. Present year.	Suits filed during present year. Value.	Suits *re* landed property.	Suits for money transaction.	Suits for other rights.	Number of suits under Rs. 100.	Number of suits above Rs. 100 and under Rs. 500.	Number of suits above Rs. 500 and under Rs. 1,000.	Number of suits above Rs. 1,000 and under Rs. 5,000.	Number of suits above Rs. 5,000.	Suits disposed of during present year. *Exparte.*	Admitted and compromised.	Struck off the file.	Otherwise disposed of.	Value.	Average duration.	Suits not estimable in money.	Remarks.
											Rs. a. p.													*Rs a. p.*	*Y.m.d.*		
Khas Adalat Original side	49	48	26	17	75	65	27	14	48	51	35,414-6-0	3	10	4	0	0	0	13	0	0	1	5	8	31,961-1-6	0-8-2	4	
Sadar Dewani Adalat	262	306	728	667	990	973	684	663	306	310	32,331-9-0	254	335	78	352	170	7	0	0	366	28	106	163	64,113-8-6	0-0-27	138	
Sonamura "	82	51	246	200	328	251	277	199	51	52	13,721-14-6	28	106	66	100	32	2	0	0	118	20	43	18	12,439-0-6	0-2-27	66	
Bilonia "	48	32	176	162	224	194	192	152	32	42	11,784-5-0	24	133	5	111	23	3	0	0	94	17	31	10	8,512-9-9	0-1-17	25	
Kailashahar "	154	175	189	163	343	338	168	217	175	121	11,304-15-3	14	113	36	104	21	3	0	0	84	39	8	86	16,005-1-6	0-6-4	35	
Khowai "	85	35	59	71	144	106	109	73	35	33	9,118-12-8	3	60	8	50	13	6	0	0	27	6	11	29	7,208-2-3	0-9-3	2	
Dharmanagar "	75	80	117	115	192	195	112	125	80	70	9,050-15-0	16	60	39	68	33	2	0	0	16	22	37	50	10,081-2-6	0-2-3	12	
Udaipur "	143	120	226	211	369	331	249	233	120	98	12,424-9-3	43	135	33	160	46	1	0	0	103	20	39	71	14,211-4-6	0-1-2	4	
Sabrum "	8	2	33	25	41	27	39	25	2	2	2,236-10-0	17	7	1	19	5	0	0	0	19	0	1	5	2,036-10-0	0-4-0	1	
Total ...	906	849	1,800	1,631	2,706	2,480	1,857	1,701	849	779	1,37,388-0-8	402	959	270	964	343	24	13	0	827	153	281	440	1,66,568-9-0	0-4-0	287	

XII.

Civil Work.—Results of applications for Execution of Decrees, 1344 T.E.

Tribunal.	Opening balance.		Value of opening balance for present year.	Applications brought to the Register.			Total.			Disposed of.			Closing balance.			Nature of applications pending disposal at the close of the year.			Remarks.
	Past year.	Present year.		Past year.	Present year.	Value for present year.	Past year.	Present year.	Value for present year.	Past year.	Present year.	Value for present year.	Past yaer.	Present year.	Value for present year.	Below 6 months.	Below 12 months.	Above 12 months.	
			Rs. a. p.			Rs. a. p.			Rs. a. p.			Rs. a. p.			Rs. a. p.				
Khas Adalat (Original side)	34	37	33,461-4-0	13	15	8,654-6-0	47	52	42,115-10-0	10	22	20,889-6-3	37	30	21,226-3-9	0	9	21	
Sadar Dewani Adalat ...	200	200	32,714-12-0	252	297	47,524-5-6	452	497	80,239-1-6	252	255	51,342-9-3	200	242	28,896-8-3	123	68	61	
Sonamura Ditto ...	62	40	7,610 15-0	116	105	15,366-9-11	178	145	22,977-8-11	138	103	14,884-8-11	40	42	8,003-0-0	32	5	5	
Bilonia Ditto ...	19	26	3,605 10-6	73	60	8,017-6-3	92	86	11,623-0-9	66	57	8,879-11-9	26	29	2,743-5-0	23	1	5	
Kailashahar Ditto ...	153	119	20,763-2-9	67	97	17,563-4-9	220	216	38,326-7-6	101	104	14,871-7-6	119	112	23,455-0-0	34	21	57	
Khowai Ditto ...	26	30	6,315-3-0	47	37	6,215-10-3	73	67	12,530-13-3	43	45	9,204-7-0	30	22	3,326-6-3	12	6	4	
Dharmanagar Ditto ...	30	27	4,259-5-6	30	50	9,757-12-6	60	77	14,017-2-0	33	28	4,920-5-6	27	49	9,096-12-6	16	22	11	
Udaipur Ditto ...	162	130	19,779-9-9	164	173	23,579-3-0	326	303	43,358-12-9	196	187	25,020-11-9	130	116	18,338-1-0	61	25	30	
Sabrum Ditto ...	4	2	375-9-3	10	4	389-5-3	14	6	764-14-6	12	3	435-9-3	2	3	329-5-3	3	0	0	
Total ...	690	611	1,28,835-7-9	772	838	1,37,067-15-5	1,462	1,449	2,65,953-7-2	871	804	1,50,448-13-2	611	645	1,15,504-10-0	304	147	194	

XIII.

Civil Work—Number and results of appeals in civil suits, 1344 T. E.

Tribunal.	Opening balance.		Filed during.		Total.		Disposed of during.		Closing balance.		Value of appeales filed during.		How disposed of.										Average duration.	
													Decisions confirmed.		Decisions reversed.		Decisions amended.		Cases remanded for retrial.		Cases compromised and otherwise disposed of.			
	Past year.	Present year.	Past year.	Present year.	Past year.	Present year.	Past year.	Present year.	Past year.	Present year.	Past year.	Present year.	Past year.	Present year.	Past year.	Present year.	Past year.	Present year.	Past year.	Present year.	Past year.	Present year.	Past year.	Present year.
											Rs. a. p.	*Rs. a. p.*											*Y.m.d.*	*Y m.d.*
Khas Adalat	118	106	147	108	265	214	159	142	106	72	8,627-5-9	10,571-7-6	72	62	31	31	18	21	12	8	26	29	0-4-12	0-5-3

XIV.

Statement showing the number of persons confined in the jails and lock-ups in the Tripura State during the year 1344 T. E.

Stations.	Number of prisons.	NUMBER OF PRISONERS.				DAILY AVERAGE.		Number of prisoners remaining at the end of the year.	Cost of jails and prisoners.	Average period in days of stay of accused under-trial.	Remarks showing mortality among convicts in jail.
		Remaining from last year.	Admitted during the year.	*Total.*							
				Past year.	Present year.	Past year.	Present year.				
									Rs.		
Agartala	1	108	307	438	415	103·7	135·29	149	15,347	42	One convict died of typhoid and pneumonia during the year.
Sonamura	1	24	143	268	167	·74	·46	4	1,365	29·96	
Bilonia	1	7	156	247	163	14·36	6·32	12	1,059	18·83	
Kailashahar	1	7	116	131	123	4·56	6·30	3	1,299	19·13	
Dharmanagar	1	2	119	72	121	3·49	7·54	14	1,212	26·10	
Udaipur...	1	8	84	107	92	11·36	11·73	10	1,111	11·6	
Sabrum	1	6	45	51	51	·13	5·41	2	956	48·93	
Khowai	1	4	56	79	60	4·48	3·11	4	965	22·1	
TOTAL ...	8	166	1026	1393	1192	142·82	176·16	198	23,314	27·33	

XV.

Registration of documents in the Tripura State during the year 1344 T.E.

Name of State.	Documents presented for registration including pending from the last year.		Nature of documents presented.										Documents registered.		Value of documents registered.		Documents of which registration has been refused.		Documents remaining unregistered at the end of the year.		Remarks.
			Mortgages.		Sale deeds.		Wills.		Money bonds.		Miscellaneous.										
	Past year.	Present year.	Past year.	Present year.	Past year.	Present year.	Past year.	Present year.	Past year.	Present year.	Past year.	Present year.	Past year.	Present year.	Past year.	Present year.	Past year.	Present year.	Past year.	Present year.	
1	2	3	4	5	6	7	8	9	10	11	12	13	14	15	16	17	18	19	20	21	22
															Rs.	Rs.					
Tripura State	6,265	6,615	1,202	1,192	3,513	3,964	1	—	47	53	1,406	1,309	6,118	6,457	6,79,981	8,32,679	50	131	97	27	

XVI.

Statement showing the receipts and expenditure on account of Registration during the year 1344 T.E.

Description.	Past Year.			Present Year			Remarks.
	Number of deeds.	Value of property.	Fees realised.	Number of deeds.	Value of property.	Fees realised.	
		Rs.	Rs.		Rs.	Rs.	
Mortgages	1,202	1,43,948	961	1,192	3,11,026	1,181	
Sale deeds	3,513	3,72,998	3,008	3,964	3,79,018	3,329	
Wills	1	—	5	—	—	—	
Money bonds	47	8,710	82	53	5,054	43	
Miscellaneous	1,406	1,67,239	1,645	1,309	1,38,246	1,477	
Total ...	6,169	6,92,895	5,701	6,518	8,33,344	6,030	
Total Expenditure ...	—	—	3,574	—	—	3,555	
Net Income ...	—	—	2,127	—	—	2,475	

XVII.

Receipts and expenditure of the Municipalities in the Tripura State during the year 1344 T.E.

NAME.	Opening balance.	RECEIPTS DURING THE YEAR.				Total Receipt		EXPENDITURE DURING THE YEAR.		Balance at the close of the year.	REMARKS.
		State grant.	Tax.	Miscellaneous.	Total.	Past year.	Present year	Past.	Present.		
1	2	3	4	5	6	7	8	9	10	11	12
	Rs. A. P.	Rs. A. P.	Rs. A. P.	Rs. A. P.	Rs. A. P.	Rs. A. P.	Rs. A. P.	Rs. A. P.	Rs. A. P.	Rs. A. P.	
Agartala Municipality. ...	39,629-1-6 a	9,000	5,376-15-0	7,818-5-6 b	22,195-4-6	60,891-2-3	61,821-6-0	21,262-0-9	17,446-6-6 c	44,377-15-6 d	a. Including Rs. 39605-0-9 of the Bazar Improvement fund and Rs. 24-0-9 of the municipality. b. Including Rs. 6827-0-0 of the Bazar Improvement fund. c. Including Rs. 2264-14-6 as expenditure on the Bazar improvement. d. Including Rs. 44167-2-3 of the Bazar Improvement fund and Rs. 210-13-3 of the municipality.

XVIII.

Statement of rainfall in the Tripura State during the year 1344 T. E.

STATE.	Baisak.	Jaisth.	Asar.	Sravan.	Bhadra.	Asvin.	Kartik.	Agrahayan.	Pous.	Magh.	Falgoon.	Chait.	Total.	Total of past year.	Average of past 5 years.	REMARKS.
Tripura State ...	8·18	22·22	18·90	14·05	9·27	11·88	2·91	·28	—	·20	1·17	2·24	91·3	83·02	84·04	

Maximum in Kailashahar—113·66″ Minimum in Amarpur—70·72″

XIX.

Statement as to the prices of staple food-grains for the year 1344 T. E.

Articles.	Price per maund during Chait, 1343 T. E.			Price per maund during chait, 1344 T. E.			REMARKS.
	Rs.	*a.*	*p.*	*Rs.*	*a.*	*p.*	
(1) RICE							
Maximum	4	8	0	4	8	0	
Minimum	2	4	0	2	0	0	
(2) PADDY							
Maximum	2	8	0	2	4	0	
Minimum	1	0	0	1	0	0	

XX.

Expenditure on Public Works during the year 1344 T.E.

Description of work.	State Funds.			Local Funds.			Total.	Remarks.
	Original.	Repairs.	Total.	Original.	Repairs.	Total.		
	Rs.	*Rs.*	*Rs.*	*Rs.*	*Rs.*	*Rs.*	*Rs.*	
Buildings—								
Ordinary Budget ...	12,253	50,466	62,729	16,00	—	1,600	64,329	
Improvement „ ...	61,277	—	61,277	—	—	—	61,277	
Roads and Bridges—								
Ordinary Budget ...	1,839	10,307	12,146	2,790	1,000	3,790	15,936	
Improvement „ ...	39,611	—	39,611	—	—	—	39,611	
Tanks and Tubewells—								
Ordinary Budget ...	162	754	916	450	—	450	1,366	*Out of the total expenditure of Rs. 2,14,552, Rs. 1,10,033 was spent for Ordinary Public Works and Rs. 1,04,519 was spent for improvement works.
Improvement „ ...	250	—	250	—	—	—	250	
Miscellaneous works—								
Ordinary Budget ...	1,929	3,791	5,720	3,188	185	3,373	9,093	
Improvement „ ...	3,381	—	3,381	—	—	—	3,381	
Total ...	1,20,712	65,318	1,86,030	8,028	1,185	9,213	1,95,243	
Minor works at the Rajbari (*Karkhana*)	—	999	999	—	—	—	999	
Establishment charges ..	—	—	18,310	—	—	—	18,310	
Grand Total ...	1,20,712	66,317	2,05,339	8,028	1,185	9,213	2,14,552*	

XXI.

Statement showing the number of excise shops and excise revenue of the Tripura State during the year 1344 T. E.

Name of State.	Country spirit.		Country spirit, Opium and Ganja.		Opium and Ganja.		Tari		Total		Remarks.
	Number of shops.	Revenue demand.	Number of shops.	Revenue demand.	Number of shops.	Revenue demand.	Number of shops.	Revenue demand.	Number of shops.	Revenue realised.	
				Rs.						Rs.	
Tripura State	—	—	33	41,409	—	—	—	—	33	42,901	

XXII.

Statement of Medical Relief afforded in the Tripura State during the year 1344 T.E.*

Dispensary.	Number of patients treated. (new)		Results of in-door patients. (new)				Expenditure.	Daily average. (old + new)			No. of surgical operations performed.			No. of persons vaccinated during the year.			Remarks.
	Outdoor.	Indoor.	Discharged cured.	Relieved or discharged otherwise.	Died.	Remaining under treatment.		Outdoor.	Indoor.	Total.	Major.	Minor.	Total.	Successfully.	Unsuccessfully.	Total.	
							Rs.										
1. Victoria Memorial Hospital...	24,805	579	408	122	27	22	9,665	131·08	20·61	151,69	4	292	296	1,103	467	1,570	
2. Palace Dispensary	6,376	0	0	0	0	0	6,590	37·91	0	37·91	0	0	0	0	0	0	
3. Homœopathic	18,966	0	0	0	0	0	2,322	96·06	0	96·06	0	0	0	0	0	0	
4. Dhaleswar	5,553	0	0	0	0	0	1,422	44·9	0	44·9	0	33	33	0	0	0	* This Statement excludes figures regarding Kaviraji treatment.
5. Kunjaban	1,493	290	272	18	0	0	2,060	12·3	6·3	18·6	0	12	12	0	0	0	
6. Old Agartala	5,335	0	0	0	0	0	1,625	46·05	0	46·05	0	78	78	1,011	105	1,116	† This figure shows the actual number of outdoor patients treated, the total outdoor attendance during the year being 2,55,303 against 2,46,246 in the year before.
7. Bishalgar	8,203	0	0	0	0	0	1,532	33·23	0	33·23	1	46	47	923	3	926	
8. Sonamura	7,502	6	1	5	0	0	2,037	34·71	·15	34·86	2	192	194	402	13	415	
9. Radhakishorpur	11,095	0	0	0	0	0	1,536	43·63	0	43·63	9	116	125	538	76	614	
10. Amarpur	2,637	0	0	0	0	0	1,097	12·98	0	12·98	1	26	27	219	36	255	
11. Sabroom	2,880	5	1	4	0	0	1,469	17·48	·34	17·82	0	28	28	430	97	527	
12. Bilonia	8,004	5	4	1	0	0	1,980	44·25	·27	44·52	0	105	105	548	54	602	
13. Khowai	6,618	0	0	0	0	0	1,714	23·42	0	23·42	0	61	61	495	22	517	
14. Kailashahar	7,344	5	1	4	0	0	1,854	44·49	·15	44·64	4	91	95	319	37	356	
15. Kamalpur	4,415	0	0	0	0	0	1,274	23·65	0	23·65	4	66	70	306	184	490	
16. Kulai Howar	2,790	0	0	0	0	0	369	10·4	0	10·4	0	15	15	0	0	0	
17. Kalyanpur	1,507	0	0	0	0	0	667	5·56	0	5·56	0	5	5	221	39	260	
18. Dharmanagar...	6,710	16	5	11	0	0	1,304	37·32	·42	37·74	0	98	98	437	52	489	
Total	†1,32,243	906	692	165	27	22	40,517	699·42	28·24	727·66	25	1,264	1,289	6,952	1,185	8,137	

XXIII.

Vital statistics of the Tripura State for the year 1344 T. E. *

STATE.	Population.	BIRTHS.				DEATHS.				RATIO PER 1,000 OF POPULATION.				REMARKS.
										BIRTHS.		DEATHS.		
		Past year.	Present year.	Increase.	Decrease.	Past year.	Present year.	Increase.	Decrease.	Past year.	Present year.	Past year.	Present year.	
Tripura State ...	3,81,243	3,406	3,248	—	158	3.753	3,866	113	—	8·91	8·51	9·81	10·13	

* The figures show the number of births and deaths so far as registered.

XXIV.

Education Return (A)—Particulars as to the schools maintained during the year 1344 T.E.

Number of Schools.		Class of Schools.	Number of Pupils on the rolls on the last day of Chait.		Average Daily Attendance.		Remarks.
Past year	Present year.		Past year.	Present year.	Past year.	Present year.	
6	6	High English Schools ... ... (including one Branch H. E. School).	1,488	1,597	1,150·15	1,186·46	
9	9	Middle English Schools for boys ...	1,092	1,132	883·58	847·06	* In some of these schools boys and girls read together.
1	1	Middle English School for girls ...	77	68	62·81	59·16	
26	26	* Lower Vernacular Schools for boys	1,255	1,243	1,013·7	1,010·11	
76	76	*Pathsalas for boys	2,183	2,519	1,733·04	1,918·18	
9	9	Do for girls	319	329	240·11	248·70	
		Special Schools :—					
4	4	Compulsory Free Primary Schools	508	585	282·61	388·94	
7	5	Madrassas and Muktabs	235	178	183·60	135·88	
5	5	Sanskrit *Tols*	50	47	38·27	34·18	
1	1	Artisan School & Silpasram ...	22	28	10·25	11·75	[1] Excluding students of private Schools.
1	1	Jail Reformatory School	20	20	19·45	19·45	
Total 145	143		7,249	7,746[1]	5,617·57	5,859·87*	

XXV.

Education Return (B) Race of Students, 1344 T. E.

Names of Divisions.	No. of Schools.				No. of Students.					Race.												Average daily attendance.		REMARKS.
										Hindus.														
	For boys.	For girls.	Total.	Private schools.	Boys.	Girls.	Total.	Students of private schools.	Total.	Rajkumars.	Thakurs.	Manipuris.	Tripuras.	Bengalees.	Others.	Reangs.	Chakmas.	Kukis.	Lusais.	Musalmans.	Christians.	Boys.	Girls.	
1. Sadar Division ...	48	2	50	3	2,714	419	3,133	87	3,220	7	281	135	618	1,342	28	0	0	0	0	722	0	1,977·77	296·97	
2. Kailashahar "	23	3	26	18	1,085	179	1,264	516	1,780	0	1	314	15	671	1	0	0	0	0	262	0	819·67	132·29	
3. Sonamura "	19	1	20	2	866	78	944	81	1,025	0	3	1	64	246	0	0	0	0	0	630	0	682·04	56·73	
4. Bilonia "	8	1	9	4	621	51	672	116	788	0	1	1	27	419	3	0	0	0	0	221	0	501·81	30·25	
5. Khowai "	5	1	6	5	279	16	295	98	393	0	0	42	150	77	11	0	0	0	0	15	0	222·64	12·94	
6. Dharmanagar "	13	1	14	12	624	84	708	296	1,004	0	0	80	2	466	11	0	0	0	1	148	0	454·16	66·81	
7. Udaipur "	10	1	11	3	484	15	499	126	625	0	3	0	87	148	0	0	0	0	0	261	0	399·70	41·73	
8. Sabrum "	6	0	6	0	198	9	207	0	207	0	0	0	42	105	2	10	0	0	0	48	0	134·83	6·25	
9. Amarpur Sub-division ...	1	0	1	3	22	2	24	40	64	0	1	0	2	7	0	8	0	0	0	6	0	21·28	2·00	
TOTAL ...	133	10	143	50	6,893	853	7,746	1,360	9,106	7	290	573	1,007	3,481	56	18	0	0	1	2,313	0	5,213·90	645·97	

N. B.—In the Sub-columns under "Race" the number of students of private schools is not included.

APPENDIX XXVI. (A)

Statement of Audited Receipts for the year 1344 T. E.

State.

Heads of Revenue.	1343 T. E.		1344 T. E.		REMARKS.
	Revised Estimate.	Actuals.	Revised Estimate.	Actuals.	
1. Land Revenue ...	4,38,000	4,50,707	6,05,000	6,44,452	
2. Rents of markets ..	6,000	6,137	6,500	6,180	
3. Family tax in the hills	45,000	46,960	53,000	52,593	
4. Toll on Forest Produce	3,28,000	3,20,852	3,10,000	3,02,907	
5. Do on the Feni River	28,000	27,073	27,000	27,155	
6. Elephant and Buffalo grazing mehals ...	6,000	8,041	7,000	6,678	
7. Thatching grass mehals	8,300	2,858	3,000	2,906	
8. Reserved *Sal* trees ...	3,500	3,094	3,000	3,070	
9. Tax on cotton and Oil seeds ...	1,17,000	1,06,839	1,32,000	1,35,224	
10 Royalty on elephants caught ...	3,000	2,616	2,000	2,315	
11. *Adda* mehal ...	23,000	24,435	24,500	25,533	
12. Excise ...	48,000	41,654	43,000	42,901	
13. Stamps and Court fees	64,000	61,514	64,000	64,240	
14. Law and Justice (fines)	2,200	2,356	2,500	2,172	
15. Process Fees ...	10,500	10,154	11,000	10,396	
16. Registration ...	5,500	6,095	5,500	5,555	
17. Jail ...	5,000	4,770	2,500	2,237	
18. Cattle pounds ...	4,000	3,747	4,000	3,826	
19. *Nazars* ...	28,000	29,620	32,000	31,918	
20. School Fees ...	14,000	14,566	15,500	15,034	
21. Duty on Tea ...	11,000	12,580	24,000	27,723	
22. Duty on jute ...	31,000	31,964	28,000	27,112	
23. Personal *Howlats* recovered	—	—	—	—	
4. Miscellaneous ...	45,000	43,154	59,000	59,411	
25 Depreciation Contribution ...	81,000	77,224	81,000	78,071	
Toatl ...	13,50,000	13,39,810	15,45,000	15,79,009	
26. Deposits ...	1,87,000	2,14,494	2,64,182	2,63,746	
27. Contribution from Chakla ...	2,80,000	2,80,000	1,35,000	1,35,000	
28 Loan from Government	9,00,000	9,00,000	—	—	
Total ...	27,17,000	27,34,304	19,44,182	19,78,355	
Opening Balance :— Cash ...	1,56,879	1,44,444	1,88,197	1,88,197	
Advances ...	2,45,632	2,46,408	1,73,407	1,73,407	
Loans ...	2,74,982	2,75,231	2,75,428	2,75,428	
Working Balance ...	—	—	4,15,182	4,15,182	
Total ...	6,77,493	6,66,083	10,52,214	10,52,214	
Grand Total ...	33,94,493	34,00,387	29,96,396	30,30,569	

APPENDIX XXVI. (B)

Statement of Audited Expenditure for the year 1344 T. E.

State.

Heads of Expenditure.	1343 T. E.		1344 T. E.		REMARKS.
	Revised estimate.	Actuals.	Revised Estimate.	Actuals.	
1. Controlling Charges	86,196	84,862	82,874	82,216	
2. Revenue General ...	99,750	88,886	80,366	78,441	
3. Survey & Settlement	37,315	36,545	20,242	20,119	
4. Tahasil ...	47,650	46,007	49,602	47,739	
5. Registration ...	3,832	3,574	3,946	3,555	
6. Police ...	87,690	86,836	88,786	87,340	
7. Judicial ...	33,335	32,056	35,511	33,992	
8. Jail ...	23,733	23,364	26,558	26,321	
9. Forest ...	47,973	46,159	48,328	46,436	
10. Medical ...	65,899	65,329	68,932	67,638	
11. Municipality ...	8,000	8,000	9,000	9,000	
12. Education General ...	1,30,798	1,25,021	1,26,237	1,23,867	
13. (a) Public Works ...	93,454	92,498	1,01,000	1,00,820	
(b) Improvement ...	72,250	71,841	1,07,000	1,04,519	
14. Electric Light ...	16,332	15,002	16,452	16,299	
15. Small Donations ...	325	318	300	288	
15. Relief to distressed subjects ...	300	282	300	—	
17. Purchase of Landed Property ...	10,260	10,021	7,000	6,845	
18. Repayment of Deposits ...	60,000	59,311	83,500	77,171	
19. Interest on Deposits	30,000	28,848	30,000	29,339	
20. Unforeseen charges...	7,500	7,263	7,000	6,644	
21. Pension ...	49,500	49,465	52,000	51,508	
22. Chief Secretary's Office & H. H.'s Tour	1,42,724	1,41,747	1,58,618	1,57,650	
23. Palace Sultanat ...	45,813	45,714	36,127	36,095	
24. Zoo ...	3,769	3,769	3,094	3,094	
25. Agriculture, Commerce and Industries	8,165	7,929	8,117	7,859	
26. Publicity, Reclamation & Immigration ...	3,030	2,843	9,028	6,965	
27. H. H.'s Private Secretary's Office ...	8,900	8,866	9,284	9,171	
28. Rajmala Office ...	5,200	4,435	4,000	3,520	
29. Military Secretary's Office ...	3,240	3,220	3,480	3,460	
30. Military ...	1,18,222	1,06,626	1,13,222	1,01,039	
31. Nijtahabil ...	1,00,000	1,00,000	1,00,000	1,00,000	
32. Adjustment of irrecoverable advances...	940	924	10,000	5,577	
33. Census ...	500	370	—	—	
34. Repayment of old Debts ...	5,50,000	4,84,818	96,500	96,439	
35. Sansar Charges ...	4,18,849	4,16,619	3,86,865	3,86,015	
36. Expenditure for the treatment of Maharaj Kumari Basanta Prava ...	32,919	32,500	—	—	
37. H. H.'s special donation .	5,000	5,000	—	—	
38. Sanitation ...	1,400	1,305	1,500	629	
Total ...	24,60,763	23,48,173	19,34,799	19,37,610	
Closing balance :—					
Cash ...	1,05,000	1,88,197	1,02,000	1,88,879	
Advances ...	2,03,061	1,73,407	2,17,415	2,10,799	
Loans issued ...	2,75,669	2,75,428	2,77,000	2,78,099	
Working balance ...	3,50,000	4,15,182	4,15,182	* 4,15,182	* Cash— 2,25,000 Advance—1,90,182
Total ...	9,33,730	10,52,214	10,11,597	10,92,959	
Grand Total ...	33,94,493	34,00,387	29,96,396	30,30,569	

APPENDIX XXVII. (A)

Statement of Audited Receipts for the year 1344 T. E.

Chakla Roshnabad Estates.

Heads of Receipts.	1343 T. E.		1344 T. E.		Remarks.
	Revised Estimate.	Actuals.	Revised Estimate.	Actuals.	
1. Rent and Cess ...	8,38,000	8,88,198	8,79,000	9,66,610	
2. Cess for Rent free holdings ...	8,000	8,217	6,500	8,483	
3. Law charges recovered	54,000	38,576	47,000	46,963	
4. Miscellaneous receipts including deposits ...	94,000	46,911	69,707	54,985	
5. Refund of loans and advances ...	1,000	987	1,000	1,176	
Total ...	9,95,000	9,82,889	10,03,207	10,78,217	
Opening Balance :—					
Cash ...	98,936	97,853	1,04,342	1,04,342	
Advance ...	1,05,000	1,11,259	1,15,477	1,15,477	
Loans issued ...	73,057	80,435	78,859	78,859	
Bank deposits ...	31,331	49,651	51,542	51,542	
Total ...	3,08,324	3,39,198	3,50,220	3,50,220	
Grand Total ...	13,03,324	13,22,087	13,53,427	14,28,437	

APPENDIX XXVII. (B)

Statement of Audited Expenditure for the year 1344 T. E.

Chakla Roshnabad Estates.

Heads of Expenditure.	1343 T. E. Revised Estimate.	1343 T. E. Actuals.	1344 T. E. Revised Estimate.	1344 T. E. Actuals.	Remarks.
i 1. Revenue and Cess ...	2,95,835	2,88,830	2,86,835	2,85,540	
2. Establishment ...	1,44,523	1,38,759	1,42,189	1,42,169	
3. Settlement ...	1,440	1,188	1,203	916	
4. Legal Expenses ...	1,17,899	1,17,193	1,37,314	1,36,800	
5. Education ...	9,354	8,962	9,318	9,075	
6. Medical ...	12,864	11,737	12,310	11,469	
7. Public Works ...	61,200	60,335	51,064	50,996	
8. Religious Expenses	6,800	6,339	6,800	6,111	
9. Miscellaneous ...	6,000	5,629	5,000	3,615	
10. Loans and Advances	1,000	600	1,000	999	
11. Pension and Gratuity	10,500	9,980	11,000	10,915	
12. Forest ...	700	599	700	576	
13. Purchase of property	2,000	1,374	7,000	6,573	
14. Unforeseen ...	1,000	671	7,200	7,109	
ii. Sansar ...	12,960	12,960	12,960	12,960	
iii. Donation ...	6,750	6,746	7,050	7,046	
iv. State Contribution	2,80,000	2,80,000	1,35,000	1,35,000	
v. Repayment of debts etc ...	20,000	19,965	31,000	30,066	
vi. Advance to Niz Tahabil ...	—	—	1,87,000	1,87,000	
Total ...	9,90,825	9,71,867	10,51,943	10,44,935	
Closing Balance :— Cash ...	1,02,719	1,04,842	55,606	1,11,086	
Advances ...	1,04,780	1,15,477	1,10,200	1,14,873	
Loans issued ...	73,000	78,859	35,678	71,050	
Bank deposits ...	32,000	51,542	50,000	86,493	
Total ...	3,12,499	3,50,220	3,01,484	3,83,502	
Grand Total ...	13,03,324	13,22,087	13,53,427	14,28,437	

MINISTER'S OFFICE,
TRIPURA STATE,
POLITICAL DEPARTMENT.

To

His Highness The Bisama-Samara-Bijayee Mahamahodaya
Pancha-Srijukta Maharaja Manikya
SIR BIR BIKRAM KISHORE
DEV BARMAN BAHADUR, K. C. S. I.,
Maharaja of Tripura.

Dated, Agartala, the 9th December, 1936.

MAY IT PLEASE YOUR HIGHNESS,

I have the honour to submit the accompanying Report on the General Administration of the State and the attached Zemindaries for the year 1345 T. E., extending from the 14th April, 1935 to the 13th April, 1936.

The reports on the administration of the Military Department as well as of the Departments of Agriculture, Commerce and Industries and Immigration under the control of the Chief Secretary to Your Highness, have been incorporated in the Report.

I have the honour to be
Your Highness's most obedient servant,
Jyotis Chandra Sen,
MINISTER.

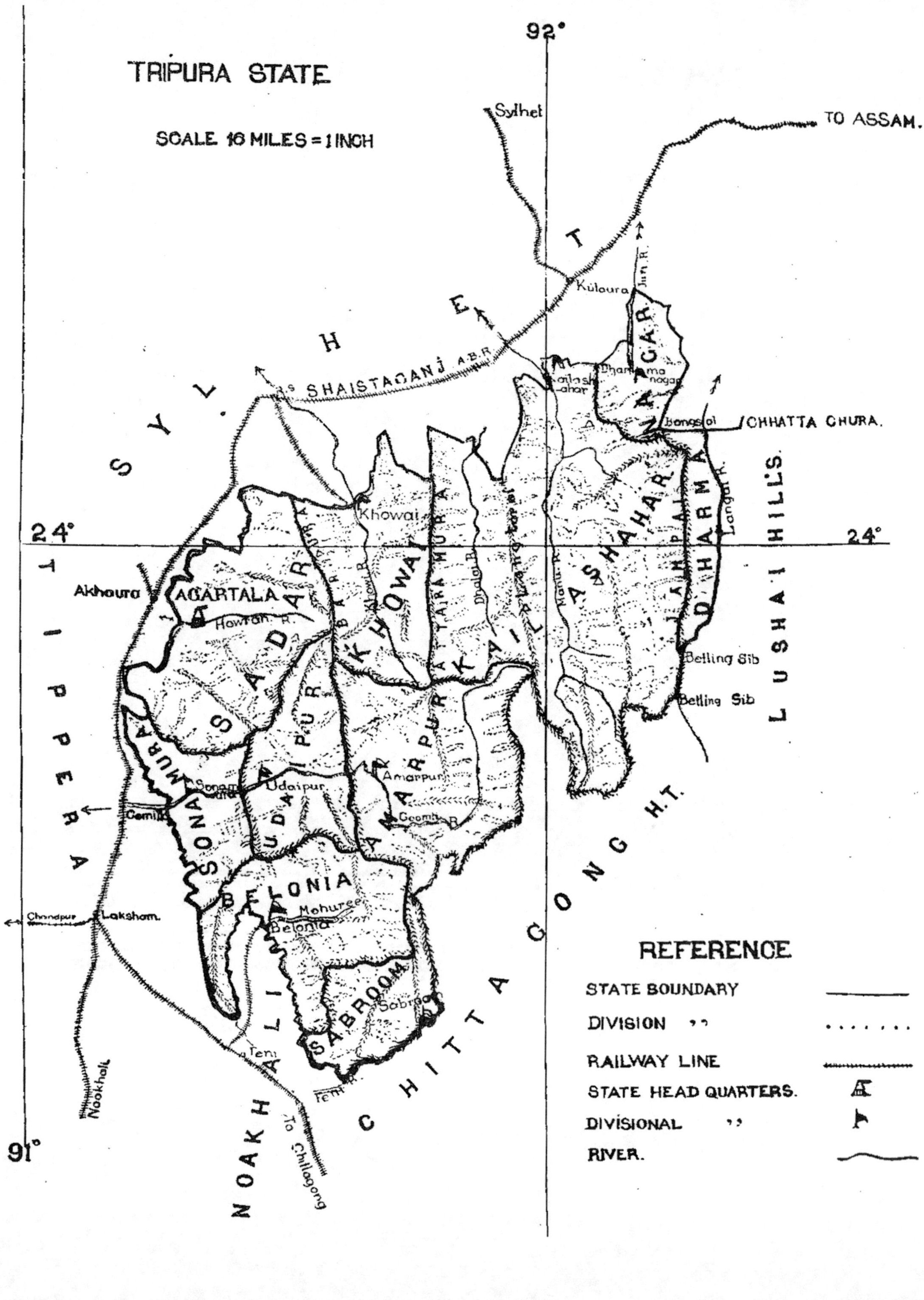

TRIPURA STATE
SCALE 16 MILES = 1 INCH
92°
24°
24°
91°
Sylhet
TO ASSAM.
SYLHET
SHAISTAGANJ
A.B.R.
Kuloura
Juri R.
Dharma nagar
Kailash ahar
Bongsol
CHHATTA CHURA.
LUSHAI HILLS
Langai R.
Khowai
Akhoura
AGARTALA
Howrah R.
SADAR
KHOWAI
KAILASAHAR
DHARMA NAGAR
Manu R.
Dhalai R.
Belling Sib
TIPPERA
Sonamura
SONAMURA
Udaipur
UDAIPUR
Amarpur
AMARPUR
Goomti R.
Comilla
BELONIA
Belonia
Mohuree
Chandpur
Laksham.
SABROOM
Sabroom
Feni
Feni R.
Nookhali
NOAKHALI
To Chittagong
CHITTAGONG H.T.
REFERENCE
STATE BOUNDARY
DIVISION ,,
RAILWAY LINE
STATE HEAD QUARTERS.
DIVISIONAL ,,
RIVER.

Book Twenty-seven

Report on the Administration of the Tripura State for 1345 T. E. (1935-1936 A.D.)

REPORT ON THE ADMINISTRATION

OF

THE TRIPURA STATE

FOR

1345 T. E. (1935-36.)

CHAPTER I—GENERAL AND POLITICAL.

Area of the State—4,116 sq. miles.
Population—3,82,450.
Gross Revenue (based on the average of five years) :—

(*a*) State	Rs. 20,98,129.
(*b*) Zemindaries	Rs. 10,18,357.

Tribute—Nil.

Ruler of the State—His Highness The Bisama-Samara-Bijayee Mahamahodaya Pancha-Srijukta Maharaja Manikya Sir Bir Bikramkishore Dev Barman Bahadur, K. C. S. I. *Age*—28 years. (Born—19th August, 1908). *Caste*—*Kshatriya* (of the Lunar race).

The year and the people.

During the year under review there was a further relaxation of the economic strain which had been such a prominent feature of the preceding years. The tide appears to have turned at last, and it is noticeable that the level of prices as well as the out-turn of most of the indigenous crops have been slowly but steadily rising in the State, with an appreciable alleviation of the conditions of the people, both in the hills and the plains, the cultivating classes, as might be expected, coming in, to a marked extent, for their legitimate share in the general improvement ; while there is also in evidence in the Zemindaries attached to the State, a similar lifting of the strain and a conspicuous advance in the economic situation.

2. The rainfall of the year was more than twelve inches below the total for the preceding year and was unevenly distributed. Kailasahar had the maximum fall of 110 inches, and the minimum *viz* 47 inches, was that of Belonia, where there was, besides, a serious outbreak of rinderpest, during the year, which brought on heavy cattle mortality. Harvesting, however, was generally satisfactory all round, and in this Bilonia proved no exception.

3. There was some rise in the price of food grains throughout the State and the condition of the middle classes continued to be as it was in the previous year.

The finances of the year.

4. The year opened with a balance of Rs. 14,76,461 against Rs. 14,02,434 in the year before. The total revenue from permanent sources was Rs. 16,96,043 against Rs. 15,79,609 in the preceding year in the State, and Rs. 11,07,653 against Rs. 9,87,261 in the Zemindaries. With deposits, the total receipts from all sources came to Rs. 30,55,435 against Rs. 29,21,572 the total sum available for expenditure being thus Rs. 45,31,896 as against Rs. 43,24,006 in the preceding year. The results of land revenue collection were encouraging, and the increase in the duty on cotton and oilseeds was satisfactory.

II.

5. Their Highnesses the Maharaja Manikya Bahadur and the Maharani Saheba returned to Agartala from Calcutta, where they had been staying for sometime, on the 15th Baisakh and remained at the Capital till the month of Jaistha.

6. On the occasion of His Imperial Majesty the King Emperor's Birthday in June, 1935, His Highness the Maharaja Manikya Bahadur was appointed to be a Knight Commander of the Most Exalted Order of the Star of India. The announcement was received with joyous acclamation throughout the State and public meetings were held at the Capital under the Presidency of Maharajkumar Brajendrakishore Deb Barman Bahadur and at Divisional headquarters in the interior at which congratulatory resolutions were passed and conveyed to His Highness.

Visit to Shillong.

7. The hot weather of the year under report was spent by Their Highnesses at Shillong. On the 19th July Their Highnesses the Maharaja Manikya Bahadur, and the Maharani Saheba, the Baby Princes and party left Agartala for Shillong via Sylhet and reached there the next day. On arrival at Sylhet Their Highnesses were received and cheered by thousands of people who assembled at the river ghat to have their '*Dursan*'.

Visit to Mussoorie.

8. During the stay at Shillong His Highness paid a flying visit to Mussoorie for the purpose of meeting his sister—the late Maharajkumari Basantaprava Devi, Yubarani Saheba of Kotla on the eve of her departure for Switzerland. Leaving Shillong on the 8th August, His Highness arrived at Calcutta next day and stopping there for one day, started for Mussoorie arriving there on the 13th August. His Highness stayed at Mussoorie at the Savoy Hotel for 4 days and returned to Shillong on the 19th idem.

9. At Shillong His Highness gave a Dinner party at Pinewood Hotel in which His Excellency the Acting Governor of Assam, Lady Laine, some of the Executive Councillors and Ministers of the Province and other leading people of the place participated.

10. On the eve of their departure for Agartala, His Highness with Her Highness the Maharani Saheba went on pilgrimage to the holy shrine of Kamakhya Devi on the 16th September.

Visit to Kamakhya Devi's Temple.

11. Their Highnesses returned to Agartala on the 20th September (3rd Asvin) by the Shillong–Sylhet route.

12. His Highness the Maharaja Manikya Bahadur accompanied by Her Highness left for Calcutta on the 18th of Agrahayan (4th December) and arrived there the following evening.

13. On being invited by the Khairagarh Durbar, His Highness with staff, left Howrah by Bombay mail on the 8th December to attend the Investiture Ceremony of the Raja Bahadur of Khairagarh which was fixed for the 10th December and arrived at Khairagarh the next afternoon.

Visit to Khairagarh, C. P.

14. On arrival at the Guest House at Khairagarh His Highness the Maharaja Manikya Bahadur was received with a Guard-of-Honour and a salute of 13 guns was fired. During the stay at Khairagarh His Highness graced all functions relating to the Investiture Ceremony by his presence and wherever he went he was accorded a hearty reception by the Ruler and people alike.

15. His Highness returned to Calcutta on the 12th December from Khairagarh.

16. In Calcutta His Highness had private interviews as usual, with Their Excellencies the Viceroy and His Excellency the Governor of Bengal on the 18th and 19th December respectively.

17. On the 21st December a party was given at Tripura House by His Highness to meet Their Excellencies the Viceroy and the Countess of Willingdon at which many distinguished ladies and gentlemen including Their Highnesses the Dowager Maharani Saheba, Maharaja Bhup Bahadur of Cooch Behar, and the Jubraj Saheb of Patiala were present.

Party at Tripura House to meet the Viceroy.

18. On the 7th of January, 1936, His Highness gave a Dinner Party at Tripura House to meet His Excellency the Governor of Bengal. Many higher officials of the Government and also leading gentlemen of the City participated in the Dinner.

Dinner Party to meet the Governor.

19. His Highness attended functions both at the Viceroy's and Government Houses as usual. Besides these he also performed some public functions as noted below :—

Public functions in Calcutta.

(i) presiding over the prize distribution ceremony of the Central Badminton Club on the 16th December,

(ii) presiding over the 5th Memorial anniversary of Srila Jagabandhu Bhattacharjee at Sri Gaudiya Math on the 23rd December, and

(iii) presiding over the Opening Ceremony of the new Vaidya Shastra Pith Hospital Building on the 5th January, 1936, of which he himself had laid the foundation stone a few years ago.

20. During the season the Raja Saheb of Khairagarh, the Raja Bahadur and Jubraj Saheb of Sakti, the Jubraj Saheb and Maharajkumar Pushpendra Singhjee of Panna, General Rana Parakram Jung Bahadur, Major Rana Jodha Jung Bahadur, Rajkumar Gajendra Pal Singhjee came to stay at Tripura House with His Highness as his guests.

Distinguished guests at Tripura House.

21. His Highness the Mahendra Maharaja Saheb of Panna, Raja Saheb of Nilgiri and the Jubraj Saheb of Patiala came to dine with His Highness at Tripura House on the 22nd December.

22. Maharaja Srish Chandra Nundy Bahadur of Cossimbazar and Raja Bhupendra Narain Singh Bahadur of Nashipur had Tea at Tripura House on the 6th January, 1936.

23. Their Highnesses the Maharaja Manikya Bahadur and the Maharani Saheba left Calcutta for Panna on the 9th January, 1936 and arrived at the latter place on the following day where he stayed for sometime.

Visit to Panna.

24. During his stay at Panna, His Highness with a few of his staff, went to Allahabad on the 13th January for the "*Makar Sankrant Snan*" where he honoured General Rana Parakram Jung Bahadur by staying with him at Phapamow Castle.

Visit to Allahabad.

25. His Highness returned to Panna on the 16th January and after a few more days' rest there, returned with Her Highness to Calcutta and thence to Agartala on the 14th February, 1936, corresponding to the 1st of Falgoon, 1345 T. E.

Return to Agartala.

26. His Highness remained at the Capital for about a month and a half, when, on the 26th February, he again left for Delhi being invited to the Investiture Ceremony to receive the insignia associated with his new distinction of the order of K. C. S. I.

27. His Highness stopped enroute in Calcutta to grace by his presence the marriage ceremony of Kumari Bhaktiprova Devi, daughter of Manyabara Rana Bodhjung Bahadur with Rajkumar Ananta Protap Singh Deo of Dharakote (Ganjam) which was performed on the 29th of February.

28. Leaving Howrah on the 3rd March His Highness reached Delhi on the 4th idem and stopped at the Maiden's Hotel.

Visit to Delhi.

29. At the Investiture Durbar at the Viceroy's House on the 7th March, His Highness received the Star and Badge of the order of K. C. S. I. from His Excellency the Viceroy. He also had lunch with Their Excellencies and left Delhi the same afternoon, arriving in Calcutta on the 9th and after a few days' rest there, returned to Agartala on the 15th of March.

30. At the end of the year under review, Their Highnesses the Maharaja Manikya Bahadur and the Maharani Saheba paid a short private visit to Mainamati, near Comilla. Their Highnesses left Agartala on the 6th and returned on the 12th of April (30th Chait). The outward journey was covered by motor car via Sonamura along the new road passing by Rudijala Lake.

Visit to Mainamati.

31. A very sad event of the year that overtook the Royal Family nay the whole State, was the premature death following a brief illness of the 2nd Maharajkumar Pradeep Bikram Kisore Dev Varman Bahadur at Tripura House, Calcutta, at 10–15 P. M. on the 28th of December, 1935. All offices and other Institutions of the State and the Zemindaries were closed for half a day as a mark of respect to the memory of our beloved Baby Prince who passed away at the age of 10 months only.

Death of Maharajkumar Pradeep Bikram Kisore Dev Varma Bahadur.

III

32. A very notable and important happy event of the year was Their Majesties' Silver Jubilee which was celebrated throughout the State with great eclat.

Royal Silver Jubilee.

33. 6th, 7th and 8th of May, 1935, were through a notification in an Extraordinary issue of the State Gazette declared public holidays on account of this happy and memorable occasion. With the dawn of 6th May a Royal Salute of 31 guns was fired announcing the auspicious day on which His Imperial Majesty began his glorious reign, 25 years ago. Police and Military parades were held on the Military grounds. Prayers were offered in places of worship for the long life and ever prosperous reign of Their Imperial Majesties.

34. At a meeting convened under the auspices of the Chairman of the Agartala Municipality the citizens of Agartala assembled and passed resolutions recording its heartfelt joy and thankfulness on the completion of the 25th year of Their Majesties' glorious reign and assuring Their Majesties of their respectful loyalty and devotion to Their Majesties' throne and persons.

35. The teachers, students and their guardians also assembled in a meeting to express their heartfelt joy and to pray for the long, peaceful and glorious reign of Their Majesties on this occasion and passed suitable resolutions.

36. A Grand Durbar was held at the Ujjayanta Palace at 8 P. M. on the 7th of May at the end of which there was a fireworks display befitting the occasion. The whole town wore a gala appearance by the successive two evenings' illumination. Some 5,000 poor were sumptuously fed and sweets were distributed among boys and girls of the various schools of the State. There was a garden party in which princes, officers and other elite of the town took part.

37. His Highness the Maharaja Manikya Bahadur sent the following cable to His Majesty the King Emperor :—

"I beg to send my loyal and sincere felicitations on this auspicious and memorable occasion of Your Majesties' Silver Jubilee. May Providence shower choicest blessings on both of Your Majesties and grant long life and prosperous reign", to which the following reply was received by His Highness from His Majesty.

"It has given me much pleasure to receive your congratulations and good wishes on my Silver Jubilee for which I wish to express my sincere thanks".

38. The entire State was plunged in grief on receipt of an intimation on the 21st January, 1936, of the most lamentable untimely death of His Most Gracious Majesty King George V. State Proclamation was issued immediately closing all offices and other institutions of the State and the Zemindaries for three days. Members of the Ruling family, officers and the public assembled in a meeting and passed resolutions expressing their deep sense of grief at the sad demise of His late Most Gracious Majesty King George V and Emperor of India and offering their condolence to and sympathy with the bereaved Royal family and offering sincere prayers for the enternal peace of the great departed soul and joining with the rest of the Empire in mourning. 70 minute guns were fired and alms distributed among the poor.

Demise of His Most Gracious Majesty King George V.

39. A notification was issued through an Extraordinary issue of the State Gazette on the 26th January, 1936 closing all the offices and other institutions of the State for one day on account of the funeral day. Prayers were offered in all places of public worship.

40. On receipt of an announcement of the accession of His Most Gracious Majesty King Edward VIII State Proclamation was issued through an Extraordinary issue of the State Gazette.

His Most Gracious Majesty King Edward the Eighth's accession to the throne.

41. A Durbar was held at the head of the Grand Stair-case of the Ujjayanta Palace with all the Durbaris, Sardars and the officials of the State at which the Proclamation of the accession was read out.

42. A sum of Rs. 27,229 was announced to be the allotment for the year 1935–36 as the State's share of the Excise duty on matches.

State's share in Excise duty on Matches.

43. The second instalment of Rs. 92,666 due on 21st September, 1935, towards the repayment of loan of Rs. 9, lacs was duly paid to the Accountant-General, Bengal, through the Lloyds Bank, Calcutta.

Repayment of loans from Government.

44. Mr. E. W. Holland, I. C. S., District Magistrate of Tipperah continued to be the Political Agent (Ex-officio) till 9th March, 1936, when Mr. S. N. Ray, I. C. S. took over charge of the office of the Political Agent on the afternoon of the same date.

Political Agent.

45. Rai J. C. Sen Bahadur, B. A., B. C. S. (Retd.) continued as Minister who was also the Manager of the Chakla Roshnabad Estates. He was out on tour for 47 days.

Minister.

CHAPTER II—LAND ADMINISTRATION.

46. Thakur K. K. Singh, Naib Dewan, continued to be in charge of the Revenue & General Departments.

Charge.

47. As shown in the subjoined statement, the total area under settlement and borne on the *toujis* at the close of the year was 621 sq. miles as against 630 sq. miles in the previous year.

Area held under settlement.

Kinds of settlement.	Area in square miles.		Increase.	Decrease.	REMARKS.
	1345 T.E.	1344 T.E.			
Jotes ...	324	328	—	4	
Taluks ...	297	302	—	5	
Total ...	621	630	—	9	

48. Permission was granted by the Durbar to open a tea garden in *Taluki* land in Sadar Division comprising 157 *drones* after realisation of Rs. 1,300 as *Nazar* and Rs. 400 as penalty for cultivating tea without obtaining previous permission of the Durbar. Two other cases of resettlement of *Khas* purchased gardens were in progress at the end of the year.

Tea Settlement.

49. Several petitions for relinquishment of portions of tea garden lands were pending from the year previous and relinquishment of 223 *drones* of land was accepted in one case during the year.

Tea Industry.

50. The Durbar has been continuing the policy of giving relief to the proprietors of tea gardens by way of granting remission of interest and easy instalments for payment of revenues and other State dues. Tea gardens of this State have not been permitted to extend cultivation since the inauguration of the restriction scheme. As the tea industry in the State is still in its infancy, the urgency of extension of plantation is keenly felt by the gardens concerned and the Durbar evinced its anxiety and interest in representing the case to the Government of India without success. They have however given the Durbar assurance that consideration of the special circumstances for an extension of tea area in Tripura State will be made if the tea restriction scheme is extended beyond March 1938.

51. With a view to control the cultivation and export of tea in and from the State the Durbar have passed the Tripura Tea Control Act No. 1 of 1345 T. E.

52. The Indian Tea Licensing Committee has been appointed Licensing Authority of the State until further orders. A joint inspection of State gardens by the nominees of the Indian Tea Licensing Comittee and the Durbar has been agreed to during the latter part of the year under review.

53. The current demand from the tea grants amounted to about Rs. 64,000. The total realisation from them was Rs. 1,04,061 including Rs. 38,990 on account of current demand.

54. Both the outturn and export of tea increased during the year under review.

55. The arrear demand up to the end of 1345 T. E. still amounts to about two *lakhs*.

56. The average *jama* per *kani* of *jote* lands in *khash mehals* (exclusive of cesses) stood at Rupee 1 and 4 pies against 1 Rupee, 1 anna and 3 pies in the previous year. The maximum rate for *jote* was Rs. 25 per *kani* while the minimum was 3 annas and those for *taluks* Rs. 3 and annas 1–9 p. respectively. For *Takshishi Taluks* in Agartala town the maximum rate was Rs. 70 per *kani*.

Rates of *Jama*.

57. The different sources of land revenue demand with the collection under each head are detailed below :—

Sources of Land Revenue.

Sources.	Current demand.		Arrear demand up to the end of		Realization up to the end of		REMARKS.
	1345 T.E.	1344 T.E.	1344 T.E.	1343 T.E.	1345 T.E.	1344 T.E.	
Taluks ...	1,58,493	1,62,675	4,00,804	4,52,368	1,98,972	1,97,877	
Khas Mehal jotes	5,31,756	5,36,255	19,00,953	17,72,543	4,10,818	4,02,891	
Bazars ...	8,293	6,414	4,079	3,781	6,534	6,052	
Cesses ...	43,554	43,896	1,55,903	1,50,011	35,767	36,771	
Total ...	7,42,096	7,49,240	24,61,739	23,78,703	6,52,091	6,43,591	

58. The above statement shows that the current demand under all heads was Rs. 7,42,096 and with the arrear demand of Rs. 24,61,739 the total demand of the year was Rs. 32,03,835 against Rs. 31,27,943 in the previous year.

Demand.

59. The total collection in round figures under all heads during the year amounted to Rs. 6,52,091 being Rs. 2,02,157 under current and Rs. 4,49,934 under arrear, as against the total collection of 6,43,591 in the previous year. The percentage of current collection was 27·24 against 26·83 and that of the arrears 18·27 against 18·6. In the *khas mehal*, the percentage of current collection was 12·18 against 11·08 and in *taluki mehal* the percentage was 76·21 against 77·24 in the previous year. The percentage of collection on the whole was not satisfactory.

Collection

60. Altogether 6,391 certificate cases covering a demand of Rs. 3,49,150 were instituted during the year. With 5,672 cases valued at Rs. 6,82,643 pending from the previous year, the total number of cases awaiting final orders on disposal of preliminary notices issued on debtors was 12,063 covering a total demand of Rs. 10,31,793. Of these, 30 cases with a demand of Rs. 12,385 were rejected or struck off and Rs. 8,096 in 816 cases with a total value of Rs. 7,52,825 remained pending at the end of the year.

Coercive measures—Certificates.

61. Orders under the provisions of the State Certificate Act were passed during the year in 5,594 cases with a total value of Rs. 2,58,487 making the demand absolute.

Execution.

62. With 13,874 cases to the value of Rs. 8,39,601 pending in execution from the previous year, the total number of cases dealt with was 19,468 covering a demand of Rs. 10,98,088. Out of the total

demand Rs. 14,470 was remitted or written off and of the remainder Rs. 1,49,678 was actually realised leaving a balance of Rs. 9,33,940. Of the amount realised Rs. 1,36,777 represents land revenue and Rs. 12,901 miscellaneous demands. In view of the accumulation of the arrear demand strict measures appear to be called for. In Sonamura Division 1 debtor was confined in jail for 3 months but nothing could however be realized from him.

Operation of the Sunset law.

63. The number of defaulting *taluks* brought under the operation of the Sunset law (including 40 pending from the previous year) was 129. Of these 69 were released on payment of dues with penalty while 17 were sold by auction and 43 remained undisposed of at the close of the year.

Survey.

64. The results of the survey (including resurvey) operations are given in the statement below. It will be seen that an area of 2958 *drones* comprising 948 *drones* of Taluk and 2010 *drones* of *Khas mahal* was surveyed as against a total of 3987 *drones* in the previous year.

Names of Divisions.	Quantity of land in *drones* surveyed in 1345 T. E.			Quantity of land in *drones* surveyed in 1344 T. E.			REMARKS.
	Taluki land.	*Khas mehal* land.	Total.	*Taluki* land.	*Khas mehal* land.	Total.	
1. Sadar Division ...	948	467	1,415	—	236	236	
2. Kailashahar ,, ...	—	42	42	—	25	25	
3. Sonamura ,, ...	—	91	91	32	86	118	
4. Bilonia ,, ...	—	509	509	—	1,259	1,259	
5. Khowai ,, ...	—	318	318	—	721	721	
6. Dharmanagar ,, ...	—	138	138	—	867	867	
7. Udaipur ,, ...	—	296	296	—	195	195	
8. Sabroom ,, ...	—	149	149	—	566	566	
9. Amarpur Sub ,, ...	—	—	—	—	—	—	
TOTAL ...	948	2,010	2,958	32	3,955	3,987	

Map Compilation.

65. This work continued under the direction of Babu Kamini Kumar Kar, Superintendent of Surveys. Compilation of *Mouzmil* maps of the Divisions on a scale of one inch to the mile from the Revenue survey maps of villages and *Taluks* was in progress.

66. Maps of twelve villages were reduced to one inch scale and compiled in the *Mouzmil* and five maps of villages out of 30 reduced maps remaining uncompiled were also compiled this year.

67. The Divisional maps were also corrected following above additions. Three copies of *mouzmil* maps for distribution to the Divisions and 14 copies of State map showing positions of Excise shops were traced.

68. Four case maps in connection with the boundary disputes along the British border lines were prepared and 20 copies of them were traced.

69. Three maps of boundary and connected award, 28 maps of *khash* villages and *Taluks*, and 17 other maps were traced, and the area

of two maps checked with Planimeter by the same staff. The total expenditure incurred was Rs. 101-1-0 only.

70. The No. 12 Survey party, Government of India, completed their survey operation within the State this year. The boundary dispute regarding the trijunction point on the Longai river between the District Sylhet, Lushai Hills and this State is under enquiry. The Superintendent of Surveys has selected a peak after re-connoitering in the Longai valley which almost agrees with the description of features mentioned in the report of Mr. Jones in 1865 and the matter is now under correspondence. The boundary disputes regarding the course and the source of the Feni river are also under correspondence.

71. Pucca pillars have been erected on some temporary marks left on the watershed line during the Topographical survey operation between the Myani Head water Reserve forest and the Gumti valley ; and Thakur Kshirode Lal Deb Barman, Surveyor, attended the erection of pillars by a British Sub-Surveyor at the selected sites.

72. The Superintendent of Surveys was on tour for 82 days. He attended a conference at Shillong about Excise matters and discussion with the Chief Secretary, Assam about the disputed site of Bongsul pillar. He toured to find out a more suitable site of Bongsul peak as agreed upon by both parties in the discussion and to enquire about the boundary of some *Taluk*s within the State.

Settlement.

73. There was *Taskhichi taluki* settlement of an area of 50 *drones* of waste land. It will be seen that settlement operations in respect of 4,358 *drones* of *jote* lands were completed against 1,156 *drones* in the previous year.

Nature of Settlement.	1345 T. E.		1344 T. E.		REMARKS.
	Area in *drones.*	*Jama* in whole rupees.	Area in *drones.*	*Jama* in whole rupees.	
1. Permanent *taluki* settlement of cultivated land ...	—	—	—	—	
2. Permanent *taluki* settlement of waste land ...	—	—	—	—	
3. *Taskhichi taluki* settlement of cultivated land ...	3 *kanis* & 9 *gandas*	91	—	—	
4. *Taskhichi taluki* settlement of waste land ...	50	400	90	722	
5. *Jotedari* re-settlement of cultivated land	4,125	44,265	1,093	13,506	
6. *Jotedari* settlement of waste land	233	2,171	63	1,167	
TOTAL ...	4,408	46,927	1,246	15,395	

Taluki Settlement.

74. There was a *Taskhichi* settlement of 50 *drones* of waste land in Kailashahar Division. The lessee wants to undertake sugarcane cultivation on the grant as a new industrial enterprise in the State.

75. A *Selami* of Rs. 400 was realised in this case. *Tashkhichi* settlement of 3½ *kanis* of *Bazar* land in the capital with the original owners was concluded during the year but no *selami* was realised.

Resettlement of *Jote* land.

76. A net increase of Rs. 13,074 in *jama* was secured by resettlement of *abadi jote* land, the *Nazarana* being Rs. 37,228. The average *jama* per *kani* was 10 annas 8 pies against 12 annas 9 pies in the previous year.

Jotedari settlement of waste land.

77. During the year an area of 233 *drones* of waste land was settled for a prospective rental of Rs. 2,171 the average *jama* per *kani* obtained being 9 annas 3 pies against Rs. 1-2-6 pies in the previous year. The maximum and minimum rates were Rs. 2-4 and 4 annas respectively. The *Nazarana* realized was Rs. 2,311, the rent-free period allowed, ranging from 1 to 3 years.

Settlement work.

78. No whole time settlement officer was employed in any Division but the Divisional Officers and Second Officers were entrusted with the settlement work within their respective jurisdictions. The total expenditure in the settlement operations was Rs. 3,169.

79. It will be seen that the *Nazarana* obtained and obtainable by settlement of *abadi jote land* and settlement of waste land as *jotes* amounted to Rs. 39,539 (Rs. 37,228 + Rs. 2,311).

Private Estates under State management.

80. As detailed below, there were altogether 17 private Estates under State management during the year under report.

Class.	Name of Estate.	Area.	Revenue.
Encumbered	1. Kakrabon Estate	283 *drones*.	1,871
	2. Jogendranagar Trust Estate	64 ,,	163
	3. Kamalnagar and Mahendranagar Estate	51 ,,	255
	4. Gouranga Tripura's Estate	13 ,,	57
	5. Maharam Ali Chaudhuri Khanje Khan Bahadur's Estate—*Taluk*	236 ,,	1,230
	Jote	6 ,,	149
	6. Thakur Nalini Mohan Deb Barma's Estate	68 ,,	170
	7. Brajendra Kumar Das's Estate	408 ,,	1,936
	8. Brajapur Estate (Kamala Kanta Deb Barman and others)	246 ,,	982
	9. Kalimulla's Estate	124 ,,	863
	10. Mahammadali Chaudhuri's Estate	24 ,,	76
Unencumbered	11. Prabhu Goswamis' Estate	31 ..	61
	12. Dowager Maharanee's Estate	169	765
	13. Late Girish Chandra Chaudhuri's Estate	36 ,,	254
	14. Late Brajakumar Thakur's Estate	47 ..	297
	15. Late Naba Kumar Chakrabarty's Estate—*Taluk*	32 ,,	225
	Jote	5 ,,	19
	16. Nilkantha Sen's Estate	75 ..	374
Endowment	17. Taranagar Estate	140 ,,	52

81. The subjoined table shows the demands and collections of the estates during the year under review. Compared with the previous

year, collections improved in 9 estates and fell in 6 estates. Nos. 12 and 16 came under State management during the latter part of 1344 T. E.

Estate No.	Demand			Collection			P. C. of collection
	Current	Arrear	Total	Current	Arrear	Total	
1.	5,788	42,296	48,084	789	3,797	4,586	9·53
2.	1,233	8,142	9,375	75	454	529	5·60
3.	1,275	2,941	4,216	85	752	837	20·2
4.	203	156	359	75	125	200	55·70
5.	3,364	19,077	24,110	230	2,063	2,312	9·50
	Jote 345	1,324			19		
6.	1,163	5,377	6,540	39	933	972	14·86
7.	3,602	11,099	14,701	2,758	168	2,926	19·80
8.	4,217	8,069	12,286	407	1,235	1,643	13·37
9.	2,459	6,280	8,739	8	424	832	4·96
10.	1,203	3,025	4,228	128	825	953	22·50
11.	912	4,871	5,783	46	183	229	3·90
12.	243	459	702	174	105	279	39·70
13.	1,149	5,457	6,606	284	1,309	1,593	24·10
14.	1,637	4,195	5,832	147	1,326	1,473	25·20
15.	619	4,163	4,782	—	123	123	2·6
16.	678	2,779	3,457	28	244	272	7·8
17.	3,116	13,404	16,520	423	1,900	2,323	14·06

CHAPTER III—PROTECTION.

I. Legislation.

82. The Tripura Tea Control Act of 1345 T. E. (Act No. 1 of 1345 T. E.) was passed during the year.

83. The following important regulations were promulgated during the year under review :—

(1) A Regulation for realisation of tax on bullock carts.

(2) A Regulation for realisation of toll on motor vehicles running between Agartala and Akhaura.

(3) A Regulation for destruction of papers in accordance with Act No. 1 of 1323 T. E. (Sec. 4).

(4) Notification No. 19 appointing the Indian Tea Licensing Committee as the Licensing Authority of the State tea gardens according to the Tripura Tea Control Act.

(5) Notification No. 20 vesting the Indian Tea Licensing Committee with power to inspect tea gardens in this State.

II. Military.

84. Charge. Dewan Saheb Kamala Prasad Dutt, M. A. B. L., F. R. E. S., M. R. A. S. and Major Kumar Dina Mohan Dev Varman Bahadur continued to be in charge of the Military Department and the Military Forces respectively.

85. The total strength of the Forces at the end of the year was
Strength. 398 against 368 of the preceding year.

86. F. T. Cox, Esqr., Civil Chief Master of Armourers inspected
Inspection all the rifles with the 1st Tripura Bir and 2nd Tripura Bikram Companies in July, 1935.

87. One N. C. O. from 1st Tripura Bir Company attended the
Training. 3rd Qualifying Course at the Army Signal School, Poona. His result was satisfactory. Two N. C. O's. from both the 1st Tripura Bir and 2nd Tripura Bikram Companies attended the Small Arms School, Gwalior and their results were very satisfactory. Armourer Sushil Chandra Dev Barman was sent to Ferozepur Arsenal for 2nd Class Armourer's training and the result was good. In this year, both the Companies had Individual and Collective Training, etc.

88. Some ordinary improvements and petty repairs of the
Cantonment. Barracks were made during the year.

89. The health of the Forces was generally good as in the
Health. previous year.

90. The total expenditure for the year excluding the Public
Expenditure. Works amounted to Rs. 1,08,263 against Rs. 1,01,039 of the previous year.

91. During the year, an N. C. O. Cadre Course on the subject
Camping and Tactical Practice by Military Forces during the year. of T. E. W. T. for all N. C. O's. and selected riflemen of the 1st Tripura Bir Coy. was held from the 16th Baishakh for 3 weeks under the Platoon Commanders of the said Coy. in order to give them full idea of of the subject. From the 23rd Kartik, the Forces pitched their camps at Jhagariamura two miles off to the South of the Cantonment for more than a week. On 19. 10. 45, on receiving news of the disturbances at Kailasahar, a detachment of one Gurkha Platoon was at once moved to the locality and placed on outpost work on the border, for the preservation of peace and order till the end of the year.

92. Besides the above both the Companies had to do Sentry duties at the Palace as well as in the General Treasury. They had also to perform Ceremonial Parades on ceremonial occasions.

III. Police

93. Rai Saheb A. C. Gupta continued as Superintendent of
Charge. Police during the whole of the year.

94 Babu Naresh Kumar Bhattacharjee, B. Sc., also continued as
A. S. P. Assistant Superintendent of Police, but he having fallen ill, the senior most Inspector Babu N. N. Bose, B. A., acted in his place from 8th Sraban to 30th Magh.

96. The total numerical strength of the Police force during the
Strength. year was 492 against 515 of the previous year, decrease being due to reduction of 1 Sub Inspector, 1 Naib Daroga, 1 Writer Naib Daroga and 20 ordinary constables in the budget for the year under review.

Rural Police.

97. The total number of village choukidars was 176 as in the previous year.

Inspecting Staff.

98. There were 4 Inspectors of Police as before, their main duties being supervision of important cases, inspection of thanas and Court offices, exercising control and maintaining discipline amongst the subordinates.

Investigating and Prosecuting Staff.

99. During the year there were 23 Sub-Inspectors and 21 Naib Darogas against 24 Sub-Inspectors and 22 Naib Darogas in the previous year.

100. The officers continued to show their detective ability in investigation of cases. More attention is being paid to smuggling of liquor and Ganja. Preventive measures to run down a large number of notorious bad characters u/s 109 and 110 Cr. P. C. were taken and patrol system was introduced in the affected areas, as a result of which crime was checked to a considerable extent, as will appear from the details in the para under the heading "crime".

101. Taking advantage of the loneliness and dense jungles of the Sabroom P. S. jurisdiction several highway mail robberies were committed there during the last few years. The present Officer-in-charge of Sabroom P. S. Ananda Chandra Majumder was able to detect the last mail robbery case which occured on 2-9-45 and great credit is due to him for the same. Some other officers, who were responsible for detection of several burglary and theft cases, including one gun theft case, also deserve credit. The behaviour of the Police and their dealings with the public were generally satisfactory and not a single case of ill-treatment was reported against any Police officer during the year under review.

C. I. D. & Intelligence Staff.

102. One Sub-Inspector, 5 Naib Darogas and 5 Constables were employed in the C. I. D. as in the previous year.

Crime.

103. The total number of cases reported during the year under review was 674 as against 894 in the previous year. The decrease is as has been stated in the para under the heading 'Investigating and prosecuting staff', due to institutions of cases u/s 109 and 110 Cr. P. C. and introduction of successful patrol system and also check in regard to unnecessary institution of non-cognizable cases.

104. The result of cases is as follows :—

Number of cases reported
674

- Enquiry refused 3
- Number investigated 640
  - True 528
    - Charge-sheet 288
    - Finally reported 240
  - Intentionally false 46
  - Mistake of law 7
  - Mistake of fact 31
  - Noncog-nizable 28
  - Doubtful 0
- Number pending 31

Result of Prosecution.

105. Altogether 516 persons were arrested in connection with various offences and 708 persons were sent up for trial by Police, as against 675 and 819 respectively in the previous year. Of the number sent up 139 were convicted and 113 acquitted (including 54 on compromise and 8 on withdrawal of cases), while 1 died and 455 (including the absconding accused) awaited trial. The percentage of conviction was 26·94 as against 30·96 of the previous year.

106. Of 472 accused awaiting trial at the end of the previous year, 153 were convicted, 147 acquitted (including 32 on compromise and 40 on withdrawal of cases,) and 172 were pending trial at the end of the year under report.

Bad livelihood cases.

107. In the previous year 5 cases of bad livelihood were started against 9 persons, of whom 8 were bound down and 1 acquitted, while in the year under report so many as 15 cases were started against 49 persons, of whom 18 were bound down, 1 acquitted and 30 were awaiting trial at the end of the year.

Arms Act cases.

108. Five Arms Act cases were instituted against 6 persons, of whom 2 were convicted and 5 were awaiting trial as the year closed.

Recovery of stolen properties

109. Total value of property stolen during the year amounted to Rs. 10,193-14-9 against Rs. 14,675-4-9 of the previous year. Of this amount Rs. 2,322-5-0 was recovered against Rs. 1,721-11-6 in the previous year. The percentage of recoveries was 22·78 against 11·73 of the previous year.

Dacoity.

110. There were 11 cases of dacoity during the year against 28 in the previous year and 5 persons were sent up in charge sheet in connection with 1 case, which ended in acquittal in the Court of Sessions.

Unnatural death.

111. Seventy-one cases of unnatural death were reported during the year. Regular enquiries were held by Police into all these cases. No foul play was detected in any of them.

Rewards and punishment.

112. One Inspector, 13 Sub-Inspectors, 8 Naib Darogas, 4 Writer Naib Darogas, 1 Armed Sub-Inspector, 2 Jamaders, 2 armed and 18 civil Constables received money rewards, while 3 Jamaders, 3 Naiks, 25 armed Constables, 62 civil Constables and 4 Choukidars were fined or degraded.

Tour.

113. The Superintendent of Police was out on tour for 63 days against 53 days in the previous year and the Assistant Superintendent of Police for 22 days (Babu N. K. Bhattacharjee, B. SC., for 5 days and Babu N. N. Bose, B. A., for 17 days)

Co-operation Meeting.

114. The relation with the police of the neighbouring districts in British India continued to be satisfactory. A big co-operation meeting was held at Agartala with the Police officers of this State, and of Tippera, Noakhali, and Sylhet Districts.

115. The system of musketry and revolver practice was continued in the year under review and the result of the Examination is a clear indication of a marked and gradual improvement of the force in this respect.

Musketry practice.

116. The expenditure amounted to Rs. 82,754 against Rs. 87,340 in the previous year.

Expenditure.

IV. Justice.

117. There were 17 courts of justice in the State during the year under report, exercising both civil and criminal jurisdiction, viz :—Khas Adalat (High Court) with its original and appellate sides, and 16 courts of Magistrate-Munsiffs exercising original jurisdiction only.

Courts.

118. Babu Jnanendra Mohan Das, B. L., continued as Chief Judge, Thakur Hriday Ranjan Dev Barman as Puisne Judge (appellate side) and Babu Ramani Mohan Goswami, M. A., B. L., as Civil and Sessions Judge (Original Side) during the year.

Khas Adalat (High Court).

119. Altogether 1,974 criminal cases were instituted during the year under report as against 2,023 of the previous year. With the balance of 788 pending from the previous year, the total number of cases for disposal before the several subordinate courts was 2,762 as against 2,674 of the previous year as detailed below ; and out of these 2,762 cases, 2,026 were disposed of as against 1,886 of the preceding year, leaving 736 cases pending at the close of the year. Thus in the year under report, the number of cases for disposal increased from that of the previous year by 88 cases and there was also an increase in disposal by 140.

Number of original criminal cases.

DESCRIPTION OF OFFENCES.	1344 T.E.	1345 T.E.
Offences against the State and public tranquillity	92	102
Offences against person	676	788
Offences against property	1,304	1,436
Other offences	602	436
TOTAL	2,674	2,762

120. Altogether extradition of 107 persons was asked for during the year under report, of whom 43 persons were arrested by the British Indian Police and surrendered to the State and 50 persons appeared of their own accord or were subsequently arrested within the State territory.

Extradition from British India.

121. The number of persons brought to trial within the year under report was 2,432; the number awaiting trial from the preceding year was 963; the total number of persons thus brought to trial in the year under report was 3,395 as against 3,106 of the previous year. Out of the aforesaid 2,432 persons, 584 were arrested by the police, 629 were produced on warrant, 903 appeared on summons, 312 appeared voluntarily and 4 persons were arrested in presence of Magistrates.

Persons brought to trial.

122. Out of the aforesaid 3,395 persons brought to trial before the several courts including the Sessions Court, 1,234 persons were discharged, 618 were acquitted, 574 were convicted, 13 died and 956 persons were awaiting trial at the close of the year. Out of the convicted persons, 253 were sentenced to various terms of imprisonment extending from less than one month to 5 years and above, 282 were sentenced to fine only, 22 were bound down and 17 persons were warned for the future. The number of persons actually tried was 1,192 (excluding those discharged) as against 1,263 of the previous year and the percentage of convictions was thus 48·15 against 53·84 of the previous year.

Results of cases.

123. Out of 2,762 cases for disposal as stated above, the number of cases in which British subjects were concerned either as complainants or accused, was 447 as against 439 of the previous year. Out of these, 342 cases were cognizable and 105 non-cognizable. In 41 cases British subjects were complainants and in 406 cases they were the accused. In 113 cases both the parties were British subjects. In all, 572 persons were actually brought under trial in those cases during the year under report as against 527 of the previous year. Out of these 572 persons, 213 persons were convicted, 205 acquitted or discharged, 3 died and 151 remained under trial at the close of the year.

Cases concerning British subjects.

124. The following statement will show the number of original criminal cases instituted during the last two years.

DESCRIPTION OF OFFENCES.	1344 T.E.	1345 T.E.	Increase.	Decrease.
Offences against the State and public tranquillity ...	67	79	12	0
Offences against person	508	591	83	0
Offences against property	963	995	32	0
Other offences	485	309	0	176
TOTAL	2,023	1,974	127	176

Decreased by 49.

125. 23 cases were committed to the Sessions during the year under report and 4 cases were pending from the previous year. Out of these 27 cases, 25 were disposed of during the year as detailed below. The number of persons

Sessions cases.

involved in those 27 cases was 64, of whom 22 were convicted, 37 were acquitted and 5 remained under trial at the close of the year.

Description of cases.	Number of cases.	Disposed of.	Pending.	REMARKS.
Murder	5	5	0	
Culpable homicide not amounting to murder	5	4	1	
Grievous hurt	1	1	0	
Rape	1	1	0	
Dacoity	1	1	0	
Robbery	6	5	1	
Destroying evidence of murder ...	1	1	0	
Unlawful assembly	1	1	0	
Wrongful confinement	1	1	0	
Arson	1	1	0	
Perjury	1	1	0	
Forgery	1	1	0	
Keeping gun-powder in possession without license	1	1	0	
Keeping coining tools in possession for the purpose of counterfeiting coins ...	1	1	0	
Total	27	25	2	

126. There were altogether 247 criminal appeals as against 236 of the previous year. These appeals were disposed of as shown below :—

Criminal appeals.

Rejected	8
Judgment affirmed	119
Modified	27
Reversed	23
Further enquiry ordered	14
	191
Pending	56
Total	247

127. The percentage of judgments affirmed and modified was 79·78 as against 76·35 of the previous year.

128. The number of original civil suits instituted during the year under report was 1,553 as against 1,631 of the preceding year. With the balance of 779 suits pending from the previous year, the total number of suits for disposal was 2,332 as against 2,480 of the preceding year. These suits were disposed of as shown below :—

Original civil suits.

Exparte	708
Admitted and compromised	152
Dismissed for want of prosecution ...	199
Disposed of on contest...	432
	1,491
Pending	841
Total	2,332

129. The average duration of suits in the civil courts was 4 months and 24 days as against 4 months of the previous year.

Duration of suits

130. The total value of civil suits instituted during the year was Rs. 4,26,173-3-6 as against Rs. 1,37,388-0-8 of the previous year, which gives an average of Rs. 274-6-9 per case. Out of 1,553 suits, instituted during the year under review, 337 related to land, 884 to money transactions and 332 suits were of other classes. 821 suits were of the value of Rs. 100 and under; 382 suits were of the value between Rs. 100 and Rs. 500; 24 suits of value between Rs. 500 and Rs. 1,000; 10 suits of value between Rs. 1,000 and Rs. 5,000, 1 suit was of value above Rs. 5,000, and 315 suits were not estimable in money value.

Nature and value of suits.

131. The number of applications for the execution of decrees filed during the year was 799 and there were 645 pending from the previous year. The total number for disposal was thus 1,444 as against 1,449 of the preceding year. The aggregate value of the new applications was Rs. 1,35,810-6-3 and that of the pending applications was Rs. 1,15,504-10-0, the total value thus amounting to Rs. 2,51,315-0-3. The number of applications disposed of was 789, the value of which was Rs. 1,38,962-14-3. The number of execution cases pending at the close of the year was 655, the value thereof being Rs. 1,12,352-2-0.

Execution of decrees.

132. There were 169 civil appeals filed during the year as against 108 of the previous year. With the balance of 78 from the previous year, the total number of civil appeals for disposal was 247 as against 214 of the preceding year. Out of these cases, 150 were disposed of during the year under report as against 136 of the previous year, leaving a balance of 97 cases at the close of the year.

Civil appeals.

133. The following figures will show the result of appeals in civil suits :—

Result of civil appeals

Decisions confirmed	73
" reversed	29
" modified	9
Remanded	10
Compromised and otherwise disposed of ...	29
	150

134. The percentage of judgments wholly or partly upheld, excluding those in the cases compromised, was 67·77 against 65·49 of the preceding year.

Percentage.

135. The total value of civil appeals filed during the year under review was Rs. 8,000-5-6 and the average duration of each appeal was 5 months as against 5 months and 3 days of the previous year.

Value and duration of appeals

136. 21 civil suits were instituted in the original side, Khas Adalat, during the year under report as against 17 of the previous year. With the balance of 51 suits pending from the preceding year, the total number for disposal was 72 as against 65 of the previous year. Of these, 13 suits were disposed of against 14, leaving 59 suits pending at the

Cases of the original side.

close of the year. There were 37 execution cases during the year, including 30 cases pending from the previous year. Of these, 15 were disposed of and 22 remained pending at the close of the year. There were 11 applications for succession and other certificates during the year under report; with the balance of 14 of the previous year, the total number of such applications was 25, out of which 20 were disposed of as shown below and 5 remained pending at the close of the year :—

Description of cases.	Total.	Disposed of.	Pending.
Probate cases	3	3	0
Succession certificate	8	8	0
Guardianship	14	9	5
Total	25	20	5

137. The total number of civil and criminal appeals including the number of cases pending from the previous year, was 494 as against 450 of the preceding year. Out of these appeals, 341 were disposed of as against 334 of the previous year. It may be mentioned here that, through mistake, the number of appeals disposed of last year was shown as 350 civil 142 and criminal 208) instead of *334 (civil 136 and criminal 198).

Total number of appeals.

138. In comparison with the preceding year, the total number of appeals for disposal increased by 44 and there was also an increase in disposal by 7 only.

Description of appeals.	Number of appeals.		Disposed of.	
	Past year.	Present year.	Past year.	Present year.
Civil	214	247	136	150
Criminal	236	247	198	191
Total	450	494	*334	341

V. Prisons.

139. As before, the State maintained 8 Jails including the Central Jail at the Capital with Dr. M. M. Majumdar, Chief Medical Officer as its Superintendent during the year under review.

Number of Jails.

140. The Jail population during the year under report totalled 1173 as against 1192 in the previous year with the daily average of 179·11 against 176·16. Of them, 577 were convicts, 586 under-trials, 4 civil prisoners, 4 lunatics and 2 detenus.

Jail population.

141. Two detenus continued to remain in the Central Jail. Two Political convicts were made over to the British Police after their release and two others remained during the year under report.

Detenu and Political convicts.

142. The following statement shows the actual number of prisoners undergoing imprisonment for more than two years, the total number being 99 as against 90 in the year before. Their offence and occupation are noted below.

Long-term prisoners.

Class of offence.	Number of prisoners.	Occupation.	REMARKS.
Murder	18	They were employed in brick manufacturing. oilmills, wheat grinding, *soorki* pounding, *khoa* breaking, weaving, gardening, bamboo and cane work, tailoring and paddy husking etc.	71 had sentences of 2 to 5 years, 9 of 5 to 10 years, 6 of 10 to 14 years and 13 for life i. e. 20 years.
Culpable homicide not amounting to murder... ...	18		
Grievous hurt	1		
Robbery	3		
Theft	6		
Dacoity	21		
Counterfeiting coin	5		
Kidnapping	2		
Rape	5		
Forgery	1		
Attempt to commit suicide ...	1		
Section 110 (security for good behaviour for habitual offenders) ...	12		
Keeping Revolver in possession without license ...	2		
Criminal trespass and rioting	4		
Total	99		

143. One convict in the Central Jail died of intestinal tuberculosis during the year under report. The health of all the jails was on the whole good.

Jail health.

144. 23 convicts underwent training in the Reformatory School attached to the Central Jail. 2 of them appeared at the Pathshala Scholarship Examination and passed in the first division. Religious instructions were also imparted to the prisoners by honorary Hindu and Mahammadan instructors as before.

Education.

145. 1 convict and 2 under-trials escaped from the Kailasahar Jail during the year under review—but the convict was re-arrested after a few days and one under-trial surrendered himself to the Court.

Escape

146. On the happy occasion of the Birth-day ceremony of His Highness the Maharaja Manikya Bahadur, 10 convicts were released during the year as against 6 in the previous year.

Special release.

147. 10 Senior Warders and 60 Warders were employed in all the Jails during the year under review. At the beginning of the year, 8 Warders had to be discharged as Military sepoys replaced them. 10 Warders were fined for negligence of their duties, 3 were warned for the future and 1 was dismissed.

Warders.

148. The total income of the Central Jail amounted to Rs. 4029-1 as against Rs. 2237 in the preceding year.

Income.

149. The total expenditure during the year under report stood at Rs. 29,658 against Rs. 26,321.

Expenditure.

VI. Registration.

Charge.

150. Mr. S. C. Deb Barman, M. A. (Harvard), Senior Naib Dewan, remained in charge of the Department till 31st Ashad and thereafter the charge remained with Thakur K. K. Singh, Naib Dewan, for the rest of the year.

Registration Offices.

151. The number of Registration Offices continued to be 9 as in the previous year—there being one at the head-quarters station of each of the Divisions and Sub-division. In the Mofussil, the Divisional and Sub-divisional Officers and in certain divisions the Second Officers acted as Registrars. For the Sadar Division there was a separate Registrar at Agartala.

Registration and Disposal.

152. The total number of documents presented for registration during the year including 27 documents pending at the end of the previous year was 7,398 against 6,615. Of this number, 60 deeds were refused registration on different grounds and 190 remained pending at the end of the year against 27 pending at the end of the previous year.

Value of deeds presented and registered.

153. The total value covered by the documents amounted to Rs. 11,06,147 as against 8,33,344 of the previous year, while the total value covered by the documents actually registered was Rs. 10,98,306 as against Rs. 8,32,679 in the year before.

Suits and appeals.

154. With 6 suits pending from the previous year, the total number of suits brought before the Registration Department in respect of documents, the registration of which had been refused in various Registration Offices, was 18, out of which 4 were disposed of and 14 remained pending at the end of the year. There were 2 appeals in the year under review which remained pending as the year closed.

Income and expenditure.

155. The total income of the Department from fees and fines amounted to Rs. 7,444 against Rs. 6,030 and the expenditure to Rs. 3,564 against Rs. 3,555 in the previous year. The net income thus amounted to Rs. 3,880 in the year under report against Rs. 2,475 in the previous year.

VII. Municipality and Sanitation.

Municipality.

156. As before, the capital town of Agartala was the only municipality in the State with a population of about 10,000 according to the last census.

Municipal Committee.

157. Municipal Administration of the Capital town was carried on by a Committee of 9 nine members including an official Chairman and a non-official Vice-Chairman. Mr. S. C. Deb Barman, M. A. (Harvard) Senior Naib Dewan, Accounts Department, Minister's Office and Babu Haridas Bhattacherjee continued to be the Chairman and Vice-Chairman respectively during the year under review.

158. The Committee held 4 four meetings—average attendance of members being 5·2 against 6·1 of the previous year.

Income.

159. The realization on account of Municipal and Latrine taxes was Rs. 5,079-2-0 as against Rs. 5,376-15-0 of the preceding year. The total demand inclusive of arrears was Rs. 9,781-3-0 of which Rs. 439-10-9 was irrecoverable.

160. Both Municipal and Latrine taxes amounting to Rs. 1,889-4-9 due by His Highness's family members living out side the Palace proper and Prabhu Goswamis of Sreepat have still remained outstanding. Had the amount been realized, the collection under the above heads would have undoubtedly been more satisfactory.

161. The income under miscellaneous head including deposits amounted to Rs. 585-8-6 as against Rs. 991-5-6 of the year previous. The fall is due to the transfer of cart license from the Municipality to the Sadar Collectorate—the income thereof being deposited in the State.

162. The State grant for the year under report was Rs. 9,000. Thus the total income of the Municipality came up to Rs. 14,664-10-6 as against Rs. 15,368-4-6 of the preceding year.

Expenditure.

163. The total expenditure of the Municipality amounted to Rs. 14,834-4-0 as against Rs. 15,181-8-0 in the year previous.

Ishangunja Bazar.

164. The control and management of the Bazar at the capital remained, as before, with the Municipal Committee. The total demand including the arrear demand was Rs. 13,084-7-3 of which Rs. 2,795-6-9 was irrecoverable. The total receipts including Rs. 578-13-0 as advances recovered from the Municipality came up to Rs. 6,762-1-3 as against Rs. 6,827 of the previous year.

165. After meeting the necessary expenditure of Rs. 2,241-0-3, the Bazar Improvement Fund stood at Rs. 48,688-3-3 at the close of the year.

166. During the last few years occasional fires caused great damage to the permanent stall-holders of the Bazar. To save them from such loss and replace them by permanent structures, His Highness the Maharaja Manikya Bahadur was pleased to prepare personally a design for Bazar buildings with a view to its improvement all round. The Stall-holders readily fell in with the project and started construction in right earnest. The works have been progressing rapidly and the shopkeepers have received financial help in the shape of loans from the State at a nominal interest. The buildings, when completed, will surely add to the grandeur of the town on its æsthetic side.

167. Two tanks were excavated side by side at a cost of Rs. 1,331-8-0 in the plot previously acquired for the removal of the Ishangunja Bazar the cost being met from the Bazar Fund.

168. The site for the daily market has been selected at a suitable place close to the north bank of the Howrah river. A spacious circular shaped structure with well arranged stalls inside as designed by

His Highness is now under construction under the supervision of the P. W. Office. The total cost will also be met from the Bazar Fund.

Health.

169. The health of the town was not quite satisfactory. Towards the beginning and latter part of the year under review cholera prevailed in the town sporadically. The Municipality reserved some tanks for drinking water as a safeguard against probable contamination during the epidemic.

170. The epidemic was mainly due to the scarcity of pure drinking water supply in the town. The water of most of the reserved tanks turned bad and un-drinkable and many private tanks were almost dried up owing to the long drought. With a view to prevent such occurrence in the future it has been proposed to sink tube-wells in different parts of the town in the next year.

171. There were 43 cases of cholera with 16 deaths and one case of small-pox which was cured by the small-pox doctor of the State.

Sanitation.

172. Some minor sanitary works were undertaken within the town proper under the direct supervision of the Officer-in-charge of the Sanitation Department at a cost of Rs. 662-3-6.

Charge.

173. Dr. M. M. Majumdar, Chief Medical Officer of the State, remained as before, officer-in-charge of both the Municipal and Sanitation Departments.

CHAPTER IV—PRODUCTION AND DISTRIBUTION.

I. Weather and Crops—Agriculture

Charge of the Department.

174. Manyabara Rana Bodhjung Bahadur, F. R. G. S., Chief Secretary to His Highness the Maharaja Manikya Bahadur of Tripura continued to be in charge of the Department assisted by Mr. J. C. Choudhury S. E., M. S. A. (Tokyo), M. R. A (Agri) S. (London) as Superintendent of Agriculture.

Staff.

175. The staff of the Department continued to be the same as in the previous year except that the services of the Poultry Expert were transferred to the Revenue Department and Babu Santi Kumar Ray appointed in his place to assist the Superintendent of Agriculture in agricultural marketing survey and general propaganda.

Propaganda.

176. Special propaganda was made in connection with the improved varieties of sugarcane, cereals, English vegetables and groundnuts.

Seed distribution. Coimbatore sugarcane, Groundnuts.

177. Improved variety of sugarcane fairly spread over Sadar Division. Nearly 44,000 cuttings of Coimbatore No. 213 were distributed in Sadar *Elaka*. Five maunds of groundnut seeds were also distributed in the localities.

Rainfall.

178. The average rainfall of the year was 79·48 inches against 91·3 inches in the previous year. The quinquennial average was 81·42 inches. Kailashahar Division had the maximum fall of 110·46 inches and Belonia the minimum of 47·04 inches. Heaviest rainfall averaging 17·72 was registered in the month of Jaista.

Temperature.

179. The highest temperature was 96 degree and lowest 54 degree in the year under report.

Crops.

180. The principal crops in the State were paddy, jute, mustard, *til*, sugarcane and cotton. The cultivation of pine-apple is increasing year after year in the State. Potatoes, tobacco, chillies and pulses of various types were also grown in some parts of the State.

Labour and Wages.

181. Male labourers earned from 4 annas to 8 annas, female labourers from 2 to 5 annas. Gharamies earned from 5 annas to 8 annas and carpenters and masons from annas 6 to Re. 1 only. Most of the labourers were outsiders from the neighbouring British Districts as well as up-country coolies

Prices.

182. Prices of food-grains varied very little from that in the neighbouring British districts. Rice sold from Rs. 2 to Rs. 4-8 and paddy sold from Re. 1 to Rs. 2 per maund.

Tea Industry.

183. The Tea industry showed appreciable progress and tea produced in the State fetched good prices. Nearly 48 gardens were in running condition during the year.

Taccavi.

184. A Taccavi advance of Rs. 1,250 only was given to the Mugh immigrants at Belonia Division.

Bengal Marketing Survey Conference.

185. The Superintendent of Agriculture was deputed to attend the Bengal Marketing Survey Conference held in Calcutta.

Agro-Industrial Exhibition, Brahmanbaria.

186. The State Agriculture Department opened a stall with agro-industrial exhibits for the State which was much appreciated by the public.

Veterinary.

187. There was an outbreak of Rinderpest in epidemic form in some parts of Belonia and Sonamura Divisions which swept away a great number of cattle. An extra Veterinary Assistant Surgeon was appointed for applying goat tissue vaccine in the affected areas after which the epidemic subsided. 1,275 animals in the Veterinary Dispensary and 1,035 animals in moffusil were treated by the Veterinary Surgeon.

Tour of the Staff.

188. The Superintendent of Agriculture was out on tour for 36 days and the Veterinary Surgeon for 40 days in all.

II. Immigration and Emigration.

189. Manyabara Rana Saheb Bodhjung Bahadur, F. R. G. S., Chief Secretary to His Highness the Maharaja Manikya Bahadur assisted by Mr. B. C. Dev Barman, Assistant, continued to be in charge of these Departments.

Charge of the Department.

190. The reclamation work in Kulaihaor during the year under report made satisfactory progress as the major portion of the lands had already been reclaimed. Some more men from different places came to settle down in Kulai and they were given lands according to their requirements.

Kulaihaor.

191. The condition of the road from Kamalpur to Salema was good and the temporary bamboo bridges over the same were fully repaired. Besides this the river route which was not so long accessible was also cleared and became suitable for boats carrying loads for Salema Bazar. This was very helpful towards the progress of the bazar at Salema.

Condition of the Kamalpur-Salema Road.

192. The tank at Salema supplied pure good drinking water to the inhabitants of the bazar and also to the neighbouring villages.

Supply of drinking water.

193. Salema Bazar kept up the progress throughout the year. The total number of permanent shops rose to 12. Weekly bazar on Saturday began to meet regularly and some 40 to 60 temporary shopkeepers from different places such as Bhanugach, Srimangal etc. come to the Bazar for merchandise on the bazar day, the number of men attending the weekly bazar being from 350 to 500. This was of great relief to the inhabitants and their long-felt want has thus been removed.

Salema Bazar.

194. Special arrangement was made there for the sale of *Sidal* and dry fish at the prescribed rate and this arrangement proved very successful.

195. The Agricultural produces of the inhabitants are now sold in the bazar which they could not do in the past and thus all facilities for their economic uplift have been afforded as never before.

196. Everything necessary for every day life excepting fresh fish is now available in the said bazar and the people are quite happy.

197. The total number of patients who received treatment in the Salema Dispensary was 3128, the number of new and old cases being 2196 and 932 respectively against 3799 in the previous year and the average of daily attendance being 9.12. Besides these there were 14 minor operation cases with success. The total expenditure amounted to Rs. 374-6 only during the year under report.

Salema Dispensary.

198. During the year under review nearly 32 *drones* of *Abadi* and 10 *drones* of jungle lands were settled, and a *nazar* of Rs. 548 was realised on this account.

Settlement.

199. Relinquishment of nearly 10 *drones* of land was accepted from different classes of tenants.

Relinquishment.

200. No *Namjari* was effected during the year under review.

Namjari.

201. The staff consisted of 1 office Moharer, 1 *Amin* and a *Nali*. Besides these several temporary *Amins* were engaged during winter for survey work. Thakur Ramkumar Dev Barman was of great help in settlement work as in the past in the Reserve area.

Staff.

202. The net expenditure towards Kalyanpur Reserve work amounted to Rs. 837-2 against Rs. 1,413-12 in the previous year.

III. Forests.

203. Babu Jatindra Nath Mitra, Naib Dewan, remained in charge of the Department during the year under review. With the exception of a few *Mahals* which were let out in *Ijara*, all the forests were under *Khas* management as before.

Charge and management.

204. Including the Patrol staff consisting of a Forester, three Head Guards and twenty guards, the Department had a staff of one Station Officer, three Forest Circle Inspectors, fourteen Foresters, seventeen Assistant Foresters, four Rangers, Moharers, twenty-four Head Guards, twelve Literate guards, one hundred and fifty one guards and six boatmen.

Staff.

205. During the year under review the patrol staff had been out on tour in three sections. They patrolled in Sadar Division for 2 months and 7 days, in Belonia Division for 6 months and twenty three days, in Sabroom Division for five days, in Kailasahar Division for 2 months and 13 days and in Sonamura Division for 11 months and 21 days.

206. There were 159 commissioned agents for the sale of the forest permits for the shoulder-borne export of minor forest produce by land routes.

Permits.

207. There were 52 forest stations for collection of duty and prevention of forest offences, including one new Range Office with one Ranger and two guards, which was established at Teliamura during the year under report for the protection of the newly declared forest Reserve at Teliamura in Khowai Division.

Forest stations.

208. The Reserved *Sal* forests of the Sonamura Division continued to be worked under the System of coppice with standards and those of the Udaipur Division under the Improvement Method, while the open unclassed forests were worked under the State Forest Rules of 1323 T. E. For the Feni river *Mohal*, the working rules of the Bengal Forest Department were followed.

Working of the Forests.

209. A joint conference regarding the future management of the Amlighat Toll Station was held at Chittagong during the year under report, and it was agreed by both the Governments that a Ranger from the Bengal Forest Department will be deputed to Amlighat every alternate year from the next session.

Future management of the Amlighat Toll station.

210. 2692·46 acres of forests have been declared "Reserved" during the year :—

Forest Reserves.

(*a*) Khowai Division—
Gulichhera Reserve and Teliamura Reserve–area 885·12 and 847·34 acres respectively.

(*b*) Bilonia Division—
Muhuripur Reserve–area 960 acres.

211. During the year under report three *kheda* operations were undertaken—2 in the Kailasahar and one in the Sonamura–Udaipur Division. 17 elephants were caught in the Sonamura–Udaipur Division, while the operations in the Kailasahar Division were unsuccessful.

***Kheda* operations.**

212. The Toll Station at Amlighat continued to be under the management of the State Forest Department. The total revenue collected at the station in the year under review was Rs. 48,186 against Rs. 39,655 in the previous year showing an increase of Rs. 8,531 which is due to the efficient management of the Station. The total expenditure incurred in running the Station in the year under report was Rs. 4,082-11-3 against Rs. 3,767-3-6 in the previous year.

Feni river mohal.

213. As before, a doctor of the Sub-Assistant Surgeon class was appointed temporarily for four months from December to March last for giving medical relief to the Station staff and to the cutters and exporters of forest produce.

214. As in the previous year, the forest produce from the Fee Simple Lots above the Amlighat Toll Station was exported under passes granted by the Collector of Chittagong.

Fee Simple Lots.

215. During the year under review there were 165 forest cases against 361 persons including 77 cases against 189 persons pending from the previous year. The offences were mainly for export of forest produce without payment of duty.

Forest offences.

216. Of the above 165 cases—(*a*) 104 cases against 235 persons were tried ; (*b*) 19 cases against 38 persons were compounded ; (*c*) 2 cases against 2 persons were disposed of without trial—in one case the only accused died before trial, and the other was taken up on an anonymous petition against one person but as the allegations were proved to be false, there was no trial ; (*d*) 40 cases against 86 persons remained pending at the close of the year.

Results.

217. Of the 235 persons tried, 27 persons were sentenced to imprisonment only ; 173 were punished with fine only ; 3 imprisoned and fined ; 2 were warned and 30 acquitted.

218. One Head Guard and two guards were rewarded for intelligent detection of cases of smuggling of forest produce. One Forester was fined and two guards were dismissed from service for misconduct.

Rewards & punishment.

219. The health of the staff was generally good. Only one guard died of pneumonia during the year.

Health of the staff.

220. The following table shows the results of the collection of forest revenue under different heads with all variations.

Sources of income.

Heads of Revenue.	1345 T.E.	1344 T.E.	Increase.	Decrease.	REMARKS.
	Rs.	Rs.			
I. Unclassed open forests :—					
(a) Toll on forest produce exported by the river mehals	2,32,253	2,39,056	—	6,803	
(b) Toll on forest produce exported by land route under permits	70,285	63,851	6,434	—	
(c) Toll collection (State share) of the Feni river mehal...	31,314	27,155	4,159	—	
(d) Grazing mehal ...	5,537	6,678	—	1,141	
(e) Thatching grass mehal	2,574	2,906	—	332	
II. Reserved Forests :— Sale of *Sal* etc	4,134	3,070	1,064	—	
III. Elephant Kheddas	2,522	2,315	207	—	
IV. Match Excise duty	16,595	—	16,595	—	
TOTAL ...	3,65,214	3,45 031	28,459	8,276	

221. Details of collections in the year under report are given below :—

Heads of Revenue.	Quantity of produce exported.	Duty realised thereon.	REMARKS.
	Cft.	Rs.	
1. Timber other than Sal...	3,33,821·1	56,331	
2. *Sal*	13,338·1	4,134	
3. Produce other than timber.			
(a) Exported by *bhatials*	—	1,75,922	
(b) Exported by land routes under permits	—	70,285	
4. Toll collection (State share) of the Feni river			
(a) Timber	13,205	2,286	
(b) Other produce ...	—	29,028	
5. Grazing *Mahal* ...	—	5,537	
6. Thatching grass *Mahal*	—	2,574	
7. Elephant Khedas ...	—	2,522	
8. Match Excise duty ...	—	16,595	
Total quantity of timber in Cft.	3,60,364·2	3,65,214	

222. **Receipts.** The total forest revenue in the year under report was Rs. 3,65,214 against Rs. 3,45,031 in the previous year showing an increase of Rs. 20,183 including Rs. 16,595 received as Match Excise duty during the year.

223. **Receipts from Matches.** During the year under report the Maharaja Match Factory manufactured 3,454½ gross of finished matches and paid Rs. 25-7-6 as duty on the timber used in making these matches. The State received Rs. 16,595 from the India Government as its share of Match Excise duty.

224. **Plantation.** Plantation of *Sal, Sonal, Manogany* and *Gamair* were continued during the year.

225. **Tour.** The Naib Dewan was out on tour for 79 days against 82 days in the previous year.

IV. Trade and Manufacture.

226. The principal exports were timber and other forest produce of various kinds, cotton, oil-seeds, (*til* and mustard seed), paddy, jute, tea, rice and *Gur* (molasses). Some homespun cotton fabrics manufactured by the hill people and specially by the Manipuries were also exported. The principal exports for the year under review and of the previous year are shown below :—

	1343 T. E.	1344 T. E.	1345 T. E.
Cotton ...	43,290 mds.	30,837 mds.	1,07,236 mds.
Til ...	9,898 ,,	54,640 ,,	21,374 ,,
Mustard seeds	19,704 ,,	34,986 ,,	31,851 ,,
Jute ...	44,162 ,,	72,274 ,,	82,009 ,,
Tea ...	17,70,097 lbs.	24,66,331 lbs.	24,88,529 lbs.

V. Public Works.

227. **Charge.** Dewan Saheb K. Dutt, M. A. B. L., M. R. A. S., F. R. E. S., Private Secretary to His Highness the Maharaja Manikya Bahadur was in charge of the Public Works Department during the year. Honorary Lt. J. N. Bhaduri, B. A., B. E., continued as State Engineer during the year.

228. **Expenditure.** The Statement XX in the ~~appendix gives~~ details of the works executed during the year, the total expenditure including improvement works being Rs. 2,01,925 as detailed below against Rs. 2,14,552 in the previous year.

Description of works.	Ordinary Public works.	Improvement works.	TOTAL.
Buildings...	60,953	53,080	1,14,033
Roads & Bridges	21,044	28,822	49,866
Tanks & Tube Wells ...	1,807	780	2,587
Miscellaneous Works ...	3,554	13,419	16,973
Minor works at Rajbari (*Karkhana*) ...	994	—	994
Establishment charges ...	17,472	—	17,472
TOTAL ...	1,05,824	96,101	2,01,925

229. The following major works were done during the year :—

1. The *Baithakkhana* of His Highness the Maharaja Manikya Bahadur is almost complete.
2. Constructing a C. I. shed on masonry wall for Kumar Probir Kishore Deb Barman Bahadur.
3. Constructing an arched Culvert on Agartala Bisalgarh road (near Carmichæl Bridge.)
4. Excavating 2 tanks at Shibnagar.
5. Constructing an Andar-Portico with 2 Guard sheds and roadway.
6. Constructing Pavilion on the north bank of the Palace west tank.
7. Improvement of Sonamura Melagarh road.
8. Constructing Sadar Collectorate Building.
9. Re-roofing Malanchabas with Melthoid.
10. Constructing Sal Bridge over the Kachi River.
11. Excavating a tank for Maharajkumar Ranabirkisore Deb Barman Bahadur's new House.
12. Constructing Palace East Road.
13. Constructing Cross Road extension.
14. Widening and straightening the Durgabari Road.
15. Substantial improvement of A. D. C. Room and Motor Garage at Rajbari.
16. Substantial improvement of *Baithakkhana* court yard at Rajbari.
17. Constructing a pucca bridge on Agartala Bisalgarh road near Bisalgarh.
18. Constructing Sal wood bridge over the Rangapania River on Bisalgarh Udaipur road.
19. Constructing a bridge over the Dhanara River on Birendranagar Road.
20. Re-metalling Akhaura Road (State Portion.)
21. Substantial improvement of the masonry railing by Akhaura road and Prasad Protoli.
22. Constructing a pucca bridge over Katakhal on Prasad Protoli.
23. Constructing Jasmine court at Malanchabas.
24. Constructing a new diversion on Udaipur Road near Behary Choudhury House.
25. Constructing a new diversion on Udaipur Road at Barakuchi.
26. Laying Marble stone on the floor of H. H's *Baithakkhana* first floor.
27. Ceiling and door lining of H. H's *Baithakkhana*.
28. Special repaires of the Kunjaban Palace.
29. Considerable progress of Kunjaban Well.
30. Buying one double-tier fountain with D. C. Pump for Moghal Garden.

31. Substantial Progress of Chooner Stone works at Moghal Garden.

32. Considerable progress of Rajbari compound wall.

33. Substantial progress of Kailasahar Thana Building.

34. Special repairs of Kailasahar Muraichera Road.

35. Constructing Fatikroy Thana (Tin shed).

36. Constructing Checking office, Forester's Quarters at Dhalai. (Tin shed.)

37 Improvement of Fatikuli Bazar at Dharmanagar.

38. Dak Bunglow at Kalyanpur.

39. Tube well at Khowai.

40. Excavating a tank at Champaknagar.

41. Constructing Kamalasagar magazine house.

42. Constructing Jail lock-up at Sabroom. (Tin shed).

43. Salgara Tahasil Kutchery. (Tin shed).

44. Making a new alignment for Udaipur–Amarpur Road.

230. The total expenditure in connection with Electric supply was Rs. 16,433 against Rs. 16,299 in the previous year.

CHAPTER V—REVENUE AND FINANCES.

I. Revenue.

231. The total collection in the year was Rs. 16,96,043 against Rs. 15,79,609 in the previous year.

232. The details of income under different heads with all variations are given in the tsatement below.

Serial number.	Heads of Revenue.	1345 T.E.	1344 T.E.	As compared with 1344 T.E.		Remarks.
				Increase.	Decrease.	
1.	Land Revenue	6,53,693	6,44,452	9,241	—	
2.	Rents of markets	6,717	6,180	537	—	
3.	Family Tax in the hills	59,850	52,593	7,257	—	
4.	Toll on forest produce	3,02,538	3,02,907	—	369	
5.	Do. Do. on the Feni Rivers	31,314	27,155	4,159		
6.	Elephant & buffalo grazing Mehal	5,537	6,678	—	1,141	
7.	Thatching grass Mehal	2,574	2,906	—	332	
8.	Reserved *Sal* Forests	4,134	3,070	1,064	—	
9.	Tax on cotton and oil-seeds ..	2,17,722	1,35,224	82,498	—	
10.	Royalty on elephants caught ...	2,522	2,315	207	—	
11.	Adda Mehal	24,300	25,533	—	727	
12.	Excise	40,057	42,901	—	2,844	
13.	Stamps and Court fees	62,874	64,240	—	1,366	
14.	Law and Justice (Fines)... ...	2,014	2,172	—	158	
15.	Process fees	9,683	10,396	—	713	
16.	Registration	7,444	5,555	1,889	—	
17.	Jail	4,235	2,237	1,998	—	
18.	Cattle pounds	4,489	3,826	663	—	
19.	Nazars	32,812	31,918	894	—	
20.	Education...	14,548	15,034	—	486	
21.	Tea Export duty	21,452	27,723	—	6,271	
22.	Jute Export duty	30,423	27,112	3,311	—	
23.	Depreciation Contribution ...	76,943	78,071	—	1,128	
24.	Miscellaneous	61,067	59,411	1,656	—	
25.	Duty on matches	16,595	—	16,595	—	Net increase—Rs. 1,16,434
	Total	16,96,043	15,79,609	1,31,969	15,535	

233. It will be seen that there was an increase in respect of 14 heads of income aggregating Rs. 1,31,969 against decrease under 11 heads amounting to Rs. 15,535: which resulted in a net increase of Rs. 1,16,434.

234. The increase under head Toll on the Feni rivers, Reserved *Sal* Forests and Royalty on elephants caught, Duty on matches and decrease under head Toll on Forest produce and elephant and buffalo grazing *mehal* will be explained in the section relating to the Forest Department.

235. The income under head Land Revenue exceeded the figures of 1340, 1341, 1342, 1343, 1344 T. E. by Rs. 2,23,513, Rs. 2,66,035, Rs. 2,44,868, Rs. 2,12,986 and Rs. 9,241 respectively.

236. Tea garden land revenue contributed Rs. 1,04,061 and exceeded the figures of 1343 and 1344 T. E. by Rs. 57,888 and Rs. 18,645 respectively. The increase under the head Land Revenue is due to better income from Tea Garden land revenue and in view of this collection under this head can hardly be taken to be satisfactory.

237. The increase under the head Family Tax in the hills may be attributed to the improved paying capacity of the hill people and that under tax on cotton & oil-seeds was due to the increased export of cotton to the extent of more than 3 times of the previous year, although export of oil-seeds fell down to less than half the quantity of the previous year. The tax under this head exceeded the figures of 1342, 1343 and 1344 T. E. by Rs. 77,682, Rs. 1,10,883 and Rs. 82,498 respectively.

238. A slight increase under head jute export duty will be perceived but the income under this head was less than that of the years 1342 T. E. and 1343 T. E., difference being Rs. 965 and Rs. 1,541 respectively.

239. The decrease under the head *Adda* denotes unsatisfactory condition of people in the plains.

240. The Excise revenue in the year under review witnessed a fall of Rs. 1,597 and Rs. 2,844 in comparison with 1343 and 1344 T. E. respectively and almost coincided with the income of 1342 T. E. under this head, the difference being a decrease of Rs. 222.

241. The increase under the head *Nazar* is attributable to greater collection of *nazars* by settlement operations.

242. The decrease under head Tea export duty in comparison with 1344 T. E. may be attributable to better realizations in 1344 T. E. of arrears but it exceeded the figures for 1343 T. E. by Rs. 8,872.

II. Finances.

243. A consolidated abstract account of the financial transactions of the State and the attached Zemindaries as compared with those of the previous year is given below :—

Receipts.	1344 T. E.	1345 T. E.
1. Opening balance :—		
(1) State ...	10,52,214	10,92,959
(2) Zemindaries ...	3,50,220	3,83,502
Total ...	14,02,434	14,76,461
2. Income :—		
(1) State ...	15,79,609	16,96,043
(2) Zemindaries ...	9,87,261	11,07,653
Total ...	25,66,870	28,03,696
3 Law charges recovered :—		
(1) Zemindaries ...	46,963	65,060
4. Refunds and compensation for lands acquired :—		
(1) Zemindaries ...	4,417	3,732
5. Deposits :—		
(1) State ...	2,63,746	1,31,004
(2) Zemindaries ...	39,576	51,943
Total ...	3,03,322	1,82,947
GRAND TOTAL ...	43,24,006	45,31,896

Expenditure.	1344 T. E.	1345 T. E.
1. General Administration charges :—		
(a) State	5,42,469	5,44,627
(b) Zemindaries :—		
1. Cost of management	1,42,745	1,37,956
2. Cost of litigation	1,36,800	1,59,230
	2,79,545	2,97,186
Total ...	8,22,014	8,41,813
2. Revenue and Taxes on account of the Zemindaries	2,85,540	2,81,546
3. Public Works—(a) State	2,09,062	2,00,017
(b) Zemindaries ...	50,996	50,912
Total ..	2,60,058	2,50,929
4. Electric Light—State	16,299	16,433
5. Municipality—State	9,000	9,000
6. Education—(a) State	1,23,867	1,22,027
(b) Zemindaries	9,075	8,557
Total ...	1,32,942	1,30,584
7. Medical and Sanitation :—(a) State ...	67,638	66,513
(b) Zemindaries ...	11,469	12,001
Total ...	79,107	78,514
8. Survey and Settlement—(a) State ...	20,119	13,835
(b) Zemindaries ...	916	1,097
Total ...	21,035	14,932
9. Agriculture, Commerce and Industries—State	7,859	8,031
10. Religious Expenses—(a) State ...	64,971	55,724
(b) Zemindaries ...	6,111	6,716
Total ...	71,082	62,440
11. Sultanat—State	62,951	56,962
12. Purchase of Land Tenures :—		
(a) State	6,845	11,522
(b) Zemindaries	6,573	6,278
Total ...	13,418	17,800
13. Pension and Gratuity—(a) State ...	59,268	56,148
(b) Zemindaries ...	10,915	11,943
Total ...	70,183	68,091
14. Ordinary *Sansar* charges :—		
(a) His Highness's own and the late Maharaja's family	85,293	82,291
(b) Other branches of the Raj family ...	1,15,454	96,142
(c) Thakurs	31,675	33,197
(d) *Sansar* office establishment ...	13,608	12,587
(e) Miscellaneous	66,670	73,250
Total ...	3,12,700	2,97,467
15. Charity and Donation :—(a) State ...	13,769	29,007
(b) Zemindaries ...	7,046	8,551
Total ...	20,815	37,558
16. His Highness's Nij Tahabil :—State ...	1,00,000	1,00,000
17. His Highness's tour—State	1,25,000	1,20,500
18. Payment of liabilities and deposits :—		
(a) State	77,171	79,860
(b) Zemindaries	30,066	13,183
Total ...	1,07,237	93,043
19. Miscellaneous—(a) State	10,164	5,901
(b) Zemindaries ...	11,723	14,225
Total ...	21,887	20,126
20 Writing off irrecoverable advances :— State ...	5,577	3,000
21. Repayment of old debts State ...	96,502	1,00,668
22. Interest on deposits—State	29,339	30,910
23. Advance to *Nijtahabil*— Zemindaries ...	1,87,000	79,591
24 Silver Jubilee	—	17,638
Total ...	28,47,545	27,37,576
25. Closing Balance :—		
(a) State		
In Cash	1,85,411	2,28,970
At Bank	3,468	72,408
Working balance :—		
In Cash	12,299	36,192
At Bank	2,12,701	1,88,808
In advances	1,90,182	1,90,182
In bonds and advances	4,88,898	5,20,616
Total ...	10,92,959	12,37,176
(b) Zemindaries :—		
In Cash	1,11,086	2,28,090
At Bank	71,050	1,08,629
In bonds and advances	2,01,366	2,20,425
Total ...	3,83,502	5,57,144
Total of State & Zemindaries' balances ...	14,76,461	17,94,320
Total of State & Zemindaries' expenditure ...	28,47,545	27,37,576
GRAND TOTAL ...	43,24,006	45,31,896

244. The year opened with a balance of Rs. 14,76,461 against Rs. 14,02,434 in the year before. During the year under report, the total receipts from all sources, including deposits, loans and law charges recovered amounted to Rs. 30,55,435 against Rs. 29,21,572 in the previous year. Thus the total sum available for expenditure was Rs. 45,31,896 against Rs. 43,24,006. The actual income amounted to Rs. 28,72,488 against Rs. 26,18,250 showing an increase of Rs. 2,54,238.

Receipts.

245. The total expenditure incurred during the year amounted to Rs. 27,37,576 against Rs. 28,47,545 in the previous year, showing a decrease of Rs. 1,09,969.

Expenditure.

246. The year closed with a balance of Rs. 17,94,320 of which Rs. 4,93,252 represented cash in the treasuries, Rs. 3,69,845 was held in Banks while the balance of Rs. 9,31, 223 was held in loans and advances.

Closing balance.

247. A quinquennial statement of the receipts and expenditure of the State and the attached Zemindaries is given below :—

Quinquennial Review of Receipts and Expenditure.

Serial No.	Year.	State.		Zemindary		Remarks.
		Receipts.	Expenditure.	Receipts.	Expenditure.	
1.	1341 T. E.	17,90,258	17,40,914	8,72,924	8,29,784	The figures for the year 1343 T. E. for the State include on the receipt side the loan of Rs. 9,00,000 (Rupees nine lacs) taken from the Government of India and on the debit side the expenditure incurred for liquidation of old debts.
2.	1342 T. E.	19,10,680	18,95,612	9,29,366	10,04,308	
3.	1343 T. E.	27,34,304	23,48,173	9,82,889	9,71,867	
4.	1344 T. E.	19,78,355	19,37,610	10 78,217	10,44,936	
5.	1345 T. E.	20,77,047	19,32,830	12,28,388	10,54,746	
	Total ...	104,90,644	98,55,139	50,91,784	49,05,635	
	Average ...	20,98,129	19,71,028	10,18,357	9,81,127	

248. The world-wide economic depression which made itself felt in the State accounts for the decline in receipts in the year 1341 T. E.. Signs of gradual recovery from the slump became however perceptible in the year 1342 T. E. and the year under report shows a marked improvement of the situation. A cautious policy was, however, followed as regards expenditure which had to be cut down to keep it within the receipts.

249. The noticeable variations in expenditure are explained below :—

i. ADMINISTRATIVE CHARGES :—

STATE—The increase was Rs. 2,158. This was mainly due to time scale increment of pay.

ZEMINDARIES—The increase was Rs. 17,641. This was due to increased litigation charges.

ii. REVENUE AND TAXES :—

The decrease of Rs. 3,994. was due to the reduced payment made on account of income-tax.

iii. Public Works :—

State—The decrease was Rs. 9,045. This was due to the reduction of expenditure for improvement works.

Zemindaries—The decrease was Rs. 84 only.

iv. Electric Light :—

The increase was Rs. 134 only.

v. Municipality :—

The amount of grant was the same as in the previous year.

vi. Education :—

State—The decrease was Rs. 1,840. This was due to curtailment of expenditure.

Zemindaries—The decrease was Rs. 518 only.

vii. Medical :—

State—The decrease was Rs. 1,125. Some special kind of miscellaneous expenditure, which was incurred in the previous year, was not necessary in the year under report. This accounts for the decrease.

Zemindaries—The increase was Rs. 532 only.

viii. Survey and Settlement :—

State—The decrease was Rs. 6,284. The expenditure incurred in the previous year in connection with the Topographical Survey of the State was not necessary in the year under report. This accounts for the decrease.

Zemindaries—The increase was Rs. 181 only.

ix. Agriculture, Commerce and Industries :—

The increase was Rs. 172 only.

x. Religious Expenditure :—

State—The decrease was Rs. 9,247. This was due to curtailment of expenditure.

Zemindaries :—The increase was Rs. 605 only.

xi. Sultanat :—

State—The increase was Rs. 4,011. This was mainly due to purchase of a new motor car and some miscelleneous expenditure relating to the Motor Department.

xii. Purchase of Land Tenures :—

State—The increase was Rs. 4,677. This was due to payment of some arrear compensation for lands brought under *Khas Mahal.*

Zemindaries—The decrease was Rs. 295 only.

xiii. Pension and Gratuity :—

State—The decrease was Rs. 3,120. The decrease was mainly due to the death of some pensioners.

Zemindaries—The increase was Rs. 1,028.

xiv. Ordinary Samsar Charges :—

The decrease was Rs. 15,233. This was mainly due to the reduction of the provision of Late Maharaj Kumar Samarendra Chandra Deb Barman Bahadur on account of his demise.

xv. Charity and Donation :—

State—The increase was Rs. 15,238. This was due to the marriage ceremony of some Kumars and Kumaris.

Zemindaries—The increase was Rs. 1,505. This was due to payment of some donations sanctioned by His Highness the Maharaja Manikya Bahadur at the time of his visit to Feni.

xvi. His Highness's Nijtahabil :—
The expenditure was the same as in the previous year.

xvii. His Highness's Tour :—
The decrease was Rs. 4,500.

xviii. Payment of Liabilities and Deposits :—
State—The increase was Rs. 2,689. This was due to, payment of some provident funds deposits and some old liabilities.

Zemindaries—The decrease was Rs. 16,883. There was some increase of expenditure in the previous year owing to refund of some deposits to the Tripura Raj Central Co-Operative Bank; but no such refund was necessary in the year under report, This accounts for the decrease.

xix. Miscellaneous :—
State—The decrease was Rs. 4,263.

Zemindaries—The increase was Rs 2,502. This was due to the purchase of a Motor Boat.

xx. Writing off Irrecoverable Advances :—
State—The decrease was Rs. 2,577.

xxi. Repayment of Old Debts :—
State—The increase of Rs. 4,166 was due to payment of some old debts.

xxii. Payment of Interest on deposits :—
The increase of Rs. 1,571 was due to payment of some outstanding interests on deposits.

xxiii. Advance to His Highness's Nijtahabil :—
Zemindaries—The decrease was Rs. 1,07,409. This was due to reduction of provision in the year under report.

xxiv. Silver Jubilee of Their Majesties :—
This was a special expenditure in the year under report.

250. Two comparative statements of Receipts and Expenditure of the State and the Zemindaries with the respective Revised Estimates are given in appendices XXV and XXVI.

251. In the State the total receipts showed an increase of Rs. 1,67,047 and Rs. 76,547 in comparison with the original and the revised Budget estimates respectively.

252. In the Zemindaries, the total receipts showed an increase of Rs. 1,54,888 and Rs. 4,588 in comparison with the original and the Revised Budget estimates respectively.

253. Thakur Kamini Kumar Singh, Naib Dewan, continued to be incharge of the Department till the 13th Jaistha. With effect from the 14th Jaistha Thakur S. C. Deb Barman M. A. (Harvard), Senior Naib Dewan, was placed in charge of the Department.

CHAPTER VI—MEDICAL.

254. The year under review opened with 18 dispensaries inclusive of the V. M. Hospital at the capital town but ended with 19—the dispensary at Muhuripur in the Belonia Division being restarted in the middle of the year.

255. The total number of new patients treated in the above Hospital and dispensaries and their daily average as compared with those of the previous year are shewn in the following statement.

New patients.

	1344 T. E.			1345 T. E		
	Outdoor.	Indoor.	Total.	Outdoor.	Indoor.	Total.
PATIENTS.	1,32,243	906	1,33,149	1,46,610	997	1,47,607
Daily average	362·3	2·48	364·78	400·57	2·72	403·29

256. 2,92,779 patients (new + old) were treated outdoor as against 2,55,303 in the preceding year—the daily average being 813·09 against 699·42.

Outdoor attendance.

257. Inclusive of last year's balance of 22, the in-patients totalled 997 as against 906 in the year previous: of them 778 were cured, 168 were relieved or otherwise discharged, 20 died and 31 remained under treatment at the close of the year.

Indoor patients.

258. In all 1281 surgical operations including 35 major were performed as against 1289 and 25 respectively of the year before.

Surgical operations.

259. The total number of Police cases admitted during the year under review was 160 against 162 of which post mortem cases were 18 against 13 in the preceding year.

Police cases.

260. The outdoor attendance of new patients in the Victoria Memorial Hospital numbered 28089 as against 24805 in the last year, the daily average of new and old patients being 173·84 against 131·08 thus shewing an increase of 3284 and 42·76 respectively.

V. M. Hospital.

261. The total number of in-patients was 723 as against 579 with the daily average (new + old) of 22 against 20·61. Of these 528 were cured 148 were relieved or otherwise discharged 19 died and 28 remained over.

262. Altogether Rs. 9,425-2-9 was expended on this Institution as against Rs 10,110-9-9 in the preceding year.

263. As before, Dr. N. Deb Barman, M. B. was incharge of this Department. 16 human cases were treated during the year under review against 29 of the year previous. The total cost amounted to Rs. 340-4 as against Rs. 317-4-6 in the previous year.

Antirabic Treatment centre.

264. As previously, Kaviraj Surendra Chandra Bhattacharjee Baidyaratna remained incharge of this Department during the year under report. 31 patients were treated by him as against 32 of the last year.

Ayurvedic Department.

265. The expenditure due to his salary and the price of medicines came up to Rs. 2,475 as against Rs. 2,392-3.

266. Under the control and supervision of Dr. M. M. Majumdar, Chief Medical Officer, two Assistant Homoeopaths continued to run the only dispensary at the Capital and treated 19,126 patients during the year as against 18,966, the daily average (new + old) being 96·84 against 96·06 of the year preceding.

Homoeopathic Department

267. The total expenditure in this Department amounted to Rs. 2,366-3 as against Rs. 2,280-12-9 of the last year.

268. 6,730 persons were successfully vaccinated out of 8,687 operations performed, the preceding year's figures being 6,952 and 8,137 respectively.

Vaccination.

269. 29 Vaccinators worked in the hills & plains. Two Small-pox doctors and 2 Inspectors inspected their works. The total cost on this account came upto Rs. 1,650-6 as against Rs. 1,543-10-3 in the previous year.

270. Dr. A. Sen Gupta, M. B., State Bacteriologist continued incharge of the Laboratory. During the year 465 samples were clinically examined as against 504 of the year before.

Clinical Laboratory.

271. The Kala-azar centre at Tilla Bazar in the Kailashahar Division was abolished in the first part of the year under report. The Centre at the Capital was worked regularly. In both 249 patients were treated. Of them 80 were cured, 1 died, 136 left treatment and 32 remained over.

Kala-azar.

272. Rs. 1,066–4–6 was expended on this head as against Rs. 1,280 in the year preceding.

273. Dr. P. Sen, M. B., having left service, the work of the Leprosy Clinics at the Capital and at Khowai Division was carried on by Dr. J. M. Bose and Dr. S. C. Dey respectively—who had received special training at the hands of Dr. Sen. They treated 28 new patients as against 54 in the last year—the average attendance in both the Clinics was ·55 against 1·08. Rs. 80-1-6 was spent on this account as the price of the medicine only as against Rs. 455-6 of the previous year.

Leprosy.

274. Cholera appeared at Sadar, Khowai, Sabroom and Kailashahar Divisions and raged rather virulently 202 deaths were reported out of 226 seizures.

Public health.

275. 2,000 persons were inoculated with anti-cholera vaccine as against 3,723 of the year before.

276. Small-pox broke out in Udaipur and Sadar Divisions. 27 persons were attacked of whom 5 died and 22 recovered under the treatment of Small-pox doctor. The question of compulsory secondary vaccination free, where necessary, is under consideration.

277. As before, Dr. M. M. Majumdar, L. M. S., Chief Medical Officer held charge of the Medical Department assisted by Dr. S. K, Dutt, L. M. S., Assistant State Physician, Dr. A. Sen Gupta, M. B., Dr. N. Deb Barman, M. B. Besides, there was a regular staff of Medical subordinates maintained for the

Staff

different dispensaries in the State as well as two Midwives at the Capital.

Tour.

278. Dr. S. K. Dutt, Dr. A. Sen Gupta and Dr. N. Deb Barman were out on tour for 22 days and inspected Dharmanagar, Kailashahar, Kamalpur, Sabroom, Khowai and Kalyanpur dispensaries.

Total Expenditure.

279. The total expenditure in the Medical Department during the year under review stood at Rs. 66,513 as against Rs. 67,638 of the previous year.

CHAPTER VII—PUBLIC INSTRUCTION.

Charge.

280. Under order of His Highness dated 10.2.45 T. E. the Public Instruction Portfolio hitherto held by the Minister was transferred to that of the Chief Secretary—Manyabara Rana Bodhjung Bahadur, F. R. G. S., and Mr. Satyaranjan Bose, B. A., Under Secretary, was entrusted with the charge of the Education Department, in the year under report. Dewan Saheb K. Dutt, M. A., B. L., F. R. E. S., M. R. A. S., Private Secretary—held the Portfolio of Public Instruction in absence of the Chief Secretary.

Number of Schools.

281. The total number of schools (including private schools) during the year under review was 181 against 193 in the previous year, and the total numerical strength 7,520 against 9,106 including 1,464 pupils reading in private institutions numbering 49 as against 50 in the preceding year.

H. E. Schools.

282. There were 5 H. E. Schools as before and one Branch H. E. School in the State. All the H. E. Schools are permanently affiliated to the Calcutta University. Class IX was opened provisionally in the Branch H. E. School at Udaipur, on condition that the Public would agree to bear the additional cost of maintaining extra staff. The total number of pupils in all these institutions were 1,584 against 1,597 in the previous year, and the average daily attendance stood at 1,155·13 against 1,186·46.

Matriculation Examination

283. Agartala, the capital of the State, continued to be a centre for the Matriculation Examination. The State H. E. Schools are allowed to send up candidates to this centre. One private student and eleven candidates from Devagram H. E. School sat for the Examination in this centre in the year under report, in addition to the candidates from the State Schools. Besides these, two female candidates—one private and the other from Kailasahar B. K. Institution, where co-education was allowed, sat for the same.

284. The Examination was conducted under the direct control and supervision of Dewan Saheb K. Dutt, M. A., B. L.; F. R. E. S., M. R. A. S., Chief Secretary-in-charge with the assistance of Mr. S. Roy, M. A., Sadar Collector, in-charge of the Education Department, as

Mr. Satyaranjan Bose, B. A., Under Secretary, was away on leave. The Department looked after the convenience of the candidates coming from *Mofussil*, in respect of accommodation and other necessary matters.

Result of the Matriculation Examination.

285. Altogether 73 candidates were sent up for the Matriculation Examination from the State H. E. Schools against 64 in the previous year. The result of the Examination is given below :—

	No. sent up.	passed.	1st Division.	2nd Division.	3rd Division.
1. U. K. Academy	23	18	5	12	1
2. R. K. Institution	20	10	4	2	4
3. B. K. Institution	16	6	2	3	1
4. B. B. Institution	5	5	4	1	0
5. N. C. Institution	9	5	2	3	0
Total ...	73	44	17	21	6

286. The result on the whole was satisfactory, percentage of successful candidates being 60·27 against 89·06 in the previous year. The percentage of passes in the 1st Division on the total number of passes was the highest for B. B. Institution *viz.* 80. and lowest for the U. K. Academy *viz* 27·77.

287. The three successful candidates topping the list, the first belonging to N. C. Institution, the second and the third belonging to U. K. Academy and B. B. Institution were awarded Scholarships of Rs. 10, Rs. 8 and Rs. 8 respectively per month.

M. E. Schools for boys.

288. In the year under review, there were 10 Middle English Schools for boys with 1,166 pupils on the rolls against 9 with 1,132 pupils in the previous year. The average daily attendance was 850·49 against 847·06 in the previous year.

M. E. Schools for girls.

289. There was one M. E. School for girls at Agartala, namely the Maharani Tulsibati Girls' School, the numerical strength of which was 74 against 68 in the previous year and the average daily attendance was 62·83 against 59·16. By special permission of this Department, some girls were allowed to continue higher studies in this School under the tuition of the Head Mistress. For conveyance of the girls, Motor Bus Service was continued as before.

L. V. Schools.

290. The total number of Lower Vernacular Schools for boys was 24 against 26 in the previous year. The total numerical strength was 1,239 against 1,243 and the average daily attendance was 938·24 against 1010·11 in the previous year. In some of these schools, boys and girls read together.

Pathshalas for boys.

291. There were 70 *Pathshalas* for boys against 76 in the previous year. The total number of boys was 2,249 against 2,519 and the average daily attendance was 1,745·34 against 1,918·18. In some of these schools, boys and girls read together. Under special orders of the Education Department, some boys of some of these institutions were allowed to read the Lower Vernacular standard.

Pathshalas for girls.

292. There were 5 *Pathshalas* for girls in the year under review against 9 in the previous year. The total numerical strength was 138 against 329 and the average daily attendance was 132·01 against 248·70 in the year preceding. In some

of these schools, some girls were allowed, under special orders, to read the Lower Vernacular standard.

Scholarship Examination.

293. Altogether 824 candidates appeared at the different Scholarship examinations of the State against 803 in the previous year. Of these 623 candidates including 95 girls came out successful. The result on the whole was satisfactory. 56 students including 8 girls passed the M. E. Examination and 2 girls passed the H. V. Examination this year. In the L. V. Examination, the number of successful candidates was 161 including 30 girls, and in the *Pathshala* Examination the number was 404 including 55 girls. Amongst these 14 candidates appeared from different *Moktab* and *Madrassas* of the State. On the results of the Examination 14 boys and 5 girls were awarded monthly scholarships varying from Rs. 2 to Rs. 5 tenable for one to four years.

Schools for special training.

294. In the year under review, there were 11 schools for special training, consisting of 5 Sanskrit *Tols*, 5 *Madrassas* and *Moktabs* and one *Silpasram* (Artisan School). The Snaskrit *Tols* had 62 students on the rolls against 47 in the previous year and the average daily attendance was 45·58 against 34·18.

295. The *Madrassas* and *Moktabs* had 347 students on the rolls as against 178 in the previous year and the average daily attendance was 318·70 against 135·88.

Compulsory Free Primary Schools.

296. There were, as before, 4 Free Primary Schools with 623 pupils including girls against 585 in the previous year. The subjoined statement will show the number of students, their classes and the average daily attendance.

Compulsory Free Primary Schools.	No. of Students. Boys.	Girls.	Average daily attendance. Boys.	Girls.	Kumars.	Thakurs.	Tripura.	Laskar.	Manipuri.	Bengali Hindu.	Mahommedan.	Others.
1. No. 1 U. K. Academy ...	160	120	167	113	0	9	20	0	0	233	18	0
2. No. 2 Tulsibati	43	100	21	122	0	29	7	0	0	103	5	0
3. No. 3 Bejoy Kumar ...	332	83	7	69	1	12	18	0	0	71	14	0
4. No. 4 Thakur Pally ...	84	0	84	7	0	22	11	0	0	34	17	0
	320	303	319	304	1	72	56	0	0	440	54	0

297. The comparative statement below will show the number of Non-Bengalee students receiving education in the several schools of the State :—

Serial number.	Nationality.	Number of students. Past year.	Present year.	Remarks.
1.	Rajkumars...	7	5	
2.	Thakurs	290	216	
3.	Manipuris	573	704	
4.	Tripuras	1,007	985	
5.	Reangs	18	9	
6.	Kukis...	0	0	
7.	Chakmas	0	1	
8.	Lushais	1	0	
9.	Others	56	121	
10.	Christians	0	2	
	Total	1,952	2,043	

298. The Maharajkumaries received their education as before under a graduate lady teacher and a Pandit.

Education of Princes and Princesses.

299. Maharajkumar Mohan Kishore Dev Barman Bahadur continued the same in the College of Engineering and Technology, Jadavpur, as before.

Education of other Kumars.

300. The young Maharajkumars received their education under a Tutor.

301. The Rajkumar Boarding House at Comilla had 11 inmates of whom 8 were from the different branches of the Ruling family and the remaining 3 were Rana Bahadurs, related to the Raj Family. 8 of the inmates were reading in the Comilla Zilla School and 3 in the Comilla Victoria College. In the year under review 1 Kumar Bahadur passed the Matriculation Examination. The boarders were placed under the charge of a Superintending tutor who in addition to his tutorial works looked after the management of the Boarding House. There was also one Assistant Graduate Resident Tutor. Besides the above, one Graduate teacher and a Pandit were engaged for coaching some of the Boarders both in the morning and evening.

Kumar Boarding House at Comilla.

302. 10 Thakur boys receiving higher education in various Colleges and technical schools were awarded stipends from the Education Department.

Education of Thakur boys.

303. The number of Boarders in the Thakur Boarding House was 30 against 32 in the preceding year. The staff consisted of one Graduate Guardian Superintendent, one Under Graduate Resident Tutor and one Manager Tutor. The average daily attendance of the boarders was 26·5 against 26·2 in the previous year. One Thakur boy appeared at the Matriculation Examination and came out successful in the 2nd division.

Thakur Boarding House at Agartala.

304. There were altogether 17 boarders from Class IV to Matriculation class in the old Tripura Boarding House against 16 in the previous year. All the boarders were allowed free boarding and stipends. A whole time graduate Superintending Tutor looked after the boys as well as the boarding management as before. Another Tutor was engaged to coach the boys in the morning. There was a small library in the Boarding House and the boys were encouraged in Agricultural pursuits within the Boarding Compound. There was a newly started Boarding House with 31 Tripura boys reading in higher and lower classes against 35 in the previous year. A tutor was engaged to coach the boys both in the morning and evening and was entrusted with the management of the Boarding. The Boarders were allowed a piece of ground in front of the Boarding House for agricultural pursuits.

Tripura Boarding House at Agartala.

305. There were 46 boarders in the Tripura Boarding House at Khowai against 60 in the previous year. The graduate Superintending Tutor and one Assistant Tutor were engaged as before for coaching the boys both in the morning and evening. The Superintending Tutor looked after the Boarding management in addition to his tutorial work.

Tripura Boarding House at Khowai.

306. There were 40 boarders on the roll in the Ramkumar Boarding School against the same number in the previous year and the average daily attendance was 23·56 against 23·42 in the preceding year. Two Tutors were engaged as before to coach the boarders and one of them looked after the Boarding management in addition.

Ramkumar Boarding School at Kalyanpur.

307. There were 22 convicts reading in the Primary Schools in the Central Jail of whom 2 appeared in the *Pathshala* Scholarship Examination in the year under report and both of them came out successful in the first division.

Schools for convicts.

308. The Woodburn Artisan School and Silpasram continued to be under the direct control of Manyabara Rana Bodhjung Bahadur F. R. G. S., the Chief Secretary to His Highness the Maharaja Manikya Bahadur. The School had on the roll 16 students against 28 in the preceding year. In the year under review the average daily attendance was 9·09 against 11·75 in the previous year. 12 students were awarded monthly stipends varying from Rs 1-8 to Rs. 8 each. There were 11, 5, 4 students in the Carpentry, Black-smith and Brass-smith Sections respectively.

Woodburn Artisan School & Silpasram.

309. The sub-joined statement will show the number of students, their classes (castes) and their average attendance in the year under report :—

Name of School.	Number of Students.	Thakurs.	Tripura.	Laskar.	Manipuri	Bengali Hindu.	Mahomedan.	Others.	Average attendance.
Woodburn Artisan School and Silpasram	20	5	—	2	2	9	2	—	9·09

310. 4 Lushai boys were awarded Lushai stipends in the year under report, of whom one read in the Victoria College, one read in the Bengal Survey School at Mainamati and the other two prosecuted their studies in M. C. College, Sylhet.

Lushai Stipends.

311. 20 students were awarded special stipends in the year under review, of whom 10 read in different schools of this State and the remaining 10 prosecuted their studies elsewhere in different schools, colleges and technical institutions.

Special Stipends.

312. There were three Sub-Inspectors of Schools as before who inspected all the schools other than the H. E. schools within their respective jurisdictions in Sadar, Khowai, Kailasahar and Dharmanagar Divisions. Revenue Inspectors of Sonamura and Belonia inspected some Schools in their respective Division.

Inspection Works.

313. Maharajkumar Norottam Kishore Deb Barman Bahadur continued to be the Librarian of the Bir Chandra Library at Agartala which was maintained in two separate sections as before, *viz.*, 1. The English Section, located in the Ujjayanta Palace, and 2. the Vernacular section in the building, near the local H. E. School. The latter section was open to the Public.

Library.

The number of English books (including foreign literature) were 5027 against 5025 in the previous year. The number of Bengali and Sanskrit books were 2250 against 2249 in the previous year. There were 4 daily newspapers, 2 weeklies and 7 monthlies against the same in the preceding year. The average daily attendance in the vernacular section of the library was 9 against 7 in the previous year and the total number of books issued to the public was 3,028 against 2,076.

Expenditure.

314. The total expenditure on public instruction in the year under report amounted to Rs. 1,22,027 against Rs. 1,23,867. Details of expenditure are noted below :—

1.	Primary Education	Rs. 27,839
2.	Secondary Education	,, 46,607
3.	Schools for special Training	,, 1,631
4.	Compulsory Free Primary Education ...	,, 2,217
5.	Boarding Institutions for Thakur boys ...	,, 6,201
6.	Education for Kumars and Kumaris ...	,, 20,682
7.	Scholarships and stipends	,, 5,100
8.	Library	,, 1,855
9.	Tripura Boarding	,, 3,916
10.	Miscellaneous...	,, 5,979

Income.

315. The total receipts from the schools amounted to Rs. 14,548 against Rs. 15,034 in the previous year.

CHAPTER VIII—ZEMINDARIES.

Chakla Roshnabad Estates.

Management.

316. The management of His Highness's Zemindaries in British India continued in the hands of Manyabar Rai J. C. Sen Bahadur, B. A., B. C. S. (Retired) for the whole year. He was, as usual, assisted by a Deputy Manager posted at Comilla and three Assistant Managers posted at Feni, Mogra and Srimangal.

The year and the tenantry.

317. The economic depression of previous years continued though in a less acute form during the year under report. Relief was given to the Talukdars and the tenants, as in previous years, in the shape of general remission of interest and damages almost throughout the whole year and the policy of allowing petty demands to be time-barred was also continued.

Demand.

318. The gross demand of the year was Rs. 10,13,059 against Rs. 10,21,090 in the previous year.

319. Total receipt amounted to Rs. 12,28,388 (including Rs. 586 on account of the Tripura Raj Central Co-operative Bank Ltd. and Rs. 2,096 on account of Debottar Mohal) against Rs. 10,78,217 in the previous year. Increase in receipt is mainly due to realisation of law charges and deposits.

Receipt.

320. The total expenditure in the year under review was Rs. 10,54,746 including payment of old debts and deposits to the extent of Rs. 13,183 and a contribution of Rs. 2,50,000 to the State and advances of Rs. 79,591 to Nij Tahabil. Total expenditure during the previous year was Rs. 10,44,935.

Expenditure.

321. Of the total expenditure during the year under review Rs. 2,81,546 was on account of Land Revenue, taxes and cesses while the total administration charges of the Zemindaries including Public works and Law charges amounted to Rs. 3,73,404 against Rs. 3,53,096 in the previous year.

322. The following items of expenditure aggregating Rs. 3,99,796 are noticeable :—

1.	Education	Rs. 8,557
2.	Medical charges	„ 12,001
3.	Religious ceremonies	„ 6,716
4.	Purchase of property	„ 6,278
5.	Loans and advances	„ 1,959
6.	Sansar stipends	„ 12,960
7.	Donations	„ 5,851
8.	Repayment of old debts and deposits	„ 13,183
9.	Advance to Nij Tahabil	„ 79,591
10.	Contribution to the State	„ 2,50,000
		Rs. 3,99,796

323. The result of the year's settlement operations will appear from the figures noted below :—

Settlement.

	Kinds of settlement.	Addition to rental.	Nazar.
1.	Railway relinquished land	—	—
2.	*Kaimi* and *Takshishi* Settlement in the Comilla Town	Rs. 11	Rs. 546
3.	Ordinary Town Settlement ...	„ 87	„ 1,410
4.	*Khas Patit* land	„ 240	„ 1,638
5.	Enhancement of rent	„ 153	„ 1,691
6.	Re-settlement of auction purchased holdings ...	„ 245	„ 21,995
7.	Settlement of rent-free holding	—	—
8.	*Takshishi Taluki* settlement in the *Moffusil* ...	„ 4	„ 221
9.	*Ijara* settlement	—	—
		Rs. 740	Rs. 27,501

324. The corresponding figures for the previous year were Rs. 1,532 and Rs. 21,206 respectively.

CHAPTER IX—MISCELLANEOUS.

325. Manyabara Rana Bodhjung Bahadur, F. R. G. S., Chief Secretary, was in camp with His Highness the Maharaja Manikya Bahadur during all his tours in the year under review.

326. Thakur K. K. Singh, Naib Dewan, was out on tour for 11 days.

327. The tours of the Divisional Officers and their assistants are noted below :—

State.

1. Sadar—
   - Sadar Collector—Babu Sashanka Bhusan Roy, M. A. ... 49 days.
   - Asst. „ Kumar Narsingh Chandra Deb Barman Bahadur ... —
   - Asst. Collector—Thakur Kamal Krishna Deb Barman ... 5 „
   - Probationer Collector—Thakur Hiran Kumar Deb Barman ... 2 „
2. Kailashahar—
   - Divisional Officer—Babu Akhil Chandra Mazumdar, M. A., B. L. ... 20 „
   - Second Officer—Babu Jyotirmay Ghosh, M. A. ... 9 „
3. Sonamura—
   - Divisional Officer—Thakur Rebati Mohan Deb Barman ... 4 „
   - Second „ Thakur Jyotilal Deb Barman, B. L. ... 16 „
4. Belonia—
   - Divisional Officer—Thakur Gokul Chandra Deb Barman ... 9 „
   - Probationer—Thakur Hiran Kumar Deb Barman ... 34 „
5. Khowai—
   - Divisional Officer—Babu Prabharanjan Das Gupta, M. A., B. L ... 66 „
   - Probationer—Babu Narendra Narayan Choudhuri, B. L. ... 44 „
6. Dharmanagar—
   - Divisional Officer—Babu Sarada Charan Sarkar, M. A., B. L. ... 21 „
   - Probationer—Babu Chandrahas Singh, B. L. ... 15 „
7. Udaipur—
   - Divisional Officer—Babu Suresh Chandra Chakravarty, B. L. ... 41 „
   - Probationer—Babu Mahendra Kumar Roy, B. L. ... 55 „
8. Sabroom—
   - Divisional Officer—Babu Jogendra Lal Ganguly, B. L. ... 82 „
9. Amarpur—
   - Sub Divisional Officer—Thakur Joysingh Deb Barman, B. A. ... 29 „

Zemindaries.

1. Babu Pramada Ranjan Bhattacharjee, B. A., Deputy Manager, Comilla ... 77 days.
2. Babu Jagadish Chandra Majumdar, M. A., B. L., Assistant Manager, Feni ... 70 „
3. Babu Bisweswar Guha, B. A., Assistant Manager, Mogra ... 67 „
4. Babu Surendra Chandra Guha, B. A., Assistant Manager, Srimangal ... 87 „

DATED, AGARTALA,
The 9th December, 1936.

Jyotis Chandra Sen,
MINISTER.

APPENDIX.

List of the principal Laws and Regulations in force in the Tripura State during 1345 T.E.

Description.	Whether adapted from British Indian Acts.	Whether introduced during the year under report.
CRIMINAL.		
1. Regulation No. III. of 1280 T. E.		
2. Regulation No. I. of 1283 T. E.		
3. Jail Regulation, 1283 T. E.		
4. Regulation No. IV. of 1283 T. E. (Cattle trespass and pound).		
5. Regulation No. III. of 1296 T. E. (Police Regulation).		
6. Act No. IV. of 1321 T. E.–Penal Laws (an amending Act)		
CIVIL.		
1. Civil Law of 1284 T. E.		
2. Rules regarding *chit* suits (small causes) 1287 and 1300 T. E.		
3. Act No. II. of 1313 T. E.—an Act for the regulation of interest on debts.		
4. Act No. II. of 1314 T. E.—Limitation Act	Partly adapted.	
5. Succession Act II of 1339 T. E.		
REVENUE.		
1. Act No. I. of 1290 T. E.—Sale Law		
2. Act No. I. of 1296 T. E.—Tenancy Act.		
3. Act No. II. of 1296 T. E.—*Abkari*		
4. Act No. II. of 1297 T. E.—Reserved forests.		
5. Act No. I. of 1304 T. E.—Duties on *til* and cotton.		
6. Act No. I. of 1306 T. E.—Registration	Do.	
7. Survey and Settlement Act, 1309 T.E.	Do.	
8. *Tuccavi* Regulation, 1310 T. E.		
9. Act No. I. of 1313 T. E.—Forests.		
10. Act No. I. of 1314 T. E.—(amending the above)		
11. A Law imposing export duty on jute and mustard-seed, 1317 T. E.		
12. Act No. II. of 1321 T.E.– Ghasuri Act		
13. P. W. & Road Cess Act IV of 1339 T. E.		
MISCELLANEOUS.		
1. An Act promulgating certain rules as Law, 1283 T. E.		
2. Regulation for the record of judicial decisions &c., 1284 T. E.		

Description.	Whether adapted from British Indian Acts.	Whether introduced during the year under report.
3. Municipal Regulation, 1284 T. E.		
4. Legal Practitioners' Regulation.		
5. Act No. I. of 1297 T. E.—an Act for the regulation of commissions for the examination of witnesses.		
6. Regulation against cow slaughter		
7. Rules of evidence		
8. Act I. of 1318 T. E.—Constitution of Courts —(an amending Act).		
9. Leave and allowance Rules	Do.	
10. Act No. I. of 1321 T. E.—Arms Act	Do.	
11. Act No. III. of 1321 T. E.—Constitution of Courts (an amending Act)		
12. Municipal Act No. I of 1322 T. E.		
13. Revenue Sale Amendment Act—1323 T.E.		
14. An Act for the destruction of old records—1323 T. E.		
15. Act I of 1326 T. E.—Regulation regarding Privy Council Appeals.		
16. Act II of 1326 T. E.—Registration of Births and Deaths		
17. Act III of 1326 T. E.—Vaccination Act	Partly adapted.	
18. Act IV of 1326 T. E.—Public Demands Recovery Act	Do.	
19. Act V of 1326 T. E.—Excise Amendment Act	Do.	
20. Act I of 1327 T. E.—Settlement of lands for tea cultivation		
21. Rules of Import and Sale of Opium—1327 T. E.		
22. Regulation No. 1 of 1328 T. E.—regarding Registration of Coolies		
23. Regulation No. 2 of 1328 T. E.—regarding Export of Tea		
24. Act I of 1329 T. E.—(Absconding sepoys Act)		
25. Act II of 1329 T. E.—(Control of prices of food stuff)		
26. Act III of 1329 T. E.—(Elephants and buffaloes grazing Act)		
27. Act IV of 1329 T. E. (House tax on Hill tribes)		
28. Act V of 1329 T. E.—(Legal practitioners, Act)	Do	
29. Act I of 1332 T. E.—Encumbered Estates Act.		
30. Act III of 1332 T. E.—The Opium and Intoxicating Drugs Act.		

Description.	Whether adapted from British Indian Acts.	Whether introduced during the year under report.
31. Rules and Regulations under the Opium and Intoxicating Drugs Act III of 1332 T. E.		
32. Act I of 1336 T. E.—(Hackney Carriages)	Partly adapted.	
33. Act II of 1336 T. E.—(Amending Act I of 1327.)		
34. Act III of 1336 T. E.—(Amending the Survey & Settlement Regulation)		
35. Act IV of 1336 T. E.—(Prevention of gambling).		
36. Act I of 1337 T. E.—(Amending the State Tenancy Act I of 1296 T. E.)		
37. Land Acquisition Rules under Act I of 1337 T. E.		
38. State Motor Vehicles Act I of 1338 T. E.		
39. Act II of 1338 T. E. for prevention of smuggling of elephant tusks.		
40. State Stamp Act III of 1338 T. E.		
41. Tripura State Bank Act I of 1339 T. E.		
42. Census Act III of 1339 T. E.		
43. Act I of 1342 T. E.—providing for trial of certain criminal cases by Special Tribunal.		
44. Compulsory Primary Education Act II of 1342 T. E.	Do	
45. Tripura Tea Control Act. (Act I of 1345 T. E.)		
46. A Regulation for realization of tax on bullock carts.		
47. A Regulation for realization of toll on Motor Vehicles plying between Agartala & Akhaura.		
48. A Regulation for destruction of papers in accordance with Act No. I of 1323 T. E. (Sec. 4)		

II

Statement showing the strength, cost and other particulars of the Military Force in Tripura State for 1345 T. E.

Arm of service.	Number of fighting officers and men.						Details of force at the end of the current year.						Bugiers.	Total cost on account of pay and allowances of the force, including followers.	Remarks.
	At the end of last year	Recruited this year.	Casualities.			At the end of the current year.	Number of regiments, battalions, or Batteries.	Number of guns.	Number of men.						
			Died.	Invalided.	Discharged, deserted, &c.				Commisioned Officers. European.	Commisioned Officers. Indian.	Non-commissioned officers.	Fighting men.			
1	2	3	4	5	6	7	8	9	10	11	12	13	14	15	16
Infantry ...	349	109	3	—	76	379	1	616	4	16	57	293	9		
Band Party	19	3	—	—	3	19	—	—	—	—	3	16	—		
Total ...	368	112	3	—	79	398	1	616	4	16	60	309	9	Rs. 1,07,181	

III.

Statement showing the strength, cost, discipline, and education of the Police for the year 1345 T. E.

Description of office.	Number.	Grade of pay.	Total cost.	Punishments. Dismissed.	Punishments. Fined, degraded or suspended departmentally.			Punishments. Punished judicially.	Rewards. By promotion.	Rewards. By money.	Education. Number able to read and write.	Education. Number under instruction.	Remarks.
1	2	3	4	5	6			7	8	9	10	11	12
		Rs.			*F.*	*D.*	*S.*						
Superintendent of Police	1	250-0-0	Rs. 82,754	—		—		—	—	—	1	—	F.=Fined.
Asst. Superintendent „	1	100-5-125		—		—		—	—	—	1	—	D.=Degraded.
Inspectors	4	2 65-5/2-90 2 55-2-65		—		—		—	—	1	4	—	S.=Suspended.
Sub-Inspectors (*a*)	23	25-2-45		—		—		—	—	13	23	—	(*a*) One retrenched in the budget. One Prob. S. I. confirmed.
Naib Darogas (*b*)	21	15-1-25		—		—		—	—	8	21	—	(*b*) Including 5 C. I. D. Naib Darogas. One retrenched in the budget.
Writer Naib Darogas (*c*)	16	15-0-0		—		—		—	—	4	16	—	(*c*) One reduced in the budget.
Subedar	1	25-2-45		—		—		—	—	—	1	—	
Armed S. I.	1	25-2-45		—		—		—	—	1	1	—	
Jamadars (civil)	6	15-1-25		—	3	0	0	—	—	2	6	—	
Jamadar (Armed)	1	20-1-30		—		—		—	—	—	1	—	
Havildar	1	19-1-25		—		—		—		—	1	—	
Naiks	4	15-1-20			3	0	0	—	—	—	3	—	(*d*) Extra sanction of 5 for the year 1344 were reduced this year.
Constables (Armed) (*d*)	33	14-1-15		4	16	9	0	--	—	2	25	—	
Constables (Civil) (*e*)	200	10 to 13		1	55	7	0	—	—	18	120	—	(*e*) 20 reduced in the budget.
Chaukidars	176	5-0-0		5	4	0	0	—	—	—	10	—	
Spies	3	20 and 15		—		—		—	—	—	3	—	
Total ...	492			10	81	16	0	—	—	49	237	—	

IV.

Statement showing the working of the Police in the Tripura State during the year 1345 T. E.

State.	Number of offences.		Number of accused arrested.		Number of accused sent up for trial.		Number of accused convicted.		Number of accused acquitted or discharged.		Percentage convicted of accused arrested.		Percentage convicted of accused sent up for trial.		REMARKS.
	Past year.	Present year	Pas year.	Present year.	Past year.	Present year.	Past year.	Present year.	Past year.	Present year.	Past year.	Present year.	Past year.	Present year.	
1	2	3	4	5	6	7	8	9	10	11	12	13	14	15	16
Tripura State	894	674	675	516	819	708	209	139	137	114	30·96	26·94	74·38	* 73·16	* Excluding :— Pending trial— 455 Withdrawal— 8 Compromise— 54 Dead— 1 518

V.

Statement showing the value of property stolen and amount of recoveries in the Tripura State during the year 1345 T. E.

State.	Amount stolen.		Amount recovered.		Percentage of recoveries of property stolen.		REMARKS.
	Past year.	Present year.	Past year.	Present year.	Past year.	Present year.	
1	2	3	4	5	6	7	8
Tripura State	Rs 14,675-4-9	Rs 10,193-14-9	Rs 1,721-11-6	Rs 2,322-5-0	11·73	22·78	

VI.

Statement showing the number of crimes committed, number of cases disposed of, and cases awaiting trial in the Tripura State during the year 1345 T. E.

Description of offences.		Number of Offences. Balance from past year.	Number of Offences. Committed during the present year.	Number of Offences. Total.	Number of cases disposed of during the past year.	Number of cases disposed of during the present year.	Number of cases awaiting trial.	Number of persons apprehended.	Number of persons convicted.	Number of Persons Sentenced. Imprisonment. Simple.	Imprisonment. Rigorous.	Imprisonment and fine. Simple.	Imprisonment and fine. Rigorous.	Fine only.	Whipping.	Capital punishment.	Total.	Number of persons acquitted or discharged.	Number of persons confined being insane.	Number of persons died during or before trial.	Term of Imprisonment. Under one month.	From 1 to below 2 months.	From 2 to below 3 months.	From 3 to below 6 months.	From 6 to below 12 months.	From 1 to below 2 years.	From 2 to below 3 years.	From 3 to below 5 years.	5 years and above.	Imprisonment for life.	Capital punishment.	Persons awaiting trial.	Remarks.
1		2	3	4	5	6	7	8	9	10	11	12	13	14	15	16	17	18	19	20	21	22	23	24	25	26	27	28	29	30	31	32	33
Class I. Offences against the State, public tranquillity, safety and justice &c.	cognizable ...	9	34	43	17	24	19	94	*a*30	4	14	0	0	6	0	0	24	12	0	0	5	9	0	2	2	0	0	0	0	0	0	52	(*a*) 5 persons were bound down.
	non-cognizable	14	45	59	52	49	10	34	3	0	3	0	0	0	0	0	3	25	0	0	0	3	0	0	0	0	0	0	0	0	0	6	
Class II. Offences against person.	cognizable ...	142	345	487	282	354	133	715	*b*90	6	29	3	19	30	0	0	87	398	0	6	14	1	10	5	9	9	2	4	2	1	0	221	(*b*) 3 persons were warned for the future.
	non-cognizable	55	246	301	197	207	94	352	30	2	7	0	0	21	0	0	30	244	0	1	3	3	2	1	0	0	0	0	0	0	0	77	
Class III. Offences against property.	cognizable ...	321	776	1097	672	815	282	1517	*c*325	5	94	1	32	174	0	0	306	682	0	4	29	28	20	42	6	2	2	2	1	0	0	506	(*c*) 7 persons were warned for the future and 12 bound down.
	non-cognizable	120	219	339	191	279	60	311	*d*41	1	9	0	0	26	0	0	36	207	0	0	2	1	7	0	0	0	0	0	0	0	0	63	
Class IV. Other offences.	cognizable ...	64	93	157	251	105	52	237	37	0	19	0	3	15	0	0	37	185	0	2	2	6	4	2	2	5	1	0	0	0	0	13	(*d*) 5 persons were warned for the future.
	non-cognizable	63	216	279	224	193	86	135	*e*18	1	1	0	0	10	0	0	12	99	0	0	1	1	0	0	0	0	0	0	0	0	0	18	
Total cognizable ...	...	536	1248	1784	1222	1298	486	2563	482	15	156	4	54	225	0	0	454	1277	0	12	50	44	34	51	19	16	5	6	3	1	0	792	(*e*) 2 persons were warned for the future and 4 bound down.
Total non-cognizable ...	...	252	726	978	664	728	250	832	92	4	20	0	0	57	0	0	81	575	0	1	6	8	9	1	0	0	0	0	0	0	0	164	
GRAND TOTAL ...	...	788	1974	2762	1886	2026	736	3395	574	19	176	4	54	282	0	0	535	1852	0	13	56	52	43	52	19	16	5	6	3	1	0	956	

VII.

Statement showing the number of offences reported and dealt with by the various Courts in the Tripura State during the year 1345 T.E.

Name of Court.	Number of offences reported during.		Number of persons dealt with.								Persons disposed of.					Persons remaining at the end of the year.	Remarks
				Brought to trial during present year.					Total.								
	Last year.	Present year.	Remaining at the end of last year.	Arrested by Police.	Upon warrant.	On summons.	Voluntary.	Arrested in presence of the Magistrate.	Last year.	Present year.	Discharged without trial.	Acquitted.	Convicted.	Committed or referred.	Died, escaped, or transferred &c.		
1	2	3	4	5	6	7	8	9	10	11	12	13	14	15	16	17	18
Sadar Magistracy	607	578	178	164	156	212	57	—	680	767	272	237	73	26	—	159	
Sonamura " ...	219	242	108	47	63	104	89	1	425	412	104	58	119	3	2	126	
Bilonia " ...	219	179	64	100	50	90	44	—	306	348	164	40	107	6	—	31	
Kailashahar " ...	307	298	116	65	137	136	12	2	457	468	125	79	66	1	3	194	
Khowai " ...	204	206	53	39	23	70	82	.	209	267	129	34	58	2	1	43	
Dharmanagar " ...	248	219	250	102	130	155	14	—	569	651	283	54	50	5	7	252	
Udaipur " ...	176	216	172	32	49	119	7	—	366	379	131	68	50	9	—	121	
Sabrum " ...	43	36	10	35	21	17	7	1	91	91	26	11	29	—	—	25	
TOTAL ...	2,023	1,974	951	584	629	903	312	4	3,103	3,383 *a*	1,234	581	552	52 *b*	13	951	

a. Excluding 12 persons pending before the Court of Sessions at the close of the previous year.

b. The total number of persons for trial before the Court of Sessions, (including 12 persons pending from the last year) was 64, of whom 22 persons were convicted, 37 acquitted and 5 remained under trial at the close of the year.

VIII.

Statement of Criminal cases in which British Subjects were concerned for 1345 T. E.

Description of Offences.		Cases pending since the previous year.	Cases instituted during the year.	Total number of cases.	Cases in which complainants were British subjects.	Cases in which both parties were British subjects.	Cases in which defendants were British Subjects: Cases pending since the previous year	Cases instituted during the year.	Total number of cases.	Cases disposed of: Rejected, compromised without enquiry.	Cases disposed of: Tried.	Cases pending at the close of the year.	Persons under trial at the close of the previous year.	Persons brought to trial during the year.	Total number of persons under trial.	Convicted.	Acquitted or discharged.	Died or escaped &c.	Under trial at the close of the year.
Class I. Offences against the State &c.	cognizable ...	3	8	11	0	0	3	8	11	2	4	5	3	18	21	9	4	0	8
	non-cognizable ...	0	2	2	2	0	0	0	0	0	0	0	0	0	0	0	0	0	0
Class II. Offences against person.	cognizable ...	14	34	48	7	14	12	29	41	10	11	20	22	78	100	30	38	0	32
	non-cognizable ...	8	30	38	5	7	8	25	33	15	3	15	10	20	30	2	15	0	13
Class III. Offences against property.	cognizable ...	61	197	258	13	53	59	186	245	74	109	62	72	280	352	158	115	2	77
	non-cognizable ...	13	34	47	4	27	10	33	43	17	10	16	8	27	35	4	16	0	15
Class IV. Other offences	cognizable ...	14	11	25	3	6	13	9	22	10	8	4	8	22	30	9	16	1	4
	non-cognizable ...	4	14	18	7	6	1	10	11	9	1	1	1	3	4	1	1	0	2
Total cognizable ...		92	250	342	23	73	87	232	319	96	132	91	105	398	503	206	173	3	121
Total non-cognizable ...		25	80	105	18	40	19	68	87	41	14	32	19	50	69	7	32	0	30
GRAND TOTAL ...		117	330	447	41	113	106	300	406	137	146	123	124	448	*572	213	205	3	151

REMARKS.

*Of this number, 95 persons were discharged without trial, the cases being compromised or struck off etc.

Excluding 3 persons dead and 151 remaining under trial at the close of the year; the actual number of persons tried was 323, of whom 213 persons were convicted; the percentage of conviction was thus 65·94 during the year under report as against 63·85 of the preceding year.

IX.

Statement of Extradition Cases for the year 1345 T. E.

Names of Courts.	Nature of cases.	NUMBER BORNE ON THE REGISTER.				NUMBER BROUGHT TO TRIAL.			RESULT.		Number at large at the close of the year.	Number of persons awaiting trial (after arrest) at the close of the year.	REMARKS.
		Number of persons at large at the close of the previous year.	Number of persons awaiting trial at the close of the previous year.	Number of persons against whom warrants were applied for during the year.	Total.	Number of persons arrested and surrendered within the year.	Number of persons who appeared of their own accord or were subsequently arrested in the State within the year.	Total (Columns 4+7+8).	Convicted.	Acquitted or discharged.			
Sadar Magistracy	Theft ...	2	5	25	32	0	21	26	0	1	6	25	‡ Discharged.
	Criminal breach of trust	1	2	2	5	0	0	2	0	2	3	0	
	Kidnapping ...	2	0	1	3	1	0	1	0	0	2	1	
	Mischief ...	1	0	0	1	0	0	0	0	0	1	0	
	Dacoity ...	0	5	5	10	3	1	9	9 *	0	1	0	
	Causing grievous hurt ...	0	0	2	2	0	2	2	0	0	0	2	
	Desertion from the army ...	0	0	2	2	1	0	1	0	0	1	1	
Sonamura „ ...	Theft ...	51	12	13	76	2	15	29	19	7	47	3	
	Rioting and causing grievous hurt ...	1	0	1	2	0	0	0	0	0	2	0	
	Murder ...	0	0	8	8	0	3	3	0	0	5	3	
Bilonia „ ...	Theft ...	8	8	10	26	10	0	18	17	0	8	1	
	Culpable homicide not amounting to murder ...	0	0	8	8	5	0	5	5 †	0	3	0	
Khowai „ ...	Theft ...	1	2	1	4	0	1	3	2	1	1	0	† Committed to Sessions.
	Kidnapping ...	1	0	0	1	0	0	0	0	0	1	0	
	Cheating ...	1	1	0	2	0	0	1	0	1	1 ‡	0	
	Criminal breach of trust ...	0	0	1	1	0	0	0	0	0	1	0	
	Dishonest misappropriation of property ...	0	0	1	1	0	0	0	0	0	1	0	
Kailashahar „ ...	Theft ...	1	0	8	9	5	0	5	1	1	4	3	
	Kidnapping ...	1	0	0	1	0	0	0	0	0	1	0	
	Criminal breach of trust ...	1	0	0	1	0	0	0	0	0	1	0	
	Causing grievous hurt ...	5	0	0	5	0	0	0	0	0	5	0	
	Lurking house trespass by night ...	0	0	1	1	1	0	1	0	0	0	1	
Sabroom „ ...	Theft ...	11	0	14	25	6	6	12	5	0	13	7	* Committed to Sessions.
	Resistence to arrest ...	4	0	4	8	4	0	4	0	0	4	4	
	Dacoity ...	2	0	0	2	0	0	0	0	0	2	0	
Dharmanagar „ ...	Abduction ...	6	0	0	6	5	1	6	0	6	0	0	
	Total ...	100	35	107	242	43	50	128	58	19	114	51	

X.

Statement showing the result of appeals against decisions passed by the Criminal Courts in the Tripura State during the year 1345 T. E.

Tribunal.	Number of applications	Number of persons and cases.																Remarks
		Applications rejected.		*Sentences.*						Proceedings quashed.		Referred.		Further enquiry &c, ordered.		Pending		
				Confirmed.		Modified.		Reversed.										
		Persons.	Cases.	Persons.	Cases.	Persons.	Cases.	Persons.	Cases.	Persons.	Cases.	Persons.	Cases.	Persons.	Cases.	Persons.	Cases.	
Khas Adalat ...	247	10	8	142	119	62	27	35	23	—	—	—	—	19	14	103	56	

XI.

Civil Work—Nature and value of original suits filed and disposed of during the year 1345 T. E.

Tribunal.	Opening balance.		Filed during the year, received by transfer or on remand.		Total.		Disposed of during the year.		Closing balance.		Suits filed during present year.									Suits disposed of during present year.						Suits not estimable in money.	Remarks.
	Past year.	Present year.	Past year.	Present year.	Past year.	Present year.	Past year.	Present year.	Past year.	Present year.	Value.	Suits *re* landed property.	Suits for money transaction.	Suits for other rights.	Number of suits under Rs. 100.	Number of suits above Rs. 100 and under Rs. 500.	Number of suits above Rs. 500 and under Rs. 1,000.	Number of suits above Rs. 1,000 and under Rs. 5,000.	Number of suits above Rs. 5,000.	*Exparte.*	Admitted and compromised.	Struck off the file.	Otherwise disposed of.	Value.	Average duration.		
											Rs. a. p.													*Rs. a. p.*	*Y.m.d.*		
Khas Adalat Original side	48	51	17	21	65	72	14	13	51	59	3,21,033-0-0	5	6	10	0	0	0	10	1	1	2	2	8	11,099-10-6	0-9-4	10	
Sadar Dewani Adalat	306	310	667	553	973	868	663	548	310	320	31,517-9-6	211	239	108	237	194	11	0	0	301	48	56	143	58,217-9-3	0-0-29	116	
Sonamura ,,	51	52	200	182	251	234	199	189	52	45	14,631-9-6	6	141	35	111	33	2	0	0	114	32	7	36	15,220-12-6	0-5-18	36	
Bilonia ,,	32	42	162	185	194	227	152	190	42	37	14,970-5-3	4	131	50	90	49	2	0	0	98	8	60	24	12,343-14-0	0-3-11	44	
Kailashahar ,,	175	121	163	214	338	335	217	173	121	162	14,712-6-3	19	143	52	130	36	3	0	0	43	25	2	103	14,039-4-3	0-8-6	45	
Khowai ,,	35	33	71	64	106	97	73	62	33	35	7,260-3-6	6	21	37	44	16	2	0	0	18	14	14	16	5,841-2-8	0-7-1	2	
Dharmanagar ,,	80	70	115	80	195	150	125	79	70	71	6,839-1-3	15	46	19	42	23	2	0	0	12	8	15	44	5,143-0-6	0-1-26	13	
Udaipur ,,	120	98	211	211	331	309	233	200	98	109	12,090-11-0	37	153	21	136	25	1	0	0	86	14	42	58	11,889-6-9	0-6-25	49	
Sabrum ,,	2	2	25	38	27	40	25	37	2	3	3,118-5-3	34	4	0	31	6	1	0	0	35	1	1	0	2,197-3-3	0-0-9	0	
Total ...	819	779	1,631	1,553	2,480	2,332	1,701	1,491	779	841	4,26,173-3-6	337	884	332	821	382	24	10	1	708	152	199	432	1,35,991-15-8	0-4-24	315	

XII.

Civil Work.—Results of applications for Execution of Decrees, 1345 T.E.

Tribunal.	Opening balance.		Value of opening balance for present year.	Applications brought to the Register.			Total.			Disposed of.			Closing balance.			Nature of applications pending disposal at the close of the year.			Remarks.
	Past year.	Present year.		Past year.	Present year.	Value for present year.	Past year.	Present year.	Value for present year.	Past year.	Present year.	Value for present year.	Past year.	Present year.	Value for present year.	Below 6 months.	Below 12 months.	Above 12 months.	
			Rs. a. p.			Rs. a. p.			Rs. a. p.			Rs. a. p.			Rs. a. p.				
Khas Adalat (Original side)	37	30	21,226-3-9	15	7	24,171-5-0	52	37	45,397-8-9	22	15	30,305-5-0	30	22	15,092-3-9	6	4	12	
Sadar Dewani Adalat ...	200	242	28,896-8-3	297	258	33,129-7-3	497	500	62,025-15-6	255	259	36,684-7-9	242	241	25,341-7-9	118	37	86	
Sonamura Ditto ...	40	42	8,093-0-0	105	80	12,410-10-9	145	122	20,503-10-9	103	74	11,294-9-9	42	48	9,209-1-0	32	6	10	
Bilonia Ditto ...	26	29	2,743-5-0	60	78	8,546-2-6	86	107	11,289-7-6	57	77	7,778-0-0	29	30	3,511-7-6	29	0	1	
Kailashahar Ditto ...	119	112	23,455-0-0	97	102	16,774-0-6	216	214	40,229-0-6	104	112	16,449-0-6	112	102	23,780-0-0	36	18	48	
Khowai Ditto ...	30	22	3,326-6-3	37	28	4,525-3-6	67	50	7,851-9-9	45	29	3,715-13-9	22	21	4,135-12-0	17	2	2	
Dharmanagar Ditto ...	27	49	9,096-12-6	50	26	5,250-9-6	77	75	14,347-6-0	28	36	5,374-11-9	49	39	8,972-10-3	11	6	22	
Udaipur Ditto ...	130	116	18,338-1-0	173	195	28,617-6-6	303	311	46,955-7-6	187	169	25,939-8-3	116	142	21,015-15-3	96	17	29	
Sabrum Ditto ...	2	3	329-5-3	4	25	2,385-8-9	6	28	2,714-14-0	3	18	1,421-5-6	3	10	1,293-8-6	9	0	1	
Total ...	611	645	1,15,504-10-0	838	799	1,35,810-6-3	1,449	1,444	2,51,315-0-3	804	789	1,38,962-14-3	645	655	1,12,352-2-0	354	90	211	

D

XIII.

Civil Work—Number and results of appeals in civil suits, 1345 T. E.

Tribunal.	Opening balance.		Filed during.		Total.		Disposed of during.		Closing balance.		Value of appeales filed during.		How disposed of.										Average duration.	
													Decisions confirmed.		Decisions reversed.		Decisions amended.		Cases remanded for retrial.		Cases compromised and otherwise disposed of.			
	Past year.	Present year.	Past year.	Present year.	Past year.	Present year.	Past year.	Present year.	Past year.	Present year.	Past year.	Present year.	Past year.	Present year.	Past year.	Present year.	Past year.	Present year.	Past year.	Present year.	Past year.	Present year.	Past year.	Present year.
											Rs. a. p.	Rs. a. p.											Y.m.d.	Y.m.d.
Khas Adalat	106	73	108	169	214	247	136	150	78	97	10,571-7-6	8,000-5-6	62	73	31	29	12	9	8	10	23	29	0-5-3	0-5-0

XIV.

Statement showing the number of persons confined in the jails and lock-ups in the Tripura State during the year 1345 T. E.

Stations.	Number of prisons.	Number of prisoners.				Daily average.		Number of prisoners remaining at the end of the year.	Cost of jails and prisoners.	Average period in days of stay of accused under-trial.	Remarks showing mortality among convicts in jail.
		Remaining from last year.	Admitted during the year.	Total.							
				Past year.	Present year.	Past year.	Present year.				
									Rs.		
Agartala	1	149	305	415	454	135·29	133·11	139	20,313	39	One convict died of intestinal tuberculosis.
Sonamura	1	4	127	167	131	·46	·35	8	837	24·61	
Bilonia	1	12	125	163	137	6·32	9·2	5	1,584	41·36	
Kailashahar	1	3	135	123	138	6·30	6·56	5	956	17·71	
Dharmanagar	1	14	143	121	157	7·54	13·31	14	1,481	32·4	
Udaipur...	1	10	51	92	61	11·73	9·04	—	1,579	9·31	
Sabrum	1	2	34	51	36	5·41	2·14	1	862	23·04	
Khowai	1	4	55	60	59	3·11	5·4	11	1,127	41·9	
TOTAL ...	8	198	975	1192	1173	176·16	179·11	183	28,739	28·66	

XV.

Registration of documents in the Tripura State during the year 1345 T.E.

Name of State.	Documents presented for registration including pending from the last year.		Nature of documents presented.										Documents registered.		Value of documents registered.		Documents of which registration has been refused.		Documents remaining unregistered at the end of the year.		Remarks.
			Mortgages.		Sale deeds.		Wills.		Money bonds.		Miscellaneous.										
	Past year.	Present year.	Past year.	Present year.	Past year.	Present year.	Past year.	Present year.	Past year.	Present year.	Past year.	Present year.	Past year.	Present year.	Past year.	Present year.	Past year.	Present year.	Past year.	Present year.	
1	2	3	4	5	6	7	8	9	10	11	12	13	14	15	16	17	18	19	20	21	22
															Rs.	Rs.					
Tripura State	6,615	7,398	1,192	1,313	3,964	4,307	—	2	53	63	1,309	1,553	6,457	7,148	8,33,679	10,98,306	131	60	170	190	

XVI.

Statement showing the receipts and expenditure on account of Registration during the year 1345 T.E.

Description.	Past Year.			Present Year.			Remarks.
	Number of deeds.	Value of property.	Fees realised.	Number of deeds.	Value of property.	Fees realised.	
		Rs.	Rs.		Rs.	Rs.	
Mortgages	1,192	3,11,026	1,181	1,313	4,07,780	1,397	
Sale deeds	3,964	3,79,018	3,329	4,307	4,47,910	3,663	
Wills	—	—	—	2	—	10	
Money bonds	53	5,054	43	53	8,566	41	
Miscellaneous	1,309	1,38,246	1,477	1,553	2,41,891	2,330	
Total ...	6,518	8,33,344	6,030	7,228	11,06,147	7,444	
Total Expenditure ...	—	—	3,555	—	—	3,564	
Net Income ...	—	—	2,475	—	—	3,880	

XVII.

Receipts and expenditure of the Municipalities in the Tripura State during the year 1345 T.E.

NAME.	Opening balance.	RECEIPTS DURING THE YEAR.				Total Receipt		EXPENDITURE DURING THE YEAR.		Balance at the close of the year.	REMARKS.
		State grant.	Tax.	Miscel-laneous.	Total.	Past year.	Present year	Past.	Present.		
1	2	3	4	5	6	7	8	9	10	11	12
	Rs. A.P.	Rs. A.P.	Rs. A.P.	Rs. A.P.	Rs. A.P.	Rs. A.P.	Rs. A.P.	Rs. A.P.	Rs. A.P.	Rs. A.P.	
Agartala Municipality. ...	44,377-15-6 *a*	9,000	5,079-2-0	7,347-9-9 *b*	21,426-11-9	61,824-6-0	65,804-11-3	17,446-6-6 *c*	17,075-4-3	48,729-7-0 *d*	*a.* Including Rs. 44,167-2-3 of the Bazar Improvement fund and Rs. 210-13-3 of the municipality. *b.* Including Rs. 6,762-1-3 of the Bazar Improvement fund. *c.* Including Rs. 2,241-0-3 as expenditure on the Bazar improvement. *d.* Including Rs. 48,688-3-3 of the Bazar Improvoment fund and Rs. 41-3-9 of the municipality.

XVIII.

Statement of rainfall in the Tripura State during the year 1345 T. E.

STATE.	Baisak.	Jaisth.	Asar.	Sravan.	Bhadra.	Asvin.	Kartik.	Agrahayan.	Pous.	Magh.	Falgoon.	Chait.	Total.	Total of past year.	Average of past 5 years.	REMARKS.
Tripura State ...	4·44	17·46	11·35	17·72	12·29	3·91	·92	—	·10	·12	2·44	8·73	79·48	91·30	81·42	

Maximum in Kailashahar--110·46″ **Minimum in Belonia—47·04″**

XIX.

Statement as to the prices of staple food-grains for the year 1345 T. E

Articles.	Price per maund during Chait, 1344 T. E.			Price per maund during chait, 1345 T. E.			REMARKS.
	Rs.	*a.*	*p.*	*Rs.*	*a.*	*p.*	
(1) RICE							
Maximum	4	8	0	4	8	0	
Minimum	2	0	0	2	8	0	
(2) PADDY							
Maximum	2	4	0	2	4	0	
Minimum	1	0	0	1	0	0	

XX.

Expenditure on Public Works during the year 1345 T.E.

Description of work.	State Funds.			Local Funds.			Total.	Remarks.
	Original.	Repairs.	Total.	Original.	Repairs.	Total.		
	Rs.	*Rs.*	*Rs.*	*Rs.*	*Rs.*	*Rs.*	*Rs.*	
Buildings—								
Ordinary Budget ...	12,142	48,326	60,468	485	—	485	60,953	
Improvement „ ...	53,080	—	53,080	—	—	—	53,080	
Roads and Bridges—								
Ordinary Budget ...	1,751	15,512	17,263	1,543	2,238	3,781	21,044	
Improvement „ ...	28,822	—	28,822	—	—	—	28,822	
Tanks and Tubewells—								
Ordinary Budget ...	652	635	1,287	520	—	520	1,807	*Out of the total expenditure of Rs. 2,01,925, Rs. 1,05,824 was spent for Ordinary Public Works and Rs. 96,101 was spent for improvement works.
Improvement „ ...	780	—	780	—	—	—	780	
Miscellaneous works—								
Ordinary Budget ...	968	2,122	3,090	464	—	464	3,554	
Improvement „ ...	13,419	—	13,419	—	—	—	13,419	
Total ...	1,11,614	66,595	1,78,209	3,012	2,238	5,250	1,83,459	
Minor works at the Rajbari (*Karkhana*)	—	994	994	—	—	—	994	
Establishment charges ...	—	—	17,472	—	—	—	17,472	
Grand Total ...	1,11,614	67,589	1,96,675	3,012	2,238	5,250	2,01,925*	

XXI.

*Statement showing the **number** of excise shops and excise revenue of the Tripura State during the year 1345 T. E.*

Name of State.	Country spirit.		Country spirit, Opium and Ganja.		Opium and Ganja.		Tari		Total		Remarks.
	Number of shops.	Revenue demand.	Number of shops.	Revenue demand.	Number of shops.	Revenue demand.	Number of shops.	Revenue. demand.	Number of shops.	Revenue realised.	
				Rs.						*Rs.*	
Tripura State	—	—	33	41,363	—	—	—	—	33	40,057	

XXII.

Statement of Medical Relief afforded in the Tripura State during the year 1345 T.E.*

Dispensary.	Number of patients treated. (new)		Results of in-door patients. (new)				Expenditure.	Daily average. (old + new)			No. of surgical operations performed.			No. of persons vaccinated during the year.			Remarks.
	Outdoor.	Indoor.	Dis-charged cured.	Relieved or dis-charged otherwise.	Died.	Remain-ing under treatment.		Outdoor.	Indoor.	Total.	Major.	Minor.	Total.	Success-fully.	Unsuc-cessfully.	Total.	
							Rs.										
1. Victoria Memorial Hospital...	28,089	723	528	148	19	28	9,238	173·84	22	195·84	14	314	328	503	361	864	
2. Palace Dispensary	6,749	0	0	0	0	0	6,947	39·62	0	39·62	0	0	0	0	0	0	
3. Homœopathic	19,126	0	0	0	0	0	2,304	96·84	0	96·84	0	0	0	0	0	0	* This Statement excludes figures regarding Kaviraji treatment.
4. Dhaleswar	6,581	0	0	0	0	0	1,536	44·8	0	44·8	0	25	25	0	0	0	
5. Kunjaban	1,227	241	229	9	0	3	2,087	13·14	5·21	18·35	0	4	4	0	0	0	
6. Old Agartala	6,562	0	0	0	0	0	1,863	53·58	0	53·58	0	54	54	761	108	869	
7. Bishalgar	8,344	0	0	0	0	0	1,419	35·22	0	35·22	0	50	50	853	88	941	
8. Sonamura	7,296	7	6	0	1	0	1,976	31·18	·11	31·29	0	220	229	589	98	687	
9. Radhakishorpur	9,749	0	0	0	0	0	1,466	46·45	0	46·45	3	68	71	759	661	1,420	† This figure shows the actual number of outdoor patients treated, the total outdoor attendance being 2,92,779 against 2,55,303 in the previous year.
10. Amarpur	3,850	0	0	0	0	0	1,245	17·4	0	17·4	5	56	61	161	32	193	
11. Sabroom	2,421	1	1	0	0	0	1,485	14·15	·06	14·21	0	17	17	185	62	247	
12. Bilonia	7,844	5	5	0	0	0	1,964	45·02	·07	45·09	0	103	103	716	97	813	
13. Khowai	8,092	0	0	0	0	0	1,322	29·63	0	29·63	1	37	38	402	44	446	
14. Kailashahar	9,993	8	1	7	0	0	1,692	63·71	·18	63·89	0	87	87	728	203	931	
15 Kamalpur	5,119	0	0	0	0	0	1,319	25·54	0	25·54	1	55	56	469	133	602	
16. Kulai Howar	2,196	0	0	0	0	0	390	8·54	0	8·54	0	14	14	0	0	0	
17. Kalyanpur	2,711	2	0	2	0	0	913	10·99	·07	11·06	2	25	27	267	30	297	
18. Dharmanagar	8,166	10	8	2	0	0	1,550	40	·21	40·21	0	96	96	337	40	377	
19. Muhoripur	2,495	0	0	0	0	0	694	23·44	0	0	0	21	21	0	0	0	The Dispensary was opened on the 21st Kartic 1345 T. E.
Total	†1,46,610	997	778	168	20	31	41,410	813·09	27·91	841	35	1,246	1,281	6,730	1,957	8,687	

XXIII.

Education Return (A)—Particulars as to the schools maintained during the year 1345 T.E.

Number of Schools. Past year	Number of Schools. Present year.	Class of Schools.	Number of pupils on the rolls on the last day of Chait. Past year.	Number of pupils on the rolls on the last day of Chait. Present year.	Average daily attendance. Past year.	Average daily attendance. Present year.	Remarks.
6	6	High English Schools ... ... (including one Branch H. E. School).	1,597	1,584	1,186·46	1,155·13	
9	10	Middle English Schools for boys ...	1,132	1,166	847·06	850·49	* In some of these schools boys and girls read together.
1	1	Middle English Schools for girls ...	68	74	59·16	62·83	
26	24	* Lower Vernacular Schools for boys	1,243	1,239	1,010·11	938·24	
76	70	*Pathsalas for boys	2,519	2,249	1,918·18	1,745·34	
9	5	Do for girls	329	138	248·70	132·01	
		Special Schools:—					
4	4	*Compulsory Free Primary Schools	585	623	388·94	373·93	
5	5	Madrassas and Muktabs	178	347	135·88	318·70	
5	5	Sanskrit *Tols*	47	62	34·18	45·58	
1	1	Artisan School & Silpasram ...	28	16	11·75	9·09	
1	1	Jail Reformatory School	20	22	19·45	21	
TOTAL 143	132		7,746	7,520	5,859·87	5,652·34	

XXIV.

Education Return (B) Race of Students, 1345 T. E.

Names of Divisions.	No. of Schools.				No. of Students.					Race.												Average daily attendance.		REMARKS.
										Hindus.														
	For boys.	For girls.	Total.	Private schools.	Boys.	Girls.	Total.	Students of private schools.	Total.	Rajkumars.	Thakurs.	Manipuris.	Tripuras.	Bengalees.	Others.	Reangs.	Chakmas.	Kukis.	Lusais.	Musalmans.	Christians.	Boys.	Girls.	
1. Sadar Division ...	45	2	47	2	2,678	417	3,095	57	3,152	5	204	287	601	1,419	43	0	1	0	0	533	2	1,967·72	331·33	
2. Kailashahar „	20	3	23	18	1,032	157	1,189	506	1,695	0	0	295	19	633	14	0	0	0	0	228	0	802·17	116·77	
3. Sonamura „	16	1	17	1	819	82	901	49	950	0	6	1	68	248	1	0	0	0	0	577	0	625·93	68·77	
4. Bilonia „	8	1	9	3	650	42	692	84	776	0	1	1	28	445	7	3	0	0	0	207	0	482·43	31·74	
5. Khowai „	6	1	7	5	314	13	327	128	455	0	1	33	166	85	18	0	0	0	0	24	0	241·76	11·47	
6. Dharmanagar „	13	1	14	15	600	78	678	492	1,170	0	0	86	0	425	12	0	0	0	0	155	0	449·15	42·84	
7. Udaipur „	7	1	8	3	382	16	398	123	521	0	3	1	77	119	0	0	0	0	0	198	0	271·10	36·09	
8. Sabrum „	5	0	5	0	161	7	168	0	168	0	0	0	13	102	0	0	0	0	0	53	0	118·24	5·36	
9. Amarpur Sub-division ...	2	0	2	2	65	7	72	25	97	0	1	0	13	13	26	6	0	0	0	13	0	55·52	3·95	
TOTAL ...	122	10	132	49	6,701	819	7,520	1,464	8,984	5	216	704	985	3,489	121	9	1	0	0	1,988	2	5,004·02	648·32	

N. B.—In the Sub-columns under "Race" the number of students of private schools is not included.

APPENDIX XXV. (A)

Statement of Audited Receipts for the year 1345 T. E.

State.

Heads of Revenue.	1344 T. E.		1345 T. E.		Remarks.
	Revised Estimate.	Actuals.	Revised Estimate.	Actuals.	
1. Land Revenue ...	6,05,000	6,44,452	6,65,000	6,53,693	
2. Rents of markets ...	6,500	6,180	6,000	6,717	
3. Family tax in the hills	53,000	52,593	55,000	59,850	
4. Toll on Forest Produce	3,10,000	3,02,907	3,25,000	3,02,538	
5. Do on the Feni River	27,000	27,155	31,000	31,314	
6. Elephant and Buffalo grazing mehals ...	7,000	6,678	6,000	5,537	
7. Thatching grass mehals	3,000	2,906	3,000	2,574	
8. Reserved *Sal* trees ...	3,000	3,070	3,000	4,134	
9. Tax on cotton and Oil seeds ...	1,32,000	1,35,224	1,75,000	2,17,722	
10 Royalty on elephants caught ...	2,000	2,315	2,500	2,522	
11. *Adda* mehal ...	24,500	25,533	25,000	24,806	
12. Excise ...	43,000	42,901	43,000	40,057	
13. Stamps and Court fees	64,000	64,240	63,000	62,874	
14. Law and Justice (fines)	2,500	2,172	2,000	2,014	
15. Process Fees ...	11,000	10,396	10,000	9,683	
16. Registration ...	5,500	5,555	7,000	7,444	
17. Jail ...	2,500	2,237	3,000	4,235	
18. Cattle pounds ...	4,000	3,826	4,000	4,489	
19. *Nazars* ...	32,000	31,918	32,000	32,812	
20. School Fees ...	15,500	15,034	15,000	14,548	
21. Duty on Tea ...	24,000	27,728	25,000	21,452	
22. Duty on jute ...	28,000	27,112	30,000	30,423	
23. Depreciation Contribution ...	81,000	78,071	78,000	76,943	
24. Miscellaneous ...	59,000	59,411	55,000	61,067	
25. Duty on matches ...	—	—	16,500	16,595	
Total ...	15,45,000	15,79,609	16,80,000	16,96,043	
26. Deposits ...	2,64,182	2,63,746	60,000	1,20,504	
27. Contribution from Chakla ...	1,35,000	1,35,000	2,50,000	2,50,000	
28 Silver Jubilee ...	—	—	10,500	10,500	(to be included in deposits.)
Total ...	19,44,182	19,78,355	20,00,500	20,77,047	
Opening Balance :— Cash ...	1,88,197	1,88,197	1,88,879	1,88,879	
Advances ...	1,73,407	1,73,407	2,10,799	2,10,799	
Loans ...	2,75,428	2,75,428	2,78,099	2,78,099	
Working Balance ...	4,15,182	4,15,182	4,15,18?	* 4,15,182	* Cash— 2,25,000 Advance— 1,90,182
Total ...	10,52,214	10,52,214	10,92,959	10,92,959	
Grand Total ...	29,96,396	30,30,569	30,93,459	31,70,006	

APPENDIX XXV (B)

Statement of Audited Expenditure for the year 1345 T. E.

State.

Heads of Expenditure.	1344 T. E.		1345 T. E.		Remarks.
	Revised estimate.	Actuals.	Revised Estimate.	Actuals.	
1. Controlling Charges	82,874	82,216	78,377	76,415	
2. Revenue General ...	80,366	78,441	80,373	78,777	
3. Survey & Settlement	20,242	20,119	15,166	13,835	
4. Tahasil ...	49,602	47,739	50,402	49,122	
5. Registration ...	3,946	3,555	4,129	3,564	
6. Police ...	88,786	87,340	83,931	82,754	
7. Judicial ...	35,511	33,992	33,915	33,380	
8. Jail ...	26,558	26,321	32,142	29,658	
9. Forest ...	48,328	46,436	50,237	48,928	
10. Medical ...	68,932	67,638	67,788	66,513	
11. Municipality ...	9,000	9,000	9,000	9,000	
12. Education General ...	1,26,237	1,23,867	1,24,681	1,22,027	
13. (a) Public Works ...	1,01,000	1,00,820	1,03,352	1,00,574	
(b) Improvement ...	1,07,000	1,04,519	96,554	96,101	
14. Electric Light ...	16,452	16,299	16,500	16,433	
15. Small Donation ...	300	288	300	295	
16. Relief to distressed subjects ...	300	—	300	—	
17. Purchase of Landed Property ...	7,000	6,845	12,000	11,522	
18. Repayment of Deposits ...	83,500	77,171	80,000	79,860	
19. Interest on Deposits	30,000	29,339	32,000	30,910	
20. Unforeseen charges...	7,000	6,644	5,500	4,792	
21. Pension ...	52,000	51,508	49,500	48,832	
22. Chief Secretary's Office & H. H.'s Tour	1,58,648	1,57,650	1,57,897	1,57,827	
23. Palace Sultanat ...	36,127	36,095	36,959	36,264	
24. Zoo ...	3,094	3,094	3,352	3,342	
25. Agriculture, Commerce and Industries	8,117	7,859	8,295	8,031	
26. Publicity, Reclamation & Immigration ...	9,028	6,965	5,008	3,667	
27. H. H.'s Private Secretary's Office ...	9,284	9,171	10,890	10,852	
28. Rajmala Office ...	4,000	3,520	2,468	1,109	
29. Military Secretary's Office ...	3,480	3,460	3,720	3,700	
30. Military ...	1,13,222	1,01,039	1,13,570	1,07,181	
31. Nijtahabil ...	1,00,000	1,00,000	1,00,000	1,00,000	
32. Adjustment of irrecoverable advances...	10,000	5,577	10,000	3,000	
33. Repayment of old Debts ...	96,500	96,439	1,00,500	1,00,109	
34. Sansar Charges ...	3,86,865	3,86,015	3,86,303	3,76,818	
35. Silver Jubilee ...	—	—	18,000	17,638	
36. Sanitation ...	1,500	629	—	—	(Included in controlling charges.)
Total ...	19,84,799	19,37,610	19,83,109	19,32,830	
Closing balance :—					
Cash ...	1,02,000	1,88,879	1,62,368	3,01,378	
Advances ...	2,17,415	2,10,799	2,32,800	2,19,356	
Loans issued ...	2,77,000	2,78,099	3,00,000	3,01,260	
Working balance ...	4,15,182	4,15,182	4,15,182	* 4,15,182	* Cash— 2,25,000 Advance—1,90,182
Total ...	10,11,597	10,92,959	11,10,350	12,37,176	
Grand Total ...	29,96,396	30,30,569	30,93,459	31,70,006	

APPENDIX XXVI. (A)

Statement of Audited Receipts for the year 1345 T. E.

Chakla Roshnabad Estates.

Heads of Receipts.	1344 T. E.		1345 T. E.		REMARKS.
	Revised Estimate.	Actuals.	Revised Estimate.	Actuals.	
1. Rent and Cess ...	8,79,000	9,66,610	10,77,300	10,85,652	
2. Cess for Rent free holdings ...	6,500	8,483	7,751	9,797	
3. Law charges recovered	47,000	46,963	66,488	65,060	
4. Miscellaneous receipts including deposits ...	69,707	54,985	70,761	66,510	
5. Refund of loans and advances ...	1,000	1,176	1,500	1,369	
Total ...	10,03,207	10.78.217	12,23,800	12,28,388	
Opening Balance :—					
Cash ...	1,04,342	1,04,342	1,11,086	1,11,086	
Bank deposits ...	51,542	51,542	71,050	71,050	
Advance ...	1,15,477	1,15,477	1,14,873	1,14,873	
Loans issued ...	78,859	78,859	86,493	86,493	
Total ...	3,50,220	3,50,220	3,83,502	3,83,502	
Grand Total ...	13,53,427	14,28,437	16,07,302	18,11,890	

APPENDIX XXVI. (B)

Statement of Audited Expenditure for the year 1345 T. E.

Chakla Roshnabad Estates.

Heads of Expenditure.	1344 T. E.		1345 T. E.		REMARKS.
	Revised Estimate.	Actuals.	Revised Estimate.	Actuals.	
i. 1. Revenue and Cess ...	2,86,835	2,85,540	3,00,227	2,81,546	
2. Establishment ...	1,42,189	1,42,169	1,40,143	1,37,363	
3. Settlement ...	1,203	916	1,440	1,097	
4. Legal Expenses ...	1,37,314	1,36,800	1,63,000	1,59,230	
5. Education ...	9,318	9,075	9,318	8,557	
6. Medical ...	12,310	11,469	12,395	12,001	
7. Public Works ...	51,064	50,996	89,927	50,912	
8. Religious Expenses	6,800	6,111	7,094	6,716	
9. Purchase of property	7,000	6,573	44,000	6,278	
10. Miscellaneous ...	5,000	3,615	11,500	9,585	
11. Pension and Gratuity	11,000	10,915	13,000	11,943	
12. Forest ...	700	576	712	593	
13. Unforeseen ...	7,200	7,109	3,500	2,681	
14. Loans and Advances	1,000	999	2,000	1,959	
ii. Sansar ...	12,960	12,960	12,960	12,960	
iii. Donation ...	7,050	7,046	8,625	8,551	
iv. Repayment of debts etc ...	31,000	30,066	25,000	18,183	
v. Advance to Nij Tahabil ...	1,87,000	1,87,000	80,000	79,591	
vi. State Contribution	1,35,000	1,35,000	2,50,000	2,50,000	
Total ...	10,51,943	10,44,935	11,74,841	10,54,746	
Closing Balance :—					
Cash ...	55,606	1,11,086	1,73,045	2,28,090	
Bank deposits ...	50,000	86,493	72,050	1,08,629	
Advances ...	1,10,200	1,14,873	1,01,078	1,25,343	
Loans issued ...	85,678	71,050	86,288	95,082	
Total ...	3,01,484	3,83,502	4,32,461	5,57,144	
Grand Total ...	13,53,427	14,28,437	16,07,302	16,11,890	

MINISTER'S OFFICE,
TRIPURA STATE,
POLITICAL DEPARTMENT.

To

Captain His Highness The Bisama-Samara-Bijayee Mahamahodaya
Pancha-Srijukta Maharaja Manikya
SIR BIR BIKRAM KISHORE
DEV BARMAN BAHADUR, K. C. S. I.,
Maharaja of Tripura.

Dated, Agartala, the 18th September, 1938.

MAY IT PLEASE YOUR HIGHNESS,

I have the honour to submit the accompanying Report on the General Administration of the State and the attached Zemindaries for the year 1346 T. E., extending from the 14th April, 1936 to the 13th April, 1937.

The reports on the administration of the Military Department, of the Departments of Education, Agriculture, Commerce and Industries and Immigration under the control of the Chief Secretary to Your Highness and of the Public Works Department under the control of the Private Secretary to Your Highness, have been incorporated in the Report.

I have the honour to be
Your Highness's most obedient servant,
Jyotis Chandra Sen,
MINISTER.

MAP
OF
TRIPURA STATE

Scale $\frac{1}{1\ \text{Million}}$ or 1 Inch to 15·783 Miles.

Miles 10 5 0 10 20 30 40 Miles

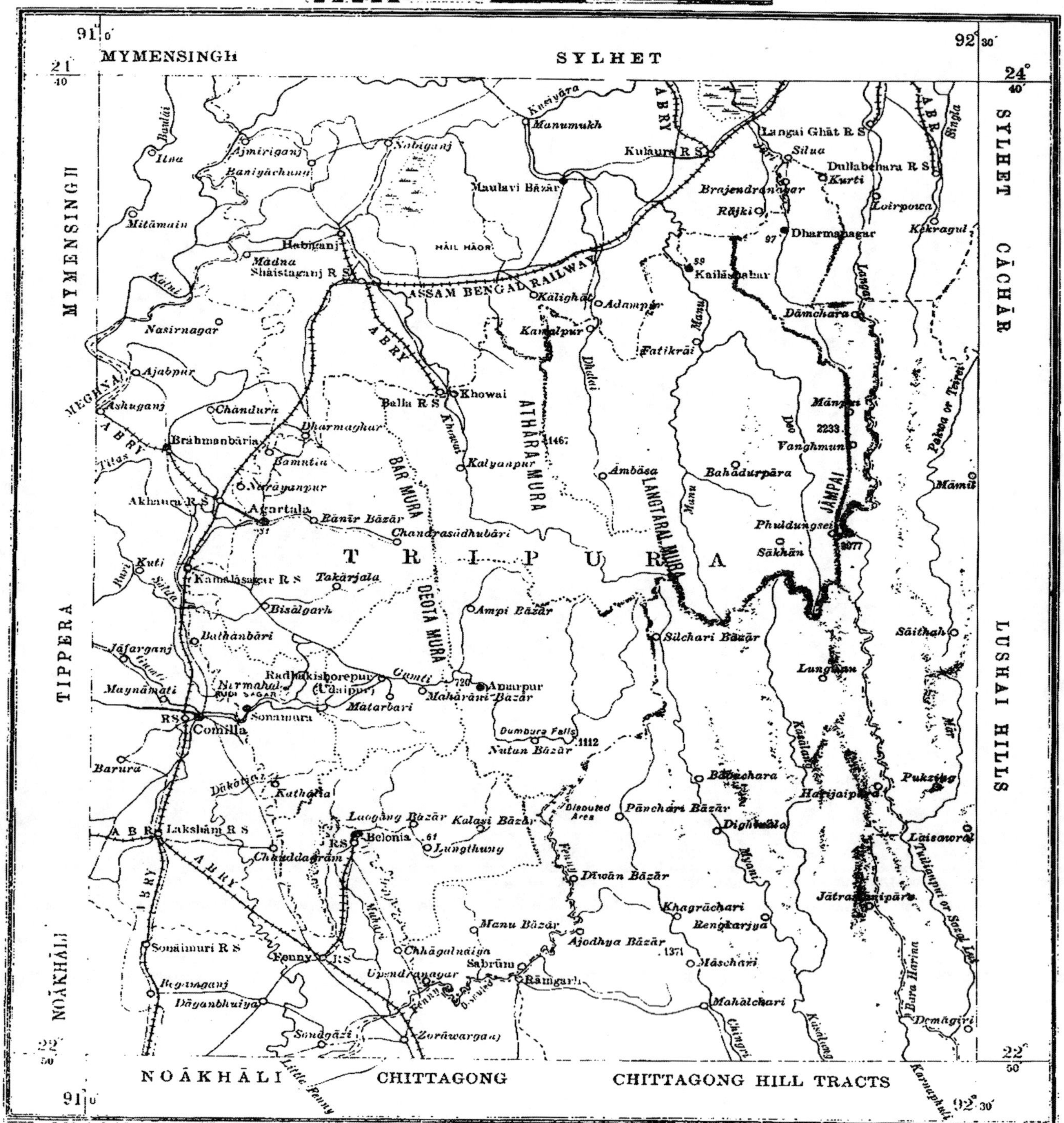

Based upon Survey of India Maps & Published with the Permission of the Surveyor General of India, 1936.

Rtc. No. 1441. E 37 -1000

Helio. S. I. O. Calcutta

Head quarters: Districts or States	...	Agartala
Ditto Sub-divisions	...	Amarpur
Other Towns or Large Villages	...	Maynamati
District Names	...	TIPPERA
Boundaries, State & District	...	
Ditto Sub-division	...	
Railways, Metre gauge	...	
Roads, Metalled, Others	...	

1st Edition 1937.

Book Twenty-eight

Report on the Administration of the Tripura State for 1346 T. E. (1936-1937 A.D.)

REPORT ON THE ADMINISTRATION

OF

THE TRIPURA STATE

FOR

1346 T. E. (1936-37.)

CHAPTER I—GENERAL AND POLITICAL.

Area of the State—4,116 sq. miles.

Population—3,82,450.

Gross Revenue (based on the average of five years):—

(*a*) State ... ... Rs. 22,23,277.

(*b*) Zemindaries ... . Rs. 11,18,827.

Tribute—Nil.

Ruler of the State—Captain His Highness The Bisama-Samara-Bijayee Mahamahodaya Pancha-Srijukta Maharaja Manikya Sir Bir Bikram Kishore Dev Barman Bahadur, K. C. S. I. *Age—29* years. (Born—19th August, 1908). *Caste—Kshatriya* (of the Lunar race.)

The year and the people.

During the year under report the improvement in the economic condition of the people noticed in the previous year's report was maintained except in the case of the people in the uplands where the outturn of the principal crops suffered to a noticeable extent compared with the year preceding. In the plains, not only was the outturn of paddy, jute and mustard larger but their prices also maintained a steadily upward tendency. The yield of cotton and sesamum was much below the normal but these fetched, to the relief of the growers, a slightly higher price. The demand for forest produce increased during the year and with it went up the prices of various forest products as well. The output of tea made a rapid advance by about two *lakh* pounds while its price also was satisfactory.

2. In the Zemindaries, there was perceptible improvement in the economic condition of the tenantry in general.

3. There was no material change in the condition of the middle class people. The wages of the skilled and unskilled labour remained at the same level as in the previous year.

4. Towards the close of the year, cholera and small-pox broke out in the Khowai Division but prompt preventive measures succeeded in checking their spread. In the Dharmanagar Division cholera made its appearance in epidemic form. There was an epidemic of rinderpest in some parts of the Sadar, Bilonia and Sabroom Divisions and this caused a large number of deaths in the Bilonia Division.

5. The rainfall during the year was more than that in the previous year by about 4 inches, being 83·19″ against 79·43″ and was unevenly distributed, the maximum being 108·81″ in the Sadar Division and the minimum 69·24″ in the Amarpur Sub-Division. The monsoon rainfall proved favourable to the principal crops in the plains but its effect on the outturn of the crops in the hilly tracts was adverse.

Rainfall.

6. The finances of the State and the attached Zemindaries were, on the whole, satisfactory during the year. The year opened with a total balance of Rs. 17,94,320 against Rs. 14,76,461 in the year preceding. The total revenue of the State from the permanent sources was Rs. 18,75,373 against Rs. 16,96,043 and that of the Zemindaries Rs. 12,48,973 against Rs. 11,07,653, in the previous year. With deposits the total receipts in the State amounted to Rs. 19,86,001 and with deposits, law charges recovered and compensation for lands acquired, the total receipts of the Zemindaries came to Rs. 13,75,274. The combined receipts of the State and the Zemindaries were thus Rs. 33,61,275 against Rs. 30,55,435 in the preceding year.

Finances of the year.

II.

7. The first notable event that closely followed the advent of the year under review was the second European tour of His Highness the Maharaja Manikya Bahadur, who was accompanied, for the first time, by Her Highness the Maharani Saheba.

8. The main object His Highness had in view in undertaking the tour was to see his sister, Yubrani Saheba of Kotla (Maharaj Kumari Basanta Prava Devi) who, on medical advice, was staying in Switzerland and whose indifferent health was causing great anxiety to His Highness and Her Highness the Dowager Maharani Saheba.

9. The staff accompanying Their Highnesses to Europe consisted of Manyabara Rana (now Raja) Saheb Bodhjung Bahadur, F. R. G. S., Chief Secretary and Capt. Kumar B. L. Dev Varma Bahadur, Aide-de-Camp.

10. His Highness, on the eve of his departure from the capital, received an address of farewell given by the State employees which contained touching expression of their hearty wishes for bon voyage and safe return to the State to which His Highness gave a suitable reply.

European Tour.

11. Their Highnesses the Maharaja Manikya Bahadur and the Maharani Saheba with party left Agartala on the 14th Baisakh corresponding to 27th April, 1936, for Bombay and stopped at Calcutta *en route* for a week.

12. During the short stay at Bombay, His Highness paid a flying visit to Maharastra visiting many historical places including Poona, Satara, Bhor and Mahabaleswar.

Continental Tour Programme.

13. Their Highnesses sailed from Bombay on the 2nd Jaistha (16th May, 1936) by the P. & O. Mail Boat "Viceroy of India" and reaching Marseilles on the 27th May, visited, during the continental tour, the following places according to the programme as set forth below :—

16th May	...	...	Sailed from Bombay.
20th ,,	...	...	Left Aden.
23rd ,,	...	...	Left Port Said.
27th ,,	...	...	Reached Marseilles.
28th ,,	...	...	Left Marseilles for Davos Platz.
29th ,,	...	...	Reached Davos Platz and stayed there till the 3rd June.
4th June	...	...	Left Davos Platz for London.
5th ,,	...	...	Reached London and stayed there till the 13th June visiting places of interest in the country and the town.
14th ,,	...	...	His Highness accompanied by the Chief Secretary flew from London to Zurich *en route* for Davos Platz.
16th ,,	...	...	Flew back to London from Davoz Platz and stayed in London till the 24th June.
26th ,,	...	...	Flew again to Davos Platz from London hearing about the grave condition of the Yubrani Saheba of Kotla.
28th ,,	...	...	Flew back to London from Davos Platz and stayed in London till the 13th July.
14th July	...	...	Their Highnesses flew to Paris from London and stayed in Paris till the 26th July.
27th ,,	...	...	Left Paris for Berlin.
28th ,,	...	...	Reached Berlin and stayed there till the 10th August.
11th August	...	...	Arrived in Vienna and stayed there till the 15th, visiting the country around.
16th ,,	...	...	Reached Lido (Venice) and stayed there till the 20th.
21st ,,	...	...	Left Lido and reached Milan the same evening.
22nd ,,	...	...	Reached Nice (French Reviera) and motored to Cannes and stayed there till the 26th.
27th ,,	...	...	Left Cannes and reached Marseilles the same evening.
28th ,,	...	...	Sailed from Marseilles for Bombay by the P. & O. boat "Mooltan."
10th Sept.	...	...	Returned to Bombay at 5 P. M.

14. His Highness the Maharaja Manikya Bahadur, accompanied by an Aide-de-Camp, had an audience with His Majesty the King Emperor at the Buckingham Palace at 3. 30 P. M. on the 23rd June, 1936. The day being His Majesty's birthday, His Highness had the honour of personally offering his loyal congratulations on the auspicious occasion. Their Highnesses were at-home that evening at which many distinguished guests were present.

Audience with H. M. the King Emperor

15. Their Highnesses and party arrived in Berlin on the 28th July and stayed there at Hotel Adlon.

16. On the 5th of August, His Highness the Maharaja Manikya Bahadur was received by the German Chancellor, His Excellency Herr Adolf Hitler at his residence in Berlin. His Highness, on his arrival at, and departure from, the Chancellor's residence, was presented with a Guard-of-Honour and he had a pleasant interview with Herr Hitler who received him very cordially.

Interview with the German Chancellor, Herr Hitler.

17. While in Berlin, Their Highnesses also attended a reception given by His Britannic Majesty's Ambassador.

18. Their Highnesses were also present at the opening and subsequent events of the eleventh session of the World Olympic Games which were being then held in Germany.

19. In Vienna, His Highness had some hunting in the famous Lainzer Animal Park and shot some very beautiful specimens of stags etc.

20. The European tour came to a successful close. But for a sad bereavement caused by the death of His Highness's sister, Yubrani Saheba of Kotla, which will be noticed in the relative chapter, the tour was thoroghly enjoyed as a very pleasant and interesting one.

21. Their Highnesses the Maharaja Manikya Bahadur and the Maharani Saheba with party returned to Bombay at 5 P. M. on the 10th September by the P. & O. Mail Boat "Mooltan" and were accorded enthusiastic reception by Swami B. H. Bon of the Gaudiya Math and by the Bengalee community of Bombay. His Highness was subsequently presented with an address of welcome at a public meeting at which Mr. Jumnadas Mehta, the then Mayor of Bombay, presided.

Return to Bombay.

22. Leaving Bombay on the 11th September Their Highnesses and party reached Calcutta on the morning of the 13th September and took rest there till the 20th.

Return to Calcutta.

23. On their way back to Agartala, Their Highnesses paid a visit to Darjeeling to see the Maharaj-Kumar Bahadur and the Maharaj-Kumari Saheba who were staying at Darjeeling during Their Highnesses' absence in Europe. Their Highnesses reached Darjeeling on the 22nd September and remained there at Hotel Mount Everest till the 25th. During the stay at Darjeeling, Their Highnesses attended a dinner party and a ball

Visit to Darjeeling.

at the Government House and subsequently gave a dinner party at the Hotel Mount Everest to which His Excellency the Governor of Bengal and many leading European and Indian residents of the station were invited.

Return to Agartala.

24. Their Highnesses with the baby Maharaj-Kumar and the baby Maharaj-Kumari left Darjeeling for Calcutta *en route* to Tripura on the 26th September and returned to Agartala on the morning of the 2nd October, 1936. Their Highnesses' safe return to the State from the foreign tour was marked by the display of hearty rejoicings by the people. On alighting from the train at Akhaura, His Highness inspected a Guard-of-Honour consisting of State troops while the crowd that assembled from far and near in thousands cheered their beloved Ruler enthusiastically.

Public Reception

25. Thereafter, Their Highnesses proceeded to Agartala and at the town entrance, were received by the Chairman and the Commissioners of the Agartala Municipality. The procession then moved on towards the Installation Pandal where a civic reception, on behalf of the citizens of Agartala, was accorded to Their Highnesses including the presentation of an address of welcome to His Highness the Maharaja Manikya Bahadur by Mahamanyabara Maharaj Kumar Brajendra Kishore Dev Varma Bahadur, Chairman of the Reception Committee which was specially formed for the purpose. His Highness in a neat little speech gave a very suitable and impressive reply.

26. Illumination in the town, afternoon party, feeding of the poor and sports by school boys were some of the features of the happy occasion.

Cold weather tour to Calcutta.

27. His Highness the Maharaja Manikya Bahadur remained at the capital till the 24th Agrahayan and, on the night of the 24th Agrahayan corresponding to the 10th December, 1936, left for Calcutta accompanied by Her Highness the Maharani Saheba and staff.

28. While in Calcutta, His Highness had private interviews with Their Excellencies the Viceroy and the Governor of Bengal on the 24th December and 17th December respectively.

Discussions with the Viceroy's Special Representative.

29. His Highness the Maharaja Manikya Bahadur accompanied by Manyabara Rai J. C. Sen Bahadur, Minister, was present at, and took part in, the conference of the Princes of the Eastern States Agency and the Honourable Mr. A. C. Lothian, C. I. E., I. C. S., Viceroy's Special Representative, to discuss matters relating to the Accession of the Indian States to Federation, at the Legislative Council House on the 28th and 29th December, besides, the separate discussions which His Highness had with Mr. Lothian on the 30th idem.

30. On the 18th December, Herr Edwart von Selzam, Consul General for Germany delivered a portrait of His Excellency the German Chancellor, Herr Hitler, to His Highness the Maharaja Manikya

Bahadur at Tripura House as a souvenir of His Highness's meeting the German Chancellor in Berlin.

31. His Highness gave some parties at Tripura House and elsewhere during the season amongst which the following may be mentioned :—

Tripura House parties.

(1) Luncheon party on the 28th December in which the principal guests included Lieut.-Col. A. S. Meek, C. M. G., the then Agent to the Governor General for the Eastern States and the Honourable Mr. A. C. Lothian, C. I. E., I. C. S., Viceroy's Special Representative for Federation matters.

(2) His Exalted Highness the Nizam of Hyderabad and Berar accompanied by staff had tea with His Highness the Maharaja Manikya Bahadur at Tripura House, on the 29th December.

(3) His Highness was at-home to a distinguished company of guests at Tripura House on the 2nd January, 1937. Over 200 guests including Their Highnesses the Maharaja Scindia of Gwalior, Maharani of Cooch Behar, Maharaja of Cooch Behar and the daughters of His Excellency the Viceroy were present at the party.

(4) His Highness the Maharaja Scindia of Gwalior and staff came to tea at Tripura House on the 8th and the 11th January, 1937.

(5) A dinner party to meet His Excellency the Governor of Bengal was given by His Highness at Tripura House on the 7th January, 1937, which was attended by many high officials of Government and distinguished gentlemen of the city.

(6) His Highness entertained the Agent to the Governor General and his staff at a luncheon party at Firpos' on the 6th January, 1937.

32. Besides attending the usual functions both at the Viceroy's House and at the Government House, His Highness, during his stay in Calcutta, accepted invitations to parties coming from many other important personages including those from His Exalted Highness the Nizam of Hyderabad and Berar, Their Highnesses the Maharani and Maharaja of Cooch Behar, the Maharaja Scindia of Gwalior and His Excellency the Naval Commander-in-Chief.

33. The cold weather tour of His Highness came to a close on the 16th January and, leaving Sealdah on the morning of the 17th His Highness returned to Agartala the same night—Her Highness the Maharani Saheba remaining in Calcutta with the babies.

Return to Agartala.

34. His Highness remained at the capital till the 12th February (30th Magh) and on the same night left again for Calcutta to reach there the following evening.

35. Her Highness the Maharani Saheba who was staying in Calcutta left for Panna on the 15th February in connection with the auspicious marriage of her brother, Raja Bahadur Shree Narendra Singh Ju Dev, Yuvraj of Panna, with Rajkumari Saheba Shreemati Durga Rajya Luxmi, the eldest daughter of His Excellency Supr

Manyabara Suprasidha Prabal Gorkha Dakshina Bahu General Singha Shum Shree Jung Bahadur Rana of Nepal, which auspicious ceremony was fixed to be celebrated at Katmandu on the 24th February, 1937.

Visit to Panna & Nepal to attend the marriage of the Yuvraj of Panna.

36. On being specially invited by the Panna Durbar, His Highness the Maharaja Manikya Bahadur accompanied by the staff left Calcutta on the 19th February and joined the Panna Party at Benares *en route* for Nepal. His Highness entrained the special train at Benares with the "Barat" on the evening of the 20th February and reached Katmandu via Raxaul-Bhimpedi-Thankot route on the evening of the 22nd February.

Stay in Nepal.

37. During the stay in Nepal, His Highness, besides attending the various ceremonies relating to the auspicious marriage, visited the places of interest in the beautiful valley of Nepal and enjoyed the visit very much. His Highness was received with all the due courtesy accorded by the Nepalese Government on his arrival at, and departure from, Katmandu and, during his stay there, was cordially received by His Majesty the King of Nepal, His Highness the Maharaja of Nepal, the Nepalese Commanding Generals and the British Ambassador of His Majesty the King Emperor at the Court of Nepal, at their respective residences.

38. His Highness with the *Barat* party left Katmandu for India at 8 A. M. on the 28th February and reached Raxaul at 12. 30 P. M. on the following day, and taking the special train in the afternoon, arrived at Panna in the evening of the 2nd March.

Stay at Panna.

39. In connection with some other functions relative to the marriage, His Highness had to stay at Panna till the 8th March and left the place for Calcutta with Her Highness the Maharani Saheba and babies by special train on the 9th March reaching Howrah at 5 P. M. the following day.

Return to Agartala.

40. Their Highnesses left Calcutta for Tripura on the 11th March (27th Falgoon) and returned to Agartala the same night in connection with the private visit of His Excellency The Right Honourable Sir John Anderson, P. C., G. C. B., G. C. I. E., Governor of Bengal, on the 15th March, 1937.

Opening ceremony of The Agartala State Guaranteed Electric Supply Co's Power House.

41. On invitation by the Board of Directors, His Highness the Maharaja Manikya Bahadur graciously performed the opening ceremony of the Power House of The Agartala State Guaranteed Electric Supply Company, on the 13th March and switched the lights on at 6–30 P. M.

Visit to Calcutta.

42. On receiving information that Her Highness the Dowager Madhyama Maharani Saheba had not been keeping good health for some time, His Highness left for Calcutta on the 27th March (13th Chaitra) to see her, and reached Sealdah on the 28th. Her Highness the Dowager Maharani Saheba, by the grace of God, was improving and after seeing her restored to

46. Her body was duly cremated at Davos Platz and the ashes borne to India for performing the last rites. All the offices and other institutions throughout the State and the Zemindaries were closed for three days.

III.

Abdication of H. M. King Edward VIII.

47. A fateful event of the year was the abdication, on the 10th December, 1936, after a brief reign, of His Most Gracious Majesty King Edward VIII, in favour of His Royal Highness the Duke of York.

Accession of H. M. King George VI.

48. A notable and happy event of the year that followed was the accession, on the 10th December 1936, of His Most Gracious Majesty King George VI, in circumstances which were without parallel in the history of the country.

49. On receipt of an announcement of the accession of His Most Gracious Majesty, a State proclamation was made in an extraordinary issue of the official gazette. The proclamation of the accessien was read out at a Durbar held at the head of the Grand Staircase of the Ujjayanta Palace with all the Durbaries, Sardars and officials to which the public also joined. All offices and institutions were closed for a day.

H. E. the Governor of Bengal's visit.

50. His Excellency the Right Honourable Sir John Anderson, P.C., G. C. B., G. C. S. I., Governor of Bengal, paid a visit to the State on the 15th March, 1937.

Transfer of political agency.

51. In the year under report the political relation of the State with the Government of Bengal was transferred to the Agent to the Governor General, Eastern States, with effect from the 1st December, 1936.

Agent to the Governor-General.

52. Lieutenant-Colonel A. S. Meek, C. M. G., was the Agent to the Governor-General from 1st December 1936 to the 9th March, 1937 and Lieutenant-Colonel H. W. C. Robson, O. B. E. from the 29th March 1937 till after the close of the year, Colonel Murphy acting as the Agent to the Governor General during the intervening period.

53. Lieutenant-Colonel Meek paid an official visit to the State on the 4th February 1937 and following days.

Political Agent.

54. Mr. S. N. Ray, I. C. S, District Magistrate, Tippera, was the ex-officio Political Agent till the transfer of the State to the Eastern States Agency and thereafter Mr. G. H. Emerson, I. C. S., Secretary to the Agent to the Governor-General, was the Political Agent for the Bengal States from the 1st December 1936 till after close of the year under review.

State Council during H. H's absence.

55. A State Council consisting of (1) Mahamanyabara Maharajkumar B. K. Dev Barman Bahadur (2) Rai J. C. Sen Bahadur, Minister and (3) Dewan Bahadur K. Dutt, M. A. B. L., Private Secretary to His Highness, exercised full powers of the Ruler during his tour in Europe and disposed of all matters except such as could wait till His Highness's return.

56. His Excellency the **Viceroy** and Governor-General of India conferred the title of **Raja**, as a personal distinction, upon Rana Saheb Bodhjung Bahadur, Chief Secretary to His Highness the Maharaja Manikya Bahadur, on the occasion of the New Year, 1937.

State official receiving British Indian title.

57. A sum of Rs. 27,270 was received from the Government of India, on account of the State's share in the general pool of the excise duty on matches for the year 1935–36 against Rs. 16,595 in the year before.

State's share in the excise duty on matches.

58. The third equated instalment of Rs. 92,666 due on the 21st September, 1936, towards the repayment of the loan of Rs. 9 lakhs was duly paid.

Repayment of loan to Govt.

59. Rai J. C. Sen Bahadur, B. A., B. C. S. (retired) continued as the Minister who was also the Manager of the Chakla Roshnabad Estate and other Zemindaries and properties in British India. He was out on tour for 104 days.

Minister.

60. In the year under review, the Indian Tea Licensing Committee which had previously been appointed to be the Licensing Authority for the State was further empowered to grant license for the plantation of tea on land not planted with tea on the last day of Chaitra, 1342 T. E.

Tea Licensing Committee.

CHAPTER II—LAND ADMINISTRATION.

61. Thakur K. K. Singh, Naib Dewan, continued to be in charge of the Revenue and General Department.

Charge.

62. As shown in the subjoined statement, the total area under settlement and borne on the *toujis* at the close of the year was 619 square miles against 621 square miles in the previous year.

Area held under settlement.

Kinds of settlement.	Area in square miles. 1346 T.E.	1345 T.E.	Increase.	Decrease.	REMRKS.
Jotes ...	324	324	—	—	
Taluks ...	295	297	—	2	
Total ...	619	621	—	2	

63. No new settlement was granted during the year under review but four cases of resettlement of *Khas* purchased gardens were in progress. 2 of them were pending since 1345 T. E.

Tea Settlement.

64. Several petitions for relinquishment of portions of tea garden lands were pending since 1345 T. E. for want of agreement to terms.

Tea Industry.

65. The Durbar has been continuing the policy of giving relief to the proprietors of the gardens by way of granting remission of interest and easy instalments for payment of arrear revenues and other

State dues. As the Tea Industry in the State is still in its infancy extension of tea cultivation is essentially necessary for most of the tea estates. But owing to the Tea Restriction scheme, the State tea gardens could not be permitted to extend their cultivation.

66. 36 tea gardens were inspected jointly by a nominee of the Indian Tea Licensing Committee and a nominee of the State during the year under review and all facilities for inspection were afforded to them by the Durbar as well as by the gardens concerned. In 2 gardens, one in the Sadar and the other in Kailashahar Divisions, tea plants on 8 acres of lands had to be uprooted on the ground of illicit plantation.

67. The current demand against tea grants amounted to about Rs. 60,000 while the realisation from them was Rs. 75,726 including Rs. 37,194 on account of current demand.

68. Both the outturn and export of tea increased during the year under review.

69. The arrear demand up to the end of 1344 T. E. still amounted to more than Rs. 1,50,000.

Rates of *Jama.*

70. The average *jama* per *kani* of *jote* lands in *khash mahals* (exclusive of cesses) stood at Re. 1 and pies 6 against 1 Rupee and 4 pies in the previous year. The maximum rate for *jote* was Rs. 20 per *kani* while the minimum was 3 annas and those for *taluks* Rs. 3 and anna 1–9 pies respectively. For *Takshishi taluk* at Agartala town the maximum rate was Rs. 100 per *kani.*

Sources of Land Revenue.

71. The different sources of land revenue demand with the collection under each head are detailed below.

Sources.	Current demand.		Arrear demand up to the end of		Realization up to the end of		REMARKS.
	1346 T.E.	1345 T.E.	1345 T.E.	1344 T.E.	1346 T.E.	1345 T.E.	
Taluks ...	1,57,236	1,58,493	3,58,478	4,00,804	1,65,883	1,98,972	
Khas Mehal jotes	5,36,685	5,31,756	20,16,869	19,00,953	6,10,578	4,10,818	
Bazars ...	8,949	8,293	5,481	4,079	7,685	6,534	
Cesses ...	45,120	43,554	1,62,307	1,55,903	49,391	35,767	
Total ...	7,48,290	7,42,096	25,43,135	24,61,739	8,33,537	6,52,091	

Demand.

72. The above statement shows that the current demand under all heads was Rs. 7,48,290 and with the arrear demand of Rs. 25,43,135 the total demand of the year was Rs. 32,91,425 against Rs. 32,03,835 in the previous year.

Collection.

73. The total collection in round figure under all heads during the year amounted to Rs. 8,33,530, being Rs. 2,43,010 under current and Rs. 5,90,520 under arrear as against the total collection of Rs. 6,52,090 in the previous year. The percentage of collection of the current demand was 32·47 against 27·24 and of the arrears 23·22 against 18·27. In the *khas mehal,* the percentage of collection of the current demand was 18·78 against 12·18 and in Taluki

mahal the percentage was 78·08 against 76·21 in the previous year. The percentage of collection on the whole was satisfactory.

Coercive measures—Certificates.

74. Altogether 13,593 certificate cases covering a demand of Rs. 7,18,619 were instituted during the year. With 6123 cases valued at Rs. 7,52,825 pending from the previous year, the total number of cases awaiting final orders on disposal of preliminary notices issued on debtors was 19,716 covering a total demand of Rs. 14,71,435. Of these, 12 cases with a demand of Rs. 5174 were rejected or struck off and Rs. 27,796 in 605 cases was realised before decree, while 8,563 cases with a total value of Rs. 9,77,576 remained pending at the end of the year.

Execution.

75. Orders under the provision of the Certificate Act were passed during the year in 10,536 cases with a total value of Rs. 4,60,889 making the demand absolute.

76. With 16,347 cases to the value of Rs. 9,33,940 pending in execution from the previous year, the total number of cases dealt with was 26,883 covering a demand of Rs. 13,94,829. Out of the total demand, Rs. 7,663 was remitted or written off and of the remainder, Rs. 1,81,254 was actually realised leaving a balance of Rs. 12,05,912.

77. Of the amount realised, Rs. 1,65,994 represents land revenue and Rs. 15,260 miscellaneous demands.

78. In view of the heavy accumulation of the demand strict measures appear to be called for.

Operation of the Sunset law.

79. The number of defaulting *taluks* brought under the operation of the Sunset law (including 43 pending from the previous year) was 299. Of these, 236 were released on realization of dues with penalty while 24 were sold by auction and 39 remained undisposed of at the close of the year.

Survey.

80. The results of the survey (including resurvey) operations are given in the statement below. It will be seen that an area of 3,497 *drones* comprising 171 *drones* of *Taluk* and 3,326 *drones* of *khash mehal* was surveyed as against a total of 2,958 *drones* in the previous year.

Names of Divisions.	Quantity of land in *drones* surveyed in 1346 T. E.			Quantity of land in *drones* surveyed in 1345 T. E.			REMARKS.
	Taluki land.	*Khas mehal* land.	Total.	*Taluki* land.	*Khas mehal* land.	Total.	
1. Sadar Division ...	—	472	472	948	467	1415	
2. Kailashahar " ...	—	84	84	—	42	42	
3. Sonamura " ...	—	91	91	—	91	91	
4. Bilonia " ...	—	1,233	1,233	—	509	509	
5. Khowai " ...	171	52	223	—	318	318	
6. Dharmanagar " ...	—	138	138	—	138	138	
7. Udaipur " ...	—	1,037	1,037	—	296	296	
8. Sabroom " ...	—	219	219	—	149	149	
9. Amarpur Sub " ...	—	—	—	—	—	—	
TOTAL ...	171	3,326	3,497	948	2,010	2,958	

81. This work was not taken up during the year as the published sheet maps of the Survey of India on one inch to the mile scale was found to serve the purpose partly and as there were not many new village-maps forthcoming. This work may now be diverted to marking out the village boundaries according to Revenue Survey on the published sheet maps which would serve the purpose better.

Map Compilation.

82. Revenue Survey maps of Agartala town on scale of 32″ to 1 mile were reduced to 16″, 8″ and 1″ to the mile scale and 33 copies traced.

83. 30 copies of various sheet maps showing roads on different sides were traced and issued to various departments.

84. 6 case maps in connection with boundary disputes concerning the British border were prepared and 30 copies traced.

85. 12 copies of *Taluki* maps and 32 copies of village and other maps were traced and the area of 3 maps checked with planimeter by the same staff. The total expenditure incurred was Rs. 158-6.

86. The disputes about portions of boundary between this State and the Districts of Sylhet in Assam and Chittagong and the Chittagong Hill Tracts in Bengal were under correspondence. The Superintendent of Surveys was on tour for 20 days. He held discussions with Mr. Creed, Superintendent of Surveys, Assam, in connection with the disputed boundaries along the Districts of Sylhet and Noakhali.

87. The statement subjoined shows the result of the settlement work of the year.

88. There were permanent and *Taskhichi taluki* settlements of an area of 170 *drones* of waste land and 3 *drones* and 6 *kanis* of cultivated land respectively. Settlement operations in respect of 3,987 *drones* of *jote* lands were completed against 4,358 *drones* in the previous year.

Settlement.

Nature of Settlement.	1346 T. E.		1345 T. E.		REMARKS.
	Area in *drones.*	*Jama* in whole rupees.	Area in *drones.*	*Jama* in whole rupees.	
1. Permanent *taluki* settlement of cultivated land ...	—	—	—	—	
2. Permanent *taluki* settlement of waste land ...	170	577	—	—	
3. *Taskhichi taluki* settlement of cultivated land ...	3–6	77	3 *kanis* & 9 *gandas*	91	
4. *Taskhichi taluki* settlement of waste land ...	—	—	50	400	
5. *Jotedari* re-settlement of cultivated land	3,807	25,064	4,125	44,265	
6. *Jotedari* settlement of waste land	180	1,560	233	2,171	
TOTAL ...	4,160	27,278	4,408	46,927	

89. A net increase of Rs. 5,925 in *jama* was secured by resettlement of *abadi jote* lands, the *Nazarana* being Rs. 35,353. The average *jama* per *kani* was 6 annas and 8 pies against 10 annas and 8 pies in the previous year.

Resettlement of *jote* lands.

90. During the year, an area of 180 *drones* of waste land was settled for a prospective rental of Rs. 1,560, the average *jama* per *kani* obtained being annas 8 and pies 8 against 9 annas and 3 pies in the previous year. The maximum and minimum rates were annas 8 and annas 4 respectively. The *Nazarana* realised was Rs. 2,003, the rent-free period allowed ranging from 1 to 3 years.

Jotedari settlement of waste land.

91. No whole-time settlement officer was employed in any division but Divisional Officers and Second Officers were entrusted with the settlement work within their respective jurisdictions. The total expenditure in the settlement operations was Rs. 1,553.

Settlement work.

92. It will be seen that the *Nazarana* obtained and obtainable by settlement of *abadi jote* land and settlement of waste land as *jotes* amounted to Rs. 37,356 (Rs. 35,353 + Rs. 2003).

93. As detailed below there were altogether 17 private estates under State management during the year under report.

Private Estates under State management.

Class.	Name of Estate.	Area.	Revenue
Encumbered	1. Kakraban Estate	283 *drones.*	1,871
	2. Jogendranagar Trust Estate	30 „	163
	3. Kamalnagar and Mahendranagar Estate	51 „	255
	4. Maharam Ali Chaudhuri Khanje Khan Bahadur's		..
	Estate—*Taluk*	236 „	1,230
	Jote	6 „	149
	5. Thakur Nalini Mohan Deb Barma's Estate	68 „	170
	6. Brajendra Kumar Das's Estate	408 „	1,936
	7. Brajapur Estate (Kamala Kanta Deb Barman and others)	246 „	982
	8. Kalimulla's Estate	124 „	863
	9. Mahammadali Chaudhuri's Estate	24 „	76
Unencumbered	10. Prabhu Goswamis' Estate	31 „	61
	11. Dowager Maharanee's Estate	169	766
	12. Late Girish Chandra Chaudhuri's Estate	36 „	254
	13. Late Brajakumar Thakur's Estate	47 „	297
	14. Late Naba Kumar Chakrabarty's		
	Estate—*Taluk*	32 „	225
	Jote	5 „	19
	15. Nilkantha Sen's Estate	75 „	374
	16. Gouranga Tripura's Estate	13 „	57
Endowment	17. Taranagar Trust Estate	140 „	52

94. It will not be out of place to mention here that the area of No. 2 Jogendranagar *Taluk* decreased from 64 *drones* to 30 *drones* as a result of survey settlement operation during the year under review, the balance of 34 *drones* having been decided as *Khas* land.

95. The subjoined table shows the demand and collection of the estates during the year under review. Compared with the previous year, collections improved in 10 estates and fell in 7 estates.

Estate No.	Demand			Collection			P. C. of collection
	Current	Arrear	Total	Current	Arrear	Total	
1.	6,101	43,486	49,587	988	4,267	5,255	10·57
2.	724	8,142	8,866	76	372	448	5·05
3.	1,286	3,419	4,705	149	1,195	1,344	28·56
4.	3,364	19,077	22,441	331	2,223	2,554	10·84
	Jote 345	1,650	1,995	—	95	95	
5.	1,163	5,377	6,540	108	1,209	1,317	20·13
6.	3,602	10,034	13,636	3,047	1,575	4,622	33·89
7.	4,217	10,643	14,860	690	2,202	2,892	19·46
8.	2,443	8,307	10,750	45	335	380	3·53
9.	1,256	3,277	4,559	133	788	921	20·20
10.	912	4,871	5,783	105	529	634	10·94
11.	107	424	531	44	54	98	18·45
12.	1,149	13,318	14,467	336	1,372	1,708	11·80
13.	1,606	4,386	5,992	95	1,172	1,267	21·14
14.	784	4,658	5,442	184	1,263	1,447	26·58
15.	694	2,820	3,514	69	168	237	6·74
16.	204	160	364	111	152	263	72·25
17.	3,116	13,443	16,559	502	2,002	2,504	15·12

CHAPTER III—PROTECTION.

I. Legislation.

96. No legislation was undertaken during the year and there was no sitting of the Legislative Council.

97. The following important regulations were promulgated during the year under review :—

(1) A Regulation for settlement of land in the capital town of Agartala.

(2) Notification No. 12, vesting the Indian Tea Licensing Committee with power to grant extension to tea gardens in the State.

(3) Notification No. 13, vesting the Indian Tea Licensing Committee with power to grant licenses to tea gardens in the State to extend their plantations up to 25 acres in all.

(4) Notification No. 14 prescribing the form of application for extension of tea cultivation.

II. Military.

98. Dewan Bahadur Kamala Prasad Dutt, M. A., B. L., F. R. E. S., M. R. A. S., continued to be in charge of the Military Department. Lt.-Col. Kumar Dina Mohan Dev Varman Bahadur, Commandant, Tripura State Forces, retired on pension on the 11th November, 1936 (25. 7. 46 T. E.) and in his place Major Rana Jodha Jung Bahadur, M. B. E., M. C., (Retired Indian Army) was appointed Commandant, Tripura State Forces.

Charge.

99. The total strength of the Forces at the end of the year was 396 against 398 of the preceding year.

Strength.

100. His Highness the Maharaja Manikya Bahadur was pleased to inspect both the units on 27th April. Major-General A. M. Mills, C. B., D. S. O. Military Adviser-in-Chief, Indian States Forces, accompanied by Major J. A. Blood, Military Adviser, C. I. S. Forces, inspected both the units from the 24th to the 28th November, 1936. Lt.-Col. A. S. Meek, C. M. G., Agent to the Governor-General, Eastern States, and His Excellency the Governor of Bengal, accompanied by His Highness the Maharaja Manikya Bahadur visited the cantonment on 3rd February and 15th March, 1937 respectively.

Inspections.

101. One N. C. O. from the 2nd Tripura Bikram Company attended the 5th (Infantry) N. C. Os' Course at Small Arms School, Pachmarhi (India.) His result was very satisfactory. Three N. C. O.s from both the 1st Tripura Bir and 2nd Tripura Bikram Companies attended the Small Arms School, Gwalior and their results were also satisfactory. Two N. C. O.s attended the District Preparatory Physical Training Course at Shillong with good results. One Indian Officer and 2 N. C. O.s (Piper and Bugler) were attached to the 1/8th Gurkha Rifles, Shillong, for training and they came out successful. During the latter part of the year, Classification Test of the Signallers of both Companies was held under Lt. H. B. Hulton, Signalling Officer, 2/2, K. E. Gurkha Rifles, Chittagong, on the 9th and 10th February, 1937.

Training.

102. Some ordinary improvements and petty repairs of the barracks were effected during the year.

Cantonment.

103. The health of the forces was generally good as in the previous year.

Health.

104. The total expenditure for the year excluding the public works amounted to Rs. 1,18,728 against Rs. 1,07,181 of the previous year.

Expenditure.

105. During the year, an Officers' Cadre Course on the subject of T. E. W. T. for all officers was held under the Company Commanders. Officers and other ranks received more practice in night operations. Besides these, both the companies went out of the cantonment in the early morning of every Saturday in each month of the year for Route March. Both the companies, including recruits, fired table A and B in the

Camping and Tactical Practice by Military Forces during the year.

musketry practice in their range. Major Rana Jodha Jung Bahadur, M. B. E., M. C., Commandant and his orderly, No. 87 U/P, L/NK., Durga Charan Deb were selected by His Highness to represent the Tripura State Forces at the London Coronation of His Majesty the King Emperor who personally presented them with Coronation Medals at the Buckingham Palace.

III. Police.

Charge.

106. Rai Saheb A. C. Gupta continued as Superintendent of Police during the whole of the year.

A. S. P.

107. Babu Naresh Kumar Bhattacharjee, B. SC., continued to be sick during the year. Babu Narendra Nath Bose, B. A. acted in his place as Assistant Superintendent of Police during the second half of the year.

Strength.

108. The total numerical strength of the Police force during the year was 496 as against 492 of the previous year, the increase being due to sanction of 4 extra constables (civil) in the budget.

Rural Police.

109. The total number of village choukidars was 176 as in the previous year.

Inspecting Staff.

110. There were 4 Inspectors of Police as before, their main duties being to exercise control over, and maintain discipline amongst, their subordinates, supervision of important cases and inspection of thanas and Court Sub-Inspectors' offices.

Investigating and Prosecuting Staff.

111. During the year, there were 23 Sub-Inspectors and 21 Naib-Darogas, as in the previous year. The officers continued to show their detective ability in the investigation of cases. As a result of keen attention towards prevention of smuggling of liquor and *ganja*, a few cases were detected. Preventive measures to run down a large number of notorious bad characters were taken and the patrol system in affected areas continued, as a result of which crime was checked to some extent. Credit is due to some officers for detection of some theft and burglary cases including one gun theft case. The behaviour and dealings of the Police with the public were generally satisfactory and no case of ill-treatment was reported against any Police officer during the year under review.

C. I. D. & Intelligence Staff.

112. One Sub-Inspector, 5 Naib Darogas and 5 Constables were employed in the C. I. D. as in the previous year.

Crime.

113. The total number of cases reported during the year under review was 663 as against 674 in the previous year. The decrease is due to, as has been stated in the paragraph under the heading "Investigating and Prosecuting Staff,"

institution of cases under sections 109 and 110 Cr. P. C. and successful patrol work.

114. The result of cases is as follows :—

Number of cases reported
663

- Enquiry refused 2
- Number investigated 624
  - True 545
    - Charge-sheet 313
    - Finally reported 232
  - Intentionally false 27
  - Mistake of law 3
  - Mistake of fact 29
  - Noncognizable 20
  - Doubtful 0
- Number pending 37

Result of Prosecution.

115. Altogether 560 persons were arrested and sent up for trial by the Police in connection with various offences as against 516 arrested and 708 sent up in the previous year.

116. Of the persons sent up, 138 were convicted and 118 acquitted (including 45 on compromise and 30 on withdrawal of cases), while 5 died and 299 (including the absconding accused) awaited trial. The percentage of conviction was 24·64 as against 26·94 of the previous year.

117. Of 455 accused awaiting trial at the end of the previous year, 99 were convicted, 144 acquitted (including 38 on compromise and 33 on withdrawal of cases), while 3 died and 209 were awaiting trial at the close of the year under report.

Bad Livelihood cases.

118. Six cases of badlivelihood were started against 17 persons of whom 8 were bound down and 9 were awaiting trial as the year closed. As many as 15 cases were started against 49 persons in the previous year of which 30 persons were awaiting trial at the close of the year and 28 persons were bound down during the year under review. Nineteen persons of the aforesaid 49 were prosecuted in one case.

Arms Act Cases.

119. Three Arms Act cases were instituted against 3 persons, of whom 2 were convicted and 1 acquitted during the year under report.

Gun theft Cases.

120. 5 guns were stolen during the year under report against 8 in the previous year, of which 2 and 1 respectively were recovered from the neighbouring British territory. Only one gun stolen during the year under review was recovered in a jungle in the State territory.

Recovery of stolen properties.

121. The total value of the properties stolen during the year amounted to Rs. 15,487-9-3 against Rs. 10,193-14-9 of the previous year. Of this amount, Rs. 2,057-1-9 were recovered against Rs. 2,322-5-0 in the previous year. The percentage of recovery was 13·28 against 22·78 of the previous year.

Dacoity.

122. There were 17 cas... of dacoity during the year against 11 in the previo year. Eight persons were sent up in chargesheet in connection with 3 cases which ended in acquittal.

Unnatural death.

123. Eighty-... e cases of unnatural death were reported during the year. Regular enquiries were held by the Police into all these cases. No foul play was detected in any of them.

Rewards and Punishments.

124. Thirteen Sub-Inspectors, 5 Naib Darogas, 1 Armed S. I., 1 Jamadar, 24 Civil Constables and three Choukidars received money rewards, while 11 armed Constables, 50 civil Constables and 1 Choukidar were fined or temporarily degraded.

Tours.

125. The Superintendent of Police was out on tour for 58 days against 63 days in the previous year and the acting Assistant Superintendent of Police, Babu N. N. Bose, B. A., for 5 days against 22 days in the previous year.

Co-operation.

126. The relation of the State police with the police of the neighbouring districts in British India continued to be satisfactory.

Musketry Practice.

127. Musketry and revolver practice was continued in the year under review and the force was found to be satisfactorily progressing in this direction.

Expenditure.

128. The expenditure amounted to Rs. 85,092 against Rs. 82,754 in the previous year.

IV. Justice.

Courts.

129. There were 17 courts of justice in the State during the year under report, exercising both civil and criminal jurisdiction, *viz.* :—Khas Adalat (High Court) with its original and appellate sides, and 16 courts of Magistrate-Munsif exercising original jurisdiction only.

Khas Adalat (High Court).

130. Babu Jnanendra Mohan Das, B. L., continued as Chief Judge. Thakur Hriday Ranjan Dev Barman as Puisne Judge (appellate side) and Babu Ramani Mohan Goswami, M. A., B. L., as Civil and Sessions Judge (Original side) during the year.

Number of original criminal cases

131. Altogether 2,077 criminal cases were instituted during the year under report as against 1,974 of the previous year. With the balance of 736 pending from the previous year, the total number of cases for disposal before the several subordinate courts was 2,813 as against 2,762 of the previous year as detailed below ; and out of these 2,813 cases, 1,978

were disposed of as against 2,026 of the preceding year, leaving 835 cases pending at the close of the year. Thus in the year under report, the number of cases for disposal increased from that of the previous year by 51, and there was a decrease in disposal by 48.

DESCRIPTION OF OFFENCES.	1345 F. E.	1346 F. E.
Offences against the State and public tranquillity	102	138
Offences against person	788	844
Offences against property	1,436	1,302
Other offences	436	529
TOTAL	2,762	2,813

132. Altogether extradition of 96 persons was asked for during the year under report, of whom 48 persons were arrested by the British Indian Police and surrendered to the State and 17 persons appeared of their own accord or were subsequently arrested within the State territory.

Extradition from British India.

133. The number of persons brought to trial within the year under report was 2,477; the number awaiting trial from the preceding year was 956; the total number of persons thus brought to trial in the year under report was 3,433 as against 3,395 of the previous year. Out of the aforesaid 2,477 persons, 477 were arrested by the police, 575 were produced on warrant, 1,053 appeared on summons, 368 appeared voluntarily and 4 persons were arrested in the presence of Magistrates.

Persons brought to trial.

134. Out of the aforesaid 3,433 persons brought to trial before the several courts including the Sessions Court, 1,231 persons were discharged, 618 were acquitted, 438 were convicted, 17 died and 1,129 persons were awaiting trial at the close of the year. Out of the convicted persons, 189 were sentenced to various terms of imprisonment extending from less than one month to 5 years and above, 236 were sentenced to fine only, 11 were bound down and 2 persons were warned for the future. The number of persons actually tried was 1,056 (excluding those discharged) as against 1,192 of the previous year and the percentage of conviction was thus 41·48 against 48·15 of the previous year.

Result of cases.

135. Out of 2,813 cases for disposal as stated above, the number of cases in which British subjects were concerned either as complainants or accused, was 382 as against 447 of the previous year. Out of these, 285 cases were cognizable and 97 non-cognizable. In 40 cases British subjects were complainants and in 342 cases they were the accused. In 87 cases both the parties were British subjects. In all, 487 persons were actually brought under trial in those cases during the year under report as against 572 of the previous year. Out of these 487 persons, 139 persons were convicted, 147 acquitted or discharged, 3 died and 198 remained under trial at the close of the year.

Cases concerning British subjects.

136. The following statement will show the number of original criminal cases instituted in the year under review and the year before.

DESCRIPTION OF OFFENCES.	1345 T.E.	1346 T.E.	Increase.	Decrease.
Offences against the State and public tranquillity ...	79	109	30	0
Offences against person	591	617	26	0
Offences against property	995	959	0	
Other offences	309	392	83	0
TOTAL	1,974	2,077	139	36

Increased by 103.

137. 18 cases were committed to the Sessions during the year under report and 2 cases were pending from the previous year. Out of these 20 cases, 18 were disposed of during the year as detailed below. The number of persons involved in those 20 cases was 67, of whom 14 persons were convicted, 48 were acquitted and 5 remained under trial at the close of the year.

Sessions cases.

Description of cases.	Number of cases.	Disposed of.	Pending.	REMARKS.
Murder	3	2	1	
Murder and destroying evidence of murder	1	0	1	
Culpable homicide not amounting to murder	3	3	0	
Attempt to murder	1	1	0	
Grievous hurt	1	1	0	
Rape	2	2	0	
Rioting	1	1	0	
Robbery	4	4	0	
Arson	2	2	0	
Using forged currency notes... ...	1	1	0	
Forgery and using forged documents ...	1	1	0	
Total	20	18	2	

138. There were altogether 256 criminal appeals as against 247 of the previous year. These appeals were disposed of as shown below :—

Criminal appeals.

Rejected	10
Judgment affirmed	104
Modified	43
Revised	15
Further enquiry ordered	7
	179
Pending	77
Total	256

139. The percentage of judgments affirmed and modified was 86·98 as against 79·78 of the previous year.

140. The number of original civil suits instituted during the under report was 1,370 as against 1,553 of the preceding year. With the balance of 841 suits pending from the previous year, the total number of suits for disposal

Original civil suits.

was 2,211 as against 2,332 of the preceding year. These suits were disposed of as shown below :—

Exparte	671
Admitted and compromised	165
Dismissed for want of prosecution ...	233
Disposed of on contest	410
	1,479
Pending	732
Total	2,211

141. The average duration of suits in the civil courts was 3 months and 26 days as against 4 months and 24 days of the previous year.

Duration of suits.

142. The total value of civil suits instituted during the year was Rs. 1,47,531-13-7 as against Rs. 4,26,173-3-6 of the previous year, which gives an average of Rs. 107-11-0 per case. Out of 1,370 suits, instituted during the year under review, 371 related to land, 693 to money transactions and 306 suits were of other classes. 693 suits were of the value of Rs. 100 and under ; 357 suits were of the value between Rs. 100 and Rs. 500 ; 20 suits of value between Rs. 500 and Rs. 1,000 ; 10 suits of value between Rs. 1,000 and Rs. 5,000 ; 1 suit was of value above Rs. 5,000, and 289 suits were not estimable in money value.

Nature and value of suits.

143. The number of applications for the execution of decrees filed during the year was 601 and there were 655 pending from the previous year. The total number for disposal was thus 1,256 as against 1,444 of the preceding year. The aggregate value of the new applications was Rs. 96,860-0-0 and that of the pending applications was Rs. 1,12,352-2-0, the total value thus amounting to Rs. 2,09,212-2-0. The number of applications disposed of was 727, the value of which was Rs. 1,07,334-12-0. The number of execution cases pending at the close of the year was 529, the value thereof being Rs. 1,01,877-6-0.

Execution of decrees.

144. There were 149 civil appeals filed during the year, as against 169 of the previous year. With the balance of 97 from the previous year, the total number of civil appeals for disposal was 246 as against 247 of the preceding year. Out of these cases, 136 were disposed of during the year under report as against 150 of the previous year, leaving a balance of 110 cases at the close of the year.

Civil appeals.

145. The following figures will show the result of appeals in civil suits :—

Result of civil appeals.

Decisions confirmed	66
Decisions reversed	24
Decisions modified	18
Remanded	5
Compromised, and otherwise disposed of ...	23
	136

146. The percentage of judgments wholly or partly upheld, excluding those in the cases compromised, was 74·34 against 67·77 of the preceding year.

Percentage.

147. The total value of civil appeals, filed during the year under review, was Rs. 1,13,872-8-6 and the average duration of each appeal was 7 months and 15 days as against 5 months of the previous year.

Value and duration of appeals.

148. 15 civil suits were instituted in the original side, Khas Adalat, during the year under report as against 21 of the previous year. With the balance of 59 suits pending from the preceding year, the total number for disposal was 74 as against 72 of the previous year. Of these, 33 suits were disposed of as against 13 of the preceding year, leaving 41 suits pending at the close of the year. There were 26 execution cases during the year, including 22 cases pending from the previous year. Of these, 8 were disposed of and 18 remained pending at the close of the year. There were 20 applications for succession and other certificates during the year under report; with the balance of 5 of the previous year, the total number of such applications was 25, out of which 21 were disposed of as shown below and 4 remained pending at the close of the year :—

Cases in the Original Side, Khas Adalat.

Description of cases.	Total.	Disposed of.	Pending.
Probate cases	3	2	1
Succession certificate	6	5	1
Guardianship	16	14	2
Total	25	21	4

149. The total number of civil and criminal appeals including the number of cases pending from the previous year, was 502 as against 494 of the preceding year. Out of these appeals, 315 were disposed of as against 341 of the previous year.

Total number of appeals.

150. In comparison with the preceding year, the total number of appeals for disposal increased by 8 and there was a decrease in disposal by 26.

Description of appeals.	Number of appeals.		Disposed of.	
	Past year.	Present year.	Past year.	Present year.
Civil	247	246	150	136
Criminal	247	256	191	179
Total	494	502	341	315

V. Prisons.

151. Exclusive of the Central Jail at the capital, there were 7 sub-jails in the State during the year under report. Dr. M. M. Majumdar, Chief Medical Officer continued to be the Superintendent of the Central Jail.

Number of Jails

152. The total jail inmates during the year under review was 1117 as against 1173 in the year before—the daily average being 184·43 against 179·11. Of them, 520 were convicts, 591 under-trials, 4 civil prisoners and 2 detenus. Altogether 163 prisoners remained at the close of the year in all the jails as against 183 in the year previous.

Jail population.

153. As in previous years two detenus were kept under restraint in the Central Jail throughout the year.

Detenu.

154. 98 prisoners were under more than 2 years' imprisonment as against 99 in the preceding year. Their offence, sentence and occupation are detailed in the following statement.

Long-term prisoners.

Class of offence.	Number of prisoners.	Occupation.	REMARKS.
Murder	17	They were employed in brick manufacturing. oilmills, wheat grinding, *soorki* pounding. *khoa* breaking, weaving. gardening. bamboo and cane work. tailoring and paddy husking etc.	68 had sentences of 2 to 5 years, 10 of 5 to 10 years, 8 of 10 to 14 years, and 12 for life *i. e.* 20 years.
Culpable homicide not amounting to murder... ...	11		
Grievous hurt	9		
Robbery	3		
Theft	3		
Dacoity	26		
Counterfeiting coin	4		
Picking pocket	1		
Arson	1		
Rape	5		
Keeping in possession counterfeit Currency note	1		
Section 110 (security for good behaviour for habitual offenders) ...	15		
Keeping Revolver in possession without license ...	2		
Total	98		

155. One convict and one undertrial died of cholera and tuberculosis respectively in the Central Jail during the year under report. The health of all the jails was generally good.

Jail health.

156. 27 convicts had primary school training under a paid tutor at the Reformatory School in the Central Jail. Three of them appeared at the Pathsala School scholarship examination and all came out successful. As in the preceding year, religious sermons were also given to the convicts weekly by honorary instructors.

Education.

157. One under-trial from the Kailashahar sub-jail and 2 under trials from the Dharmanagar sub-jail escaped during the year under review. But one of the two of the Dharmanagar jail was re-arrested.

Escape.

158. On the auspicious occasion of the birthday of His Highness
Special release. the Maharaja Manikya Bahadur, 10 convicts were set at liberty before the expiry of their sentence during the year under report—the same number as in the year before.

159 The total warder staff was 70 strong. Of them, 10 were
Jail staff Jamadars (Head warders) and 60 warders. The two jails at Sonamura and Kailashahar were under military watch as arranged in the year previous. Owing to the negligence of their duties, 17 warders were fined, 3 discharged from their services, 1 suspended and 4 warned for the future.

160. His Excellency the Right Honourable Sir John Anderson,
Visit. P. C., G. C. B., G. C. I. E., Governor of Bengal, paid a visit to the Central Jail at the capital towards the end of the year under review and laid the foundation stone of a big 2 storied building there on the 17th March, 1937, which, when completed, will greatly improve the jail accommodation with classification of prisoners. Lt. Col. A. S. Meek, C. M. G., Agent to the Governor General, Eastern States, was also pleased to pay a visit to the Central Jail on the 3rd February, 1937.

161. The income of the Central Jail alone totalled Rs. 7932-15-0
Income. as against Rs. 4029-1-0 in the year before.

162. The total expenditure amounted to Rs. 29,668 as against
Expenditure. Rs. 29,658 in the preceding year.

VI. Registration.

163. Thakur K. K. Singha, Naib Dewan, continued to be in charge of the Registration Department.

164. The number of Registration offices continued to be 9 as
Registration Offices. in the previous year—there being one at the head quarters station of each of the Divisions and subdivision. In the Mofussil, the Divisional and Sub-divisional Officers and in certain divisions the Second Officers acted as Registrars. For the Sadar Division there was a separate Registrar at Agartala.

165. The total number of documents presented for registration
Registration and disposal. during the year including 190 documents pending at the end of the previous year, was 7,819 against 7,398. Of these, 45 deeds were refused registration on different grounds and 457 remained pending at the end of the year against 90 pending at the end of the previous year.

166. The total value covered by the documents amounted to Rs. 9,25,694/- as against Rs. 11,06,147/- of the previous year, while the total value covered by the documents actually registered was Rs. 9,17,873 as against Rs. 10,98,306 in the year before.

167. With 14 suits pending from the previous year, the total number of suits brought before the Registration Department in respect of documents, the registration of which had been refused in various Registration offices, was 22, out of which 12 were disposed of and 10 remained pending at the end of the year. With 2 appeals pending from the previous year the total number of appeals for disposal was 5, out of which 2 were disposed of and 3 remained pending as the year closed.

Suits and Appeals.

168. The total income of the Department from fees and fines amounted to Rs. 7,243 against Rs. 7,444 and the expenditure to Rs. 3,993 against Rs. 3,564 in the previous year. The net income thus amounted to Rs. 3,250 in the year under report against Rs. 3,880/- in the previous year.

Income and Expenditure.

VII. Municipality and Sanitation.

169. As before, the State had the only municipality at the Capital town of Agartala during the year under report with a population of about 10,000 according to the last census of 1340 T. E. It may be mentioned here that the population of the town has been steadily and appreciably increasing due to expansion and improvements effected during the last few years.

Municipality.

170. The Municipality, on behalf of the citizens of Agartala, takes this opportunity to record its high appreciation of, and thanks for, the very kind visit of Lt.-Col. A. S. Meek, C. M. G., Agent to the Governor General, Eastern States, and also of His Excellency The Right Honourable Sir John Anderson, P. C., G. C. B, G. C. I. E., Governor of Bengal, to Agartala, the State capital, on the 3rd February 1937 and on the 15th March, 1937 respectively.

171. His Excellency the Governor of Bengal was graciously pleased to accept an address of welcome from the Chairman on behalf of the Municipal Commissioners and citizens of Agartala at "Malanchabas" to which he kindly responded eulogising our present beloved Ruler for his sincere and manifold activities in beautifying and improving the general condition of the town. For this kindness the Municipality expresses its sincere thanks to His Excellency.

172. A committee of 9 members—all nominated, administered the Municipality with Thakur S. C. Deb Barma, M. A. (Harvard) Senior Naib Dewan, Accounts Department, Minister's Office, as the official Chairman and Babu Haridas Bhattacharjee as non-official Vice-Chairman elected by the members, during the year under report.

Municipal Committee.

173. The committee held 3 meetings—average attendance of members being 4·3 as against 5·2 of the previous year. It was found

difficult to hold meetings regularly due to protracted illness of certain members.

174. Apart from the State grant of Rs. 9000, the total realization from Municipal and latrine taxes amounted to Rs. 5,069-8-0 as against Rs. 5,079-2-0 of the previous year. The total demand under this head inclusive of arrears was Rs. 9,352-1-6 of which Rs. 486-8-9 was irrecoverable.

Income.

175. Both Municipal and latrine taxes to the amount of Rs. 2,281-1-6 due by the members of His Highness's family living outside the palace proper and Prabhugoswamis of Sreepat still remained outstanding. Had the above amount been realized, the collection would have been more satisfactory.

176. The miscellaneous income from all sources including deposits recovered amounted to Rs. 1,716-14-9 as against Rs. 585-8-6 of the preceding year. This figure includes the amount of Rs. 1,074-7-3 being the depreciation contribution of the Municipal staff which was transferred and credited to Municipal fund.

177. Thus the total income of the Municipality came up to Rs. 15,786-6-9 as against Rs. 14,664-10-6 of the preceding year.

178. The total expenditure of the Municipality excluding the amount spent on the Bazar improvements amounted to Rs. 15,793-8-0 as against Rs. 14,834-4-0 of the previous year.

Expenditure.

179. The control and management of the bazar continued to be in the hands of the Municipal Committee. The total demand including the arrear demand was Rs. 15,558-0-6, of which Rs. 2,900-13-6 was irrecoverable. The total receipts including Rs. 100 as advance recovered from the Municipality were Rs. 8,404-4-3 as against Rs. 6,762-1-3 of the previous year. After necessary expenditure of Rs. 12,585-6-6, the Bazar improvement fund stood at Rs. 44,507-1-0 at the close of the year.

Ishanganja Bazar

180. The well-thought-out plan for the improvement of the town as ordered by His Highness the Maharaja Manikya Bahadur was pushed on and showed considerable progress during the year. When the whole scheme is worked out the citizens of Agartala will have ample reasons to be proud of its wide roads, better water-supply and lighting arrangement—not to speak of the splendid Bazar structure which has considerably added to the grandeur of the town.

Town Roads.

181. The construction of straight and broad roads of considerable length throughout the length and breadth of the town and further on has immensely improved the aesthetic aspect of the town and made communications much easier.

182. The scheme for the supply of electrical energy to the town submitted by the present Chairman and approved by His Highness the Maharaja Manikya Bahadur took definite shape and by the end of the year under report, the Agartala State Guaranteed Electric Supply Co. was entrusted

Electric street-light.

with it. Practically all the main roads were lighted with electricity within the municipal area. Such arrangement has already given impetus to new industries now being established in and about the town. The electrical energy was available to the Municipality and the State at -/2/- two annas per unit. The cost of lighting was met from the Municipal and Bazar funds. It is expected that with the growing importance of the town, all the roads including katcha roads will soon be electrically lighted in the near future.

Bazar Buildings construction.

183. The construction of Bazar buildings on pretty design with running verandahs and round pillars in front was on the verge of completion during the year under review. Apart from the beauty and grandeur of the town, such construction of masonry buildings has practically solved the problem of fire hazards which so often caused a great havoc and loss to the local traders.

Daily Market.

184. On the site for the daily market selected on the north bank of the Howra river, a stupendous circular building with broad gates and turrets is nearing its completion. It will have ample space within its walls to accommodate the daily and weekly markets leaving sufficient ground for future expansion outside. The Bazar fund is contributing to the cost of construction which is expected to run up to Rs. 35,000 or more.

Tube-wells.

185. So long the citizens experienced the greatest scarcity of pure drinking water within the town which seldom failed to invite epidemic diseases like cholera dysentery and others. The public have greatly been relieved of the havoc and trouble due to want of pure water-supply on a number of tube-wells being sunk in different parts of the town and bazar area during the year under review. The sinking of these tube-wells both by Municipality and Sanitation Department cost Rs. 2,459 3-0 in all.

Road watering.

186. His Highness was pleased to grant Rs. 9,346 for the purchase of two road watering lorries supplied by Messrs. French Motor Car & Co. for this Municipality. These lorries are specially fitted with fire-fighting accessories and rendered valuable services on two occasions, besides appreciable service in watering both katcha and pucca roads. The public greatly appreciated this arrangement and the Municipality records its grateful thanks to His Highness for such a grant.

Sanitation.

187. The Department concerned had some works of minor nature for sanitary purposes done at a cost of Rs. 661-8-3.

Health.

188. The general health of the town was on the whole not quite satisfactory. Towards the first part of the year under review cholera prevailed in the town epidemically.

189. There were 87 cases of cholera with 23 deaths and 10 cases of small-pox with 3 deaths. Most of the cholera and small-pox cases were imported from outside. Small-pox cases were attended to and cured by the Small-pox specialists of the State.

190. Dr. M. M. Majumdar, Chief Medical Officer of the State continued to be in charge of both the Municipal and Sanitation Departments as before.

Charge.

CHAPTER IV—PRODUCTION AND DISTRIBUTION.

1. Weather and Crops—Agriculture.

191. Manyabara Raja Rana Bodhjung Bahadur, F. R. G. S., Chief Secretary to His Highness the Maharaja Manikya Bahadur continued to be in charge of the Department and during his absence while on tour with His Highness, the charge of the Department remained with Dewan Bahadur K. Dutt M. A. B. L., F. R. Econ. S., M. R. A. S., Private Secretary to H. H. the Maharaja Manikya Bahadur.

Charge of the Department.

192. The staff of the Department continued to be the same as in the previous year with Mr. J. C. Choudhury, S. E., M. S. A. (Tokyo), M. R. A. (Agri) S. (London) as Superintendent of Agriculture at its head. But the services of the General Assistant, Babu Smarajit Chakrabarty, B. SC., was utilised during most part of the year by the Secretary of the Tripura Charity Lottery.

Staff.

193. The Propaganda Office at the local market served the purpose of general propaganda as in previous years.

Propaganda Office.

194. The Agricultural Propagandist carried on general propaganda in connection with the improved varieties of sugarcane, cereals, English vegetables and ground-nuts in the State with special attention to Kamalpur, Bishalgarh, Kalyanpur and Khowai. The problem of improving the cattle-breeding in the State, was taken up by the Department, in all seriousness and vigorous propaganda was made in Sadar and Bishalgara Elaka on this line.

Propaganda tours.

195. Various leaflets in connection with ground-nut manures, ericulture and napier grass cultivation were distributed among the public and market rates of different goods were given publicity to on the publicity-board twice a week.

Publicity.

196. Arrangements were made from the Department to distribute seeds of ground-nut, grown from the seeds distributed from the Department in the previous year, and in addition to this, a few maunds of fresh seeds of ground-nut and English vegetable seeds of good quality were distributed. That ground-nut grows satisfactorily in the State and yields a profitable crop is now a proved fact.

Seed distribution and seed crops.

197. The Agricultural Survey work was taken up by this Department and necessary information regarding lands and crops of some places was gathered.

Agricultural Survey.

198. In co-operation with the Government of Bengal, the Department took up the Marketing Survey work and necessary reports regarding all commodities available in the State, were sent to the Senior Marketing Officer, Bengal.

Marketing Survey.

199. The spread of eri-culture in the State was gradually increasing and a few pieces of cloth were also woven.

Eri-culture.

200. The Kashipur Farm was leased on *Borga* system and departmental seeds of experimental crops were also grown there.

Kashipur Farm on *Borga* system.

201. Average rainfall of the year was 83·19 inches against 79·48 inches in the previous year. The quinquennial average was 81·50 inches. Sadar Division had the maximum fall of 108·81 inches. Heaviest rainfall of 20·94 inches was registered in the month of Sraban.

Rainfall.

202. Maximum temperature recorded was 96 degrees and minimum 46 degrees during the year under report.

Temperature.

203. The principal crops in the State were paddy, jute, mustard, *til*, sugarcane and cotton. Cultivation of pine-apple and ground-nut is increasing gradually. Potatoes, tobacco, chillies and pulses of various types were also grown in some parts of the State.

Crops.

204. Male labourers earned from 4 annas to 8 annas per day, female labourers from 3 to 5 annas. Gharamis earned from 4 to 10 annas and carpenters and masons from 8 annas to Re 1 only. Most of the labourers came from bordering British Districts.

Labour and Wages.

205. Rice sold from Rs. 2-4 to Rs. 4-8 and paddy sold from Re. 1 to Rs. 2 per maund. The slight differences of these prices from those of the neighbouring British districts are only due to transport charges.

Prices

206. Nearly 50 gardens were in running condition during the year, and production of tea increased by nearly 2,00,000 lbs in comparison with the previous year. A statement of production will be found in Section IV.

Tea Industry.

207. There was an outbreak of rinderpest in epedemic form in some parts of the Sadar, Sonamura, Bilonia and Sabroom Divisions and the State Veterinary Surgeon was deputed to apply Goat Tissue Vaccine.

Veterinary.

208. Superintendent of Agriculture was out on tour for 37 days only.

Tour of the staff.

II. Immigration and Emigration.

209. The charge of the Department continued to be with Raja Saheb Manyabara Rana Bodhjung Bahadur, F. R. G. S., Chief Secretary to His Highness the Maharaja Manikya Bahadur with the exception of the period when he was out on tour with His Highness the Maharaja

Charge of the Department.

Manikya Bahadur when Dewan Bahadur K. Dutt M. A., B. L. Private Secretary to His Highness the Maharaja Manikya Bahadur held the charge. Mr. B. C. Dev Barman continued as Assistant during the year under review.

210. During the year under review, 1533 persons immigrated into and 1267 persons emigrated out of the State.

Immigration & Emigraton.

211. Reclamation work in Kulaihaor made satisfactoy progress during the year.

Reclamation in Kulai.

212. Some Khasias came to the area with a view to cultivate *Pan* (betel) and the forecast of the same is very satisfactory.

Khasias.

213. Some Mags from British Districts came to settle down in Nalichhera and they were given lands there.

Mags.

214. Salema Bazar kept up the progress during the whole year. Weekly bazar is held there on every Saturday as usual.

Salema Bazar.

215. The natural waterflow and the tank at Salema supplied pure drinking water to the inhabitants.

Drinking water.

216. The-Primary School made satisfactory progress, the number of students during this short period being over 50. There was also a Boarding House with nearly 20 students but to the misfortune of the inhabitants both the school and the boarding house were burnt down during the latter part of the year by jungle fire and this caused much inconvenience and stood in the way of further progress. However, inhabitants with the greatest difficulty, made a temporary house for the school although it is not suitable for the purpose.

217. The *Dak Bungalow* of Salema with its attached cooksheds was also burnt down by jungle fire and there is no *Dak Bungalow* at present.

Dak Bungalow

218. Salema Dispensary rendered medical help throughout the whole year as before.

Dispensary.

219. The staff continued to be as it was in the previous year except in the winter when a temporary staff was engaged for the survey of Pulinpur Mouza.

Kalyanpur Reserve.

220. During the year under review a Kayemi Taluk of 22 Drones of land was granted and a Nazar of Rs. 469 was realised thereby.

221. Cultivated jotes covering 22 Drones, 5 Kanis and 13 Gandas and cultivated jungle lands of nearly 17 drones were setteled and Nazars of Rs. 216 and Rs. 148 respectively were realised.

222. The total expenditure on Reserve work amounted to Rs. 1266-14-9 against Rs. 837-2 in the previous year,

223. During the year under report Mr. B. C. Dev Barman, Assistant, was out on tour for 45 days.

III. Forests.

Charge and Management.

224. Babu Jatindra Nath Mitra, Naib Dewan, remained in charge of the Department during the year under review With the exception of a few Mahals which were le out on *Ijara*, all the forests were under khas management as before.

Staff.

225. Including the Patrol staff consisting of a Forester, three Head Guards and twenty guards, the Department had a staff of one Station Officer, four Forest Circle Inspectors, fourteen Foresters, eighteen Assistant Foresters, four Rangers, six Moharers, twentyfive Head Guards, thirteen Literate guards, one hundred and fiftynine guards and six boatmen.

226. During the year under review, the Patrol staff was out on tour in three sections. They patrolled in batches in Sadar Division for two months and fifteen days, in Belonia Division for four months and twenty days, in Kailasahar and Sonamura Divisions for twelve months.

Permits.

227. There were 145 commissioned agents for the sale of the forest permits for the shoulder-borne export of minor forest produce by land routes.

Forest Stations.

228. There were fiftyfive forest stations for collection of duty and prevention of forest offences including one new Forest Office at Samru in the Kailashahar Division, with one Assistant Forester and three guards and another at Muhuripur in the Bilonia Division, with one Head Guard and one guard.

Working of the Forests.

229. The working of the Sal forests was stopped during the year under review. The open unclassed forests were worked under the State Forest Rules of 1323 T. E. but for the Feni river mahal the working rules of the Bengal Forest Department were followed.

New Forest Reserves.

230. 65·91 square miles of forests detailed below were declared reserve during the year under report.

(*a*) Kailashahar Division—
Kulai Head water Reserve—area 26·25 square miles.

(*b*) Udaipur Division—
Garjichhera Reserve—area 39·66 square miles.

Kheda Operation.

231. No *Kheda* operation was undertaken during the year under report.

Management of the Amlighat Toll Station.

232. As agreed to by both the State and the Bengal Government, a Ranger from the Bengal Forest Department was deputed to Amlighat as Station Officer during the year under report. He remained there for about a year.

Feni river mahals.

233. The Toll Station at Amlighat continued to be under the management of the State Forest Department. A Ranger of the Bengal Forest Department worked as Station Officer of the Toll Station. The total revenue collected at the Station in the year under review was Rs. 36,519 against Rs. 48,186 in the previous year showing a decrease of Rs. 11,667. The total

expenditure incurred in running the Station was Rs. 3,676 against Rs. 4,082-11-3 in the previous year.

234. As before, a doctor of the Sub-Assistant Surgeon class was appointed temporarily for four months from December to March for giving medical relief to the Station staff and to the cutters and exporters of forest produce.

Fee Simple Lots.

235. As in the previous year, the forest produce from the Fee Simple Lots above the Amlighat Toll Station was exported free of duty under passes granted by the Collector of Chittagong.

Forest offences.

236. In the year under review, there were 143 forest cases against 258 persons including 40 cases against 86 persons pending from the previous year. The offences were mainly for export of forest produce without payment of duty.

Results.

237. Of the above 143 cases—(*a*) 73 cases against 120 persons were tried; (*b*) 12 cases against 28 persons were compounded and (*c*) 58 cases against 110 persons remained pending at the close of the year.

238. Of the 120 persons tried, 14 persons were sentenced to imprisonment only, 81 persons were punished with fine only; 6 were warned for the future and 19 were acquitted.

Rewards & punishment.

239. One Assistant Forester and one Ranger were fined for their neglect of duty during the year under review.

Health of the staff.

240. The health of the staff was generally good.

Sources of income.

241. The following table shows the results of the collection of forest revenue under different heads with all variations :—

Heads of Revenue.	1346 T.E.	1345 T.E.	Increase.	Decrease.	REMARKS.
	Rs.	Rs.			
I. Unclassed open forests :—					
(*a*) Toll on forest produce exported by the river mehals...	2,77,246	2,32,253	44,993	—	
(*b*) Toll on forest produce exported by land route under permits	69,637	70,285	—	648	
(*c*) Toll collection (State share) of the Amlighat Toll Station	26,877	31,314	—	4,437	
(*d*) Grazing mehal ...	6,183	5,537	646	—	
(*e*) Thatching grass mehal	2,221	2,574	—	353	
II. Reserved Forests :— Sale of *Sal* etc	1,039	4,134	—	3,095	
III. Elephant Kheddas	—	2,522	—	2,522	
TOTAL ...	3,83,203	3,48,619	45,639	11,055	
Match Excise duty	27,229	16,595	10,634	—	

242. Details of collection in the year under report are given below :—

Heads of Revenue.	Quantity of produce exported.	Duty realised thereon.	REMARKS.
	Cft.	Rs.	
1. Timber other than Sal...	5,06,820·6	85,791	
2. *Sal*	1,822·8	1,039	
3. Produce other than timber.			
(*a*) Exported by *bhatials*	—	1,91,455	
(*b*) Exported by land routes under permits	—	69,637	
4. Toll collection (State share) of the Feni river	—	26,877	
5. Grazing *Mahal* ...	—	6,183	
6. Thatching grass *Mahal*		2,221	
7. Elephant Khedas ...	—	—	
Total ...	—	3,83,203	
Excise Duty on Matches ...	—	27,229	

243. The total forest revenue in the year under report was Rs. 3,83,203 against Rs. 3,48,619 in the previous year showing an increase of Rs. 34,584.

Receipts.

244. During the year under report the Maharaja Match Factory manufactured 1098 gross of finished matches and paid Rs. 5-12-6 as duty on the timber used in making these matches. The State received Rs. 27,229 from the Government of India as its share of the Match Excise Duty against Rs. 16,595 in the previous year.

Receipt from Matches.

245. Plantation of *Gamair* and *Sonal* were continued during the year under report.

Plantation.

246. The Naib Dewan was out on tour for 64 days against 79 days in the previous year.

Tour.

IV. Trade and Manufacture.

247. The principal exports were timber and other forest produce of various kinds, cotton, oil-seeds (*til* and mustard) and *Gur* (molasses). Some homespun cotton fabrics manufactured by the hill people and specially by the manipuries were also exported. The principal exports of the year under review and two previous years are shown below :—

	1344 T. E.	1345 T. E.	1346 T. E.
Cotton ...	30,837 mds.	1,07,236 mds.	34,011 mds.
Til ...	54,640 ,,	21,374 ,,	33,323 ,,
Mustard seeds	34,986 ,,	31,851 ,,	36,027 ,,
Jute ..	72,274 ,,	82,009 ,,	1,50,032 ,,
Tea ...	24,66,331 lbs.	24,88,529 lbs.	26,56,780 lbs.

V. Public Works.

248. Dewan Bahadur K. Dutt, M. A., B. L., M. R. A. S., F. R. E. S., Private Secretary to His Highness the Maharaja Manikya Bahadur was in charge of the Public Works Department as before. Honorary Capt. J. N. Bhaduri, B. A., B. E., continued as State Engineer during the year.

Charge.

249. The Statement XX in the appendix gives details of the works executed during the year, the total expenditure including improvement works being Rs. 2,80,009 as detailed below against Rs. 2,01,925 in the previous year.

Expenditure.

Description of works.	Ordinary Public works including Local fund.	Improvement works.	TOTAL.
Buildings...	89,407	87,744	1,77,151
Roads & Bridges	24,961	38,261	63,222
Tanks & Tube-wells ...	4,240	2,646	6,886
Miscellaneous Works ...	3,849	8,379	12,228
Minor works at Rajbari (*Karkhana*) ...	1,175	—	1,175
Establishment charges ...	18,113	1,234	19,347
TOTAL ...	1,41,745	1,38,264	2,80,009

250. The following works were done during the year :—

1. Constructing a tin-shed for Fuel Reserve forest at Tulakona.
2. Constructing a tin-shed for forest Beat Office at Rishyamukh.
3. Constructing a tin-shed for *Tehsil Katchari* at Takarjala.
4. Jail lock-up at Kailashahar.
5. Jail lock-up at Sabroom.
6. Sinking two tube-wells at Sabroom—one at Maharagunj Bazar and another at Puran Bazar.
7. Sinking a tube-well at the Minister's House.
8. Sinking a tube-well in the Sadar Collectorate compound and another at Kunjaban.
9. Sinking a *Pucca* well at Kunjaban.
10. Excavating a tank at Kailashahar near the police station.
11. Constructing a road from Sadar to Takarjala.
12. Improvement of Dharmanagar Divisional Office.
13. Re-excavation of Amarsagar tank at Udaipur.
14. Constructing A. D. C's room & motor garage at Rajbari.
15. Constructing *Baithakkhana* court-yard.
16. Masonry railing by the Akhaura Road.
17. Raising of the *Prasad Pratoli*.
18. Constructing a cause-way on the Agartala-Bishalgarh Road at Batadhepa.
19. His Highness's bath and swimming bath.
20. His Highness's water-closet.
21. Main fountain of the Mogal Garden.

22. Lowering the bazar road at Sadar.
23. Laying marble stone on the floor of His Highness's *Baithakkhana* 1st floor.
24. Substantial improvement of the circular Bazar Building.
25. Flooring and ceiling of His Highness's bath room.
26. Laying marble stone on the floor of Her Highness the Mata Maharani's dressing room.
27. Palace compound-wall partly.
28. Raising of the Andharmanik *Bundh.*
29. Excavating a tank behind the Palace Compound.
30. Constructing a *pucca verandah* of the building wherein lions were previously kept.
31. Constructing a *pucca* building for lions and tigers.
32. Substantial improvement of Chief Justice's quarters.
33. Constructing a *pucca verandah* attached to the Studio and Studio extension building.
34. Constructing a bridge at Jangalia on the Bishalgarh road.
35. Constructing a bridge at Charilam on the Bishalgarh road.
36. Substantial progress of X'ray building.
37. Improvement of Sonamura-Melaghar road.
38. Driving piles for protection of the Andharmanik *Bundh.*
39. Re-inforced concrete slab decking on bridge No. 1, 2, 3, 4, 5 on the Bishalgarh road.
40. Mosaic and plaster works in the Mogal Garden canal.
41. Constructing two wards in the Sadar Jail.
42. Supplying cold bitumen on the Akhaura Road, near the Police Reserve.
43. Substantial progress of Akhaura road metalling.
44. Cement concrete and chunar stone works on Mogal Garden roads.
45. Improvement of Melaghar to Kakraban road.
46. Constructing a road from Andharmanik to Lemboo cherra.
47. Constructing a road from Lemboo cherra to Fatikcherra Tea garden.
48. Constructing a road from Bagbari to Devendranagar.
49. Improvement of Bisalgarh-Udaipur Road.
50. Thorough and special repairs of Agartala Sadar Jail.
51. Escape canals of Rudisagar.
52. Substantial progress of armourer's workshop at the Kunjaban Cantonment.
53. Improvement of the Mogra road.
54. Painting works and ceiling of *Svet Mahal.*
55. Substantial progress of Ghoramara bridge on the Ranirbazar road.
56. Earth-work on the road from Agartala to Chandra Sadhu Para.
57. Constructing one wooden bridge on the road betwen the Durgabari and Narsinggarh Tea garden.
58. Constructing wooden bridges on the Sylhet road.
59. Opening out a road-way to Durgabari tea garden.

60. Constructing a bathing platform and vats in Sadar Jail.
61 Constructing a sanitary latrine for females at the V. M. Hospital.
62. Metalling the Hospital road.
63. Constructing a dome of *Abdarkhana*.
64. Laying whiteglazed marble tiles on the Palace extension building.
65. Installation of electric wiring in servants' quarters attached to *Svet Mahal*.
66. Installation of electric wiring in the V. M. Hospital.
67. Contructing 6 suites in Studio extension building.
68. Ceiling and painting works of the Palace Library.
69. Thorough repairs and pinting of the Administration Building.

251. The total expenditure in connection with Electric Supply was Rs. 26.748 against Rs. 16,433 in the previous year.

CHAPTER V—REVENUE AND FINANCES.

I. Revenue.

252. The total collection in the year was Rs. 18.75,373 against Rs. 16,96,043 in the previous year.

253. The details of income under different heads with all variations are given in the statement below :—

Serial number.	HEADS OF REVENUE.	1346 T.E.	1345 T.E.	As compared with 1345 T.E.		REMARKS.
				Increase.	Decrease.	
1.	Land Revenue	8,32,454	6,53,693	1,78,761	—	
2.	Rents of markets	7,357	6,717	640	—	
3.	Family Tax in the hills	53,698	59,850	—	6,152	
4.	Toll on forest produce	3,46,883	3,02,538	44,345	—	
5.	Do. Do. on the Feni Rivers	26,877	31,314	—	4,437	
6.	Elephant & buffalo grazing Mehal	6,183	5,537	646	—	
7.	Thatching grass Mehal	2,221	2,574	—	353	
8.	Reserved *Sal* Forests	1,039	4,134	—	3,095	
9.	Tax on cotton and oil-seeds ..	1,06,518	2,17,722	—	1.11,204	
10.	Royalty on elephants caught ...	—	2,522	—	2,522	
11.	Adda Mehal	25,470	24,806	664	—	
12.	Excise	39,705	40,057	—	352	
13.	Stamps and Court-fees	67,627	62,874	4,753	—	
14.	Law and Justice (Fines)... ..	2,269	2,014	255	—	
15.	Process fees	10,726	9,683	1,043	—	
16.	Registration	7,243	7,444	—	201	
17.	Jail	7,968	4,235	3,733	—	
18.	Cattle pounds	3,745	4,489	--	744	
19.	Nazars	59,426	32,812	26,614	—	
20.	Education...	15,078	14,548	530	—	
21.	Tea Export duty	42,685	21,452	21,233	—	
22.	Jute Export duty	56,338	30,423	25,915	—	
23.	Depreciation Contribution ...	58,915	76,943	—	18,028	
24.	Miscellaneous	62,776	61,067	1,709	—	
25.	Duty on matches	27,270	16,595	10,675	—	
26.	Public Works	4,902	—	4,902	—	Net increase—Rs. 1,79,330
	TOTAL	18,75,373	16,96,043	3,26,418	1,47,088	

254. It will be seen that there was an increase in respect of 16 heads of income aggregating Rs. 3,26,418 against a decrease under 10 heads amounting to Rs. 1,47,088 which resulted in a net increase of Rs. 1,79,330.

255. The decrease under the heads Toll on the Feni river, Thatching grass *mahal*, Reserved *Sal* Forests, and Royalty on Elephants Caught is explained in the section relating to the Forest Department.

256. The income under the head Land Revenue exceeded the income of 1345 T. E. by Rs. 1,78,761 and the income under this head in 1345 T. E. was never reached before. The unprecedented increase in 1346 T. E. is attributable to satisfactory collection in the Sadar Division resulting in an excess of Rs. 27,642 and Rs. 1,08,736 against current and arrear demands respectively and to an excess of Rs. 42,383 realised in other Divisions, in comparison with 1345 T. E.

257. Tea garden land revenue contributed Rs. 75,726 showing a fall of Rs. 9,690 and Rs. 28,335 in comparison with 1344 and 1345 T. E. Realisation of current demand in 1345 and 1346 T. E. stood at Rs. 38,990 and Rs. 37,194 while that of arrear demand in 1345 T. E. and 1346 T. E. at Rs. 65,071 and Rs. 38,532.

258. The Tea duty doubled in comparison with the previous year showing an excess of Rs. 14,962 in comparison with 1344 T. E. The increase under the head "Jute Export Duty" is remarkable as it almost doubled in comparison with the previous years.

259. The increase under head *Nazar* has also been unprecedented in comparison with previous years.

260. The decrease under the head Family Tax in the Hills needs some explanation. The income under this head in 1340 was Rs. 37,204 but gradually it rose to Rs. 59,850 in 1345 T. E. against Rs. 52,593 in 1344 T. E. causing an unprecedented increase of Rs. 7257. The figure for the year under review exceeded the figure of 1344 T. E. by Rs. 1105. The income from Tax on Cotton and Oil-seeds showed a deficit of Rs. 1,11,204 in comparison with the year previous.

261. The excise revenue in the year under review witnessed a fall of Rs. 352 and Rs. 3,196 in comparison with 1345 and 1344 T. E. respectively.

262. The decrease under other heads is not noticeable.

II. Finances.

263. Thakur S. C. Deb Barman, M. A. (Harvard) Senior Naib Dewan, continued to be in charge of the Department.

264. A consolidated abstract account of the financial transactions of the State and the attached Zemindaries as compared with those of the previous year is given below :—

Receipts.	1345 T.R.	1346 T.R.
1 Opening balance :—		
(1) State ...	10,92,959	12,37,176
(2) Zemindaries ...	3,83,502	5,57,144
Total ...	14,76,461	17,94,320
2. Income :—		
(1) State ...	16,96,043	18,75,373
(2) Zemindaries ...	11,07,653	12,48,973
Total ...	28,03,696	31,24,346
3. Law charges recovered :—		
(1) Zemindaries ...	65,060	67,443
4. Refunds and compensation for lands acquired :—		
(1) Zemindaries ...	3,732	4,472
5. Deposits :—		
(1) State ...	1,31,004	1,10,628
(2) Zemindaries ...	51,943	54,386
Total ...	1,82,947	1,65,014
GRAND TOTAL ...	45,31,896	51,55,595

Expenditure.	1345 T.R.	1346 T.R.
1. General Administration charges :—		
(a) State	5,44,827	5,76,687
(b) Zemindaries :—		
1. Cost of management	1,37,956	1,39,290
2. Cost of litigation	1,59,230	1,26,609
	2,97,186	2,65,899
Total ...	8,41,813	8,42,586
2. Revenue and Taxes on account of the Zemindaries	2,81,546	2,84,317
3. Public Works—(a) State	2,00,017	2,60,797
(b) Zemindaries ...	50,912	76,889
Total ..	2,50,929	3,37,686
4. Electric Light—State	16,433	26,748
5. Municipality—State	9,000	9,000
6. Education—(a) State	1,22,027	1,31,956
(b) Zemindaries	8,557	8,932
Total ...	1,30,584	1,40,888
7. Medical and Sanitation :—(a) State ...	66,513	71,950
(b) Zemindaries ...	12,001	12,138
Total ...	78,514	84,088
8. Survey and Settlement—(a) State ...	13,835	12,296
(b) Zemindaries ...	1,097	1,964
Total ...	14,932	14,260
9. Agriculture, Commerce and Industries—State	8,031	4,902
10. Religious Expenses—(a) State ...	55,724	55,235
(b) Zemindaries ...	6,716	6,565
Total ...	62,440	61,800
11. Sultanat—State	56,962	1,15,850
12. Purchase of Land Tenures :—		
(a) State	11,522	6,616
(b) Zemindaries	6,278	5,871
Total ...	17,800	12,487
13. Pension and Gratuity—(a) State ...	56,148	56,689
(b) Zemindaries ...	11,943	11,806
Total ...	68,091	68,495
14. Ordinary *Sansar* charges :—		
(a) His Highness's own and the late Maharaja's family	82,291	95,763
(b) Other branches of the Raj family...	96,142	88,997
(c) Thakurs	33,197	30,569
(d) *Sansar* office establishment ...	12,587	13,099
(e) Miscellaneous	73,250	94,481
Total ...	2,97,467	3,22,909
15. Charity and Donation :—(a) State ...	29,007	24,618
(b) Zemindaries ...	8,551	9,865
Total ...	37,558	34,483
16. His Highness's Nij Tahabil :—State ...	1,00,000	1,20,000
17. His Highness's tour—State	1,20,500	94,175
18. Payment of liabilities and deposits :—		
(a) State	79,860	98,908
(b) Zemindaries	13,183	16,554
Total ...	93,043	1,15,462
19. Miscellaneous—(a) State	5,901	5,926
(b) Zemindaries ...	14,225	9,428
Total ...	20,126	15,354
20. Writing off irrecoverable advances :— State ...	3,000	—
21. Repayment of old debts—State ...	1,00,668	99,685
22. Interest on deposits State	90,910	92,761
23. Advance to *Nijtahabil*— Zemindaries	79,591	40,984
24. Silver Jubilee	17,638	—
25. Governor's Visit	—	29,201
Total ...	27,37,576	29,11,130
26 Closing Balance :—		
(a) State		
In Cash	2,28,970	2,01,939
At Bank	72,408	29,384
Working balance :—		
In Cash	36,192	10,199
At Bank	1,88,808	2,14,801
In advances	1,90,182	1,90,182
In bonds and advances	5,20,616	8,69,539
Total ...	12,37,176	15,16,044
(b) Zemindaries :—		
In Cash	2,28,090	2,36,813
At Bank	1,08,629	1,90,898
In bonds and advances ...	2,20,425	3,00,710
Total ...	5,57,144	7,28,421
Total of State & Zemindaries' balances ...	17,94,320	22,44,465
Total of State & Zemindaries' expenditure ...	27,37,576	29,11,130
GRAND TOTAL ...	45,31,896	51,55,595

265. The year opened with a balance of Rs. 17,94,320 against Rs. 14,76,461 in the year before. During the year under report, the total receipts from all sources, including deposits, loans and law charges recovered amounted to Rs. 33,61,275 against Rs. 30,55,435 in the previous year. Thus the total sum available for expenditure was Rs. 51,55,595 against Rs. 45,31,896. The actual income amounted to Rs. 31,96,261 against Rs. 28,72,488 showing an increase of Rs. 3,23,773.

Receipts.

266. The total expenditure incurred during the year amounted to Rs. 29,11,130 against Rs. 27,37,576 in the previous year showing an increase of Rs. 1,73,554.

Expenditure.

267. The year closed with a balance of Rs. 22,44,465 of which Rs. 4,48,951 represented cash in the Treasuries, Rs. 4,35,083 was held in banks while the balance of Rs. 13,60,431 was held in loans and advances.

Closing balance.

268. A quinquennial statement of the receipts and expenditure of the State and the attached Zemindaries is given below :—

Quinquennial Review of Receipts and Expenditure.

Serial No.	Year.	State.		Zemindary		Remarks.
		Receipts.	Expenditure.	Receipts,	Expenditure.	
1.	1342 T. E.	19,10,680	18,95,612	9,29,366	10,04,303	The figures for the year 1343 T. E. for the State include on the receipt side the loan of Rs. 9,00,000 (Rupees nine lacs) taken from the Government of India and on the debit side the expenditure incurred for liquidation of old debts.
2.	1343 T. E.	27,34,304	23,48,173	9,82,889	9,71,867	
3.	1344 T. E.	19,78,355	19,37,610	10,78,217	10,44,935	
4.	1345 T. E.	20,77,047	19,32,830	12,28,388	10,54,746	
5.	1346 T. E.	24,16,001	21,87,133	13,75,274	12,03,997	
	Total ...	1,11,16,387	1,02,51,358	55,94,134	52,79,848	
	Average ...	22,23,277	20,50,271	11,18,827	10,55,970	

269. The gradual recovery from the economic depression accounts for the increased receipts and the year under report shows a marked improvement of the situation. The restrictions imposed on expenditure in previous years were also relaxed to some extent and consequently expenditure on constructive works increased.

270. The noticeable variations in expenditure are explained below :—

i. ADMINISTRATIVE CHARGES :—

STATE—The increase was Rs. 32,060. This was mainly due to the following reasons.

(1) Time scale increment of pay and other increments of pay.
(2) Sinking of tube-wells by the Sanitation Department.
(3) Award of service prize medals,
(4) Contribution to the King George Memorial Fund.
(5) Purchase of a motor car for the Superintendent of Police.
(6) Extra expenditure on account of pleader's fees.

(7) Establishment of two new forest offices at Samaru and Muhuri pur and extra expenditure on account of Sal plantation.

(8) Purchase of rifles by the Military Department.

(9) Other miscellaneous expenditure :—

ZEMINDARIES—The decrease was 31,287. This was due to reduced expenditure on account of litigation charges as compared with the previous year.

ii. REVENUE AND TAXES :—

ZEMINDARIES—The increase was Rs. 2,771. This was due to payment of some arrear dues.

iii. PUBLIC WORKS :—

STATE—The increase was Rs. 60,780. This was due to substantial repairs to roads and bridges and some special improvement works.

ZEMINDARIES—The increase of Rs. 25,977 was mainly due to expenditure in connection with the *Nirmahal* Palace in Sonamura.

iv. ELECTRIC LIGHT :—

The increase was Rs. 10,315 only. The increase was due to new wiring work done in the year.

v. MUNICIPALITY :—

The amount of grant was the same as in the previous year.

vi. EDUCATION :—

STATE—The increase was 9,929. This was due to time-scale increment, extra expenditure on account of the education of some Kumars, provision for special training, and also to the inclusion of the expenditure on account of the controlling establishment of the Education Department and the *Silpasram* (school for technical training) within the budget provision for educational expenses.

ZEMINDARIES—The increase of Rs. 375 was due to payment of some outstanding expenditure for the previous year in the year under report.

vii. MEDICAL :—

STATE—The increase was Rs. 5,437. This was due to purchase of a motor car for the Chief Medical Officer, provision for medical staff at Samaru and Muhuripur, provision for the Lady Doctor for the whole year, time-scale increment and purchase of medicines.

ZEMINDARIES—The increase was Rs. 137.

viii. SURVEY AND SETTLEMENT :—

STATE—The decrease was Rs. 1,539.

ZEMINDARIES—The increase was Rs. 867.

ix. AGRICULTURE :—

The decrease was Rs. 3,129. This was due to the provision for *Silpasram* being transferred to the education budget.

x. RELIGIOUS EXPENDITURE :—

STATE—The decrease was Rs. 489.

ZEMINDARIES—The decrease was Rs. 151.

xi. SULTANAT :—

STATE—The increase was Rs. 58,897. This was due to purchase of new motor cars, furniture and other articles for the Palace.

xii. PURCHASE OF LAND TENURES :—

STATE—The decrease was Rs. 4,906.

ZEMINDARIES—The decrease was Rs. 407.

xiii. PENSION AND GRATUITY :—

STATE—The increase was Rs. 541.

ZEMINDARIES—The decrease was Rs. 137.

xiv. ORDINARY SANSAR CHARGES :—

The increase was Rs. 25,442. This was mainly due to expenditure in connection with the prospective marriage ceremony of Maharajkumari Kamal Prova Debi and also to provision of new monthly allowances for some Maharajkumars and Maharajkumaries.

xv. CHARITY AND DONATION :—

STATE—The decrease was Rs. 4,389.

ZEMINDARIES—The increase was Rs. 1,314. This was due to the donations sanctioned by His Highness the Maharaja Manikya Bahadur for some educational institutions and temples of Feni as also for the Brahmanbaria Rural Reconstruction fund.

xvi. HIS HIGHNESS'S NIJTAHABIL :—

The increase was Rs. 20,000.

xvii. HIS HIGHNESS'S TOUR :—

The decrease was Rs. 26,325.

xviii. PAYMENT OF LIABILITIES AND DEPOSITS :—

STATE—The increase was Rs. 19,048. This was mainly due to repayment of deposits on account of the Agartala Bazar Improvement Fund and that of the Silver Jubilee Fund of Their Mejesties.

ZEMINDARIES—The increase was Rs. 3,371. This was due to payment of interest on some interest-bearing deposits.

xix. MISCELLANEOUS :—

STATE—The increase was Rs. 25,

ZEMINDARIES—The decrease was Rs. 4,797. This was due to extra expenditure incurred in the previous year on account of purchase of a motor boat being not necessary in the year under report.

xx. WRITING OFF IRRECOVERABLE ADVANCES :—

No adjustment was effected on this account in the year under report.

xxi. REPAYMENT OF OLD DEBTS :—

STATE—The decrease was Rs. 983.

xxii. PAYMENT OF INTEREST ON DEPOSITS :—

STATE—The increase was Rs. 1,851.

xxiii. ADVANCE TO HIS HIGHNESS'S NIJTAHABIL :—

ZEMINDARIES—The decrease was Rs. 29,607. This was due to reduction of provision on this account

xxiv. Silver Jubilee of Their Majesties :—
State—No expenditure was incurred in the year under report.

xxv. Visit of His Excellency the Governor of Bengal :—
State—This was a special expenditure in the year under report.

271. Two comparative statements of receipts and expenditure of the State and the Zemindaries with the respective Revised Estimates are given in appendices XXV and XXVI.

272. In the State the total receipts showed an increase of Rs. 4,01,001 and Rs. 65,001 in comparison with the Original and the Revised Budget Estimates respectively.

273. In the Zemindaries the total receipts showed an increase of Rs. 2,19,274 and Rs. 25,274 in comparison with the Original and the Revised Budget Estimates respectively.

III. Tripura State Bank.

274. Tripura State Bank has an interesting history behind it. From time immemorial, monied men of the locality, for safety, would keep their hoarded money with the General Treasury and the State authority kept those moneys as custodian only. In course of time, a plan of utilising the money crept into the mind of the authorities and they began to think how to benefit the depositors with interest on their sterile deposits and at the same time to benefit the poor State employees with loans at a very low interest, at a time when they were suffering under heavy interest for their loans from the local banks. The State Bank is the outcome of this plan. Thus on the 4th July 1934, the Tripura State Bank was formed by the gracious order of H. H. the Maharaja Manikya Bahadur of Tripura.

275. It is a State-owned institution run by the State itself with the Minister as the authority to control all its transactions through Accounts Department; the General Treasury Officer works as its ex-officio Secretary.

276. During the year under review the total amount of Fixed Deposits received by the Bank was Rs. 1,02,451 as against Rs. 21,450 in the previous year.

277. The total amount of loans issued during the year amounted to Rs. 87,243 as against Rs. 38,425 in the previous year. Out of this, advances as loans to the P. W. contractors amounted to Rs. 23,500. During the year, 476 persons received the benefit of loans from the Bank, as compared with 297 persons in the previous year. With a view to help the local trade, Rs. 10,000 was invested as deposits in two local banks. Besides this, Rs. 10,000 was advanced to the Town Improvement Loan Fund of the State.

278. During the year under report, after meeting all sorts of working expenses and also providing for the interest payable on Fixed Deposits for the period, depreciation on furniture and reserves for Bad and Doubtful Debts etc the Bank made a net profit of Rs. 730-6-9 as against Rs. 411-9-9 in the previous year.

CHAPTER VI—MEDICAL.

279. As in the year before, 18 State dispensaries worked during the year under report, the Victoria Memorial Hospital at the capital town excluded.

New patients.

280. The total number of patients treated new in the above hospital and dispensaries as well as their daily average for the year under review and that preceding it are comparatively stated below.

	1345 T. E.			1346 T. E.		
	Outdoor.	Indoor.	Total.	Outdoor.	Indoor.	Total.
PATIENTS.	1,46,610	997	1,47,607	1,33,515	806	1,34,321
Daily average	400·57	2·72	403·29	365·79	2·2	367·99

Outdoor attendance.

281. The out-patients (old and new) numbered 2,57,788 as against 2,92,779 in the previous year—the daily average being 706·17 against 813·09.

Indoor attendance.

282. Together with the balance of 31 from the previous year, 806 patients were admitted for indoor treatment during the year under review as against 997 of the preceding year. Of them, 637 were discharged cured, 116 were relieved or left of their own accord, 28 died and 25 remained under treatment at the end of the year. The noticeable decrease in the number of both indoor and outdoor attendance is attributed to the comparatively better general health prevailing throughout the year—particularly at the capital town.

Surgical operations.

283. The total number of operations performed during the year under review was 1174 with 33 major cases. The previous year's figures were 1281 and 35 respectively.

Police cases.

284. The Police cases attended to during the year numbered 154 against 160 in the preceding year—including 21 post-mortem cases against 18.

V. M. Hospital.

285. The new patients treated outdoor in the Victoria Memorial Hospital totalled 20,482 as against 28,089 in the year previous, the daily attendance of new and old patients averaging 115·73 against 173·84. The total number of in-patients was 537 against 723 with the daily average (new + old) of 19·51 against 22.

286. Of the number, 393 were discharged cured, 101 were discharged otherwise or relieved, 27 died and 16 remained over for treatment in the next year. Rs. 9478-10-3 were expended on this institution as against Rs. 9425-2-9 in the preceding year.

287. Lt. Col. A. S. Meek, C. M. G., Agent to the Governor General, Eastern States, paid a visit to the Hospital on 4th February, 1937. His Excellency The Right Honourable Sir John Anderson, P. C., G. C. B., G. C. I. E., Governor of Bengal also honoured the institution with a visit accompanied by His Highness the Maharaja Manikya Bahadur and performed the opening ceremony of the King George V X-Ray Installation Building on 16th March, 1937.

Antirabic centre.

288. Dr. N. C. Deb Barma, M. B., continued to be in charge of this centre. The total number of persons treated during the year was 23 against 16 in the year before. The expenditure on this account was Rs. 271 as against Rs. 340-4-0 in the previous year.

Clinical Laboratory.

289. As before Dr. A. Sen Gupta, M. B., State Bacteriologist, held charge of the laboratory and examined 450 samples of sorts as against 465 in the preceding year.

Leprosy.

290. The previous two leprosy clinics—one at the capital and the other at Khowai Division—were kept up under the charge of Dr. J. M. Bose and Dr. S. C. Dey respectively. 8 new patients were treated by them as against 28 of the year before. The daily attendance (new + old) in both was 18·11 against 24·22 on the average. The total cost on account of the price of medicines only was Rs. 32-0-0 as against Rs. 80-1-6 in the preceding year.

Kala-azar.

291. 120 patients were treated at the Kala-azar centre at the capital as against 249 of the year previous. Of them 45 were cured, 70 left treatment and 5 remained under treatment at the close of the year. Rs. 828-0-0 was spent on the treatment of this malady as against Rs. 1066-4-6 in the previous year.

Ayurvedic Department.

292. Kaviraj Surendra Chandra Bhattacharjee, Baidyaratna, assisted by a young Kaviraj newly appointed, continued to be in charge of the Department during the year under report and treated 40 patients as against 31 in the previous year.

293. The expenses incurred in this Department on account of the salary of the Kavirajes and cost of medicines amounted to Rs. 2678-1-0 as against Rs. 2475-0-0 in the year preceding.

Homœpathic Department.

294. Three Assistant Homœopaths under the control and supervision of Dr. M. M. Majumdar, Chief Medical Officer, carried out the work of this Department. As in the previous year there was only one dispensary at the capital town. Altogether 19833 patients were treated by them during the year under review as against 19126 in the year before with the daily average (new + old) of 91·25 against 96·84. The total amount expended on this account was Rs. 2735-15-6 as against Rs. 2366-3-0

12

295. The total number of persons vaccinated was 13557 of which 10336 were successful as against 8687 and 10336 respectively.

Vaccination.

296. 29 vaccinators were employed for the above purpose under two Small-pox doctors and two inspectors. The total cost on this item was Rs. 1690-13-0 against Rs. 1650-6-0.

Public health.

297. Cholera broke out in the Sadar, Kailashahar, Amarpur, Bilonia and Sabroom Divisions during the year under report and made a toll of 201 victims out of 631 attacks. Two temporary epidemic doctors were posted at Kailasanar for its treatment. In all, 8000 persons were inoculated with anti-cholera vaccine as against 2000 in the previous year.

298. Small-pox appeared at Sadar, Khowai, Sabroom, Amarpur, Sonamura and Bilonia Divisions. But its virulence was felt in the Bilonia Division and it accounted for 387 deaths out of 1169 attacks. Four small-pox doctors were sent out for treatment to the affected areas and treated 226 patients of whom 219 were cured and 7 died. Rs. 423-4-0 was spent on this account as the price of medicines for the persons treated.

Staff.

299. As in the previous year, Dr. M. M. Majumdar, L. M. S., remained in charge of the Medical Department with Dr. S. K. Dutta, L. M. S. Assistant. State Physician, Dr. A. Sen Gupta, M. B., Dr N. Deb Barma, M. B., Dr. S. Bhattacharjee, M. B., as his assistants at the capital. Apart from there—the dispensaries maintained by the State in different places had one medical subordinate in each. A lady doctor, Mrs. S. Gore, was appointed at the beginning of the year under review. She worked at the V. M. Hospital at the capital with the assistance of two midwives.

Inspection

300. Dr. A. Sen Gupta, M. B., was out on tour for 14 days and inspected 4 dispensaries. The inspection was inadequate.

Total expenditure.

301. The total expenditure incurred for the Medical Department in the year under report came up to Rs. 71,950 as against Rs. 66513-0-0 in the preceding year.

CHAPTER VII—PUBLIC INSTRUCTION.

Charge.

302. The Public Instruction portfolio was held by the Chief Secretary, Manyabara Raja Rana Bodhjung Bahadur, F. R. G. S., and Mr. Satya Ranjan Bose, B. A., Under Secretary, was entrusted with the charge of the Education Department in the year under report, as in the preceding year. Dewan Bahadur K. Dutt, M. A., B. L., F. R. E. S., M. R. A. S., Private Secretary, held the portfolio of Public Instruction in the absence of the Chief Secretar y.

303. The total number of schools (including private schools) during the year under review, was 181 against the same number in the previous year and the total numerical strength 8766 against 7520 including 1321 pupils reading in private institutions numbering 46 as against 49 in the preceding year.

Number of Schools.

304. There were 5 H. E. Schools as before and one branch H. E. School in the State. All the H. E. Schools are permanently affiliated to the Calcutta University. Class IX was opened provisionally in the branch H. E. School at Udaipur, on condition that the public would agree to bear the additional cost of maintaining extra staff. The total number of pupils in all these institutions were 1527 against 1584 in the previous year and the average daily attendance stood at 1,160·70 against 1,155·13.

H. E. Schools.

305. Agartala, the capital of the State, continued to be a centre for the Matriculation Examination. The State H. E. schools are allowed to send up candidates to this centre. Thirteen candidates from the Devagram H. E. School sat for the examination at this centre in the year under report, in addition to the candidates from the State schools. Besides these, four female private candidates sat for the same.

Matriculation Examination.

306. The examination was conducted under the direct control and supervision of Dewan Bahadur K. Dutt, M. A., B. L., F. R. E. S., M. R. A. S., Chief Secretary-in-charge, with the assistance of Kumar Bhupendra Chandra Dev Barman Bahadur B. A., Personal Assistant to the Minister and Mr. S. C. Mukherjee, B. A., Secretary, Nij-Tahabil Office, as Mr. Satya Ranjan Bose, B. A., Under Secretary, was engaged in other State business. The Department looked after the convenience of the candidates coming from Mofussil, in respect of accommodation and other necessary matters.

307. Altogether 70 candidates were sent up for the Matriculation Examination from the State H. E. Schools against 73 in the previous year. The result of the examination is given below :

Result of the Matriculation Examination.

	No. sent up.	passed.	1st Division.	2nd Division.	3rd Division.
1. U. K. Academy	17	13	6	6	1
2. R. K. Institution	11	10	2	7	1
3. B. K. Institution	21	15	4	8	3
4. B. B. Institution	9	7	2	5	0
5. N. C. Institution	12	7	1	5	1
Total ...	70	52	15	31	6

308. The result on the whole was satisfactory, percentage of successful candidates being 74·2 against 60·27 in the previous year. The percentage of passes in the 1st division on the total number of passes, was the highest for U. K. Academy viz. 46·1 and lowest for the N. C. Institution, Sonamura, viz., 14·2.

309. The three successful candidates topping the list, the first belonging to U. K. Academy, the second to R. K. Institution, Kailashahar and the third from U. K. Academy, were to be awarded scholarships

of Rs. 10, Rs 8 and Rs. 8 respectively per month. But as the first boy won a Bengal Government's scholarship of Rs. 10 per month he was granted an extra monthly stipend of Rs. 6 only. The Department distributed the scholarships of Rs. 10, Rs. 8 and Rs. 8 among the boys who stood 2nd, 3rd and 4th from the State schools. Thus the 1st scholarship went to Kailshaahar school, 2nd and 3rd to U. K. Academy, Agartala.

M. E. Schools for boys.

310 In the year under review, there were 10 Middle English Schools for boys with 1205 pupils on the rolls against the same number of schools with 1,166 pupils in the previous year. The average daily attendance was 821·59 against 850·49 in the previous year.

M. E. Schools for girls.

311. There was one M. E. School for girls at Agartala, namely the Maharani Tulsibati Girls' School, the numerical strength of which was 121 against 74 in the previous year, and the average daily attendance was 73·35 against 62·83. By special permission of this Department, some girls were allowed to continue higher studies in this school under the tuition of the Head Mistress. For conveyance of the girls, motor bus service was continued as before.

L. V. Schools.

312. The total number of Lower Vernacular Schools for boys was 22 against 24 in the previous year. The total numerical strength was 1287 against 1239 and the average daily attendance was 1,049·58 against 938·24 in the previous year. In some of these schools, boys and girls read together.

Pathshalas for boys.

313. There were 71 *Pathshalas* for boys against 70 in the previous year. The total number of boys was 2,089 against 2249 and the average daily attendance was 1,614·21 against 1,745·34. In some of these schools, boys and girls read together. Under special orders of the Education Department, some boys of some of these institutions were allowed to read the Lower Vernacular Standard.

Pathshalas for girls.

314. There were 9 *Pathshalas* for girls in the year under review against 5 in the previous year. The total numerical strength was 278 against 138 and the average daily attendance was 219·23 against 132·01 in the year preceding. In some of these schools, some girls were allowed, under special orders, to read the Lower Vernacular Standard.

Scholarship Examination.

315. Altogether 961 candidates appeared at the different Scholarship Examinations of the State against 824 in the previous year. Of these, 732 candidates including 146 girls came out successful. The result on the whole was satisfactory. 67 students including 9 girls passed the M. E. Examination. 2 girls passed the H. V. Examination, this year. In the L. V. Examination the number of successful candidates was 231 including 38 girls and in the *Pathshala* Examination the number was 573 including 99 girls. Amongst these candidates, 12 appeared from different *Moktabs* and

Madrassas of the State. On the results of the Examinations 13 boys and 5 girls were awarded monthly scholarships varying from Rs. 2 to Rs. 5 tenable for one to four years.

Schools for special training.

316. In the year under review, there were 11 schools for special training, cansisting of 5 Sanskrit *Tols*, 5 *Madrassas* and *Moktabs* and one *Silpasram* (Artisan School). The Sanskrit *Tols* had 74 students on the roll against 62 in the previous year and the average daily attendance was 56·45 against 45·58.

317. The *Madrassas* and *Moktabs* had 203 students on the rolls as against 347 in the previous year and the average daily attendance was 136·88 against 318·70.

Compulsory Free Primary Schools.

318. There were, as before, 4 Free Primary Schools with 612 pupils including girls against 623 in the previous year. The subjoined statement will show the number of students, their classes and the average daily attendance :–

Compulsory Free Primary Schools.	No. of Students.		Average daily attendance		Kumars.	Thakurs.	Tripura.	Laskar.	Manipuri	Bengali Hindu.	Mahommedan.	Others
	Boys.	Girls.	Boys	Girls.								
1. No. 1 Umakanta ...	219	96	136·30	63·73	0	14	0	0	0	277	24	0
2. No. 2 Tulsibati ...	61	81	24·50	45·	0	3	0	0	6	132	0	1
3. No. 3 Bejoy Kumar ...	51	73	40·90	57·50	0	16	21	0	0	73	14	0
4. No. 4 Thakur Pally ..	31	0	9·81	0	0	21	0	0	0	4	0	6
	362	250	211·51	166·23	0	54	21	0	6	486	38	7

319. The comparative statement below will show the number of non-Bengalee students receiving education in the several schools of the States :–

Serial number.	Nationality.	Number of students.		Remarks.
		Past year.	Present year	
1.	Rajkumars...	5	2	
2.	Thakurs	216	203	
3.	Manipuris	704	697	
4.	Tripuras	985	917	
5.	Reangs	9	9	
6.	Kukis...	0	0	
7.	Chakmas	1	1	
8.	Lushais	0	1	
9.	Others	121	112	
10.	Christians	2	5	
	Total	2,043	1,947	

Education of Princes and Princesses.

320. Maharajkumar Mohan Kishore Dev Barman Bahadur passed the First Engineering Examination and was promoted to the Mechanical and Electrical Engineering 3rd year class in the College of Engineering and Technology, Jadavpur.

321 The Maharajkumaries received their education, as before, under a graduate lady teacher and a Pandit.

322. The young Maharajkumars received their education under a tutor.

13

323. The Rajkumar Boarding House at Comilla had 11 inmates of whom 9 were from the different branches of the Ruling family and the remaining 2 were Rana Bahadurs, related to the Raj Family. 6 of the inmates were reading in the Comilla Zilla School and 5 in the Comilla Victoria College. In the year under review, Maharajkumar Hemanta Kishore Dev Barman Bahadur passed the B. A. Examination. The Boarders were placed under the charge of a Superintending tutor who in addition to his tutorial works, looked after the management of the Boarding House. There was also one graduate Assistant Resident tutor. Besides the above, one graduate, a Pandit and a professor were engaged for coaching some of the boarders both in the morning and evening.

Kumar Boarding House at Comilla.

324. 14 Thakur boys receiving higher education in various colleges and technical schools were awarded stipends from the education Department.

Education of Thakur boys.

325. The number of boarders in the Thakur Boarding House were 28 against 30 in the preceding year. The staff consisted of one graduate Guardian Superintendent, one under-graduate Resident Tutor and one Manager Tutor. The average daily attendance of the boarders was 24 against 26·5 in the previous year.

Thakur Boarding House at Agartala.

326. There were altogether 16 boarders of Class V to Matriculation class in the old Tripura Boarding House against 17 in the previous year. All the boarders were allowed free boarding stipends. A whole-time graduate Superintending tutor looked after the boys as well as the boarding management as before. Another tutor was engaged to coach the boys in the morning. There was a small library in the Boarding House and the boys were encouraged in agricultural pursuits within the boarding compound. There was another boarding house called "New Tripura Boarding House" with 19 Tripura boys reading in higher and lower classes against 31 in the previous year. A tutor was engaged to coach the boys both in the morning and evening and was entrusted with the management of the boarding. The boarders were allowed a piece of ground in front of the boarding house for agricultural pursuits.

Tripura Boarding House at Agartala.

327. There were 60 boarders in the Tripura Boarding House at Khowai against 46 in the previous year. One graduate Superintending tutor and one assistant tutor were engaged as before for coaching the boys both in the morning and evening. The Superintending tutor looked after the boarding management in addition to his tutorial work.

Tripura Boarding House at Khowai.

328. There were 52 boarders on the roll in the Ramkumar Boarding School against 40 in the previous year and the average daily attendance was 38·71 against 23·56 in the preceding year. Two tutors were engaged as before to coach the boarders one of whom looked after the boarding management in addition.

Ramkumar Boarding School at Kalyanpur.

329. There were 27 convicts reading in the Primary School in the Central Jail, out of which 3 appeared in the *Pathshala* Scholarship Examination in the year under report and all of them came out successful—one in the 1st, one in the 2nd and the other in the third divisions.

Schools for convicts.

330. The Woodburn Artisan School and Silpasram continued to be under the direct control of Education Department. The school had 22 students on the roll against 16 in the preceding year. In the year under review the average daily attendance was 10·75 against 9·09 in the previous year. 14 students were awarded monthly stipends varying from Rs. 1-8 to Rs. 8 each. There were 13, 5, 3, students in the Carpentary, Black-smith and Brass-smith Sections respectively.

Woodburn Artisan Schools & Silpasram.

331. The subjoined statement will show the number of students, their classes (castes) and their average attendance in the year under report :—

Name of School.	Number of Students.	Thakurs.	Tripura	Laskar.	Manipuri	Bengali Hindu.	Mahomedan	Others.	Average attendance.
Woodburn Artisan School and Silpasram	22	5	—	1	2	13	—	1	10·75

332. 5 Lushai boys were awarded Lushai stipends in the year under report of whom one was reading B. A. 3rd year in the Victoria College, one in M. A 5th year of the Calcutta University and the others were reading in different schools of the State.

Lushai Stipends

333. 30 students were awarded special stipends in the year under review, of whom 11 read in different schools of this State and the remaining 19 prosecuted their studies elsewhere in different schools, colleges and technical institutions.

Special Stipends.

334. There were three Sub-Inspectors of schools as before whc inspected all the schools other than the H. E. Schools, within their respective juridictions in Sadar, Khowai Kailashahar and Dharmanagar Divisions. Revenue Inspectors o Sonamura and Beloniya inspected some schools in their respective divisions.

Inspection Works.

335. Maharajkumar Narottam Kishore Dev Barman Bahadur continued to be the Librarian of the Bir Chandra Library at Agartala which was maintained in two separate sections as before Viz. (1) English section, located in the Ujjayanta Palace, and (2) the Vernacular Section in the building near the local H. E. School. The latter section was opened to the public The number of English books (including foreign literature) were 503[illegible] against 5027 in the previous year. The number of Bengali and Sanskrit books were 2253 against 2250 in the previous year. There were 5 daily newspapers, 4 weeklies and 13 monthlies against 4, 4, 7 respectively in the preceding year. The average daily attendance in the vernacular

Library.

section of the library was 8 against 9 in the previous year and the total number of books issued to the public was 1636 against 3028.

Expenditure.

336. The total expenditure on public instruction in the year under report amounted to Rs. 1,31,956 against Rs. 1,22,027. Details of expenditure are noted below :—

1.	Education Department	Rs.	1,556
2.	Primary Education	„	31,336
3.	Secondary Education	„	48,198
4.	Schools for special Training	„	1,605
5.	Compulsory Free Primary Education ...	„	2,330
6.	Boarding Institutions for Thakur boys ...	„	6,256
7.	Education for Kumars and Kumaris ...	„	20,678
8.	Scholarships and stipends	„	5,086
9.	Library	„	1,959
10.	Tripura Bo rding	„	4,111
11.	Miscellaneous	„	5,734
12.	Silpasram	„	3,107

Income.

337. The total receipts from the schools amounted to Rs. 15,078 against Rs. 15,034 in the previous year.

CHAPTER VIII—ZEMINDARIES.

Chakla Roshnabad Estates.

Management

338. The management of His Highness's Zemindaries in British India continued in the hands of Manyabara Rai J. C. Sen Bahadur, B. A., B. C. S. (Retd.) for the whole year. He was, as usual, assisted by a Deputy Manager posted at Comilla and three Assistant Managers, posted at Feni, Mogra and Srimangal.

The year and the tenantry.

339. The Talukdars in general and the majority of the tenants not having recovered from the economic depression of previous years relief had to be given to them, as in previous years, in the shape of general remission of interests and damages almost throughout the year and the policy of allowing petty demands to be time-barred was also continued.

Demand.

340. The gross demand of the year was Rs. 10,13,969 against Rs. 10,13,059 in the previous year.

Receipt.

341. Total receipts amounted to Rs. 13,75,274 including Rs. 383 on account of Debottar mahal, against Rs. 12,28,388 in the previous year. The year's collection is a record one in the annals of Chakla Roshnabad Estates. The increase was mainly due to realisation of arrear rents, land lord's fees, law charges recovered and deposits.

Expenditure.

342. Total expenditure in the year under review was Rs. 12,03,997 including payment of old debts and deposits to the extent of Rs. 16,554 and a contribution of Rs. 2,80,000 to the State, Rs. 1,50,000 towards His Highness's European Tour and advances of Rs. 49,984 to Niz Tahabil. Total expenditure in the previous year was Rs. 10,54,746.

343. Of the total expenditure during the year under review Rs. 2,84,317 was on account of Land Revenue, taxes and cesses while the total administration charges of the Zemindaries including Public works and Law charges amounted to Rs. 3,64,044 against Rs. 3,73,404 in the previous year.

344. The following items of expenditure aggregating Rs. 5,55,636 are noticeable :—

1.	Education	Rs.	8,932
2.	Medical Charges	,,	12,138
3.	Religious Ceremonies	,,	6,565
4.	Purchase of property	,,	5,871
5.	Loans and advances	,,	1,942
6.	Sansar Stipends	,,	13,785
7.	Donations	,,	9,865
8.	Payment of old debts and deposits ...	,,	16,554
9.	Advance to Niz Tahabil	,,	49,984
10.	Contribution to the State	,,	2,80,000
11.	His Highness's European Tour ...	,,	1,50,000
		Rs.	5,55,636

Settlement.

345. The result of the year's settlement operations will appear from the figures noted below :—

	KINDS OF SETTLEMENT.	ADDITION TO RENTAL.		NAZAR.	
1.	Railway relinquished land		—		—
2.	*Kaimi* and *Takshishi* Settlement of the Comilla Town	Rs.	14	Rs.	2,189
3.	Ordinary Town Settlement	,,	46	,,	241
4.	*Khas Patit*	,,	346	,,	1,204
5.	Enhancement of rent ...	,,	179	,,	2,912
6.	Re-settlement of auction purchased holding ...	,,	508	,,	21,068
7.	Settlement of rent-free holding	,,	9		—
8.	*Takshishi Taluki* settlement in the *Moffusil* ...		—		—
9.	*Ijara*	,,	1,738		—
		Rs.	2,840	Rs.	27,614

346 The corresponding figures for the previous year were Rs. 740 and Rs. 27,501 respectively.

CHAPTER IX—MISCELLANEOUS.

347. Thakur K. K. Singha, Naib Dewan, was out on tour for 19 days.

348. The tours of the Divisional Officers and their assistants are noted below :—

State.

1. Sadar—
   Sadar Collector—Babu Sashanka Bhusan Roy, M. A., B. L. ... 93 days.
   Asst. " Kumar Narsingh Chandra Deb Barman Bahadur ... —
   " " Thakur Joysingh Deb Barman, B. A. ... 36 "
   " " Thakur Kamal Krishna Deb Barman ... 6 "
2. Kailashahar—
   Divisional Officer—Babu Akhil Chandra Mazumdar, M. A., B. L. ... 31 "
   Second Officer—Babu Jyotirmay Ghosh, M. A. ... 20 "
3. Sonamura—
   Divisional Officer—Thakur Rebati Mohan Deb Barman ... 24 "
   Second Officer—Thakur Jyotilal Deb Barman, B. L. ... 1 day.
   Asst. Collector—Thakur Kamal Krishna Deb Barman ... 19 days.
4. Belonia—
   Divisional Officer—Thakur Gokul Chandra Deb Barman ... 11 "
   Asst. Collector—Thakur Kamal Krishna Deb Barman ... 6 "
5. Khowai—
   Divisional Officer—Babu Prabha Ranjan Das Gupta, M. A., B. L ... 46 "
   Second Office—Babu Narendra Narayan Choudhury, B. L. ... 44 "
6. Dharmanagar—
   Divisional Officer—Babu Sarada Charan Sarkar, M. A., B. L. ... 12 "
   Second Officer—Thakur Hiran Kumar Deb Barman, B. A. ... 22 "
7. Udaypur—
   Divisional Officer—Babu Suresh Chandra Chakravarty, B. L. ... 23 "
   Second Officer—Babu Mahendra Kumar Roy, B.L. ... 13 "
   Divisional Officer—Kumar Pramode Chandra Deb Barman Bahadur ... 8 "
   Second Officer—Babu Chandrahas Singha, B. L. ... 18 "
8. Sabroom—
   Divisional Officer—Babu Jogendra Lal Ganguli, B. L. ... 70 "
9. Amarpur—
   Sub Divisional Officer—Babu Mahendra Kumar Roy ... 102 "

Zemindaries.

1.	Babu P. R. Bhattacharjee, B. A., Deputy Manager	...	...	146 days.
2.	,, J. C. Majumdar, M. A., B. L. Asst. Manager, Feni	...	...	62 ,,
3.	,, B. Guha, B. A. Asst. Manager, Mogra	...	...	54 ,,
4.	,, S. C. Guha, B. A. Asst. Manager, Srimangal	...	...	79 ,,

DATED, AGARTALA,
The 18th September, 1938.

Jyotis Chandra Sen,
MINISTER.

APPENDIX.

List of the principal Laws and Regulations in force in the Tripura State during 1346 T. E.

Description.	Whether adapted from British Indian Acts.	Whether introduced during the year under report.
CRIMINAL.		
1. Regulation No. III. of 1280 T. E.		
2. Regulation No. I. of 1283 T. E.		
3. Jail Regulation, 1283 T. E.		
4. Regulation No. IV. of 1283 T. E. (Cattle trespass and pound).		
5. Regulation No. III. of 1296 T. E. (Police Regulation).		
6. Act No. IV. of 1321 T. E.–Penal Laws (an amending Act)		
CIVIL.		
1. Civil Law of 1284 T. E.		
2. Rules regarding *chit* suits (small causes) 1287 and 1300 T. E.		
3. Act No. II. of 1313 T. E.—an Act for the regulation of interest on debts.		
4. Act No. II. of 1314 T. E.—Limitation Act	Partly adapted.	
5. Succession Act II of 1339 T. E.		
REVENUE.		
1. Act No. I. of 1290 T. E.—Sal[illegible] Law		
2. Act No. I. of 1296 T. E.—Tenancy Act.		
3. Act No. II. of 1296 T. E.—*Abkari*		
4. Act No. II. of 1297 T. E.—Reserved forests.		
5. Act No. I. of 1304 T. E.—Duties on *til* and cotton.		
6. Act No. I. of 1306 T. E.—Registration	Do.	
7. Survey and Settlement Act, 1309 T.E.	Do.	
8. *Tuccavi* Regulation, 1310 T. E.		
9. Act No. I. of 1313 T. E.—Forests.		
10. Act No. I. of 1314 T. E.—(amending the above)		
11. A Law imposing export duty on jute and mustard-seed, 1317 T. E.		
12. Act No. II. of 1321 T.E.—Ghasuri Act		
13. P. W. & Road Cess Act IV of 1339 T. E.		
MISCELLANEOUS.		
1. An Act promulgating certain rules as Law, 1283 T. E.		
2. Regulation for the record of judicial decisions &c., 1284 T. E.		

Description.	Whether adapted from British Indian Acts.	Whether introduced during the year under report.
3 Municipal Regulation, 1284 T. E.		
4. Legal Practitioners' Regulation.		
5. Act No. I. of 1297 T. E.—an Act for the regulation of commissions for the examination of witnesses.		
6. Regulation against cow slaughter		
7. Rules of evidence		
8. Act I. of 1318 T. E.—Constitution of Courts—(an amending Act).		
9. Leave and allowance Rules	Do.	
10. Act No. I. of 1321 T. E.—Arms Act	Do.	
11. Act No. III. of 1321 T. E.—Constitution of Courts (an amending Act)		
12. Municipal Act No. I of 1322 T. E.		
13. Revenue Sale Amendment Act—1323 T.E.		
14. An Act for the destruction of old records—1323 T. E.		
15. Act I of 1326 T. E.—Regulation regarding Privy Council Appeals.		
16. Act II of 1326 T. E.—Registration of Births and Deaths		
17. Act III of 1326 T. E.—Vaccination Act	Partly adapted.	
18. Act IV of 1326 T. E.—Public Demands Recovery Act	Do.	
19. Act V of 1326 T. E.—Excise Amendment Act	Do.	
20. Act I of 1327 T. E. Settlement of lands for tea cultivation		
21. Rules of Import and Sale of Opium—1327 T. E.		
22. Regulation No. 1 of 1328 T. E.—regarding Registration of Coolies		
23. Regulation No. 2 of 1328 T. E.—regarding Export of Tea		
24. Act I of 1329 T. E.—(Absconding sepoys Act)		
25. Act II of 1329 T. E.—Control of prices of food stuff)		
26. Act III of 1329 T. E. (Elephants and buffaloes grazing Act)		
27. Act IV of 1329 T. E. (House tax on Hill tribes)		
28. Act V of 1329 T. E. (Legal practitioners, Act)	Do	
29. Act I of 1332 T. E.—Encumbered Estates Act.		
30. Act III of 1332 T. E.—The Opium and Intoxicating Drugs Act.		

Description.	Whether adapted from British Indian Acts.	Whether introduced during the year under report.
31. Rules and Regulations under the Opium and Intoxicating Drugs Act III of 1332 T. E		
32. Act I of 1336 T. E.—(Hackney Carriages)	Partly adapted,	
33. Act II of 1336 T. E.– (Amending Act I of 1327.)		
34. Act III of 1336 T. E.– (Amending the Survey & Settlement Regulation)		
35. Act IV of 1336 T. E.—(Prevention of gambling)		
36. Act I of 1337 T. E.—(Amending the State Tenancy Act I of 1296 T. E.)		
37. Land Acquisition Rules under Act I of 1337 T. E.		
38. State Motor Vehicles Act I of 1338 T. E.		
39. Act II of 1338 T. E. for prevention of smuggling of elephant tusks.		
40. State Stamp Act III of 1338 T. E.		
41. Tripura State Bank Act I of 1339 T. E.		
42. Census Act III of 1339 T. E.		
43. Act I of 1342 T. E.—providing for trial of certain criminal cases by Special Tribunal.		
44. Compulsory Primary Education Act II of 1342 T. E.	Do	
45. Tripura Tea Control Act. (Act I of 1345 T. E.)		
46. Regulation for realization of tax on bullock carts.		
47. Regulation for realization of toll on Motor Vehicles plying between Agartala and Akhaura.		
48. Regulation for destruction of papers in accordance with Act No. I of 1323 T. E. Sec. 4)		

II

Statement showing the strength, cost and other particulars of the Military Forces in Tripura State for 1346 T. E.

Arm of service.	Number of fighting officers and men.						Details of force at the end of the current year.						Buglers.	Total cost on account of pay and allowances of the force, including followers.	Remarks
	At the end of last year	Recruited this year.	Casualties.			At the end of the current year.	Number of regiments, battalions, or Batteries.	Number of guns.	Number of men.						
									Commisioned Officers.		Non-commissioned officers.	Sepoy and others.			
			Death.	Desertion.	Discharge &c.				British Commissioned.	Indian Commissioned.					
1	2	3	4	5	6	7	8	9	10	11	12	13	14	15	16
Infantry ...	379	112	3	35	82	371	1	724 (a)	4	16	58	287	6		
Band Party	19	9	—	—	3	25	—	—	—	—	3	22	—		(a) 412 old and unserviceable.
Total ...	398	121	3	35	85	396	1	724	4	16	61	309	6	Rs. 1,18,728	

III.

Statement showing the strength, cost, discipline, and education of the Police for the year 1346 T. E.

Description of office	Number.	Grade of pay.	Total cost.	PUNISHMENTS.					REWARDS.		EDUCATION.		REMARKS
				Dismissed.	Fined, degraded or suspended departmentally.			Punished judicially.	By promotion.	By money.	Number able to read and write.	Number under instruction.	
					F.	D.	S.						
1	2	3	4	5	6			7	8	9	10	11	12
		Rs.											
Superintendent of Police	1	250-0-0		—		—		—	—	—	1	—	F. = Fined. D. = Degraded. S. = Suspended.
Asst. Superintendent "	1	100-5-125		—		—		—	—	—	1	—	
Inspectors	4	2 65 5/2-90 2 55-2-65		—		—		—	—	—	4	—	
Sub-Inspectors	23	25-2-45		—		—		—	—	15	23	—	Including 5 C I. D. Naib Darogas.
Naib Darogas	21	15-1-25		—		—		—	—	5	21	—	
Writer Naib Darogas	16	15-0-0	Rs. 85,092	—		—		—	—	—	16	—	
Subedar	1	25-2-45		—		—		—	—	—	1	—	
Armed S. I.	1	25-2-45		—		—		—	—	1	1		
Jamadars (civil)	6	15-1-25		—		—		—	—	1	6	—	
Jamadar (Armed)	1	20-1-30		—		—		—	—	—	1	—	
Havildar	1	19-1-25		—		—		—		—	1	—	
Naiks	4	15-1-20				—		—	—	—	4	—	
Constables (Armed)	33	14-1-15		5	10	1	0	—	—	—	25	-	
Constables (Civil)	204	10 to 13		3	42	8	0		-	24	120	—	4 constables increased in the budget.
Chaukidars	176	5-0-0		2	1	0	0	—	—	3	10	—	
Spies	3	20 and 15		—		—		—	—	—	3	—	
Total ...	496			10	53	9	0	—	—	47	238	—	

IV.

Statement showing the working of the Police in the Tripura State during the year 1346 T. E.

State.	Number of offences.		Number of accused arrested.		Number of accused sent up for trial.		Number of accused convicted.		Number of accused acquitted or discharged.		Percentage convicted of accused arrested.		Percentage convicted of accused sent up for trial.		REMARKS.
	Past year.	Present year.	Pas year.	Present year.	Past year.	Present year.	Past year.	Present year.	Past year.	Present year.	Past year.	Present year.	Past year.	Present year.	
1	2	3	4	5	6	7	8	9	10	11	12	13	14	15	16
Tripura State	674	663	516	560	708	560	139	138	114	123	26·94	24·64	73·16	* 69·35	* Excluding :— Pending trial— 281 Withdrawal— 30 Compromise— 45 Dead— 5 361

V.

Statement showing the value of property stolen and amount of recoveries in the Tripura State during the year 1346 T. E.

State.	Amount stolen.		Amount recovered.		Percentage of recoveries of property stolen.		REMARKS.
	Past year.	Present year.	Past year.	Present year.	Past year.	Present year.	
1	2	3	4	5	6	7	8
Tripura State	Rs 10,193-14-9	Rs 15487-9-3	Rs 2322-5-0	Rs 2,057-1-9	22·78	13·28	

VI.

Statement showing the number of crimes committed, number of cases disposed of, and cases awaiting trial in the Tripura State during the year 1346 T. E.

Description of offences.	Number of offences.			Number of cases disposed of during the last year.	Number of cases disposed of during the present year.	Number of cases awaiting trial.	Number of persons apprehended.	Number of persons convicted.	Number of persons sentenced.								Number of persons acquitted or discharged.	Number of persons confined being insane.	Number of persons died during or before trial.	Term of imprisonment.											Persons awaiting trial.	Remark.
									Imprisonment.		Imprisonment and fine.																					
	Balance from past year.	Committed during the present year.	Total.						Simple.	Rigorous.	Simple.	Rigorous.	Fine only.	Whipping.	Capital punishment.	Total.				Under one month.	From 1 to below 2 months.	From 2 to below 3 months.	From 3 to below 6 months.	From 6 to below 12 months.	From 1 to below 2 years.	From 2 to below 3 years.	From 3 to below 5 years.	5 years and above.	Imprisonment for life.	Capital punishment.		
1	2	3	4	5	6	7	8	9	10	11	12	13	14	15	16	17	18	19	20	21	22	23	24	25	26	27	28	29	30	31	32	33
Class I. Offences against the State, public tranquillity, safety and justice &c. — cognizable ...	19	44	63	24	43	20	130	a30	0	13	0	6	2	0	0	21	50	0	0	0	6	1	1	6	5	0	0	0	0	0	50	(a) 9 persons were bound down.
non-cognizable	10	65	75	49	58	17	36	0	0	0	0	0	0	0	0	0	15	0	0	0	0	0	0	0	0	0	0	0	0	0	21	
Class II. Offences against person. — cognizable ..	133	354	487	353	365	122	738	b65	7	27	1	12	17	0	0	64	453	0	3	6	8	4	2	10	13	0	0	3	1	0	217	(b) 1 person was warned for the future.
non-cognizable	94	263	357	206	266	91	374	43	3	4	0	0	36	0	0	43	248	0	0	0	4	0	3	0	0	0	0	0	0	0	83	
Class III. Offences against property. — cognizable ...	282	727	1009	814	701	308	1533	c230	4	74	3	10	138	0	0	229	728	0	12	14	24	14	9	26	3	1	0	0	0	0	563	(c) 1 person was warned for the future.
non-cognizable	61	232	293	285	202	91	367	23	1	10	0	0	12	0	0	23	235	0	1	0	6	3	2	0	0	0	0	0	0	0	108	
Class IV. Other offences. — cognizable ...	52	133	185	107	114	71	120	28	1	10	0	0	17	0	0	28	57	0	1	0	5	2	1	1	2	0	0	0	0	0	34	(d) 2 persons were bound down.
non-cognizable	85	259	344	138	229	115	135	d19	0	3	0	0	14	0	0	17	63	0	0	0	1	2	0	0	0	0	0	0	0	0	53	
Total cognizable	486	1258	1744	1298	1222	521	2521	353	12	124	4	28	174	0	0	342	1288	0	16	20	43	21	13	43	23	1	0	3	1	0	864	
Total non-cognizable	250	819	1069	728	755	314	912	85	4	17	0	0	62	0	0	83	561	0	1	0	11	5	5	0	0	0	0	0	0	0	265	
GRAND TOTAL	736	2077	2813	2026	1975	835	3433	438	16	141	4	28	236	0	0	425	1849	0	17	20	54	26	18	43	23	1	0	3	1	0	1129	

VII.

Statement showing the number of offences reported and dealt with by the various Courts in the Tripura State during the year 1346 T.E.

Name of Court	Number of offences reported during.		Number of persons dealt with.								Persons disposed of.					Persons remaining at the end of the year.	Remarks
			Remaining at the end of last year.	Brought to trial during present year.					Total.								
	Last year.	Present year.		Arrested by Police.	Upon warrant.	On summons	Voluntary.	Arrested in presence of the Magistrate.	Last year.	Present year	Discharged without trial.	Acquitted.	Convicted.	Committed or referred.	Died, escaped, or transferred &c.		
1	2	3	4	5	6	7	8	9	10	11	12	13	14	15	16	17	18
Sadar Magistracy	578	570	159	137	123	189	54	—	767	662	224	196	71	12	—	159	
Sonamura „ ...	242	2[illegible]8	1[illegible]6	42	58	164	95	2	412	487	150	60	62	9	3	203	
Bilonia „ ...	179	190	31	60	34	53	50	—	348	228	1[illegible]1	17	69	3	—	38	
Kailashahar „ ...	298	329	194	65	101	135	62	2	468	559	181	95	65	14	3	201	
Khowai „ ...	206	183	43	12	38	93	6[illegible]	[illegible]	267	247	104	58	23	22	2	38	
Dharmanagar „ ...	219	311	252	105	153	183	27	—	651	7[illegible]0	257	59	72	—	7	325	
Udaipur „ ...	216	223	121	45	61	233	14	—	379	474	197	71	44	2	2	158	
Sabrum „ ...	36	30	25	11	7	3	5	—	91	51	17	14	18	—	—	2	
TOTAL ...	1,974	2,077	951	477	575	1,053	368	4	3,383	3,428 *a*	1,231	570	424	62 *b*	17	1,12[illegible]	

a. Excluding 5 persons pending before the Court of Sessions at the close of the previous year.

b. The total number of persons for trial before the Court of Sessions, (including 5 persons pending from the last year) was 67, of whom 14 persons were convicted, 48 acquitted and 5 remained under trial at the close of the year.

VIII.

Statement of Criminal cases in which British Subjects were concerned in 1346 T. E.

Description of Offences.		Cases pending since the previous year.	Cases instituted during the year.	Total number of cases.	Cases in which complainants were British subjects.	Cases in which both parties were British subjects.	Cases in which defendants were British Subjects.														Remarks.
							Cases pending since the previous year	Cases instituted during the year.	Total number of cases.	Cases disposed of.		Cases pending at the close of the year.	Persons under trial at the close of the previous year.	Persons brought to trial during the year.	Total number of persons under trial.	Convicted.	Acquitted or discharged.	Died or escaped &c.	Under trial at the close of the year.	
										Rejected, compromised without enquiry.	Tried.									
Class I. Offences against the State &c.	cognizable ...	5	3	8	0	1	5	3	8	1	4	3	8		13	3	2	0	8	*Of this number, 79 persons were discharged without trial, the cases being compromised or struck off etc. Excluding 3 persons dead and 198 remaining under trial at the close of the year; the actual number of persons tried was 207, of whom 139 persons were convicted; the percentage of conviction was thus 67·15 during the year under report as against 65·94 of the preceding year.
	non-cognizable ...	0	1	1	1	0	0	0	0	0	0	0	0	0	0	0	0	0	0	
Class II. Offences against person.	cognizable ...	21	31	52	9	17	20	23	43	10	13	20	32	62	94	14	34	1	45	
	non-cognizable ...	18	20	38	10	6	15	13	28	7	13	8	13	25	38	7	16	0	15	
Class III. Offences against property.	cognizable ...	50	157	207	12	36	62	133	195	52	76	67	77	189	266	103	69	2	92	
	non-cognizable ...	13	21	34	6	14	16	12	28	7	15	6	15	27	42	6	13	0	23	
Class IV. Other offences	cognizable ...	4	14	18	0	1	4	14	18	10	4	4	4	20	24	2	11	0	11	
	non-cognizable ...	2	22	24	2	12	1	21	22	13	3	6	2	8	10	4	2	0	4	
Total cognizable ...		80	205	285	21	55	91	173	264	73	97	94	121	276	397	122	116	3	156	
Total non-cognizable ...		33	64	97	19	32	32	46	78	27	31	20	30	60	90	17	31	0	42	
GRAND TOTAL ...		113	269	382	40	87	123	219	342	100	128	114	151	336	*487	139	147	3	198	

IX.

Statement of Extradition Cases for the year 1346 T. E.

Names of Courts.	Nature of cases.	Number Borne on the Register.				Number Brought to Trial.			Result.		Number at large at the close of the year.	Number of persons awaiting trial (after arrest) at the close of the year.	Remarks.
		Number of persons at large at the close of the previous year.	Number of persons awaiting trial at the close of the previous year.	Number of persons against whom warrants were applied for during the year.	Total.	Number of persons arrested and surrendered within the year.	Number of persons who appeared of their own accord or were subsequently arrested in the State within the year.	Total (Columns 4+7+8).	Convicted.	Acquitted or discharged.			
Sadar Magistracy	Theft ...	3	25	17	45	18	2	45	1	44	0	0	
	Kidnapping	0	1	0	1	0	0	1	1	0	0	0	
	Criminal breach of trust	2	1	0	3	2	0	3	2	1	0	0	
	Dacoity	1	0	0	1	1	0	1	1	0	0	0	
	Causing mischief	0	2	2	4	2	0	4	0	4	0	0	
Sonamura „ ...	Theft ...	47	3	9	59	2	0	5	3	2	54	0	
	Murder	5	3	0	8	2	3	8	5	2	0	1	
	Rioting and causing grievous hurt ...	2	0	0	2	0	1	1	1	0	1	0	
Bilonia „ ...	Theft	8	1	0	9	0	0	1	1	0	8	0	
	Cheating	0	0	1	1	1	0	1	0	1	0	0	
	Rape ...	0	0	4	4	1	0	1	1 *	0	3	0	
	Theft and causing hurt	0	0	7	7	1	0	1	0	0	6	1	
	Culpable homicide not amounting to murder	3	0	0	3	0	2	2	0	2	0 †	0	
Khowai „ ...	Theft ...	1	0	0	1	1	0	1	0	1	0	0	
	Criminal breach of trust etc.	1	0	0	1	0	0	0	0	0	1	0	
	Dishonest misappropriation of property	1	0	0	1	0	0	0	0	0	1	0	
	Arson ...	0	0	1	1	0	0	0	0	0	0 ‡	0	
	Kidnapping	1	0	2	3	0	1	1	1	0	2	0	
Kailashahar „ ...	Rioting and causing grievous hurt ...	5	0	0	5	0	0	0	0	0	0 $	0	
	Criminal breach of trust	1	0	0	1	1	0	1	1	0	0	0	
	Theft ...	4	3	3	10	4	0	7	2	2	3	3	
	Kidnapping	1	0	1	2	1	0	1	0	0	1	1	
	House breaking by night etc.	0	1	0	1	0	0	1	0	1	0	0	
	Causing grievous hurt etc.	0	0	30	30	0	2	2	0	0	28	2	
	Voluntarily causing grievous hurt and kidnaping	0	0	1	1	0	0	0	0	0	1	0	
Sabroom „ ...	Dacoity	5	0	4	9	4	0	4	3	1	5	0	
	Theft ...	2	7	5	14	0	0	7	4	3	7	0	
	Escape from lawful custody	0	0	1	1	1	0	1	1	0	0	0	
	Resistence to arrest ...	12	4	0	16	6	6	16	4	8	0	4	
Dharmanagar „ ...	Theft ...	1	1	7	9	0	0	1	1	0	8	0	
	Escape from lawful custody	0	0	1	1	0	0	0	0	0	1	0	
	Total ...	106	52	96	254	48	17	117	33	72	130	12	

* Committed to Sessions. † One died. ‡ Extradition refused.
$ Extradition warrants cancelled by Assam Government.

X.

Statement showing the result of appeals against decisions passed by the Criminal Courts in the Tripura State during the year 1346 T. E.

Tribunal.	Number of applications.	Number of persons and cases.																Remarks.
		Applications rejected.		Sentences.						Proceedings quashed.		Referred.		Further enquiry &c. ordered.		Pending		
				Confirmed.		Modified.		Reversed.										
		Persons.	Cases.	Persons.	Cases.	Persons.	Cases.	Persons.	Cases.	Persons.	Cases.	Persons	Cases.	Persons	Cases.	Persons.	Cases.	
Khas Adalat ...	256	10	10	145	104	83	43	28	15	—	—	—	—	9	7	121	77	

XI.

Civil Work—Nature and value of original suits filed and disposed of during the year 1346 T. E.

Tribunal.	Opening balance.		Filed during the year, received by transfer or on remand.		Total.		Disposed of during the year.		Closing balance.		Suits filed during present year.									Suits disposed of during present year.						Suits not estimable in money.	Remarks.
	Past year.	Present year.	Past year.	Present year.	Past year.	Present year.	Past year.	Present year.	Past year.	Present year.	Value.	Suits *re* landed property.	Suits for money transaction.	Suits for other rights.	Number of suits under Rs. 100.	Number of suits above Rs. 100 and under Rs. 500.	Number of suits above Rs. 500 and under Rs. 1,000.	Number of suits above Rs. 1,000 and under Rs. 5,000.	Number of suits above Rs. 5,000.	*Exparte.*	Admitted and compromised.	Struck off the file.	Otherwise disposed of.	Value.	Average duration.		
											Rs. a. p.													*Rs a. p.*	*Y.m.d.*		
Khas Adalat Original side	51	59	21	15	72	74	13	33	59	41	50,454-0-0	3	8	4	0	0	0	10	1	3	2	4	24	22,913-10-6	0-5-21	4	
Sadar Dewani Adalat	310	320	558	511	868	831	548	563	320	268	30,191-7-6	216	202	93	213	187	7	0	0	318	72	77	96	49,316-13-9	0-0-28	104	
Sonamura „	52	45	182	150	234	195	189	150	45	45	15,189-8-1	10	107	33	81	34	4	0	0	68	28	34	20	14,256-4-11	0-5-27	31	
Bilonia „	42	37	185	152	227	189	190	140	37	49	7,878-2-3	2	83	68	59	25	1	0	0	57	11	34	38	7,299-1-0	0-2-22	67	
Kailashahar „	121	162	214	179	335	341	173	208	162	133	14,583-11-6	14	114	51	102	35	2	0	0	84	22	12	90	17,156-14-6	0-5-3	40	
Khowai „	33	35	64	51	97	86	62	59	35	27	4,972-10-0	2	24	25	32	17	0	0	0	11	10	19	19	9,027-4-0	0-7-18	2	
Dharmanagar „	70	71	80	107	150	178	79	118	71	60	7,562-4-6	14	66	27	60	24	1	0	0	16	4	15	83	8,592-2-6	0-1-15	22	
Udaipur „	98	109	211	170	309	279	200	172	109	107	13,793-12-9	82	83	5	119	28	4	0	0	84	14	36	38	11,110-14-6	0-5-5	19	
Sabrum „	2	3	38	35	40	38	37	36	3	2	2,900-5-0	28	7	0	27	7	1	0	0	30	2	2	2	3,662-8-6	0-0-7	0	
Total ...	779	841	1,553	1,370	2,332	2,211	1,491	1,479	841	732	1.47,531-13-7	371	693	306	693	357	20	10	1	671	165	233	410	1,43,335-10-2	0-3-26	289	

XII.

Civil Work.—Results of applications for Execution of Decrees, 1346 T.E.

Tribunal.	Opening balance.		Value of opening balance for present year.	Applications brought to the Register.			Total.			Disposed of.			Closing balance.			Nature of applications pending disposal at the close of the year.			Remarks.
	Past year.	Present year.		Past year.	Present year.	Value for present year.	Past year.	Present year.	Value for present year.	Past year.	Present year.	Value for present year.	Past year.	Present year.	Value for present year.	Below 6 months.	Below 12 months.	Above 12 months.	
			Rs. a. p.			Rs. a. p.			Rs. a. p.			Rs. a. p.			Rs. a. p.				
Khas Adalat (Original side)	30	22	15,092-3-9	7	4	5,967-0-9	37	26	21,059-4-6	15	8	3,265-9-9	22	18	17,793-10-9	0	4	14	
Sadar Dewani Adalat ...	242	241	25,341-7-9	258	213	31,613-11-6	500	454	56,955-3-3	259	241	35,341-9-6	241	213	21,613-9-9	103	39	71	
Sonamura Ditto ...	42	48	9,209-1-0	80	60	11,988-14-3	122	108	21,197-15-3	74	72	12,307-1-0	48	36	8,890-14-3	27	1	8	
Bilonia Ditto ...	29	30	3,511-7-6	78	59	9,715-14-3	107	89	13,227-5-9	77	64	7,129-5-0	30	25	6,098-0-9	22	2	1	
Kailashahar Ditto ...	112	102	23,780-0-0	102	76	10,187-6-0	214	178	33,967-6-0	112	96	16,263-8-0	102	82	17,703-14-0	2	30	50	
Khowai Ditto ...	22	21	4,135-12-0	28	25	2,085-5-0	50	46	6,221-1-0	29	25	2,600-4-6	21	21	3,620-12-6	5	6	10	
Dharmanagar Ditto ...	49	39	8,972-10-3	26	29	6,628-3-6	75	68	15,600-13-9	36	36	6,436-10-6	39	32	9,164-3-3	11	5	16	
Udaipur Ditto ...	116	142	21,015-15-3	195	118	15,324-5-9	311	260	36,340-5-0	169	167	21,731-5-9	142	93	14,608-15-3	44	13	36	
Sabrum Ditto ...	3	10	1,293-8-6	25	17	3,349-3-0	28	27	4,642-11-6	18	18	2,259-6-0	10	9	2,383-5-6	7	1	1	
Total ...	645	655	1,12,352-2-0	799	601	96,860-0-0	1,444	1,256	2,09,212-2-0	789	727	1,07,334-12-0	655	529	1,01,877-6-0	221	101	207	

XIII.

Civil Work Number and results of appeals in civil suits, 1346 T. E.

Tribunal.	Opening balance.		Filed during.		Total.		Disposed of during.		Closing balance.		Value of appeales filed during.		How disposed of. Decisions confirmed.		Decisions reversed.		Decisions amended.		Cases remanded for retrial.		Cases compromised and otherwise disposed of.		Average duration.	
	Past year.	Present year.	Past year.	Present year.	Past year.	Present year.	Past year.	Present year.	Past year.	Present year.	Past year.	Present year.	Past year.	Present year.	Past year.	Present year.	Past year.	Present year.	Past year.	Present year.	Past year.	Present year.	Past year.	Present year
											Rs. a. p.	*Rs. a. p.*											*Y.m.d.*	*Y m.d.*
Khas Adalat	78	97	169	149	247	246	150	136	97	110	8,000-5-6	1,13,872-8-6	73	66	29	24	9	18	10	5	29	23	0-5-0	0-7-15

XIV.

Statement showing the number of persons confined in the jails and lock-ups in the Tripura State during the year 1346 T. E.

Stations.	Number of prisons.	Number of prisoners.				Daily average.		Number of prisoners remaining at the end of the year.	Cost of jails and prisoners.	Average period in days of stay of accused under-trial.	Remarks showing mortality among convicts in jail.
		Remaining from last year.	Admitted during the year.	Total.							
				Past year.	Present year.	Past year.	Present year.				
									Rs.		
Agartala	1	139	358	454	497	133'11	153'01	128	20,956	33'6	One convict died of cholera.
Sonamura	1	8	107	131	115	'35	'3	3	697	19'39	One undertrial died of tuberculosis.
Bilonia	1	5	115	137	120	9'2	4'7	1	1,086	14'76	
Kailashahar	1	5	124	138	129	6'56	5'9	5	700	20'01	
Dharmanagar	1	14	104	157	118	13'31	12'06	6	1,437	42'92	
Udaipur...	1	—	44	61	44	9'04	3'14	12	967	29'59	
Sabrum	1	1	30	36	31	2'14	1'58	3	909	23'15	
Khowai	1	11	52	59	63	5'4	3'74	5	964	24'34	
Total ...	8	183	934	1173	1117	179'11	184'43	163	27,716	25'97	

XV.

Registration of documents in the Tripura State during the year 1346 T.E.

Name of State	Documents presented for registration including pending from the last year.		Nature of documents presented. Mortgages.		Sale deeds.		Wills.		Money bonds.		Miscellaneous.		Documents registered.		Value of documents registered.		Documents of which registration has been refused.		Documents remaining unregistered at the end of the year.		Remarks.
	Past year.	Present year.	Past year.	Present year.	Past year.	Present year.	Past year.	Present year.	Past year.	Present year.	Past year.	Present year.	Past year.	Present year.	Past year.	Present year.	Past year.	Present year.	Past year.	Present year.	
1	2	3	4	5	6	7	8	9	10	11	12	13	14	15	16	17	18	19	20	21	22
															Rs.	Rs.					
Tripura State	7,398	7,819	1,313	1,228	4,307	4,707	2	3	53	38	1,553	1,653	7,148	7,317	10,98,306	9,17,873	131	45	190	457	

XVI.

Statement showing the receipts and expenditure on account of Registration during the year 1346 T.E.

Description.	Past Year.			Present Year.			Remarks.
	Number of deeds.	Value of property.	Fees realised.	Number of deeds.	Value of property.	Fees realised.	
		Rs.	Rs.		Rs.	Rs.	
Mortgages	1,313	4,07,780	1,397	1,228	2,66,550	7,243	
Sale deeds	4,307	4,47,910	3,663	4,707	4,34,137		
Wills	2	—	10	3	300		
Money bonds	53	8,566	41	38	5,723		
Miscellaneous	1,553	2,41,891	2,330	1,653	2,18,983		
Total ...	7,228	11,06,147	7,444	7,629	9,25,693	7,243	
Total Expenditure ...	—	—	3,564	—	—	3,993	
Net Income ...	—	—	3,880	—	—	3,250	

E

XVII.

Receipts and expenditure of the Municipalities in the Tripura State during the year 1346 T.E.

NAME.	Opening balance.	RECEIPTS DURING THE YEAR.				Total Receipt		EXPENDITURE DURING THE YEAR.		Balance at the close of the year.	REMARKS.
		State grant.	Tax.	Miscel-laneous.	Total.	Past year.	Present year	Past.	Present.		
1	2	3	4	5	6	7	8	9	10	11	12
	Rs. A.P.	Rs. A.P.	Rs. A.P	Rs. A.P	Rs. A.P.	Rs. A.P.	Rs. A.P.	Rs. A.P.	Rs. A.P.	Rs. A.P.	
Agartala Municipality. ...	48,729-7-0 *a*	9,000	5,069-8-0	10,121-3-0 *b*	24,190-11-0	65,804-11-3	72,920-2-0	17,075-4-3	28,378-14-6 *c*	44,541-3-6 *d*	*a.* Including Rs. 48,688-3-3 of the Bazar Improvement fund and Rs. 41-3-9 of the municipality. *b.* Including Rs 8,404-4-3 of the Bazar Improvement fund *c.* Including Rs. 12,585-6-6 as expenditure on the Bazar improvement. *d* Including Rs. 44,507-1-0 of the Bazar Improvement fund and Rs. 34-2-6 of the municipality.

XVIII.

Statement of rainfall in the Tripura State during the year 1346 T. E.

STATE.	Baisak.	Jaisth.	Asar.	Sravan.	Bhadra.	Asvin.	Kartik.	Agrahayan.	Pous.	Magh.	Falgoon.	Chait.	Total.	Total of past year.	Average of past 5 years.	REMARKS.
Tripura State ...	6·83	18·87	14·13	20·94	11·28	7·89	·60	·15	·03	·19	·58	1·70	83·19	79·48	81·50	

Maximum in Sadar—108·81″ Minimum in Amarpur—69·24″

XIX.

Statement as to the prices of staple food-grains for the year 1346 T. E

Articles.	Price per maund during Chait, 1345 T. E.			Price per maund during Chait, 1346 T. E.			REMARKS.
	Rs.	*a.*	*p.*	*Rs.*	*a.*	*p.*	
(1) RICE							
Maximum	4	8	0	4	8	0	
Minimum	2	8	0	2	4	0	
(2) PADDY							
Maximum	2	4	0	2	0	0	
Minimum	1	0	0	1	0	0	

XX.

Expenditure on Public Works during the year 1346 T.E.

Description of work.	State Funds.			Local Funds.			Total.	Remarks.
	Original.	Repairs.	Total.	Original.	Repairs.	Total.		
	Rs.	*Rs.*	*Rs.*	*Rs.*	*Rs.*	*Rs.*	*Rs.*	
Buildings—								
Ordinary Budget ...	9,125	61,547	70,672	18,735	—	18,735	89,407	
Improvement „ ...	87,744	—	87,744	—	—	—	87,744	
Roads and Bridges—								
Ordinary Budget ...	1,102	23,759	24,861	—	100	100	24,961	
Improvement „ ...	38,261	—	38,261	—	—	—	38,261	
Tanks and Tubewells—								
Ordinary Budget ...	1,174	1,566	2,740	—	1,500	1,500	4,240	Of the total expenditure of Rs. 2,80,009, Rs. 1,19,275 was spent for ordinary Public Works, Rs. 1,38,264, was spent for improvement works from the State and Rs. 22,470 was spent for ordinary Public Works from the local funds.
Improvement „ ...	2,646	—	2,646	—	—	—	2,646	
Miscellaneous works—								
Ordinary Budget ...	—	1,714	1,714	2,135	—	2,135	3,849	
Improvement „ ...	8,379	—	8,379	—	—	—	8,379	
Total ...	1,48,431	88,586	2,37,017	20,870	1,600	22,470	2,59,487	
Minor works at the Rajbari (*Karkhana*)	—	1,175	1,175	—	—	—	1,175	
Establishment—								
Ordinary Budget ...	—	—	18,113	—	—	—	18,113	
Improvement „ ...	—	—	1,234	—	—	—	1,234	
Grand Total ...	1,48,43	89,761	2,57,539	20,870	1,600	22,470	2,80,009	

F

XXI.

Statement showing the number of excise shops and excise revenue of the Tripura State during the year 1346 T. E.

Name of State.	Country spirit.		Country spirit, Opium and Ganja.		Opium and Ganja.		Tari		Total.		Remarks.
	Number of shops.	Revenue demand.	Number of shops.	Revenue demand.	Number of shops.	Revenue demand.	Number of shops.	Revenue, demand.	Number of shops.	Revenue realised.	
				Rs.						Rs.	
Tripura State	—	—	33	41,348	—	—	—	—	33	39,705	

XXII.

Statement of Medical Relief afforded in the Tripura State during the year 1346 T.E.*

Dispensary.	Number of Patients Treated. (new) Outdoor.	Indoor.	Results of In-door Patients. (new) Dis-charged cured.	Relieved or dis-charged otherwise.	Died.	Remain-ing under treatment.	Expenditure.	Daily Average. (old + new) Outdoor.	Indoor.	Total.	No. of Surgical Operations Performed. Major.	Minor.	Total.	No. of Persons Vaccinated during the Year. Success-fully.	Unsuc-cessfully.	Total.	Remarks.
							Rs.										
1 Victoria Memorial Hospital ...	20,482	537	393	101	27	16	9,277	115·73	19·51	135·24	17	223	240	1,347	872	2,219	
2. Palace Dispensary	5,698	0	0	0	0	0	8,453	34·88	0	34·88	0	0	0	0	0	0	
3. Homœopathic	19,833	0	0	0	0	0	2,780	91·25	0	91·25	0	0	0	0	0	0	* This Statement excludes figures regarding Kaviraji treatment
4. Dhaleswar	4,918	0	0	0	0	0	1,658	37·36	0	37·36	0	18	18	0	0	0	
5. Kunjaban	1,118	250	236	6	0	8	2,119	10·93	4·89	15·82	0	12	12	0	0	0	
6. Old Agartala	5,231	0	0	0	0	0	1,858	46·69	0	46·69	1	22	23	935	292	1,227	
7. Bishalgar	9,645	0	0	0	0	0	1,763	40·94	0	40·94	0	40	40	696	24	720	
8. Sonamura	6,715	2	1	1	0	0	1,924	30·35	·06	30·41	0	194	194	897	312	1,209	
9. Radhakishorpur	9,460	0	0	0	0	0	1,435	43·5	0	43·5	4	75	79	103	15	118	† This figure shows the actual number of outdoor patients treated, the total outdoor attendance being 2,57,788 against 2,92,779 in the year before.
10. Amarpur	3,655	0	0	0	0	0	1,308	18·41	0	18·41	2	70	72	1,142	130	1,272	
11. Sabroom	2,472	0	0	0	0	0	1,596	13·16	0	13·16	0	20	20	2,337	804	3,141	
12. Bilonia	8,179	3	3	0	0	0	1,973	47·2	·02	47·22	1	83	84	67	10	77	
13. Muhuripur	4,055	0	0	0	0	0	1,446	17·33	0	17·33	0	65	65	1,006	301	1,307	
14. Khowai	5,93.	0	0	0	0	0	1,218	25·6	0	25·6	0	18	18	176	22	198	
15 Kalyanpur	2,833	0	0	0	0	0	850	12·05	0	12·05	2	38	40	220	49	269	
16. Kailashahar	8,980	14	4	8	1	1	1,700	51·82	·4	55·22	3	104	107	739	279	1,018	
17 Kamalpur	4,114	0	0	0	0	0	1,374	20·36	0	20·36	3	43	46	406	79	485	
18. Kulai Howar	3,302	0	0	0	0	0	398	12·46	0	12·46	0	1	1	0	0	0	
19 Dharmanagar	6,975	0	0	0	0	0	1,581	33·15	0	33·15	0	115	115	265	32	297	
Total	†1,33,515	806	637	116	28	25	44,711	706·17	24·88	731·05	33	1,141	1,174	10,336	3,221	13,557	

XXIII.

Education Return (A)—Particulars as to the schools maintained during the year 1346 T.E.

Number of Schools.		Class of Schools.	Number of pupils on the rolls on the last day of Chait.		Average daily attendance.		Remarks.
Past year	Present year.		Past year.	Present year.	Past year.	Present year.	
6	6	High English Schools ... ... (including one Branch H. E. School).	1,584	1,527	1,155·13	1,160·70	
10	10	Middle English Schools for boys ...	1,166	1,205	850·49	821·59	* In some of these schools boys and girls read together.
1	1	Middle English Schools for girls ...	74	121	62·83	73·35	
24	22	* Lower Vernacular Schools for boys	1,239	1, 87	938·24	1,049·58	
70	71	*Pathsalas for boys	2,249	2,089	1 745·34	1,614·21	
5	9	Do for girls	138	278	132·01	219·23	
		Special Schools :—					
4	4	*Compulsory Free Primary Schools	623	612	373·93	377·74	
5	5	Madrassas and Muktabs	347	203	318·70	136·88	
5	5	Sanskrit *Tols*	62	74	45·58	56·45	
1	1	Artisan School & Silpasram ...	16	22	9·09	10·75	
1	1	Jail Reformatory School	22	27	21	25·40	
Total 132	135		7,520	7,445	5,652·34	5,545·88	

XXIV.

Education Return (B) Race of Students, 1346 T. E.

Names of Divisions.	No. of Schools.				No. of Students.					Race.												Average daily attendance.		REMARKS.
										Hindus.														
	For boys.	For girls.	Total.	Private schools.	Boys.	Girls.	Total.	Students of private schools.	Total.	Rajkumars.	Thakurs.	Manipuris.	Tripuras.	Bengalees.	Others.	Reangs.	Chakmas.	Kukis.	Lusais.	Musalmans.	Christians.	Boys.	Girls.	
1. Sadar Division ...	45	2	47	3	2,430	479	2,909	78	2,987	2	187	228	547	1,334	39	0	1	0	0	566	5	1,765·69	301·65	
2. Kailashahar „	22	3	25	18	1,056	147	1,203	525	1,728	0	0	335	18	629	15	0	0	0	0	206	0	842 59	104·51	
3. Sonamura „	17	1	18	2	864	72	936	57	993	0	8	0	57	259	0	0	0	0	0	612	0	667·30	64·01	
4. Bilonia „	8	1	9	3	647	54	701	75	776	0	3	1	24	447	9	4	0	0	0	213	0	498·02	34·44	
5. Khowai „	6	1	7	5	360	15	375	123	498	0	0	57	175	100	19	0	0	0	0	24	0	267·32	11·20	
6. Dharmanagar „	13	1	14	12	595	61	656	394	1,050	0	1	75	1	407	9	0	0	0	1	162	0	450·73	47·90	
7. Udaipur „	7	1	8	1	364	21	385	47	432	0	4	1	68	154	0	0	0	0	0	158	0	249·41	13·96	
8. Sabrum „	5	0	5	0	178	17	195	0	195	0	0	0	10	127	1	0	0	0	0	57	0	153·64	13·25	
9. Amarpur Sub-division ...	2	0	2	2	79	6	85	22	107	0	0	0	17	14	20	5	0	0	0	29	0	55·70	4·56	
TOTAL ...	125	10	135	46	6,573	872	7,445	1,321	8,766	2	203	697	917	3,471	112	9	1	0	1	2,027	5	4,950·40	595·48	

N. B.—In the sub-columns under "Race" the number of students of private schools is not included.

APPENDIX XXV. (A)

Statement of Audited Receipts for the year 1346 T. E.

State.

Heads of Revenue.	1345 T. E.		1346 T. E.		Remarks.
	Revised Estimate.	Actuals.	Revised Estimate.	Actuals.	
1. Land Revenue ...	6,65,000	6,53,693	8,20,000	8,32,454	
2. Rents of markets ...	6,000	6,717	8,000	7,357	
3. Family tax in the hills	55,000	59,850	50,000	53,698	
4. Toll on Forest Produce	3,25,000	3,02,538	3,45,000	3,46,883	
5. Do on the Feni River	31,000	31,314	25,000	26,877	
6. Elephant and Buffalo grazing mehals ...	6,000	5,537	6,000	6,183	
7. Thatching grass mehals	3,000	2,574	2,500	2,221	
8. Reserved *Sal* trees ...	3,000	4,134	2,000	1,039	
9. Tax on cotton and Oil seeds ...	1,75,000	2,17,722	1,15,000	1,06,518	
10 Royalty on elephants caught ...	2,500	2,522	—	—	
11. *Adda* mehal ...	25,000	24,806	24,000	25,470	
12. Excise ...	43,000	40,057	42,000	39,705	
13. Stamps and Court fees	63,000	62,874	68,000	67,627	
14. Law and Justice (fines)	2,000	2,014	2,500	2,269	
15. Process Fees ...	10,000	9,688	11,000	10,726	
16. Registration ...	7,000	7,444	7,500	7,243	
17. Jail ...	3,000	4,235	8,500	7,968	
18. Cattle pounds ...	4,000	4,489	3,500	3,745	
19. *Nazars* ...	32,000	32,812	51,500	50,426	
20. School Fees ...	16,000	14,518	15,000	15,078	
21. Duty on Tea ...	25,000	21,452	35,000	42,685	
22. Duty on jute ...	30,000	30,423	57,000	56,338	
23. Depreciation Contribution ...	78,000	76,943	59,000	58,915	
24. Miscellaneous ...	55,000	61,067	61,000	62,776	
25. Duty on matches ...	16,500	16,595	27,000	27,270	
26. Public Works ...	—	—	5,000	4,902	
Total ...	16,80,000	16,96,043	18,51,000	18,75,373	
27. Deposits ...	60,000	1,20,504	70,000	1,10,628	
28. Contribution from Chakla ...	2,50,000	2,50,000	2,80,000	2,80,000	
29 Silver Jubilee ...	10,500	10,500	—	—	
30. Contribution from Chakla to His Highness's European Tour	—		1,50,000	1,50,000	
Total ...	20,00,500	20,77,047	23,51,000	24,16,001	
Opening Balance :—					
Cash ...	1,88,879	1,88,879	3,01,378	3,01,378	
Advances ...	2,10,799	2,10,799	2,19,356	2,19,356	
Loans ...	2,78,099	2,78,099	3,01,260	3,01,260	
Working Balance ...	4,15,18	4,15,182	4,15,182	* 4,15,182	* Cash— 2,25,000 Advance— 1,90,182
Total ...	10,92,959	10,92,959	12,37,176	12,37,176	
Grand Total ...	30,93,459	31,70,006	35,88,176	36,53,177	

APPENDIX XXV. (B)

Statement of Audited Expenditure for the year 1346 T. E.

State.

Heads of Expenditure.	1345 T. E.		1346 T. E.		REMARKS.
	Revised estimate.	Actuals.	Revised Estimate.	Actuals.	
1. Controlling Charges	78,377	76,415	91,792	89,877	
2. Revenue General ...	80,373	78,777	83,152	80,948	
3. Survey & Settlement	15,166	13,835	12,590	12,296	
4. Tahasil ...	50,402	49,122	51,226	49,943	
5. Registration ...	4,129	3,564	4,034	3,993	
6. Police ...	83,931	82,754	85,665	85,092	
7. Judicial ...	33,915	33,380	37,460	36,937	
8. Jail ...	32,142	29,658	30,886	29,668	
9. Forest ...	50,237	48,928	53,190	50,177	
10. Medical ...	67,788	66,513	72,315	71,950	
11. Municipality ...	9,000	9,000	9,000	9,000	
12. Education General ...	1,24,681	1,22,027	1,35,496	1,31,956	
13. (*a*) Public Works ...	1,03,352	1,00,574	1,21,420	1,19,275	
(*b*) Improvement ...	96,554	96,101	1,40,228	1,38,264	
14. Electric Light ...	16,500	16,433	26,919	26,748	
15. Small Donation ...	300	295	500	479	
16. Relief to distressed subjects ...	300	—	300	—	
17. Purchase of Landed Property ...	12,000	11,522	7,000	6,616	
18. Repayment of Deposits ..	80,000	79,860	1,00,000	98,908	
19. Interest on Deposits	32,000	30,910	35,000	32,761	
20. Unforeseen charges...	5,500	4,792	5,000	4,893	
21. Pension ...	49,500	48,832	50,000	49,742	
22. Chief Secretary's Office & H. H.'s Tour	1,57,897	1,57,827	3,30,536	1,57,623	
23. Palace Sultanat ...	36,959	36,264	69,406	66,523	
24. Zoo ...	3,352	3,342	3,452	3,258	
25. Agriculture, Commerce and Industries	8,295	8,031	4,910	4,902	
26. Publicity, Reclamation & Immigration ...	5,608	3,667	3,745	3,068	
27. H. H.'s Private Secretary's Office ...	10,890	10,852	11,679	11,664	
28. Rajmala Office ...	2,468	1,109	2,468	1,033	
29. Military Secretary's Office ...	3,720	3,700	3,960	2,430	
30. Military ...	1,13,570	1,07,131	1,26,918	1,18,728	
31. Nijtahabil ...	1,00,000	1,00,000	1,80,000	1,20,000	
32. Adjustment of irrecoverable advances...	10,000	3,000	1,000	—	
33. Repayment of old Debts ...	1,00,500	1,00,109	1,00.000	99,398	
34. Governor's Visit ...	—	—	23,500	23,201	
35. Sansar Charges ...	3,86,303	3,76,818	4,30,058	3,95,732	
36. Silver Jubilee ...	18,000	17,638	—	—	
Total ...	19,83,109	19,32,830	24,44,805	21,37,133	
Closing balance :—					
Cash ...	1,62,368	3,01,378	1,60,675	2,31,323	
Advances ...	2,32,800	2,19,356	2,60,000	5,61,419	
Loans issued ...	3,00,000	3,01,260	3,07,514	3,08,120	
Working balance ...	4,15,182	4,15,182	4,15,182	* 4,15,182	* Cash— 2,25,000 Advance—1,90,182
Total ...	11,10,350	12,37,176	11,43,371	15,16,044	
Grand Total ...	30,93,459	31,70,006	35,88,176	36,53,177	

APPENDIX XXVI. (A)

Statement of Audited Receipts for the year 1346 T. E.

Chakla Roshnabad Estates.

Heads of Receipts.	1345 T. E.		1346 T. E.		REMARKS.
	Revised Estimate.	Actuals.	Revised Estimate.	Actuals.	
1. Rent and Cess ...	10,77,300	10,85,652	11,95,500	12,28,689	
2. Cess for Rent free holdings ...	7,751	9,797	10,000	10,814	
3. Law charges recovered	66,488	65,060	70,000	67,443	
4. Miscellaneous receipts including deposits ...	70,761	66,510	73,000	66,688	
5 Refund of loans and advances ...	1,500	1,369	1,500	1,610	
Total ...	12,23,800	12,28,388	13,50,000	13.75.274	
Opening Balance :—					
Cash ...	1,11,086	1,11,086	2,28,090	2,28,090	
Bank deposits ...	71,050	71,050	1,08,629	1,08,629	
Advance ...	1,14,873	1,14.873	1,25,343	1,25,343	
Loans issued ...	86,493	86,493	95,082	95,082	
Total ...	3,83,502	3,83,502	5,57,144	5,57,144	
Grand Total ...	16,07,302	16,11,890	19,07,144	19,32,418	

APPENDIX XXVI. (B)

Statement of Audited Expenditure for the year 1346 T. E.

Chakla Roshnabad Estates.

Heads of Expenditure	1345 T. E. Revised Estimate.	1345 T. E. Actuals.	1346 T. E. Revised Estimate.	1346 T. E. Actuals.	REMARKS.
i. 1. Revenue and Cess ...	3,00,227	2,81,546	2,96,474	2,84,317	
2. Establishment ...	1,40,143	1,37,363	1,40,915	1,38,703	
3. Settlement ...	1,440	1,097	2,968	1,964	
4. Legal Expenses ...	1,63,000	1,59,230	1,28,000	1,26,609	
5. Education ...	9,318	8,557	9,294	8,932	
6. Medical ...	12,395	12,001	12,383	12,138	
7. Public Works ...	89,927	50,912	1,68,363	76,889	
8. Religious Expenses	7,094	6,716	7,079	6,565	
9. Purchase of property	44,000	6,278	8,000	5,871	
10. Miscellaneous ...	11,500	9,585	8,000	6,851	
11. Pension and Gratuity	13,000	11,943	13,000	11,806	
12. Forest ...	712	593	712	587	
13. Unforeseen ...	3,500	2,681	3,500	635	
14. Loans and Advances	2,000	1,959	2,000	1,942	
ii. Sansar ...	12,960	12,960	13,860	13,785	
iii. Donation ...	8,625	8,551	9,945	9,865	
iv. Repayment of debts etc ...	25,000	13,183	20,000	16,554	
v. Advance to Nij Tahabil ...	80,000	79,591	50,000	49,984	
vi. State Contribution	2,50,000	2,50,000	2,80,000	2,80,000	
vii. State Contribution to His Highness's Tour of Europe	—	—	1,50,000	1,50,000	
Total ...	11,74,841	10,54,746	13,24,493	12,03,997	
Closing Balance :—					
Cash ...	1,73,045	2,28,090	1,76,726	2,11,813	
Imperial Bank ...	72,050	1,08,629	1,00,500	1,00,000	
State Bank ...	—	—	—	30,000	
Sinking Fund ...	—	—	25,000	25,000	
Advances ...	1,01,073	1,25,343	1,25,343	2,05,523	
Loans issued ...	86,293	95,082	95,082	95,187	
Total ...	4,32,461	5,57,144	5,82,651	7,28,421	
Grand Total ...	16,07,302	16,11,890	19,07,144	13,32,418	

CHIEF MINISTER'S OFFICE.
TRIPURA STATE.

To

Major His Highness Bisama-Samara-Bijoyee Mahamahodaya
Pancha-Srijukta Maharaja Manikya
SIR BIR BIKRAM KISHORE DEV BARMAN
BAHADUR, K. C. S. I.,
Ruler of Tripura.

Dated, Agartala, the 27th February, 1943.

MAY IT PLEASE YOUR HIGHNESS,

On behalf of the *Mantri Parishad*, I have the honour most respectfully to submit the accompanying consolidated Administration Report of the State for the three years 1347, 1348 and 1349 T. E., covering the period from 14th April 1937 to 13th April, 1940, as compiled and edited by the Political Department of the State.

2. Owing to various untoward circumstances, the practice of publishing a general Administration Report annually in English, on the basis of departmental Reports, had to be discontinued for a time after the issue of 1346 T. E.; but it has been decided to make the series up-to-date, and it is hoped that the gap will now be filled up without delay.

3. There have been important administrative changes since the period under report closed. Rai J. C. Sen Bahadur, B. A., B. C. S. (Retd.), who controlled the Administration during the first two years of the triennium as the sole Minister, and was the Chief Minister after the inauguration of the Reforms in 1349 T. E., has unfortunately retired owing to failing health, and so has Dr. M. M. Majumdar, L. M. S., Minister for Public Health and Sanitation. Rai J. M. Chatterjee Bahadur M. A., B. C. S. (Retd.), who held the important portfolios of Finance and Revenue, is no longer—it is sad to mention—in the land of the living, while Dr. Majumdar's successor in office, Thakur R. M. Dev Barman, I am sorry to add, has likewise passed away. Rai Dewan K. P. Dutt Bahadur, M. A. B. L., M. R. A. S., F. R. E. S., Chief Secretary to Your Highness, who was in charge of important departments during the period has also retired.

4. All these changes constitute a more or less serious handicap in the matter of turning out this report, to which have been added the difficulties caused by the world war, notably those in the shape of scarcity of paper and press materials, in view of which it has been decided to omit the usual statistical index, though steps have been taken to make the narrative portion self-contained and in some respects more comprehensive.

I have the honour to be
Your Highness's most obedient servant,

Rana Bodhjung,

CHIEF MINISTER AND PRESIDENT,
MANTRI PARISHAD.

MAP
OF
TRIPURA STATE

Scale $\frac{1}{1\ \text{Million}}$ or 1 Inch to 15·783 Miles.

Miles 10 5 0 10 20 30 40 Miles

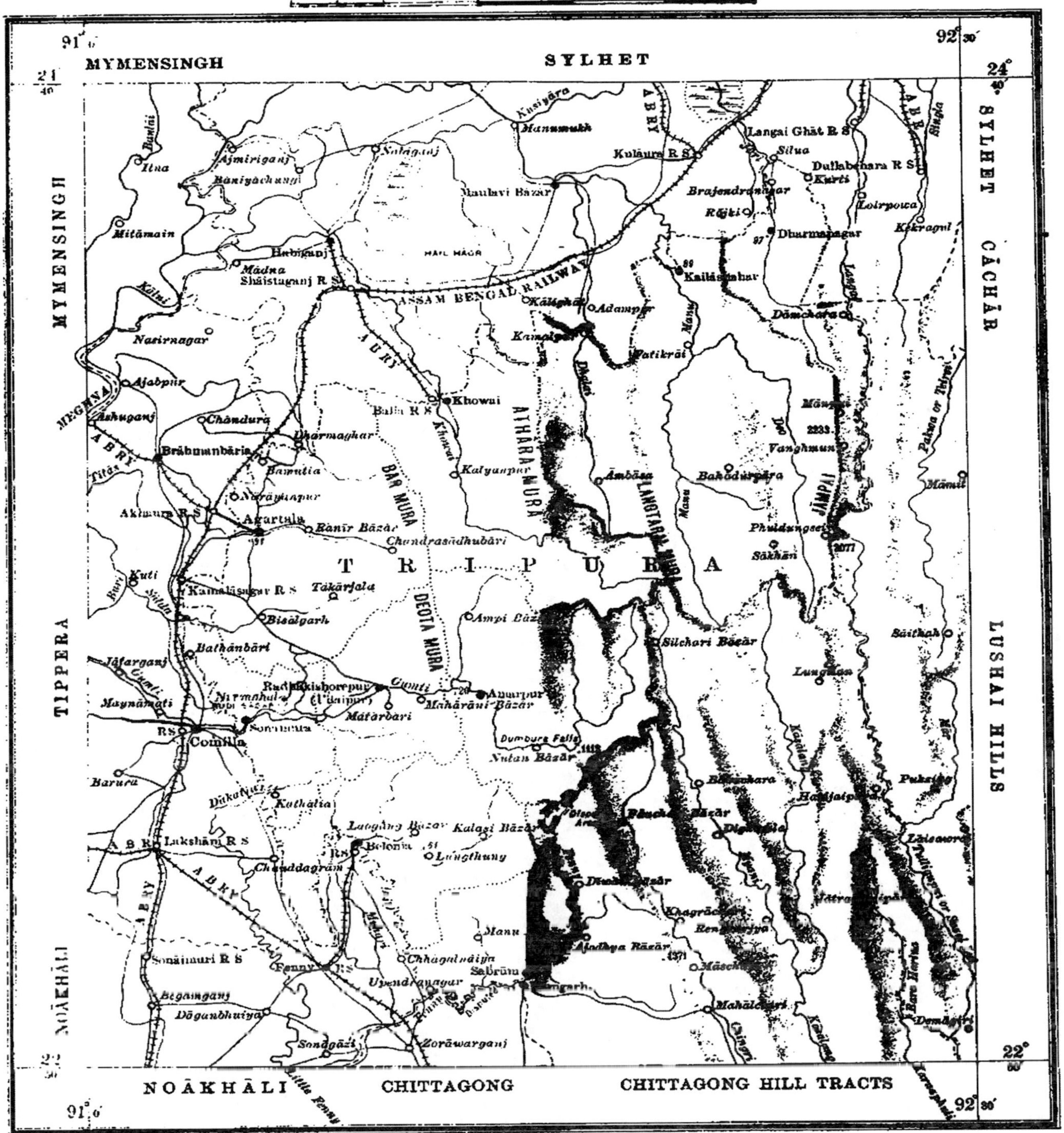

Based upon Survey of India Maps & Published with the Permission of the Surveyor General of India, 1936.

REG NO 1441. E 37 – 1000. HELIO. S. I. O. CALCUTTA

Head quarters: Districts or States	● Agartala	Boundaries, State & District	
Ditto Sub-divisions	• Amarpur	Ditto Sub-division	
Other Towns or Large Villages	○ *Maynāmati*	Railways, Metre gauge	
District Names	TIPPERA	Roads, Metalled, Others	

1st Edition 1937.

Book Twenty-nine
Consolicated Administration Report of the Tripura State for 1347-49 T. E. (1937-1940 A.D.)

REPORT ON THE ADMINISTRATION OF THE TRIPURA STATE FOR 1347 T. E.—1349 T. E. (1937-1940.)

CHAPTER I—GENERAL AND POLITICAL.

Area of the State—4,116 sq. miles.

Population (Census 1941—provisional)—5,13,952.

Gross income—(1) Total for the triennium—Rs. 1, 11, 42, 994.
Annual average of the triennium—Rs. 37,14,331.
(2) Annual based on the average for previous five years, i. e. 1342—1346 T. E. (inclusive)—Rs. 30,73,104.

Tribute—Nil.

Ruler—Major His Highness The Bishama-Samara-Bijayee Mahamahodaya Pancha-Srijukta Maharaja Manikya Sir Bir Bikramkishore Dev Barman Bahadur, K. C. S. I., Maharaja of Tripura. *Born*—19th August, 1908. *Caste*—*Kshatriya* of the Lunar Race.

Jubraj—Sreela-Sreejukta Maharajkumar Kirit Bikram Kishore Dev Barman, Jubraj Goswami Bahadur. *Born*—12th December 1933.

I.

The TRIENNIUM under report commenced under good auspices in the State.

2. There was of course no indication at its advent of the approaching world-conflagration which was to break out towards its close in Europe under the garb of a mere local war. The improvement noticeable in the general economic condition at the end of the year preceding, continued, and the masses looked forward to better times in view of the apparent upward tendency of prices of indigenous crops, while some fall-off in the prices of jute and cotton in evidence was counteracted by increased demand for exports, specially of forest produce. The rainfall was not, however seasonable, and floods affected portions of the State and contiguous parts of the attached Zemindaries, mainly in the Gumti and Fenny valleys, with a serious breach in the embankment of the Gumti early in 1349 T. E. On the outbreak of the European war in the same year

Economic condition and health.

prices of some imported necessaries suddenly shot up, taking away a good deal from the expectations of the agricultural population and worsening the position of the middle classes, which was more or less unsatisfactory throughout. No definite rise in the wages of labour was also noticeable. There were outbreaks, mostly sporadic, of cholera and small-pox in some Divisions, with high mortality from the first-named disease for a time in Kailashahar, saving which public health in the triennium was on the whole good.

The finances of the year.

3. The period under review started with an aggregate opening balance in the State proper and the Zemindaries, of Rs. 22,44,465, inclusive of unadjusted advances and bonds, against Rs. 14,02,434, the corresponding figure for the previous three years. With the above opening balance of Rs. 22,44,465, and the gross receipts which stood at Rs. 1,11,42,994, the total amount available for expenditure during the period was Rs. 1,33,87,459, against Rs. 1,07,40,716, of the preceding three years, while the total expenditure amounted to Rs. 1,16,32,308, against Rs. 84,96,251. The closing balance left was thus Rs. 17,55,151, against Rs. 22,44,465.

II.

HIS HIGHNESS AND THE TRIENNIUM.

4. The period under report was characterised by intense personal activities on the part of His Highness the Maharaja Manikya Bahadur, both in respect of Administrative measures and Tours which included an extensive world tour.

ADMINISTRATIVE REFORMS.

The Vidyapattan Scheme.

5. On the 24th Baisakh, 1347 T. E. corresponding to the 7th May, 1937, His Highness laid the foundation-stone of the Maharaja Manikya College building near Agartala in furtherance of the "Vidyapattan Scheme" previously sanctioned.

Municipal reforms.

6. At the *Bijaya Dashami Darbar* held on the 29th Aswin (15th October, 1937) of the same year, His Highness was pleased to announce Municipal reforms in the State on the basis of popular franchise, which received grateful appreciation all round. A law has since been passed and the Agartala Municipality reconstituted after election.

Nagar Samities.

7. At the *Mahanavami Darbar* on the 16th Aswin, 1348 T. E. (3rd October, 1938) there was an announcement of the establishment of *Nagar Samities* or Town Councils in all Divisional headquarters in the interior of the State, pending the constitution of full-fledged municipalities. This announcement has also since been given effect to by legislation.

8. At the same Darbar His Highness announced the introduction of compulsory Free Primary education in the Howrah Valley as the first step towards initiation of the policy throughout the State.

Compulsory Free Primary Education.

9. The 1st Baisakh, 1349 T. E. (14th April, 1939) which was the new year's day in the State according to the local era, must be regarded as a red letter day in its annals, as at a largely attended *Darbar* on that day His Highness was pleased to proclaim amidst popular rejoicings the grant of a written Constitution to the people on the basis of a policy of their increased association with the Government, and embracing the subjoined administrative reforms, namely :

The State Constitution—Popular franchise.

(*i*) The establishment of a *Rajsava* or Privy Council as an advisory body, executive and judicial, consisting of experienced and noted persons, official and non-official ;

(*ii*) The improvement and reorganisation of the High Court ;

(*iii*) The establishment of a Council of Ministers consisting of a Chief Minister, and other Ministers not exceeding four in number ;

(*iv*) The establishment of a Legislative Assembly possessing adequate legislative and recommendatory powers with a popular majority and a more or less wide franchise ;

(*v*) The establishment on elective principle of village unions or *Mandalis* as territorial electoral units with powers, executive and judicial ;

(*vi*) The introduction of an improved system of financial administration and audit with a complete separation of the Ruler's personal budget from the State Budget, on an allocation to the former of ten per cent. of the annual income of the State.

The peroration of the Proclamation was worthy of the subject and the occasion :

"It is my earnest prayer to God Almighty", Observed His Highness, addressing the vast gathering, "that the governing and the governed in this ancient State may now by His Grace join hands in a new spirit of co-operation and enhanced amity, and restore to it by combined efforts all its pristine glory, no longer indeed the glory of a conquering Military State as in the olden times, but the abiding glory and prestige of an organised State, where traditional Indian culture harmonises with modern thought in shaping the guiding principle, and rendering it invulnerable in the prosperity, happiness and contentment of the people."

10. Anxious to provide for a strong Executive to conduct the administration of the State and to give speedy effect to the reforms indicated in the Proclamation, His Highness was pleased to constitute and appoint under his *Robakari* dated the 9th Baisakh, 1349 T. E., a Mantri Parishad (or Council of Ministers), consisting of the marginally noted five Ministers to be in charge of the Executive Government of the State with wide powers of joint and individual disposal, delegated and defined.

Mantri Parishad or Council of Ministers.

1. Manyabara Rai Jyotish Chandra Sen Bahadur, B. A., B. C. S., (Retd.) Chief Minister
2. Manyabara Raja Rana Bodhjung Bahadur, F. R. G. S., Minister-in-charge, Reforms, Education and other Depts.
3. Rai Jatindra Mohan Chatterjee Bahadur, M. A., B. C. S., (Retd.) Finance Minister.
4. Thakur Kamini Kumar Singh, Minister-in-charge, Village Uplift, Agriculture and other Deptts.
5. Doctor Manimay Majumdar, L. M. S. Minister-in-charge, Public Health, Medical and other Deptts.

11. Towards the close of 1348 T.E. (1938–39 A.D.) His Highness was pleased to recall to Agartala for assistance in the work of the formulation of a scheme of Reforms Development, Dewan Bahadur B. K. Sen, M. A., B. L., Ex-Dewan of the State, who had already been co-operating in matters relating to the proposed All-India Federation. On the constitution of the Council of Ministers, the Dewan Bahadur was placed in charge of all spade work towards the initiation of measures of reform in co-operation with it.

Special machinery for Reforms work.

12. Another important measure of the period was the creation of a separate fund exclusively for Road Development, under His Highness's order of the 17th Agrahayan, 1347 T. E. (3rd December, 1937). The cultivated areas in the State generally fringing its frontiers, the lack of suitable communication with the interior stood in the way of proper distribution of agricultural produce—a fact that operated to provide an artificial stimulus for export to the detriment of the people including the growers themselves, who were often placed at the mercy of outside traders. With a view to prevent this uneconomic exploitation, and with the object of financing the opening out of the country by development of communications, the Government of the State imposed a duty on rice and paddy exported for trade purposes, and earmarked the amount thereof for road construction. A substantial portion of the income from Road cess, and the receipts from Road traffic monopolies have also been added to the fund since, and a qualified Road Engineer appointed to be in charge of all constructions, with Advisory committees in Divisions to co-operate.

Road Fund and Road Development.

III.

TOURS AND NOTABLE INCIDENTS.

13. His Highness's tours during the first year of the triennium commenced with a visit to Ranchi, extending from the 12th Asharh, 1347 T. E. (26th June 1937) to the 5th Bhadra (21st August) following, in the course of which His Highness, who was accompanied by Her Highness the

Summer tour in 1347—Ranchi.

Maharani Saheba, paid flying visits to some other places, including one to Bombay in July to receive His Highness's sister the Jubrani Saheba of Baria and her father-in-law, His Highness the Maharaja Saheb of Baria, on their return from Europe. A week's shooting excursion in the Ker forests in Palamau followed, and on the 6th Bhadra (22nd August), His Highness returned to Calcutta with the intention of joining a frontier regiment on active service in Waziristan, as arranged at his request by the Political Department, though unfortunately the trip had to be abandoned owing to a bad attack of fever with which His Highness was laid up at the last moment. His Highness went back to Ranchi thereafter for change, returning ultimately to Agartala via Panna and Calcutta on the 21st Aswin (7th October).

Visit to Darjeeling.

14. On being invited by His Excellency the Right Honourable Sir John Anderson, P. C., G. C. B., G. C. S. I., the then Governor of Bengal, on the eve of his departure from India, His Highness visited Darjeeling on the 12th Kartick, 1347 T. E. (29th October, 1937), and after a stay of a couple of days at the Government House returned to Agartala on the 18th Kartick (4th November).

Tour in the interior.—Military camping.

15. His Highness was pleased to camp out with some State troops at Melaghar in the Sonamura Division from the 30th Kartick to the 3rd Agrahayan, 1347 T. E. (16th to 19th November, 1937) and later on in Khowai and Kalyanpur from the 25th to the 29th Falgun (9th to 13th March, 1938).

Winter tour.

16. There was the usual cold weather visit to Calcutta from the 26th Agrahayan to the 28th Poush (12th December, 1937 to 12th January, 1938), a very important function in connection with which was an At-Home party at the Tripura House attended by 250 guests, foremost among whom were His Highness Maharaja Sir Sayaji Rao Gaekwad, G. C. S. I., G. C. I. E., (the late lamented) Ruler of Baroda, Her Highness the Maharani Saheba of Baroda, Her Highness the Maharani Saheba of Cooch Behar, Their Highnesses the Maharajas of Jaipur, Bhavnagar and Panna, and the Rulers of Mayurbhanj, Bamra, Khandpara, Nilgiri and Nayagarh, as also His Excellency Vice Admiral Sir Alexander Ramsay the Naval Commander in Chief, and Rear Admiral and Mrs. Fitzherbert. His Highness attended, on invitation, all functions of the season at the Belvedere and the Government House, as well as those arranged by His Highness the Maharaja of Jaipur, Her Highness the Maharani Saheba of Cooch Behar, His Excellency the Naval Commander in Chief, and Rear Admiral and Mrs. Fitzherbert. His Highness the Maharaja and Her Highness the Maharani Saheba of Bhavnagar, the Raja Saheb of Khairagarh and the Raja Bahadur of Bonai with his younger brother were guests of His Highness at the Tripura House for sometime during the season.

17. Another visit to Calcutta about the close of the year followed from 16th Chaitra 1347 T. E. (30th March, 1938) and His Highness was in residence at the Tripura House with Her Highness the Maharani Saheba for sometime thereafter.

Tours and incidents in 1348 T. E.—the birth of a Maharajkumari.

18. The very first happy event of the year 1348 T. E. was the birth at the Tripura House, of a second daughter to His Highness on the 10th Baisakh, (23rd April, 1938) which led to universal rejoicings in the State. His Highness the Maharaja Saheb of Panna came to stay with Their Highnesses in Calcutta for some time on the auspicious occasion.

Grihaprabesh ceremony of Nirmahal Palace.

19. His Highness returned to the State on the 28th Baisakh (11th May) and proceeded to perform on the 29th idem (12th May) the *Grihaprabesh* ceremony of the newly-built lake view Palace 'Nirmahal' on the Rudrasagar in Sonamura Division.

Visit to Shillong.

20. His Highness with Her Highness the Maharani Saheba visited and stayed at Shillong thereafter throughout the summer season, and had the pleasure, during the stay, of entertaining at dinner, His Excellency the Governor of Assam and the Resident for the Eastern States, and of joining His Excellency's Dinner party at the Pinewood Hotel. His Highness also visited Digboi on the 30th Sraban (15th August, 1938) on the invitation of the management of the Assam Oil Company and received a most cordial reception.

Bombay Conference of Princes and Ministers.

21. On the 5th Agrahayan, 1348 (21st November, 1938) His Highness left with Her Highness the Maharani Saheba for Calcutta *en route* to Bombay to attend a conference of Princes and Ministers arranged by the Chamber of Princes for the 25th November, 1938. His Highness was present at all the meetings of the session and achieved signal success in securing adequate representation of the Eastern Group of States and a revision of the constitution of the Chamber for the purpose. His Highness's efforts were highly appreciated by all concerned.

Visit to Rajpipla.

22. On the 15th Agrahayan (1st December) following, His Highness visited Rajpipla on invitation, and attended the marriage ceremony of Maharajkumar Heerasingji of Baria, proceeding therefrom to Devgarh Baria for a couple of days as the guest of His Highness the Maharaja Maharawal Saheb of Baria.

Calcutta and the Xmas season.

23. His Highness spent as before the Christmas season in Calcutta attending a number of functions of the occasion, including those at the Belvedere and the Government House, and had the honour of His Excellency the Viceroy and the Marchioness of Linlithgow's company at a luncheon party at the Tripura House on the 4th Pous (20th December, 1938) while His Excellency (the late lamented) Lord Brabourne, Governor of Bengal, was pleased to join him at dinner at the Tripura House on the 20th Pous (5th January, 1939), another interesting function being, as before His Highness's At-Home party attended by 300 distinguished guests.

24. On the 13th Pous, (29th December, 1938) His Highness had the pleasure of presiding over the Calcutta session of the *Kshatriya Mahasabha* on the invitation of the Reception Committee, and had a befitting ovation as a Ruling Prince representing the great and historic Lunar Race of kings, while His Highness's presidential address was heard with rapt attention.

The Kshatriya Mahasabha

25. A unique event that followed was His Highness's visit of two days to the Santiniketan and the Viswabharati at Bolpur, on the 22nd Poush, corresponding to the 7th January 1939, on the invitation of the great poet, the late lamented Dr. Rabindranath Tagore. His Highness received a most enthusiastic welcome from the august host, the Governing Body of the Viswabharati, as well as the local public, and at the Reception held, host and guest feelingly recalled and referred to the most intimate relations that had prevailed between the poet and four generations of Rulers of Tripura over half a century, while His Highness gave expression to his sense of profound satisfaction at the fulfilment of his long-cherished desire to meet the revered Poet at the centre of his activities, and to his high appreciation of the aims and objects of the famous international seat of learning, so ably inaugurated by the poet.

Visit to the Santiniketan.

A TOUR ROUND THE WORLD.

26. The closing year of the triennium witnessed His Highness's third European tour which later on developed into a world tour under peculiar circumstances, and took a sensational turn owing to the outbreak of the European war.

The world tour of 1349 T. E

27. The original object of the tour was confined mainly to a temporary residence by His Highness, on grounds of health, at one of the Spas of South France and a short trip to America. His Highness who was accompanied in the tour by his sister the *Jubrani Saheba* of Baria and a personal staff consisting of Captain Maharajkumar Durjay Kishore Dev Barman Bahadur, Private Secretary, Captain Kumar Ramendra Kishore Dev Barman Bahadur, Assistant Military Secretary, (Captain) Thakur Jogendra Chandra Dev Barman, Staff Officer, Mr. Dwijendra Chandra Dutta, Personal Assistant, and Lieutenant-Colonel O. C. Pulley, I. A., Emeritus Chief Staff Officer, left Agartala with Her Highness the Maharani Saheba on the 9th Jaistha 1349 T. E. (23rd May, 1939) reaching Bombay via Calcutta and Panna on the 31st May, and sailed for Marseilles on the 3rd June by the P & O Mail Boat S. S. Comorin, arriving in London on the 30th June via Paris. Her Highness stayed on at Panna pending a visit to Mussoorie during His Highness's absence, while the *Jubrani Saheba* of Baria and Colonel Pulley joined His Highness, respectively, at Bombay and Paris.

His Highness leaves India and reaches London.

28. On the eve of departure, His Highness was pleased to constitute and appoint a State Council, under His *Robakari*, dated the 1st Jaistha 1349 T. E., composed of the subjoined members, to carry on with full powers the administration of the State during his absence ;

A State Council set up.

Mahamanyabara Maharajkumar Brajendra Kishore Dev Barman Bahadur,
President.

Manyabara Raja Rana Bodhjung Bahadur, F. R. G. S.,
Minister, Vice President.

Manyabara Rai J. C. Sen Bahadur, B. A., B. C. S. **(Retd.),**
Chief Minister.

Rai Dewan Kamala Prasad Dutt Bahadur, M. A., B. L., F. R. **Econ.** S., M. R. A. S.,
Chief Secretary to His Highness.

Dewan Bahadur B. K. Sen, M. A., B. L.,
Ex-Dewan, Tripura State.

29. On the 12th July His Highness left London and set out on the trans-Atlantic trip planned, hoping to return to France shortly to settle down there for some time, as previously contemplated. This hope was not however destined to be fulfilled.

30. His Highness reached New York on the 17th July, and after paying flying visits to Washington, Mount Vernon, and Chicago in the United States, as well as Toranto, the Niagara Falls, Ottwa and Montreal in Canada, returned to New York, and left for France on the 16th August, reaching Aix Les Banes on the 22nd idem. The only item of interest on return to France was a visit to the League of Nations at its seat on the 28th August, but hardly the visit was over, an alarming development in the international situation necessitated a hurried journey to London on advice on the 31st idem.

First American trip & return to France.

31. The entire programme was thereafter upset, and His Highness started immediately on the 1st September on a trans-Pacific return journey to India. Barely two days after His Highness sailed, the European war broke out on the 3rd September 1939, and the voyage continued amidst the grave perils of the situation till His Highness reached America again on the 12th September.

His Highness starts on the return journey.

32. There was a stay in America with more or less extensive movements in the interior, after which His Highness left San Francisco on the 13th October, 1939, arriving at Calcutta ultimately on the 8th Pous (24th December, 1939), seven months after his departure from India.

The trans-Pacific voyage and return to Calcutta.

33. During the Pacific voyage, His Highness visited all the places of importance *en route* and it will suffice to say briefly, that the world tour covered, on the whole, visits to France, England, the United States, Canada, New Zealand, Australia, Java, Bali, Malaya, Singapore and Burma, with trips to many important centres in the interior of these countries—an itinerary too long to detail.

34. A few of the numerous notable events of the great tour are summarised below :—

Notable incidents of the world tour.

(1) While in New York, His Highness was accorded an official reception at the World's Fair, where he reviewed the march past staged by the U. S. A. Marines in his honour, and afterwards had tea with the management of the Fair at the Federal Pavilion.

Reception at the World's Fair in New York.

(2) Mr. Franklin Delano Roosevelt, President of the United States of America, received His Highness at a private interview in the White Hall at Washington, D. C. at 3 P. M. on the 31st July, 1939. President Roosevelt received His Highness very cordially and later on presented His Highness with his autographed portrait as a souvenir. Captain Kumar R. K. Dev Varma Bahadur, and Mr. Mallet, Counsellor to the British Embassy at Washington, accompanied His Highness to the interview.

Meeting with President Roosevelt.

(3) His Highness, who was *en route* when war was declared against Germany, cabled immediately on arrival in New York to His Excellency the Viceroy, placing, towards the successful prosecution of the war, at the disposal of His Majesty the King Emperor, His Highness's personal services as well as the entire resources of the State—an offer that was thankfully acknowledged by His Excellency on His Majesty's behalf.

Outbreak of the great war,—His Highness's offer to His Majesty.

(4) On arrival at Los Angeles, California, His Highness broadcast a speech over the California Radio System expatiating on his expectations about the sure victory of Britain and the great part that India was destined to play in the war. His Highness's speech was appreciated by the American Press.

Broadcast speech from Los Angeles.

(5) His Highness was entertained at a Dinner Party given in his honour by Mr. Paul D. Butler, British Consul General, and Mrs. Butler, on the 9th October at San Francisco.

Dinner Party given by the British Consul General at San Francisco.

(6) On the 11th October, His Highness was given an official reception, elaborately arranged, at the Golden Gate Exposition at San Francisco, where all the customary honours due were accorded to His Highness. A salute of 13 guns were fired, and a guard of honour furnished by American troops presented arms on arrival of His Highness, who was then shown round the Exposition and entertained at a Luncheon Party.

Reception at the Golden Gate Exposition at San Francisco.

(7) On his way to Australia, His Highness, on invitation, lunched on the 24th October, with Mr. Hansen, Governor of American Samoa (South Seas) at the Government House at Pago Pago.

Luncheon at the Government House at Pago Pago, (Samoa.)

Reception in the Fiji Islands.

(8) His Excellency Sir Harry Luke, Governor of the Fiji Islands entertained His Highness at a luncheon party at the Government House at Suva on the 27th October, 1939, during His Highness's short stay there.

Reception by the Indian Community.

(9) On board the S. S. Maripose, as the ship arrived, the Indian community in the Fiji Islands represented by Mr. Vishnu, member of the Fiji Legislative Assembly, Mr. Raghvanand, District Commissioner, as well as Dr. and Mrs. Gopalam, accorded their cordial welcome to His Highness on his auspicious visit to the Fiji Islands.

Reception in Australia.

(10) On arrival at Sydney on the 2nd November, His Highness was received likewise on board the S. S. Maripose, by representatives both of the Federal Government of Australia, and the Provincial Government of New South Wales. His Highness lunched with His Excellency Lord Gowrie, V. C., Governor General of Australia on the 3rd November at the Admiralty House, Sydney, and in the same afternoon, had a private interview with His Excellency Lord Wakehurst, Governor of New South Wales, at the Government House.

Meeting with a Balinese Chief.

(11) During his stay in Bali, His Highness met the Chief of Gianjar, Zelf Bestuurder (Home Ruler), Anak Agoeng Ngorah Agoeng, at the latter's Puri (Palace) at Gianjar on the 28th November. Mr. Van Romondt, Controller of Gianjar introduced His Highness to the Zelf Bestuurder and acted as interpreter. His Highness was very cordially received by the Zelf Bestuurder and was treated to light refreshments at the Palace.

Return to Calcutta.

35. Thus ended, in any case, the forty-four thousand mile tour round the world, and His Highness the Maharaja Manikya Bahadur was enthusiastically received, as soon as the S. S. Amra pulled up alongside the Outram Ghat, by the members of the Ruling Family, many of the leading officials of the State, and the public including a representative gathering of the Tripura Hitasadhini Sabha. Heartfelt delight mixed with a sense of great relief was noticeable on every face on His Highness's safe return after a most perilous voyage.

His Highness's return to the State.

36. His Highness remained in Calcutta for a fortnight, and returned to Agartala on the 11th of Magh (25th January, 1940). The deep sense of popular relief on His Highness's safe return to the State manifested itself in many a loyal demonstration that followed, and His Highness was the recipient of a number of addresses from public bodies including one from the Agartala Municipality.

IV.

OTHER NOTEWORTHY MATTERS.

Coronation of His Majesty King George VI.

37. A unique event of the period demanding foremost mention, was the Coronation in London of His most gracious Majesty King Geroge VI, Emperor of India, and Her Majesty Queen Elizabeth, on the 12th May, 1937. His Highness the Maharaja Manikya Bahadur cabled to His Majesty offering his loyal and respectful congratulations on the happy occasion, with earnest prayers for Their Majesties' long and prosperous reign. In reply His Majesty was graciously pleased to cable to His Highness in the following terms—"It has given the Queen and Myself much pleasure to receive your congratulations and good wishes on the occasion of Our Coronation for which We wish to express Our sincere thanks."

38. In celebration of the great event in the State, there were military and police parades, prayers offered in temples, churches and mosques throughout, with illumination and attendant festivities, including refreshments arranged for school children, while the auspicious day was observed as a public holiday. A proclamation covering the announcement of the Coronation was published in an extraordinary issue of the State Gazette and Major (now Lieut.-Colonel) Rana Jodha Jung Bahadur, M. B. E., M. C., Commandant of the State Forces, attended the ceremony in London.

Ruling Princes' visit to Tripura.

39. On being invited by His Highness the Maharaja Manikya Bahadur, His Highness Mahendra Maharaja Sir Yadvendra Singhji, K. C. S. I., K. C. I. E., Maharaja of Panna, Raja Birendra Bahadur Singhji, Ruler of Khairagarh, Raja Bahadur Narendra Singhji and Maharajkumar Puspendra Singhji of Panna, Diwan Bahadur Chandrabhan Singhji, Chief of Garrauli and a few other guests paid a visit to the State, arriving at Agartala with Their Highnesses from Calcutta on the 30th Pous 1347 T. E. (14th January, 1938).

40. The honoured guests were accorded a most befitting and cordial welcome by all sections of people, irrespective of caste and creed, on arrival at Agartala and during visits that followed to different places, including the Rudrasagar, Debendranagar, Khowai and Kalyanpur in the State, as also Comilla and Mainamati in the Zemindaries. Special mention may be made of the civic address, the State Banquet, and the parties in their honour at Agartala, the capital of the State, as well as the addresses presented and functions arranged, in particular, at Comilla, the headquarters station of His Highness's Zemindaries and of the British District of Tippora, by the Municipality, the District Board, the European Club, the Hindu Mahasabha, the Maharaja Beerchandra Public Library, and the general public of the town. At Kalyanpur the guests had a magnificient reception from thousands of people gathering from far and near, and had an enjoyable Shikar, in the course of which a rogue tusker was shot. The distinguished visitors left Agartala for Calcutta on the 9th Magh, 1347 T. E. (23rd January, 1938) amidst a hearty send-off.

41. A happy event of the triennium was the appointment of His Highness the Maharaja Manikya Bahadur to the honorary rank of Captain in His Majesty's Regular Army in June, 1937, all offices and institutions being closed for a day on the occasion.

His Highness's military honours.

42. An interesting item of the programme of the Navami Darbar, 1347 T. E. (14th October, 1937) was the presentation by His Highness to Manyabara Rana Bodhjung Bahadur, (then Chief Secretary to His Highness) with the *Sanad* and *Khilat* of the title of "Raja" conferred on him by the Viceroy.

Rana Bodhjung Bahadur's new honours.

43. Lieutenant-Colonel H. W. C. Robson, O. B. E., continued as Agent to the Governor General, Eastern States, up to the forenoon of the 11th April, 1939, where-after he was relieved by Lieutenant-Colonel L. E. Barton. The designation of the office was changed to "Resident for the Eastern States" and the headquarters transferred from Ranchi to Calcutta with effect from the 1st July, 1937. Lieutenant-Colonel Robson visited the State from 2nd to 5th February, 1938, and again from the 24th to 26th March, 1939, and was pleased during the visits to go round the Central Jail, the Victoria Memorial Hospital, the Administration Secretariat, the Agartala U. K. Academy and the High Court. His successor, Lieutenant-Colonel Barton, was at Agartala on official visit from the 27th to 29th March, 1940, in the course of which he visited the Central Jail, the V. M. Hospital, the Secretariat, the High Court and the Cantonment, and was pleased to lay the foundation-stone of the King Emperor's Anti-Tuberculosis Hospital, as also to open the New Mogra road. A very interesting event of the occasion was the Resident's visit to Mogra (accompanied by His Highness) where he received a magnificent welcome from the Talukdars and other tenants of His Highness's Zemindaries. Another notable function was a Darbar held at the Ujjayanta Palace in which Colonel Barton presented His Highness's Private Secretary Rai Dewan Kamala Prasad Dutt Bahadur with the badge and *Sanad* of "Rai Bahadur".

Agent to the Governor General—Resident for the Eastern States.

44. On the 6th April, 1940, the Hon'ble Maharaja Srish Chandra Nandy of Cossimbazar, Minister, Government of Bengal, paid an official visit to Agartala, accompanied by Mr. S. C. Majumdar Chief Engineer, Irrigation, to discuss with the Government of Tripura the question of introduction of measures in control of the floods of the river Gumti, in connection with the general problem on the subject under consideration.

Visit of a Bengal Minister.

45. The subjoined Administrative measures and changes of the period are noticeable :—

Some important measures and events.

(1) A Geological Department was created under His Highness's order, dated the 7th September, 1937, and organised during the triennium under report, with appointment of a Geologist and of an expert Geological Advisor.

Vidyapattan Governing Committee.

(2) A committee designated "Vidyapattan Governing Committee," consisting of 10 members with the Minister as its President, was appointed under His Highness's order, dated the 7th Jaistha, 1348 T. E. (21st May, 1938) to carry out the Vidyapattan Scheme of education, and a sum of Rs. 50,000 was placed at its disposal at the first instance. Construction of the college buildings was undertaken during that year.

Charter for Maharaja Match Factory.

(3) A Charter incorporating the Maharaja Match Factory was granted during the year 1348 T. E. The factory formerly belonged to a private person.

Prospecting license for petroleum.

(4) A prospecting license for natural petroleum including natural gas in respect of 250 square miles of State territory was granted to The Burmah Oil Company Ltd. (Scotland) for a period of 3 years.

Excise arrangement.

(5) The excise vendors in the State were formerly subject to payment of excise duty to the Government of Bengal for import of opium, *ganja* and *bhang* into the State through that Government. During the year 1347 T. E. (1937–38) the Government agreed, on the representation of the State, to supply the drugs duty free, with effect from the month of August, 1937, on condition that an equal amount of duty was levied on the drugs by the State.

Extradition.

(6) A reciprocal arrangement was entered into during the same year with the Government of India for extradition of persons accused of being concerned in traffic in opium and other dangerous drugs.

Tea control.

(7) To implement the agreement entered into with the Government of India, for a further period of five years, in respect of matters of control over extension of cultivation, production and export of tea, the Tripura Tea Control Act 1848 T. E. was passed in supercession of certain interim rules on the subject previously promulgated.

King Emperor's Anti-Tuberculosis Fund.

(8) Out of the contribution of Rs. 25,806-4-6 by the State to the King Emperor's Anti-Tuberculosis Fund, Rs. 24,515 was received back in March, 1940 for works in the State in furtherance of the object of the scheme, and a hospital building has been constructed, since, on a suitable site pending the establishment of a full-fledged Anti-Tuberculosis hospital.

Administrative changes—Chief Justice of the High Court.

(9) Mr. J. M. Das, B. L., Chief Judge of the Khas Adalat, (High Court) resigned early in the triennium after over 7 years' of meritorious service, highly appreciated all round ; Mr. K. C. Nag, B. A., M. B. E., Bar.-at-law, for sometime a Judge of the Calcutta High Court, was thereafter appointed in his place under the designation of Chief Justice of the State High Court.

(10) Rai Bahadur J. M. Chatterjee, M. A., B. C. S., a retired District Magistrate of Bengal (since deceased) joined, on appointment as Finance Minister of the State, on the 24th Magh, 1348 T. E. (7th February, 1939) and became a member of the Cabinet later on, as mentioned above.

Finance Minister.

(11) Rai Bahadur G. R. Dutt, a retired Deputy Superintendent of Police, Bengal, joined on 3rd Baisak, 1348 T. E. (16th April, 1938) on appointment as the Superintendent of Police, in succession to Rai Saheb A. C. Gupta, resigned, the designation of the office having, since, been changed to that of "Commissioner of the State Police."

Commissioner of Police.

(12) A very sad event of the period occurring on the 27th Pous, 1348 T. E. (12th January, 1939) was the accidental and untimely death, while on a railway journey to Lucknow, of Mr. S. C. Dev Barman, M. A. (Harvard), Senior Naib Dewan, one of the Departmental heads of the Administration, as the result of the derailment of the 9 Up Dehra Doon Express between Chicheki and Hazaribagh Road stations. In him the Government of Tripura has lost a most promising officer recruited from a noble family of the State, educated and specially trained overseas.

Accidental death of Senior Naib Dewan.

46. The discussions between His Excellency the Viceroy and the Rulers of Indian States regarding the establishment of the proposed all India Federation and the accession of the States thereto, were nearing completion, when in view of the outbreak of the war the matter had to be indefinitely postponed, as it was not possible for His Majesty's Government in the midst of the preoccupations caused by the war, to give active attention to the question—a decision that was communicated to the State in September, 1939.

All India Federation.

THE GREAT WAR AND TRIPURA'S INITIAL WAR ACTIVITIES.

47. As already mentioned in para 34 above, His Highness who was *en route* to America when War was declared against Germany on the 3rd September, 1939, wired to the Viceroy immediately on arrival in New York, placing his personal services and the entire resources of the State at the disposal of His Majesty's Government.

Offer of His Highness wired en voyage.

48. Towards the end of 1349 T. E. (1939–40) offers were made and announced of annual contributions of (i) Rs. 30,000 from the State to the Viceroy's War Purposes Fund, (ii) Rs. 15,000 from His Highness's personal funds to the Red Cross Society and the St. John's Ambulance Association, and (iii) Rs. 5,000 from the same source to the St. Dunstan's Fund. It was also decided to increase the strength of the Armed Police and the Militia at an estimated expenditure of Rs. 50,000 in view of the possible

Financial contributions and reorganisation of the forces.

utilisation of the regular State troops on duty outside the State, for which offer had promptly been made. A War Committee was also established under His Highness's orders dated the 19th Magh, 1349 T.E. (2nd February, 1940) more or less for the same purpose for which District War Committees in British India were formed.

49. All this however was only a small beginning, and nobody in this part of the world perhaps imagined at the time that the European War was destined to develop soon into a world conflagration, with a ruthless enemy thundering at India's very door. Yet the unforeseen has happened, and it has devolved upon Tripura, since, to extend considerably and intensify her War efforts, as future records will show.

CHAPTER II—LAND ADMINISTRATION.

Charge.

50. Rai J. C. Sen Bahadur B. A., B. C. S., (Retd.), Minister, controlled all the Departments of the Government of Tripura up to 9th Baisakh, 1349 T. E. (22nd April 1939) after which date, on the constitution of the *Mantri Parishat*, he was appointed Chief Minister, and the Revenue and General Department was transferred to the portfolio of Minister Rai J. M. Chatterjee Bahadur M. A., B. C. S., (Retd.). Thakur K. K. Singha continued to be the Departmental head under the Minister till the 9th Baisakh, 1349 T. E., when he was appointed as a Minister-Member of the Cabinet, and Thakur R. M. Deb Barma assumed charge of the Department as Secretary to the Minister.

Area held under Settlement.

51. As shown in the subjoined statement, the total area held under settlement and borne on the *toujis* at the close of 1349 T. E. was 606 sq. miles as against 603 sq. miles in 1347, and 619, in 1346, the closing year of the previous triennium. There was thus an abrupt and substantial fall in 1347 T. E., as compared with the previous triennium, which was due, *inter alia*, to the fact that in the Sadar Division alone a large number of new certificate cases had been instituted in 1346, for realisation of heavy arrears and all disposed of within the year, with the result that about 10 Sq. miles of land came over to Khas possession for the time being, under auction-purchase by the State. It is noticeable however that the figure which was abnormally low in 1347 T. E., was apparently rising again on a progressive scale through the succeeding years.

Kinds of settlement.	Area in square miles.			
	1346 T.E. *i. e.* at the close of the previous triennium.	1347 T.E.	1348 T.E.	1349 T.E.
Jote ...	324	311	311	313
Taluks ...	295	292	293	293
Total ...	619	603	604	606

Average rates of *jama*.

52. The average *Jama* per *kani* of jote lands in *khasmahals* exclusive of cesses stood at Rs. 1/0/11 pies against Rs. 1/1/11 pies in the previous triennium. The maximnm rate for jotes was Rs. 20/– though, it may be mentioned, that this high rate, while technically coming under the class, was exclusively confined to some small settlements of bazar or town land of advantagous position in great demand. The minimum rate was Annas 3 only as before. The corresponding maximum and minimum rates for *Taluks* practically continued to be Rs. 3/- and Rs. 0/1/6 per *kani*, excluding higher rates secured in some *Takshisi* settlements, generally of small area, in the capital town.

Sources of Land Revenue.

53. The different sources of land revenue demand and the collection under each head are detailed below :—

		Taluks.	*Khasmahal jotes.*	Bazar.	Cesses.	TOTAL.
Current demand. ...	1347 T. E.	1,54,037	5,21,086	8,572	66,940	7,50,635
	1348 T. E.	1,54,294	5,27,471	8,042	85,381	7,75,188
	1349 T. E.	1,54,365	5,30,246	7,397	74,719	7,66,727
Arrear demand upto the end of ...	1346 T. E.	3,57,601	19,36,312	5,864	1,81,732	24,81,509
	1347 T. E.	3,68,198	19,68,998	6,410	2,15,291	25,58,897
	1348 T. E.	3,83,027	20,67,219	4,112	2,16,149	26,70,507
Realisation upto the end of ...	1347 T. E.	1,45,400	4,79,476	8,045	62,812	6,95,733
	1348 T. E,	1,40,571	4,29,877	7,270	63,783	6,41,501
	1349 T. E.	1,43,622	4,76,906	6,756	60,282	6,87,566

Demand.

54. The above statement shows that the demand in 1349 T. E. under all heads was Rs. 7,66,727, and with the arrear demand of Rs. 26,70,507, the total demand stood at Rs. 34,37,234, against Rs. 33,34,085, and Rs. 22, 32, 144, in 1348 and 1347 T. E. respectively.

Collection.

55. The total collection in round figures under all heads in 1349 T. E. amounted to Rs. 6,87,566 (viz. Rs. 2,64,346 under current and Rs. 4,23,220 under arrear), against Rs. 6,41,501 (*i.e.* Rs. 2,51,565 current and Rs. 3,89,936 arrear) in 1348, and Rs. 6,95,733 (*i.e.* Rs. 2,50,863 current and Rs. 4,44,870 arrear) in 1347 T. E. The percentage of collection, as detailed in the subjoined statement, was for various reasons unsatisfactory.

	Current Collection.			Arrear Collection.		
	1347	1348	1349	1347	1348	1349
Khas Mahal ...	18·56	18·13	19·76	19·76	12·89	13·16
Taluki Mahal ...	78·96	77·85	80·69	6·67	5·55	4·97
Percentage of total collection	33·42	32·45	34·48	17·92	12·89	15·84

56. The average annual demand during the period was Rs. 7,64,183 against Rs, 7,46,542, of the previous triennium, and the average annual collection Rs. 6,74,938 against Rs. 7,09,739. The decline is due to an indirect cause, namely, the realisation of about a lac of rupees of the arrear demand by Certificate procedure in the Sadar Division, as a special step, in 1346 T. E., as referred to in para 51 above.

Demand and collection as compared with the previous triennium.

57. Altogether Rs. 15,496 requisitions, covering a demand of Rs. 6,83,798 were received during the three years; and 8,563 requisitions covering Rs. 9,77,572 were pending from 1346 T. E. The total number of requisitions was thus 24,059, covering a total demand of Rs. 16,61,365. Of these, 93 cases with a demand of Rs. 11,535 were rejected or struck off, and a sum of Rs. 52,955 in 1,572 cases was realised before decree ; while 6625 cases on the whole for realisation of Rs. 8,15,495 remained pending at the end of 1349 T. E.

Coercive measures—Certificates.

58. Orders under the provisions of the State Certificate Act were passed making the demands absolute, during the period, in 15,771 cases with a total demand of Rs. 7,80,465. Out of the total demand, Rs. 2,618, Rs. 4,612 and Rs. 18,017 were remitted or written off respectively in 1347, 1348 and 1349 T. E., and of the remainder, Rs. 1,77,110, Rs. 1,55,719 and Rs. 1,95,426 were actually realised, leaving a balance of Rs. 12,19,776, Rs. 12,12,557 and Rs. 14,43,379 respectively. The following table shows separately the amounts realised under heads "land revenue" and "miscellaneous" :—

Execution.

	Realisation of land revenue demands.	Realisation of miscellaneous demands.	Total.
1347 T.E.	Rs. 1,58,319	Rs. 18,791	Rs. 1,77,110
1348 T.E.	„ 1,40,890	„ 14,829	„ 1,55,719
1349 T.E.	„ 1,78,535	„ 16,891	„ 1,95,426

59. In view of the heavy accumulation of arrears, a scheme for improving collection has been drawn up and is under consideration.

Scheme for improving collection.

60. With 39 defaulting *Taluks* pending from the previous triennium, altogether 522 *Taluks* came in under the operation of the Sunset law during the period under report. Of these, 439 were released on payment of dues with penalty, and 34 *Taluks* were auctioned off, leaving a closing balance of 49. The corresponding figures for the previous triennium were as under : Balance brought forward from 1343 : 40, defaulting *Taluks* : 447, released on payment of dues and penalty : 381, auctioned : 67 and balance : 39.

Operation of the Sun-set Law.

5

61. Survey operations in respect of an area of 2,440 *drones*, comprising 361 *drones* of *taluk* and 2079 *drones* of *Khas Mahal*, were carried out in 1347 against a total of 3497 *drones* in the previous year: while an area of 3871 *drones*, comprising 644 *drones* of *taluk* and 3,227 *drones* of *Khas Mahal*, and that of 2412 *drones*, comprising 248 *drones* of *taluk* and 2164 *drones* of *Khas Mahal*, were surveyed in 1348 and 1349 T. E. respectively. Compared with the previous triennium, the total area surveyed during the period was less by 1719 *drones*.

Survey.

62. (1) The total area covered by original *Jotedari* settlement of waste land during the triennium was 483 *drones* against 476 *drones* in the previous triennium.

Settlement and re-settlement of *Jote* and *Taluk* land.

(2) The aggregate area of cultivated land brought under original settlement and re-settlement during the period stood at 5,790 *drones* against 9,025 of the preceding triennium, there being thus a marked decrease of 3,235 *drones* in respect of the operations in the triennium under report.

(3) *Taluki* settlement was effected in respect of a total area of 155 *drones*, during the triennium against 313 *drones* in the previous triennium.

Taluki settlement.

63. The following statement shows the net increase in the *jama* secured during the period by re-settlement of *Abadi jote* land as well as the *Nazarana* assessed as the result of the operations.

Results of re-settlement of *Jote* lands

	Amount		Average *Jama* (per *kani*)
	Increase in *jama*.	*Nazarana* assessed.	
1346 T.E.	Rs. 5,925	Rs. 35,353	0–6–8p.
1347 T.E.	Rs. 6,599	Rs. 30,246	0–10–9p.
1348 T.E.	„ 5,155	„ 22,177	0–10–9p.
1349 T.E.	„ 911	„ 20,616	0–14–6p.

64. During 1347 T. E., an area of 130 *drones* of waste land was settled for a prospective rental of Rs. 1,211, while in the following year 76 *drones* only were settled for Rs. 768. But in 1349 T. E. the area settled rose to 277 *drones* for a rental of Rs. 2,675. The average *jama* per *kani* obtained was 15 annas 5 pies, 10 annas 1 pie, and 9 annas 8 pies, in 1347, 1348 and 1349 T. E. respectively. In the closing year of the previous triennium the corresponding figures stood at: waste land

Results of *Jotedari* settlement of waste land.

settled, 180 *drones*, rental, Rs. 1,560, average *jama* per *kani*, 8 annas 8 pies. The maximum and the minimum rates and the *Nazarana* realised were as noted below. The rent-free period allowed ranged, as before, from 1 to 3 years.

	Maximum rate.	Minimum rate.	Amount of *Nazarana.*
1346 T.E.	0–8–0	0–4–0	Rs. 2,003–0–0
1347 T.E.	1–10–0	0–4–0	Rs. 1,799–0–0
1348 T.E.	2–8–0	0–4–0	„ 1,817–0–0
1349 T.E.	2–0–0	0–4–0	„ 3,278–0–0

Settlement Officers and Expenditure.

65. No whole time Settlement Officer was employed in any Division, during the period, but the Divisional Officers and the Second Officers were entrusted with settlement work in their respective jurisdictions. The total expenditure incurred was Rs. 1,900-12-6 p. in 1347 T. E., and Rs. 1,398 and Rs. 604 respectively in the years 1348 and 1349.

Tea Industry.

66. There were 55 tea gardens in the State during the triennium yielding a revenue of about Rs. 65,000 annually. The total area under tea was 10,938·5 acres at the close of 1349. T. E. Owing to the adoption of the Restriction Scheme several petitions for relinquishment of portions of tea gardens were received and pending consideration.

67. The tea industry in the State was suffering in the triennium from the tremendous effects of the slump that it had experienced, in spite of protective measures adopted and various concessions allowed by the Tripura Government.

The Control Scheme.

68. The first period of tea control which had come into operation under arrangement with the Government of India ended on the 1st day of Chaitra, 1347 T. E. (15th March, 1938). As the result of agreement arrived at for extension of the control scheme for a further term of five years, the Tripura Tea Control Act was ultimately passed in 1348 T. E. embodying the principles of interim rules previously promulgated, and sanctioning control of the industry for a period of 5 years with effect from 1st Baisakh 1348 T. E. (14th April, 1939).

Private estates under State management.

69. As detailed in the following statement, there were 20 private estates under State management at the close of the triennium. The percentage of collection in the estates during the period was not satisfactory, having ranged between 54·42 (maximum) to 2·78 (minimum). The low percentage was however due to exceptional circumstances affecting the estates concerned.

PRIVATE ESTATES UNDER STATE MANAGEMENT.

Class.	Names of Estates.	Area in *drones.*	Revenue	Remarks.
Encumbered	1. Kakraban Estate	283	1,871	*N.B.*—The maximum percentage of Collection during the period as a whole was 54·42 and the minimum 2·79.
	2. Jogendranagar Trust Estate	30	163	
	3. Kamalnagar & Mahendra nagar Estate	51	255	
	4. Maharamali Choudhuri Khanje Khan Bahadur's Estate *Taluk*	236	1,230	
	Jote	6	149	
	5. Thakur Nalini Mohan Deb Barma's Estate	68	170	
	6. Brajendra Kumar Das's Estate	408	1,936	
	7. Brajapur Estate (Kamalakanta Dev Barma & others)	246	982	
	8. Kalimulla's Estate	124	863	
	9. Mahammad Ali Choudhury's Estate	24	76	
Unencumbered	10. Prabhu Goswami's Estate	31	61	
	11. Dowager Maharani's Estate	169	766	
	12. Late Girish Chandra Choudhuri's Estate	36	254	
	13. Late Braja Kumar Thakur's Estate	47	297	
	14. Late Nava Kumar Chakraborty's Estate *Taluk*	32	225	
	Jote	5	19	
	15. Nil Kantha Sen's Estate	75	374	
	16. Gouranga Tripura's Estate	13	57	
Endowment	17. Taranagar Trust Estate	140	52	
Encumbered	18. Prabin Chandra Choudhuri's Estate	14	74	
	19. Iswar Chandra Bhowmic Roy's Estate	25	850	
Unencumbered	20. Dowager Bara Maharani's Estate	529	11,564	

CHAPTER III—PROTECTION.

1. LEGISLATION.

70. The subjoined enactments, Orders (ordinances) and Rules promulgated during the triennium are noticeable :

1347 T. E.

1. Rules regarding the State Bank, dated 4. 5. 46 T. E.
2. His Highness's Order of 19. 2. 47 prohibiting grazing in *Sal* forests.

3. His Highness's Order No. 127 of 17. 8. 47 T. E. imposing a small duty on export of rice and paddy under certain conditions for purposes of road development.

4. Rules under the above Order.

1348 T. E.

1. His Highness's Order No. 139, dated 10. 2. 48 T. E. regarding registration of cycles.

2. Amended Rules for Motor Vehicles, dated 5. 6. 48 T. E.

3. Act I of 1348 T. E. (The Tripura Tea Control Act.)

4. Rules for organisation of Village Mandalis (Memo No. 11, dated 3. 8. 48 T. E. of Revenue and General Department).

1349 T. E.

1. Proclamation of His Highness, dated 1. 1. 49 T. E. announcing the grant of a written Constitution to the State and various Administrative Reforms.

2. Act I of 1349 T. E. in definition of the term "*Rajmantri*".

3. Act II of 1349 T. E. (Municipal Act.)

4. Rules regarding the working of the *Mantri Parishad* or Council of Ministers.

5. His Highness's Order No. 190, dated 9. 2. 49 T. E. regarding Grazing Tax.

6. His Highness's Order No. 196, dated 9. 2. 49 T. E. regarding Money-lending business.

7. His Highness's Order, dated 9. 2. 49 T. E. in amendment of Revenue Rules of 1290 T. E.

8. Rule No. 1 of 1349 T. E. re Registration and Licencing of money-lenders.

9. Order No. 1 of 1349 T. E. regarding registration of Foreigners.

10. Order, dated 8. 5. 49 T. E. regarding arrest of potentially hostile foreigners.

11. Order No. II of 1349 T. E. in adoption of the Defence of India Ordinance No. V of 1939.

12. Order No. III of 1349 T. E. in adoption of the Defence of India Rules 1939.

13. Order No. VI of 1349 T. E. in prevention of profiteering.

14. Registration of Foreigners Rules, 1349 T. E. (Notification, dated 7th September, 1939).

15. The Enemy Foreigners Rules, 1349 T. E. (Order, dated 15. 8. 49).

II. MILITARY.

71. Charge. Rai Dewan Kamala Prasad Dutt Bahadur, M. A., B. L., M. R. A. S., and Major Rana Jodha Jung Bahadur, M. B. E., M. C. (Retd. I. A.) continued to be in charge of the Military Department and the Tripura State Forces respectively, during

the year 1347 T. E, and 1348 T. E. ; while during the year following Captain Maharajkumar Durjoy Kishore Dev Varma Bahadur was appointed Officer-in-charge, Military Department, and Lt.-Colonel Rana Jodha Jung Bahadur continued to be in charge of the Tripura State Forces.

72. Strength. The actual strength of the Forces was 386 at the end of the year 1347 T. E., against 396 of the previous year, while at the end of the years 1348 T. E. and 1349 T. E. the actual strength was 382 and 420 respectively. During the year 1349 T. E. the State Army consisted of the following forces :—

Indian State Forces.

1. Headquarters.
2. Infantry—1st Tripura B. B. M. Rifles.
3. Band party.

Other Forces.

4. Infantry—one company.

73. Arms. At the close of the triennium the troops were armed with ·303 Rifles, revolvers and pistols, Vickers and Lewis guns, M. H. muskets, D. P. guns, Sniders, breech-loaders and muzzle loaders.

74. Inspections. The Technical Adviser, Signalling, Central India States Forces, held a classification test of the Signallers during the 1st week of December 1937 (1347 T. E). The Chief Civil Master Armourer inspected the arms of the forces in the week following. The Millitary Adviser, Central India States Forces, Gwalior Residency, inspected the 1st Tripura Rrifles in February 1938, (1347 T. E). Major-General Sir Arthur M. Mills, C. B., D. S. O., Military Adviser-in-Chief, Indian States Forces, and Major W. A. Windsor Aubrey, Military Adviser, Central India States Forces, inspected the forces from the 19th November, 1938 to 21st idem (1348.T.E.). Lt.-Colonel L. E. Barton, Resident for the Eastern States, accompanied by His Highness the Maharaja Manikya Bahadur, visited the Cantonment on the 27th March 1940, (1349 T. E). Major-General (Since Lieutenant-General) Sir Frederick Gwatkin, C. B., D. S. O., M. C., Military Adviser-in-Chief, Indian States Forces, and Captain J. C. Lewis, Military Adviser, Central India States Forces, inspected the troops from the 15th to the 23rd February 1940 (1349 T. E).

75. Training. In 1347 T. E. (1937) two State Officers were attached to the 1/8th Gurkha Rifles, Shillong, for three months' training. Two I. O's were attached to the 1/7th Gurkha Rifles, Shillong, for $1\frac{1}{2}$ months for Preliminary Weapon Training. One N. C. O. attended the Junior Instructor's course, Army school of

Education, India, Belgaum. Six N. C. O's. qualified themselves from the Small Arms School, Gwalior. One N. C. O. qualified himself as Assistant Instructor (Indian) from the Army School of Physical Training, Ambala.

76. In the year 1348 T. E. (1938–39), one I. O. qualified himself from the S. A. S. Pachmarhi Wing—Pachmarhi. One State Officer was attached to the 1/7th Gurkha Rifles, Shillong, for Signalling Training. After completing his training there, he proceeded to attend the Signal Training Course at Alwar. The result was very satisfactory. Two I. O's were attached to the 1/7th Gurkha Rifles, Shillong for Platoon Commander's training. One S. O. and two N. C. O's were attached to the 1/6th Sikh Regiment, Chittagong, for training. One S. O. was attached to the 2/4th Punjab Regiment, Dacca, for training.

77. During the year 1349 T. E. (1939–40), one State Officer attended the first qualifying Signalling course at Poona and Alwar, and another S. O. was attached to the 1/11th Sikh Regiment, Comilla, for officers' Tactical Course. After completing his training at Comilla, he proceeded to attend the Small Arms School, Gwalior. The results were good. One I. O. was attached to the 1/11th Sikh Regiment, Comilla and two I. O's. to the 2/14th Punjab Regiment at Dacca for general training. One I. O. was attached to the 4th Gwalior M. B. Battalion for M. G. training. One I. O. attended the S. A. S. at Saugor. Two N. C. O's attended the preliminary Signalling Course and L. G. training at Gwalior. One N. C. O. attended the courses of Instruction, Indian Armourers, at Ishapur. The results were also satisfactory.

Camping and Tactical training.

78. In the year 1347 T.E. (1937–38) the State Forces were out in camps at Melaghar, a distance of about 34 miles, from Headquarters, for ten days from 14th November, 1937 (1347 T. E.), and one platoon went to Kalyanpur on duty during the visit of the Ruling Princes. The troops were called out three times during the year to extinguish fire at the Palace.

79. During the year 1347 T. E. (1937–38), the forces were out in camp at Mainamati, Comilla, for 10 days. They did, besides their routine works such as musketry firing, route march, tactical exercises.

80. In 1349 T. E. (1939–40) ten days' camping (liaison march and collective training) was done at Fajilpur from 22nd January 1940 (1349 T. E.) with the 1 Sikh Regiment. The Officers and men had besides practices in various military operations such as Field works, Field firing and Anti-aircraft training, under the supervision of Lt.-Col. Rana Jodha Jong Bahadur, M. B. E., M. C., Commandant, Tripura State Forces.

Cantonment.

81. The Cantonment was supplied with electric light during the year 1347 T. E. (1937–38), and some ordinary improvements and petty repairs of the barracks were carried through during the three years under review.

82. The health of the forces during the triennium was generally
Health. good.

83. Excluding the expenditure on the public works, the total
Expenditure. expenditure stood at Rs. 1,35,368 for the year 1347 T. E., Rs. 1,64,167 for the year 1348 T. E. and Rs. 1,55,594 for the year 1349 T. E., against Rs. 1,18,728 of the year 1346 T. E., (the closing year of the previous triennium). A special expenditure of Rs. 18,338 was besides incurred in 1349 T. E. (1939) for war purposes.

III. POLICE.

84. Rai Sahib A. C. Gupta continued as Superintendent of Police
Charge. till the 24th Chaitra, 1347 T. E. (1937–38) and as he resigned, Rai G. R. Dutt Bahadur joined as Superintendent of Police and held charge during the rest of the triennium, the designation of the office having subsequently been changed to "Commissioner of Police."

85. Babu Naresh Kumar Bhattacharjee, B. Sc. resumed office on
A. S. P. afterwards Dy. Commissioner. the 18th Kartick, 1347 T. E. (1937–38) and Babu N. N. Bose, B. A., who was acting in his place reverted to his own rank.

86. The total numerical strength of the Police Force was 498 in
Strength. 1347 and 1348 T. E. (1938–39) and 522 in 1349 T. E. (1939–40) against 496 in 1346 T. E. (1936–37), the increase in 1349 T. E. being due to the appointment of 15 permanent and 9 temporary armed constables during the year.

87. The total number of village choukidars throughout the period
Rural Police. continued to be 177 as against 176 in the year 1346 T. E.

88. There were 4 Inspectors of Police during the period as before,
Inspecting Staff. their main duties being to exercise control over and maintain discipline amongst the subordinate staff, besides supervision of cases and inspection of Police Stations and Courts.

89. During the period there were 23 Sub-Inspectors and 21 Naib
Investigating and Prosecuting Staff. Darogas on the police establishment as in the previous triennium. Their behaviour with the public were generally satisfactory throughout.

90. One Sub-Inspector, 5 Naib Darogas and 5 Constables were
C. I. D and Intelligence Staff. employed in the C. I. D., as before.

91. The total number of cases reported during the years under review was 2,245 as against 2,231 in the previous three years.

Crime.

92. The results of the cases are detailed below :—

Number of cases reported
2,245

- Enquiry refused — 36
- Number investigated — 2,117
  - True — 1,682
    - Charge-sheet — 858
    - Finally reported — 824
  - Intentionally false — 163
  - Mistake of law — 34
  - Mistake of fact — 98
  - Noncognizable — 140

93. The above table shows only institutions from year to year with their disposal and does not include pending cases, the number of which was as subjoined :—

Pending from 1346 T. E. (*i. e.* previous triennium)—	37	96
,, ,,	1347 T. E.–30	
,, ,,	1348 T. E.–29	
Pending from 1349 T. E. (*i. e.* close of the triennium)–	33	

All the above 96 cases were disposed of within the triennium, the percentage of disposal thereof under each head in the table being almost identical.

94. Altogether 1,534 persons were arrested and 1,872 persons (including absconders) were sent up for trial by the Police in connection with various offences during the period under review, as against 1,539 arrested and 1,765 sent up in the previous triennium. Of the persons sent up 613 were convicted and 642 acquitted against 486 and 368, the corresponding figures for the previous triennium, while 617 (including absconding accused) awaited trial, against 299.

Results of prosecution.

95. Nine cases of bad livelihood in which 30 accused were involved were started during the period, against 26 cases and 75 persons of the previous triennium. Only one case was pending at the close of the period against 9.

Bad livelihood cases.

96. Two Arms Act cases were instituted against two persons in 1347 T. E. both of whom were convicted during the triennium. There were no such cases in the two years following.

Arms Act Cases.

97. Altogether 20 guns were stolen during the period against 7 of the previous triennium, of which 3 were recovered—1 within the State territory and 2 from the neighbouring British territory.

Theft of guns.

98. The total value of properties stolen during the three years under review amounted to Rs. 43,035–6–3p against Rs. 40,356–12–9 p of the preceding triennium. Of this amount, Rs. 11,024–13–6 was recovered within the period against Rs. 6,101–2–3p in the previous three years. The percentage of recovery was 25·58 against 15·27.

Recovery of stolen property.

99. There were 30 cases of dacoity during the triennium against 56 in the previous three years. Charge-sheets against 58 persons in 8 cases were sent up, with the result that 4 persons were convicted and 11 acquitted, while 43 awaited trial at the end of the period. The corresponding figures for the previous triennium were as under : charge-sheet—37 persons ; convicted 5 ; acquitted 17 ; pending trial 16.

Dacoity.

100. Altogether 194 cases of unnatural death were reported during the period against 233 of the previous three years. As before, enquiries were held by the Police into all these cases and no foul play was detected in any of them.

Unnatural death.

101. Two Inspectors of Police, 15 Sub-Inspectors, 12 Naib Darogas, 3 Writer Naib Darogas, 34 civil constables, 4 armed constables, and 5 Choukidars received money rewards, while 1 Sub-Inspector, 1 Armed Sub-Inspector, 2 Naib Darogas, 1 Jamadar, 1 Havildar, 2 civil Jamadars, 2 Writer Naib Darogas, 33 armed constables, 151 civil constables, and 7 Choukidars were fined or temporarily degraded. 1 Havildar, 10 armed constables, 27 civil constables and 9 Choukidars were dismissed for varying degrees of delinquency.

Rewards and Punishments.

102. The Commissioner of Police was out on tour for 84 days against 174 days in the previous three years, and the Deputy Commissioner of Police for 25 days against 53 days.

Tours.

103. The relation of the State Police with the Police of the neighbouring districts in Bengal and Assam continued to be satisfactory.

Co-operation.

104. Musketry and revolver practice were continued and the result showed improvements in marksmanship.

Musketry practice.

105. The Expenditure during the three years under review amounted to Rs. 2,55,869 against Rs. 2,55,186 in the previous triennium.

Expenditure.

IV. JUSTICE.

Courts.

106. There were 17 courts of justice in the State during the year 1347 T. E., consisting of the High Court with its original and appellate sides, and 16 courts of Magistrate-Munsiff, while in the following two years there were 18 courts of justice viz., the High Court—Appellate Side, 2 Courts (including an Additional Court) in the Original Side of the High Court, and 15 courts of Magistrate-Munsiff exercising original jurisdiction only.

High Court.

107. Mr. Jnanendra Mohan Das, B. L., continued as Chief Judge till the 13th Ashadh, 1347 T. E. and as he resigned, Mr. K. C. Nag, B. A., M. B. E., Barrister-at-law, a retired District and Sessions Judge of the Selection Grade, Bengal, and sometime Judicial Secretary and Legal Remembrancer to the Government of Bengal, and later on a Judge of the High Court of Calcutta, was appointed as Chief Justice of the High Court and assumed charge on the 6th Sraban, 1347 T. E.. In the Original Side Mr. Ramani Mohan Goswami, M. A., B. L., continued as Civil and Sessions Judge during the period, while Thakur Hriday Ranjan Dev Barman continued as a Judge of the Appellate Side till the 9th Pous, 1348 T. E. when he retired. Mr. Sarada Charan Sarkar, M. A., B. L. acted temporarily as the Additional Civil and Sessions Judge for sometime during the year 1348 T. E. till he succeeded Thakur Hriday Ranjan Dev Barman with effect from the 17th Pous of that year.

Number of original criminal cases.

108. Altogether 6,830 criminal cases were instituted during the three years under review. With the balance of 835 pending from the year 1346 T. E., the total number of cases for disposal before the several subordinate courts was 7,665 as against 6,725 cases of the previous triennium, as detailed below ; out of these 7,665 cases, 6,682 were disposed of during the period against 5,890 in the preceding three years, leaving 983 cases pending at the end, against 835 of the previous triennium.

DESCRIPTION OF OFFENCES.	During previous 3 years (1344–46.)	During three years (1347–49) under review.
Offences against the State and public tranquillity ...	276	174
Offences against person	3,392	2,304
Offences against property	1,682	3,753
Other offences	1,375	1,434
TOTAL ...	6,725	7,665

Persons brought to trial.

109. The number of persons brought to trial during the triennium under review was 7,347 ; the number awaiting trial from the preceding year was 1,129 ; the total number of persons thus brought to trial in the years under report was 8,476, the corresponding figure for the previous three years being 8,015. Out of the aforesaid 7,347 persons, 1,812 were arrested by the Police, 1,806 were produced on warrant, 2,787 appeared on summons, 936 appeared voluntarily, and 6 persons were arrested in the presence of Magistrates.

110. Out of the total of 8,476 persons brought to trial before the several Courts including the Sessions Court, 4,195 persons were discharged, 1,771 were acquitted, 1,314 were convicted, 19 died, 3 escaped, and 1,174 persons were awaiting trial at the close of the triennium. Out of the convicted persons, 553 were sentenced to various terms of imprisonment extending from less than one month to 5 years and above, 700 were sentenced to fine only, 30 were bound down and 31 persons were warned for the future. The number of persons actually tried was 3,085 (excluding those discharged), as against 3,511 of the previous triennium, and the percentage of convictions was thus 42·59 against 48·19 of the previous three years.

Results of cases.

111. Out of 7,665 cases for disposal as stated in para 108 above, the number of cases in which British Indian subjects were concerned either as complainants or accused, was 1,113 as against 1,268 of the previous triennium. Out of these, 829 cases were cognizable, and 284 non-cognizable. In 154 cases British Indian subjects were complainants and in 959 cases they were the accused. In 362 cases both parties were British Indian subjects. In all, 1,499 persons were actually brought under trial in these cases during the period under report, as against 1,586 of the previous triennium. Out of these 1,499 persons, 495 persons were convicted, 858 acquitted or discharged, 3 died 2 escaped and 141 remained under trial at the close of the period.

Cases concerning British subjects.

112. In all 52 cases were committed to the Sessions during the three years under review and 2 cases were pending from the preceding year. Out of these 54 cases, 53 were disposed of during the period as detailed below. The number of persons involved in these 54 cases was 251, of whom 62 persons were convicted, 109 acquitted and 80 remained under trial at the close of the year,

Sessions cases.

Description of cases.	Number of cases.	Disposed of.	Pending.	REMARKS.
Murder	10	10	0	
Murder and destroying evidence of murder	1	1	0	
Dacoity with murder	1	1	0	
Attempt to murder	1	1	0	
Dacoity	2	2	0	
Culpable homicide not amounting to murder	12	12	0	
Conspiracy, unlawful assembly rioting, causing grievous hurt, kidnapping etc.	1	1	0	
Rioting and causing hurt	1	1	0	
Grievous hurt.	1	1	0	
Rape	4	3	1	
Robbery	8	8	0	
Criminal breach of trust	1	1	0	
Tampering with judicial record, making false statement on oath, etc.	1	1	0	
Arson	2	2	0	
Unlawful assembly and criminal intimidation.	2	2	0	
House trespass by night accompanied by grievous hurt. ...	1	1	0	
Forgery and using forged documents.	2	2	0	
Lodging false information	2	2	0	
Making false document	1	1	0	
Total	54	53	1	

113. There were altogether 655 criminal appeals during the period under review including those pending from 1346 T. E., against 739 of the previous triennium. These appeals were disposed of as shown below :—

Criminal appeals.

Rejected	... ...	26
Judgment affirmed	... ...	378
Modified	... ...	64
Reversed	... ...	138
Further enquiry ordered.	... ...	22
		628
Pending	... ...	27
Total	... ...	655

The percentage of judgments affirmed and modified was 71·97 against 60·62 of the previous three years.

114. The number of original civil suits instituted during the period was 4,105, as against 4,554 of the preceding period. With the balance of 732 pending from the previous triennium, the total number of suits for disposal was 4,837, as against 5,403 of the previous triennium. These suits were disposed of as follows :—

Original Civil suits.

Exparte	... ...	1,818
Admitted and compromised	... ...	381
Dismissed for want of prosecution	...	726
Disposed of on contest	... ...	1,235
Pending	... ...	677
Total	... ...	4,837

The average duration of suits in the civil courts was 4 months and 10 days, as against 4 months and 7 days of the previous triennium.

115. The total value of civil suits instituted during the three years was Rs. 3,31,987–3–3p. as against 7,11,093–1–9p. of the previous triennium. Out of 4,105 suits instituted during the three years under review, 1,106 related to land, 2,016 to money transactions, and 983 suits were of other classes. 2,252 suits were of the value of Rs. 100 and under ; 972 suits were of the value between Rs. 100 and Rs. 500 ; 61 suits of value between Rs. 500 and Rs. 1,000 ; 38 suits of value between Rs. 1,000 and Rs, 5,000 ; 1 suit was of value above Rs. 5,000, and 781 suits were not estimable in money value.

Nature and value of suits.

116. The number of applications for the execution of decrees filed during the period was 1,865, and there were 529, applications pending from the previous triennium. The total number for disposal was thus 2,394, as against 2,849 of the previous three years. The aggregate value of the new applications was Rs. 2,90,315-8-3p. and that of the pending applications was Rs. 1,01,877–6–0p. the total value thus amounting to Rs. 3,92,192–14–3p. against Rs. 4,98,623–13–5p. of the previous triennium. The number of applications disposed of was 2,012, the value of which was Rs. 3,11,812–1–0p. The number of execution cases pending at the close of the year was 382. the value thereof being Rs. 80,380–13–3p.

Execution of decrees.

Civil appeals.

117. There were 433 civil appeals filed during the years, as against 426 of the previous triennium. With the balance of 110 of the previous triennium, the total number of civil appeals for disposal was 543 as against 532 of the preceding triennium. Out of these cases, 481 were disposed of within the period under report, as against 428 of the previous three years, leaving a balance of 62 cases at the close of the period as against 104.

Result of civil appeals.

118. The following figures will show the result of appeals against civil suits :—

Decisions confirmed	236
Decisions reversed	140
Decisions modified	26
Remanded	18
Compromised and otherwise disposed of ...	61
	481

The percentage of judgments wholly or partly upheld excluding those in the cases compromised, was 62·38 as against 69·17 of the preceding period of three years.

Value and duration of appeals.

119. The total value of civil appeals filed during the three years under review was Rs. 25,464-11-9 and the average duration of each appeal was 6 months and 10 days, as against 5 months and 26 days of the preceding triennium.

Cases in the Original Side of the High Court.

120. In all 64 suits were instituted in the Original Side, High Court, during the three years, as against 53 of the previous three years. With the balance of 41 suits pending from the preceding year, the total number for disposal was 105 as against 101 of the previous triennium. Of these, 78 suits were disposed of as against 60 of the previous triennium, leaving 27 suits pending at the close of the period, as against 41. There were 56 execution cases during the period under report, including 18 cases pending at the close of the previous triennium. Of these, 43 were disposed of and 13 remained pending at the close of the period. There were 57 applications for succession and other certificates during the period ; with the balance of 4 of the previous triennium, the total number of such applications was 61, out of which 57 were disposed of as shown below and 4 remained pending at the close of the triennium :—

Description of cases.	Total.	Disposed of.	Pending.
Probate cases	4	4	0
Succession certificate	25	24	1
Guardianship	32	29	3
Total	61	57	4

Total number of appeals.

121. The total number of civil and criminal appeals including the number of cases pending from the previous year was 1,198 against 1,177 of the previous triennium. Out of these appeals, 1,109 were disposed of, as against 990 of the previous triennium, and 89 remained pending as against 187. In comparison with the preceding triennium the total

number of appeals for disposal increased by 12 and there was also an increase in the disposals by 119 cases.

V. PRISONS.

Number of Jails.

122. Together with the Central Jail at the Capital under the superintendence of Dr. M. M. Majumdar, L. M. S., Chief Medical Officer, as before, 8 jails were maintained by the State during the years under review.

Jail population.

123. In 1347 T. E. 525 convicts, 451 under-trials, 7 civil prisoners and 2 detenus–in all 985–constituted the total jail population, against 1,117 of 1346 T. E., while in 1348 the total was 930 consisting of 444 convicts, 479 under-trials, 4 civil prisoners and 3 lunatics, and in 1349 T.E., 962, consisting of 361 convicts, 594 under-trials, 3 civil prisoners, 2 lunatics and 2 detenus. The daily average was 152·64, 163·71 and 138·76, respectively, against 184·3 of 1346 T. E. ; 154 prisoners remained in the jails at the end of the period.

Long term prisoners.

124. Prisoners undergoing imprisonment for more than 2 years, totalled 101 in 1347 T. E., 97 in 1348 T. E., and 96 in 1349 T. E., against 98 in the year 1346 T. E.. A statement detailing offences, periods of sentence and occupation is given below with the corresponding figures at the end of the previous triennium.

Class of offence	Number of prisoners.				Occupation.	REMARKS.
	1346 T.E.	1347 T.E.	1348 T.E.	1349 T.E.		
Murder ...	17	20	20	20	They were employed in brick manufacturing, oilmills, wheat grinding, soorki pounding, *khowa* breaking, weaving, gardening, bamboo and cane work, tailoring and paddy husking etc.	69 had sentences of 2 to 5 years, 14 of 6—10 years, 6 of 11—14 years and 12 for life *i. e.*, 20 years in 1347 T. E. 66 of 2 to 5 years, 16 of 6—10 years, 3 of 11—14 years and 12 for life in 1848 T. E. 61 of 2 to 5 years, 18 of 16—10 years, 6 of 11—14 years and 11 for life in 1849 T. E.
Culpable Homicide not amounting to murder ...	11	14	15	19		
Grievous hurt ...	9	11	6	10		
Robbery ...	3	2	2	2		
Theft	3	7	4	3		
Dacoity ...	26	9	10	14		
Counterfeiting coin ...	4	1	—	—		
Picking pocket ...	1	1	—	2		
Arson	1	1	1	—		
Keeping in possession counterfeit currency note ...	1	1	1	1		
Section 110 Cr. P. C. (Security for good behaviour for habitual offenders) ...	15	14	—	—		
Escape from lawful custody ...	—	2	3	—		
House trespass ...	—	1	1	11		
Unlawful assembly ...	—	9	9	8		
Keeping revolver & gun in possession without license ...	2	2	1	—		
Rape	5	2	1	1		
Kidnapping ...	—	2	21	2		
Adultery ...	—	1	1	2		
Breach of trust ...	—	1	1	1		
TOTAL ...	98	101	97	96		

125. One convict suffering from chronic diarrhoea and dropsy died of heart failure in the Central Jail in the year 1347 T. E.. Two undertrials died in 1349 T. E., one of bronchitis (tubercular) and the other of septic pneumonia from throat cut wound.

Jail Health.

126. The Reformatory school in the Central Jail continued to work satisfactorily. 18 convicts were trained in the year 1347 T. E.. Of them, one sent up for the Pathshala Scholarship Examination passed in the second division. 14 convicts were trained in 1348 T. E., and one passed the Pathshala Scholarship Examination in the 3rd division. The number of convict students was 19 in the year 1349 T. E.. The Muslim convicts were also imparted religious instruction by the Maulavi of the local mosque.

Education.

127. One undertrial effected his escape from the Sonamura Jail but was re-arrested in 1347 T. E.. Two undertrials escaped from the Kailashahar Jail in 1349 T. E. but one was re-arrested during the year.

Escape.

128. On the occasion of the auspicious birth-day ceremonies of His Highness the Maharaja Manikya Bahadur, 12 convicts were released on the 14th Bhadra 1347 T. E., 10 convicts on the 3rd Bhadra of 1348 T. E., and 8 convicts on the 22nd Bhadra of 1349 T. E. The number of convicts released during on the occasion in 1346 T. E. was 10.

Special release.

129. Ten Jamadars and 57 warders were employed in the Jail during the years under report.

Jail Staff.

130. Two Jamadars were discharged, 8 warders dismissed, 14 warders fined and 7 warders warned for the future in the year 1347 T. E.; while 16 warders were fined, 2 warders discharged and 2 warders warned in 1348 T. E.; in 1349 T. E. 24 warders were fined, 1 warder discharged and 1 warder was warned.

Punishment.

131. His Highness the Maharaja Manikya Bahadur was pleased to show Lieutenant-Colonel H. W. C. Robson, O. B. E., ~~the Agent to the Gove~~rnor-General, Eastern States, round the Central Jail on 3rd February 1938, during his first visit to the State. Lieutenant-Colonel H. W. C. Robson, O. B. E. was also good enough to visit the Central Jail on the 24th March 1939. Lieutenant-Colonel L. E. Barton, Resident for the Eastern States, was pleased to visit the Central Jail on the 27th March 1940.

Visits.

132. The total income of the Central Jail came upto Rs. 6884, Rs. 4357 and Rs. 7391, respectively, during the years 1347, 1348, and 1349 under report. The income in the year 1346 T. E. was Rs. 7968.

Income.

133. The total expenditure in the jails amounted to Rs. 28,884, Rs .29,249 and Rs. 29,755, respectively, in 1347 T. E., 1348 T. E. and 1349 T. E., as against Rs. 29,688 in 1346 T. E.

Expenditure.

VI. REGISTRATION.

134. Thakur K. K. Singh, Naib Dewan was in charge of the Registration Department during the years 1347 T. E. and 1348 T. E., and Thakur Rebati Mohan Deb Barman, thereafter, during 1349 T. E.

Registration Offices.

135. The number of Registration offices continued to be 9, there being one at the headquarters station of each of the Divisions and Sub-Divisions. In the Mofussil the Divisionai and the Sub-Divisional Officers and in certain Divisions the Second Officers acted as Registrars. For the Sadar Division there was a separate Registrar at Agartala.

Registration & disposal.

136. The total number of documents (including the previous year's balance) awaiting registration during the year 1347 T. E. was 7,659 against 7,819 of the previous year, while such documents in 1348 T. E. and 1349 T. E. totalled 8,070 and 9,413 respectively. Of these, 81, 49 and 81 documents were refused registration on different grounds and 362, 953 and 1,448 remained pending at the end of the years 1347, 1348 and 1349 T. E. respectively, the corresponding figures for 1346 T. E. being 45 and 457.

137. The aggregate value carried by the documents in 1347, 1348 and 1349 T. E. amounted, respectively, to Rs. 10,75,062, Rs. 10,21,205 and Rs. 10,67,149, against Rs. 9,25,693 of the year 1346 T. E., while the total value of the documents actually registered was Rs. 10,66,718, Rs. 9,76,423 and Rs. 9,88,218, respectively, against Rs. 9,17,873 of the year 1346 T. E.

Suits and appeals

138. With suits pending from the previous year, the total number of suits brought before the Registration Department in respect of documents the registration of which had been refused in various registration offices, respectively, in the years 1347, 1348 and 1349 T. E., were 17, 48, and 53, out of which 4, 6 and 22 were disposed of, and 13, 42 and 31 remained pending, at the end of the years.

139. The total number of appeals for disposal including balances from year to year, was 3 in 1347 T. E., 7 in 1348 T. E., and 8 in 1349 T. E., out of which 3, 1 and 4 respectively were disposed of, and 6 and 4 remained pending at the end of 1348 and 1349 T. E. against 3 in 1346 T. E. No appeal was pending at the end of the year 1347 T. E.

Income and Expenditure.

140. The total income from fees and fines in the years 1347, 1348 and 1349 T. E., respectively, was Rs. 7,609, Rs. 7,551 and Rs. 9,078, and the expenditure, Rs. 4,030, Rs. 3,958 and Rs. 3,634, the net income thus amounting to Rs. 3,579, Rs. 3,593 and Rs. 5,444 respectively. The corresponding figures for 1346 T. E. were as under :—

Income—Rs. 7,968 ; expenditure—Rs. 3,993 ; net income—Rs. 3,975.

VII. MUNICIPALITY.

Municipality.

141. In the period under report, the capital town of Agartala had the only Municipality in the State with a population of about 20,000 (twenty thousand) according to the census of 1941.

Municipal Committee.

142. The Municipal Committee consisted of 9 nominated members, including an official Chairman and a non-official Vice-Chairman, who were appointed with the approval of His Highness the Maharaja Manikya Bahadur. Both in the years 1347 and 1348 T. E. Mr. S. C. Deb Barman, M. A. (Harvard), Senior Naib Dewan, and Babu Haridas Bhattacharjee continued to be the Chairman and Vice-Chairman respectively. During the latter part of the year 1348 T. E., the office of Chairman having fallen vacant on the death of Mr. S. C. Deb Barman, the Vice-Chairman, Babu Haridas Bhattacharjee, acted as Chairman till the vacancy was filled up by the appointment of Thakur K. K. Singh, Naib Dewan. Early in 1349, he was succeeded by Thakur L. M. Deb Barman, M. A. B. L., Sadar Magistrate, who continued to be the Chairman during the year. Babu Haridas Bhattacharjee continued as Vice-Chairman throughout the triennium.

143. During the year 1347 T. E. the Municipal Committee held 3 meetings, the average attendance of members being 6·6 against 4·3 of the previous year. In the year 1348 T. E. there were 5 meetings, with an average attendance of 5·6, and in the year 1349 T. E. 13 sittings, with an average attendance of 8·1.

Income.

144. The realisations on account of Municipal and Latrine taxes were Rs. 4,775-15-0p in the year 1347 T. E., Rs. 4,075-13-0p in 1348 T. E. and Rs. 4,925-6-6 in 1349 T. E., as against Rs. 5,069-8-0 in 1346 T. E.. On account of financial stringency an advance of Rs. 2,650 was obtained from the Municipal Bazar Fund in 1347 T. E. and a loan of Rs. 3,000 from the State arranged in the year following.

145. The receipts under miscellaneous head in the year 1347 T. E. including advances from the Bazar fund was Rs. 3,612-1-3p, in the year 1348 T. E., including loans obtained from the State, Rs. 3,827-4-3p, and in the year 1349 T. E. Rs. 1,126-9-6p, as against Rs. 1,716-14-9p in 1346 T. E.. The State grants for the years 1347, 1348 and 1349 T. E. were Rs. 12,600, Rs. 10,000, and Rs. 11,000 respectively, against Rs. 9,000 in 1346 T. E.

Expenditure.

146. The total expenditure amounted in the year 1347 T. E. to Rs. 20,831-12-0p, in the year 1348 T. E. to Rs. 17,392-5-9p and in the year 1349 T. E. to Rs. 17,719-10-0p, as against Rs. 15,793-8-0p in 1346 T. E..

Bazar at Agartala.

147. The management of the Ishanganj Bazar at the Capital town was in the hands of the Municipal Committee as before. The total realisation from the Bazar amounted to Rs. 7,923-14-9p in 1347 T. E., Rs. 7,794-0-0p in 1348 T. E.,

and Rs. 7,798-11-0p in 1349 T. E., as against Rs. 8,404-4-3p in 1346 T. E.. The expenditure towards improvement and maintenance of the Bazar amounted to Rs. 25,948-7-9p in 1347 T. E., Rs. 16,190-8-6p in 1348 T. E. and Rs. 13,606-12-0p in 1349 T. E., the excess expenditure having been met from the accumulated Bazar fund earmarked for the purpose. In 1346 T. E. the expenditure amounted to Rs. 12,585-6-6p.

Health.

148. The general health of the town was on the whole satisfactory. In the year 1347 T. E. there were 59 cases of cholera with 9 deaths and 3 cases of small-pox all cured. In the year 1348 T. E. there were 59 cases of cholera, most of them imported from outside, with 14 deaths, and 2 cases of small-pox with 1 death. In the year 1349 T. E. there was no case of small-pox and other contagious diseases.

Charge.

149. Dr. M. M. Majumder, Chief Medical Officer and later on Minister Public Health and Sanitation, continued to be in charge of the Municipal Department during the period under review.

CHAPTER IV—PRODUCTION AND DISTRIBUTION.

I. WEATHER AND CROPS—AGRICULTURE.

Charge of the Department.

150. The charge of the Department during the triennium was with Manyabara Raja Rana Bodhjung Bahadur, F. R. G. S., Chief Secretary to His Highness the Maharaja Manikya Bahadur, till transferred to Thakur K. K. Singh, Minister, Development Departments in 1349 T. E.

Staff.

151. In the years 1347 T. E. and 1348 T. E., the departmental executive staff continued to be the same as in the previous years, with Mr. J. C. Choudhury, S. E., M. S. A. (Tokyo), M. R. Agri. S. (London) as Superintendent of Agriculture at the head. In the year 1349 T. E. the Department of Agriculture was reorganised with the opening of the allied Departments of Rural Uplift, Factory, Labour and Employment, Co-operative and Marketing. With the expansion of departmental activities, due to the re-organization, the Superintendent of Agriculture was promoted to the post of Director of Agriculture with Mr. S. Chakrabarty, B. Sc., promoted to the post of Assistant Agricultural Officer, and Mr. P. Das Gupta M. A. (Com.) newly appointed as Co-operative Officer. One Field Assistant and two probationer Fieldmen were also employed during the year 1349 T. E.

Propaganda Office.

152. The Propaganda Office at the Agartala market served the purposes of general propaganda work during the years 1347 T. E. and 1348 T. E., while in the year 1349 T. E. the office of the Nursery ground was used as a hall, where a number of propaganda meetings were held and lantern lectures delivered.

153. In addition to general propaganda on agriculture, the propagandists held meetings and delivered lectures with lantern in

different parts of the State on various subjects, such as Social service, Crop extension, Cattle improvement, Cottage Industries, Co-operation, Hygiene and Sanitation, Child welfare and Maternity, Education, Temperance, Moral reconstruction etc. Altogether 32 such meetings were held during the year 1349 T. E. in Sadar and other Divisions.

Nursery.

154. A nursery with a small store of seeds and chemical manures was opened in 1349 T. E. in the heart of the Capital town with a view to distribute good seeds and seedlings and to demonstrate the utility thereof, as well as of chemical manures and fertilizers, and improved agricultural implements.

Publicity.

155. Leaflets on fodder, compost and preservation of manures, Groundnuts, Ericulture, Napier grass, Cotton, indigenous treatment of cattle diseases etc. were distributed all over the State among the rural population.

Seed distribution.

156. Arrangements were made to distribute seeds of groundnuts, potatoes, different kinds of English vegetables and *Rabi* crops during the period.

Marketing Survey.

157. Necessary information regarding different indigenous commodities was supplied to the Senior Marketing Officer to the Government of Bengal during all the three years.

Ericulture.

158. Special attention was given by the Department to the spread of Ericulture and to establish it as a cottage industry. A vigorous propaganda was carried on for the purpose. During the year 1349 T. E. Castor seeds were distributed to 311 families and Eri-rearing was introduced in 180 families, while 33 families learnt from practical demonstration how to spin Eri thread. Some of them were already weaving cloths from this thread at the close of the period. Special prizes and medals were awarded to the finest spinners and weavers by the Department. Great enthusiasm was in evidence amongst the people in the plains, both urban and rural, and some hill people as the result of these activities.

Labour and wages.

159. During the years 1347 T. E., 1348 T. E. and 1349 T. E., male labourers generally earned from 4 annas to 6 annas, and female labourers from 3 annas to 6 annas a day which *Gharamies* (thatchers) earned from 6 annas to 10 annas and carpenters and masons from 8 annas to Re 1 per day. Blacksmiths earned from 8 annas to Re 1 only. Most of the labourers came from the neighbouring British districts.

Food Crops.

160. The subjoined table shows the average prices of rice and paddy during the triennium.

Years.	Rice per maund.	Paddy per maund	REMARKS.
1347 T. E.	Rs. 2–4 to Rs. 5	Re. 1–2 to Rs. 2–4	
1348 ,,	,, 2–8 to Rs. 5	,, 1–4 to Rs. 2–8	
1349 ,,	,, 3 to Rs. 6	,, 1–6 to Rs. 3	

161. No Taccavi loan was issued during the triennium except one of Rs. 1,222 only allowed in the Sadar Division in 1348 T. E.

Taccavi.

162. A Canning plant was bought in the year 1347 T. E. and the services of an expert in that line were secured for nearly a month for demonstrations. The work of preservation of fruits, making jams, jelly, sauce, syrup etc. and canning and bottling them, was carried on for six months thereafter by the Department under the guidance of Mr. S. Chakrabarty B. Sc., General Assistant. On financial consideration however the Fruit Preservation Laboratory was closed indefinitely in 1348 T. E.

Fruit Preservation Laboratory.

163. Mr. Chakrabarty was deputed to the Alipore Observatory for a month's training in 1347 T. E.. The Department also secured necessary instruments for installation of an Observatory at Agartala.

Meteorology.

164. There was no outbreak of cattle disease worth mention during the year 1347 T. E., but rinderpest and foot and mouth disease prevailed during 1348 T. E. and 1349 T. E., the former having taken a rather heavy toll in 1349 T. E. in some parts of the State. Proper help was rendered by the Veterinary staff.

Veterinary

165. The Veterinary staff consisted of Doctor Prabhat Chandra Laskar, G. B. V. C., Veterinary Surgeon, one Compounder, and one peon. A student was sent to the Bengal Veterinary College, Calcutta, in 1349 T. E. for necessary training with a view to strengthen the staff.

166. During the year 1347 T. E., the Superintendent of Agriculture was out on tour for 12 days and the Veterinary Surgeon for 17 days. In 1348 T. E. the Veterinary Surgeon toured for 30 days, and in 1349 T. E. the Director of Agriculture toured for 26 days, while the Co-operative Officer, the Assistant Agricultural Officer, and the Veterinary Surgeon were out for 34, 35 and 26 days respectively.

Tour

167. Mr. Purnendu Das Gupta, M. A. (Com.) was appointed as Co-operative Officer in Agrahayan 1349 T. E. During the period from Agrahayan to Chaitra, he toured in four Divisions, viz.,—Khowai, Kailashahar, Sonamura and Udaipur, and took stock of the assets and liabilities of villagers and made a preliminary economic survey of their financial condition with a view to ascertain the types of Co-operative organisations that would suit the State. He drew up drafts of a Co-operative Societies Act and bye-laws for Co-operative Rural Credit Societies, and also prepared schemes for Co-operative Cattle Breeding Societies and Co-operative stores.

Co-operative movement.

168. The work of Rural Reconstruction was also taken up and possibilities of all-round improvement of the rural areas examined.

169. The subjoined statements show the rainfall and temperature in the State during the period, as a whole. The rainfall was however occasionally unseasonable and in some localities excessive for a time.

Rainfall & Temperature.

Rainfall.

Serial No.	Years under Review	Total average rainfall	Quinquennial average	Maximum fall	Minimum fall	Monthly average heaviest fall
1.	1347 T. E.	79·37"	83·25"	99·25" (Khowai)	59·07" (Udaipur)	19·78"
2.	1348 ,,	84·"	83·44"	97·85" (Khowai)	66·06" (Amarpur)	14·38"
3.	1349 ,,	85·32"	82·25"	107·56" (Dharmanagar)	68·51" (Amarpur)	23·80"

Temperature.

Years under Review.	Maximum temperature.	Minimum temperature.	REMARKS.
1347 T. E.	98°	51°	
1348 ,,	98°	50°	
1349 ,,	94°	52°	

170. The staple crops in the State in these three years were paddy, jute, sugarcane, til, cotton and mustard. Cultivation of pineapple and groundnuts increased during these years. Among other crops grown in various parts of the State, chillies, potatoes, tobacco and pulse of various kinds are worth mention.

Crops.

II. IMMIGRATION AND RECLAMATION.

171 The charge of the Department was held by Manyabara Raja Rana Bodhjung Bahadur, F. R. G. S., Chief Secretary to His Highness the Maharaja Manikya Bahadur till 1348 T. E. With the administrative changes made in the year 1349 T. E., the charge was placed with Thakur K. K. Singh, Minister, except in respect of the Kalyanpur Reserve, which continued to be under the control of the Raja Bahadur, as Minister. During this period both the Chief Secretary and the Ministers were assisted by Thakur Bharat Chandra Deb Barman, Colonisation Officer and Under Secretary.

172. Reclamation work in Kulai Haor was on a satisfactoryway of progress. In many cases the rent-free period having been over, rents were realised.

173. Cultivation of *pan* (betel) by the *Khasias* in Duluchhera block made very good progress during the years under report. The commodity was sold in Kamalpur, Halhali and Chhellengma bazar and it is gratifying to note that the production was more than sufficient to meet the local requirement, the surplus being exported to the adjoining British district.

174. Many *Mag* families have taken to plough cultivation and their number is growing. Chhellengma bazar made satisfactory progress, the number of permanent shops having considerably increased.

175. Water-supply from natural sources being insufficient the authorities were considering steps to remove the difficulty by re-excavation of the existing tank. The L. V. School at Chhellengma made good progress.

Kalyanpur Reserve.

176. To give impetus to plough cultivation among hill people who were habituated to *juming*, an area of eleven thousand *drones* of land was set apart as a Reserve. Many families have since permanently settled in the Reserve area and taken to ploughing, though the area actually brought under cultivation during the period was not encouraging. It was however found that the people fully understood the utility of the new method. It is hoped that in a short time the whole area will be under settlement and there will growup a number of populated villages in the Reserve. In the year 1347 T. E. 16 *drones* and 15 *kanis*, and in the year 1348 T. E. 10 *drones* and 3 *kanis* of land came under actual settlement in the area.

Survey.

177. Survey operations were carried on in 1347 T. E., within the Reserve in respect of 125 *drones* and 8 *kanis* of land.

Expenditure.

178. The total expenditure incurred in the year 1347 T. E., in furtherance of the Scheme, amounted to Rs. 1,239-10-9 pies only, there being no expenditure in the following two years.

III. FOREST AND CUSTOMS.

Charge and Management.

179. Mr. Jatindra Nath Mitra, Naib Dewan, held the charge of the Department during the years under review. His designation was changed to Secretary on 9th Jaistha, 1840 T. E. With the exception of a few Mahals which were let out in *Ijara*, all the forests were under *Khas* management as before.

180. In 1349 T. E. a new Department designated "Customs Department" was created mainly to deal with the collection of duty on commodities exported from the State, and this new Department was put under the charge of the Forest Secretary, who managed both the Forest and the Customs Departments together.

181. Kumar Nanda Lal Dev Varma Bahadur joined this Department on 19. 7. 48 T. E. as Officer-in-charge, Forest Reserves and Afforestation, and worked in that capacity till 19. 12. 49 T. E. after which on 20. 12. 49 T. E. by an order of His Highness the Maharaja Manikya Bahadur his designation was changed to "Conservator of Forests."

182. During the years under review, the strength of the Patrol Staff, consisting of one Forester, three Head guards and twenty guards, continued to be the same as in the previous year. During the period, the Department had at its disposal the undermentioned executive staff including the Patrol.

Staff.

		1347 T. E.	1348 T. E.	1349 T. E.
1.	Station Officer	1	1	1
2.	Forest Circle Inspectors or Customs Officers	3	4	5
3.	Foresters	14	14	14
4.	Assistant Foresters	18 }	18 }	25
	or Rangers	4 }	4 }	
5.	Moharers	6	6	10
6.	Head Guards	29	29	52
7.	Literate guards	18	18	11
8.	Guards	169	170	268
9.	Boatmen	6	6	8

With the creation of the Customs Department, the designation "Forest Circle Inspector" was changed to "Customs Officer" and 24 Customs Offices were newly established in 1349 T. E.

183. During the years under review the Patrol staff was out on tour throughout the State in four sections.

Permits.

184. The number of agents for the sale of forest permits on commission for shoulder borne export of minor forest produce by land routes, was 138 in 1347 T. E., 135 in 1348 T. E. and 150 in 1349 T. E.

Forest and customs Stations.

185. For collection of duty and prevention of offences there were fiftynine forest stations in the years 1347 and 1348 T. E. but in 1349 T. E., on the establishment of 24 new Customs stations and one Reserve forest Office, there were altogether 84 Forest and Customs stations.

working of the Forest.

186. The working of the Sal forests was kept in abeyance during the years under review, except to the extent of the removal and disposal of damaged and uprooted trees. The open unclassed forests were worked under the State Forest Rules of 1323 T. E. and the Feni river Mahal under the Rules of the Bengal Forest Department.

New Forest Reserves.

187. The forest areas that were provisionally declared Reserves under His Highness the Maharaja Manikya Bahadur's orders during 1347, 1348 and 1349 T. E. are detailed below :—

1347 T. E.

1. Muhuripur Reserve—11 square miles, in Belonia Division.
2. Betaga Ludhua Reserve—44.5 square miles in Sabroom Division.

1348 T. E.

1. South Sonamura Reserve—21.5 sq. miles.
2. Tulatalibari Forest Reserve—21.5 sq. miles in Sonamura Division.
3. Karcha-khola Forest Reserve—29 sq. miles in Sonamura Division.
4. Pathalia Reserve—18 square miles in Sadar Division.

1349 T. E.

1. Kasari Reserve—52 sq.miles in Belonia Division.
2. Jagannathdighi Reserve—41 sq. miles in Belonia Division.
3. Trishna Parbat Forest Reserve—25 sq. miles in Belonia Division.
4. Radhakishorepur North Reserve—20 sq. miles in Udaipur Division.
5. Kachigang protected Forest—20 sq. miles in Udaipur Division.
6. Chandrapur Reserve—65 sq. miles in Udaipur Division.
7. Charilam Forest Reserve—11 sq. miles in Sadar Division.
8. North Sonamura Reserve—42 sq. miles in Sonamura Division.

The total forest area reserved upto 1349 T. E. was 530.05 sq. miles.

Keeda Operation.

188. No lease for *kheda* operations was granted during the years 1347 and 1348 T. E. but in 1349 T. E. operations were undertaken in four places with 3 *khedas* in Kailasahar and 1 in Dharmanagar. 50 elephants were caught in Kailasahar and 2 in Dharmanagar Division.

Management of the Amlighat toll Station

189. The Toll Station at Amlighat continued to be under the management of the State Forest Department during the years under review. But according to the terms of agreement with the Bengal Government, a Ranger from the Bengal Forest Department was deputed to be in charge of the station during 1348 T. E. for a year. In 1347 and 1349 T. E. a Customs Officer was posted as Station Officer from the Forest and Customs Department of the State.

190. The total revenue collected and the expenditure incurred at the station during the years under report were as follows :—

	Revenue.	Expenditure.
1937–38 A. D. (1347)	Rs. 54,403	Rs. 3,949
1938–39 A. D. (I348)	,, 50,270	,, 3,678
1939–40 A. D. (1349)	,, 56,007	,, 3,620

191. As before, a Doctor of the Sub Assistant Surgeon class was appointed temporarily each year for four months, from December to March, for giving medical relief to the Station staff and to the cutters and exporters of forest produce.

Fee simple lots.

192. As in the previous years, the forest produce from the Fee Simple Lots above the Amlighat Toll Station was exported free of duty under passes granted by the Collector of Chittagong.

Forest offences and Results.

193. Altogether 249 cases against 486 persons were instituted during the period. With 58 cases against 110 accused pending from the previous triennium, the total number of cases for disposal stood at 307 involving 596 persons. The cases were disposed of as under —(i) Tried—238, (ii) Compounded—27, (iii) Struck off—6, and (iv) pending—36. Of 307 persons convicted, (i) 20 were imprisoned, (ii) 260 were fined, (iii) 5 received punishments of both inprisonment and fine, and (iv) 16 were warned for the future. 127 persons were acquitted or discharged, 1 died, and 91 persons were awaiting trial while the 6 cases struck off involved 11 persons.

Punishment and rewards.

194. In 1347 T. E. one first class Forester and one guard were dismissed from service ; one Assistant Forester, one Literate guard and four guards were fined for misconduct. In 1348 T. E. one second class Forester and one guard were dismissed from service for disobedience and misconduct and one Assistant Forester was suspended from service for a few months. In 1349 T. E. no forest subordinate was punished for any offence.

Sources of income and receipts.

195. The following table shows the results of collection of Forest and Customs Revenue under different heads during the year under report as compared with 1346 T. E.

Heads of revenue.	1346 T. E.	1347 T.E.	1348 T.E.	1349 T.E.
	Rs.	Rs.	Rs.	Rs.
I. Unclassed open forests :—				
(a) Toll on forest produce exported by the river Mahals ..	2,77.246	3,46,623	3,62,488	3,55,990
(b) Toll on forest produce exported by land routes under permits	69,637	74,903	77,037	81,268
(c) Toll collection (State share of the Amlighat Toll Station)...	26,877	36,200	30,433	38,680
(d) Grazing Mahals ...	6,183	5,629	6,050	9,739
(e) Thatching grass Mahal ...	2,221	2,203	3,812	4,180
II. Reserved Forests—sale of *Sal* etc ...	1,039	1,271	135	1,928
III. Elephant Khedas ...	—	—	—	3,951
IV. Match Excise Duty	27,229	1,564	56,918	37,674
V. Tax on cotton & oil seeds	—	—	—	1,42,707
VI. Duty on jute ...	—	—	—	90,292
VII. Duty on Tea ...	—	—	—	49,414
VIII. Duty on Rice & paddy	—	—	—	59,467
TOTAL ...	4,10,432	4,68,393	5,36,873	8,75,290

196. The increase of revenue in 1349 T. E. was mainly due to (i) improvements in heads I—III and (ii) transfer of the income under

heads V—VII to this major head from the head Revenue owing to the amalgamation of the Customs and Forest Departments. During this year, grazing fees were levied on animals from across the frontiers for check and protection of crops and forests.

Timber.

197. The quantity of timber exported during the years under report with the amount of duty realised is shown below :—

	1347 T. E.		1348 T. E.		1349 T. E.		REMARKS
	Quantity (in c. ft.)	Duty (in Rs.)	Quantity (in c. ft.)	Duty (in Rs.)	Quantity (in c. ft.)	Duty (in Rs.)	
1. Timber other than Sal	6,05,155·5	1,17,849.	6,93,239·5	1,36,522.	6,24,545	1,15,268	
2. *Sal*	1,992	1,271	432	135	6,162	1,928.	
3. Timber exported by the Feny river (State share)	16,772·5	1.750	20.538	2,110	21,446	2,981	

Receipts from matches.

198. The Maharaja Match Factory manufactured 7,150, 11,309 and 17,485 gross of finished matches and paid Rs. 39-3-9, Rs. 59-2-6 and Rs. 54-14-3p respectively as duty on timber used in making these matches during the years under report. The State received Rs. 1,564 in 1347 T. E., Rs. 56,918 in 1348 T. E. and Rs. 37,674 in 1349 T. E. from the Government of India as its share of the Match Excise duty. The difference between the receipts of 1347 and 1348 T. E. was due to the fact that a substantial portion of the share allotted to the State for the year 1347 was received in 1348 T. E.

Plantation.

199. Plantation of Gamair (Gmelina arborea), Sonal (Cassia fistula) and Jarul (Lagerostromia Flos-reginae) was continued during the years under review and out of the 3 species of trees, the first-named one looked most promising.

Tour.

200. The Secretary and the Conservator of Forests were out on tour for the following days :—

	1347 T. E.	1348 T. E.	1349 T. E.
Secretary	64 days	69 days	86 days
Conservator	—	12 ,,	28 ,,

IV. PUBLIC WORKS.

Charge.

201. Dewan Bahadur K. Dutt, M. A., B. L., M. R. A. S., F. R. ECON. S., Private Secretary to His Highness the Maharaja Manikya Bahadur was in charge of the Public Works Department during the years 1347 and 1348 T. E., and Manyabara Raja Rana Bodhjung Bahadur, F. R. G. S. was Minister in charge of the Department in the year 1349 T. E. Honorary Capt. J. N. Bhaduri, B. E., C. E., M. I. E. (India), M. R. San. I. (London), continued as State Engineer.

Mr. K. P. Roy, M. A., C. E., Hydro-Electric and Irrigation Engineer, appointed for a big Hydro-Electric Scheme in Bangeswar valley worked during the years 1347 to 1349 T. E., while Mr. A. K. Sen, B. E., Road Engineer, appointed for Road works of the State, worked during **the years 1348 and 1349 T. E.**

202. The total expenditure incurred during the years under review on Public works including Improvement works, amounted to **Rs. 10,06,588** as detailed below, against Rs. 6,96,486 of the previous triennium.

Description of works.	Ordinary Public works.	Improvement works including local Fund.	Road Improvement works.	TOTAL.
Buildings. 1347 T. E.	51,390	1.69,637	—	2,21,027
1348 „	46,909	1,03,178	—	1,50.087
1349 „	47,378	80,569	—	1,27,947
Roads & Bridges.				
1347 T. E.	19.039	48,542	21.243	88,314
1348 „	3,739	5,434	1,09.525	1.18,698
1349 „	8,660	6.552	1,26,585	1,41,797
Tanks & Tube Wells.				
1347 T. E.	3,205	640	—	3,845
1348 „	1,515	—	—	1,515
1349 „	500	—	—	500
Miscellaneous.				
1347 T. E.	2,507	22,650	—	25,157
1348 „	691	15,295	—	15,986
1349 „	1,344	36,482	—	37,826
Minor Works at *Rajbari Karkhana.*				
1347 T. E.	887	—	—	887
1348 „	998	—	—	998
1349 „	946	—	—	946
Establishment.				
1347 T. E.	19,315	—	1,597	20,912
1348 „	18,420	—	4,759	23,179
1349 „	14,904	—	11.563	26,467
	2,42,337	4,88,979	2,75,372	10,06,588

203. The following works (major) were carried through during the years :—

1. Construction of X-ray Building.
2. Construction of armourers' work-shop at the Kunjaban Cantonment.
3. Construction of the Circular Bazar Building.
4. Construction of Ghoramara Bridge on the road from Agartala to Chandra Sadhu Para.
5. Construction of the Andharmanik Bundh.
6. Construction of the Chief Justice's Quarters.
7. Construction of the Hydro-Electric & Irrigation Engineer's Quarters.
8. Survey works of Bangeswar Hydro-Electric works Scheme.
9. Improvement of the Akhaura Road.
10. Substantial work in the Agartala—Ranirbazar Road.
11. Bituminizing road from Jackson Gate to Dharmasala.
12. Road metalling from Bazar to Municipal limit in the eastern side of the Capital town.
13. Construction of a new road from Padmanagar to Jumerdhepa
14. Improvement of Ujjyanta Palace.
15. Construction of the Chief Commandant's Quarters.

16. Construction of Indian Officers' Quarters at Kunjaban.
17. Improvement of *Prasad Pratolee*.
18. New Road from Birendranagar to Mandai Bazar.
19. Improvement of the Police Commissioner's Quarters.
20. Construction of a garage and record room in Minister's Office Compound.
21. Construction of a Bund between Mahadev Bari & Kunjaban Tila.
22. Improvement of Bisalgarh Road.
23. Sanitary fittings and bathroom fittings to the Palace.
24. Extension of Bazar Road at Agartala.
25. Construction of a building for a Prabhu Goswami at *Sreepat*.
26. Khosal Pushkarni diversion of Udaipur road.
27. Construction of an Additional Sessions Court in the compound of the Khas Adalat.
28. Sinking a Tube-well at Sibnagar.
29. Sinking 2 Tube-wells at *Sreepat*.
30. Sinking a Tube-well in the Guest House compound.
31. Sinking a Tube-well near Maharaj Kumar N. K. Dev Varman Bahadur's residence.
32. Sinking a Tube-well in Mohanpur Tahasil Office compound.
33. Sinking a Tube-well at Bisalgarh.
34. Sinking a Tube-well at Charilam Tahasil Kuchery.
35. Sinking a Tube-well at Sidhai Thana.
36. Sinking a Tube-well in Sabroom Divisional Office compound.
37. Sinking a Tube-well at Chandra Sadhu Para.
38. Sinking a Tube-well at Dhaleswar.
39. Sinking a Tube-well at Krisnanagar Thakur Palli.
40. Construction of a Tinshed with pucca plinth and wall in the H. E. School compound at Sadar.
41. Construction of 5 Tinshed Bunglows in the Rajbari compound with pucca plinths and walls.
42. Construction of houses and fencings in the Guest House compound.
43. Special improvement and reconstruction of Buildings occupied by the Chief Secretary and several Kumars necessary after a fire during the last part of the year 1346 T. E.
44. Construction of a Godown in the Guest House Compound.
45. Special improvement of Sylhet–Devendranagar Road.
46. Construction of Fatikchera–Dharmagarh Road.
47. Construction of one four-seated Sanitary Latrine in the Office componnd.
48. Repairs to Sadar Sonamura Road (Motorable) between Bisramganj and Melagarh.

49. Repairs to Agartala–Bisalgarh Road.
50. Construction of Bazar Building at Agartala.
51. Construction of Golaghati–Salda Road.
52. Construction of a Tinshed for Radhanagar Beat Office.
53. Construction of a Tinshed for Fatikroy Tahasil Kuchery in Kailashahar.
54. Construction of a Tinshed for Dharmanagar Dak Bunglow.
55. Construction of Gate and Guard rooms in front of Sadar Jail.
56. Improvement of Military Barracks at Kunjaban.
57. Construction of a pucca Railing round the Kunjaban Palace Tila.
58. Construction of Quarters for Examiner of Accounts.
59. Construction of a Tahasil Kuchery at Rajdhar nagar.
60. Construction of Belonia–Loongthung Road.
61. Construction of Belonia H. E. School building.
62. Construction of a Motor Road from the Bisalgarh Road to Bangeswar.
63. Construction of a bridge in the Akhaura–Agartala Road with R. C. decking and R. S. Joists.
64. Improvement of Mogra Road.
65. Addition and alteration to the Finance Minister's Quarters.
66. Digging of a tank near Gol-Bazar.
67. Improvement of Kakraban Road from Melagarh to Kakraban.

Electric and water-works.

203. The total expenditure in connection with Electric and water works was Rs. 36,474 in 1347 T. E., Rs. 22,921 in 1348 T. E. and Rs. 25,387 in 1349 T. E. against Rs. 26,748 in 1346 T. E.

V. GEOLOGICAL.

Charge.

204. A new Geological Department was created in 1347 T. E. (1937). Mr. S. C. Deb Barman, M. A. (Harvard), Senior Naib Dewan, who was assisted by Mr. D. C. Nag, B. SC. (Mining), L. C. E., Geological Adviser and Mr. K. L. Das, M. SC., M. M. G. I., F. G. M. S., State Geologist, was in charge of the Department, till Mr. Deb Barman's unfortunate death in 1348 T. E., after which the charge was transferred to Thakur K. K. Singh Naib Dewan, since Minister Development Departments.

The Geologist's operations

205. During the winter season of 1347 T. E., the Geologist carried on mineral prospecting works in the Barmura, Deotamura and Atharamura ranges and discovered some oil structures. The area under survey was about 200 Sq.

miles. Some indications of coal were also observed, and Calcareous sandstones, suitable for building materials and road-ballasts, noted. The broad synclinal valleys were studied for Artesian well conditions. Invertebrate and Verterbrate fossils of high scientific value were discovered on the occasion for the first time in the State and numerous fossil-woods noticed.

206. After submitting his field report for the year 1347 T. E. the Geologist carried on analytical works on the specimens collected in Calcutta. In 1348 T. E., prospecting works in the Unakoti, Sakhan and Jampui Ranges in the Kailashahar Division were undertaken by him, covering altogether about 300 Sq. miles. Mainly three anticlinal structures, suitable for the accumulation of Petroleum, were discovered. Four bands of fossiliferous limestone were noticed in the Jampui Range. Indications of the existence of Pottery Clay, Building materials, Road ballast, Coal, etc. were observed and soil samples from waste lands in the interior were collected with a view to studying their physical and chemical properties and suitability for different types of crops. Phuldungsei on the Jampui hills near the highest peak of the Range, Betting sib, was studied for its suitability as a Hill Station. During the year, the Burmah Oil Company Ltd. was granted a Prospecting License for Natural Petroleum and Natural gas for three years in respect of an area of 250 Sq. miles.

207. After submittng his field report for the year 1348. T. E., the Geologist went to Calcutta in the month of Ashad 1349 T. E. (1939) for his Laboratory works. In the month of Agrahayan (November) he again went out for the field works in the Jampui Range for a month, and thereafter inspected the works of the Geological staff of the Burmah Oil Company Ltd. in the Sonamura Division. The rest of the winter season he devoted to prospecting of Pottery clay and glass-sand deposits in the Champamura area of the Sadar Division.

Outings on field work

208. The State Geologist was out for his field works altogether for 141 days in 1347 T. E., 158 days in 1348 T. E. and for 69 days in 1349 T. E.

Expenditure.

209. The following table will show the actual Income and Expenditure of the years under review :—

YEAR.	INCOME.	EXPENDITURE.	REMARKS.
1347 T. E.	—	Rs. 2405.	*This figure includes (a) *Nazar* Rs. 70,000 (b) acreage fee Rs. 30,000 (c) deposit Rs. 25,000 and (d) Renewal fee for certificate of approval Rs. 10 realised from the B. O. C.
1348 T. E.	Rs. 1,25010.*	Rs. 5040.	
1349 T. E.	Rs. 10. †	Rs. 5750.	†Renewal fee for certificate of approval Rs. 10 from B. O. C.

VI. TRADE AND MANUFACTURE.

210. The principal exports were timber and other forest produce of various kinds, such as, Cotton, Oil-seeds, (*Til* and Mustard seeds), Paddy, Jute, Rice and *Gur* (Molasses). Some home-spun cotton fabrics manufactured by the hill people and specially by the Manipuris were also exported. The principal export figures during the years under review as compared with 1346 T. E., are given below :—

	1346 T. E.	1347 T. E.	1348 T. E.	1349 T. E.
Cotton	34,011 Mds.	46,986 Mds.	46,367 Mds.	68,964 Mds
Til	33,323 ,,	16,674 ,,	13,979 ,,	10,774 ,,
Mustard ...	36,627 ,,	45,047 ,,	37,106 ,,	32,917 ,,
Jute	1,50,032 ,,	1,61,360 ,,	86,897 ,,	2,37,430 ,,
Tea	26,56,780 lbs.	27,41,421 lbs.	32,41,916 lbs.	32,05,263 lbs

---

CHAPTER V—REVENUE & FINANCE.

I. REVENUE.

211. The following table shows the total collection in each of the years under different heads as compared with 1346 T. E.

Serial No.	Heads of Revenue.	1346 T.E.	1347 T.E.	1348 T.E.	1349 T.E.	Remarks.
1.	Land Revenue ... ... } ...	8,32,454	6,29,697	6,02,917	6,27,569	
2.	Road Cess ... ... } ...	—	39,284	36,811	40,420	
3.	Road Improvement Fund ...	—	92,182	1,09,642	1,03,986	
4.	Rents of markets	7,357	8.023	7,724	7,015	
5.	Family Tax in the hills ...	53,698	45,617	49,079	77,366	
6.	Toll on forest produce } ...	3,46,883	4,21,526	3,62,488	3,55,990	
7.	Income from permit sale } ...	—	—	77,037	81,268	
8.	Feni River Tolls	26,877	36,200	31,905	40,325	
9.	Elephant & buffalo grazing Mahal	6,183	5,629	6,050	9,739	
10.	Thatching grass Mahal	2,221	2,203	3,812	4,180	
11.	Reserve *Sal* Forests	1,039	1,171	135	1,928	
12.	Tax on cotton and oil-seeds ..	1,06,518	93,192	88,157	1.42,707	
13.	Adda Mahal	25,470	22,942	22,285	24,696	
14.	Excise	39,705	74.778	94,533	91,453	
15.	Stamps and Court-fees	67,627	67,727	61,596	65,660	
16.	Law and Justice (Fines) ...	2,269	2,375	1,469	1,006	
17.	Process fees	10,726	10,293	8,235	6,930	
18.	Registration	7,243	7,609	7,551	9,078	
19.	Jail	7,968	6,884	4,357	7,391	
20.	Cattle pounds	3,745	3,516	3,157	3,406	
21.	Nazars	59,426	40,823	1,10,458	61,507	
22.	Education...	15,078	14,208	14,375	15,111	
23.	Tea Export duty	42,685	41,638	22,586	49,414	
24.	Depreciation Contribution ...	58,915	40,380	—	—	
25.	Jute Export duty	56,338	60,717	66,032	90.292	
26.	Duty on matches	27,270	1,564	56,918	37,674	
27.	Miscellaneous	62,776	67,409	75,581	89,956	
28.	Public Works	4,902	6,118	—	—	
29.	Kheda Operation	—	—	—	3,951	
30.	Money Lenders' License fees ...	—	—	—	5,577	
	TOTAL ...	18,75,373	18,43,305	19,24,890	20,55,595	

212. The total collections in the year 1349 T. E. were Rs. 20,55,595, in 1348 T. E. Rs. 19,24,890, and in 1347 T. E., Rs. 18,43,805 ; against Rs. 18,75,373 in 1346 T. E. The net increase in collection in the year 1348 T. E. was Rs. 81,085 in comparison with that of the previous year ; while in 1349 T. E. there was an increase of Rs. 1,30,705 in comparison with the collection in 1348 T. E., and that of Rs. 1,80,922 in comparison with 1346 T. E.

213. The income in 1347 T. E. under head Land Revenue decreased by Rs. 1,63,473 in comparison with that of the previous year. It may be noted that there was a remarkably satisfactory collection specially in the Sadar Division in 1346 T. E. when arrear revenue amounting to more than a lac of rupees was realised.

214. As already noted in para 12 above, the income under head Road Improvement Fund was new, being the result of a scheme of development of communications. The noticeable increase in *Nazar* in 1348 T. E. was mainly attributable to realisation of Rs. 70,000 from the Burma Oil Co. Ltd. as premium for prospecting license.

215. The marked increase under the head Excise in 1347 T. E. was due to the new arrangement for realisation by the State of Excise duty on *opium, ganja* and *bhang* which was being previously realised by the Government of Bengal. The comparative increase under this head in 1348 is ascribable to competition amongst rival bidders during resettlement under the new conditions.

216. The decrease under head Depreciation Contribution was due to the discontinuance towards the end of 1347 T. E. of economic cuts and deductions from salary.

II. FINANCES.

Charge.

217. During the three years under review, Rai Bahadur J. C. Sen, B. A., B. C. S. (Retd.), Minister, controlled the Department, till Rai Bahadur J. M. Chatterjee, M. A., B. C. S. (Retd.), assumed charge on appointment as Finance Minister on the 24th Magh, 1348 T. E., and held charge thereafter throughout the remaining part of the period under report.

218. Mr. S. C. Dev Barman, M. A. (Harvard) continued as the Departmental Head till his sad death on the 27th Pous, 1348 T. E., whereafter Rai Sahib S. C. Dutt (Examiner of Accounts) assumed charge, first as Officer-in-Charge of the Department, and later on, with the establishment of the *Mantri Parisad,* as Secretary to the Minister.

219. Subjoined is a consolidated abstract account of the Financial transactions of the State and the attached Zemindaries from 1344 T. E. to 1349 T. E.

A consolidated abstract account of the Receipts of the State and the attached Zemindaries from the year 1344 T. E. to 1349 T. E.

Receipts.	1344 T. E.	1345 T. E.	1346 T. E.	TOTAL.	1347 T. E.	1348 T. E.	1349 T. E.	TOTAL.	REMARKS.
1. Opening Balance :–				Opening Balance for 1344 T. E.				Opening Balance for 1347 T. E.	
(1) State	10,52,214	10,92,959	12,37,176	10,52,214	15,16,044	16,53,890	1,99,187	15,16,044	
(2) Zemindaries ...	3,50,220	3,83,502	5,57,144	3,50,220	7,28,421	10,64,966	11,63,951	7,28,421	
TOTAL ...	14,02,434	14,76,461	17,94,320	14,02,434	22,44,465	27,18,856	13,63,138	22,44,465	
2. Income :–									
(1) State	15,79,609	16,96,043	18,75,373	51,51,025	17,51,623	18,15,248	19,82,428	55,49,299	
(2) Zemindaries ...	9,87,261	11,07,653	12,48,973	33,43,887	12,65,702	11,79,575	13,89,133	38,34,410	
TOTAL ...	25,66,870	28,03,696	31,24,346	84,94,912	30,17,325	29,94,823	33,71,561	93,83,709	
3. Law charges recovered :–									
(1) Zemindaries ...	46,963	65,060	67,443	1,79,466	73,024	48,812	40,658	1,62,494	
4. Refunds and compensation for lands acquired :–									
(1) Zemindaries ...	4,417	3,732	4,472	12,621	3,25,081	1,582	16,326	3,42,989	
5. Deposits :–									
(1) State	2,63,746	1,31,004	1,10,628	5,05,378	3,04,711	2,80,601	2,51,228	8,36,540	
(2) Zemindaries ...	39,576	51,943	54,386	1,45,905	64,798	29,229	17,425	1,11,452	
TOTAL ...	3,03,322	1,82,947	1,65,014	6,51,283	3,69,509	3,09,830	2,68,653	9,47,992	
6. Road Fund –									
(1) State	–	–	–	–	92,182	1,09,642	1,03,986	3,05,810	
GRAND TOTAL ...	43,24,006	45,31,896	51,55,595	1,07,40,716	61,21,586	61,88,545	51,64,322	1,33,87,459	

A consolidated abstract account of Expenditure of the State and the attached Zemindaries from the year 1344 T. E. to 1349 T. E.

Expenditure.	1344 T. E	1345 T. E.	1346 T. E.	Total.	1347 T. E.	1348 T. E.	1349 T. E.	Total.	REMARKS.
1. General Administration charges :—									
(a) State	5,42,469	5,44,627	5,76,687	16,63,783	6,86,318	6,31,046	7,09,865	19,77,223	
(b) Zemindaries :—									
1. Cost of management	1,42,745	1,37,956	1,39,290	4,19,991	1,42,174	1,37,557	1,39,873	4,19,604	
2. Cost of litigation	1,36,800	1,59,230	1,26,609	4,22,639	1,11,176	1,07,570	1,13,456	3,32,202	
Total ..	8,22,014	8,41,813	8,42,586	25,06,413	8,89,668	8,76,172	9,63,194	27,29,029	
2. Revenue and Taxes on account of the Zemindaries	2,85,540	2,81,546	2,84,317	8,51,403	2,62,041	3,45,211	3,78,969	9,86,221	
3. Public Works—(a) State	2,09,062	2,00,017	2,60,797	6,69,876	3,15,871	1,94,253	1,89,101	6,99,225	
(b) Zemindaries ...	50,996	50,912	76,889	1,78,797	4,42,556	1,60,847	1,00,740	7,04,143	
Total ...	2,60,058	2,50,929	3,37,686	8,48,673	7,58,427	3,55,100	2,89,841	14,03,368	
4. Electric Light—State	16,299	16,433	26,748	59,480	36,474	22,921	25,387	84,782	
5. Municipality—State	9,000	9,000	9,000	27,000	12,600	10,000	17,750	40,350	
6. Education—(a) State	1,23,867	1,22,027	1,31,956	3,77,850	1,30,817	1,30,783	1,24,215	3,85,815	
(b) Zemindaries ..	9,075	8,557	8,932	26,564	9,103	4,130	4,149	17,382	
Total ...	1,32,942	1,30,584	1,40,888	4,04,414	1,39,920	1,34,913	1,28,364	4,03,197	
7. Medical and Sanitation :—									
(a) State	67,638	66,513	71,950	2,06,101	87,812	76,984	84,791	2,49,587	
(b) Zemindaries	11,469	12,001	12,138	35,608	11,831	10,199	10,227	32,257	
Total ...	79,107	78,514	84,088	2,41,709	99,643	87,183	95,018	2,81,844	
8. Survey and Settlement—(a) State...	20,119	13,835	12,296	46,250	12,000	14,355	13,923	40,278	
(b) Zemindaries ...	916	1,097	1,964	3,977	2,201	2,523	2,324	7,048	
Total ...	21,035	14,932	14,260	50,227	14,201	16,878	16,247	47,326	
9. Agriculture, Commerce and Industries—State ...	7,859	8,031	4,902	20,792	9,565	4,483	12,733	26,781	
10. Religious Expenses—(a) State ...	64,971	55,724	55,235	1,75,930	56,592	54,158	56,881	1,67,631	
(b) Zemindaries ...	6,111	6,716	6,565	19,392	6,845	6,340	6,779	19,964	
Total ...	71,082	62,440	61,800	1,95,322	63,437	60,498	63,660	1,87,595	
11. Sultanat—State	52,951	56,962	1,15,859	2,25,772	98,418	69,242	52,816	2,20,476	
12. Purchase of Land Tenures :—									
(a) State	6,845	11,522	6,616	24,983	14,310	6,717	3,184	24,211	
(b) Zemindaries	6,573	6,278	5,871	18,722	20,134	675	42,444	63,253	
Total ...	13,418	17,800	12,487	43,705	34,444	7,392	45,628	87,464	

Expenditure.	1344 T. E.	1345 T. E.	1346 T. E.	Total.	1347 T. E.	1348 T. E.	1349 T. E.	Total.	Remarks.
13. Pension and Gratuity—(*a*) State ...	59,268	56,148	56,689	1,72,105	88,492	93,721	98,478	2,80,691	
(*b*) Zemindaries ...	10,915	11,943	11,806	34,664	12,605	17,098	16,073	45,776	
Total ...	70,183	68,091	68,495	2,06,769	1,01,097	1,10,819	1,14,551	3,26,467	
14. Ordinary *Sansar* charges :—									
(*a*) His Highness's own and the late Maharaja's family—State...	85,293	82,291	95,763	2,63,347	1,01,388	72,513	72,273	2,46,174	
(*b*) Other branches of the Raj family—State & Zemindaries ...	1,15,454	96,142	88,997	3,00,593	89,229	85,880	85,396	2,60,505	
(*c*) Thakurs—State	31,675	33,197	30,569	95,441	—*	—	—	—	*Expenditure in respect of head 14 (*c*) transferred to head 13(*a*) with effect from 1347 T. E.
(*d*) *Sansar* office establishment :— State	13,608	12,587	13,099	39,294	15,080	13,957	5,440	34,477	
(*e*) Miscellaneous—State	66,670	73,250	94, 81	2,34,401	83,825	29,672	21,880	1,35,377	
Total ...	3,12,700	2,97,467	3,22,909	9,33,07	2,89,522	2,02,022	1,84,989	6,76,533	
15. Charity and Donation :—									
(*a*) State	13,769	29,007	24,618	67,394	17,736	14,142	16,682	48,560	
(*b*) Zemindaries	7,046	3,551	9,865	25,462	3,026	11,892	14,963	29,881	
Total ...	20,815	37,558	34,483	92,856	20,762	26,034	31,645	78,441	
16. His Highness's Nij Tahabil :— State...	1,00,000	1,00,000	1,20,000	3,20,000	1,20,000	1,94,591	1,98,418	5,13,009	
17. His Highness's tour—State ...	1,25,000	1,20,500	94,175	3,39,675	1,04,657	20,000	30,000	1,54,657	
18. Payment of liabilities and deposits—									
(*a*) State	77,171	79,860	98,908	*2,55,939	1,05,102	79,999	99,994	2,85,095	
(*b*) Zemindaries	30,066	13,183	16,554	59,803	61,854	1,25,312	25,744	2,12,910	
Total ...	1,07,237	93,043	1,15,462	3,15,742	1,66,956	2,05,311	1,25,738	4,98,005	
19. Miscellaneous—(*a*) State	10,164	5,901	5,926	21,991	7,892	4,761	17,763	30,416	
(*b*) Zemindaries ...	11,723	14,225	9,428	35,376	11,152	10,084	5,640	26,876	
Total ...	21,887	20,126	15,354	57,367	19,044	14,845	23,403	57,292	
20. Coronation of King Emperor—Zemindaries	—	—	—	—	302	—	—	302	
21. Writing off irrecoverable advances—State	5,577	3,000	—	8,577	782	—	—	782	
22. Payment of old debts—State ...	96,502	1,00,668	99,685	2,96,855	96,941	1,57,609	1,53,520	4,67,030	
23. Interest on deposits—State ...	29,339	30,910	32,761	93,010	22,059	36,901			
24. Advance to *Nijtahabil*—Zemindaries	1,87,000	79,591	49,984	3,16,575	—	—	—	—	
25. Silver Jubilee	—	17,638	—	17,638	—	—	—	—	
26. Governor's Visit	—	—	23,201	23,201	6,490	—	—	6,490	

Expenditure.	1344 T. E.	1345 T. E.	1346 T. E.	Total.	1347 T. E.	1348 T. E.	1349 T. E.	Total	REMARKS.
27. Marriage Ceremony of Renuka Kumari—State ...	—	—	—	—	12,445	—	—	12,445	
28. Road Fund—State	—	—	—	—	22,840	1,14,284	1,38,148	2,75,272	
29. Geological Department	—	—	—	—	—	6,040	5,750	11,790	
30. His Highness's Official entertainments—State ...	—	—	—	—	—	20,000	30,000	50,000	
31. Contribution to His Highness's *Nijtahabil*—Zemindaries ...	—	—	—	—	—	2,05,715	2,60,000	4,65,715	
32. Purchase of share of Electric Supply Co. Ltd.—State ...	—	—	—	—	—	23,000	—	23,000	
33. King Emperor's Anti Tuberculosis Fund—State ...	—	—	—	—	—	25,000	—	25,000	
34. Loans—State	—	—	—	—	—	—	4,000	4,000	
35. Advance—State	—	—	—	—	—	—	1,064	1,064	
36. War Expenditure—State	—	—	—	—	—	—	18,338	18,338	
Total ...	25,47,545	27,37,576	29,11,130	84,96,251	34,02,730	33,52,164	34,09,171 14,68,243 48,77,414	1,01,64,065 14,68,243 † 1,16,32,308	†Adjusted and excluded under circumstances explained below.
Closing Balance :—(a) State—				Closing balance for the year 1346 T. E.				Closing balance for the year 1349 T. E.	
In Cash ...	1,85,411	2,28,970	2,01,939	2,01,939	1,23,171	1,38,191	2,57,092	2,57,692*	*Including Bank balances Rs. 23,448.
At Bank ...	3,468	72,408	29,384	29,384	4,992	14,427	—	—	
Working balance :— In Cash ...	12,299	36,192	10,199	10,199	412	4,15,182	—	—	
At Bank ...	2,12,701	1,88,808	2,14,801	2,14,801	29,588				
In advances ...	1,90,182	1,90,182	1,90,182	1,90,182	3,85,182				
In bonds and advances	4,88,898	5,20,616	8,69,539	8,69,539	10,41,208	10,34,929	—	—	
Road Fund Balance	—	—	—	—	69,342	64,701	12,407	12,407 *	*Including Rs. 1,004 in Bank.
Total ...	10,92,959	12,37,176	15,16,044	15,16,044	16,53,890	16,67,430	2,70,099	2,70,099	
(b) Zemindaries :—In Cash ...	1,11,086	2,28,090	2,36,813	2,36,813	2,56,482	2,00,217	1,78,558	1,78,558	
At Bank ...	71,050	1,08,629	1,90,898	1,90,898	4,00,595	4,27,506	7,27,406	7,27,406	
In bonds and advances ...	2,01,366	2,20,425	3,00,710	3,00,710	4,07,889	5,36,228	5,79,088	5,79,088	
Total ...	3,83,502	5,57,144	7,28,421	7,28,421	10,64,966	11,63,951	14,85,052	14,85,052	
Total of State & Zemindaries' balances	14,76,461	17,94,320	22,44,465	22,44,465	27,18,856	28,31,381	17,55,151	17,55,151	
Total of State & Zemindaries' expenditure	28,47,545	27,37,576	29,11,130	84,96,251	34,02,730	33,52,164	48,77,414	1,16,32,308	
GRAND TOTAL ...	43,24,006	45,31,896	51,55,595	1,07,40,716	61,21,586	61,83,545	66,32,565	1,33,87,459	

N. B.—The slight discrepancy in certain cases between figures in Departmental sections and those in this financial statement is due to the fact that in this statement audited figures have been used, arranged under major Budget heads, after final debit and adjustment.

220. The period under report started with an opening balance of Rs. 22,44,465 against Rs. 14,02,434 in the previous triennium.

221. The total receipts during the period from all sources, including deposits, law charges recovered, refunds and compensations for lands acquired, as well as Road Fund, amounted to Rs. 1,11,42,994 against Rs. 93,38,282 in the previous three years (1344-46 T. E.). The total sum available for expenditure, including the opening balance, thus stood at Rs. 1,33,87,459 against Rs. 1,07,40,716. The actual income, excluding receipts under head Deposits, amounted to Rs. 1,01,95,002 against Rs. 86,86,999, showing an increase of Rs. 15,08,003. This was mainly due to increased receipts, under various heads owing to normal expansion (Rs. 8,89,000) ; under the head Refunds and Compensation for Lands acquired, consequent on adjustment in 1347 T. E. of advances made in 1344, 1345 and 1346 T. E. (Rs. 3,30,000) ; and under Road Fund opened for the first time in 1347 T.E, for improvement of communications in the State (Rs. 3,06,000).

222. The total expenditure incurred during the years under report (1347–49 T. E.) amounted to Rs. 1,16,32,308 against Rs. 84,96,251 in the previous three years (1344–46 T. E.), showing an increase of Rs. 31,36,057.

223. The year 1349 closed with a balance of Rs. 17,55,151 as per details below :—

Actual Cash Balance,

In the Treasuries	Rs. 4,24,205
In Banks	Rs. 7,51,858
Held in Loans and Advances, (Zemindaries) ...	Rs. 5,79,088
	Rs. 17,55,151.

224. The period in question thus ended with a balance of Rs. 17,55,151 against Rs. 22,44,465. The big drop in the starting balance in 1349 T. E., as compared with that in 1346 T. E., was due mainly to the exclusion of the advances granted from year to year in the past for specific expenditure pending final adjustment on submission of details and vouchers, and partly to non-inclusion of loans granted by the State from the opening balance of 1349 T. E. According to the past practice these advances and loans, though treated as final expenditure, were included in the balances. The amount of Rs. 13,63,138 represents under the circumstances the actual opening Cash Balance of 1349 T. E. in the Treasuries.

225. The noticeable variations in the expenditure are explained below :—

i. Administration Charges :—

State :—1. Sinking of a number of Tube wells by the Sanitation Department.

2. Purchase of three Motor Cars one for the Superintendent of Police and the other two for watering of the roads at Agartala.

3. Extra expenditure on account of Pleader's Fees.
4. Establishment of some new Reserve Forest Offices.
5. Purchase of Rifles by the Military Department and new appointments in that Department.
6. Time scale increment of pay and other increments of pay.
7. The constitution of the Mantri Parishad in 1349 T. E. with five Ministers, involving extra expenditure on Salaries and incidental charges.

ZEMINDARIES :—The decrease was Rs. 90,437. This was due to reduced litigation charges on the whole.

ii. REVENUE AND TAXES :—

ZEMINDARIES :—The increase of Rs. 1,34,818 was due to the payment of Education Cess and of some arrear Bills.

iii. PUBLIC WORKS :—

ZEMINDARIES :—The increase of Rs. 5,25,346 was due to expenditure in connection with the Tripura House in Calcutta and the Nirmahal Palace at Sonamura.

iv. ELECTRIC LIGHT :—

STATE :—The increase of Rs. 25,302 was due to the new Electric installation in State Buildings and other important places and also to the payment of some outstanding bills.

v. MEDICAL :—

STATE :—The increase of Rs. 43,486 was due to the purchase of an X'-Ray Machine and increments of pay, establishment of two new Charitable Dispensaries at Dumburnagar and Fatikroy, and appointments of some new Midwives and Taluas for some Divisions.

vi. AGRICULTURE :—

STATE :—The increase was Rs. 5,989. This was due to village reconstruction work and introduction of Co-operative system of Agriculture and some increased expenditure on Veterinary and Agricultural purposes.

vii. PURCHASE OF LAND TENURES :—

ZEMINDARIES :—The increase of Rs. 44,531 was due to purchase of Cromeen House, Shillong.

viii ROAD FUND :—

STATE :—A Road Fund was opened for the first time in 1347 T. E. and the expenditure of Rs. 2,75,272 was due to construction of a number of new roads in the State and improvements of old roads carried out during the period.

III. THE TRIPURA STATE BANK.

Management.

226. The management of the Bank was in the hands of the late Mr. S. C. Deb Barman till the month of Pous, 1348 T. E., and on his death, with Rai Saheb S. C. Dutt (now Finance Minister), Thakur Jogesh Chandra Deb Barman, B. com., continuing as Secretary throughout the period.

Progress.

227. The Bank maintained its popularity and progress and the total amount of deposits stood at Rs. 3,81,372 in 1349 T. E. against Rs. 1,21,901 in 1346 T. E., while the net profit during the three years under report amounted to Rs. 11,290 with an average of Rs. 3,763 a year, as against Rs. 1,142 in 1346 T. E.

CHAPTER VI—MEDICAL.

Hospitals and dispensaries.

228. Including the Victoria Memorial Hospital at the capital, there were 19 dispensaries in the year 1347 T. E. Two more dispensaries were opened, one at Fatikroy and the other at Dumburnagar, in the Kailasahar and Udaipur Divisions respectively, in the year 1348 T. E. The number of hospitals and dispensaries, thus, came up to 21 during the year 1349 T. E., against 19 in 1346 T. E.

New patients.

229. The following statement will show the actual number of new patients treated in the V. M. Hospital and the different dispensaries with their daily average, in comparison with 1346 T. E.

	1346 T. E.	1347 T. E.	1348 T. E.	1349 T. E.
PATIENTS :—				
Outdoor	1,33,515	1,35,920	1,46,296	1,53,626
Indoor	806	999	934	1,099
TOTAL	1,34,321	1,36,919	1,47,230	1.54,725
DAILY AVERAGE :—				
Outdoor	365·79	372·38	400·81	420·89
Indoor	2·2	2·73	2·55	3·01
TOTAL	367·81	375·11	403·36	423·90

Out-door attendance.

230. The out-door patients (new & old) during the years under review numbered 2,65,681 ; 2,82,895 and 3,04,338, the daily average being 727·88, 795·56 and 831·73 respectively. The number of patients and their daily average in 1346 T. E. were 2,65,681 and 727·88 respectively.

231. Including the balance of 26 from the year 1346 T. E. in-patients totalled 999 in the year 1347 against 806 of the year before. Out of the total, 809 were discharged cured, 141 relieved or discharged otherwise, 23 died and 26 remained in the hospitals at the close of the year.

Indoor patients.

232. In 1348 T. E. the total number was 934, with 659 cured, 217 relieved, 32 dead and 26 remaining under treatment.

233. The in-patients numbered 1,099 in the year 1349 T. E.; out of the number, 862 were cured, 180 relieved, 30 died and 27 remained in the hospitals at the end of the year.

234. Altogether 1329 operations including 29 major cases were performed during the year 1347 T. E. against 1,141 and 33 of the previous year.

Surgical operations.

235. In 1348 T. E., 1328 operations were performed, of which 32 were major. The total number of operation cases was 1,408 including 32 major cases in 1349 T. E.

236. The total number of Police cases was 138 in 1347 T. E., as against 154 in the year 1346 T. E. of which 17 were postmortem cases against 21.

Police cases.

237. In 1348 T. E., there were 155 Police cases with 29 postmortems, as against 179 cases with 33 postmortems in 1349 T. E.

238. Only 9 new patients came in for treatment in the two Leprosy clinics, one at the capital and the other at Khowai Divisional town and were treated by Dr. J. M. Bose and Dr. P. Sen Gupta, respectively, in the year 1347 T.E. The number of new patients was 11 and 14 during the years 1348 and 1349 T. E. respectively. Two Doctors were sent to Calcutta for Leprosy treatment training during the year 1348. Leprosy Propaganda Officer Dr. Isac Santra came to see the works of the leprosy clinics on 3rd December 1938 (1348).

Leprosy Clinic.

239. There was only one out-door Kala-azar centre at the V. M. Hospital, in charge of Dr. S. Bhattacherjee. The number of patients treated and results thereof are shown below, as compared with 1346 T. E.

Kala-azar.

Year	No. of patients treated	Cured	Relieved	Left treatment	Died	Remained for treatment
1346 T. E.	120	45	—	70	—	5
1347 T. E.	87	19	—	61	—	7
1348 T. E.	175	75	32	47	3	18
1349 T. E.	186	83	27	59	7	10

240. Outdoor patients treated new numbered 20,539 during the year 1347 T. E., as against 20,482 of the previous year, the daily average of new and old patients being 119·46 against 115·73. The number of patients in the two successive years was 20,039 with a daily average of 109·14 and 213·73 with a daily average of 115·86. The total number of in-patients was 647, 717 and 828. The total cost incurred in this Institution amounted to Rs. 9,579–6, Rs. 9,951–14–9 and Rs. 10,419 respectively during the years 1347, 1348 and 1349 T. E., against Rs. 9,478–11–3p in 1346 T. E.

V. M. Hospital.

241. Dr. N. Deb Barman remained in charge of this centre at the Capital. 18 persons and 2 dogs were treated in 1347 T. E. The number of patients treated in 1348 and 1349 T. E. stood at 23 and 17 respectively. The total expenditure on this account was Rs. 412 on average. The corresponding figures in 1346 T. E. were :—persons 23 ; dogs—nil ; expenditure Rs. 271.

Antirabic centre.

242. The charge of the clinic remained with Dr. A. Sen Gupta M. B., during the triennium ; Dr. N. Deb Barman M. B. also worked during the absence of the former. 645, 578 and 566 samples of different kinds were examined by them during the years under report against 450 in 1346 T. E.

Clinical Laboratory.

243. An X-Ray Power plant with equipments was installed at Agartala in the early part of the year 1347 T. E. Dr. N. Deb Barman, the State Radiologist, was put in charge of this Institute. The cost of the machine with equipments amounted to Rs. 12,638. Altogether 47 cases were examined in this section in 1348 T. E. and 22 in 1349 T. E. The recurring expenditure on this Institution was Rs. 603 on an average.

The King George V X-Ray Installation.

244. Dr. M. M. Majumdar, Chief Medical Officer, continued to be in charge of this Department in the year 1347 T. E. Three Assistant Homœopaths performed their normal duties. The total number of patients treated in 1347 T. E. was 21,490 against 19,833 of the previous year, the daily average (new + old) being 107·39 against 91·25. Dr. K. B. Ghosh B. A., H. M. B. was appointed to the post of the State Homœopath in the early part of the year 1348, in which year 24,718 patients were treated with a daily average of 125·48. The number of new patients treated in 1349 T. E. was 26,434, the daily average being 161·08. The total cost came to Rs. 2,897, Rs. 3,443 and Rs. 4,344, respectively, during the years under report, against Rs. 2,735-12-5 in 1346 T. E.

Homœopathic Dept.

245. As in the year before, Kabiraj Surendra Chandra Bhattacharjee Vaidyaratna was in charge of this Department. The number of patients treated during the three years under report was 110. The average annual expenditure, covering the price of medicines and the annual salary of the Kabiraj during the 3 years, was Rs. 3,229 as against Rs. 2,678–1–0 in 1346 T. E.

Ayurvedic Dept.

246. Altogether 14,934 persons were successfully vaccinated out of 18,848 operations performed during the year 1347 T. E. The corresponding figures in the year 1348 T. E. were 11,805 and 13,726 respectively. In 1349 T. E., 16,119 persons were vaccinated, 12,907 cases proving successful. The total cost on this account for the 3 years was Rs. 6,711. The corresponding figures in 1346 T. E. were—total cases—13,577 ; successful 10,336 ; expenditure Rs. 1,690–13–0.

Vaccination.

247. In 1347 T. E. cholera broke out in Sadar and Kailasahar Divisions and raged rather virulently in the latter Division for some time. 507 seizures with 295 deaths were reported. Three temporary Doctors were employed for Kailasahar Division. 9,500 anti-cholera inoculations were performed.

Public Health.

248. Small-pox also broke out more or less in all the Divisions of the State. As reported, there were 340 deaths out of 971 seizures. Four Small-pox specialists were engaged for treatment. The total cost of the treatment amounted to Rs. 500. During the year 1348, cholera broke out sporadically in the Sadar, Kailasahar, Sonamura and Khowai Divisions. 70 deaths out of 137 seizures were reported. 9,000 persons were inoculated with anti-cholera vaccine. The total amount spent was Rs. 301.

249. Small-pox also broke out in Sadar Division during the year 1349 T. E. There were 124 attacks with 3 deaths. 115 of the number were treated by Small-pox specialists. The cost of medicines amounted to Rs. 331–12–0.

250. Lieutenant-Colonel H. W. C. Robson, O. B. E., Resident for the Eastern States kindly visited the V. M. Hospital and the X-Ray installation on 24th march 1339.

Visit.

251. Dr. M. M. Majumdar L. M. S. Chief Medical Officer (later on Minister, Public Health) remained in charge of the Medical Depeartment with his assistants, Dr. S. K. Dutta L. M. S., Asst. State Physician, Dr. A. Sen Gupta M. B., State Bacteriologist, Dr. N. Deb Barman M. B. State Radiologist, and Dr. S. Bhattacharjee M. B., General Assistant at the capital town, during the years under report.

Staff.

252. In addition to this, there was a regular staff of medical subordinates in charge of the *Mofussil* Dispensaries. A Lady Doctor, 9 midwives and 6 nurses were also employed at the V. M. Hospital and the different Dispensaries.

253. In 1347 T. E., Doctor A. Sen Gupta went out on inspection for 7 days and visited 2 Dispensaries. He was out on tour for 9 days and inspected 4 Dispensaries during the year 1348 T. E.

Inspection.

254. Dr. N. Deb Barman M. B. was on tour for 5 days and inspected 2 Dispensaries and Dr. Sen Gupta was out for 11 days and inspected 3 Dispensaries in 1349 T. E.

255. The total expenditure amounted to Rs. 87,812, Rs. 76,984, Rs. 84,791 respectively, during the years under review, against Rs. 71,950 in 1346 T. E.

Expenditure.

CHAPTER VII—PUBLIC INSTRUCTION.

257. The Department of Public Instruction was under the portfolio of Manyabara Raja Rana Bodhjung Bahadur, F. R. G. S., Chief Secretary to His Highness the Maharaja Manikya Bahadur during the years 1347 T. E. and 1348 T. E. On the inauguration of Reforms in 1349 T. E. the portfolio continued to be held by the Raja Bahadur, as Minister in charge. In 1347 T. E. and 1348 T. E. Mr. Satya Ranjan Bose, B. A., as Under Secretary, and later on, Officer-in-charge, Education Department, and in 1349 T. E. Mr. Janesh Kumar Bhattacharjee, M. SC., Inspector of Schools and later on, Secretary, Education Department, assisted the Raja Bahadur.

Charge.

258. The total number of Schools during the years under review was 138, 132 and 141 with an aggregate numerical strength of 7,176, 7,786 and 8,955 respectively, as against 135 schools and 7,445 students in 1346 T. E. Besides, there were private schools numbering 31, 33 and 33 against 46 in 1346 T. E.

Number of Schools.

259. In the years 1347 T. E. and 1348 T. E. there were 6 permanently affiliated High Schools and 1 Branch for boys and in 1349 T. E. 7 permanently affiliated H. E. Schools for boys. The total number of pupils in these institutions was 1,832, 1,923 and 1,947 respectively and the average daily attendance stood at 1,371·68, 1,408·60 and 1504·30 respectively, against 1,167·70 in the preceding year.

H. E. Schools.

260. Agartala, the capital of the State continued to be a centre for the Matriculation Examination. The State H. E. Schools sent up candidates to this Centre. Candidates from schools in British India were also allowed at it. In 1347, 4 female candidates and 2 teachers, in 1348, 8 female candidates and 1 teacher, and in 1349, 6 female candidates and 3 teachers sat for the Examination at this Centre. In 1349, the Matriculation Examination was held twice, once in December, 1939 (Supplementary Matriculation Examination) and again in March 1940 A. D.

Matriculation Examination.

261. The subjoined statement will show the results of the examination during the period under review :

	No. sent up.	Passed.	1st Division.	2nd Division.	3rd Division.
1. U K. Academy					
1347 T. E.	22	19	10	8	1
1348 T. E.	28	19	10	4	5
1349 T. E.	30	19	0	3	16
2. R. K. Institution					
1347 T. E.	26	23	3	16	4
1348 T. E.	18	10	4	5	1
1349 T. E.	7	4	0	1	3
3. B. K. Institution					
1347 T. E.	21	15	1	13	1
1348 T. E.	25	18	2	8	8
1349 T. E.	15	10	1	1	8
4. B. B. Institution					
1347 T. E.	7	7	3	3	1
1348 T. E.	13	9	2	5	2
1349 T. E.	6	5	1	1	3
5. N. C. Institution					
1347 T. E.	11	10	1	6	3
1348 T. E.	20	9	1	2	6
1349 T. E.	7	3	1	0	2
6. K. B. Institution					
1348 T. E.	7	5	0	3	2
1349 T. E.	7	5	0	0	5
	270	190	40	79	71

262. The result on the whole was satisfactory, the percentage of success being 85·05, 63·06 and 67·65 respectively.

263. The subjoined statement will show the mothly Scholarships awarded to the students of the State H. E. Schools on the results of the Matriculation Examinations, each being tenable for 2 years.

	1347 T. E.	1348 T. E.	1349 T. E.
1st—Rs. 10 ...	U. K. Academy.	R. K. Institution	B. B. Institution
2nd—Rs. 8 ...	R. K. Institution.	U. K. Academy.	N. C. Institution.
3rd—Rs. 8 ...	U. K. Academy. and B. K. Institution.	U. K. Academy.	B. K. Institution.

M. E. Schools for boys.

264. During the years under review there were 10, 10, and 11, M. E. Schools for boys with a total strength of 1172, 1153, and 1290 respectively, against 10 schools and 1205 students in 1346 T. E., and the average daily attendance stood at 857·31, 897·76 and 990·09 respectively, against 821·59 of the year 1346 T. E.

M. E. Schools for girls.

265. The Maharani Tulsibati Girls' School at Agartala had a numerical strength of 153, 143 and 373 respectively against 121 in the year 1346 T. E. Under special permission of the Department some girls were allowed to continue higher studies in this school under the tuition of the Head Mistress. For conveyance of the girls a motor bus service was maintained as bofore. In 1349 T. E. there were 3 other M. E. Schools for girls besides Maharani Tulsibati Girls' School.

L. V. Schools for boys.

266. During the period under review there were 22, 20 and 19 L. V. Schools respectively for boys, with a total strength of 1217, 1033 and 1111 respectively, against 22 schools and 1087 students in 1346 T. E.

L. V. Schools for girls.

267. During the years 1348 and 1349 T. E. there were 8 and 5 L. V. Schools respectively for girls with a total strength of 270 and 155 students, and the average daily attendance stood at 214·16 and 106·33 respectively.

Pathsalas for boys.

268. In the years under report there were 74, 70 and 79 pathsalas for boys against 71 in the preceding year. The total number of pupils stood at 2272, 2251 and 2946 against 2089 in the preceding year, and the average daily attendance was 1911·50, 1619·20 and 2523·60 respectively in the years under review, against 1614·21 in 1346 T. E.

Pathsalas for Girls.

269. There were 9, 1 and 1 *Pathsalas* for girls respectively in the years 1347, 1348 and 1349 T. E. against 9 in 1346 T. E. The total number of students were 286, 44 and 59 as against 278, while the average daily attendance stood at 232·48, 22·88 and 38·25 respectively against 219·23.

Scholarship Examinations.

270. Altogether 900, 1062 and 1097 candidates appeared at the different Scholarship Examinations of the State against 961 in 1346 T. E. Of these, 670 including 146 girls, 812 including 140 girls and 856 including 166 girls respectively in the years 1347, 1348 and 1349 T. E. came out successful, as against 732 inclusive of 146 girls. The results on the whole were satisfactory.

271. In 1347 T. E., 61 students including 8 girls passed the M. E. Examination and 3 girls passed the H. V. Examination ; in the L. V. Examination, the number of successful candidates was 135 including 35 girls, and in the *Pathsala* Examination, the number was 471 including 82 girls. Amongst these candidates 25 appeared from different *Maktabs* and *Madrassas* of the State.

272. In 1348 T. E., 85 students including 16 girls passed the M. E. Examination, and 4 girls passed the H. V. Examination. In the L. V. Examination the number of successful candidates was 173 including 38 girls, and in the *Pathsala* Examination, the number of successful candidates was 550 including 82 girls. Amongst these candidates 29 caadidates appeared from different *Maktabs* and *Madrassas* of the State.

273. In 1349 T. E., 51 students including 13 girls passed the M. E. Examination and 1 girl the H. V. Examination. In the L. V. Examination the number of successful candidates was 198 including 47 girls, and in the *Pathsala* Examination the number was 605 including 105 girls. Amongst these candidates 20 appeared from different *Maktabs* and *Madrassas* of the State.

274. On the results of the examinations 12 boys and 6 girls, in 1347, 13 boys and 5 girls in 1348, and 14 boys and 5 girls in 1349 T. E. were awarded monthly scholarships varying from Rs. 2 to Rs. 5 per month tenable for two to four years.

Schools for special training.

275. In the years under review there were 10 schools for special training consisting of 5 Sanskrit *Tols*, 4 *Maktabs* and *Madrassas* and 1 *Silpasram* (Artisan School).

276. The Sanskrit *Tols* had 71, 57 and 65 students respectively in 1347, 1348 and 1349 T. E. on the roll, against 74 in the preceding year, and the average daily attendance stood at 53·27, 39·37 and 47·08 against 56·45.

277. The *Maktabs* and *Madrassas* had 142, 144 and 116 students respectively on the roll, and the average daily attendance stood at 95·47, 101·37 and 95·57 against 136·88 in 1346 T. E.

Compulsory Free Primary Schools.

278. In the years under review there were, as before, 4 compulsory Free Primary Schools with 694, 732 and 856 pupils including girls, as against 612 in 1346 T. E.

279. The subjoined statement will show the number of students, their nationality and the average daily attendance in these Free Primary Schools :

Compulsory Free Primary Schools	No. of Students		Average daily attendance		Kumars	Thakurs	Manipuris	Tripuras	Reangs	Bengalees	Mahomedans	Others
	Boys	Girls	Boys	Girls								
No. 1 U. K. Academy—												
1347 ...	·230	116	144·30	88·73	—	17	—	–	0	297	30	2
1348 ...	193	101	136·21	79·62	—	7	–	2	1	253	31	2
1349 ...	237	128	128·20	74·60	—	10	—	1	0	317	35	2
No. 2 Tulsibati—												
1347 ...	68	98	29·50	55·00	—	5	0	9	—	142	7	3
1348 ...	88	101	49·73	62·11	—	5	8	1		174	1	—
1349 ...	99	·112	70·80	77·60	—	11	6	8	—	182	4	—
No. 3 Bejoykumar—												
1347 ...	57	88	44·90	62·50	—	19	26	–	—	78	11	11
1348 ...	86	93	57·41	61·51	1	32	-	—	—	135	9	1
1349 ...	100	87	59·60	53·90	3	44	—	—	—	130	9	1
No. 4 Thakurpalli—												
1347	37	—	12·81	—	—	23	2	2	—	9	—	1
1348 ...	51	19	40·32	7·13	—	53	—	1	—	8	8	—
1349 ...	54	39	39·30	25·80	—	56	5	7	—	18	3	4

280. The comparative statement below will show the number of non-Bengalee students receiving education in the several schools of the State :

Serial No.	Nationality	Number of students			
		1346 T. E.	1347 T. E.	1348 T. E.	1349 T. E.
1.	Rajkumars ...	2	2	1	6
2.	Thakurs ...	203	320	279	370
3.	Manipuris ...	697	673	825	1220
4.	Tripuras	917	983	845	1023
5.	Reangs	9	20	19	39
6.	Kukis	—	—	1	1
7.	Chakmas	1	2	1	3
8.	Lushais	1	3	6	6
9.	Others	112	153	139	231
10.	Christians ...	5	–	—	10

281. The Maharajkumaris received their education as before under a graduate lady teacher and a *Pandit*.

Education of Princes and Princesses.

282. Maharajkumar Mohan Kishore Dev Barman Bahadur continued his studies in the College of Engineering and Technology, Jadavpur. After passing the Matriculation Examination in First Division from the Comilla Zilla School in 1347 T. E. Maharajkumar Chandrama Kishore Dev Barman Bahadur prosecuted his studies, I. A. Standard, in the St. Edmund's College, Shillong. Maharajkumar Sukumar Kishore Dev Barman Bahadur also prosecuted his studies in the same Institution (School Department). Both of them were placed under the guardianship and coaching of a Professor of the St. Edmund's College.

Education of other Kumars.

283. The young Maharajkumar Bahadurs received their education under a tutor.

284. In the years under report Thakur boys numbering 14, 19 and 13 respectively were receiving Higher Education in various Colleges and Technical Schools and they were awarded stipends from the Education Department.

Education of Thakur boys.

285 In the years under review the number of boarders in the Thakur Boarding House were 30, 24 and 29 respectively against 28 in the year 1346 T. E. The staff consisted of one graduate Guardian Superintendent, one under graduate Resident Tutor and one Manager-Tutor. The average daily attendance stood at 27·80, 22·90 and 25·00 against 24·00 in the preceding year.

Thakur Boarding House at Agartala.

286. In the years under review there were in the Tripura Boarding House boarders numbering 35, 27 and 33 against 48 in the year 1346 T. E. All the boarders were allowed free Boarding stipends. A wholetime graduate Superintending tutor looked after the boys as well as the boarding management as before. Two other tutors were engaged to coach the boys in the morning and evening.

Tripura Boarding House at Agartala.

287. In the years under review, there were 60, 41 and 55 boarders in the Tripura Boarding House at Khowai against 60 in the year 1346 T. E. One graduate Superintending Tutor and one Assistant Tutor were engaged, as before, for coaching the boys both in the morning and evening. The Superintending tutor looked after the Boarding management in addition to his work.

Tripura Boarding House at Khowai.

288. In the years under review there were 30, 34 and 44 boarders in the Ramkumar Boarding School, against 52 in the preceding year, and the average daily attendance stood at 21·71, 21·68 and 29·02 against 38.71 in the previous year. Two tutors were engaged as before to coach the boarders and one of them looked after the Boarding management in addition.

Ramkumar Boarding School at Kalyanpur

Schools for convicts.

289. In the years under report there were 18, 15 and 19 convicts reading in the Primary School in the Central Jail. In 1347 T. E. one passed the L. V. Scholarship Examination, and in 1348 T. E. one passed the *Pathsala* Scholarship Examination.

Silpasram.

290. The *Silpasram* continued to be under the direct control of the Education Department. In the years under report there were 19, 19 and 18 students respectively on the roll against 22 in the preceding year, and the average daily attendance stood at 10·53, 11·55 and 9·50 against 10·75 in the preceding year. 14 students were awarded monthly stipends varying from Rs. 1/8/- to Rs. 8/- each.

291. The subjoined statement will show the number of students in the *Silpasram*, their nationality and their average daily attendance in the years under report :—

Name of the School	Years	No. of students	Thakurs	Tripuras	Manipuris	Bengalees	Mahommedans	Others	Average daily attendance
Silpasram	1347 T. E.	19	3	1	2	12		1	10·53
	1348 T. E.	19	4	5	1	8		1	11·55
	1349 T. E.	18	2	7	2	6		1	9·50

Lushai stipends.

292. In the years under report 5, 6 and 9 Lushai boys were awarded Lushai stipends. Of them some prosecuted their studies in different Colleges and the others in different schools of the State.

Special stipends.

293. In the years under review, 30, 27 and 25 students were awarded special stipends. Some of them prosecuted their studies in different schools of this State and others elsewhere in different Colleges and Technical Institutions.

Inspection works.

294. There were 3 Sub-Inspectors of Schools, as before, who inspected all the schools other than H. E. Schools within their respective jurisdiction in Sadar, Khowai, Kailasahar and Dharmanagar Divisions. Revenue Inspectors of Sonamura and Belonia also inspected some schools in their respective jurisdictions.

Library.

295. Maharajkumar Norottam Kishore Dev Barman Bahadur continued to be the Librarian of the Bir Chandra Library at Agartala, which was maintained in two separate sections as before, viz., (1) English Section, located at the Ujjayanta Palace and (2) Vernacular Section, in the building near the local H. E. School. The latter section was open to the public. In the years under review the number of English books (including foreign literature) stood at 5037, 5039 and 5039 against 5037 in the year 1346 T. E. The number of Bengali and Sanskrit books were 2259, 2261 and 2256 against 2253 in 1346 T. E. In 1347 T. E. there were

5 dailies, 4 weeklies and 13 monthlies subscribed in the libraries against the same number in the preceding year ; in 1348 T. E. there were 4 dailies, 5 weeklies and 10 monthlies and in 1349 T. E. 3 dailies, 5 weeklies and 7 monthlies. In the years under report the average daily attendance in the Vernacular section of the library was 11, 6 and 5, against 8 in the previous year, and the total number of books issued to the public was 1673, 1580 and 893, against 1636 in 1346 T. E.

Expenditure.

296. The total expenditure on public instruction in the years under report amounted to Rs. 1,30,817, Rs. 1,30,783 and Rs. 1,24,215 against Rs. 1,31,956 in the preceding year, as detailed below.

	1347 T. E.	1348 T. E.	1349 T. E.
1. Education Department	Rs. 2,147	Rs. 6,311	Rs. 5,447
2. Primary Education	,, 27,413	,, 32,168	,, 27,043
3. Secondary Education	,, 52,834	,, 58,415	,, 55,017
4. Schools for special training	,, 1,250	,, 1,225	,, 1,177
5. Compulsory Free Primary Education	,, 3,020	,, 3,000	,, 3,214
6. Boarding Institutions for Thakur Boys	,, 6,501	,, 6,075	,, 6,118
7. Education of Kumars and Kumaris	,, 7,970	,, 8,417	,, 6,657
8. Scholarships and stipends	,, 6,180	,, 5,949	,, 4,360
9. Library	,, 1,894	,, 1,800	,, 1,799
10. Miscellaneous	,, 14,780	,, 5,906	,, 7,209
11. Silpasram	,, 3,029	,, 3,045	,, 2,986
12. Tripura Boarding	,, 3,799	,, 3,472	,, 3,188
	Rs. 1,30,817	Rs. 1,30,783	Rs. 1,24,215

Income.

297. The total receipt from the schools in the years under review amounted to Rs. 14,208, Rs. 14,375 and Rs. 15,111 respectively against Rs. 15,078 in the previous year.

CHAPTER VIII—REFORMS.

Charge.

298. The portfolio of Reforms was held by ***Manyabara*** Raja Rana Bodhjung Bahadur with effect from his appointment as Minister and the establishment of the ***Mantri Parishad*** in 1349 T. E. The Minister was assisted in the Department as well as in the Local Self Government Department by Mr. Satya Ranjan Bose, B. A., as Officer-in-charge and later on as Secretary.

Work.

299. The first item of work undertaken was territorial reorganisation and establishment of a number of Village Mandalis or unions on elective basis as electoral units for election to the ***Vyavasthapak Sava*** of the State and with powers to administer certain local affairs. This work was pushed on during 1349 T. E. on the strength of His Highness's provisional order on the subject. A law has since the close of the triennium, been passed as the Village Mandali Act or Act I of 1350 T. E.

Scope of the Reforms.

300. The scope of the reforms undertaken has already been dealt with in Chapter I.

CHAPTER IX—ZEMINDARIES.

CHAKLA ROSHNABAD AND OTHER ESTATES.

Chakla Roshnabad.

301. The zemindaries of His Highness, attached to the State, and known as the Chakla Roshnabad and other Estates, consist principally of the following *Toujis* in different collectorates—the properties extending over the Tippera, Noakhali and Sylhet Districts.

Touji and other Particulars	Annual Revenues and cesses payable to British India			
	Revenue	Road Cess	Education Cess	Total
The Central Division.				
TIPPERA COLLECTORATE.				
(1) Touji No. 252 Chakla Roshnabad Estates ...	1,52,408	74,032	94,810	3,21,250
(2) Touji No. 355 Lakheraj Bajapti Mohal at Pargana Bagasair	261	71	93	425
(3) No. 52 Taluk Dharma Narayan	105	16	22	143
(4) No. 2053 Taluk Panchu Hazari	236	37	50	323
(5) No. 364 Taluk Kalikinkar Ghosh (Soydabad)	705	525	668	1,898
(6) 87 Lakheraj at Lalmai	—	470	587	1,057
MINOR MOHALS.				
(7) Touji Nos. 1190, 669, 671, 2205, 4303, 88, 119, 120, 123, 126, 127, 128, 129, 130, 131, 133, 139, 113, 111, 114, 137, 138.	162	665	833	1,660
	1,53,877	75,816	97,063	3,26,756
The Southern Division.				
NOAKHALI COLLECTORATE.				
(1) Touji No. 209 Taluk Kripa Kishore ...	3,928	2,125	2,718	8,771
(2) Tauji No. 229 Mohal Asharkota ...	193	22	31	246
(3) Touji No. 12 Darara Hishya 3 as. 5 karas-2½ krantas ...	1,721	2,321	2,929	6,971
(4) Touji No. 204 Char Shaha Bhikari Hishya 4 annas	1,402	281	373	2,056
MINOR MOHALS.				
(5) Touji Nos. 535/1, 829/1, 148/1, 92/B, 34799, 1679.	196	52	68	316
	7,440	4,801	6,119	18,360

Particulars	Annual Revenues & Cesses Payable to British India			
	Revenue	Road Cess	Education Cess	Total
The Northern Division. *	—	—	—	—
The Srimangal Division (MAULAVI BAZAR COLLECTORATE.)				
(1) Touji No. 51168/1 Taluk Golamali Hishya no. 1	2,686	1,054	—	3,740
(2) Touji No. 51168/1 Golamali parent Mohal ...	215	73	—	288
(3) Touji No. 51483/325 Taluk Golam Rasul ...	120	33	—	153
(4) Touji No. 51783/1 Golamali Hishya No. 5 Jubaraj Birchandra ...	839	369	—	1,208
(5) Touji No. 51783/1 Golamali parent Mohal ...	271	115	—	386
MINOR MOHALS				
(5) Touji Nos. 51168/1, 51169/2, 51169/3, 51169/4, 51169/2 (Parent Mohal), 51171/4, 51171/2, 51192/25, 51230/63, 51326/162, 51349/185, 51351/188, 51364/20, 51368/205, 51384/223, 51390/228, 51402/240.	754	381	—	1,135
	4,885	2,025	—	6,910
Srimangal Division (KARIMGANJ COLLECTORATE)				
(1) Touji No. 16361/6 Taluk Bodoruddin Ahmed.	10	5	—	15
HABIGANJ COLLECTORATE.				
(1) Touji No. 55835/1081 Ramprasad	1,167	1,698	—	2,865
(2) Touji No. 56087/1335 Sarbamongola ...	168	260	—	428
(3) Do. No. 55949/1196 Taluk Shed Ramjan Ali...	62	10	—	72
(4) Do. No. 252 Chakla Roshnabad (in respect of Local rate of Montala only)	—	1,551	—	1,551
	1,397	3,519	—	4,916

* Revenue etc of this Division are paid in the Comilla Collectorate along with the Revenue etc of the Central Division, the properties being included in Touji. No. 252.

302. Most of the above properties are situated in an unbroken line contiguous to the western boundary of the Tripura State and having once been part and parcel of the kingdom of the ancient Rulers of Tripura. They form now an indivisible appange of the State.

Administrative Divisions.

303. For administrative purposes, the Zemindaries are divided into four units, viz :—

(1) The Central Division with headquarters at Comilla, comprising properties within the jurisdiction of the Police stations Kotwali, Burichang, Chauddagram and Laksam in the District of Tippera.

(2) The Southern Division with headquarters at Feni, comprising properties within the jurisdiction of the Police stations Feni, Parasuram and Chhagalnaiya in the District of Noakhali.

(3) The Northern Division with headquarters at Mogra (Gangasagar) comprising properties within the jurisdiction of police stations Kasba, Brahmanbaria and Nabinagar under the Brahmanbaria Subdivision in the District of Tippera.

(4) The Srimangal Division with headquarters at Srimangal comprising properties under the jurisdiction of police stations Srimangal, Chunarughat, Madhabpur and Patharkandi in the District of Sylhet.

Management.

304. The management of the zemindaries continued in the hands of Manyabara Rai J. C. Sen Bahadur B. A. B. C. S. (Retd.) during the three years under review in this report i. e. the years 1347 to 1349 T. E. He was assisted as in previous years, by a Deputy Manager posted at Comilla and three Assistant Managers, posted at Feni, Mogra and Srimangal.

Relief to tenants.

305. As in previous years, relief had to be given to the Talukdars and the tenants in the shape of general remission of interest and damages almost throughout the years, while the policy of allowing petty demands of the jote lands to be time barred was also continued.

The demand of the period.

306. The gross demands of the years with arrears were as follows :—

1347 T. E.	...	...	...	Rs. 36,91,940
1348 T. E.	...	...	...	,, 36,08,921
1349 T. E.	...	...	...	,, 34,85,761

Decrease in demand.

307. The demand of 1346 T. E. with arrears was 36,78,747. The decrease in demand in 1349 T. E. was mainly due to deduction of rents and cesses etc. from the rent-rolls owing to large number of Taluks and jotes having been purchased in rent sales on behalf of the Raj.

308. Total receipts in the above mentioned years were :—
Realisation.

1347 T. E.	...	...	Rs. 17,28,605
1348 T. E.	...	...	Rs. 12,59,198
1349 T. E.	...	...	Rs. 14,63,542

309. Total receipts in the preceding year viz. 1346 T. E. amounted to Rs. 13,75,274. The increase in 1347 T. E. was mainly due to adjustment of previous advances amounting to Rs. 3,23,000 made for Nirmahal Palace at Rudrasagar.

A conference with tenants—concessions allowed.

310. To give special relief to the jotedars, a Conference of the delegates, nominated by the tenants was held at Agartala in Chaitra 1348 T. E. under direction of His Highness the Maharaja Manikya Bahadur. After discussion with the delegates a scheme, approved by His Highness, was circulated amongst the tenants in the shape of a memorandum (Memo no. 21 of 1348 T. E.). The main object of the scheme was to give opportunities to the tenants to pay up arrear dues within 9 years by easy instalments without any interest. Opportunities were also given to the tenants to pay decretal dues excluding damages and interests with remission of Rs. 20/– per cent. of the actual claim, provided they paid up such dues by Aswin 1349 T. E. The auction purchased jotes were also ordered to be restored to the judgment-debtors and their heirs who paid up all decretal and subsequent dues less 20% p. c. by Aswin 1349 T. E.

311. The Memo. had certain effect upon the collection of 1348 T. E. But its full effect was in evidence in 1349 T. E. in which year the collection was a record one.

312. Total expenditure of each of the years under review was as follows :—
Expenditure.

1347 T. E.	...	...	Rs. 13, 92, 060
1348 T. E.	...	...	Rs. 11, 60, 213
1349 T. E.	...	...	Rs. 11, 42, 441

313. The total expenditure in 1346 T. E. was Rs. 12,03,997. The expenditure mentioned above includes payments of old debts and deposits P. W. D. expenses, and contributions to the State. In 1347 T. E. expenditure under head P. W. D. rose to Rs. 4,42,556, owing to part payment of the cost of construction of the Nirmahal Palace being made this year.

314. Of the total expenditure during the years under review Rs. 2,62,041, Rs. 3,45,211 and Rs. 3,78,969, respectively were for Land Revenue, Taxes and Cesses, while the Administration charges including public works and Law charges were Rs. 7,21,864, Rs. 4,35,679 and Rs. 3,78,106. The increase in administrative charges in 1347 T. E. was due to the adjustment of Rs. 3,16,575 advanced in previous years and debit of the amount to the proper head, viz. P. W. D.

315. The following items of expenditure are noticeable :—

		1347 T. E.	1348 T. E.	1349 T. E.	Remarks.
1.	Education ...	Rs. 9,103	4,180	4,149	
2.	Medical	11,831	10,199	10,227	
3.	Religious ceremony...	6,845	6,340	6,779	
4.	Purchase of property	20,134	675	42,444	
5.	Sansar stipends ...	15,060	15,0,60	15,060	
6.	Donation	3,026	11,892	14,963	
7.	Repayment of old debts and deposits	61,854	1,25,312	25,744	
8.	Contribution to the State	2,30,000	2,05,715	2,66,000	
9.	Donation to Coronation fund	302	—	—	
	Rs. ...	4,08,155	3,79,323	3,85,366	

316. The result of the three years' Settlement operations will appear from the table below :—

Settlement.

Kinds of settlement	1347 T. E.		1348 T. E.		1349 T. E.		REMARKS
	Addition to rent roll	*Nazar* realised	Addition to rent roll	*Nazar* realised	Addition to rent roll	*Nazar* realised	
Railway relinquished land	69	—	—	—	—	—	
Kaimi and *Takshishi* settlement at Comilla Town	21	1,043	100	5,949	152	12,010	
Ordinary Town settlement ...	19	140	10	54	28	510	
Khas patit	919	3,664	419	2,986	441	3,966	
Enhancement of rent...	180	2,575	94	282	227	3,523	
Resettlement of auction purchased holdings	265	16,841	313	49,113	515	43,604	
Settlement of rent free holding	—	—	—	—	—	—	
Takshishi settlement in the *Moffusil* ...	5	250	3	048	[illegible]	911	
Ijara settlement ...	274	—	16,471	—	31,860	—	
Rs. ...	1,752	24,513	17,416	58,732	33,228	64,557	

317. The corresponding figures for the year 1346 T. E. were Rs. 2,840 and Rs. 27,614 respectively.

318. **Subjoined is a Statement of tours of the officers in-charge of the Administrative Divisions of the Zemindaries :—**

Tours.

		1347 T. E.	1348 T. E.	1349 T. E.
1.	Babu P. R. Bhattacharjee, B. A., Deputy Manager.	105	64	35
2.	,, J. C. Majumdar, M. A. B. L., Assistant Manager, Feni.	92	95	83
3.	,, B. Guha, B. A. Assistant Manager, Mogra.	76	85	30
4.	,, S. C. Guha, B. A., Assistant Manager, Srimangal.	106	103	61

CHAPTER X—MISCELLANEOUS.

319. **Rai J. C. Sen Bahadur, Minister, and on the establishment of the Council of Ministers, Chief Minister, was out on tour for 101 days, in the course of which he visited Calcutta, Shillong, Delhi, Bombay, Comilla, and Feni, in some cases as representative of the State to various committees and conferences of the Chamber of Princes and other public bodies. Noticeable tours of other Ministers during 1349 T. E. were as under :— Manyabara Raja Rana Bodhjung Bahadur, Minister, Local Self-Government and other departments—41 days ; the late Rai J. M. Chatterjee Bahadur, Minister, Finance and other departments—51 days ; Thakur K. K. Sing, Minister Agriculture and other departments—10 days.**

Tours of Ministers.

320. **Altogether extradition of 77 persons from British India was granted by the Political Agent during the years under report, of whom 16 persons were arrested and surrendered to the State Courts concerned, and 37 persons appeared of their own accord, or were subsequently arrested within the State.**

Extradition between British India & Tripura.

321. **Surrender of 44 persons from the State territory to British Indian Courts was allowed during the period. Out of them, 32 persons were arrested by the State Police ; 2 surrendered themselves before the trying Courts ; 1 was released ; proceedings against 2 persons were dropped on the cases being withdrawn, and 7 persons were absconding.**

The State Press.

322. There were one electric printing press, one treddle press and three hand presses, during the years under review, which sufficed to meet the growing demands on the press and for printing of all Government publications, forms as also question papers for various school examinations. Judicial Stamps were printed at the treddle press. Soon after the close of the period, a calamity overtook the press in the shape of heavy floods which inundated the whole of the town of Agartala and seriously damaged the presses and all accessories.

Stationery and Forms Department.

323. As in previous years, the Stationery Department stocked all stationery articles as also forms, and issued them to various Departments as indents were received.

DATED, AGARTALA.
The 27th February, 1943.

Rana Bodhjung,
Chief Minister.

B. K. Sen,
Political Minister.

S. Goswami,
Revenue Minister.

K. K. Singh,
Minister. Public health & Sanitation.

S. C. Dutt,
Finance Minister.

**CHIEF MINISTER'S OFFICE,
TRIPURA STATE.**

To

Major His Highness Bisama-Samara-Bijoyee Mahamahodaya
Pancha-Srijukta Maharaja Manikya
SIR BIR BIKRAM KISHORE DEV BARMAN
BAHADUR, K. C. S. I.,
Ruler of Tripura

Dated, Agartala, the 26th December, 1944.

MAY IT PLEASE YOUR HIGHNESS,

On behalf of the *Mantri Parishad,* I have the honour most respectfully to submit the accompanying consolidated Administration Report of the State for the three years 1350, 1351 and 1352 T. E., covering the period from 14th April 1940 to 13th April, 1943, as compiled and edited by the Political Department of the State.

2. In spite of serious difficulties experienced, the gap of six years has, I am glad to be able to say, now been bridged up, and the previous practice of publishing a general Administration Report of the State in English, year by year, will henceforth be resumed.

I have the honour to be
Your Highness's most obedient servant,
Rana Bodhjung,
CHIEF MINISTER AND PRESIDENT,
MANTRI PARISHAD.

Book Thirty
Consolidated Administration Report of the Tripura State for
1350-52 T. E. (1940 1943 A.D.)

REPORT ON THE ADMINISTRATION

OF

THE TRIPURA STATE

FOR

1350 T. E.—1352 T. E. (1940—1943.)

CHAPTER I—GENERAL AND POLITICAL.

Area of the State—4,116 sq. miles.

Population (*Census 1941*)—5,13,010.

Gross income—(1) Total for the triennium—Rs. 1,10,89,700
Annual average of the triennium—Rs. 36,96,566

(2) Annual based on the average for previous five years, i. e. 1345—1349 T. E. (inclusive)—Rs. 35,09,940.

Tribute—Nil.

Ruler—Major His Highness The Bishama-Samara-Bijayee Mahamahodaya-Pancha-Srijukta Maharaja Manikya Sir Bir Bikramkishore Dev Barman Bahadur, K. C. S. I., Maharaja of Tripura. *Born*—19th August, 1908. *Caste*—*Kshatriya* of the Lunar Race.

Jubraj—Sreela-Sreejukta Maharajkumar Kirit Bikram Kishore Dev Barman, Jubraj Goswami Bahadur. *Born*—12th December, 1933.

I.

The War and the economic condition. The repercussions of the great war on the State constitute a special and noticeable feature of the triennium under report. With the advent of Japan in the arena, about the close of 1941, the European War turned into a world--conflagration, and it was not long before the war-front in the east vis-a-vis India, came to the very gates of the State. The dangers of the situation were soon amply in evidence, and were unfortunately accentuated for a time by hostile forces of nature at work—with unsettled weather conditions, heavy floods, land-slides and loss of crops, the hill sections in particular being practically in the throes of famine.

High prices. 2. Prices of rice rose gradually from the second year of the triennium till they reached abnormal proportions towards its end, those of other commodities also evincing a substantial rise, while shortage of stock and high prices in the adjoining British districts had their reaction in the State and gave strong impetus to export and smuggling. The changed condition of the rice market came in, no doubt, as a matter of relief to the agricultural population—and perchance of gain to middlemen and traders, but the landless classes with a limited income were soon thrown on the verge of break-down. Wages of labour also went up, in spite of a rapid influx of labour population, the normal demand being considerably affected by new and attractive sources of diversion.

Public health.

3. To add to the trouble, public health turned unsatisfactory, with malaria, cholera, dysentery, and small-pox constantly rampant all round, though a comparatively low mortality presented a silver lining, and the virulence with which cattle diseases raged causing havoc in places, proved a grave menace in the complications of the economic situation.

The finances of the triennium.

4. The finances of the triennium, however, were on the whole steady and, to all intents and purposes, normal. It will be seen that with an opening balance of Rs. 17,55,151 (inclusive of unadjusted advances and bonds) against Rs. 22,44,465 of the previous triennium, and the gross receipts standing at Rs. 1,10,89,700 against Rs. 1,11,42,994, the total consolidated amount available for expenditure during the period under review in the State and attached Zemindaries, aggregated Rs. 1,28,44,851 against Rs. 1,33,87,459, while the expenditure totalled Rs. 1,05,11,989 against Rs. 1,16,32,308, leaving a closing balance of Rs. 23,32,862 against Rs. 17,55,151.

II.

CONSTITUTIONAL REFORMS.

Development of the Reforms Scheme.

5. The development of the Constitutional Reforms inaugurated by His Highness the Maharaja Manikya Bahadur in 1349 T. E. continued under the control of Dewan B. K. Sen Bahadur, M. A., B. L. in co-operation with the *Mantri Parishad*, Manyabara Raja Rana Bodhjung Bahadur, F. R. G. S., Minister, holding the corresponding administrative portfolio.

The Constitution Act, and its salient features.

6. The Constitution of the Tripura Government deserves foremost mention. The Government of Tripura Act (or Act I of 1351 T. E.), embodying the Constitution received His Highness's assent on the 20th Asharh 1351 T. E. and came into force with effect from 1st Sravan following. Subjoined are the main features of the Act :—

(i) Raj Sava or Privy Council.

To assist the Ruler of the State in matters connected with the due exercise of his rights and authority, a *Raj-Sava* or Privy Council composed of not less than 5 and more than 15 notable persons, official and non-official, as members, appointed by the Ruler for a term not exceeding 5 years, is to be set up as an advisory body with functions both executive and judicial, the latter function being exercisable with appellate jurisdiction only by a Judicial Committee of three to five members, likewise appointed by the Ruler, its recommendations coming direct to the Ruler for final orders.

(ii) The Executive.

The executive authority of the Government of Tripura is to be exercised to the extent of powers delegated by His Highness, by a *Mantri Parishad* or Council of Ministers, consisting of a Chief Minister and other Ministers not exceeding four in number, each Minister holding independent charge of a portfolio, with specified individual powers of disposal in respect of such Departments of the Government as His Highness may from time to time be pleased to direct, the Chief Minister functioning as the President of the *Mantri Parishad*, with advisory powers over the work of his colleagues in cases of difficulty, complication or inter-departmental conflict, all matters beyond the individual powers of Ministers being disposed of by the *Parishad* as a Cabinet on the basis of joint responsibility.

(iii) The Legislature.

A Legislature is to be established comprising the Ruler as the final sanctioning authority and a unicameral Chamber, styled the "Tripura *Vyavasthapak Sava*" or Legislative Assembly, with a President and the Ministers as ex-officio members, and 49 other members, of whom (a) 29 are to be elected by constituencies detailed below and (b) 20 nominated, including not less than 7 non-officials appointed to represent minorities and labour :—

(1)	*Talukdars* and *Jaigirdars*	3
(2)	Village *Mandalis* as constituted under Act I of 1350 T. E.	12
(3)	Municipalities and notified urban areas ...	3
(4)	Tea Planting interests	2
(5)	Business Communities	3
(6)	Legal Practitioners, graduates with bonafide residence in the State, and under-graduates being State subjects	2
(7)	Backward Communities	3
(8)	A special Community of historic importance selected by the Ruler	1

Besides legislative functions, the *Vyavasthapak Sava* is to have recommendatory powers in respect of certain matters including the annual budget which has to be presented before it, and it may exercise powers of final disposal in certain cases if so authorised by the Ruler.

(iv) The High Court of Judicature.

The supreme Judicial tribunal of the State named Khas Adalat is to be reorganised and styled "the High Court of Judicature, Tripura", and composed of one Chief Justice and not less than two other Judges, appointed by His Highness in his discretion, and is to exercise both Appellate and Original civil and criminal jurisdiction, a Court of two or more Judges appointed by the Chief Justice constituting an Appellate Bench and two Judges, also nominated by the Chief Justice, presiding over the Original Civil Side and the Sessions Division respectively. All appeals from the Original Sides of the High Court as well as those from the Magistrate-Munsiffs are to be heard by the Appellate Bench (there being no Sessions Judge or Civil Judge empowered to hear appeals from decisions of subordinate courts), while the jurisdiction of the Civil Original Side is to cover all civil matters beyond the jurisdiction of the Munsiffs, that of the Original Criminal Side being restricted to trial of Sessions cases only.

(v) Finance and Audit.

An improved system of Financial Administration and Audit is to be introduced under a Finance Minister, and strengthened if necessary by the appointment by the Ruler, of a Controller of Accounts under him, as an adviser to the Finance Minister and with special responsibility in respect of audit and expenditure.

Territorial reorganisation and the Village Mandali Act.

7. The reorganisation and grouping of villages so as to convert each group into a territorial electoral unit of the *Vyavasthapak Sava* and at the same time a basic unit of the Government, was pushed on early as one of the most essential steps towards the introduction of the Reforms, with the result that the Village *Mandali* Act (or Act I of 1350 T. E.) received His Highness's assent on the 9th Asharh 1350 T. E. and came into force on the 15th idem.

The leading features of the Mandali Act.

8. Under Act I of 1350 T. E. a Village *Mandali* is deemed constituted on promulgation of a proclamation by the appropriate Department of the *Mantri Parishad* detailing its boundaries. Each *Mandali* is generally to consist of 9 *Mahallas* and each inhabitant with the requisite qualifications prescribed is to be a primary voter. The details below will indicate the other features of the Act.

(i) Electorates and Elections.

(*a*) The primary voters of each *Mahalla* are to elect, under the procedure laid down in the Act, from their number one *Sardar* for the *Mahalla*, and the *Sardars* of the *Mahallas* in their turn are to elect for the *Mandali* a *Pradhan* (or Headman) who has to appoint an assistant to be styled "Assistant *Pradhan*" from amongst the *Sardars*.

(*b*) The *Pradhans* are to represent the Boards as voters for election of members of the *Vyavasthapak Sava*.

(ii) The Mandali Board.

A *Mandali* Board is to be composed of the *Pradhan* as the President, the Assistant *Pradhan* as the Vice President, and the *Sardars* of the *Mandali* as members.

(iii) The powers, privileges and functions of the Board.

Each Board is to be deemed a Corporate body with franchise as an Electorate for return of members to the *Vyavasthapak Sava*, empowered also to deal, subject to certain conditions, with all petty local concerns, executive, administrative or judicial, the village Police, primary education, ferries, pounds, agricultural development and *Mandali* property, forming its special charge, while it is to have control over its own finances with rights of imposition and realisation of taxes for the purpose and authority to frame bye laws for local improvement. The functions, powers and privileges of the Board are detailed and explained in Chapter VII of the Act.

(iv) Powers—Magisterial and Judicial.

The *Pradhan*, or if need be some other member of the Board, may be vested with executive Magisterial powers, and a Bench consisting either of (a) three members, one of whom is to be the President, or (b) one Stipendiary Magistrate-Munsiff as President with two members of the Board, is to constitute a Court, styled the *Mandali Adalat*, for trial of petty civil and criminal cases of the locality with jurisdiction as prescribed, and under a summary procedure detailed, in the Act.

Rules promulgated under Section 25 of Act I of 1351 T. E. (Constitution).

9. The following Rules were promulgated during the triennium under Section 25 of Act I of 1351 T. E. in furtherance of the work of establishment of the *Vyavasthapak Sava*.

(1) ELECTORATE RULES—defining Electorates and prescribing detailed procedure for their formation and function.

(2) ELECTION RULES—detailing procedure for election of members to the *Vyavasthapak Sava* by Electorates.

Rules awaiting promulgation.

10. The undernoted draft Rules and Regulations were also framed, but kept in abeyance (in view of changes that may be called for in the practical field) pending prompt promulgation as soon as the preliminary work connected with the constitution of the *Vyavasthapak Sava* was finished.

(1) RULES FOR THE CONDUCT OF THE BUSINESS of the *Vyavasthapak Sava*.

(2) CORRUPT PRACTICES REGULATION.

11. It may be added that RULES FOR THE CONDUCT OF BUSINESS OF THE *Mantri Parishad*, with powers of Secretaries (the Reforms envisaging a Secretariat form of Administration) and other high officers of government defined, had already been promulgated towards the close of the previous triennium after the constitution of the *Mantri Parishad* under His Highness's New Year's Day Proclamation of 1349 T. E.

Rules for the conduct of business of the Mantri Parishad.

12. His Highness was pleased to appoint, under his *Robakari* No. 256, dated the 7th Jaistha 1351 T. E., twelve persons—high officials, pensioners, and non-officials—as members of the Privy Council with two Advisers of local affairs from the masses, six of the members designated constituting a panel as a Judicial Committee from which three or more were to be selected by the President to form a Bench for hearing appeals in matters appealable under law to the Ruler.

The Privy Council and the Judicial Committee.

13. On the 28th Kartik 1351 T. E. His Highness was also pleased to inaugurate the *Raj Sava* personally at the Palace, and to address the members according all a most cordial welcome and giving expression to his expectations of assistance from them in the arduous task of leading the Administration to its ultimate goal which—to quote His Highness's own language—"was to lie in an ideal of traditional Indian culture harmonising with modern thought in shaping the guiding principle of the government, calculated to render the State invulnerable in the prosperity, happiness and contentment of the people". Mahamanyabara Maharajkumar B. K. Dev Barman Bahadur who presided, offered His Highness on behalf of the *Sava*, the grateful thanks of the members, and assured him of the deep sense of allegiance and eagerness for loyal service to His Highness and the State, shared by all present. Later on under His Highness's order No. 280, dated the 13th Agrahayan 1351 T. E. Maharajkumar Brajendra Kishore was formally appointed as the President of the *Raj Sava* and the Judicial Committee.

Inauguration of the Raj Sava by His Highness.

14. A MANUAL OF RULES FOR THE CONDUCT OF THE BUSINESS OF THE *Raj Sava* AND THE JUDICIAL COMMITTEE as drawn up under the Scheme of Reforms was considered by the *Raj Sava* and received His Highness's sanction on the 10th Agrahayan 1351 T. E.

Rules for the conduct of business of the *Raj Sava* and the Judicial Committee.

15. To sum up the net position, the progress of the Constitutional Reforms at the close of the triennium, stood as under :—

The position of the Reforms at the close of the Triennium.

(1) The *Raj Sava* in function with Rules promulgated ;

(2) The *Mantri Parishad* functioning with five Ministers and with Rules of conduct of business passed and in force ;

(3) All spade works for the establishment of the Legislative Assembly completed and all necessary Rules either promulgated or ready ;

(4) The *Mandali* Act passed and the territorial reorganisation under it almost carried through, with 150 *Mandalis* constituted on elective basis.

(5) The *Khas Adalat* reorganised and converted into a High Court with a Chief Justice and two Puisne Judges and a better scale of pay provided.

(6) An improved system of Financial Administration and audit initiated under a separate Finance Minister.

The emergent situation and postponement of Reforms measures.

16. Owing to practical difficulties consequent on the adverse situation, it was however considered advisable to defer the outstanding portion of the Reforms till the war was at an end, or at least till its keenness as a disturbing factor in the State was gone.

III.

ADMINISTRATIVE CHANGES AND MEASURES.

Reorganisation Committee.

17. In view of an apprehended financial depression, and the expected introduction of a new and more or less costly system of Government, His Highness was pleased to appoint a Committee in 1350 T. E., composed of five members outside the *Mantri Parishad*, to submit independent suggestions for reorganisation of the State machinery, the members selected being the Chief Justice and another Judge of the High Court, the Deputy Manager of the Chakla Roshnabad Zemindaries, the Officer in charge of His Highness's Nijtahabil, and the Secretary to the Finance Department. The Committee submitted a number of recomendations, some of which were accepted by the Government in 1351 T. E.

Important Administrative changes.

18. The subjoined administrative changes during the triennium are noticeable as far-reaching in their bearing on the Administration :—

(1) The untimely and sad death on 18th Baisakh 1350 T. E. of Rai J. M. Chatterjee Bahadur, M. A., D. C. S.—the first Revenue and Finance Minister of the new Cabinet and an officer of great promise with a brilliant past.

(2) The retirement on 7th Magh 1351 T. E. of Rai J. C. Sen Bahadur, B. A., B. C. S., Chief Minister, after a record of 15 years' service (excluding an intervening gap of four years)—an able, popular and disinterested administrator who came first as the Vice President of the late Minority Council, to be appointed thereafter as (sole) Minister, and on the inauguration of the Reforms, Chief Minister.

(3) The retirements on 7th Jaistha 1351 T. E. and 1st Asharh 1352 T. E., respectively, after about forty years of service each, characterised by zeal and devotion to His Highness and the State,

of Dr. M. M. Majumdar L. M. S., Minister, Public Health and formerly Chief Medical Officer, and Rai Dewan K. P. Dutt Bahadur M. A., B. L., M. R. E. S., Chief Secretary to His Highness and Manager, Chakla Roshnabad Zemindaries.

(4) The retirement on 8th Sravan 1352 T. E. after 23 years of successful career of Captain J. N. Bhaduri, B. A., B. E., State Engineer;

The resultant vacancies were filled up finally by the appointments detailed below, namely of,

(1) Manyabara Raja Rana Bodhjung Bahadur, Minister, Public Works and other Departments, on 8th Magh 1351 T. E. as Chief Minister;

(2) Mr. Satyadas Goswami, B. A., A. C. S. on 25th Falgoon 1351 T. E. as Revenue Minister;

(3) Rai Saheb S. C. Dutt, Secretary Finance Department on 7th Jaistha 1351 T. E. as Finance Minister;

(4) Thakur R. M. Deb Barman, Secretary Revenue Department on 7th Jaistha 1351 T. E. as Medical Minister, his incumbency being unfortunately cut short by illness, followed by death on 16th Sravan 1352 T. E., leading to the assumption of the portfolio by Thakur K. K. Singh Minister, Agriculture and other Departments;

(5) Mr. P. R. Bhattacharjee, B. A., with effect from 1st Baisakh 1352 T. E. as Chief Secretary to His Highness and Manager, Chakla Roshnabad Estates;

(6) Captain J. M. Ghosh, M. B., (Cal), D. T. M. & H (Cant.), D. P. H. (Lond), C. L. S. T. M. on 2nd Pous 1351 T. E. as Chief Medical Officer;

(7) Captain A. K. Sen, B. E., C. E., Road Engineer, on 15th Bhadra 1352 T. E. as State Engineer.

A new portfolio—appointment of a Political Minister.

19. An administrative measure of importance was the creation by His Highness of a separate portfolio for the Political Department, in view of the growingly heavy work of political and legal character incident to the emergency, Dewan B. K. Sen Bahadur, M. A., B. L., Ex-Dewan, in charge of the Reforms, being appointed as Political Minister, with effect from 1st Chaitra 1351 T. E.

Other noticeable measures.

20. Among other noticeable measures of the period may be mentioned (1) the apportionment of the portfolio of the Judicial Department so as to admit of a control of the subordinate Judicial machinery by the Chief Justice of the High Court from outside the cabinet, the mainly executive functions of the department being left included in the portfolio of the Chief Minister; (2) the acceptance of the principle of retirement on lines in vogue in British India with a reduced standard of maximum pension, the *Mantri Parishad* being empowered to sanction all ordinary pensions and (3) the promulgation of a scheme for and introduction of a General Provident Fund.

IV.

NOTABLE EVENTS.

21. A most important event of the triennium was the *Tika* or investiture ceremony of the Heir Apparent, Maharajkumar Kirit Bikram Kishore Dev Barman Bahadur, as Jubraj, with which came to be associated another notable function, the marriage of Maharajkumari Bina Devi, sister of His Highness with Maharajkumar Shree Nirmalkumar Singhji, brother of His Highness the Maharaja Saheb of Bhavnagar, both being synchronised and celebrated at Agartala with befitting *eclat* in Agrahayan 1350 T. E. (December 1940). Among the distinguished guests who graced the occasion with their presence were :

Noticeable functions.

His Highness the Maharaja Saheb of Panna
His Highness the Maharaj Rana Saheb of Dholpur
His Highness the Maharaja Saheb of Bhavnagar
His Highness the Thakor Saheb of Palitana
His Highness the Maharaja Saheb of Mayurbhanj
The Raja Saheb of Khairagarh
The Raja Saheb of Sakti
Maharajkumar Joydeep Singhji Saheb, Jubraj of Baria

22. For a time Agartala assumed a festive look in marked relief to the shadow cast by the developing emergent situation, added to anxieties caused by the lingering illness of Her Highness the Dowager Maharanee Arundhati Mahadevi (mother of His Highness), and after customary religious rites on the previous day, the *Tika Darbar* came off at the Ujjayanta Palace on the 26th Agrahayan (12th December) in which His Highness's *Robakari* appointing the Heir Apparent as Jubraj was read, with *Khilat* and *Nazar* exchanged, and the investing *Tika* put by His Highness amidst public rejoicings on the forehead of the Maharajkumar. A State Banquet worthy of the occasion followed on the next day, and the ceremony closed with a *Nazar Darbar* held at the Installation Pandal, where a huge gathering of enthusiastic people, respresenting all sections of the tenantry and public, accorded their loyal greetings and paid *Nazar* to the future Ruler of the State. His Highness accompanied by the Jubraj Goswami Bahadur proceeded to the *Darbar* in procession and was pleased at the end of the function to announce remission of dues of tenants to the extent of six lacs, total abolition of *Nazar Kaziana* payable to the Government during Mahomedan marriages, and release of a number of prisoners.

The Investiture ceremony of the Jubraj.

23. The wedding of the Maharajkumari came off on the 28th Agrahayan (14th December), Their Highnesses the Maharaja Saheb of Bhavnagar and the Thakor Saheb of Palitana participating as members of the bridegroom's party and honoured guests, and the function concluded with a largely attended State Banquet at the Ujjayanta Palace on the 29th Agrahayan (15th December).

The wedding of Maharajkumari Bina Devi.

24. Unfortunately Her Highness the Dowager Maharanee Sababa's illness soon took a worse and ultimately a fatal turn, and the end came at last on the 6th Chaitra 1350 T. E. (20th March 1940). A daughter of the late General Sir Padamjung Bahadur of Allahabad, the deceased Maharanee was a popular and respected figure, ever since she came to Agartala after her marriage with the late Ruler of the State, conspicuous in her strong commonsense, education, and the qualities of head and heart. She ably carried on the administrative duties of the legal guardian of His Highness during his minority, and Her untimely death at the age of only 52 was deeply and sincerely mourned all round. The ***Sradh*** ceremony which was suitably performed on the 18th Chaitra (1st April) proved in every way an appropriate sequel to the melancholy event.

Death of the Dowager Maharanee Saheba.

25. Hardly had the ceremony concluded, when the State came in for a unique experience in the sudden influx of a large body of Hindu refugees in extreme distress from the Dacca district as the result, as alleged, ot serious communal disturbances. The total number soon came up to fifteen thousand with a preponderance of females and infants, who had to be promptly accommodated, given medical help and supplied with food and clothing. The humanitarian policy followed by the State from time immemorial of helping the needy, irrespective of caste and creed, was followed with the full co-operation of the local public, Hindu and Mahomedan, while the authorities of the Bengal Government were contacted for consultation and concerted action. Every effort was made to persuade the refugees to return to their homes when peace was reported restored, and His Excellency Sir John Herbert, Governor of Bengal in his letter of the 11th April 1941 thanked His Highness as well as all concerned, and expressed his "sincere appreciation of the sympathy shown and the valuable assistance rendered" to the refugees, and for "every possible arrangement made for their safety and comfort"

Influx of a large body of refugees from Dacca.

26. On the 25th Baisakh, 1351 T. E., the eightieth birth-day of the Great poet Rabindranath, His Highness was pleased to confer on the poet the Title of "***Bharat Bhaskar***" (The Sun of India) at a ***Darbar*** held at the Ujjayanta Palace for the purpose. A deputation with a letter from His Highness visited Santiniketan and presented the Sanad to the poet, who gave eloquent expression to his high appreciation, and accepted the title as a great honour done to him by an ancient State.

Rabindra Jayanti Darbar.

27. In less than three months, however, came the sad news of the death on the 22nd Sravan (7th August 1941) of the world-famed poet and one of the foremost men of the Age, whose friendly relations and historic exchanges of cultural thought with four generations of enlightend Rulers of Tripura, have, as testified to by the Poet himself, left their indelible mark in his great literary creations. All offices and institutions in the State were closed in honour of the occasion.

The passing away of the poet.

Heavy floods at Agartala.

28. Early in Asharh 1351 T. E. (June 1941) the capital town of the State had another though a bitter experience. There was heavy rainfall for days towards the close of Jaistha and the river Howrah was in spate. Suddenly on the 2nd Asharh (16th June) high floods were in sight and in a moment entire Agartala was inundated with considerable depth of water in places and currents madly rushing on in eddies even along roads. Relief measures were at once started under the personal supervision of His Highness and though the floods lasted for four days, it is fortunate there was no loss of human life. Many domestic animals were however washed off and a considerable quantity of food stuff and other property lost. Relief measures had to be continued with free kitchens for days.

Chamber of Princes—Annual Session and Standing Committee.

29. (*a*) His Highness attended a meeting of the Standing Committee of the Chamber of Princes held at Bombay on 19th Sravan 1351 T. E. (4th August 1941) as well as the annual session of the Chamber at Delhi on the 28th Falgoon 1351 T. E. (12th March 1942), participating in all meetings and functions, formal or informal, held on both occasions.

Ministers' Committee.

(*b*) On the retirement of Rai J. C. Sen Bahadur, Chief Minister, who was a member of the Ministers' Committee of the Chamber, Dewan B. K. Sen Bahadur, Political Minister, was elected as a member by the constituency of the Eastern States Agency Group of Rulers, with effect from Sravan 1352 T. E. (August 1942).

Council of Rulers Eastern States.

30. Early in the triennium His Highness was elected President of the Council of Rulers, Eastern States, and presided over four Sessions of the Council held at the Tripura House, Calcutta, in May, July 1940 (1350 T. E.), January 1941 (1350 T. E.) and July 1941 (1351 T. E.).

National Defence Council.

31. A session of the National Defence Council was held at Delhi from 7th to 9th September 1942 (1352 T. E.) which His Highness attended as a member and was the guest of His Excellency the Viceroy during his stay.

Marriage of Maharj Kumari Sorashi Debi

32. An auspicious event in the Ruling Family towards the close of the period under report, was the marriage of Maharaj Kumari Sorashi Debi, a sister of His Highness, with Raja Saheb Chandrachur Prasad Singh Deo, Ruler of Udaipur (E. S. Agency) which was becomingly celebrated at Allahabad on the 21st Baisakh 1352 T. E. (4th May 1942) in the presence of His Highness.

His Highness' military honours.

33. In August, 1942 (1352 T. E.) His Highness was promoted to the honorary rank of Major in His Majesty's Regular Army, and received His Excellency the Viceroy's congratulations and public felicitations. All offices and institutions were closed for a day on the occasion.

Resident for the Eastern States.

84. Lieutenant-Colonel L. E. Barton continued as Resident for the Eastern States till he was relieved on the 25th October, 1941 by Lieutenant-Colonel C. P. Hancock, C. I. E., O. B. E., M. C. Colonel Barton paid his last visit to the State from 5th to 8th February, 1941 (1351 T. E.) while Colonel Hancock visited the State thrice, namely, from 25th to 28th January, 1945, 7th to 12th April, 1942 and 1st to 4th November, 1942 (1352 T. E.). Both the Residents went round certain offices and institutions at Agartala, and Colonel Hancock visited the Nirmahal Palace in Sonamura Division and Udaipur, accompanied by His Highness on the 27th January, 1942 (13th Magh 1351 T. E.).

V.

HIS HIGHNESS'S MOVEMENTS.

35. Besides tours referred to above, the triennium was characterised by extensive movements of His Highness, both in and outside the State. His Highness had to be in Calcutta and Shillong more than once for some length of time in connection with the treatment of his mother as well as some important administrative matters civil and miltary, and certain functions necessary to attend, while he had to visit Panchmari, Allahadad and other places to see to the arrangements for the stay of Her Highness the Maharani Saheba and the children and to look after certain important measures concerning the Ruling Family. His Highness's tours in the interior of the State and other war areas on Military duty extended to about a month. The following tours besides those previously mentioned are noticeable :—

(*i*) His Highness's visit to Darbhanga on the 21st Magh 1350 T. E. (3rd Feb, 1941) on the invitation of the Maharajadhiraj who with the local public accorded His Highness a most cordial welcome.

(*ii*) Visit to Puri on the 25th Jaistha 1350 T. E. (8th June 1940) where His Highness presided over the Puri *Banga Sahitya Sammilan* and the *Sangeet Sammilan.*

(*iii*) Visit to Bangalore (including Chilka *en route* on invitation of Raja Saheb of Parkudi) from the 31st Asharah to the 8th Bhadra 1351 T. E. (15th to 24th July 1941) during which His Highness went round all places of interest in the Mysore State.

(*iv*) Visits to Ooty, Madura, Trivendrum, Cape Comorin, Perriyer Lake Game Sanctuary, Rameswaram Trichinpolly and Madras from the 9th Bhadra to the 19th Bhadra 1351 T. E. (26th August to 5th September 1941).

(*v*) Visit to Travancore State from the 12th Bhadra to the 16th Bhadra (29th August to 2nd September 1942) where His Highness was the guest of Her Highness the Maharanee Saheba, and His Highness the Maharaja Saheb, and was accorded a most hearty reception, the Travancore Government making every possible arrangement to make His Highness's stay comfortable and to enable him to visit everything of interest.

(vi) Visits to Panna on 9th Chaitra, 1351 T. E. (31st March 1942), 25th Bhadra 1352 T. E. (11th September 1942) and 1st Poush, 1352 T. E. (15th January 1943) as well as to Baria on 27th Magh 1352 T. E. (10th February, 1943).

(vii) Camping, bivouacking, route marches, and inspection of troops (a) BARAMURA—25th Chaitra 1350 T. E. (8th April 1941) onwards ; and again from 21st Agrahayan 1351 T. E. (7th December 1941) ; (b) UDAIPUR—2nd Agrahayan 1351 T. E. onwards (18th November 1941) and from 4th Poush 1352 T. E. (20th December 1942), (c) KHOWAI—20th Poush 1351 T. E. (4th January 1942) onwards, (d) FORWARD AREA—30th Aswin 1352 T. E. (17th October 1942), (e) MAINAMATI—11th Jaistha 1352 T. E. (25th May 1942), (f) JAMPUI JALA—27th Falgoon 1352 T. E. (11th March 1943) onwards.

V.

WAR ACTIVITIES OF THE STATE.

36. In the first two years of the triennium under report the war was developing and the enemy had some initial success but during the last year of the period it entered on a new phase and the Allies everywhere wrested the initiative from the enemy. His Highness the Maharaja Manikya Bahadur in his messages to the people explained the position of the State and its attitude with a view to call up the full energy of the people for vigorous activities in aid of the war.

37. The Tripura State Unit of the Indian States Forces proceeded on war duty outside the State and was taking part in the operations. A training centre for its reinforcements was started and maintained in full strength. There was besides an irregular force participating in the operations, and a garrison company fully trained was on duty outside the State. The forces on active service were maintaining high traditions. For internal security and other work, a Militia of considerable strength was organized and the armed police improved with added strength and better equipments, while recruiting was pushed on vigorously with satisfactory results.

38. His Highness the Maharaja Manikya Bahadur's annual donation of Rs. 20,000 to the Indian Red Cross Society, St. John Ambulance Association and St. Dunstan's Fund continued, the total paymant during the period amounting to Rs. 60,000. The yearly State contribution of Rs. 30,000 to the Viceroy's War Purposes Fund also continued with a total paymant of Rs. 90,000 within the triennium. The other war gifts were :—

(1) Contributions paid by State, employees	Rs.	14,000
(2) East India Fund	Rs.	120
(3) Silver Trinket Fund (Assam Branch)	Rs.	82
(4) Lady Mary Herbert Fund	Rs.	550
(5) Bengal Urban Infantry	Rs.	150

39. In addition, the remission of the annual rent for the Polo-ground at Comilla occupied by Indian Army troops amounted to Rs. 9,540.

40. Investments in 3% Defence Bonds stood at Rs. 1,25,000 by the State, Rs. 1,49,000 by His Highness personally and Rs. 21,000 by local Banks.

41. The extra expenditure incurred on account of War arrangements and measures amounted to Rs. 88,755 in 1350 T. E. (1940-41), Rs. 1,26,716 in 1351 T. E. (1941-42) and Rs. 2,11,488 in 1352 T. E. (1942-43).

42. Internal Security & A. R. P. and Civil Defence Schemes were prepared and organizations initiated or set up including Civic Guards.

43. The State adopted practically all laws and rules relating to the war including those for rationing and control of various commodities and civil supplies.

44. Huge quantity of materials for extensive road constructions in and outside the State, as well as requisites for construction of houses and camps, such as murum, timber, bamboo, cane and other forest produce were supplied from the State.

CHAPTER II—LAND ADMINISTRATION.

Charge.

45. Rai J. M. Chatterjee Bahadur, M. A., B. C. S. (Retd.) Minister, controlled the Revenue & General Departments, till his death on the 13th Baisakh, 1350 T. E. whereafter Thakur K. K. Singh remained in charge, till Mr. S. Goswami, B. A., A. C. S. (Retd.) assumed charge on appointment as Revenue Minister on the 25th Falgun 1351 T. E.

Thakur R. M. Dev Barman, continued as the Revenue Secretary till he was appointed Minister, Public Health on 7.2.51 T.E. whereafter Mr. S. C. Sarker, M. A., B. L. joined with the designation changed to "Revenue Officer"

Area held under settlement.

46. As shown in the subjoined statement, the total area held under settlement and borne on the toujis at the close of 1352 T. E. was 621 sq. miles as against 622 sq miles in 1351 T. E. and 613 in 1350 T. E. The fall off in 1352 T. E. was due to the auction purchase by the State of certain defaulting *Taluks*. *Jotes* showed a marked and steady increase from year to year during the triennium.

Kinds of settlement.	Area in square miles.			
	1349 T.E.	1350 T.E.	1351 T.E.	1352 T.E.
Jote ...	313	317	323	328
Taluk ...	293	296	299	293
Total ...	606	613	622	621

47. The maximum and minium rates of *Jama* per *kani* for ordinary *Jote* settlements in *Khas Mahals* were Rs. 2/4/- and As. -/4/- respectively, though there were some cases coming technically under the class of *Jote* in respect of *Bazar* and Municipal lands which fetched higher *Jamas* ranging from Rs. 2/6/- to Rs. 7/-. The corresponding maximum and minimum rates for ordinary *Taluks* stood at Rs. 2/8/- and -/1/6 pies per *kani*. This does not include *Tashkhichi* settlements covering small areas in the capital town which generally fetched a much higher rate. The average *Jama* per *Kani* for *Jotes* stood at 1/0/11 pies against the same figure of the previous triennium and that for *Taluks* annas 5/2 pies against annas 5/3 pies.

Sources of land revenue.

48. The different sources of land revenue demand and the collection under each head are detailed below :—

		Taluks.	*Khasmahal jotes.*	Bazar.	Cesses.	TOTAL.
Current demand. ...	1350 T. E.	1,54,268	5,36,129	8,140	76,121	7,74,658
	1351 T. E.	1,56,861	5,48,083	7,220	80,577	7,92,741
	1352 T. E.	1,51,338	5,57,570	7,427	81,158	7,97,493
Arrear demand upto the end of ...	1349 T. E.	3,94,114	21,16,484	4,576	2,34,307	27,49,481
	1350 T. E.	4,25.633	22,50,136	5,210	2,54,266	29,35,245
	1351 T. E.	4,06,050	23,18,451	4,947	2,62,399	29,91,847
Realisation upto the end of ...	1350 T. E.	1,30,879	3,96,146	7,530	75,058	6,09,613
	1351 T. E.	1,35,011	4,78,245	7,504	72,477	6,93,237
	1352 T. E.	1,41,448	6,41,987	7,453	84,204	8,75,092

Demand.

49. The above statement shows that the current demand in 1352 T. E. under all heads aggregated Rs. 7,97,493, and with the arrear demand of Rs. 29,91,847, the total demand stood at Rs. 37,89.340 against Rs. 37,27,986 and Rs. 35,24,139 in 1351 T. E. and 1350 T. E. respectively.

It will be seen that the difference between the arrear demands at the end of 1350 and 1351 was substantially smaller than the difference between the corresponding figures for 1349 T. E. and 1350 T. E. This no doubt is indicative of better collection of arrears in the triennium.

Collection.

50. The total collection under all heads in 1352 T. E. amounted to Rs. 8,75,092 (viz. Rs. 3,19,224 under current and Rs. 5,55,868 under arrear) against Rs. 6,93,237 (*i. e.*, Rs. 2,60,409 under current and Rs. 4,32,828 under arrear) in 1351 T. E. and Rs. 6,09,613 (*i. e.*, Rs. 2,41,876 under current and Rs. 3,67,737 under arrear) in 1350 T. E.

Average demand and collection.

51. The average current annual demand during the period was Rs. 7,88,297 against Rs. 7,64,183 of the previous triennium and the average annual collection Rs. 7,25,981 against Rs. 6,74,933.

Coercive measures—Certificates.

52. Altogether 12,819 requisitions, covering a demand of Rs. 6,71,145 were received during the three years, and 6,625 requisitions covering Rs. 8,15,495 were pending from 1349 T. E. The total number of requisitions was thus 19,444, covering a total demand of Rs. 14,86,640. Of these, 435 cases with a demand of Rs. 35,095 were rejected or struck off, and a sum of Rs. 41,076 in 1,295 cases was realised before decree ; while 6,057 cases on the whole for realisation of Rs. 8,15,462 remained pending at the end of 1352 T. E.

Execution.

53. Orders under the provisions of the State Certificate Act were passed making the demands absolute, during the period, in 11,657 cases with a total demand of Rs. 5,95,007. Out of the total demand, Rs. 3,569, Rs. 3,713, and Rs. 4,907 were remitted or written off, respectively, in 1350, 1351 and 1352 T. E. and of the remainder, Rs. 1,68,164, Rs. 1,49,856 and Rs. 2,12,930 were actually realised leaving a balance of Rs. 14,82,832, Rs 14,81,370, and Rs. 14,95,247 respectively. The following table shows separately the amounts realised by certificates under heads "Land Revenue" and "Miscellaneous" :—

	Realisation of land revenue demands	Realisation of miscellaneous demands	Total
1350 T.E.	Rs. 1,60,240	Rs. 7,924	Rs. 1,68,164
1351 T.E.	„ 1,37,601	„ 12,255	„ 1,49,856
1352 T.E.	„ 2,02,037	„ 10,893	„ 2,12,930

Operation of the Sun-set Law.

54. With 49 defaulting *Taluks* pending from the previous triennium, altogether 325 *taluks* came in under the operation of the Sun-set Law during the period under report. Of these, 249 were released on payment of dues with penalty, and 22 *taluks* were auctioned off, leaving a closing balance of 54. The corresponding figures for the previous triennium were as under :- Balance brought forward from 1346 : 39, defaulting *Taluks* : 483, released on payment of dues with penalty : 439, auctioned : 34, and balance : 49.

Survey.

55. Survey operations in respect of an area of 1,226 *drones*, were carried out in 1350 T. E. against 2,412 *drones* in 1349 T. E. comprising both *Taluk* and *Khas Mahal* land ; while an area of 1,749 *drones*, comprising 400 *drones* of *taluk* and 1349 *drones* of *Khas Mahal*, and of 967 *drones*, comprising 371 *drones* of *taluk* and 596 *drones* of *Khas Mahal*, were surveyed in 1351 and 1352 T. E. respectively. Compared with the previous triennium, the total area surveyed during the period was less by 4,922 *drones*. No extensive operations were possible under the existing emergent situation.

Settlement and re-settlement of *Jote* and *Taluk* land.

56. (1) The total area covered by original *Jotedari* settlement of waste land during the triennium was 869 *drones* against 483 *drones* in the previous triennium.

(2) The aggregate area of cultivated land brought under original settlement and re-settlement during the period stood at 2,050 *drones* against 5,790 of the preceding triennium, there being thus a decrease of 3,740 *drones* in respect of the operations in the triennium under report, ascribable partially at least, to the policy generally followed of releasing holdings auction purchased by the State to original tenants on realisation of outstanding dues.

Taluki settlement.

(3) *Taluki* settlement was effected in respect of a total area of 370 *drones*, during the triennium, against 155 *drones* in the previous triennium.

Results of re-settlement of *Jote* lands.

57. The following statement shows the amount of *Jama* assessed during the period by re-settlement of *Abadi-jote* land as well as the *Nazarana* assessed as the result of the operations.

	Amount		Average *Jama* (per *kani*)
	Jama assessed.	*Nazarana* assessed.	
1349 T.E.	Rs. 4,968	Rs. 20,616	Rs. 0–14–6 p.
1350 T.E.	„ 3,459	„ 19,853	„ 0–15–10p.
1351 T.E.	„ 12,831	„ 28,585	„ 1–0–1 p.
1352 T.E.	„ 17,739	„ 28,339	„ 0–15–10p.

Results of *Jotedari* Settlement of wasteland.

58. During 1350 T. E. an area of 233 *drones* of waste land was settled for a prospective rental of Rs. 1,703, while in 1351 T. E., 382 *drones* only were settled for Rs. 3,293 and in 1352 T. E. 254 *drones* for Rs. 2,507 only. The average *Jama* per *kani* obtained was 9 annas and 11 pies, nine annas and 8 pies, and 10 annas and 3 pies, in 1350, 1351 and 1352 T. E. respectively. In the closing year of the previous triennium the corresponding figures stood at : waste land settled 277 *drones*, rental–Rs. 2,675, average *jama* per *kani*–9 annas 8 pies. The maximum and the minimum rates and the *Nazarana* realised were as noted below, the rent-free period ranging as before, from 1 to 3 years :—

	Maximum rate.	Minimum rate.	Amount of *Nazarana*.
1349 T.E.	2–0–0	0–4–0	Rs. 3,278–0–0
1350 T.E.	2–0–0	0–4–0	„ 3,068–0–0
1351 T.E.	2–0–0	0–4–0	„ 6,560–0–0
1352 T.E.	16–0–0	0–4–0	„ 6,109–0–0

59. No whole-time Settlement Officer was employed in any Division during the period, but the Divisional Officers were entrusted with settlement work in their respective jurisdictions. The total extra expenditure incurred was thus only Rs. 1,848 in 1350 T. E , Rs. 3,004 in 1351 and Rs. 2,475 in 1352 T. E.

Settlement Officers and expenditure.

60. There were 55 tea gardens in the State during the triennium yielding a revenue of about Rs. 65,000 annually. The total area under tea was about 11,366.86 acres at the end of 1352 T. E. Owing to the adoption of the Restriction Scheme a number of petitions for relinquishment of portions of tea gardens were received and left pending for enquiry and consideration.

Tea Industry.

61. In the original Tripura Tea Control Act, 1348 T. E. it was provided that all acts of the licensing authority appointed under the Act would be subject to the control of the Minister of the Government of Tripura who might cancel, suspend or modify any such act as he thought fit. It is noticeable that the Tripura Tea Control Amendment Order, or Order No. I of 1351 T. E. was passed during the period under which appeals from tea estates in Tripura against the orders of the Indian Tea Licensing Committee relating to crop basis and export quota, were to lie either to the Central Government or the High Court of the State, and those relating to orders of the Committee dealing with extensions, to the Minister.

Legislation.

62. Under the provisions of Clause 7 of the International Tea Agreement, the total area of land, permisssible for extensions to be made during the currency of the agreement was 52 acres. After considerable correspondence, however, it was decided (in 1940) that 200 acres out of the unutilised area of 981 acres available for extensions in Bengal would be allotted to the Tripura State. The total area available for extensions in Tripura was therefore 252 acres.

Control over extensions on virgin soil.

63. The Tripura Tea Control Act having provided for an appeal to the State Government from orders of the Indian Tea Licensing Committee in respect of the distribution of the area of 252 acres for new extensions in the State, it was suggested by the Committee and agreed to by the State Government, that out of the area, 152 acres should be distributed at the first instance, keeping 100 acres in reserve to meet the requirements of any orders passed in appeals to the State Government. An allotment was made accordingly (November, 1941) on the basis of this arrangement.

64. On the introduction of the amended Indian Tea Control Act, it was decided by the Government of Tripura to implement the Act with retrospective effect, where necessary, from the 1st April, 1943.

Tea Control Scheme.

65. As detailed in the following statement, there were 20 private estates under State management at the close of the triennium.

Private estates under State management.

PRIVATE ESTATES UNDER STATE MANAGEMENT.

Class.	Names of Estates.	Area in *drones.*	Revenue	Remarks.
Encumbered	1. Kakraban Estate	283	1,871	
	2. Jogendranagar Trust Estate	30	163	
	3. Kamalnagar & Mahendra nagar Estate	51	255	
	4. Maharamali Choudhuri Khanje Khan Bahadur's Estate *Taluk*	236	1,230	
	Jote	6	149	
	5. Thakur Nalini Mohan Deb Barma's Estate	68	170	
	6. Brajendra Kumar Das's Estate	408	1,936	
	7. Brajapur Estate (Kamalakanta Dev Barma & others)	246	982	
	8. Kalimulla's Estate	124	863	
	9. Mahammad Ali Choudhury's Estate	24	76	
	10. Prabin Chandra Choudhuri's Estate	14	74	
	11. Iswar Chandra Bhowmic Roy's Estate	25	850	
Unencumbered	12. Prabhu Goswami's Estate	31	61	
	13. Dowager Maharani's Estate	169	766	
	14. Late Girish Chandra Choudhuri's Estate	36	254	
	15. Late Braja Kumar Thakur's Estate	47	297	
	16. Late Nava Kumar Chakraborty's Estate *Taluk*	32	225	
	Jote	5	19	
	17. Nil Kantha Sen's Estate	75	374	
	18. Gouranga Tripura's Estate	13	57	
	19. Dowager Bara Maharani's Estate	941	739	
Endowment	20. Taranagar Trust Estate	140	52	

CHAPTER III—PROTECTION.

1. LEGISLATION.

66. The subjoined enactments, Orders (ordinances) and Rules promulgated during the triennium are noticeable :

1350 T. E.

1. Census Act ;
2. Notification dated the 13th September 1940 Re : Control of use of Wireless Transmitting Apparatus ;

3. **Provident Fund Rules ;**
4. **Notification dated the 22nd December 1940, Re : Certain amendments to the Enemy Foreigners' Rules.**

1351 T. E.

1. Tripura Tea Control Amendment Act (No. I of 1351 T. E.) ;
2. Cycle Registration Act ;
3. Notification No. 150–C dated the 17th July 1941, Re : Control of Foreigners ;
4. Motor Spirit Rationing Order, 1351 T. E. ;
5. Notification No. 1622–P/II–5, dated the 19th September, 1941, Re : Control of use, sale etc. of certain chemical substances under sub-rule 2 of Rule 81 of the Defence of India Rules as adopted in the Tripura State ;
6. Notification No. 1613–P/II–48, dated the 18th September, 1941, Re : Control over Financial Trade with Japan ;
7. Notification No. 2260–P, dated the 21st November, 1941, Re : Financial Trade with China ;
8. Notification No. 2258–P, dated the 21st November, 1941, Re : Reciprocal arrangement for extradition for offences against the Defence of India Rules ;
9. Notification No. 2617–P, dated the 12th December, 1941 placing 1st Tripura Rifles under the Indian Army Act as long as they are on active service with the British Indian Forces ;
10. Political Department Order No. 2618–P, dated the 12th December, 1941, notifying that all troops of the Tripura State Forces are to be considered on active service for the purpose of discipline and reporting casualties from the date on which the Tripura State Forces leave the State.
11. Indian Soldiers' (Litigation) Act, 1351 T. E. (Act II of 1351 T. E.) ;
12. Aluminium Control Order, 1351 T. E. ;
13. Chrome Compounds Control Order, 1351 T. E. ;
14. Order to provide special machinery for carrying on the administration if necessary ;
15. Notification No. 3399–P, dated the 3rd February, 1942 Re : adoption of principle that State Officials of one State may sit on courts martial, courts of enquiry, etc. concerning personnel of a unit from another State ;
16. Notification No. 4004–P, dated the 16th March, 1942, Re : Restriction on the export of tea seeds from Tripura State by land & sea to any of the French & Portuguese settlements bounded by India ;
17. Rules regulating the entry of undesirable persons into the State during the period of the present War.

1352 T. E.

1. Notification Re : Motor Spirit Rationing order (Amendment) ;
2. Tripura Special Criminal Courts Order, 1352 T. E. (Order No. I of 1352 T. E.) ;

3. Enhancement of Penalties Order, 1352 T. E. (Order No. II of 1352 T. E.) ;
4. Amendments of Chrome Compound Order, 1351 T. E. ;
5. Amendment of Limitation Act of 1314 T. E. (Order No. III of 1352 T. E.) ;
6. Notification No. 2037–P, dated the 30th August 1942, Re : Action to discourage the practice of listening to Axis Broadcasts ;
7. Tyre Rationing Order, 1352 T. E. ;
8. Adoption of the Indian Criminal Law Amendment Act, 1908—Order No. IV of 1352 T. E. ;
9. Collective Fines Order, 1352 T. E. (Order No. V of 1352 T. E.) ;
10. Sugar Control Order, 1352 T. E. ;
11. Legal Tender (inscribed Notes) Ordinance, 1352 T. E. ;
12. Amendment of Tripura Tea Control Act, 1348 T. E. ;

II. MILITARY.

Charge.

67. Lt.-Col. (now Col.) Rana Jodha Jung Bahadur, M. B. E., M. C., as Chief Commandant, Tripura State Forces, took charge of the Military Department under *Robakaris* Nos. 199 and 200, dated 27. 12. 49 T. E., with effect from 1.1.50 T. E. and from the same date Major Kumar K. Dev Varma Bahadur took over the command of the 1st Tripura B. B. M. Rifles and continued to be in charge until 14. 12. 41, when he with the 1st Tripura B. B. M. Rifles proceeded to British India to serve under the Crown, leaving charge of the Depot of the 1st Tripura B. B. M. Rifles and the Trg. Coy. with Major Kumar B. L. Dev Varma Bahadur, who again on his transfer to H. H.'s Body Guards handed over the charge to Col. Rana Jodha Jung Bahadur, M. B. E., M. C., Chief Commandant on 13. 2. 42.

Strength.

68. The actual strength of the regular Forces was 399 at the end of 1350 T. E. against 420 of the previous year, while at the end of the years 1351 T. E. and 1352 T. E. the actual strength was 492 and 732 respectively. During the year 1352 T. E. the State Army consisted of the following :—

Indian States Forces.

1. Infantry—1st Tripura B. B. M. Rifles (on active service).
2. Depot, 1st Tripura B. B. M. Rifles (including Band).
3. Training Company.

Other Forces.

1. His Highness' Bodyguard.
2. 2nd Tripura Infantry.
3. Kirit Militia.

Arms.

69. About the close of the triennium the Forces were armed mostly with ·303 Rifles, ·410 muskets, revolvers, pistols, Vickers and Lewis Guns, besides other modern weapons.

70. Asst. Military Adviser, C. I. S. F., visited Tripura State on 22.8.41. His Highness the Maharaja Manikya Bahadur was pleased to inspect the 1st Tripura Rifles on 22.4.41. The I. O. M. E. inspected the technical equipment of the 1st Tripura Rifles on 9. 1. 42. His Highness also inspected this unit again on 12. 1. 42. Lt.-General Sir Frederick Gwatkin, C. B., D. S. O., M. C., Military Adviser-in-Chief, I. S. Forces, visited and inspected this unit from 18. 1. 42 to 19. 1. 42. The Resident for the Eastern States visited the State Forces on 25. 1. 42. The M. A., C. I. S. F., the Resident for the Eastern States and Brigadier Thomas, Commander, 88 Ind. Inf. Bde, visited the State Forces from 1. 11. 42 to 5.11.42. Brigadier Felix Williams and Lt.-Col. Whyte visited Agartala and inspected the Tripura (M. B.) Legion on 26.6.42. Capt. Bore, R. E., visited this unit on 16. 2. 43 (10/52 T. E.) and gave demonstrations and lectures on explosives and Booby Traps. Brigadier Felix Williams and two other officers visited the unit on 8. 2. 43 (10/52 T. E.)

Visit and Inspection.

71. During the years under report, 12 S. O's, 9 I.O's and 18 I. O. R's underwent training in various courses in different schools and centres in British India or under attachment to different Indian Army units.

Training Courses and attachments.

72. The 1st Tripura Rifles went out on 8. 4. 41 for camping and manoeuvres at Subalsing-Para, a place 21 miles east of Agartala in the interior, and held camps there up to 11.4.41, returning to Agartala on 12.4.41.

Camps & Manoeuvres.

Depot, 1st Tripura B.B.M. Rifles, Trg. Coy. and all other Units of the Tripura State Forces held camps for 10 days at Udaipur (Tripura State) for Jungle Warfare training and other exercises.

73. General health of the forces during the years under report was good except for occasional attacks of malaria.

General Health.

74. During the month of January 1943 the 1st Tripura Rifles and the Tripura Mahabir Legion (known as Tripforce), took part in the Arakan operations very successfully and captured the Japanese position at Kyauktaw in spite of comparatively heavy casualties. They received the following Immediate Awards for their gallantry :—

War Services.

List of Personnel awarded Honours.

Sl. No.	Regtl. No.	Rank, Name.	Rank held at present.
		M. C.	
1.	4603.	Capt. Maharajkumar Arjun Kishore Dev Barman Bahadur (since deceased).	
		I. O. M.	
1.	4633.	Jem. Balbahadur Thapa (since deceased).	
2.	174.	L/NK. Bimal Chandra Dev	Jemadar.
		I. D. S. M.	
1.	4612.	Sub. Mingma Lama	Lieut.
2.	4631.	„ Ambar Prakash Sahi	
3.	4636.	Jem. Maheswar Thapa	Subedar.
4.	4640.	„ Jaikarna Rai	„

Sl. No.	Regtl. No.	Rank, Name.	Rank held at present.
5.	583.	Hav. Kulman Singh Lama	
6.	326.	,, Kartik Chandra Dev	Jemadar.
7.	84.	,, Punaram Thapa	

MENTION IN DESPATCHES.

1.	4601.	Lt.-Col. K. C. Dev Barma Bahadur (since deceased).	
2.	4007.	Lt. Hrishikes Dev Varma	A/Major.
3.		Sub. Fariduddin Choudhury	2/Lt.
4.	4633.	Jem. Balbahadur Thapa (since deceased).	
5.	4644.	,, Mangal Dev	
6.	4641.	,, Narbahadur Gurung.	
7.	4646.	,, Dhan Bahadur (Discharged).	
8.	326.	Hav. Kartik Chandra Dev	Jem.
9.	583.	,, Kulman Singh	
10.	1170.	,, Sherbahadur Chhetri	
11.	105.	NK. Abdul Shamed	
12.	423.	,, Abdul Gafur (since discharged).	
13.	720.	,, Radhakrishna Dev	Havildar.
14.	84.	,, Punaram Thapa	,,
15.	197.	,, Manibhadra Jaisi	
16.	388.	,, Ramani Das	
17.	632.	,, Biak Sanga Lushai	
18.	354.	L/Nk. Nibaran Laskar	Naik.
19.	823.	,, Hiralal	
20.		,, Ranbahadur Thapa.	
21.		Rfn. Abdul Barik	

C.-IN-C'S COMMENDATION CARDS.

1.	4644.	Jem. Mangal Ch. Dev	
2.	4646.	,, Dhan Bahadur (since discharged).	
3.		NK. Lalgopal	
4.	72.	,, Sukdeo Gurung	A/Hav.
5.		Rfn. Kanai Singh	Naik.

THE BURMA GALLANTRY MEDAL.

1.	4644.	Jem. Mangal Ch. Dev	
2.	423.	NK. Abdul Gafur (since discharged).	
3.	197.	,, Manibhadra	Havildar.
4.	720.	,, Radhakrishna Dev	,,
5.	388.	,, Ramani Das	
6.	823.	L/NK. Hiralal Das	
7.	554.	,, Nibaran Laskar	Naik.
8.	105.	NK. Abdul Shamed	Havildar.

CERTIFICATE OF GALLANTRY.

1.	EC 7864.	A/Major	W. C. L. Creech
2.	10519.	Ws/Lieut.	F. T. Maginn
3.	636.	L/Naik	Dhanbahadur Thapa
4.	195.	Naik	Chandrakanta Dev
5.	665.	RFN	Surendra Ch. Dev
6.	208.	L/Naik	Birkumar Dev

75. The following units were raised in the State from H. H's Body Guard and 2/T. Infantry and placed at the desposal of the Govt. of India during 1942. :—

Tripura Mahabir Legion (V Force).
49 Tripura Garrison Company.

76. Brigadier His Highness the Maharaja Manikya Bahadur personally raised and organised an Irregular Force of considerable strength from the hill tribes known as *Tripura Rajya Rakshi Bahini.* They manned the Picket Posts in strategical points in the State. Recce. parties were sent out occasionally as far as Burma border and they brought valuable information.

Expenditure.

77. Excluding the expenditure on public works, and some general expenditure transferred to the "War Head", the total ordinary expenditure for the forces stood at Rs. 1,66,060 for the year 1350 T. E., Rs. 1,54,881 for the year 1351, and Rs. 99,628 for the year 1352 T. E. as against Rs. 1,55,594 of the year 1349 T. E. The decrease in 1352 T. E. it will be seen is not real, being due partly to the transfer of certain items of expenditure borne on the Military budget in the year 1351 to a new Head of expenditure named "War Expenditure" in the year 1352 T. E., and partly to the decrease in the expenditure on the 1st Tripura Rifles on account of their proceeding on active service, as also to some contribution from the Government of India for the Training company.

III. POLICE.

Charge.

78. Rai G. R. Dutt Bahadur continued as Commissioner of Police during the triennium.

79. Mr. Naresh Kumar Bhattacharjee, B. Sc., continued as Deputy Commissioner of Police.

Strength.

80. The total numerical strength of the Police force was 593 in 1350 and 1351 T. E. (1940–41 & 1941–42) and 612 in 1352 T. E. (1942–43), the increase in 1352 being due to the appointment of 19 permanent armed constables.

Rural Police.

81. The total number of village choukidars throughout the period continued to be 177, as before.

Inspecting Staff.

82. There were 4 Inspectors of Police during the period as before, their main duties being to exercise control over and maintain discipline amongst the subordinate staff, besides supervision of cases and inspection of Police Stations and Courts.

Investigating and Intelligence Staff.

83. During the period there were 23 Sub-Inspectors, 21 Naib-Darogas, and 16 Writer Naib-Darogas on the Police establishment. Their behaviour with the public was generally satisfactory throughout.

C. I. D. and Intelligence Staff.

84. One Sub-Inspector, 6 Naib-Darogas and 5 constables were employed in the Criminal Investigation Department, as before.

Crime.

85. The total number of cases reported during the years under review was 2,576 as against 2,245 in the previous triennium.

86. The results of the cases are detailed below :—

Number of cases reported
2,576

- Enquiry refused 67
- Number investigated 2,509
  - True 1,973
    - Charge-sheet 1,075
    - Finally reported 898
  - Intentionally false 156
  - Mistake of law 66
  - Mistake of fact 167
  - Noncognizable 147

87. The above table shows only institutions from year to year with their disposal and does not include pending cases, the number of which was as subjoined :—

Pending from 1349 T. E. (*i. e.* previous triennium)—	33	158
,, ,, 1350 T. E.–	42	
,, ,, 1351 T. E.–	83	
Pending from 1352 T. E. (*i .e.* close of the triennium)—	95	

Almost all the above 158 cases were disposed of within the triennium.

Results of prosecution.

88. Altogether 2,107 persons were arrested and 2,506 persons (including absconders) were sent up for trial by the Police in connection with various offences during the period under review, as against 1,534 arrested and 1,872 persons sent up in the previous triennium. Of the persons sent up, 1,555 were convicted and 389 acquitted as against 613 and 642 the corresponding figures for the previous triennium, while 562 (including absconding accused) awaited trial, against 617.

Bad Livelihood cases.

89. Fourteen cases of bad livelihood in which 29 accused were involved were started during the period, against 9 cases and 30 persons of the previous triennium. Only two cases were pending at the close of the period as against one.

Arms Act cases.

90. Eight Arms Act cases were instituted against 38 persons, of whom 7 were convicted, 14 acquitted and 17 persons were awaiting trial.

Theft of Guns.

91. Altogether 8 guns were stolen during the period against 20 of the previous triennium, of which 7 were recovered.

Recovery of Stolen Property.

92. The total value of property stolen during the three years under review amounted to Rs. 52,198-6-6 against Rs. 43,035-6-3 of the preceding triennium. Of this amount Rs. 5,587-14-9 was recovered within the period against Rs. 11,024-13-6 in the previous triennium. The percentage of recovery was 10·10 against 25·58.

93. There were 83 cases of dacoity during the triennium against 30 in the previous three years. Charge-sheets against 38 persons in 13 cases were sent up, with the result that 7 persons were convicted and 1 acquitted, while 30 awaited trial at the end of the period. The corresponding figures for the previous triennium were as under :—

Dacoity.

Charge-sheets—58 persons ; Convicted—4 ;
Acquitted—11 ; Pending trial—43.

94. Altogether 217 cases of unnatural death were reported during the period against 194 of the previous three years. As before enquiries were held by the Police into all these cases and no foul play was detected in any of them.

Unnatural death.

95. One Inspector of Police, 5 Sub-Inspectors, 2 Naib-Darogas and 5 Choukidars received money rewards, while 13 Sub-Inspectors, 2 Armed Sub-Inspectors, 11 Naib-Darogas, 2 Jamadars, 14 Writer Naib-Darogas, 2 Havildars and 137 Constables were fined or temporarily degraded and also 24 Constables and 4 Choukidars were dismissed from service for varying degrees of delinquency.

Rewards and Punishments.

96. The Commissioner of Police was out on tour for 43 days against 84 days in the previous three years. The Deputy Commissioner of Police did not go out during the triennium under review as against 25 days of tour in the previous three years.

Tours.

97. The relation of the State Police with the Police of the neighbouring districts in Bengal and Assam continued to be satisfactory.

Co-operation.

98. Musketry and revolver practice were continued and the result showed improvements in marksmanship. One Havildar, one Naik and 8 Constables were rewarded for proficiency therein.

Musketry Practice.

99. The expenditure during the three years under review amounted to Rs. 2,98,790 as against Rs. 2,55,869 in the previous triennium. The former included "War Expenditure" of a sum of Rs. 30,790.

Expenditure.

IV. JUSTICE.

100. There were 17 Courts of Justice in the State during the years under report, exercising both civil and criminal jurisdiction, viz. :—High Court of Judicature, Tripura, with its Original and Appellate Sides, and 16 Courts of Magistrate-Munsiffs exercising original jurisdiction only.

Courts.

101. Mr. Khagendra Chandra Nag, Bar.-at-Law, M. B. E., continued as Chief Justice and Babu Sarada Charan Sarkar M. A., B. L., as Puisne Judge (Appellate Side), till he was succeeded by Babu Akhil Chandra Majumder M. A., B. L., on the 22nd Asharh, 1351 T. E. Babu Ramani Mohan Goswamy M. A., B. L., continued as Civil & Sessions Judge (Original Side) during the years under report.

High Court.

102. Altogether 7,923 criminal cases were instituted during the three years under review. With the balance of 983 pending from the previous triennium, the total number of cases for disposal before the several subordinate Courts was 8,906 as against 7,665 of the previous triennium as detailed below ; and out of these 8,906 cases, 7,735 were disposed of as against 6,682 of the preceding three years, leaving 1,171 cases pending at the end, against 983 of the previous triennium.

Number of original criminal cases.

DESCRIPTION OF OFFENCES.	During previous 3 years (1347-49.)	During three years (1350-52) under review.
Offences against the State and public tranquillity ...	174	459
Offences against person	2,304	2,833
Offences against property	3,753	4,050
Other offences	1,434	1,564
TOTAL ...	7,665	8,906

103. The number of persons brought to trial during the years under report was 9,348 ; the number awaiting trial from the preceding years was 1174 ; the total number of persons thus brought to trial during the triennium under review was 10,522 as against 8,476 of the previous three years. Out of the aforesaid 9,348 persons, 2,022 were arrested by the police, 2,686 were produced on warrant, 3,532 appeared on summons, 1,086 appeared voluntarily and 22 persons were arrested in presence of Magistrates.

Persons brought to trial.

104. Out of the aforesaid 10,522 persons brought to trial before the several courts including the Sessions Court, 5,522 persons were discharged, 1,851 were acquitted, 1,410 were convicted, 28 died, 2 escaped, and 1,709 persons were awaiting trial at the close of the triennium. Out of the convicted persons, 459 were sentenced to various terms of imprisonment extending from less than one month to 5 years and above, 4 persons were imprisoned for life, 892 were sentenced to fine only, 10 were bound down and 45 persons were warned for the future. The number of persons actually tried was 3,261 (excluding those discharged) as against 3,085 of the previous triennium and the percentage of convictions was thus 43·23 against 42·59 of the previous three years.

Results of cases.

105. Altogether extradition of 132 persons from British India was granted by the Political Agent during the years under report, of whom 39 persons were arrested and surrendered to the State Courts concerned, and 41 persons appeared of their own accord, or were subsequently arrested within the State.

Extradition from British India.

106. Out of 8,906 cases for disposal as stated above, the number of cases in which British subjects were concerned either as complainants or accused, was 1,082 as against 1,113 of the previous triennium. Out of these, 756 cases were cognizable and 326 non-cognizable. In 172 cases British subjects were complainants and in 910 cases they were the accused. In 360 cases both the parties were British subjects. In all 1,109 persons were actually brought under trial in those cases during the period under report, as against 1,499 of the previous triennium. Out of these 1,109 persons, 285 persons were convicted, 643 acquitted or discharged, 8 died, 11 escaped and 162 remained under trial at the close of the period.

Cases concerning British subjects.

107. 47 cases were committed to the Sessions during the three years under report and 1 case was pending from the previous triennium. Out of these 48 cases, 44 were disposed of during the period as detailed below. The number of persons involved in those 48 cases, was 141, of whom 52 were convicted, 70 were acquitted, 1 escaped and 18 remained under trial at the close of the triennium.

Sessions cases.

Description of cases.	Number of cases.	Nos. Disposed of.	Nos. Pending.	REMARKS.
Murder	5	5	0	
Murder and voluntarily causing grievous hurt by deadly weapons ...	1	1	0	
Murder with Conspiracy	1	1	0	
Murder and abetment of murder ...	2	2	0	
Murder and abduction in order that a person may be so disposed of as to be put in danger of being murdered	1	0	1	
Causing death by setting a trap ...	1	1	0	
Lurking house trespass by night, causing grievous hurt, and attempt to murder	1	1	0	
Attempt to murder	1	1	0	
Rioting with deadly weapons and kidnapping with intent to murder	1	1	0	
Culpable homicide not amounting to murder	10	9	1	
Dacoity by causing death with deadly weapons	1	1	0	
Dacoity with attempt to cause death or grievous hurt ...	1	1	0	
Dacoity	8	7	1	
House trespass by night and dacoity	1	1	0	
Robbery with grievous hurt	1	1	0	
Rape	3	3	0	
Arson	1	1	0	
Rioting and causing grievous hurt ...	1	1	0	
Causing grievous hurt	1	1	0	
Voluntarily causing grievous hurt with deadly weapons	1	1	0	
Criminal trespass and grievous hurt ...	1	1	0	
Criminal trespass and attempt to commit arson	1	1	0	
Causing miscarriage	1	1	0	
Institution of false case	1	1	0	
Picking pocket	1	0	1	
Total	48	44	4	

108. There were altogether 446 criminal appeals and motions as against 655 of the previous triennium. These appeals and motions were disposed of as shown below :—

Criminal appeals & motions.

Rejected	24
Judgment affirmed	232
Modified	52
Reversed	78
Further enquiry ordered	20
	406
Pending	40
Total	446

The percentage of judgments affirmed and modified was 74·34 as against 71·97 of the previous three years.

109. The number of original civil suits instituted during the years under report was 3,626 as against 4,105 of the preceding period. With the balance of 677 pending from the previous triennium, the total number of suits for disposal was 4,303 as against 4,837 of the preceding triennium. These suits were disposed of as shown below :

Original civil suits.

Exparte	1,584
Admitted and compromised	416
Dismissed for want of prosecution ...	603
Disposed of on contest	999
Pending	701
Total	4,303

The average duration of suits in the civil courts was 3 months and 17 days as against 4 months and 10 days of the previous triennium.

110. The total value of civil suits instituted during the three years was Rs. 3,41,644–15–7 as against Rs. 3,31,987–3–3 of the previous period of three years. Out of 3,626 suits, instituted during the three years under review, 1,018 related to land, 1,760 to money transactions and 848 suits were of other classes. 2,098 suits were of the value of Rs. 100 and under ; 771 suits were of the value between Rs. 100 and Rs. 500 ; 43 suits of value between Rs. 500 and Rs. 1,000 ; 28 suits of value between Rs. 1,000 and Rs. 5,000 ; 2 suits were of value above Rs. 5,000 and 684 suits were not estimable in money value.

Nature and value of suits.

111. The number of applications for the execution of decrees filed during tho years was 1,598, and there were 382 pending from the previous triennium. The total number for disposal was thus 1,980 as against 2,394 of the preceding period. The aggregate value of the new applications was Rs. 2,19,837–4–8 and that of the pending applications was Rs. 80,380–13–3, the total value thus amounting to Rs. 3,00,218–1–11, against Rs. 3,92,192–14–3 of the previous triennium. The number of applications disposed of was 1,552, the value of which was Rs. 2,12,381–5–0. The number of execution cases pending at the close of the period was 428 the value there of being Rs. 87,836–12–11.

Execution of decrees

112. There were 318 civil appeals and motions filed during the years, as against 433 of the previous triennium. With the balance of 62 from the previous period, the total number of civil appeals and motions for disposal was 380 as against 543 of the preceding triennium. Out of these cases, 309 were disposed of during the years under report as against 481 of the previous triennium, leaving a balance of 71 cases at the close of the period. The following figures will show the result of appeals and motions in civil suits ;—

Civil appeals & motions.

Decisions confirmed	173
Decisions reversed	61
Decisions modified	18
Remanded	22
Compromised or otherwise disposed of ...	35
	309
Pending	71
	380

The percentage of judgments wholly or partly upheld, excluding those in the cases compromised, was 69·71 against 62·38 of the preceding triennium.

113. The total value of civil appeals filed during the years under review was Rs. 21,740–11–0 and the average duration of each appeal was 7 months and 5 days as against 6 months and 10 days of the preceding triennium.

Value and duration of appeals.

114. 49 civil suits were instituted in the Original Side, High Court, during the three years under report as against 63 of the previous period. With the balance of 27 suits pending from the preceding years, the total number for disposal was 76 as against 105 of the previous years. Of these, 40 suits were disposed of against 78, leaving 36 suits pending at the close of the triennium. There were 38 execution cases during the period under report, including 13 cases pending from the previous triennium. Of these, 24 were disposed of and 14 remained pending at the close of the period. There were 76 applications for succession and other certificates during the years under report ; with the balance of 4 of the previous triennium, the total number of such applications was 80 ; out of which 78 were disposed of as shown below and 2 remained pending at the close of the period under review.

Civil cases in the Original Side of the High Court.

Description of cases.	Total.	Disposed of.	Pending.
Probate cases	2	2	0
Succession certificates	26	26	0
Guardianship	52	50	2
Total	80	78	2

115. The total number of appeals and motions, both civil and criminal, including the number of cases pending from the previous triennium, was 826 as against 1,198 of the preceding period. Out of these appeals and motions, 715 were disposed of as against 1,109 of the previous triennium and 111 remained pending as against 89.

Total number of appeals and motions.

116. In comparison with the preceding triennium, the total number of appeals and motions for disposal decreased by 372 and there was also a decrease in disposal by 394 only due to a decrease in number of institutions.

V. PRISONS.

Number of Jails. 117. The State maintained 8 Jails including the Central Jail at the Capital during the years under review as before. The Chief Medical Officer Dr. M. M. Majumdar and after him Capt. J. M. Ghosh, M. B. (Cal.) D. T. M & H. (Cantab) D. P. H. (London) C. L. S. T. M., remained as Superintendent.

Jail population. 118. The total jail population was 803 with 321 convicts, 473 under-trials, 1 civil prisoner, 4 lunatics and 4 detenus in 1350 T. E.; 1022 including 406 convicts, 600 under-trials, 4 civil prisoners, 4 lunatics and 8 detenus, in 1351 T. E., and 996 with 357 convicts, 630 under-trials, 3 lunatics and 6 detenus in 1352 T. E.

Long-term prisoners. 119. Prisoners undergoing imprisonment for more than 2 years numbered 75 in 1350 T. E., 85 in 1351 T. E., and 104 in 1352 T. E. against 96 in 1349 T. E.

120. The following statement will show their offences, periods of sentence and occupation :—

Class of offence	Number of prisoners. 1350 T.E.	1351 T.E.	1352 T.E.	Occupation.	REMARKS.
Murder ...	21	21	25	They were employed in brick manufacture, at oilmills, wheat grinding, soorki pounding, *khowa* breaking, weaving, gardening, bamboo and cane works, tailoring, and paddy husking etc.	40 had sentences of 2 to 5 years, 20 of 5 to 10 years, 3 of 10 to 14 years and 12 of 20 years in 1350 T. E. — 51 of 2 to 5 years, 8 of 5 to 10 years, 12 of 10 to—14 years, 14 of 20 years in 1351 T. E — 60 had sentences of 2 to 5 years, 14 of 5 to 10 years, 13 of 10 to 14 years and 17 of 20 years in 1352 T. E.
Culpable Homicide not amounting to murder ...	12	16	12		
Attempt to murder ...	—	1	—		
Grievous hurt ...	9	13	11		
Robbery ...	2	1	3		
Theft	3	4	4		
Dacoity	15	24	20		
Picking pocket ...	1	1			
Keeping stolen property in possession ...	—	—	1		
Security for good behaviour for habitual offence	10	1			
Keeping gun in possession without license	—	—	1		
Rape	1	1			
Kidnapping ...	—	1	18		
Breach of trust ...	1	1	1		
Desertion from cantonment ...	—	—	3	Convicted by Court martial.	Transfered to Civil Jail for custody.
Desertion from Battle Field	—	—	2		
Insubordination ...			3		
TOTAL	75	85	104		

121. In 1350 T. E. one convict died of septic almia in the Central Jail, Agartala. One convict suffering from hook-worm died in the said Jail during the year 1352 T. E.

Jail Health.

122. As before the Reformatory school in the Central Jail continued to work during the years under review. The number of convict students was 18 in 1350 T. E. In 1351 T. E. the number of students was 14 of whom 2 were sent up for the Pathshala Examination both coming out successful. The number during the year 1352 T. E. was 14.

Education.

123. One under-trial escaped from the Sabrum Jail but was re-arrested in 1350 T. E. One under-trial from the Belonia Jail, one under-trial from the Khowai Jail and two under-trials from the Dharmanagar Jail escaped during the year 1351 T. E. 3 of whom were re-arrested. During the year 1352 T. E. 22 convicts effected their escape from the Central Jail. One convict from the Sonamura Jail and one under-trial from the Khowai Jail also escaped.

Escape.

124. On the occasion of the auspicious birthday ceremony of His Highness the Maharaja Manikya Bahadur, 11,, 10 and 15 convicts were respectively released in 1350 1351 and 1352 T. E.

Special Release.

125. The staff of the jails during the years under report remained the same as in the year 1349 T. E.

Staff.

126. One Jamadar was fined and one warder was discharged from service in the Central Jail in 1352 T. E.

Punishment.

127. Lt.-Col. C. P. Hancock, Resident for the Eastern States with His Highness the Maharaja Manikya Bahadur visited the Central Jail, Agartala, on the 25th January 1942.

Visit.

128. The income of the Central Jail amounted to Rs. 7,319 in 1350 T. E., Rs. 5,330 in 1351 T. E. and Rs. 10,922 in 1352 T. E.

Income.

129. The total expenditure in the jails came upto Rs. 22,982, Rs. 20,031 and Rs. 36,006 respectively in the years under report against Rs. 29,755 in the year 1349 T. E.

Expenditure.

VI. REGISTRATION.

130. Thakur Rebati Mohan Deb Barman, Revenue Secretary was in charge of the Registration Department during the years 1350 T. E. and 1351 T. E. and Thakur Kamini Kumar Singh, Minister, thereafter during the year 1352 T. E.

131. The number of Registration offices continued to be 9, there being one at the headquarters station of each of the Divisions and Sub-Divisions. In the Mofussil the Divisional and the Sub-Divisional Officers and in certain Divisions

Registration Offices.

the Second Officers acted as Registrars. For the Sadar Division there was a separate Registrar at Agartala.

Registration & disposal.

132. The total number of documents (including previous year's balance) presented for registration during the year 1350 T. E. was 9,747 against 9,413 of the previous year, while such documents in 1351 T. E. and 1352 T. E. were 11,209 and 13,735 respectively. Of these, 63, 38 and 42 deeds respectively were refused registration on different grounds and 1,587, 2,665 and 4,101 deeds remained pending at the end of the year 1350 T. E., 1351 T. E. and 1352 T. E. respectively.

133. The total value covered by the documents in 1350, 1351 and 1352 T. E. amounted to Rs. 10,77,528, Rs. 13,75,939 and Rs. 12,96,226 respectively against Rs. 10,67,149 of the year 1349 T. E., while the total value covered by the documents actually registered was Rs. 11,54,456, Rs. 12,68,999 and Rs. 12,58,593 respectively against Rs. 9,88,218 of the year 1349 T. E.

Suits and appeals.

134. With suits pending from the previous year, the total number of suits brought before the Registration Department in respect of documents, the registration of which had been refused iu various registration offices in the years 1350, 1351 and 1352 T. E. was 57, 35 and 41, out of which 36, 13 and 21 were disposed of and 21, 22 and 20 remained pending at the end of those years respectively.

135. The total number of appeals (including balance from the previous year) was 5, 1 and 2 in 1350, 1351 and 1352 T. E. respectively, out of which 5 and 1 were disposed of in the year 1350 and 1351 respectively and 2 remained pending at the end of the year 1352 T. E. No appeal remained pending at the end of the year 1350 and 1351 T. E.

Income and Expenditure.

136. The total income from fees and fines in the years 1350, 1351 and 1352 T. E. was Rs. 8,061, Rs. 9,629 Rs. 11,497 and the expenditure Rs. 3,552, Rs. 3,306 and Rs. 3,567, the net income thus amounting to Rs. 4,509, Rs. 6,323 and Rs. 7,930, respectively. The corresponding figures for 1349 T. E. were as under : Income Rs. 9,078, Expenditure Rs. 3,634, net income Rs. 5,444.

VII. MUNICIPALITY

Municipality.

137. As before the State had the only Municipality at the capital town of Agartala during the years under report with a population of about 20,000.

Municipal Committee.

138. A Committee of 9 members—all nominated, administered the Municipality with Thakur Lalit Mohan Deb Barman, M. A., B. L. as the official Chairman and Babu Haridas Bhattacherjee as non-official Vice-Chairman elected by the Municipal Commissioners. Thakur Lalit Mohan Deb Barman acted

as Chairman till the appointment of Lt.-Col. Rana Jodha Jung Bahadur, Chief Commandant, Tripura Military Forces, as Chairman towards the end of the year 1350 T. E. The present Committee of 12 Commissioners-6 elected by the local public and 6 nominated by the State according to the new Municipal Act of 1349 T. E.—assumed the charge of municipal administration towards the beginning of the year 1351 T. E., Babu Naresh Kumar Bhattacherjee, B. Sc., Deputy Commissioner of Police, Tripura State and Babu Nripendra Mohan Bose being elected by the Commissioners, Chairman and Vice-Chairman respectively.

139. In the year 1350 T. E. the Committee held 10 meetings, average of attendance of members being 5·5 as against 8·1 of the preceding year and in the year 1351 T. E. the Committee held 13 meetings average attendance of members being 8·4 as against 5·5 of the preceding year ; in the year 1352 T. E. the Committee held 14 meetings the average attendance of members being 7·4 as against 8·4 of the preceding year.

Income.

140. The realization on account of Municipal and Latrine taxes in the year 1350 T. E. was Rs. 4,014-14-9, in the year 1351 T. E. Rs. 5,593-14-9, and in the year 1352 T. E. Rs. 7,130-10-3. Both Municipal and Latrine taxes amounting to nearly Rs. 2,000-0 due by the members of the Ruling Family living outside the palace proper and the Prabhu Goswamis of Sreepat remained outstanding. Had the above amount been realized the collection would have been more satisfactory.

141. The State grant for the year 1350 T. E. was Rs. 15,235, in the year 1351 T. E. Rs. 15,475 and in the year 1352 T. E. Rs. 10,000.

142. The Miscellaneous Collections from all sources including deposits for the three years under review were Rs. 825, Rs. 1,354 and Rs. 1,484-6-9 respectively. Thus the total receipts of the municipality year by year was Rs. 20,075 in 1350, Rs. 22,423 in 1351 and Rs. 18,615-1-0 in 1352 T. E.

Expenditure.

143. The expenditure was Rs. 20,075, Rs. 22,423 and Rs. 17,552-11 respectively in the years 1350, 1351, and 1352 T. E.

The Ishanganja Bazar.

144. The control and management of the Bazar at the capital continued to be in the hands of the Municipal Committee, the income from the Bazar being earmarked for Bazar improvement.

145. The total realization from the Bazar amounted to in the year 1350 T. E. Rs. 7,592-9-9, in the year 1351 T. E. Rs. 7,788-4-6 and in the year 1352 T. E. Rs. 7,897-12-0.

146. The expenditure against the Bazar Fund in 1350 T. E. was Rs. 17,993-8-9, in 1351 T. E. Rs. 8,334-10-9, and in 1352 T. E. Rs. 3,418-7.

Health.

147. The general health of the town was on the whole fair inspite of occasional outbreaks of malaria, influenza and other diseases.

CHAPTER IV—PRODUCTION AND DISTRIBUTION.

1. WEATHER AND CROPS—AGRICULTURE.

Charge of the Department.

148. The charge of the Department during the triennium was with Thakur K. K. Singh, Minister.

Staff.

149. Mr. J. C. Choudhury, S. E., M. S. A. (Tokyo) M. R. Agri. S. (London) continued as Director of Agriculture till his retirement in 1352 T. E. Mr. S. Chakraborty B. SC. Assistant Agricultural officer being transferred to Revenue Department in 1351 T. E. Mr. Sunil Kumar Roy, B. AG. was appointed in his place. Co-operative officer Mr. P. Das Gupta was transferred to the Revenue Department in 1351 T. E.

150. The executive staff of the Department was abolished in 1352 T. E. as a war economic measure.

Propaganda.

151. Several propaganda meetings were held in different parts of the State with the help of lantern slides on various subjects, such as, general agriculture, crop extension, cattle improvement, Poultry farming, Cottage industries, Co-operation, Hygiene, Sanitation, Child Welfare, Maternity, Temperance and Rural Reconstruction.

Publicity.

152. Leaflets on fodder, compost manures, manure preservation, ground-nuts, ericulture, on cotton and indigenous treatment of cattle, and playlets on sericulture, were distributed all over the State.

Seed distribution.

153. A large number of sugarcane cuttings of C. O. 213 were distributed at Dharmanagar Division among the cultivators. Different kinds of both English and Indian vegetable seeds and seedlings were also distributed among the people of Agartala and its suburbs.

Ericulture.

154. As a result of vigorous propaganda made by the staff of this Department the people realised fully the necessity of eri-rearing and many families took up the work in right earnest as a Cottage industry, and weaving of cloths in hand-loom from hand-spun eri-thread was gradually in progress.

Co-operation and Rural Reconstruction.

155. The Co-operative officer toured in different parts of the State and preached among the people the importance of co-operation in all economic as well as social activities and tried to organise rural areas on that line. He also carried on propaganda with the help of magic lantern on the subject of rural uplift.

Cattle farm.

156. Under the gracious direction of His Highness the Maharaja Manikya Bahadur, at Radhakishorenagar, situated at a distance of about six miles from Agartala, a hilly place was selected for starting a cattle farm, and an artificial Jheel was created by erecting a dam across some marshy lands. The work had however to be postponed in 1352 T. E. owing to the war situation.

157. At the instance of the Government of India a census of live-stock of this State was taken by this Department in January, 1940.

Cattle Census.

158. Various leaflets in connection with the "Grow More Food" Campaign were distributed to all classes of people and extensive propaganda to induce the cultivators to grow more food grains by double cropping in suitable lands, bringing all cultivable fallow lands under crops and improving yield of crops by using better and improved strains of seeds and proper manuring was carried on all through in right earnest by all possible means.

"Grow More Food" Campaign.

159. The subjoined statements show the rainfall and temperature in the State during the period as a whole. The rainfall was however occasionally unseasonable and in some localities excessive for a time.

Rainfall & Temperature.

Rainfall.

Serial No.	Years under Review.	Total average rainfall.	Quinquennial average.	Maximum fall.	Minimum fall.	Monthly average heaviest fall.
1.	1350 T. E.	70·82"	80·52"	95·28 (Sabroom)	59·92" (Udaipur)	20·90"
2.	1351 ,,	99·78"	83·83"	115·90" (Sabroom)	74·13" (Amarpur)	24·40"
3.	1352 ,,	92·19"	86·42"	118·92" (Dharmanagar)	58·31" (Belonia)	20·95"

Temperature.

Years under Review.	Maximum temperature.	Minimum temperature.	REMARKS.
1350 T. E.	96°	51°	
1351 T. E.	97°	51°	
1352 T. E.	98°	52°	

160. During the years 1350 T. E., 1351 T. E. and 1352 T. E., male labourers generally earned from 5 annas to Re. 1–4 and female labourers from 4 annas to 8 annas a day, while *Gharamies* (thatchers) earned from 8 annas to Re. 1–4 and carpenters, blacksmiths and masons from 12 annas to Rs. 2 per day. Most of the labourers came from the neighbouring British districts.

Labour and wages.

161. The subjoined table shows the average prices of rice and paddy during the triennium in the month of Chait.

Food Crops.

Years.	Rice per maund.	Paddy per maund.	REMARKS.
1350 T. E.	Rs. 3 to Rs. 5–8	Re. 1–4 to Rs. 3	
1351 T. E.	Rs. 4–8 to Rs. 7	Rs. 2–4 to Rs. 4	
1352 T. E.	Rs. 8 to Rs. 28	Rs. 4 to Rs. 18	

162. The Veterinary staff continued to be the same as in the previous years, with one Veterinary Surgeon, one Compounder Assistant and a Tolua. Rinderpest and foot and mouth diseases of cattle prevailed in some parts of the State and proper help was rendered by the staff.

Veterinary.

163. No Taccavi loan was issued during the years under review.

Taccavi.

164. Director of Agriculture was out on tour for 10 days in 1351 T. E. Veterinary Surgeon was out on tour for 45 days in 1350 T. E., 34 days in 1351 T. E. and 15 days in 1352. T. E.

Tour.

165. The staple crops in the State in these three years were paddy, jute, sugar-cane, linseed cotton and mustard. Among other crops grown in different parts of the State, pine-apple, groundnut, chilli, potatoes, tomatoes and pulse besides various kinds of ordinary vegetables are worth mention.

Crop.

II. FOREST AND CUSTOMS.

166. Mr. Jatindra Nath Mitra, as Secretary, remained in charge of the Department till 2. 3. 51 T. E. The post of Secretary having been abolished, the Department was put under the charge of Kumar Nandlal Deb Barman Bahadur, Conservator of Forests.

Charge and Management.

167. With the exception of a few mahals which were leased out, all the forests were under Khas management.

168. During the years under review the Department had at its disposal the undermentioned staff.

Staff.

	Rank.	1350 T. E.	1351 T. E.	1352 T. E.
1.	Station Officer	1	1	1
2.	Customs Officers	6	—	—
3.	Foresters	13	14	14
4.	Asst. Foresters	25	24	25
5.	Moharers	10	10	10
6.	Head Guards	49	49	51
7.	Literate Guards	18	14	14
8.	Guards	248	215	218
9.	Boatmen	9	9	9
	Patrol Staff.			
1.	Forester	1	1	1
2.	Head Guards	3	3	4
3.	Guards	20	20	26

169. In 1351 T. E. the posts of Customs Officers were abolished and their services were transferred to the Revenue Department.

170. During these years the Patrol staff was out on duty in several sections throughout the State according to necessity.

10

171. There were during the years altogether 84 stations which included offices of reserved forests and Toll Stations.

Forest and Customs Stations.

172. In these years the management of the forests was carried on according to State rules and regulations. The system followed was more or less allied to the selection system, with some modification to suit local conditions and peculiar circumstances affecting local hill population. The policy behind this system was to prepare the forests for scientific management in the near future with the least possible inconvenience to the inhabitants.

Management.

173. The toll station at Amlighat continued to be under the management of the State Forest & Customs Department during the years under report. The rules followed in the management was those of the Bengal Forest Department. According to the terms of agreement with the Bengal Government, a Ranger from Bengal Forest Department was placed in charge of the station during 1350 T. E. An officer of the State Forest Department was in charge of the Toll Station under arrangement both in 1351 T. E. and 1352 T. E.

Management of Amlighat Toll Station.

174. The total revenue collected and the expenditure incurred at the station during the years under report were as follows :—

Years.	Revenue.	Expenditure.
1940–41 (1350 T. E.)	Rs. 58,973	Rs. 4,016
1941-42 (1351 T. E,)	,, 58,346	,, 3,806
1942–43 (1352 T. E.)	,, 58,865	,, 3,861

175. In previous years a doctor of Sub Assistant Surgeon class used to be appointed each year at Amlighat for four months from December to March for giving free medical aid to the Toll Station Staff and to the cutters and exporters. But according to subsequent arrangement with the Bengal Government, a doctor of the same category was posted at the station for the whole year during the triennium.

176. As in the previous years, the forest produce from the Fee Simple Lots above the Amlighat Toll Station was exported free of duty under passes granted by the Collector of Chittagong.

Fee Simple Lots.

177. In addition to 530·5 sq. miles of reserved forest area of previous years, 630 sq. miles of forests in the following six plots were reserved during 1351 and 1352 T. E. Thus the total area of reserved forests upto 1352 T. E. came to 1160·5 sq. miles.

Forest Reserves.

1. Langtarai Reserve	...	368	Sq. miles	in Kailashahar Division.
2. Unakoti Reserve	...	72	,,	,, ,, ,,
3. Langai Machmara Reserve	...	124	,,	in Kailashahar and Dharmanagar Divisions.
4. Thal Reserve...	...	16	,,	in Dharmanagar Division.
5. Taranagar Reserve	...	20	,,	in Sadar Division.
6. Harishnagar Reserve	...	30	,,	,, ,, ,,

178. In 1350 and 1351 T. E. Kheda operations were undertaken as detailed below. But in 1352 T. E. owing to the emergent situation, no lease for kheda was granted.

Kheda operations.

Names of Divisions.	No. of kheda operation.		No. of elephants caught.	
	1350 T. E.	1351 T. E.	1350 T. E.	1351 T. E.
Kailashahar	3	3	42	5
Khowai	1	1	7	—
Dharmanagar	1	—	—	—
TOTAL ...	5	4	49	5

179. Besides the above, 11 more elephants were caught by what is known as Mela Shikar Method in 1350 T. E. The total number of elephants caught in 1350 T. E. was 60 against 5 only in 1351 T. E.

Permit Agents.

180. The number of Agents for the sale of permits on commission for shoulder-borne export of minor forest produce by land route was 148 in 1350 T. E. 149 in 1351 T. E. and 135 in 1352 T. E.

Afforestation.

181. So far upto 1352 T. E., approximately 148 acres were planted with Gamair, Sal, and Jarul. Out of this area of 148 acres, during 1350 T. E., only gamair seeds were put out over 19½ acres and in 1351 T. E. Taungya system of regeneration was first tried over 5 acres. But due to want of labour no further extension of plantation was undertaken in 1352 T. E. The regeneration of the years under report was quite satisfactory though proper tending of the new crop could not be done for want of labour.

Sources of income and receipts.

182. The following table shows the results of collection of forest and customs revenue under different heads during the years under report as compared with 1349 T. E.

Heads of revenue.	1349 T.E.	1350 T.E.	1351 T.E.	1352 T.E.
	Rs.	Rs.	Rs.	Rs.
I. Unclassed open forests :—				
(*a*) Toll on forest produce exported by river routes	3,55,990	3,32,922	3,19,127	4,72,364
(*b*) Toll on forest produce exported by land routes under permits	81,268	77,501	81,456	99,094
(*c*) Toll collection (State share) of the Amlighat Toll Station ...	38,680	39,995	41,060	42,449
(*d*) Grazing fees ...	9,739	16,385	15,477	19,128
(*e*) Thatching grass Mahals	4,180	4,392	4,758	4,702
II. Reserved Forests—sale of *Sal* ...	1,928	1,806	649	5,331
III. Elephant Khedas ...	3,951	7,607	2,288	—
IV. Match Excise Duty	37,674	9,627	34,087	43,428
V. Tax on cotton and oil seeds	1,42,707	66,422	92,597	37,612
VI. Duty on jute ...	90,292	63,212	45,136	57,501
VII. Duty on Tea ...	49,414	46,092	53,590	67,437
VIII. Duty on Rice and paddy	59,467	74,590	89,842	45,100
TOTAL ...	8,75,290	7,40,551	7,80,067	8,94,446

183. The quantity of timber exported during the years under report with the amount of duty realised, is shown below :—

Timber.

	1350 T. E.		1351 T. E.		1352 T. E.		REMARKS.
	Quantity (in c. ft.)	Duty (in Rs.)	Quantity (in c. ft.)	Duty (in Rs.)	Quantity (in c. ft.)	Duty (in Rs.)	
1. Timber other than Sal	5,34,190	1,04,157	4,94,168	96,089	5,68,985	1,31,891	
2. *Sal*	3,029	1,806	1,539	649	11,134	5,331	
3. Timber exported by the Feni river (State share)	15,174	3.107	18,313	3,202	9,935	2,486	

184. The Maharaja Match Factory manufactured 14400, 9000 and 8800 gross of finished matches and paid Rs. 60–15–0, Rs. 38–4–0 and Rs. 38–10–0 respectively as duty on timber used for the purpose during the years under report. The State share of the Match Excise Duty received from the Government of India has been shown in the table in para 182.

185. Altogether 319 cases against 764 persons were instituted during the period. With 36 cases against 91 accused pending from the previous triennium, the total number of cases for disposal stood at 355 involving 855 persons. The cases were disposed of as under—

Forest offences and results.

186. Tried—252 ; Compounded—44 ; Pending—59.

187. Of 855 persons involved, 23 were imprisoned, 344 were fined 16 received punishment of both imprisonment and fine, 68 were warned for the future, 192 were acquitted or discharged, 1 died in course of trial and 211 persons were awaiting trial.

188. In 1350 T. E. one Forester and one Literate guard were suspended from service for a few months and then fined ; one Forester and one Assistant Forester were fined ; one guard was suspended from service for some time and then let off with a warning and two guards were dismissed from service for misconduct. In 1351 T. E., no forest subordinate was punished for any offence. In 1352 T. E. one Forester, one Assistant Forester and one Literate guard were punished with fine and one guard was dismissed from service for neglect of duty.

Punishment and Rewards.

189. The Secretary and the Conservator of Forests were out on tour as under :—

Tour.

	1350 T. E.	1351 T. E.	1352 T. E.
Secretary	60 days	3 days	—
Conservator of Forests	—	45 days	24 days.

III. PUBLIC WORKS.

190. The Chief Minister, Manyabara Raja Rana Bodhjung Bahadur, F. R. G. S. was in charge of the Public Works Department as before. Honorary Capt. J. N. Bhaduri, B. E., C. E., M. I. E. (India), M. R. San I. (London), was State Engineer up to 1351 T. E. On his retirement Capt. A. K. Sen, B. E. was State Engineer in 1352 T. E.

191. The total expenditure incurred during the years under review on Public Works including Improvement works, amounted to Rs. 7,88,332 as detailed below against Rs. 10,06,588 of the previous triennium.

Description of works.	Ordinary Public works.	Improvement works including Local Fund.	Road Improvement works.	TOTAL.
Buildings. 1350 T. E.	31,315	97,258		1,28,573
1351 "	33,942	62,319		96,261
1352 "	53,973	71,785		1,25,758
Roads & Bridges.				
1350 T. E.	2,464	691	92.953	96,108
1351 "	4,392		97.799	1.02,191
1352 "	5,705		43,726	49,431
Tanks & Tube Wells.				
1350 T. E.	495	6,430		6,925
1351 "	374	6,400		6,774
1352 "	46	642		688
Miscellaneous works.				
1350 T. E.	1,270	16,706		17,976
1351 "	1,053	27,483		28,536
1352 "	1,521	19,939		21,460
Minor works at *Rajbari Karkhana*.				
1350 T. E.	991			991
1351 "	982			982
1352 "	761			761
Establishment.				
1350 T. E.	12,866	8,640	13.656	35,162
1351 "	23,070	4,300	8,000	35,370
1352 "	25,785		8,600	34,385
	2,01,005	* 3,22,593	2,64,734	7,88,332

*This includes contributions from local funds amounting to Rs. 22,101, consisting of, buildings—Rs. 6,600, tube-wells—Rs. 5,000, miscellaneous works—Rs. 10,501.

192. The following works were carried out during the years :—

Sadar.

1. Construction of Post, Telegraph and Telephone exchange office at Agartala.
2. Improvement of family quarters at the Military cantonment.
3. Constructing Military Hospital Building at the Military cantonment.
4. Construction of Barrack house for His Highness the Maharaja Manikya Bahadur's Body Guards.
5. Improvement of Tulsibati Girls' School.
6. Improvement of Tripura Boarding.
7. Improvement of Reserve Thana.
8. Constructing two buildings at T. B. Sanatorium.
9. Improvement of Jail Buildings.
10. Constructing a house for detenus in Sadar Jail.
11. Constructing Kalazar ward in V. M. Hospital.

12. Construction of Laskar Boarding.
13. Improvement of Sadar Thana.
14. Improvement of Sadar Tahasil station.
15. Improvement work in studio building and Body Guards Magazine in Palace.
16. Improvement of Bazar Buildings.
17. Clearing and cutting jungles at Jagatpur Tila for new cantonment.
18. Improvement of Chief Minister's quarters.
19. Earth work for circular park at the junction of Mantri Bari and Mogra Roads.
20. Constructing one Pucca well East of the Kunjaban palace.
21. Improvement of the Andharmanik dam.
22. Constructing an Earthquake-proof Building at the Palace.
23. Providing a 4-seated latrine with septic tank and an extra kitchen at Durgabari.
24. Gate Building in front of Pandal.
25. Constructing a Pucca Gallery at the Pandal.
26. Improvement of the Palace Compound.
27. Constructing a Motor Garage at Minister's Office.
28. Improvement of Revenue Officer's quarters.
29. Repairs and certain improvement of the quarters of the Raj family.
30. Constructing quarters for Capt. Maharaj Kumar D. K. Dev Barma Bahadur and Maharaj Kumar A. K Dev Barma Bahadur.
31. Necessary repairs to the Kunjaban Palace proper.
32. Repairs to Malanchabash.
33. Sinking Tube well at the office compound.
34. Sinking Tube well at Sessions Judge's quarters.
35. Excavating a tank within the existing ditches lying to the north of the Uzir Bari.
36. Excavation of a tank at Nagaichharah.
37. Excavation of a tank to the north of the Palace Compound.
38. Constructing a new road at Badarghat.
39. Improvement of Mogra Road.
40. Improvement of the bridge over Sakuntala Road.
41. Remodelling Madhuban Road.
42. Metalling Hospital Road.
43. Improvement of Agartala-Champaknagar Road.
44. Repairs to Akhaura Road.
45. Repairs to Kalachharah-Fatickchharah Road. (1350 T. E.)
46. Improvement of Prasad Pratoli between Katakhal Bridge and Major Kumar B. L. Deb Barma Bahadur's quarters.
47. Repairs to bridges on Bishalgarh-Melaghar Road (1350 T. E.)
48. Setting up mile-stones, sign boards etc. on the roads.
49. Constructing Salbagan diversion road. (1350 T. E.)
50. Steel work in trusses in reinforced concrete works at Gazaria on the Agartala-Mogra Road.
51. Constructing a road from Khoyajuri to Dharmagarh linking up the State with Assam Road.

52. Remodelling drain across the Puran Agartala for the drainage of Agartala Town between Jail Road and Ranir Bazar Road.
53. Improvement of Bridges on Trenching Ground Road.
54. Arboriculture on Kunjaban Road.
55. Pucca and Katcha works in the Murati Prangan.
56. Remodelling Kalapania Khal.
57. Constructing new roads in the new colonies at Durjoynagar, Ratannagar etc.
58. Substantial progress of Kashipur-Prayagpur Improvement works.
59. Constructing the western portion of the Barjala Road.
60. Experimental crete way on Agartala-Bishalgarh Road.
61. Making new by-roads in Arunduti Nagar.
62. Cement concrete approach road at the front of the Administration Building.
63. Automatic Sluice Gate to the east of the Gol Bazar.

Kailashahar.

64. Substantial progress of Kailashahar H. E. School.
65. Constructing M. E. School at Goldharpur.
66. Constructing Girls' M. E. School.
67. Constructing Thana officer's quarters at Kailashahar.
68. Improvement of Unakoti road.

Khowai.

69. Improvement of Second Officer's quarters.
70. Excavating a Tank at Khowai for the public.
71. Constructing Subal Singh Bari Road between Mohanpur and Subal Singh Bari.
72. Improvement of road from Subal Singh Bari to Khowai.
73. Constructing Culverts on Khowai-Barmura Road.
74. Improvement of Khowai-Kalyanpur Road.

Sonamura.

75. Improvement of Sonamura-Comilla Road. (1350 T. E.)
76. Raising Battali-Melaghar Road. (1351 T. E.)
77. Improvement of Melaghar-Bholamura Road.
78. Improvement of Sonamura embankment work in Durgabari Road.
79. Improvement of the west embankment of road in Rudrasagar.

Udaypur.

80. Clearing Jagannath Dighi at Udaypur.
81. Improvement of Matabari Road.
82. Improvement of Chandrapur Road.

Dharmanagar.

83. Improvement of Raghna road.

Belonia.

84 Constructing Lungthung-Muharipur Road.

IV. TRADE AND MANUFACTURE.

193. The principal exports were timber and other forest produce of various kinds, cotton, oil-seeds (Til and Mustard) Jute, Tea and Gur (Molasses). The principal exports of the years under review besides timber (mentioned in the connected section) are shown below.

	1349 T. E.	1350 T. E.	1351 T. E.	1352 T. E.
Cotton	68,964 Mds.	19,970 Mds.	33,395 Mds.	7,250 Mds.
Til	10,774 „	24,043 „	18,708 „	20,747 „
Mustard ...	32,917 „	35,511 „	38,430 „	39,358 „
Jute ...	2,37,430 „	5,05,696 „	90,272 „	4,60,008 „
Tea	32,05,263 lbs.	32,53,718 lbs.	33,17,290 lbs.	33,27,423 lbs.
Rice & Paddy ...	—	5,96,720 Mds.	7,18,736 Mds.	3,60,800 Mds

CHAPTER V—REVENUE & FINANCE.

1. REVENUE.

194. The following table shows the total collection in each of the years under different heads as compared with 1349 T. E.

Serial No.	Heads of Revenue.	1349 T.E.	1350 T.E.	1351 T.E.	1352 T.E.	Remarks.
1.	Land Revenue ... ... } ...	6,27,569	5,42,196	6,13,664	7,94,073	
2.	Road Cess ... ... } ...	40,420	34,823	39,647	50,477	
3.	Road Improvement Fund ...	1,03,986	1,30,235	1,20,604	78,714	
4.	Rents of markets	7,015	7,568	7,542	9,062	
5.	Family Tax in the hills ...	77,366	42,712	62,471	52,274	
6.	Toll on forest produce } ...	3,55,990	3,32,922	3,19,089	4,72,364	
7.	Income from permit sale } ...	81,268	77,501	81,464	99,094	
8.	Feni River Tolls*	40,825	39,995	41,060	42,449	
9.	Elephant & buffalo grazing Mahals	9,739	16,385	15,479	19,428	
10.	Thatching grass Mahals ..	4,180	4,392	4,758	4,702	
11.	Reserve *Sal* Forests	1,928	1,806	649	5,331	
12.	Tax on cotton and oil-seeds ..	1,42[illegible]7	66,422	92,556	37,612	
13.	Adda Mahal	24,696	25,299	28,864	29,007	
14.	Excise	91,453	97,339	90,910	97,880	
15.	Stamps and Court-fees	65,660	69,528	70,289	77,268	
16.	Law and Justice (Fines) ..	1,006	1,562	1,599	3,870	
17.	Process fees	6,930	8,200	7,585	8,388	
18.	Registration	9,078	8,061	9,629	11,497	
19.	Jail	7,391	7,319	5,330	10,922	
20.	Cattle pounds	3,406	3,316	2,661	3,196	
21.	Nazars	61,507	47,080	59,685	70,623	
22.	Education...	15,111	17,271	18,801	19,070	
23.	Tea Royalty	49,414	46,092	53,590	67,437	
24.	Jute Export duty	90,292	63,212	45,136	57,501	
25.	Duty on matches	37,674	9,627	34,085	43,428	
26.	Miscellaneous	89,956	75,990	70,845	1,08,799	
27.	Public Works	—	5,408	7,038	6,261	
28.	Kheda Operations	3,951	7,607	2,290	—	
29.	Money Lenders' License fees ...	5,577	3,884	4,559	4,829	
30.	Municipal Contribution ...	—	4,840	6,948	=	
	Total ...	20,55,595	17,98,592	19,18,817	22,85,556	

* State share only shown ; for total vide para 174.

195. The total collections in the year 1352 T. E. were Rs. 22,85,556, in 1351 T. E. Rs. 19,28,817, and in 1350 T. E. Rs. 17,98,592 ; against Rs. 20,55,595 in 1349 T. E. The net increase in collection in the year 1351 T. E. was Rs. 1,30,225 in comparison with that of the previous year ; while in 1352 T. E. there was satisfactory increase of Rs. 3,56,739 in comparison with the collection in 1351 T. E. and that of Rs. 2,29,961 in comparison with 1349 T. E., the closing year of the previous triennium.

196. The decrease in the total collection in 1350 T. E. was due to the gradual and remarkable fall-off under heads Tax on Cotton and Oil-seeds, as well as Jute Export Duty, mainly due to export and marketing difficulties and the economic situation in the hill sections. There was also some decline in the figures for land revenue in 1350 T.E. ascribable to the emergency, but subsequent rise is steady and noticeable.

197. The decrease under head Road Improvement Fund in the year 1352 was due to imposition of restrictions on the export of rice and paddy to avert shortage of food.

198. The collections under other heads showed substantial increase.

II. FINANCE.

199. Rai Sahib S. C. Dutt was in charge of the Department
Charge. during the three years under review.

200. Subjoined is a consolidated abstract account of the Financial transactions of the State and attached Zemindaries from 1347 T. E. to 1352 T. E.

201. The period under report started with an opening balance of Rs. 17,55,151 against Rs. 22,44,465 in the previous triennium.

202. The total receipts during the period from all sources, including deposits, law charges recovered, refunds and compensation for lands acquired as well as Road Fund amounted to Rs. 1,10,89,700 against Rs. 1,11,42,994 in the previous three years (1347–49 T. E.). The total sum available for expenditure including the opening balance, thus stood at Rs. 1,28,44,851 against Rs. 1,33,87,459. The actual income excluding receipts under the heads Deposits and Provident Fund amounted to Rs. 90,63,030 against Rs. 1,01,95,002 showing a decrease of Rs. 11,31,972. This was mainly due to decreased receipts under various heads.

203. The total expenditure incurred during the years under report (1350–52 T. E.) amounted to Rs. 1,05,11,989 against Rs. 1,16,32,308 in the previous three years (1347–49 T. E.) showing a decrease of Rs. 11,20,319.

A consolidated abstract account of the Receipts of the State and the attached Zemindaries from the year 1347 T. E. to 1352 T. E.

Receipts.	1347 T. E.	1348 T. E.	1349 T. E.	TOTAL.	1350 T. E.	1351 T. E.	1352 T. E.	TOTAL.	REMARKS.
1. Opening Balance :—				Opening Balance for 1347 T. E.				Opening Balance for 1352 T. E.	
(1) State	15,16,044	16,53,890	1,99,187	15,16,044	2,70,099	1,44,912	81,909	2,70,099	
(2) Zemindaries ...	7,28,421	10,64,966	11,63,951	7,28,421	14,85,052	17,08,884	13,55,567	14,85,052	
TOTAL ...	22,44,465	27,18,856	13,63,138	22,44,465	17,55,151	18,53,796	14,37,476	17,55,151	
2. Income :—									
(1) State ...	17,51,623	18,15,248	19,82,428	55,49,299	16,68,357	17,98,213	22,07,518	56,74,088	
(2) Zemindaries ...	12,65,702	11,79,575	13,89,133	38,34,410	12,61,887	5,65,989	11,09,386	29,37,262	
TOTAL ...	30,17,325	29,94,823	33,71,561	93,83,709	29,30,244	23,64,202	33,16,904	86,11,350	
Law charges recovered :—									
(1) Zemindaries ...	73,024	48,812	40,658	1,62,494	33,025	21,819	20,741	75,585	
4. Refunds and compensation for lands acquired :—									
(1) Zemindaries ...	3,25,081	1,582	16,326	3,42,989	9,814	1,252		11,942	
5 Deposits :—									
(1) State	3,04,711	2,80,601	2,51,228	8,36,540	6,14,609	3,97,108	7,09,984	17,21,701	
(2) Zemindaries ...	64,798	29,229	17,425	1,11,452	11,755	24,226	85,808	1,21,789	
TOTAL ...	3,69,509	3,09,830	2,68,653	9,47,992	6,26,364	4,21,334	7,95,792	18,43,490	
6. Road Fund Contribution...	—	—	—	—	8,000	8,000	8,600	24,600	
Road Fund	92,182	1,09,642	1,03,986	3,05,810	1,30,235	1,20,604	78,714	3,29,553	
7 Provident Fund ...	—	—	—	—	60,214	64,140	48,826	1,73,180	
GRAND TOTAL ...	61,21,586	61,83,545	51,64,322	1,33,87,459	55,53,047	48,75,147	57,07,929	1,28,44,851	

A consolidated abstract account of Expenditure of the State and the attached Zemindaries from the year 1347 T. E. to 1352 T. E.

Expenditure.	1347 T. E.	1348 T. E.	1349 T. E.	Total.	1350 T. E.	1351 T. E.	1352 T. E.	Total.	Remarks.
1. General Administration charges :—									
(a) State	6,36,313	6,31,045	7,09,865	19,77,223	7,18,696	6,85,455	6,45,642	20,49,793	
(b) Zemindaries :—									
1. Cost of management	1,42,174	1,37,557	1,39,873	4,19,604	1,39,292	1,43,057	1,35,430	4,17,779	
2. Cost of litigation	1,11,176	1,07,570	1,13,456	3,32,202	1,07,259	92,253	78,788	2,78,300	
Total ...	8,89,663	8,76,172	9,63,194	27,29,029	9,65,247	9,20,765	8,59,860	27,45,872	
2. Revenue and Taxes on account of the Zemindaries	2,62,044	3,45,211	3,78,969	9,86,221	3,88,609	3,13,768	4,40,377	11,42,754	
3. Public Works—(a) State	3,15,871	1,94,253	1,89,101	6,99,225	1,75,026	1,46,915	1,78,046	4,99,987	
(b) Zemindaries ...	4,42-556	1,60,847	1,00,740	7,04,143	1,33,658	72,489	88,915	2,95,060	
Total ..	7,58,427	3,55,100	2,89,841	14,03,368	3,08,684	2,19,404	2,66,961	7,95,047	
4. Electric Light—State	36,474	22,921	25,387	84,782	28,581	20,512	30,433	79,526	
5. Municipality & Sanitation—State...	12,600	10,000	17,750	40,350	23,008*	22,423	10,000	55,431*	* Included Rs 2,933 spent on sanitation work.
6. Education—(a) State	1,30,817	1,30,783	1,24,215	3,85,815	1,31,773	1,25,399	1,32,920	3,90,092	
(b) Zemindaries ...	9,103	4,130	4,149	17,382	6,598	4,156	2,993	13,747	
Total ...	1,39,920	1,34,913	1,28,364	4,03,197	1,38,371	1,29,555	1,35,913	4,03,839	
7. Medical and Sanitation :—									
(a) State	87,812	76,984	84,791	2,49,587	96,782	83,928	85,534	2,66,244	
(b) Zemindaries	11,831	10,199	10,227	32,257	9,731	9,857	8,244	27,832	
Total ...	99,643	87,183	95,018	2,81,844	1,06,513	93,785	93,778	2,94,076	
8. Survey and Settlement—(a) State...	12,000	14,355	13,923	40,278	8,890	13,423	11,113	33,426	
(b) Zemindaries ...	2,201	2,523	2,324	7,048	2,281	3,102	2,383	7,766	
Total ...	14,201	16,878	16,247	47,326	11,171	16,525	13,496	41,192	
9. Agriculture, Commerce and Industries—State ...	9,565	4,483	12,733	26,781	10,020	8,676	4,085	22,681	
10. Religious Expenses—(a) State ...	56,592	54,158	56,881	1,67,631	56,335	58,083	58,854	1,73,272	
(b) Zemindaries ...	6,845	6,340	6,779	19,964	6,689	6,527	6,897	20,113	
Total ...	63,437	60,498	63,660	1,87,595	63,024	64,610	65,751	1,93,385	
11. Sultanat—State	98,418	69,242	52,816	2,20,476	49,419	41,550	40,649	1,31,618	
12. Purchase of Land Tenures :—									
(a) State	14,310	6,717	3,184	24,211	5,764	22,149	11,242	39,155	
(b) Zemindaries	20,131	675	42,444	63,253	99	5,300	303	5,702	
Total ...	34,444	7,392	45,628	87,464	5,863	27,449	11,545	44,857	

Expenditure.	1347 T. E	1348 T. E.	1349 T. E.	Total.	1350 T. E.	1351 T. E.	1352 T. E.	Total.	Remarks.
13. Pension and Gratuity —(*a*) State	88,492	93,721	98,478	2,80,691	1,04,590	1,10,345	1,16,613	3,31,548	
(*b*) Zemindaries	12,605	17,098	16,073	45,776	15,005	16,217	18,160	49,382	
Total	1,01,097	1,10,819	1,14,551	3,26,467	1,19,595	1,26,562	1,34,773	3,80,930	
14. Ordinary *Sansar* charges :—									
(*a*) His Highness's own and the late Maharaja's family—State	1,01,388	72,513	72,273	2,46,174	74,325	71,054	69,368	2,14,747	
(*b*) Other branches of the Raj family—State	74,169	70,820	70,336	2,15,325	70,887	73,868	63,946	2,08,701	
(*c*) Thakurs—(Zemindaries)	15,060	15,060	15,060	45,180	15,060	15,060	15,060	45,180	
(*d*) *Sansar* office establishment :— State	15,080	13,957	5,440	34,477	4,941	3,936	4,211	13,088	
(*e*) Miscellaneous—State	83,325	29,670	21,880	35,377	29,950	12,480	14,269	56,699	
Total	2,89,522	2,02,022	1,84,989	6,76,533	1,95,163	1,76,398	1,66,85	5,38,415	
15. Charity and Donation :—									
(*a*) State	17,736	14,142	16,682	48,560	12,562	25,011	15,226	52,799	
(*b*) Zemindaries	3,026	11,892	14,963	29,881	5,917	5,293	1,057	12,267	
Total	20,762	26,034	31,645	78,441	18,479	30,304	16,283	65,066	
16. His Highness's Nij Tahabil :— State... 17. His Highness's tour—State	2,24,657	2,14,591	2,28,418	6,67,668	2,29,719	2,19,730	2,18,766	6,68,215	
18. Payment of liabilities and deposits—									
(*a*) State	1,05,102	79,999	99,994	2,85,095	1,00,838	1,15,190	1,74,963	3,90,991	
(*b*) Zemindaries	61,854	1,25,312	25,744	2,12,910	20,597	21,516	17,202	59,315	
Total	1,66,956	2,05,311	1,25,138	4,98,005	3,51,154	3,56,436	4,10,931	11,18,521	
19. Miscellaneous—(*a*) State	7,892	4,761	17,763	30,416	17,174	15,385	33,071	65,630	
(*b*) Zemindaries	11,152	10,084	5,640	26,876	7,659	3,880	3,409	14,948	
Total	19,044	14,845	23,403	57,292	24,833	19,265	36,480	80,578	
20. Coronation of King Emperor—Zemindaries	302	—	—	302	—	—	—	—	
21 Writing off irrecoverable advances—State	782	—	—	782	—	—	—	—	
22. Payment of old debts—State	96,941	1,57,609 }							
23. Interest on deposits—State	22,059	36,901 }	1,53,520	4,67,030	1,47,238	1,26,532	1,88,944	4,62,714	
24. Governor's Visit—State	6,490		—	6,490	—	—	—	—	
25. Marriage ceremony of Maharaj Kumari Renuka Debi—State	12,445	—	—	12,445	—	—	—	—	
26. Road fund :—(*a*) State	22,840	1,14,284	1,38,148	2,75,272	1,66,609	1,05,799	57,193	2,69,601	
(*b*) Do Advance	—	—	—	—	29,800	1,713	8,000	39,513	

Expenditure.	1347 T. E.	1348 T. E.	1349 T. E.	Total.	1350 T. E.	1351 T. E.	1352 T. E.	Total	REMARKS.
27. Geological Department	—	6,040	5,750	11,790	4,630	2,308	1,927	8,865	
28. His Highness's Official entertainments—State	—	20,000	30,000	50,000	30,000	30,000	30,000	90,000	
29. Contribution to His Highness's *Nijtahabil*—Zemindaries	—	2,05,715	2,60,000	4,65,715	2,28,195	2,48,128	—	4,76,323	
30. Purchase of share of Electric Supply Co. Ltd.—State	—	23,000	—	23,000	—	—	—	—	
31. King Emperor's Anti Tuberculosis Fund—State	—	25,000	—	25,000	—	—	—	—	
32. Loans—State	—	—	4,000	4,000	—	—	—	—	
33. Advance—State	—	—	1,064	1,064	—	—	—	—	
34. War Expenditure—State	—	—	18,338	18,338	88,755	1,26,716	2,11,488	4,26,959	
(*a*) Purchase of War Bond	—	—	—	—	65,363	60,478	—	1,25,841	
35. Advances & Loans treated as Final expenditure	—	—	14,68,243	14,68,243	—	—	—	—	
36. Expenditure of the *Sradh* ceremony of the Late Madhyama Maharani	—	—	—	—	13,000	—	—	13,000	
37. State Contribution to the War Fund	—	—	—	—	30,000	30,000	30,000	90,000	
Total	34,02,730	33,52,164	48,77,414	1,16,32,308	—	—	—	—	
38. Census—State	—	—	—	—	3,691	1,944	690	6,325	
39. Co-operative—State	—	—	—	—	831	—	—	831	
40. Immigration etc.—State	—	—	—	—	3,525	95,271	8,172	1,06,968	
41. Marriage & Jubraji Tika—State	—	—	—	—	1,36,318	—	—	1,36,318	
42. Advance—State	—	—	—	—	3,562	6,210	85,795	95,567	
43. Provident Fund—State	—	—	—	—	—	8,685	14,689	23,374	
44. State Contribution from Zemindaries	—	—	—	—	—	6,000	—	6,000	
Total	—	—	—	—	36,99,251	34,37,671	33,75,067	1,10,11,989	

Expenditure.	1347 T. E.	1348 T. E.	1349 T. E.	Total.	1350 T. E.	1351 T. E.	1352 T. F.	Total	REMARKS.
Closing Balance :—(a) State—				Closing balance for the year 1349 T. E.				Closing balance for the year 1352 T. E.	
In Cash	1,23,171	1,38,191	2,34,244	2,34,244	1,38,675	62,584	5,49,255	5,49,255	
At Bank	4,992	14,427	23,448	—	—	—	—	—	
Working balance :— In Cash	412								
At Bank	29,588	4,15,182	—	—	—	—	—	—	
In advances	3,85,182								
In bonds and advances	10,41,203	10,34,929	—	—	—	—	—	—	
Road Fund Balance	69,342	61,701	12,407	12,407	6,233	19,325	32,847	32,847	
Total	16,53,890	16,67,430	2,70,099	2,70,099	1,44,912	81,909	5,82,102	5,82,102	
(b) Zemindaries :—In Cash	2,56 482	2,00,217	1,78,558	1,78,558	1,42,726	1,32,509	82,129	82,129	
At Bank	4,00,595	4,27,506	7,27,406	7,27,406	6,39,288	1,95,243	5,53,03	5,58,034	
In bonds and advances	4,07,889	5,36,228	5,79,088	5,79,088	8,26,870	10,27,815	11,10,597	11,10,597	
Total	10,64,966	11,63,951	14,85,052	14,85,052	17,08,884	13,55,567	17,50,760	17,50,760	
Total of State & Zemindaries' balances	27,18.856	28,31,381	17,55.151	17,55,151	18,53,796	14,37,476	23,32,862	23,32,862	
Total of State & Zemindaries' expenditure	34,02,730	33,52,164	48,77,414	1,16,32,308	36,99,251	34,37.671	33,75,067	1,05,11,989	
GRAND TOTAL	61,21,586	61,83,545	66,32.565	1,33,87,459	55,53,047	48,75,147	57,07,929	1,28,44,851	

N. B.—The slight discrepancy in certain cases between figures in Departmental sections and those in this financial statement is due to the fact that in this statement audited figures have been used, arranged under major Budget heads, after final debit and adjustment.

204. The year 1352 T. E. closed with a balance of Rs. 23,32,862 as per details below :—

ACTUAL CASH BALANCE,

In the Treasuries	Rs. 6,22,686
In Banks	Rs. 5,99,579
Held in Loans and Advances, (Zemindaries) ...	Rs. 11,10,597
	Rs. 23,32,862.

205. The period under report thus ended with a balance of Rs. 23,32,862 against Rs. 17,55,151.

206. Noticeable variations in expenditure are explained below :—

i. ADMINISTRATION CHARGES :—

The increase of Rs. 72,570 was due to the following reasons.

STATE :—(a) Purchase of papers ;

(b) Purchase of Food-Stuff for the Jail population and provision for certain State detenus confined in British Jails ;

(c) Time-scale increment of pay and other increments of pay ;

(d) Increment of pay for the 1st Tripura B. B. M. Rifles and the Ration Allowance of the Training Coy. ;

(e) Extra expenditure on account of Pleader's Fees.

ZEMINDARIES :—The decrease of Rs. 55,727 was due to reduced litigation charges on the whole.

ii. REVENUE AND TAXES :—

ZEMINDARIES :—The increase of Rs. 1,56,533 was due to payment of arrears of previous years and payment of Education Cess and of some arrear bills.

iii. PUBLIC WORKS :—

STATE AND ZEMINDARIES :—Stoppage of costly public works as well as non-payment of some bills both in the State as well as in the Zemindaries were the main causes for the noticeable decrease of Rs. 6,08,321 under this head.

iv. MUNICIPALITY :—

STATE : —The increase was Rs. 15,081. In the previous triennium the Municipality was awarded a grant which was shown as expenditure under this particular head. This system was discontinued in 1350 and 1351 T. E. in which years the total income and the expenditure of the Municipality were included in the State Budget. All expenditure under the Municipality was shown in 1350 and 1351 T. E. as expenditure of the State. This accounts for the increase.

v. **Medical :—**

State :—The increase of Rs. 16,657 was due to the increase in the prices of medicines and appliances.

vi. Sultanat :—

State :—The decrease was Rs. 88,858. In the previous triennium extra expenditure was incurred on account of purchase of new motor cars and furniture. This was not necessary in the triennium under report. This accounts for the decrease.

vii. Purchase of Land Tenures :—

State :—The increase was Rs. 14,944. The increase was due to purchase of land generally under auction sale.

Zemindaries :—The decrease was Rs. 57,551. There was no remarkable purchase of lands in the triennium under report.

viii. Pension and Gratuity :—

State :—The increase was Rs. 50,857. The allowance given to the members of Thakur Families and others which had been included in the Sansar charges in the previous years was included in the pension head in the period under report. This accounts for the increase.

ix. Sansar :— The decrease was Rs. 1,38,115. This was mainly due to the allowance given to the members of Thakur Families being included in the pension head during the period under report and also to the provision for some of the establishments being transferred to other heads.

x. Charity and Donation :—

Zemindaries :—The decrease was Rs. 17,614. Some special donations were made in the previous triennium while no such donations were made in the triennium under report. This accounts for the decrease.

xi. Payment of old Liabilities and Deposits :—

State :—The increase was Rs. 1,05,896. This was mainly due to payment of some Provident Fund deposits and some old liabilities.

Zemindaries :—The decrease was Rs. 1,53,595. In the previous triennium there was extra expenditure due to repayment of deposits received, while no such expenditure was necessary in the triennium under report.

xii. Immigration & :—

State :—Includes fairly large contributions towards the relief of the distressed refugees from Dacca.

xiii. Miscellaneous :—

State :—The increase of Rs. 35,214 was due to the expenditure incurred in connection with the Kotla Succession Certificate case and some other unforeseen expenditure.

Zemindaries :—The decrease was Rs. 11,928. The decrease was due to curtailment of general expenditure.

III. THE TRIPURA STATE BANK.

Management.

207. Rai Sahib S. C. Dutt, Finance Minister of the State, continued to be in charge of the Bank. (Now Captain) Thakur Jogesh Chandra Dev Barma, B. COM., continued as Secretary of the Bank till his transfer to the State Military service in Poush 1351 T. E. when Babu Prafulla Kumar Bhattacharjee B. A., was appointed Secretary in his place and he continued as such during the remaining period of the triennium.

Progress.

208. The Bank was maintaining its popularity with continued progress and the total amount of deposits stood at Rs. 8,45,417 in 1352 T. E., against Rs. 3,81,372 in 1349 T. E., the closing year of the previous triennium.

Profit.

209. The net profit during the three years was Rs. 37,094 against Rs. 11,290 in the previous triennium, the annual average being Rs. 12,365 against Rs. 3,763 in 1349 T. E.

CHAPTER VI—MEDICAL.

Hospital & Dispensaries.

210. As in the year before, 21 Dispensaries worked during the years under report including the Victoria Memorial Hospital at the Capital town.

New Patients.

211. The total number of patients treated new during the years is shown below with their daily average in comparison with that of the year 1349 T. E.

	1349 T. E.	1350 T. E.	1351 T. E.	1352 T. E.
PATIENTS :—				
Outdoor	1,53,626	1,62,875	1,67,633	1,00,035
Indoor	1,099	1,018	1,658	1,046
TOTAL	1,54,725	1,63,893	1,69,291	1,01,081
DAILY AVERAGE :—				
Outdoor	420·89	446·23	459·26	274·06
Indoor	3·01	2·76	4·54	2·86
TOTAL	423·90	448·99	463·8	276·92

Out-door Attendance.

212. Out-patients treated old and new numbered during the years under report 3,18,334 ; 3,19,091 and 2,33,474, with a daily average of 871·72, 871·39 and 639·58 respectively, the number of patients and their daily average being 3,04,338 and 831·73 in the year 1349 T. E.

In-door Patients.

213. Together with the balance of 27 of the previous year, 1,018 patients were admitted during the year 1350 T. E. for treatment against 1,099 of the year before. Of them, 729 were discharged cured, 152 relieved, 40 died and 97 remained for treatment at the end of the year.

214. The number of patients totalled 1,658 during the year 1351 T. E. 1,398 of them were cured, 171 relieved or otherwise discharged, 72 died and 22 remained under treatment at the close of the year.

215. In 1352 T. E. the total number of patients was 1,046 of whom 694 were cured, 291 discharged, 42 died and 19 remained under treatment at the close of the year.

Leprosy Centre.

216. In the year 1350 T. E., 14 new patients against the same number in 1349 T. E., were treated in the two Leprosy Centres, one at the Capital town of Agartala and the other at Khowai Divisional town. Dr. J. M. Bose and Dr. J. K. Sarker were in charge of the centres respectively. 7 new patients came under treatment during the year 1351 T. E. The total number of new patients was 18 in the year 1352 T. E. Dr. J. K. Sarker and Dr. S. C. Dey were in charge of these centres in that year.

Kala-azar.

217. Dr. S. Bhattacharjee, M. B., remained in charge of the Out-door Kala-azar Centre at the V. M. Hospital.

218. The following statement will show the number of patients treated during the years under report as compared with that of the year 1349 T. E.

Year	No. of patients treated	Cured	Relieved	Left treatment	Died	Remained for treatment
1349 T. E.	186	83	27	59	7	10
1350 T. E.	95	20	—	69	—	6
1351 T. E.	144	35	—	94	—	15
1352 T. E.	79	34	—	38	—	7

V. M. Hospital.

219. The total number of out-door patients treated new was 19,074 during the year 1350 T. E. as against 21,373 of the year before, the daily average of old and new patients being 110·61 as against 115·86.

220. In 1351 T. E. 19,601 outpatients were treated with a daily average of 111·12 and in 1352 T. E. 11,152 out-patients were treated, their daily average being 64·32.

221. The total number of in-patients during the years under report was 842, 1487 and 790 respectively.

222. Altogether Rs. 10,048-8-9 was expended for the institution during the year 1350 T. E. as against Rs. 10,419 in the year before. The total cost in the two succeeding years amounted to Rs 24,281-7-9 and Rs. 21,667-1-0.

Antirabic centre.

223. As before Dr. N. Deb Barma, M. B., was in charge of this centre.

224. The total number of patients in this line treated during the year 1350 T. E. was 37 against in 1349 T. E., while 24 and 15 patients were treated during the years 1351 and 1352 T. E. respectively.

225. The total cost incurred on this account was on average Rs. 280-5-0 only against 412 of the previous triennium.

Surgical operations.

226. The total number of operations performed during the year 1350 T. E. was 1,419 including 47 major cases, the previous year's figures being 1,408 and 32 respectively.

227. Altogether 1,191 operations were performed in the year 1351 T. E. Of them 39 cases were major.

228. In the year 1352 T. E., the total number of operations was 1,142 including 38 major cases.

Police cases.

229. Police cases attended to during the year 1350 T. E. numberd 201 with 20 post mortem cases, as against 179 and 33 respectively in the year 1349 T. E.

230. In 1351 T. E. the total number of Police cases was 241 including 19 post mortem cases, and in 1352 T. E. the total number of Police cases was 244 of which 32 were post mortem cases.

Clinical Laboratory.

231. The charge of the clinic remained with Dr. A. Sen Gupta M. B., and after him with Dr. S. Bhattacharjee, M. B. during the years under report. 502, 663 and 1,236 samples of different kinds were examined in the clinic during the years under report respectively, against 566 samples in 1349 T. E.

The King George V X-Ray Installation.

232. As before, Dr. N. Deb Barma, M. B., remained in charge of the Ward during the years under report. In the year 1350 T. E., 32 cases were examined against 22 in 1349 T. E. and in the year 1351 T. E. 30 cases and in the year 1352 T. E. 37 cases were examined in this institution. The expenditure on this institution during the years was Rs. 497-9-6, Rs. 519-7-0 and Rs. 559-11-9 respectively against Rs. 603 the average of the previous triennium.

Ayurvedic Department.

233. As in the preceding year, Kaviraj Surendra Chandra Bhattacharjee, Vaidyaratna was in charge of this Department. The number of patients treated during the years under report totalled 114. The expenditure incurred in this section including the cost of medicines and the annual pay of the Kaviraj during the triennium on an average amounted to Rs. 2,879 as against Rs. 3,229, the previous three years' average.

Vaccination.

234. The subjoined statement will show the total number of vaccination cases during the years as compared with 1349 T. E. with the results of the operations :—

Year	Total number of operations performed	Successful
1349 T. E.	16,119	12,907
1350 T. E.	15,742	11,848
1351 T. E.	10,195	6,542
1352 T. E.	15,239	12,250

235. The total cost incurred in this section in the year 1350 T. E. was Rs. 1,036-4, in 1351 T. E. Rs. 609-9-6 and in 1352 T. E. Rs. 1,455-3-5, against Rs. 2,237 the average for the previous triennium.

Homoeopathic Department.

236. Dr. K. B. Ghosh, B. A., H. M. B., with 5 Assistant Homoeopaths performed the duties of this section under the direct supervision of the Chief Medical Officer of the State.

237. The total number of patients treated in 1350 T. E. was 35,771 against 26,434 in 1349 T. E. In the year 1351 the number of patients treated came up to 41,161 and in the year 1352 T. E. to 21,597.

238. The total cost incurred amounted to Rs. 4,292-13-6, Rs. 4,446-13-6 and Rs. 5,295-3-3 respectively during the years under review as against Rs. 4,344 in 1349 T. E.

Public Health.

239. During the triennium cholera broke out in some parts of the State—Dharmanagar, Khowai and Belonia Divisions. Small-pox also broke out more or less in all the Divisions of the State but the number of deaths was comparatively small.

Visit.

240. Lt.-Col. C. P. Hancock, Resident for the Eastern States paid a visit to the V. M. Hospital on the 25th January, 1942.

Staff.

241. Dr. M. M. Majumdar, L. M. S., Chief Medical Officer (Public Health Minister) remained in charge of the Medical Department till his retirement from service on the 8th Jaistha 1351 T. E.

242. Capt. Dr. J. M. Ghosh, M. B. (Cal.), D. T. M. & H. (Cantab.), D. P. H. (London), C. L. S. T. M. was appointed to the post of Chief Medical Officer in the month of Poush 1351 T. E. and he continued to work with Dr. A. Sen Gupta, M. B., State Becteriologist, Dr. N. Deb Barma, M. B., State Radiologist and Dr. S. Bhattacharjee, M. B., as his assistants, at the Capital town during the years under review. But it is a matter of great regret that Dr. Sen Gupta died on the 26th Falgoon in 1351 T. E.

243. There was besides a regular staff of medical subordinates in charge of the Mofussil dispensaries, while 6 Midwives and 6 Nurses were engaged at the V. M. Hospital and some Mofussil dispensaries during the years under review.

Expenditure.

244. The total expenditure amounted to Rs. 96,782, Rs. 83,928 and Rs. 85,534 respectively during the years under report, as against Rs. 84,791 in 1349 T. E.

CHAPTER VII—PUBLIC INSTRUCTION.

Charge.

245. During the years under review, the Portfolio of Public Instruction was held by Manyabara Raja Rana Bodhjung Bahadur, F.R.G.S., Chief Minister. Mr. J. K. Bhattacherjee, M. SC., was entrusted with the charge of the Department as Director of Public Instruction.

Education of Yubaraj Goswami Bahadur.

246. The education of Sreela Sreejut Yubaraj Goswami Bahadur was entrusted to the care of Mr. Janesh Kumar Bhattacherjee, M. SC. since the 8th Jaistha, 1350 T. E. The Yubaraj Goswami Bahadur was only a beginner but at the end of the year it was found that he had made considerable progress in his studies. The Yubaraj Goswami Bahadur had his education for 5 months under the care of the Tutor at Shillong and for the remaining portion of the year at Agartala.

In 1351 T. E. he had his education for some months under the care of the Tutor at Panna, Bangalore and for the remaining part of the year at Agartala.

In 1352 T. E. he had his education for some months under the care of the Tutor at Panna and Pachmaria. His progress in studies was quite satisfactory.

Number of Schools.

247. The total number of schools during the years under review was 150, 151 and 150 with an aggregate numerical strength of 6112, 8740 and 8388 as against 141 schools and 8,953 students in 1349 T. E. Besides, there were private schools numbering 42, 32 and 37 against 33 in 1349 T. E.

H. E Schools.

248. In the year 1350 T. E. there were 7 permanently affiliated High English Schools for boys and one branch H. E. School for girls, while in 1351 and 1352 T. E. there were 8 permanently affiliated H. E. Schools (7 for boys and 1 for girls). The total number of pupils in these institutions was 2104, 3106 and 2,197 respectively and the average daily attendance stood at 1,584·83, 1,703·52 and 1,645·16 against 1,504·30 in the preceding year.

Matriculation Examination.

249. Agartala, the Capital of the State, continued to be a Centre for the Matriculation Examination. The State H. E. Schools sent up candidates to this Centre. Candidates from schools in British India were also allowed to sit at it. In 1350 T. E. besides the students of the State H. E. Schools 1 candidate from Adarsha Bidyalaya, Calcutta and 7 private girl candidates sat for the examination. No Matriculation Examination was held in 1351 T. E. as the dates of the examination were shifted by the Calcutta University to the following year. In 1352 T. E. 1 candidate from Sashidal Union H. E. School, Tipperah, 1 from Bhutnath Mahamaya Institution, 2 private candidates, 3 female candidates (1 from Metropolitan Institution and 2 from Aparnacharan H. E. School for girls) and 19 private female candidates, besides the regular candidates from the State H. E. Schools appeared in the examination.

250. The subjoined statement will show the results of the examination during the period under review :—

	No. sent up.	Passed.	1st Division.	2nd Division.	3rd Division.
1. U K. Academy					
1350 T. E.	31	25	3	7	15
1352 T. E.	35	26	3	5	18
2. R K. Institution					
1350 T. E.	13	6	4	1	1
1352 T. E.	24	20	1	3	16
3. B. K. Institution					
1350 T. E.	17	6	4	1	1
1352 T. E.	21	13	2	1	10
4. B. B. Institution					
1350 T. E.	5	4	1	0	3
1352 T. E.	12	10	1	1	8
5. N. C. Institution					
1350 T. E.	6	4	1	0	3
1352 T. E.	9	3	0	1	2
6. K. B. Institution					
1350 T. E.	7	2	0	1	1
1352 T. E.	6	6	1	0	5
7. Khowai H. E. School					
1350 T. E.	6	5	1	3	2
1352 T. E	11	6	1	1	3
	203	136	23	25	88

251. The result was on the whole satisfactory, the percentage of success being 62·35 and 70·33 in 1350 and 1352 T. E. respectively.

252. The subjoined statement will show the monthly State scholarships awarded to the students of the State H. E. Schools on the results of the Matriculation Examination, each being tenable for 2 years.

	1350 T. E.	1352 T. E.
1st—Rs. 10	R. K. Institution, Kailashahar.	U. K. Academy, Agartala.
2nd—Rs. 8	R. K. Institution, Kailashahar.	Khowai H. E. School.
3rd—Rs. 8	U. K. Academy, Agartala.	B. K. Institution, Belonia.

M. E. Schools for boys and girls.

253. During the years under review, there were 11, 13 and 14 M. E. Schools for boys with a total strength of 1,306, 1,309 and 1,455 respectively against 11 schools and 1,290 students in 1349 T. E., and the average daily attendance stood at 1054·13, 1015·13 and 1,051·23 respectively against 990·09 of 1349 T. E., while there were 3, 4 and 4 M. E. Schools for girls with a total strength of 215, 267 and 287 respectively, against 4 schools and 273 students in 1349 T. E., and the average daily attendance stood at 164·01, 197·77 and 194·57 respectively against 276·14 of 1349 T. E.

L. V. Schools for boys and girls.

254. During the period there were 19, 24 and 24 L. V. Schools for boys respectively with a total strength of 1093, 1,384 and 1,112 students respectively against 19 schools and 1,111 students of 1349 T. E. and the average daily attendance stood at 909·39, 1048·81 and 841·60 against 855·02 of 1349 T. E. ; and there were 6, 5 and 5 L. V. Schools for girls with a total strength of 222, 245 and 223 respectively against 5 schools and 155 students in 1349 T. E., the average daily attendance of which was 165·73, 170·72 and 154·63 respectively against 106·33 of 1349 T. E.

Pathsalas for boys.

255. In the years under report, there were 88, 83 and 83 *Pathshalas* for boys against 79 in 1349 T. E. The total number of pupils stood at 2966, 2221 and 2,116 against 2,946 in the preceding year and the average daily attendance stood at 2446·33, 1736·29 and 1,641·12 respectively in the years under report against 2,523·60 in 1349 T. E.

Scholarship Examinations

256. In 1350 T. E., altogether 1,166 candidates appeared at the different Scholarship Examinations of the State against 1,097 in the previous year. Of these, 976 candidates including 187 girls came out successful. The results on the whole were satisfactory. 84 students including 28 girls passed the M. E. Examination. 2 girls passed the H. V. Examination. In the L. V. Examination the number of successful candidates was 235 including 42 girls and in the *Pathshala* Examination the number was 654 including 115 girls, 15 out of these candidates having appeared from different *Muktabs* and *Madrasas* of the State.

257. In 1351 T. E., altogether 1,263 cadidates appeared at the different Scholarship Examinations of the State against 1,166 in the previous year. Of these, 740 candidates including 159 girls came out successful. The results on the whole were satisfactory. 54 students including 10 girls passed the M. E. Examination. 2 girls passed tne H. V. Examination. In the L. V. Examination the number of successful candidates was 145 including 46 girls and in the *Pathshala* Examination the number was 541 including 103 girls.

258. In 1352 T. E., altogether 409 candidates appeared at the different Scholarship Examinations of the State against 1,263 in the previous year. Of these, 262 candidates including 79 girls came out successful. The results on the whole were satisfactory. 34 students including 12 girls passed tne M. E. Examination. In the L. V. Examination the number of successful candidates was 66 including 26 girls and in the *Pathshala* Examination the number was 162 including 41 girls.

259. On the results of the examinations 10 boys and 8 girls in 1350 T. E., 12 boys and 7 girls in 1351 T. E. and 10 boys and 7 girls in 1352 T. E. were awarded scholarships varying from Rs. 2 to Rs. 5 per month tenable for two to four years.

Schools for special training.

260. In the years under review, there were 11, 10 and 10 schools for special training consisting of 5 Sanskrit *Tols*, 4 *Madrasas*, 1 Artisan School and *Silpasram* and 1 Jail Reformatory School in 1350 T. E. and 5 Sanskrit *Tols*, 4 *Madrasas*, 1 Artisan School and *Silpasram* and 1 Jail Reformatory School in 1351 T. E. and 4 Sanskrit *Tols*, 4 *Muktabs* and *Madrasas*, 1 Artisan School and *Silpasram* and 1 Jail Reformatory School in 1352 T. E.

Sanskrit *Tols*.

261. The Sanskrit *Tols* had 51, 41 and 38 students on the rolls respectively in 1350, 1351 and 1352 T. E. against 65 in the preceding year and the average daily attendance stood at 38·08, 28·52 and 28·45 against 47·08 in 1349 T. E.

262. The *Muktabs* and *Madrasas* had 214, 187 and 160 students respectively on the roll against 116 in the preceding year and the average daily attendance stood at 176·25, 175·06 and 132·30 against 95·57 in the preceding year.

Muktabs and Madrasas.

263. In the years under review, there were, as before, 4 Compulsory Free Primary Schools with 903, 931 and 786 pupils against 856 in 1349 T. E. and the average daily attendance stood at 650·88, 601·14 and 486·30 against 529·80 in the preceding year.

Compulsory Free Primary Schools.

264. The subjoined statement will show the number of students, in these Free Primary Schools with their nationality and the average daily attendance :—

Compulsory Free Primary Schools	No. of Students		Average daily attendance		Raj Kumars	Thakurs	Manipuris	Tripuras	Lushais	Christians	Bengalees	Mahomedans	Others
	Boys	Girls	Boys	Girls									
No. 1 U. K. Academy—													
1350 ...	250	139	186·60	97·12	—	19	—	4	-	—	341	20	5
1351 ...	241	121	151·40	80·10	—	16	1	1	1	1	322	—	—
1352 ...	189	129	102·50	99·60	—	10	—	-	1	—	283	22	2
No. 2 Tulsibati—													
1350 ...	118	97	88·20	65·30	—	12	1	—	—	—	191	8	3
1351 ...	119	138	84·10	87·70	—	7	2	1		—	223	19	5
1352 ...	117	122	67·30	62·40	—	9	—	1	—	—	212	17	—
No. 3 Bejoykumar—													
1350 ...	104	85	73·08	57·60	—	51	—	-	—	—	127	10	1
1351 ...	105	92	69·98	65·36	—	53	-	—	—	—	138	6	—
1352 ...	83	70	54·30	44·70	—	37	—	—	—	—	111	5	—
No. 4 Thakurpalli—													
1350	61	49	42·30	40·60	—	52	5	16	—	—	15	13	9
1351 ...	58	57	31·90	30·60	—	43	7	24	—	—	21	11	5
1352 ...	41	35	29·80	25·70	—	38	7	-	—	—	29	—	2

265. The comparative statement below will show the number of non-Bengalee students receving education in several schools of the State.

Serial No.	Nationality	Number of students			
		1349 T. E.	1350 T. E.	1351 T. E.	1352 T. E.
1.	Rajkumars ...	6	4	5	5
2.	Thakurs ...	370	303	261	254
3.	Manipuris ...	1220	1095	627	863
4.	Tripuras ...	1023	1104	1102	951
5.	Reangs ...	39	45	29	34
6.	Kukis	1	17	25	5
7.	Chakmas ...	3	4	3	3
8.	Lushais ...	6	12	2	24
9.	Garoes ...	—	—	10	5
10.	Others ...	231	108	107	69
11.	Christians ...	10	-	8	—

266. The Maharajkumari Sahebas received their education as before under a graduate teacher and a Pandit.

Education of Maharajkumars and Maharajkumaris.

267. The infant Maharajkumar Bahadurs received their education under a graduate teacher. In 1350 T. E. Maharajkumar Mohan Kishore Dev Barman Bahadur completed his studies in the College of Engineering and Technology, Jadavpur. Maharajkumar Sukumar Kishore Dev Barman Bahadur, Maharajkumar Arjun Kishore Deb Barman Bahadur and Maharajkumar Chandrama Kishore Deb Barman Bahadur joined the Military on receipt of Commission after finishing their studies.

268. In the years under review :—

Education of Thakur Boys.

(*a*) Thakur boys numbering 13, 10 and 12 respectively were receiving higher education in various Colleges and Technical Schools and they were awarded stipends from the Education Department.

Thakur Boarding House at Agartala.

(*b*) The number of boarders in the Thakur Boarding House was 30, 20 and 17 respectively against 29 in 1349 T. E. The average daily attendance stood at 28·00, 27·00 and 16·50 against 25·00 in 1349 T. E.

Tripura Boarding House at Agartala.

(*c*) There were boarders in the Tripura Boarding House numbering 31, 24, and 23 respectively against 33 in 1349 T. E. All the boarders were allowed free boarding stipends. The Tripura Boarding House was managed by a graduate Superintendent who also coached the boys with the help of two other tutors.

Tripura Boarding House at Khowai.

(*d*) There were 58, 40 and 49 boarders respectively against 55 in 1349 T. E. One graduate Superintending tutor and one assistant tutor were engaged as before to coach the boys both in the morning and in the evening. The Superintendent looked after the boarding management in addition to coaching.

Ramkumar Boarding House at Kalyanpur.

(*e*) There were 53, 52 and 52 boarders in the Tripura Boarding House concerned against 44 in 1349 T. E. Two tutors were engaged as before to coach the boarders and one of them looked after the boarding management in addition.

School for Convicts.

(*f*) There were 19, 22 and 20 convicts against 19 in 1349 T. E. reading in the Primary School in the Central Jail.

Silpasram and Woodburn Artisan School.

269. The Silpasram continued to be under the direct control of the Department of Public Instruction. In the years under report there were 19, 27, and 14 students respectively on the roll against 18 in 1349 T. E. and the average daily attendance stood at 11·62, 16·47 and 6·05 against 9·50 in 1349 T. E. 13 students were awarded monthly stipends varying from Rs. 1-8 to Rs. 8 each.

16

270. The subjoined statement will show the number of students in the Silpasram, their nationality and their average daily attendance in the years under report.

Name of the School	Years	No. of students	Thakurs	Tripuras	Manipuris	Bengalees	Others	Average daily attendance
Silpasram	1350 T. E.	19	2	5	1	11	—	11·62
	1351 T. E.	27	3	6	2	16	—	16·47
	1352 T. E.	14	1	2	2	9	—	6·05

271. In the years under report :—

Lusai stipends.

(*a*) 12, 23 and 25 Lusai boys were awarded Lushai stipends. Some of them prosecuted their studies in different colleges and some in different schools of the State.

Special stipends.

(*b*) 14, 15 and 14 students were awarded special stipends. Some of them prosecuted their studies in different schools of the State and some elsewhere in different colleges and technical institutions.

Inspection works.

272. There were 3 Sub-Inspectors of Schools who inspected all the schools other than H. E. Schools. Reveune Inspectors also inspected some schools in their respective jurisdiction.

Library

273. Maharajkumar Narottam Kishore Dev Barman Bahadur continued to be the Librarian of the Birchandra Library at Agartala which was maintained in two separate sections as before Viz., (1) English Section located at the Ujjayanta Palace and (2) Vernacular Section in a building near the Local H. E. School. The latter section was open to the public. In the years under review the number of English books (including foreign literature) stood at 5,039, 5,491 and 5,521 against 5,039 in 1349 T. E. The number of Bengali and Sanskrit books was 2,256, 2,363 and 1,415 against 2,256 in 1349 T. E. In 1350 T. E. there were 3 dailies, 3 weeklies and 3 monthlies against 3, 5, and 7 respectively in the previous year ; in 1351 T. E. there were 3 dailies 5 weeklies and 4 monthlies and in 1352 T. E. there were 3 dailies, 4 weeklies and 5 monthlies.

Boy Scout Movements in Tripura.

274. Under gracious order of His Highness the Maharaja Manikya Bahadur, dated 2. 5. 50 T. E. the Tripura State Boy Scouts Local Association was formed and constituted as follows :—

1. Patron—His Highness the Maharaja Manikya Bahadur of Tripura.
2. Chief Scout—Resident, Eastern States Agency.

3. Commissioner— Raj–Sabhabhusan Manyabara Raja Rana Bodhjung Bahadur, F. R. G. S.,

4. Asst. Commissioner—Mr. K. C. Nag, M. B. E. Bar.-at-law.

5. Organising Secretary—Mr. J. K. Bhattacherjee, M. sc., (D. P. I. ex-officio)

277. It has been affiliated to the Boy Scouts Association in India through the Eastern States Agency Boy Scouts Association from the month of August 1940 A. D. No note-worthy event took place during the year 1350 T. E. save and except that four teachers from the U. K. Academy were allowed to join the Rally at Raigarh. As an experimental one, the movement was first introduced in the U. K. Academy, Agartala and then gradually the same has been given effect to in other H. E. Schools of the State.

278. In 1350 T. E. a Scoutmasters' Training Camp was organised by the Local Association with the kind permission of the Provincial Commissioner, Eastern States Agency Boy Scouts Association, who very kindly deputed two Trainers to run the camp at Indranagar (Agartala) in the garden house of Manyabara Raja Rana Bodhjung Bahadur, Chief Minister, Tripura State and District Commissioner of the Local Association. 18 teachers joined the Course and 14 came out successful. The entire expenses incurred in this connection were borne by the State. During the year, one Scouter from U. K. Academy was deputed for undergoing Cubmasters' Training Course at Ganganagar (Bengal) and he secured 1st. Class Certificate.

279. The most note-worthy event during the year 1351 T. E. was the reviewing of the Scouts and Cubs at Sadar by the Provincial Chief Scout (Resident for the Eastern States) on the grounds of the U. K. Academy. The Patron, His Highness the Maharaja Manikya Bahadur of Tripura, the Provincial Secretary, District Commissioner, Honorary Secretary, some members of the Local Association and some other high officials of the State were present on the occasion when the Scouts and Cubs gave a fine display of First Aid, Signalling and Scouting games and other activities. Besides this, the Scouts and the Cubs had pleasant camping on three or four occasions in the interior of the State.

Expenditure.

280. The total expenditure on Public Instruction in the years under report amounted to Rs. 1,31,773, Rs. 1,25,399 and Rs. 1,32,920 respectively, against Rs. 1,24,215 in the preceding year.

Receipts.

281. The total receipts from the schools in the years under review amounted to Rs. 17,271, Rs. 18,801 and Rs. 19,070 respectively against Rs. 15,111 in the preceding year.

CHAPTER VIII—CENSUS.

282. In collaboration with the first Imperial Census of the Indian Empire including the Indian States, Government of Tripura undertook its first Census in 1872, which was followed by another in 1881. Since then the operations have been regular and synchronised with the British Indian Decennial Census. The last census of 1940-41 (1350 T. E.) was the eighth one.

Census operations.

283. Manyabara Raja Rana Bodhjung Bahadur, F. R. G. S. was in charge of the operations with Mr. J. M. Sen, Statistical Officer, as his assistant.

Charge.

284. A Census Act was duly passed and urban and rural areas divided and sub-divided into centres, charges, circles and blocks, and an adequate number of special officers as well as paid enumerators appointed to work out the operations.

Divisions and sub-divisions.

285. The Minister in charge and his assistant moved about freely among the people to create interest and for inspection.

Tours and inspections.

286. As the result, the total number of houses came upto 91,592 against 72,318 in 1930 and enumeration (final census) showed a total population of 5,13,010 with 2,72,002 males and 2,41,008 females including 31,423 literate (male 26,140 and feamle 5,283). There was a net increase of 1,30,560 souls *i. e.* 34·11 per cent over the previous Census total (3,82,450) as against an increase of 78,013 *i. e.* 25·6 per cent obtained in 1921.

Results.

287 Arrangements were made with the Imperial and Provincial Census Authorities for the extraction of special figures to meet statistical requirements of the State.

Special arrangement.

288. The operations generally went on smoothly, the provisional figures were ready within the fixed time and these were intimated to the Census Commissioner for India, and the Superintendent of Census Operations, Bengal, by post on the 12th March, 1941.

289. His Highness the Maharaja Manikya Bahadur took a keen interest in the operations.

290. Special thanks of the Tripura Government are due to the Provincial Census Superintendent, Mr. R. A. Dutch, O. B. E., I. C. S., who visited the State to discuss various matters and evinced a keen interest and sympathy.

CHAPTER IX—ZEMINDARIES.

CHAKLA ROSHNABAD AND OTHER ESTATES.

Chakla Roshnabad.

291. The Zemindaries of His Highness the Maharaja Manikya Bahadur, attached to the State, and known as the Chakla Roshnabad and other Estates, consist principally of the following *Toujis* in different collectorates—the properties extending over the Tipperah, Noakhali and Sylhet Districts and comprising an area of 692 square miles (approximately).

Touji and other particulars	Annual Revenues and cesses payable to British India			
	Revenue	Road Cess	Education Cess	Total
I. The Central Division.				
TIPPERA COLLECTORATE.				
(1) Touji No. 252 Chakla Roshnabad Estates ...	1,52,408	74,032	94,810	3,21,250
(2) Touji No. 355 Lakheraj Bajapti Mahal at Pargana Bagasair ...	261	71	98	425
(3) No. 52 Taluk Dharma Narayan	105	16	22	143
(4) No. 2053 Taluk Panchu Hazari ...	236	37	50	323
(5) No. 364 Taluk Kalikinkar Ghosh (Soydabad)	705	525	668	1,898
(6) No. 87 Lakheraj Lalmai	—	470	587	1,057
MINOR MAHALS.				
(7) Touji Nos. 1190, 669, 671, 2205, 4303, 88, 119, 120, 123, 126, 127, 128, 129, 130, 131, 133, 139, 113, 111, 114, 137, 138.	162	665	833	1,660
	1,53,877	75,816	97,063	3,26,756
II. The Southern Division.				
NOAKHALI COLLECTORATE.				
(1) Touji No. 209 Taluk Kripa Kishore ...	3,928	2,125	2,718	8,771
(2) Touji No. 229 Mahal Asharkota ...	193	22	31	246
(3) Touji No. 12 Darara Hishya 3 as. 5 karas-2½ krantas ...	1,721	2,321	2,929	6,971
(4) Touji No. 204 Char Shaha Bhikari Hishya 4 annas	1,402	281	373	2,056
MINOR MAHALS.				
(5) Touji Nos. 535/1, 829/1, 148/1, 92/B, 34799, 1679.	196	52	68	316
	7,440	4,801	6,119	18,360

17

Particulars	Annual Revenues & Cesses Payable to British India			
	Revenue	Road Cess	Education Cess	Total
III. The Northern Division.*	—	—	—	—
IV. The Srimangal Division				
MAULAVI BAZAR COLLECTORATE.				
(1) Touji No. 51168/1 Taluk Golamali Hishya No. 1	2,686	1,054	—	3,740
(2) Touji No. 51168/1 Golamali parent Mahal	215	73	—	288
(3) Touji No. 51483/325 Taluk Golam Rasul ...	120	33	—	153
(4) Touji No. 51783/1 Golamali Hishya No. 5 Jubaraj Birchandra ...	839	369	—	1,208
(5) Touji No. 51783/1 Golamali parent Mahal	271	115	—	386
MINOR MAHALS				
(6) Touji Nos. 51168/1, 51169/2, 51169/3, 51169/4, 51169/2 (Parent Mahal), 51171/4, 51171/2, 51192/25, 51230/63, 51326/162, 51349/185, 51351/188, 51364/20, 51368/205, 51384/223, 51390/228, 51402/240.	754	381	—	1,135
HABIGANJ COLLECTORATE.				
(1) Touji No. 55835/1081 Ramprasad ...	1,167	1,698	—	2,865
(2) Touji No. 56087/1335 Sarbamangala ...	168	260	—	428
(3) Do. No. 55949/1196 Taluk Shek Ramjan Ali	62			
(4) Do. No. 252 Chakla		10	—	72
Roshnabad (in respect of Local rate of Mantala only)	—	1,551	—	1,551
KARIMGANJ COLLECTORATE.				
(1) Touji No. 16361/6 Taluk Badaruddin Ahmed	10	5	—	15
	6,292	5,549	—	11,841

* Revenue etc of this Division are paid in the Comilla Collectorate along with the Revenue etc of the Central Division, the properties being included in Touji. No. 252.

292. Most of the above properties are situated in almost an unbroken line contiguous to the western boundary of the Tripura State and having once been comprised in the kingdom of the ancient Rulers of Tripura. They form now an indivisible appanage of the State.

293. For administrative purposes, the Zemindaries are divided into four units, viz :—

Administrative Divisions.

(1) The Central Division with headquarters at Comilla, comprising properties within the jurisdiction of the Police stations Kotwali, Burichang, Chouddagram and Laksam in the District of Tippera.

(2) The Northern Division with headquaters at Mogra (Gangasagar) comprising properties within the jurisdiction of Police stations Kasba, Brahmanbaria and Nabinagar under the Brahmanbaria Subdivision in the District of Tippera.

(3) The Southern Division with headquarters at Feni, comprising properties within the jurisdiction of the Police stations Feni, Parsuram and Chhagalnaiya in the District of Noakhali.

(4) The Srimangal Division with headquarters at Srimangal comprising properties under the jurisdiction of Police stations Srimangal, Chunarughat, Madhabpur and Patharkandi in the District of Sylhet.

294. The management and control of the affairs of the Zemindaries continued, as in previous years, to be entrusted in the hands of one Manager with headquarters at Agartala (Capital of the State) assisted by one Deputy Manager and three Assistant Managers posted at Comilla, Mogra, Feni and Srimangal. During the period under review Manyabara Rai J. C. Sen Bahadur held the post of Manager till the month of Ashar 1351 T. E. and Rai Dewen K. Dutt Bahadur was in charge of the Manager's duties till the end of the year 1351 T. E. ; thereafter Mr. P. R. Bhattacherjea, B. A., T. C. S. was appointed as Manager and he took over charge from the beginning of the year 1352 T. E.

Management.

295. As in previous years, relief had to be given to the *Talukdars* and the tenants in the shape of general remission of interest and damages almost throughout the years, while the policy of allowing petty demands of the jote lands to be timebarred was also continued.

Relief to tenants.

296. The gross demands of the years were as follows :—

The demand of the period.

	Current	Arrears	Total
1350 T. E.	10,72,600	35,41,312	Rs. 46,13,912
1351 T. E.	11,20,168	32,13,500	,, 43,33,668
1352 T. E.	10,65,661	33,14,880	,, 43,80,541

The annual average demand of the preceding 3 years with arrears was Rs. 44,54,518.

297. The receipts in the above mentioned years were :—

Realisation.

1350 T. E.	...	...	...	Rs. 13,16,481
1351 T. E.	...	...	...	,, 6,13,286
1352 T. E.	...	...	...	,, 12,16,811

298. The annual average of total receipts during the preceding 3 years amounted to Rs. 14,83,781.

299. The total expenditure of each of the years under review was as follows :—

Expenditure.

1350 T. E.	... ...	Rs. 10,92,649
1351 T. E.	... ...	,, 9,66,608
1352 T. E.	... ...	,, 8,19,218

300. The average of total expenditure during the preceding 3 years was Rs. 12,31,571. The expenditure mentioned above includes payments of old debts and deposits, P. W. D. expenses and contribuion to the State. Of the total expenditure during the years under review Rs 3,88,609, Rs 3,13,768 and Rs. 4,40,377 respectively were for payments of Land Revenue & Cesses and Taxes, while the Administration costs including Public Works and Law Charges were Rs. 4.05,154, Rs. 3,30,998 and Rs. 3,27,085 respectively.

Education.

301. With the imposition of the Education Cess since the year 1348 T. E., involving an additional burden of Tax amounting to a huge sum of Rs. 1,03,188 annually upon the resources of the Zemindaries, the Administration was regretfully constrained to curb its expenditure in matters of educational grants which had hitherto been made to various Primary and Secondary Schools in the Zemindary area. The Estate did however make the following annual contributious during the years under review .—

1.	Viswa Bharati, Bolepur ...	...	Rs. 4,000
2.	Brahmacharyyasram, Bolepur	...	,, 1,000
3.	Comilla Victoria College ...	...	,, 1,200
4.	Feni College	...	,, 600
5.	Purbabanga Saraswat Samaj, Dacca	...	,, 400
6.	Deaf & Dumb School, Dacca	...	,, 120
7.	Bidhabasram, Dacca ...	...	,, 100
8.	Tripura Hitasadhini Sabha ...	...	,, 150
9.	Kanya Siksha Vidyalaya, Comilla ...		,, 120
10.	Two stipends of the value of Rs. 15 each tenable at the Comilla Victoria College	...	,, 360

Medical.

302. Zemindary Administration continued to maintain five Charitable Dispensaries at Comilla, Sukchail, Mogra, Subhapur and Mantala at an average annual cost of nearly Rs. 8,000 besides making annual contributions to certain Hospitals and Dispensaries etc. as mentioned below :—

1.	Chittagong Medical School and Hospital	...	Rs. 1,000
2.	Comilla Sadar Hospital ...	...	,, 360
3.	Chouddagram D. B. Dispensary	...	,, 120
4.	Razar Bazar D. B. Dispensary	...	,, 220
5.	Burichang D. B. Dispensary	...	,, 80

6.	Kasba D. B. Dispensary	,,	40
7.	Feni Charitable Dispensary	,,	120
8.	Chhagalnaiya D. B. Dispensary ...	,,	80
9.	Mangalkandi D. B. Dispensary ...	,,	80
10.	Fulgazi D. B. Dispensary	,,	40
11.	Noakhali Birendrakishore Female Hospital	,,	80
12.	Parashuram D. B. Dispensary ...	,,	60
13.	Munshirhat D. B. Dispensary ...	,,	60
14.	Srimangal L. B. Dispensary ...	,,	128
15.	Matri Sadan, Calcutta	,,	120
16.	Dacca Orphanage...	,,	120

303. The result of the three years' settlement operations will
Settlement. appear from the table below :—

Kinds of settlement	1350 T. E.		1351 T. E.		1352 T. E.		REMARKS
	Addition to rent roll	*Nazar* realised	Addition to rent roll	*Nazar* realised	Addition to rent roll	*Nazar* realised	
Railway relinquished land	—	—	—	—	—	—	
Kaimi and *Takshisi* settlement at Comilla Town	14	540	70	24,556	—	—	
Ordinary Town Settlement ...	17	943	7	25	1	80	
Khas Patit	330	1,677	548	3,737	670	4,831	
Enhancement of rent ...	50	488	30	686	63	2,387	
Resettlement of auction purchased holdings ...	538	46,969	132	32,292	188	40,431	
Settlement of rent-free Holdings	6	—	2	—	1	—	
Takshishi settlement in the *Moffusil* ...	—	—	—	—	—	—	
Ijara settlement ...	31,321	—	31,563	—	25,430	—	
Rs. ...	32,276	50,567	32,347	61,296	26,353	47,729	

304. The corresponding figures for the years 1349, 1348 and 1347 T. E. were as follows :—

	Addition to Rent Roll	*Nazar* realised
1349 T. E.	33,228	64,557
1348 T. E.	17,416	58,732
1347 T. E.	1,752	24,513

305. Subjoined is a statement of tours of the officers in charge
Tours. of the Administrative Divisions of the Zemindaries :—

Central Division, Comilla.

	1350 T. E.	1351 T. E.	1352 T. E.
Babu P. R. Bhattacherjea, B. A., Deputy Manager (at present Manager).	94	92	—
Babu J. C. Majumder, M. A. B. L., Deputy Manager.	—	—	22

18

Southern Division, Feni.

Babu J. C. Majumder, M. A. B. L., Assistant Manager (at present Deputy Manager).	81	83	5
Babu S. C. Kar, B. L., Assistant Manager.	—	—	69

Northern Division, Mogra.

Babu B. Guha, B. A., Assistant Manager.	62	5	—
Kumar B. C. Dev Barma Bahadur. B. A., Assistant Manager.	—	11	—
Babu B. M. Choudhuri, B. L., Assistant Manager.	—	—	40

Srimangal Division, Srimangal.

Babu S. C. Guha, B. A., Assistant Manager.	82	17	—
Babu N. N. Choudhury, B. L., Assistant Manager.	—	79	102

CHAPTER X—MISCELLANEOUS.

Mantri Parishad.

306. There were certain changes in the personnel of the Mantri Parishad during the period as previously noted.

307. Altogether 1089 proposals came up before the Parishad from the various Departments of the Government during the years under rivew, of which 967 were discussed and disposed of during the period, leaving 122 proposals under consideration at the close of the triennium.

308. The Parishad held 52 meetings in 1350 T. E., 75 in 1351 T. E. and 69 in the year 1352 T. E.

Tours of Ministers.

309. Rai J. C. Sen Bahadur, Chief Minister, was out on tour in 1350 T. E. for 45 days in the course of which he visited Calcutta and Shillong to participate in certain joint enquiries and conferences. Manyabara Raja Rana Bodhjung Bahadur, Minister and subsequently Chief Minister, toured for 51 days mainly in connection with the war activities of the State and also visited Shillong on duty. Dewan B. K. Sen Bahadur, Political Minister, was out in 1351 T. E. (following his appointment) and 1352 T. E. for 33 days altogether, taking part in some conferences outside the State, and visiting, in furtherance of certain emergent measures, the Khowai Division. Mr. S. Goswami, Revenue Minister was out for 18 days in 1352 T. E. visiting Sylhet, as well as Feni and Khowai Divisions of the State, while Thakur K. K. Singh, Development and Agricultural Minister, toured for 34 days in 1350 T. E., 26 days in 1351 T. E. and 54 days in 1352 T. E.

The State Press.

310. There were at work in the State Press one Electric Printing Press, one Treadle Press and three hand presses during the years under review, which just sufficed to meet the growing demands covering printing of all Government publications, forms, as also question papers for various school examinations. Judicial

stamps were printed at the treadle press installed at the General Treasury office room for the purpose, under direct supervision of the Treasury staff. The world-war seriously handicapped the usual running of the Press owing to scarcity of printing materials as well as of spare parts of Engines in the Power House. The rationing of paper by the Central Government also proved a great handicap.

311. As in previous years, the Stationery Department stocked all stationery articles including papers, as also Forms for supply to all Government offices and institutions on requisition. The Department purchased stationery articles and papers worth Rs. 8,929–11 during 1350 T. E. and Rs. 9799–15 and Rs. 11,295 during 1351 and 1352 T. E. respectively. The amount recouped during the triennium on bills sanctioned amounted to Rs. 3,942–9 in 1350 T. E. and Rs. 3,368–10 and Rs. 3,581–14 in 1351 and 1352 T. E. respectively.

Stationery and Forms Department.

312. Thakur B. C. Deb Barman was in charge both of the Stationery Department and the Press, during the period.

Charge.

313. There is a special departmental orgainastion under the control of the State Engineer for supervision and overhauling of lighting arrangements and wiring at the Palace and Government buildings as also for water supply at the Palace.

Special Electric and water supply arrangements

314. The total expenditure on account of the establishment maintatined for the purpose and purchase of materials, together with the expenditure incurred in payment of the Electric Supply Company's bills for consumption of current for the State, amounted to Rs. 79,527 during the years under report, against Rs. 84,782 in the previous triennium.

315. The working of the subjoined Departments and machinery were kept in abeyance during the triennium in view of the emergency and pending the formulation of post war requirements, while new and expensive administrative measures were generally postponed :

Measures kept in abeyance.

(1) Geological Department.
(2) Hydro-electric Department.
(3) Special Reclamation and colonisation machinery.

DATED, AGARTALA.
The 26th December, 1944.

Rana Bodhjung,
Chief Minister.

B. K. Sen,
Political and Revenue Minister.

K. K. Singh,
Minister, Public Health & Agriculture.

S. C. Dutt,
Finance Minister.

B. B. K. Manikya
17. 11. 48.

A CHARTER

FOR INCORPORATING AND CONFERRING POWERS UPON

Maharaja Match Factory Limited

1939

AND

FOR OTHER PURPOSES.

HIS HIGHNESS MAHARAJA SIR BIR BIKRAM KISHORE MANIKYA BAHADUR, K. C. S. I., MAHARAJA OF TRIPURA, IN BENGAL BY THE GRACE OF GOD RULER OF THE INDEPENDENT STATE OF TRIPURA, TO ALL TO WHOM THESE PRESENTS SHALL COME, GREETING.

WHEREAS the business on a large scale of manufacturing and trading in various substances out of raw materials found in the State would be of general interest ;

AND WHEREAS the encouragement of industrial development within the area of the State would be of public benefit ;

AND WHEREAS His Highness the Maharaja Manikya Bahadur of Tripura has been graciously pleased to allow arrangements to be made for the purpose of manufacturing of matches and other things as hereinafter described ;

AND WHEREAS the persons named in this Charter are willing and it is expedient that they should form themselves into a Company with limited liability (hereinafter referred to as the Company) with power to add to their number by sale of shares in the manner as hereinafter mentioned for the purpose of carrying on business that has for its object the acquisition of gain by the company ;

AND WHEREAS it is expedient that necessary powers should be conferred upon the Company for the regulation of its own affairs and to make contract with local authorities, persons and companies and other, for the purpose of carrying on business as stated hereinafter and for other purposes ;

AND WHEREAS in order to safeguard the interest of the industry it is expedient that Monopoly for manufacturing and exporting matches, splints and veneers and for such works within and from the State of Tripura should be given to the Company and provision made therefor ;

AND WHEREAS by the exercise of the Prerogative of His Highness the Maharaja Manikya Bahadur of Tripura it is lawful for His Highness the Maharaja Manikya Bahadur to grant this Charter under the Seal of the Tripura Durbar to the Company for the purpose of the works as aforesaid ;

NOW KNEW YE that in pursuance of His gracious promise and by virtue of His Prerogative, certain knowledge and mere motion His Highness Maharaja Sir Bir Bikram Kishore Manikya Bahadur, Maharaja of Tripura by these presents for him, His heirs and successors and for the purpose as above and of incorporation of the said Company and for proper working of the same as hereinbefore and hereinafter mentioned does give, grant, make, ordain, constitute, declare, appoint and establish this Charter in the terms as follows :—

GENERAL.

1. This Charter shall be known and be cited as the Charter for the incorporation of Maharaja Match Factory Limited, 1939 A. D.

2. The provisions contained herein shall come into operation on the signing of the Charter.

3. The name of the Company shall be Maharaja Match Factory Limited.

4. The Registered office of the Company shall be situated at Agartala, in the State of Tripura, in Bengal.

OBJECT.

5. The objects for which the company is incorporated are :—

(I) To acquire and take over as a going concern the right, title, interest, goodwill etc. of Maharaja Match Factory, situated at Tulakona Ghat, within the Jurisdiction of Sadar Division in Tripura State from Maharajkumar Ranabir Kishore Dev Barman, who purchased the same from the previous owner Babu Bejoy Basanta Ghose by a deed of sale dated 24. 5. 48. T. E. for himself and on behalf of Mahamanyabara Maharajkumar Brojendra Kishore Dev Barman, Satyaranjan Bose and Kiron Chandra Bose.

(II) To promote and establish Match Factories within Tripura State.

(a) To carry on Match manufacturing business of all descriptions in all its branches and departments, exporting and selling of Veneers and Splints,

(b) To carry on manufacturing, exporting, selling veneers and splints,

(c) To buy and sell wood required for manufacturing Matches, Veneers and Splints,

(d) To make wood pulp, making paper and to carry on business of printing in general,

(e) To manufacture, sell and carry on business of packing, ply and other woods,

(f) To indent all kinds of papers, chemicals, glue & gum, to produce same and particularly manufacturing chemicals for bleaching Match splints, chemicals for impregnating splints, chemicals for Match proper, for treatment of splints for ready inflammability (Paraffin), for friction composition, for Ignition composition, Agglutinants and Binding chemicals, chemicals for Match tips etc. etc.,

(g) To buy, sell raw materials for Matches, indenting and selling machinery,

(h) To plant and grow suitable match wood, other timbers, sell same and growing agricultural produces,

(i) To instal power plant, boilers, sell same, instal machinery, workshop together with importing and selling parts and requisites for power plant, boilers and machinery workshop,

(j) To promote and establish rice and oil mills in Tripura State or in any other parts of India ;

(k) To establish all kinds and sorts of mills, factories, godowns, plantations, offices, stores, gardens, shops, show-rooms, as well as Branches and Agencies and to appoint agents and brokers within India and in any part of the world ;

(l) To purchase, take on lease or in exchange hire or otherwise acquire or sell or dispose of in any way movable or immovable properties, plants, machinaries, patents, Licenses, rights or privileges, which the Company may think necessary or convenient, for the purpose of its business ;

(m) To purchase, sell, mortgage, hold as securities, and in any other way, deal in Government Promissory Notes, loans, bonds, Municipal or Port-trust Debentures, shares stocks and other negotiable or transferable instruments,

(n) To carry on the business of banking in all its branches and departments, including the borrowing, raising or taking up money, the lending or advancing money on securities and property, the discounting, buying, selling and dealing in bills of exchange, Promissory Notes, coupons, drafts, bills of lading, warrants, debentures, certificates, script and other instruments and securities, whether transferable or negotiable or not, the granting and issuing of letters of credit and circular notes, the buying, selling and dealing in stock funds, shares, debenture-stocks, bonds, obligations and other securities.

(o) To purchase, take on lease, or in exchange hire or otherwise acquire, or sell or let out on lease, or hire, otherwise dispose of any rolling-stock, wharves, ware-houses, ships, steam vessels, steam or motor boats, barges, launches, jetties, docks, dockyards, and other necessary machines, tools, implements and things necessary for transport of passengers, marchandise and goods of every description.

(p) To construct, maintain and improve any telegraph or telephone lines, cannals, water-courses, reservoirs, warehouses, sheds, godowns and other buildings and works calculated, directly or indirectly, to advance the interests of the Company and to pay or contribute to the expense of constructing, maintaining and improving any such works.

(q) To carry on business of general manufacturers, and to manufacture, buy, sell and deal in machineries, apparatus, building materials and articles of all kinds.

(r) To carry on the business of electricians and electrical, civil and mechanical engineers, also to carry on the business of food-crushers, food-cutters, printers, binders, bailing, house wiring, battery-charging, various jobbing and small and big repairings to motor cars and other vehicles and machinery and also electrical, mechanical and industrial plants of this Company and those of others as contractors and also to own and operate workshops of this own Company or others.

(s) To search for and to purchase or otherwise acquire from any Government, State or authority or persons or person any concessions, grants, decrees, rights, powers and privileges whatsoever which may seem to the Company capable of being turned to account and in particular any water rights or concession either for the purpose of obtaining motive power or otherwise and to work, develop, carry out exercise and turn to account the same ;

(t) To purchase or otherwise acquire and undertake the whole or any part of the business, property, rights and liabilities of any person, firm and company carrying on any business which this company is authorised to carry on or possessed of property or rights suitable for any of the purposes of the company ;

(u) To pay all the costs, charges, and expenses of and incidental to the promotion, formation, registration and establishment of the company and the issue of its capital, including any 'underwriting or other commission, brokers' fees and charges in connection therewith any premiums or salaries and to remunerate or make donations to (by cash or other assets or by the allotment of fully or partly paid up shares or by a call or option on shares, debentures, debenture stock, or securities of this or any other company or in any other manner whether out of the company's capital or profits or otherwise) any person or persons for services rendered or to be rendered in introducing any property or business to the company or in placing or assisting to place or guaranteeing the subscription of any shares, debentures, debenture-stock or other securities of the company or for any other reason which the company may think proper ;

(v) To appoint Agents, Manager, Attorney, and constituted agents of the Company in India (in or outside the Tripura State) or in any other country whatsoever and to carry on general export and import business ;

(w) To organise sale and distribution of the products of this and other companies or of person or persons or of any firm, the whole world over ;

(x) To establish and support or aid in the establishment and support of associations, institutions, funds, trusts and conveniences calculated to benefit employees or ex-employees of the company or the dependents and connections of such persons and to make payments towards insurance and to subscribe guarantee money for benevolent objects or for any exhibition or for any public, general or useful object;

(y) To grant pensions, allowances, gratuities and bonuses to employees or ex-employees of the company or the dependants of such persons and to support or subscribe to any charitable or other institutions, clubs, societies or objects ;

(z) To be appointed and act as Agents, Managing Agents, Managers, or Brokers of business concerns, Zemindary or other properties whether of Joint Stock Companies or not ;

(z 1) To purchase or otherwise acquire, patents, brevets of invention, license, concession, monopolies and the like, conferring any exclusive or non-exclusive or limited right to use any invention which may seem capable of being used for any of the purposes of the company or the acquisition of which may seem calculated to directly or indirectly benefit this company and to use, exercise, develop or grant licenses in respect of or otherwise turn to account the property and rights so acquired ;

(z 2) To carry on any other business which may seem to the company capable of being conveniently carried on in connection with the afore-mentioned business or any of them or calculated directly or indirectly to enhance the value of or render profitable any of the company's rights ;

(z 3) To enter into partnership or into any arrangement for sharing profits union of interest, co-operation, joint adventure, reciprocal conecessions or otherwise or amalgamate with any person or persons or company carrying on or engaged in or about to carry on or engage in any business or transaction capable of being carried on or conducted so as directly or indirectly to benefit this company and to lend money to and guarantee the contracts of or otherwise assist any such person or persons or company and to take or assist any such person or persons or company and to take or otherwise acquire shares and securities of any such company or in any other company having objects altogether or in part similar to those of this company and to sell, hold, reissue with or without guarantee or otherwise deal with the same.

(z 4) To enter into any arrargement with the Government of India or with any local Government or with any authorities, Municipal, local or otherwise or with any Rajahs, Zemindars, Landholders or other person or persons of any rights, privileges and concessions which the company may think it desirable to obtain and carry out, exercise or comply with any such arrangements, rights, privileges and concessions ;

(z 5) To distribute any of the property of the company among the members in specie.

(z 6) To make, accept, endorse, execute and issue promissory notes, bills of exchange, bills of lading, debentures and other negotiable and transferable instruments ;

(z 7) To invest or deposit the monies of the company not immediately required upon such securities or in such manner as may from time to time be determined by the Board of Directors and to buy, acquire, sell, exchange or deal in shares of any other company ;

(z 8) To guarantee the performance of contracts by members of or persons having dealings with the company ;

(z 9) To borrow or raise or secure the payment of money in such manner as the company may think fit and in particular by the issue of debenture or debenture-stocks perpetual or otherwise charged upon any or all of the company's property (both present and future) including its uncalled capital, if any and to supply the same and any part thereof for all or any purpose of the company and to purchase, redeem or pay off any such securities ;

(z 10) To purchase or acquire or free-hold perpetual or lease hold tenure or otherwise any suitable land ;

(z 11) To do such other things as may be, for the time being conducive to the interest of the company ;

(z12) To adopt such means of making known the objects and business, as well as the products and manufactures of the company as may seem expedient, and in particular by advertising in the press, by circulars, by purchase and exhibitions of works of art or interests, by publication of books, journals, periodicals and pamphlets, and by granting prizes, rewards, subscription and donations ;

(z 13) To establish and maintain information and investigation bureaus and to collect statistics, returns, particulars and informations likely to prove usefull for the consideration of business and financial propositions and to undertake experimental and research work ;

(z 14) To establish and support or aid in the establishment and support of associations, institutions, funds, trusts, and conveniences calculated to benefit the emplyees or ex-employees of the Company or its predecessors in business or the dependants or relatives of such persons and to grant pension and allowances and to make payments towards insurance and to subscribe or grant money for charitable or benevclent objects, or for any exhibition for any public, general or useful object ;

(z 15) To construct, lay down, establish fix, carry out, maintain, improve all necessary buildings, water-works, tanks, bridges, cooly line, officers quarters, houses, bustees and other works and convenience which may seem directly or indirectly conducive to any of the objects of the company and to contribute to, subsidise or otherwise aid or take part in any such operations ;

(z 16) To promote and establish saw mills and to carry on the business of timber trading ;

(z 17) To do all other things with the previous sanction of the Government of Tripura not mentioned herein ; and generally to do all such things as are in the opinion of the Directors of the Company incidental or conducive to the attainment of the above objects so that the object specified in each paragraph shall except when otherwise expressed in such paragraph, be in no way limited or restricted by reference to or inference from the terms of any other subclause or by the name of Company.

INCORPORATION.

6. 1. Mahamanyabara Maharajkumar Brojendra Kishore Dev Barman Bahadur.

2. Maharajkumar Ranabir Kishore Dev Barman Bahadur.

3. Manyabar Raja Rana Bodhjung Bahadur.

4. Major Kumar Prafulla Kumar Dev Barman Bahadur.

5. Mr. S. C. Dev Burman.

6. Sj. Priyanath Banerjee.

7. Dr. Manimoy Majumdar.

8. Sj. Janesh Kumar Bhattacherjee.

9. Sj. Satyaranjan Bose,

and all other persons who have already subscribed or shall hereinafter subscribe and become proprietors in the undertaking and their executors administrators and successors and assigns respectively shall be and are hereby united into a company for the purposes hereinafter mentioned and for those purposes shall be and are hereby incorporated by the name of the Maharaja Match Factory Ltd. hereinafter referred to as "The Company" and by that name shall be a body corporate with perpetual succession and a common seal and with power to purchase, take hold and dispose of land and other property and any other undertaking for the purpose of this Charter and that of the other powers and privileges as a body corporate.

7. This Charter shall be in all things valid and effective in law according to the true intent and meaning of the same and shall be recognised as valid and effective by all courts and Judges as well in the State of Tripura as in the district of Tippera in British India or in any other part of British India or foreign countries or upon the high seas or

elsewhere and to all other persons and bodies politic to whom it may concern and the same shall be taken construed and judged in the most favourable and beneficial sense for and for the best advantages of the company in the said courts or elsewhere notwithstanding any non-recital, mis-recital uncertainty or imperfection which may be found therein.

CAPITAL & LIMITATION OF LIABILITY OF SHAREHOLDERS.

8. The shares capital of the company is Rs. 1,00,000/- divided into 10,000 shares of Rs. 10/- each with power to increase and repay the capital or any portion thereof and to divide the shares in the capital for the time being into sevsral classes and to attach thereto respectively such preferential, deferred or special rights privileges and conditions as may be determined by or in accordance with the regulations of the company and to vary, modify or abrogate any such rights, privileges or conditions in such manner as may for the time being be provided or determined by or in accordance with the regulation of the company.

Each share shall ordinarily be payable in instalments of Rs. 2/- with application, Rs. 2/- on allotment within 30 days from the date of acceptance and the balance by three two-monthly instalments of Rs. 2/- each according to calls,

The admission fee of Rs. 1/- is payable with each application.

9. The liability of the members of the Company shall be limited to the amount if any, for the time being unpaid on the shares in the company held by them respectively.

10. The shares shall be under the control of the Directors who may allot or otherwise dispose of the same to such persons on such term and conditions, and at such time as they think fit, and with full power to give to any person the right to call for the allotment of any share either at par or at a premium, for such time and for such consideration as the Directors may think fit.

11. Every person whose name is entered as a member in the register of members shall, without payment, be entitled to a certificate under the common seal of the Company specifying the share or shares held by him and the amount paid up thereon ; provided that in respect of a share or shares held jointly by several persons the company shall not be bound to issue more than one certificate, and delivery of a certificate for a share to one of several joint-holders shall be sufficient delivery to all. The share certificate shall be signed by two Directors and the Managing Agents or one of the Ex-officio Directors nominated by them.

12. If a share certificate is defaced, lost or destroyed, it may be renewed on payment of such fee, if any, not exceeding rupee one, and on such terms, if any, as to evidence and indemnity as the Directors think fit.

13. The Directors at their discretion can refuse to allot any share or shares or decline to register any transfer of share or shares without assigning any reason for such refusal or denial.

14. The Managing Agents subject to the approval of the Directors shall have the power to issue the whole or any portion of the Capital for public subscription at par or at a premium or at discount at any time and may reserve the rest for issuing in future as they think fit, with full power of refusing any application for shares without assigning any reason.

15. The joint-holders of a share shall be severally as well as jointly liable for the payment of all instalments and calls due in respect of such share.

16. The company shall be entitled to treat the holder of any share as the absolute owner thereof and accordingly shall not be bound to recognise any Benami, equitable, contingent future or partial interest in any share or any other right in respect of a share on the part of any other person save as herein provided.

17. The preliminary expenses have been estimated at Rs. 3,000/- only.

18, An application for shares shall be taken to imply an acceptance of the principles, rules and resolutions contained in this Charter,

19. The Company may at any time pay a commission not exceeding 10 per cent of the shares in each case subscribed or to be subscribed to any person for subscribing or agreeing to subscribing (whether absolutely or conditionally) for any shares of the company or for procuring or agreeing to procure subscriptions (whether absolutely or conditionally) for any shares of the company.

CALLS.

20. The Managing Agents subject to the approval of the Directors may from time to time make such calls as they think fit upon the shareholders in respect of all moneys unpaid on the shares held by them respectively and not by the conditions of allotment thereof made payable at fixed times and each member shall pay the amount of every call so made on him to the persons and at the times and places appointed by the Managing Agents.

21. A call shall be deemed to have been made at the time when resolution of the Directors approving such call was made.

22. Fifteen clear days' notice at least of any call shall be given specifying the time and place of payment and to whom such call shall be paid.

23. If the sum payable in respect of any call or instalment be not paid on or before the day appointed for payment thereof, the holder for the

time being of the share in respect of which the call shall have been made or the instalment shall be due may be asked to pay interest for the same at the rate of 12 per cent per annum from the day appointed for the payment thereof to the time of actual payment.

24. The provisions of these regulations as to payment of interest shall apply in the case of non-payment of any sum which by the terms of issue of a share becomes payable at a fixed time, whether on account of the amount of share, or by way of premium, as if the same had become payable by virtue of a call duly made and notified.

25. The Directors may make arrangements on the issue of shares for a difference between the holders in the amount of calls to be paid and in the times of payment.

26. The Directors may, if they think fit receive from any shareholder willing to advance the same all or any part of the moneys due upon the share or shares held by him beyond the sums actually called for and upon the money so paid in advance or so much thereof as from time to time exceeds the amount of the calls then made upon the share or shares in respect of which such advance has been made, the company may pay interest at such rate not exceeding $7\frac{1}{2}\%$ percent per annum as the shareholder paying such sum in advance and the Directors agree upon. Money so paid in excess of the amount of calls shall not rank for dividend.

TRANSFER AND TRANSMISSION OF SHARES.

27. The instrument of transfer of any share in the company shall be executed both by the transferor and transferee, and the transferor shall be deemed to remain holder of the share until the name of the transferee is entered in the Register of members in respect thereof.

28. Shares in the Company shall be transferred in the following form, or in any usual or common form which the Directors shall approve.

I. A. B. of in consideration of the sum of Rupees paid to me by C·D of (hereinafter called "the said transferee"), do hereby transfer to the said transferee the share (or shares) numbered in the undertaking called the Company Limited, to hold unto the said transferee, his executors, administrators and assigns, subject to the several conditions on which I held the same at the time of execution thereof, and I, the said transferee, do hereby agree to take the said share (or shares) subject to the conditions aforesaid. As witness our hands the day of witnees to the signatures of, etc.

29. The Directors may decline to register any transfer of shares to a person of whom they do not approve, and may also decline to register any transfer of shares on which the Company has a lien The Directors may also suspend the registration of transfers during the fourteen days immediately preceding the ordinary General Meeting in each year. The Directors may decline to recognise any instrument of transfer unless—

(a) a fee not exceeding two rupees is paid to the Company in respect thereof and

(b) the instrument of transfer is accompanied by the certificate of the shares to which it relates, and such other evidence as the Directors may reasonably require to show the rights of the transferor to make the transfer.

If the Directors refuse to register a transfer of any shares, they shall within two months after the date on which the transfer was lodged with the company send to the Transferee and the transferor notice of the refusal.

30. The heirs, executors or administrators of a deceased sole holder of a share shall be the only persons recognised by the company as having any title to the share. In the case of a share registered in the names of two or more holders, the survivors or survivor or the executors or administrators of the deceased survivor, shall be the only persons recognised by the company as having any title to the share.

31. A person becoming entitled to a share by reason of the death or insolvency of the holder shall be entitled to the same dividends and other advantages to which he would be entitled if he were the registered holder of the share, except that he shall not, before being registered as a member in respect of the share, be entitled in respect of it to exercise any right conferred by membership in relation to meetings of the company.

32. Any committee or guardian of a lunatic or infant member, or any person becoming entitled to or to transfer shares in consequence of the death, bankruptcy or insolvency of any member upon producing such evidence that he sustains the character in respect of which he proposes to act or of his title as the Directors think sufficient which they shall not be under any obligation to give, be registered as a member in respect of such share or may, subject to the regulations as to transfer herein before contained, transfer such shares.

FORFEITURE AND LIEN.

33. If any member fails to pay any call or instalment on or before the day appointed for the payment of the same, the Managing Agents may at any time hereafter, during such time as the call or instalment remains unpaid, serve notice on such member to pay the same, together with any interst that may have accrued and expenses that may have been incurred by the company by reason of such non-payment. A Notice shall name a day (not being less than 15 days from the date of the notice) and a place on, and at which such call or instalment and such interest and expenses as aforesaid are to be paid. The notice shall also state that in the event of non-payment on or before the time and at the place appointed, the shares in respect of which such call was made or instalment is payable will be liable to be forfeited.

34. If the requirements of such notice be not complied with, any share, in respect of which such notice has been given may at any time

thereafter, before, the payments of the calls or instalments, interests and expenses due in respect thereof, be forfeited by the Managing Agents with the approval of the Directors. Such forfeiture shall include all dividends declared in respect of the forfeited shares and not actually paid before the forfeiture.

35. When any share shall have been so forfeited notice of the resolution shall be given to the member in whose name it stood immediately prior to the forfeiture, and an entry of the forfeiture, with the date thereof, shall forthwith be made in the register, but no forfeiture shall be in any manner invalidated by any omission or neglect to give such notice or to make such entry as aforesaid and as such entry as aforesaid shall be conclusive evidence of such forfeiture.

36. Any share, so forfeited, shall deemed to be the property of the company and the Directors may sell, transfer to the Reserve Fund, re-allot or otherwise dispose of the same in such manner as they think fit.

37. The Directors may, at any time before any share so forfeited is sold, re-allotted, or othewise disposed of, annul the forfeiture thereof upon such conditions as they think fit.

38 Any member whose shares have been forfeited shall notwithstanding be liable to pay and shall forthwith pay to the Company all calls or instalments, interests & expenses owing upon or in respect of such shares at the time of forfeiture, together with interest thereon from the time of forfeiture until payment at 12% per annum and the Directors may enforce the payment thereof, if they think fit.

39. The forfeiture of a share shall involve the extinction of all interest in and also of all claims and demands against the company in respect of the share and all other rights incident to the share, except only such of those rights as by the Articles are expressly saved.

40. The provisions of these regulations as to forfeiture shall apply in the case of non-payment of any sum which, by the terms of issue of a share becomes payable at a fixed time, whether on account of the amount of the share, or by way of premium, as if the same had been payble by virtue of a call duly made and notified.

41. The Company shall have the first and paramount lien upon all the shares registered in the name of each member (whether solely or jointly with others) and upon the proceeds of sale thereof for his debts, liabilities and engagements, solely or jointly with any other person to or with the Company, whether the period for the payment, fulfilment or discharge thereof shall have actually arrived or not. And such lien shall extend to all dividends from tfme to time declared in respect of such shares.

42. For the purpose of enforcing such lien the Managing Agents, subject to the approval of the Directors, may sell the shares subject thereto in such manner as they think fit, but no sale shall be made until such period as aforesaid shall have arrived, and until notice in writing of the intention to sell, shall have been served on such member, his heirs executors or administra-

tors, and default shall have been made by him or them, in payment, fulfilment or discharge of such debt liabilities or engagements for seven days after notice.

43. The net proceeds of any such sale shall be applied in or towards satisfaction of the debts, liabilities or engagements and the resedue (if any) paid to such member, his heirs executors, administrators or any other representatives.

44. Upon any sale after forfeiture or for enforcing a lien in exercise of the power herein before given, the Directors may cause the purchaser's name to be entered in the register in respect of the shares sold and the purchaser shall not be bound to see to the regularity of the proceedings nor to the application of the purchase money, and after his name has been entered in the register in respect of such shares, the validity of the sale shall not be impeached by any person and the remedy if any, of any person aggrieved by the sale shall be in damages only and against the Company exclusively.

ALTERATION OF CAPITAL.

45. The Company in General Meeting may from time to time increase the Capital by the creation of new shares of such amount as may be deemed expidient. The new shares shall be issued upon such terms and conditions and with such rights and privileges annexed thereto as the General Meeting resolving upon the creation thereof shall direct, and if no direction be given, the Directors shall determine and in particular such share may be issued with a preferential or qualified right to dividends and in the distribution of assets of the Company and with a special or without any right of voting.

46. Subject to the provision of section 105C of the Indian Companies Act of 1936 and subject to any direction to the contrary that may be given by the meeting which sanctions the increase of the capital, all new shares shall be disposed of by the Directors in such manner as they may deem to be most benificial to the Company.

47. Any capital raised by the creation of new shares shall be considered as part of the original capital in all respects so far as may be and shall be subject to the foregoing provisions with reference to the payment of calls and instalments, transfer and transmission, forfeiture, lien and surrender unless it may be otherwise resolved by the General Meeting sanctioning the increase.

48, The Company may from time to time by special Resolution reduce its Capital by paying off or cancelling Capital which has been lost or is unrepresented by available assets or reducing the liability on the shares or otherwise as may seem expedient and Capital may be paid off upon the footing that it may be called up again or otherwise.

49. The Company may, by ordinary resolution ;

(a) Consolidate and divide its share Capital into shares of larger amount than its existing shares.

(b) By sub-divisions of its existing shares or any of them, divide the whole or any part of its share Capital into shares of smaller amount than is fixed by this Charter,

(c) Cancel any shares which, at the date of passing of the resolution, have not beed taken or agreed to be taken by any person.

BORROWING POWERS.

50. The Managing Agents may from time to time with the approval of the Directors borrow from the members or other persons and may themselves lend any sum or sums of moneys for the purpose of the Company and pay interest thereon.

51. The Managing Agents may with such approval as aforesaid raise and secure payment of such money in such manner and upon such terms and conditions in all respects as they think fit and in particular by making, drawing, accepting or endorsing on behalf of the company any promissory notes or bills of exchange or giving or issuing any other security of the Company or by mortgage or charge of all or any part of the property of the Company, both present and future, including its uncalled capital for the time being and the Managing Agents with such approval as aforesaid may on behalf of the Company guarantee the whole or any part of any loans or debts incurred by the company with power for them to secure the guarantors against liability in respect of such loans by means of a mortgage or charge of the Company's property moveable or immoveable or otherwise.

MEETINGS.

52. The first ordinary General Meeting of the Company shall be held within the six months from the date of the grant of this Charter.

53. Subsequent General Meeting shall be held once at least in every year at such time not being more than fifteen months after the holding of the last preceding General Meeting and at such place as may be determined by the Directors.

54. The above-mentioned General Meetings shall be called ordinary meetings ; all other General Meetings shall be called Extra-ordinary.

55. An Extra-ordinary General Meeting may at any time be called by the Board of Directors or by the Managing Agents and shall also be called upon a requisition of not less than one-tenth of the members of the company then holding shares upon which all calls or other sums then due have been paid and stating the object of the meeting and signed by the requisitionists and left at the Office for and addressed to the Board of Directors or any other place or addressed to any other person as the

Directors may determine. The requisition may consist of several documents in like form each signed by one or more of the requisitionists.

56. If the Board of Directors fail to cause a meeting to be held within 21 days after the delivery of any such requisition, the requisitionists or a majority of them in number may call the meeting but in either case every Meeting so called shall be held within three months from the date of deposit of the requisition. The Meeting must be convened for the purpose specified in the requisition and if convened otherwise than by the Board of Dicectors for those purposes only. The Bcard of Directors, calling any General or Extraordinary meeting and the share-holders calling any Extra-ordinary General Meeting shall respectively give at least fourteen clear day's notice specifying the time and place of the Meeting.

57. A resolution shall be a special resolution when it has been passed by such a majority as is required for the passing of an extra-ordinary resolution and at a Genaral Meeting of which not less than twenty-one days notice specifying the intention to propose the resolution as a special resolution has been duly given, provided that if all the members entitled to attend and vote at any such meeting so agree, a resolution may be proposed and passed as a special resolution at a meeting of which less than twenty-one day's notice has been given.

58. The non-receipt by a shareholder of notice of a General Meeting shall not affect the validity of the procedings of the meeting.

59. It shall not be requisite in any event to give notice of a General Meeting or other meeting to any share-holder who has not a ragisted address in India.

PROCEEDINGS AT GENERAL MEETING.

60. The business of an Ordinary Meeting shall be to receive and consider the Profit and Loss Account and the Balance sheet, the report of the Directors and Auditors, to elect Directors, Auditors and other officers in place of those retiring, to declare dividends and to transact any other business which under these presents ought to be transancted at any Ordinary Meeting and any business which is brought under consideration by the report of the Directors issued with the notice convening the Meeting. All other business transacted at any Ordinary Meeting and all business transacted at an Extra-Ordinary Meeting shall be deemed special.

(a) No special Resolution or Extra-ordinary Resolution shall be allowed to be moved by the shareholder in a General Meeting of which no notice has been given at least 21 days before the date of such meeting.

61. No business shall be transacted at any general meeting unless a quorum of members is present at the time when the meeting proceeds to business. Five members personally present shall be a quorum.

62. If within half-an-hour after the time appointed for the holding of a General Meeting a quorum be not present, the meeting if convened on

the requisition of share-holders, shall be dissolved and in every other case shall stand adjourned to the same day in the next week, at the same time and place as was appointed for holding the General Meeting and if in such an adjourned meeting the qourum be not present, the members who are present and entitled to vote shall be a qourum whatever their number and the amount of shares held by them and may transact the business for which the meeting was called.

63. The Chairman with the consent of the meeting may adjourn any General Meeting from time to time and place to place but no business shall be transacted at adjourned General Meeting other than the business left unfinished at the General Meeting from which the adjournment took place, and which might have been transacted at that meeting.

64. In every General Meeting a share-holder chosen by the share-holders present and entitled to vote shall takh the chair.

65. At any General Meeting a resolution put to the vote of the Meeting shall be decided on a show of hands, unless a poll is (before or on the declaration of the result of the show of hands) demanded by at least five members present in person or by proxy, or the chairman of the Meeting or any member or members holding not less than one-tenth of the issued capital which carries voting rights and unless a poll is so demanded, a declaration by the Chairman that a resolution on a show of hands has been carried or carried unanimously, or by a particular majority or lost, and an entry to that effect in the book of the proceedings of the company shall be conclusive evidence of the fact, without proof of the number or proportion of the votes recorded in favour of, or against that resolution.

66. If a poll is duly demanded, it shall be taken in such manner as the Chairman directs and the result of the poll shall be deemed to be the resolution of the meeting at which the poll was demanded.

67. In the case of an equality of votes, whether on a show of hands or on a poll the Chairman of the meeting at which the show of hands takes place, or at which the poll is demanded shall be entitled to a second or casting vote.

68. If a poll is duly demanded as aforesaid it shall be taken in such time and place as the Chairman of the Meeting directs and either at once or after an interval or adjournment or otherwise and the result of the poll shall be deemed to be the resolution of the meeting at which the poll was demanded. The demand for a poll may be withdrawn.

69. Minutes shall be made in books provided for the purpose of all resolutions and proceedings at General Meeting and any such minutes if signed by the Chairman of the Meeting to which it related or by the Chairman of the next subsequent General Meeting shall be receivable as evidence of the facts therein stated without further proof.

70. Any poll duly demanded on the election of a Chairman of a meeting or any question of adjournment, shall be taken at the meeting and without adjournment.

71. The demand of a poll shall not prevent the continuance of meeting for the transaction of any business other than the business on which a poll has been demanden.

72. On a show of hands every member present in person shall have one vote. On a poll every member shall have one vote in respect of each share held by him.

73. If two or more persons are jointly registered as holders of any share, any one of such persons may vote at any meeting either personally or by proxy or attorney as if he were solely entitled thereto, and if more than one of such joint holders be present at any meeting personally or by proxy or by attorney then one of such persons so present whose name precedes the rest in the register in respect of such share shall alone be entitled to vote in respeet of the same. Several executors or Administrators of a deceased member in whose name any share stands shall for the purpose of this clause be deemed joint-holders.

74. Any guardian or other person entitled under the transmission clauses to transfer any shares may vote at any General Meeting in respect thereof as if he was the registered holder of such shares, provided that at least 48 hours before the holding of the meeting he shall satisfy the Board of Directors of his right to act in that capacity unless the Board of Direcrors shall have previously admitted his right to vote at such meeting in respect thereof.

75. Votes may be given either personally or by proxy or by an Agent acting under a duly executed power-of-attorney.

76. The instrument appointing a proxy shall be either printed or written or partly printed or partly written and shall be signed by the appointor or attorney or if such appointor be a corporation it shall be under its common seal. No person shall be appointed a proxy who is not a member of the company and qualified to vote, but an attorney under a power may attend and vote at meetings without being a shareholder and where a corporation is the registered holder of shares of the Company it may by resolution of its Directors appoint any of its officials or any other person to act as its representative at any meetings of this company, and the person so authorised shall be entitled to exercise the same powers on behalf of the company which he re-presents as if he were an individual shareholder of this company.

77. An instrument appointing a proxy may be in the following form or in any other form which the Directors shall approve

.... Company Limited. I .... of .... in the district of .... being a member of the ....Company Limited, hereby appoint ....of ....as my proxy to vote for me and on my behalf at the (Ordinary or Extra-ordinary, as the case may be) General Meeting of the Company to be held on the .... day of .... and at any adjournment thereof.

Signed this..................................day of ....

78. The instrument appointing a proxy and the power-of-attorney or other authority (if any), under which it is signed or a notarially certified copy of that power or authority, shall be deposited at the registered office of the Company not less than seventy-two hours before the time of holding the meeting at which the person named in the instrument proposes to vote and in default the instrument of proxy shall not be treated as valid.

79. A vote given in accordance with the term of an instrument of proxy or a power of attorney shall be valid notwithstanding the previous death of the principal or revocation of the proxy or power-of-attorney or transfer of the share in respect of which the vote is given unless an intimation in writing of the death, revocation or transfer shall have been received at the office of the company before the meeting

80. No member shall be entitled to be present, or to vote at any General Meeting either personally or by proxy or attorney or as a proxy on attorney for any other member or be received in a quorum, whilist anycall or other sum shall be due and payable to the company in respect of the shares of such manner.

DIRECTORS.

81. Until otherwise determined by a General Meeting the number of the Directors shall not be less than five nor more than eleven and one third of the whole number of Directors may be appointed by the Managing Agents.

82. The Directors appointed by the Managing Agent from their members shall be styled as Ex-officion Directors and they will not be subject to retirement by rotation. All powers exerciseable by the Managing Agents firm shall ipso facto be vested in such Ex-officio Directors on his or their being so appointed.

83. Unless otherwise determined by the general Meeting, the qualification of every Director shall be his holding at least twenty shares of the company in his own name.

The first Directors of the Company shall be the following persons who have signified their consent to act as such :----

1. Mahamanyabara Maharajkumar Brajendra Kishore Dev Burman Bahadur.

2. Maharajkumar Ranabir Kishore Dev Burman Bahadur.

3. Manyabara Raja Rana Bodhjung Bahadur Chief Secretary to His Highness the Maharaja Maniky Bahadur of Tripura.

4. Major Kumar Prafulla Kumar Dev Burman Bahadur Military Secretary to His Highness the Maharaja Manikya Bahadur of Tripura.

5. Mr. S. C. Dev Burman M. A. (Harvard), Seniar Naib Dewan, Accaunts Deprtment.

6. Sj. Priyanath Banerjee, Pleader, Khash Adalat, Tripura State.

7. Dr. Manimoy Muzumdar, Chief Medical officer Tripura State.

8. Sj. Janesh Kumar Bhattacharjee, M. Sc. Inspectors of Schools, Tripura State.

9. Sj. Satyaranjan Bose, B. A., Officer-in-charge, Education & Publicity Departments, Tripura State.

84. Each Director including the ex-officio Directors shall receive out of the funds of the Company by way of remuneration for services, the sum of Rs. 10/- or such larger sum as the company in General Meeting may sanction for each meeting attended by him and for each meeting at which he may not be present, if the Board shall deeide. The directors shall also be paid any travelling and other expenses of attending and returning from meetings of the Board (including Hotel expenses and any other expenses properly incurred in connection with the business of the Company).

85. The directors may meet together for the despatch of business, adjourn and otherwise regulate their business, as they think fit. Questions arising at any meeting shall be decided by a majcrity of votes. In case of an equality of votes, the Chajrman shall have a second or casting vote. A Director may and the Secretary on the requisition of a Director shall, at any time, summon a meeting of directors.

86. Unless otherwise determined by the Board, the quorum necessary for ths transaction of business of the Directors, shall be three.

87. The Directors may elect a Chairman of their meetings and determine thh period for which he is to hold office ; but if no such Chairman is elected, or if at any meeting the Chairman is not pesent within five minutes after the appointed for holding the same, the Directors present may choose one of their number to be chairman of the meetig.

88. The Directors may delegate any of their powers to Committees consisting of such member or members of their body as they think fit ; any committee so formed shall, in the exercise of the power so delegated, conform to any regulations that may be imposed on them by the Directors,

89. The Committee may elect a chairman of their meetings ; if no such chairman is elected, or if at any meeting, the chairman is not present within five midutes afther the time appointed for holding the same, the members present may choose one of their number to be chairman of the meeting.

90. A committee may meet and adjourn as they think proper. Questions arising at any meeting shall be determined by a majority of votes of the members present, and in case of an equality of votes, the chairman shall have a second or casting vote.

91, A resolution in writing and signed by all the Directors shall be as valid and effectual as if it had been passed in a meeting of tae Directors duly called and constituted.

92. If any Director, being willing shall be called upon to perform extra services, or to make any special exertions in going or residing away from the head-quarter for any of the purpose of the company, or giving any special attendance to the businees of the company, the Company may remunerate the Director so doing either by a fixed sum, or by percentage on profits or otherwise as may be determined by the Directors and such remuneration may be either in addition to, or in substitution for his share in the remuneration above provided for the Directors.

93. The Company in general meeting may from time to time tncrease or reduce the number of Directors and may alter their qualifications and remunerations.

94. A share-holder, not being a retiring Director, shall not unless recommended by a Director for election as a Director, be eligible to be elected as a Director, at any General Meeting unless he or some other Member intending to propose him has at least seven clear days before the meeting, left at the office of the company, a notice in writing duly signed signifying his candidature for the office or the intention of such member to propose him.

95. At the first ordinary meeting of the company, the whole of the Directors shall retire from office, and at the ordinary meeting in every subsequent year, one-third of the Directors for the time being or, if their number is not three or a multiple of three, then the number nearest to one-third shall retire from office.

96, The Directors to retire every year shall be those who have been longest in the office since their last election, but as between persons who become Directors on the same day those to retire shall (unless they otherwise agree among themselves) be determined by lot.

97. The retiring Director shall be eligible for re-election.

98. The Company at the General Meeting at which a Director retires in manner afore said may fill up the vacated office by electing a person thereto.

99. If at any meeting at which an election of Directors ought to take place the places of the vacating Directors are not filled up, the meeting shall stand adjourned, till the same day in the next week at the same time and place, and, if at the adjourned meeting the places of the vacating Directors are not filled up, the vacating Directors or such of them as have not had their places filled up shall be deemed to have been re-elected at the adjourned meeting.

100. Any casual vacancy occuring in the Board of Directors may be filled up by the Directors, but the person so chosen shall be subject to retirement at the same time as if he had become a Director on the day on which the Director in whose place he is appointed was last elected a Director.

101. The Directors shall have power at any time and from time to time, to appoint a person as an additional Director who shall retire from office at the next following Ordinary General Meeting, but shall be eligible for election by the company at that meeting as additional Director.

102. The company may by Extra-ordinary resolution remove any Director other than Ex-officio Directors before the expiration of his period of office, and may by an ordinary resolution appoint another person in his stead ; the person so appointed shall be subject to ratirement at the same time as if he had become a Director on the day on which the Director in whose place he is appointed was last elected a Director.

103. Every Director shall vacate his office on the happening of any of the events following, that is to say :—

(I) The office of a Director shall be vacated if :—

(a) he fails to obtain within the time specified in Sub-Section (I) of Section 84 or any time thereafter ceases to hold, the share qualification, if any, necessary for his appointment, or

(b) he is found to be of unsound mind by a court of competent jurisdiction, or

(c) he is adjudged an insolvent, or

(d) he fails to pay calls made on him in respect of shares held by him within six months from the date of such calls being made, or

(e) he or any firm of which he is a partner or partner of any private company of which he is a director without the sanction of the Company in General Meeting accepts or holds any office of profit under the company other than that of a Managing Director or manager or a legal or technical advisor or a banker, or

(f) he absents himself from three consecutive meetings of the Directors or from all meetings of the Director of a continuous period of three months whichever is longer without leave of absence from the Board of Directors or

(g) he or any firm of which he is a partner or any private company of which he is a Director accepts a loan or gauarantee from the Company in contravention of section 86D, or

(h) he acts in contravention of section 86F

(II) Nothing contained in this section shall be deemed to preclude a company from providing by its article that the office of director shall be vacated on grounds additional to those specified in this section.

104. All acts done by any meeting of the members or of the Directors or of any committee of the Directors or by any person acting as Managing Director or by Managing Agents purporting to act under powers delegated by the Directors or under these articles shall, notwithstanding that it shall afterwards be discovered that there was defect in the appointment of such Directors or persons acting as aforesaid or that they or any of them were disqualified, be as valid as if such person or persons had been duly qualified.

105. The Directors shall cause to be made in books provided for the purpose minutes of the proceedings of all meetings of the Directors and of the names of the Directors present at such meetings.

106. All such minutes shall be signed by the Chairman of the meeting at which the same are recorded or in case of inability from any cause of such Chairman to sign the same, then by the person who shall preside as Chairman at the next ensuing meeting and all minutes purporting to be so signed shall for all purposes whatever be prima facie evidence of the actual passing of the resolution recorded, and the actual and regular transaction or occurance of the proceedings to be so recorded and of the regularity of the meeting at which the same shall appear to have taken place.

MANAGEMENT & REMUNERATION OF MANAGING AGENTS.

107. Subject to the control and supervision of the Board of Directors of the Company the business of the compony shall be carried on by the Managing Agents hereinafter mentioned. The Managing Agents shall in relation to the management and conduct of the Company's business have and may, subject to such control and supervision as aforesaid, exercise all and singular the like powers and authorities as those which are by this Charter, expressed to be vested in the Directors.

108. Tripura Industrial Agency as it is or may hereinafter be constituted either as a partnership firm or a limited liability company shall be the first Managing Agents of the Company and shall be allowed to retain office for a period of twenty years certain from the date of the grant of this charter.

109. The rent of offices, factories, power stations, godowns etc., and salary for the office staff and all other establishment and such like

other charges including stationery, postage, printing etc., shall be paid out from the funds of the Company.

110. The Managing Agents shall subject to the approval of the Board of Directors retain the whole or part services of such expert staff as may be necessary in the Company's interest on such terms and on such remuneration as may be thought fit and may charge such remuneration to the funds of the Company in addition to the expenses mentioned in clause 109 above.

111. The Managing Agents shall provide a suitable office, an office staff to keep the books and to carry on the business of the Company, the cost of which shall be paid from the funds of the Company.

112. Without prejudice to the general power conferred upon the Managing Agents by the provisions of the Charter it is expressly declared that the Managing Agents shall subject to such general control and supervision as aforesaid have the following powers, namely the power :--

(1) To make, draw, endorse, sign, accept negotiate and give all cheques, bill of landing, drafts, orders, bills of exchange, Government of India and other promissory notes and other negotiable instruments required in the business of the Company.

(2) To appoint and at their discretion remove or suspend such local agents, assistants' clerks, officers and servants from permanent, temporary or special services as they may from time to time think fit and to determine their powers and duties and fix their salaries or emoluments and to require security in such instances to such amount as they think fit.

(3) To institute, conduct, defend, compound or abandon any legal proceedings by or against the Company or otherwise concerning the affairs of the Company and also to compound and allow time for payment or satisfaction of any debt due and of any claim or demands by or against the Company.

(4) To refer any claims or demands by or against the Company to arbitration and proceed with the same and observe and perform the award thereof.

(5) To make and give receipt, release and other discharges for money payable to the Company and for the claim and demands of the Company and for property delivered to the Company.

(6) To invest and to deal with any of the moneys of the Company including moneys from time to time carried to any Reserve fund or depreciation funds not immediately required for the purposes thereof and in such manner as they think fit and from time to time to vary or realise such investment or to place any such moneys in deposit with the Associated Bank of Tripura Ltd,. or with any ether Bank or Banks which the Managing Agents think fit.

(7) To enter into all such negotiation and contracts and rescind and vary all such contracts and execute and do all such acts deeds and things in the name and on behalf of the Company as they may consider expedient for or in relation to any of the matter aforesaid or otherwise for the pnrpose of the business of the Company.

(8) To pay the costs, charges and expenses preliminary and incidental to the promotion, formation, advertisement etc., and issuing of the Charter constituting the Company.

(9) To purchase or otherwise acquire for the Company property rights or privileges which the Company is authorised to acquire at such price and generally on such terms and condition as they think fit.

(10) From time to time to provide for the management of the affairs of the Company in such manner as they think fit and in particular to establish branch office at any other place and to appoint any person or persons to be the Attorney or Agents of the Company with such powers and upon such powers and upon such terms as may be thought fit.

(11) To invest and deal with any of the moneys of the Company not immediately required for the purposes thereof upon such securities (not being the shares in this Company) and in such manner as they think fit and from time to time to vary or realise such investments.

(12) To give to any person employed by the Company any commission for the sale of shares of the Company.

(13) To make calls for the unpaid share money from the share-holders.

(14) To give effect to and carry out all or any of the objects of the company as defined in the objects clause of this Charter.

113. The Managing Agents shall be at liberty to exercise and perform all and every powers and duties as such Managing Agents through any Member-in-charge, Manager or Managers, Secretary or Secretaries or other Officer or officers of the Managing Agents holding a full general power of attorney from the Managing Agents and every such Member-in-charge, Manager, Secretary or other officers shall be deemed to have vested in him all the powers authorities and discretions by the Charter vested in Managing Agents and all documents required to be signed by the Managing Agents of the Company shall be deemed to be sufficiently so signed if signed for and on behalf of the Managing Agents by any such Member-in-charge, Manager, Secretary or other Officer as aforesaid.

114. The Managing Agents may also in addition to their duties as Managing Agents of the Company perform any other duties and works for the company which the Directors may decide and shall receive such reasonable and proper remuneration for such work as shall be from time to time agreed upon between the Managing Agents and the Directors such

remuneration being in addition to remuneration payable to them as the Managing Agents of the Company mentioned in this Charter.

115. The remmuneration of the said first Managing Agents "Messrs Tripura Industrial Agency" shall be as follows :--

(a) A commission at the rate of ten per cent on the nett annual profits of the Company. For the purpose of this clause, nett profit shall mean the profits of the company as defined in section 87 C clause (3) of the Indian Companies Act as amended in 1936.

(b) The said Managing Agents in addition to above commission shall be entitled to get a minimum payment in the case of absence of or inadquacy of profits together with an office allowance or any further remmuneration as sanctioned by a special resolution of the Company.

(c) The said remmuneration shall be exclusive of and shall not include any remuneration, selaries, wages, which shall be payable to the Bankers, Solicitors, Engineers, Commission Agents, Dealers, Brokers, officicers, clerks, servants, workmen and other employees who may be employed by the said firm for or on behalf of the Company or for carrying on and conducting the business of the said company, nor any rent, post and telegram expenses, printing and stationery, abvsrtisements or other office expenses nor any travelling charges and expenses incurred by the said firm in connection with the business of the said company, all of which rents, remmunerations, salaries, wages, costs, charges and other expenses shall be paid by the said company.

116. The Directors and the Managing Agents shall not be disqualified by their office from contracting with company either as a vendor or purchaser or otherwise nor shall any such contract or arrangement entered into by or on behalf of the company or partnership of or in which any Director or the Managing Agents so contracting or being such member or so interested be liable to account to the company for any profit realised by any such contract or arrangement by reasons only of such Directors or Managing Agents holding that office or of the fiduciary relations thereby established by them or him at the meeting of the Board of Directors at which the contract or arrangement is determined on, if the interest then exists, or in any other case at the first meeting of the Board of Directors after acquisition of interest provided nevertheless that no Director shall vote in respect of any contract or arrangement in which he is interested and if he do so vote his vote shall not be counted. And any Director who is a Solicitor or lawyer, may act as the Solicitor or lawyer of the company and shall not be liable to account to the company for any profit realised any professional work done by him or his firm for the company.

117. The Managing Agents shall be responsible for the due and proper management of the Company's business and shall do all acts which they are entitled to do under these presents and by delegation and with the previous consent and approval of the Board of Directors.

118. The partners or Directors for the time being of the Managing Agents as the same may be constituted for the time being shall be entitled to regulate and conduct their proceedings and exercise all or any of the powers, authorities and discretions of that firm or company as the Managing Agents of this Campany in such manner as the Articles of Agreement or Articles of Association of that firm or that company may permit or direct and may delegate all or any of such powers, authorities and discretions to such of the members or officers of that Company and on such terms and conditions as the partners or Directors of the Managing Agents firm or Company may seem fit and accordingly all deeds and documents required to be signed by the Managing Agents of this Company shall be deemed to be sufficiently so signed if signed by such member or officer of the Managing Agents firm or company so properly authorised to whom the partners or Directors as the case may be may have delegated their powers in that behalf.

119. Subsequent Managing Agents shall be appointed and their remmuneration determined by the company in General Meeting, but the company may at any time or times after the vacation of the office by the first Managing Agents appoint a Manager or Managers or a Secretary or Secretaries instead of Managing Agents. In the case of emergency the Directors may subject to confirmation by the Company in General Meeting appoint subsequent Managing Agents for a period not exceeding six months. Unless and until otherwise determined by the Company in General Meeting the Managing Agents, Manager or Managers, Secretary or Secretaries so appointed shall have the like power and authorities and perform the like functions as those which are by this Charter vested in the first Managing Agents.

SEAL.

120. The Board of Directors shall provide for the safe custody of the seal. Every instrument to which the seal is affixed shall be signed by at least one Director and countersigned by the Managing Agents, provided that the signature of a Director shall not be required in documents to which the seal is affixed and which are required for use only in connection with any civil or criminal proceedings or in documents which the Managing Agents are expressly authorised by the Board of Directors or by these presents to sign, and it shall be sufficient by such documents are signed by the Managing Agents.

ACCOUNTS.

121. The Managing Agents shall cause true account to be kept of the sums of money received and expended by the Company and all matters in respect of which such receipts and expenditures take place, and of the assets, credits and liabilitles of the Company.

122. Such books of account shall be kept at the registered office of the company, or at such other place or places as the Directors think fit.

123. The Directors shall from time to time determine whether, and to what extent, and at what time and place, and under what conditions or regulations the accounts and books of the Company or any of them shall be open to the inspection of the members, and no member shall have any right of inspection of any account or book or document of the Company, except as authorised by the Directors or by a resolution of the Company in General Meeting.

124. At the Ordinary General Meeting in every year, the Directors shall lay before the Company a profit and loss account and a balance sheet containing a summary of the assets and liabilities of the Company, made upto date not more than six months before the date of the meeting.

125. Every such account and Balance sheet shall be accompanied by a report of the Directors as to the state and condition of the Company and as to the amount which they recommend to be paid out of the profits by way of dividends to the members, and the amount, if any, which they propose to carry to the Reserve Fund, according to the provision in that behalf hereinbefore contained and the report and Balance Sheet shall be signed by at least two Directors and countersigned by a member of the Managing Agents.

126. A copy of such account, Balance sheet and Report shall, seven days previous to the meeting, be kept at the office open for inspection of the members and the same shall be served on the registered holders of shares in the manner in which notices are hereinafter directed to be served.

127. A copy of such accounts, balance sheet and report shall after adoption of the same by the Company in general meeting shall be sent to the Minister of the State of Tripura within 14 days of the date of such adoption, together with a copy of the annual list of members and summary prepared in accordance with the requirements of Sec. 32 of the I. C. Act amended in 1936. If the general meeting before which a balance sheet, is laid does not adopt the balance sheet, a copy of the balance sheet with a statement of that fact and of the reasons therefor annexed to the copy shall be sent to the Minister of the State of Tripura within 14 days of the date of holding the General Meeting.

AUDITS.

128. Once at least in every year the accounts of the Company shall be examined, and the correctness of the Balance Sheet ascertained by an Auditor.

129. The company at each Ordinary General Meeting shall appoint an Auditor to hold office until the next Ordinary General Meeting. If an appointment of Auditor is not made as aforesaid the State of Tripura may on the application of any member of the Company appoint an Auditor for the current year, and fix the remmuneration to be paid to him by the Company for his service.

130. A Director or officer of the Company shall not be capable of being appointed Auditor of the Company.

131. The first Auditor of the Company may be appointed and the remmuneratien fixed by the Directors before the first Ordinary General meeting and if so appointed shall hold office until the first Ordinary General Meeting, unless previously removed by a resolution of the Shareholders in an Extra-Ordinary General Meeting in which case the shareholders at such Meeting may appoint Auditor.

132. The Directors of the Company shall fill any casual vacancy in the office of auditor, but while any such vacancy continues, the surviving or continuing Auditor (if any) may act.

133. Subject to Section 131 as above the remmuneration of Auditor of the Company shall be fixed by the Company in General Meeting.

134. Every Auditor of the Company shall have a right to access at all times to the books and accounts and vouchers of the Company, and shall be entitled to require from the Directors and the Managing Agents such information and explanation as may be necessary for the performance of the duties of the Auditor and the Auditor shall sign a certificate at the foot of the Balance sheet, stating whether or not all his requirements an Auditor have been complied with, and shall make a report to the shareholders on the accounts examined by him, and on every balance sheet laid before the company in General Meeting during his tenure of office.

DIVIDENDS AND RESERVE.

135. The Company in General Meeting may declare dividends, but no dividend shall exceed the amount recommended by the Directors.

136. The Directors may from time to time pay to the members such interim dividends as appear to the Directors to be justified by the profits of the Company.

137. No dividends shall be paid otherwise than out of profits of the year or any other undistributed profits.

138. Subjects to the rights of persons (if any) entitled to shares with special rights as to dividends, all dividends shall be declared and paid according to the amounts paid on the shares, but if and so long as nothing is paid upon any of the shares in the company, dividends may be declared and paid according to the amount of the shares. No amount paid on a share in advance of calls shall while carrying interest be treated for the purpose of this articles as paid on the share.

139. The Directors may, before, recommending any dividend, set aside out of the profits of the Comany such sums as they think proper as a reserve or reserves which shall at the discretion of the Directors be applicable

for meeting contigencies or for equalizing dividends, or for any other purpose to which the profits of the company may be properly applied, and pending such application, may at the like discretion, either be employed in the business of the Company or be invested in such investments (other than shares of the company) as the Directors may from time to time think fit.

140. If several persons are registered as joint-holders of any share, any one of them may give effectual receipts for any dividend payable on the share.

141. When any shareholder is indebted to the company for calls or otherwise all dividends payable to him or a sufficient part thereof may be retained and applied by the Directors in or towards satisfaction of the debt.

142. Unless otherwise directed by the Company in general meeting any dividend may be paid by cheque or warrant sent through the post to the registered address of the member entitled or in case of joint-holders to the registered address of that one whose name stands first on the register in respect of the joint-holding and every cheque so sent shall be made payable to the order of the persons to whom it is sent.

143. All dividends on any share not having a legal registered owner entitled to require payment of or competent to give valid receipt for the same shall remain in suspense until some competent person be registered as the holder of the share, provided that all dividends remaining for three years after declaration thereof unclaimed by some person entitled and competent to receive and give a valid receipt for the same shall at the end of that period be forfeited to the company and cease to be payable and shall be carried to such fund of the company as the Managing Agents with the sanction of the Directors may see fit, but the Managing Agents with the sanction of the Directors may remit the forfeiture whenever they may think proper.

144. Unpaid dividends shall never bear interest as against the company.

NOTICES.

145. A notice may be served by the company upon any member either personally or by sending it through the post with the certificate of posting at his registered address in the books of the company.

146. All notices shall with respect to any registered shares to which persons are jointly entitled be given to whichever of such persons is named first in the register and notice so given shall be sufficient notice to all the holders of such shares.

147. Any notice sent by post shall be deemed to have been duly served when such notice has been posted and in proving such service it shall be sufficient to prove that the card, envelope or wrapper containing

the same was properly addressed and put in the post either by a certificate of posting or registration.

148. Where a given number of days' notice, or notice extending over any other period, is required to be given the day of serving shall be included in such number of days or other period.

WINDING UP.

149. The affairs of the Company may be wound up either (a) Compulsorily, or (b) Voluntarily (c) Voluntarily under the supervision of the High Court of Tripura.

In the case of winding up the provisions similar to that under the Indian Companies Act VII of 1913 as amended by Act XXII of 1936 or any subsequent statutory modification thereof on the part of Goverment of India or rules as near to as there can be shall apply subject to this modification that the High Court referred to therein will mean the High Court of the State of Tripura under its original special jurisdiction and the Registrar of Joint Stock Company shall mean the Minister of State of Tripura, or any Officer authorised by him to act in this behalf.

150. If the affairs of the Company be wound up compulsorily such person shall be known by the name of State Liquidator. The person appointed under clause (B) and (C) herein as Liquidator for winding of the affairs of the Company shall be known by the name of Voluntary Liquidator or Voluntary Liquidator under supervision respectively. The powers of the Liquidators as above will be the same as of the Liquidators respectively under the provision of the Indian Companies Act and the said modification thereof.

151. If the affairs of the Company be wound up and the assets available for distribution among the members as such be insufficient to repay the whole of the paid up capital such assets shall be distributed so that as nearly as may be the losses shall be borne by the members in proportion to the capital paid up or which ought to have been paid up at the commencement of the winding up on the shares held by them, respectively and if in the winding up the assets available for distribution among the members shall be more than sufficient to repay the whole of the capital paid up at the commencement of the winding up the excess shall be distributed among the members in proportion to the capital at the commencement of the winding up or which ought to have been paid up on the shares held by them respectively.

AGREEMENT.

152. By virtue of an agreement made on 8. 12. 46. T. E. between Mahamanyabara Maharajkumar Brojendra Kishore Dev Barman, Maharajkumar Ranabir Kishore Dev Barman, Satyaranjan Bose and Kiron Chandra

Bose of the first part and Bejoy Basanta Ghosh of the second part, the latter did agree to sell all the right title and interest of Maharaja Match Factory owned absolutely by him including lands, goodwill, building, out-houses, fixtures, areas, ways, passages, lights, sewers, gutters, drains, appartments,.machineries, accessories, License and all sorts of assets and properties belonging or with the same now or heretofore held, used, occupied or enjoyed or reputed or known as part or parcel thereof or appartment thereto, to Maharaja Match Factory Ltd., at a price of Rs. 50,000 fifty thousand only, which would be realised by alloting 5000 fully paid up shares of the company to him. Upon this agreement, the said Bijoy Basanta Ghose delivered the possession of the Factory with all its belongings as setforth above to Mahamanyabara Maharajkumar Brojendra Kishore Dev Barman, Maharajkumar Ranabir Kishose Dev Barman, Satyaranjan Bose and Kiron Chandra Bose, who took this management and possession of the factory and advanced and took responsibility for Rs. 45,000/- forty-five thousand only, for the developement on various heads. After this, the said Bijoy Basanta Ghose made a separate arrangement in consonance with which he absolutely sold his right, title interest, goodwill etc., of Maharaja Match Factory to Maharajkumar Ranabir Kishore Dev Barman, by a deed of sale executed on 24. 5. 48. T. E. who purchased the same for himself and on behalf of Mahamanyabar Maharajkumar Brojendra Kishore De Barman, Maharajkumar Ranabir Kishore Dev Barman, Satyaranjan Bose and Kiron Chandra Bose, at a price of Rs. 22,000 - twenty-two thousand only, out of which the vendor Bijoy Basanta Ghose has been paid Rs. 11,000/- eleven thousand only in cash and the rest to be paid to him in instalments as detailed in a separate bond executed by the vendee in favour of Bijoy Basanta Ghose on the same date. Thus Mahamanyabar Maharajkumar Brajendra Kishore Dev Barman, Maharajkumar Ranabir Kishore Dev Barman, Satyaranjan Bose and Kiron Chandra Bose have become the absolute owner and possessor of the said Maharaja Match Factory.

It has been settled with Mahamanyabar Maharajkumar Brajendra Kishore Dev Barman, Maharajkumar Ranabir Kishore Dev Barman, Satyaranjan Bose ann Kiron Chandra Bose, that they will transfer their right title, interest, goodwill etc., thus owned by them to the Company after its incorporation at a price of Rs. 50,000 fifty thousand only, out of which the sum of Rs. 39,000 thirty-nine thousand only should be paid to them in cash and the rest Rs. 11,000 eleven thousand only to be paid to the said Bijoy Basanta Ghose in instalments as agreed upon by Maharajkumar Ranabir Kishore Dev Barman, in the above mentioned bond.

PRIVILEGES.

153. Inorder to enhance the credit and encouragement of the concern and to facilitate the smooth working there of His Highness the Maharaja Manikya Bahadur has been graciously pleased to grant the following licences to the Company :-

(a) The Company shall have and is hereby given the sole and exclusive right of monopoly for a period of ten years from the date of grant of this Charter to manufacture matches, splints veneers and all other allied goods within the area of Sadar and Khowai Divisions of the State of Tripura and export them outside.

Fcr this grant of exclusive right of monopoly the company should pay Rs. 100/- one hundred rupees annually to the State.

(b) If any restriction is made in future as regards the use, purchase and sale of fuel and woods, that will not affect the Company in any way, to collect, carry, grow, gather, purchase, and stock woods for the consumption within the area of the factory.

(c) If the Company so desire and apply for the purpose, the State will grant a lease of suitable plot or plots of land near the factory as sleected by the Campany not exceeding 1000/- acres in all for the plantation of growing cutting and using match wood on the terms at which the lands have been lased for tea cultivation in Sadar Division and if any portion of the said land is fouud to be owned and occupied by person or persons other than the State and if the Company so desire, to aviod difficulties, the State shall notwithstanding acquire the same by paying the bonafide owner or occupier of the land due compensation to be borne by the Company and shall lease out the same to the Company on the terms as stated above.

(d) The Company if so appply to the State, the Tulakona Fuel Reserve which is quite close to the present Factory at Agartala may be exclusively worked by the Company for the match wood and fuel required.

(e) The existing rules, orders, circulars, etc., or any modification thereof whatsoever in future in relation to the taxes, duties, rates, imposed upon the forest goods used, consumed exported, sold, purchased or otherwise taken into operation regarding the manufacture or matches, splints, veneers etc., shall stand so far as this company is directly or indirectly concerned.

MISCELLANEOUS.

154. No member shall be entitled to visit or inspect the company's power House, stations or properties or stores or factories without the permission of the Board or Managing Agents or require discovery of any information respecting any detail of the company's trading or any matter which is or may be in the nature of a trade secret process which may relate to the conduct of the business of the company and which in the opinion of the Board of Managing Agents, will be enexpedient in the interest of the member of the company to communicate to the public.

155. In all other matters to the business of the company for which any provisions similar to those contained in the Indian Companies Act 1913

(as amended by Act XXII of 1936) have not been made all the provisions similar to those contained in this Act, which are not inconsistant with the provisions of the Charter, will apply.

156. In case an interpelation in all General Meetings as to all subjects at least 10 days' notice will be given for preparation.

157. The year of the company shall be counted from 1st Baisakh to 31st Chaitra.

158. The duties of the Managing Agents shall in default of any other arrangement include the duties usually performed by a Secretary of a company.

159. In case of any dispute as to admission or regulation of a vote, the Chairman shall determine the same and such determination made in good faith shall be final and conclusive.

160. Eevery Director and member of the Managing Agents, Manager or officer of the Company shall be indemnified out of the funds of the Company against any liability incurred by him in defending any proceedings whether civil or criminal in which Judgment is given in his favour or in which he is acquitted or in connection with any application under Section 281 of the Indian Companies Act 1913 as amended by Act XXII of 1936 in which relief is granted to him by the Court.

161. The promoters will get a remunertion of Rs. 5.000/- only and this will be paid by 500 fully paid up shares of the Company.

162. The Directors shall not proceed to allotment of shares unless and until at least a minimum subscription of the face value of Rs. 10,000/- has been subscribed. The shares to be paid to the promoters shall be counted as a part and parcel of the minimum shares subscribed, defined in this clause.

163. The Court or High Court referred to in the said Act shall mean the High Court of the State of Tripura in its original jurisdiction and the Registrar of joint Stock Companies shall mean the Minister of Tripura State or any other officer authorised by him to act in this behalf.

A

CHARTER

FOR

INCORPORATING AND CONFERRING POWERS

AND

GRANTING PRIVILEGES AND CONCESSIONS

UPON

HOTEL KHOSMAHAL LIMITED. 1351 T. E

AND

FOR OTHER PURPOSES.

PRINTED AT THE STATE PRESS.
AGARTALA.
1351 T. E.

(Sd.) B. B. K. Manikya.

24. 1. 51. (T. E.).

A Charter for incorporating and conferring powers and granting privileges and concessions upon Hotel Khosmahal Limited, 1351 T. E. and for other purposes.

Captain His Highness Maharaja Sir Bir Bikram Kishore Deb Barman Manikya Bahadur, K. C. S. I., Maharaja of Tripura, in Bengal, by the grace of God Ruler of the Independent State of Tripura, to all to whom these presents shall come, greeting.

Whereas the opening and maintenance of a high class hotel in the town of Agartala is deemed necessary for the convenience and benefit of the public,

And Whereas His Highness the Maharaja Manikya Bahadur of Tripura has been graciously pleased to accord his consent to the running of such a hotel in the town of Agartala,

And Whereas the persons named in this Charter are willing to arrange for the running of such a Hotel and to construct and maintain buildings and collect things necessary for the purpose and it is expedient that they should form themselves into a Private Company with limited liability (hereinafter referred to in this Charter as the Company) with power to add to their number, total not exceeding fifty, by sale of shares in the manner as hereinafter mentioned and that necessary powers should be conferred on the Company for such purposes and for the purpose of acquiring lands, constructing buildings, collecting articles making contracts with local authorities, persons and companies and others and such other works as are necessary for the purpose of running a high class hotel in the town of Agartala and generally for the purpose of the objects and provisions of this Charter,

And Whereas it is expedient that all other powers mentioned in this Charter should be conferred on the Company and that necessary provision for the same should be made as are in this Charter contained,

And Whereas by the exercise of the Prerogative of His Highness the Maharaja Manikya Bahadur of Tripura it is lawful for His Highness the Maharaja Manikya Bahadur to grant this Charter under the seal of the Tripura Durbar to the Company for the purposes as aforesaid.

NOW KNOW YE that in pursuance of His gracious promise and by virtue of His prerogative, certain knowledge and mere motion Captain His Highness Maharaja Sir Bir Bikram Kishore Deb Barman Manikya Bahadur, K. C. S. I., Maharaja of Tripura, by these presents for Him, His heirs and successors does give, grant, make, ordain, constitute, declare and appoint and establish as follows :—

His Highness the Maharaja Manikya Bahadur of Tripura has been graciously pleased to declare and His Highness does so ordain in this Charter that until the Company incorporated herein is able to pay to its shareholders an amount of dividend equal to five per cent per annum on the paid up amount of share capital not exceeding Rupees Forty thousand only out of its net profits earned in any one year, such sums as would be necessary either for the payment of the whole of such dividend in such year, and of the balance of running expenditure, if any, in case the earning of the Company be not sufficient to meet the whole of such running expenditure in such year, or the balance to make up such dividend in such year would be guaranteed and paid by the State of Tripura out of the funds of the State of Tripura, subject only to this that such guarantee shall extend to a period of Twenty years certain from the date of first of Baisakh, 1349 T. E., and that the extent of the liability of the said State funds in respect of such guarantee shall only extend (in case the Company is unable to pay the same from its own earnings and profits) to the payment of the difference between the amount which the Company is able to pay out of its earnings after meeting all running expenditure (which expression "Running expenditure" shall mean and include the money required for repair and replacement of furniture, cutleries, crockeries, curtains, radio, gramophone with records, refriegerator, electric fittings, electric bulbs and fans, tablefans, electric charges, mosquito curtains, mattresses and other materials for beds and beddings, land revenue, Municipal and other charges, advertisement costs, lease for foreign liquor, remuneration and dress of the employees and all other establishment and such like other charges including stationery postage, telegrams printing etc.) and such dividend and the balance of running expenditure if any and of five percent due upon the said paid up share capital of the Company by way of annual dividend—

Provided that in order to get the benefit of this guaranteed dividend the Board of Directors of the Company shall prepare a budget of income and expenditure every year and submit a copy of the said budget to the Minister, Tripura State, but if any item of the budget is objected to by the Director nominated by the State of Tripura under section 31 of this Charter or by the representative of Nijtahabil Office nominated under section 51 of this Charter as a Director of the Company, then the matter relating to that particular item shall be placed before the *Mantri Parishad* of the State and the decision of the said

Parishad shall be final and conclusive as regards that particular item of the budget :

Provided also that on the completion of the nineteenth year from the date of 1st Baishakh, 1349 T. E., the State of Tripura shall have the option and shall be entitled after giving to the Company one Tripura Calendar year's notice of its intention to do so, to purchase the business, the buildings, assets, stock in trade and other materials for the purpose of the business then belonging to the Company at a price for only the buildings to be determined at the time of the expiry of the period of such notice, by an expert selected by the State of Tripura and the Company, and that the State of Tripura shall have to pay nothing in excess of the value of the buildings only at the time for the purchase of the entire properties of the Company including its good will :

Provided further that upon such exercise of the option to purchase as aforesaid by the State of Tripura the purchase price paid by the State as well as the Reserve fund, if any, of the Company at the time of the expiry of the period of such notice as aforesaid shall be distributed amongst the shareholders of the Company (including the State of Tripura if holding shares of the Company) at that time registered as such in the books of the Company in proportion to the paid up value of the shares held by them respectively.

And further His Highness the Maharaja Manikya Bahadur has been graciously pleased to ordain that the State of Tripura will have full power of supervision over the annual profit, expenditure and accounts of the Company incorporated herein, in the manner as herein contained and in the manner formulated and dictated by His Highness from time to time.

And further His Highness the Maharaja Manikya Bahadur has been pleased to ordain that the State of Tripura, shall forthwith purchase the fully paid up shares of the Company of the value equal to the amount of Nazar payable to the State by the Company for the settlement of land in permanent right for the above mentioned purpose of running a Hotel in lieu of the Cash money to be paid for Nazar, but in adjusting the same if it is found that after converting the dues to the State into fully paid up shares a balance falling short to cover one fully paid up share still remains to be settled, then such amount shall be paid by the Company in cash to the State of Tripura.

And for the purpose as above and of incorporation of the said Company and for proper working of the same as hereinbefore and hereinafter mentioned His Highness the Maharaja Manikya Bahadur of Tripura, ordains, grants, constitutes, declares, appoints and establishes this Charter in the terms as follows :—

1. This Charter shall be known and be cited as the Charter for the incorporation of Hotel Khosmahal Limited and the provisions contained herein shall come into operation with retrospective effect from 1st Baishakh, 1349 T. E.

2. The name of the Company shall be Hotel Khosmahal Limited.

3. The Registered Office of the Company shall be situated at Agartala in the State of Tripura, in Bengal.

4. The objects for which the Company is incorporated are :—

(a) To establish hotels, restaurants, manufactories and shops in Agartala or elsewhere as may be determined, and to erect, purchase or lease all necessary buildings for the purpose thereof ;

(b) To carry on the business of hotelkeepers, lodginghouse keepers, wine, beer and spirit merchants, sodawater and other aerated water dealers and manufacturers, bakers, confectioners, livery stable keepers, book-sellers, stationers, printers, provisioners, purveyors, hair-dressers, perfumers, drapers, outfitters, tailors, ice-suppliers and manufacturers, tobacco and cigar merchants and general dealers and any other business or businesses calculated to facilitate or further the general objects of the Company.

(c) To buy and sell goods, stores, consumable articles, chattels and effects, of all kinds both wholesale and retail.

(d) To carry on the business of restaurant proprietors and for that purpose to buy and sell comestibles, wine, spirits and beverages of all kinds.

(e) To manufacture, sell, deal and trade in all goods articles and things usually dealt in by provision dealers, oilmen, confectioners provisioners, warehousemen and the like.

(f) To purchase or otherwise acquire and undertake all or any of the business, property and liabilities of any person or Company carrying on any business which this Comany is authorised to carry on or possessed of property suitable for the purpose of this Company.

(g) To purchase, take on lease or in exchange, hire or otherwise acquire any moveable and immoveable property, easements, machinery, plants, stock in trade, and any patents and patents rights or privileges which the Company may think necessary and convenient for the purposes of its business.

(h) To develop and turn to account any land acquired by or in which the Company is interested, and in particular by laying out and preparing the same for building purposes, constructing, altering, pulling down, decorating, maintaining, fitting up and improving buildings and erections and by planting, paving, draining, farming, cultivating or letting on building lease or building agreement and by advancing money to and entering into contracts and arrangements of all kinds with builders, tenants or others.

(i) To sell the moveable and immoveable property of the Company, or any part thereof for such consideration as the Company may think fit and in particular for shares, debentures or securities of any other Company having objects altogether or in part similar to those of this Company.

(j) To distribute any of the property of the Company among the members in specie but so that no distribution amounting to a reduction in Capital be made without the sanction of the Tripura Durbar.

(k) To make, accept, endorse and execute promissory notes, bills of exchange and other negotiable instruments.

(l) To invest the moneys of the Company not immediately required upon such securities as may from time to time be determined.

(m) To lend money and in particular to customers of, and persons having dealings with, the Company.

(n) To raise money in such other manner as the Company shall think fit and by the issue of debentures charged upon all or any of the Company's property (both present and future) including its uncalled capital and to apply the same or any part thereof for all or any purpose of the Company.

(o) To establish and maintain circulating libraries, reading rooms, baths, lavatories, tennis courts, bowling alleys, pleasure grounds, billiard rooms, and other convenience for the recreation and use of the Company's customers.

(p) To establish agencies or branches for the purpose and sale of goods of all descriptions to the State of Tripura or elsewhere in India or foreign countries and to undertake the management of any company or companies having objects altogether or in part similar to those of this Company.

(q) To confirm or enter and execute all and every such contract or contracts, agreement or agreements, as shall or may be necessary or expedient for all or any of the purposes aforesaid.

(r) To make and carry into effect arrangements with respect to union of interests or amalgamation either in whole or in part, with any other company or person carrying on any business similar to that of this Company upon terms and conditions deemed just and suitable.

(s) And generally to do and perform all such other acts and things as may, in the opinion of the Directors of the Company for the time being, be incidental or conducive to the attainment of the above objects, or any of them.

5. (1) Maharajkumar Durjaya Kishore Deb Barman.

(2) Kumar Ramendra Kishore Deb Barman and all other persons, the total number of whom shall in no case exceed fifty, who have already subscribed and become proprietors in the undertaking and their executors, administrators and successors and assigns respectively shall be and are hereby united into a Company for the purposes hereinbefore and hereinafter mentioned and for those purposes shall be and are hereby incorporated as a private Company by the name of "Khosmahal Hotel Limited" hereinafter referred to as "the Company" and by that name shall be a body corporate with perpetual succession and a common seal and with power to purchase, take, hold and dispose

of land and other properties and any other undertaking for the purpose of this Charter and that of the other powers and privileges as a body corporate, provided that on the completion of nineteenth year from the date of 1st Baishakh, 1349 T. E. the State of Tripura shall be entitled after giving to the Company one Tripura Calendar year's notice of its intention to do so, to purchase the business, assets and stock of the Company including its goodwill and other materials then belonging to the Company at a price for only the buildings, to be determined at the time of the expiry of such notice by an expert selected by the then Minister of the State of Tripura and the Company, and the State of Tripura shall have to pay nothing in excess of the value of the buildings only at the time for the purchase of all entire moveable and immoveable properties of the Company, and the valuation made by such expert shall be accepted as final. Upon such exercise of the option to purchase as aforesaid by the State of Tripura the purchase price paid by the said State of Tripura as well as the Reserve fund of the Company at the time of expiry of such notice as aforesaid shall be distributed amongst the share-holders (including the State of Tripura) of the Company at that time registered in the books of the Company in proportion to the paid up value of the shares held by them respectively.

6. This Charter shall be in all things valid and effective in law according to the true intent and meaning of the same and shall be recognised as valid and effective by all courts and judges in the State of Tripura and in any part of British India or in Indian State or foreign countries or upon the high seas or elsewhere and to all other persons and bodies politic to whom it may concern and the same shall be taken, construed and judged in the most favourable and beneficial sense for and for the best advantage of the Company in the said courts or elsewhere notwithstanding any non-recital mis-recital, uncertainty or imperfection which may be found therein.

7. The Capital of the Company shall be Rupees Forty thousand only divided into Four hundred ordinary 5 per cent dividend guaranteed shares of Rs. 100/- each provided—

(i) that those Four hundred shares shall be divided amongst fifty members of the Company and in no case the number of members shall exceed fifty not including persons who are in the employment of the Company,

Provided that where two or more persons hold one or more shares in the Company jointly they shall, for the purpose of this clause, be considered as a single member.

(ii) that the shares of the Company shall not be transferred to a person, to a body corporate, or to a firm until and unless the proposed transferee is approved at a meeting by the majority of the members present. But this clause shall be no bar to a transfer to heirs, successors administrators and executors of a share-holder.

(iii) that the Company shall not be entitled to issue any invitation to the public to subscribe for shares or debentures by way of advertisement or otherwise.

8. The Company may with the permission of His Highness the Maharaja Manikya Bahadur of Tripura raise any further capital which it may from time to time think necessary by the creation and issue at its option, of new shares either ordinary or preference and either of one class with like privilege or several classes and with different privileges and of the same or different amount and respectively with any fixed, fluctuating, preference, terminable, deferred or other dividend or wholly or partly by one or more of these modes respectively provided always that the Company shall not issue any share of less nominal value than Rs. 100/- and the number of share-holders shall not exceed fifty as hereinbefore mentioned. In the case of new shares, the same shall not be disposed of to others before offering them in the first place to the existing shareholders at least in proportion to their existing holding.

9. The liability of the members of the Company shall be limited to the amount if any, for the time being, unpaid on the shares in the Company held by them respectively.

10. The Company shall keep at its registered office a register of the names of the share-holders and of their addresses and of the numbers of shares standing in their names and the amount paid up on such shares, and the entries in such a register shall be conclusive evidence of the facts contained therein.

11. Every person whose name is entered as a member in the register of members shall, without payment, be entitled to a certificate under the common seal of the Company specifying the share or shares held by him and the amount paid up thereon : Provided that in respect of a share or shares held jointly by several persons the Company shall not be bound to issue more than one certificate and delivery of a certificate for a share to one of several jointholders shall be sufficient delivery to all.

12. In case a share certificate is defaced, lost or destroyed, it may be renewed on payment of such fee and on such terms as to evidence and indemnity as the Directors think fit.

13. No part of the Funds of the Company shall be employed in the purchase of or in loans upon the security of the Company's shares.

14. The Company shall have first and paramount lien on every share for all moneys (whether presently payable or not) called or payable at a fixed time in respect of that share. The Company's lien, if any, on a share shall extend to all dividends payable thereon.

15. The Directors may from time to time make calls upon the members in respect of money unpaid on their shares, provided that no call shall exceed one-fourth of the nominal amount of the share, or

be payable at less than one month from the last call subject to receiving at least 14 days' notice specifying the time of payment.

16. If the amount is not paid accordingly the shares shall be liable to be forfeited at the option of the Directors.

17. The joint holders of a share shall be jointly and severally liable to pay all calls in respect thereof in the manner to be determined by them.

18. Subject to the provision hereinafter contained shares in the Company shall be transferable by written instrument in the form which the Director shall approve, executed both by the transferor and transferee and the transferor shall be deemed holder of the shares until the name of the transferee is entered in the register of members in respect thereof.

19. The Directors may in their absolute and uncontrolled discretion refuse to register any proposed transfer of shares without assigning any reason.

20. The heirs and executors or administrators of a deceased sole holder or joint-holder of a share shall be the only person recognised by the Company as having any title to the share.

21. Any person becoming entitled to a share in consequence of the death or insolvency of a member, shall upon such evidence being produced as may from time to time be required by the Directors, have the right, either to be registered as a member in respect of the share or instead of being registered himself to make such transfer of the share as the deceased or insolvency person could have made ; but the Directors shall, in either case, have the same right to decline or suspend registration as they would have had in the case of a transfer of the share by the deceased or insolvent person before the death or insolvency.

22. A person becoming entitled to a share by reason of the death or insolvency of the holder shall be entitled to the same dividends and other advantages to which he would be entitled if he were the registered holder of the share except that he shall not, before being registered as a member in respect of the share, be entitled in respect of it to exercise any right conferred by membership in relation to a meeting of the Company.

23. Except as hereinbefore provided no share in the Company shall be transferred to a non-member. Every member or a person becoming entitled to a share by reason of the death or insolvency of the holder thereof, who intends to sell his share shall notify his intention to do so to the Board and the Board shall sell those shares as his agent to any member at a price to be agreed upon, between the vendor and the intending purchaser and in default of agreement, at the market value of the shares to be fixed by the Board. In case the Board is unable to sell those shares within two months of the receipt of the notice, the vendor, after the expiry of two months, may sell the shares not sold as aforesaid to any person at any price, but subject to section 19 of

this Charter, provided that nothing in this section shall debar a shareholder from transferring his shares to a person who is already a member of the Company subject to section 19 of this Charter.

24. Save as herein otherwise provided, the Company shall not be bound by or recognise any equitable, contingent, future or partial interest in any share or any other right in respect of a share except an absolute interest of the person from time to time registered as the holder thereof.

25. The Statutory General meeting of the Company shall be held within a period of not less than one month nor more than six months from the date of the granting of this Charter in accordance with the provisions contained in the Indian Companies Act 1913 as amended in 1936 A. D.

26. The first general meeting of the Company shall be held within eighteen months from the date of granting of this Charter and thereafter once at least in every Tripura Calendar year and more than fifteen months after the holding of the last preceding general meeting at such place as may be prescribed by the Company in general meeting or in default as the Directors shall appoint.

27. The above-mentioned general meetings shall be called ordinary general meetings, all other general meetiegs shall be called extraordinary general meetings.

28. The Directors may whenever they think fit, call an extraordinary general meeting. An extraordinary general meeting shall also be called on such requisition, or in default, may be called by such requisitionists, as provided by section 78 of the Indian Companies Act.

29. At least fourteen days' notice in writing in the case of a general meeting for the passing of an ordinary or extraordinary resolution and at least twentyone clear days' notice in writing in the case of a general meeting for the passing of a special resolution specifying the time, place, the business to be transacted at the meeting and the intention to propose a resolution as an extraordinary or a special resolution as the case may be, shall be given in such manner as the Directors may from time to time prescribe, to all the registered members of the Company.

30. Two members personally present in the meeting shall form a quorum.

31. Unless a poll is demanded, a declaration by the Chairman that a resolution has been carried or carried unanimously or by a particular majority or lost and an entry to that effect in the book of the proceedings of the Company shall be conclusive evidence of the fact stated therein.

32. A poll shall be taken in such manner as the Chairman directs and the result of the poll shall be deemed to be the resolution of the meeting at which the poll is demanded.

33. On a show of hands every member present in person shall have one vote. On a poll every member shall have one vote in respect of each share held by him.

34. In the case of joint-holders, the vote of the senior who tenders a vote whether in person or by proxy shall be accepted to the exclusion of the votes of the other joint-holders: and for this purpose seniority shall be determined by the order in which the names stand in the register of members.

35. The number of the Directors shall not be less than two and not more than five, excluding the Director to be nominated by the State of Tripura as hereinafter mentioned.

36. (1) The State of Tripura shall nominate one Director on the Board who need not be a member of the Company and the rules relating to the rotation of Directors shall not be applicable to him.

(2) His Highness's Nijtahabil will also nominate one Director on the Board who need not be a member of the Company and the rules relating to the rotation of Directors shall not be applicable to him.

37. At every annual general meeting all the Directors except those nominated by the State and His Highness' Nijtahabil shall retire. A retiring Director shall be eligible for re-election.

38. The remuneration of the Directors shall be determined in the General meeting from time to time and in the absence of any such provision the decision of the Directors will be final.

(a) The first directors of the Company shall be :—

1. Manyabara Raja Rana Bodhjung Bahadur,
2. Maharajkumar Karnakishore Deb Barman Bahadur,
3. Maharajkumar Durjaya Kishore Deb Barman Bahadur,
4. (nominated by His Highness' Nijtahabil)
5. (nominated by the State of Tripura).

(b) Unless otherwise fixed by the general meeting the remuneration of each of the first Directors shall be Rs. 5/- five for attending every Directors' meeting exclusive of the travelling expenses to be paid by the Company to attend such meeting.

(c) The Office of Director shall be vacated for the reasons mentioned in article 77, Table A, of the Indian Companies Act.

39. Subject to the supervision and control of the Board of Directors, the business of the Company shall be carried on by a Managing Director or a body of Managing Directors or Managing Agents or a Manager. Maharajkumar Durjaya Kishore Deb Barman Bahadur shall hold the office of the first Managing Director with effect

from the 1st of Baishakh, 1349 T. E. and he shall continue to be in the office as aforesaid

(i) Unless :—

(a) He voluntarily resigns the same in writing

or (b) He becomes insolvent or bankrupt or he dies,

or (c) He is found lunatic or of unsound mind.

or (d He ceases to hold the required amount of shares qualifying him for Directorship.

or (e) He is concerned in or participates in the profits of any contract with the Company by using his position as Director of the Company. (But this clause shall not apply if he be a member of such companies which have entered into contract with this Company or which are concerned in or participate in the profits of any contract with this Company).

or (ii) Until :—

(a) Any defalcation of the Company's funds is proved against him.

or (b) He shall be removed therefrom by an extraordinary resolution supported by such share-holders of the Company as represent at least three-fourths of the issued Capital of the Company at a General Meeting to be convened for the express purpose and of which twelve Calendar months' notice shall be given to each share-holder at his address on the Register of the Company.

40. The Managing Director shall have power to sign and give all receipts, release and other discharges for money payable to the Company and shall have such other powers as may from time to time be delegated to him by the Directors or may otherwise be vested in him by the regulations of the Company for the time being.

41. The remuneration of the first Managing Director shall be Rs. 50/- (fifty) per month with effect from the 1st Baisakh 1349 T. E. But this remuneration may be increased from time to time by the share holders in General Meetings.

42. The Directors shall cause to be kept proper books of account with respect to :—

(a) all sums of money received and expended by the Company and the matters in respect of which the receipts and expenditure take place.

(b) all sales and purchases of goods by the Company.

(c) the assets and liabilities of the Company.

43. The Directors shall cause to be prepared and to be laid before the Campany in General Meeting profit and loss accounts, balance sheets and reports, as required by law or by the State of Tripura, made up

to a date not more than six months before such meeting. The amount recommended to be paid by way of dividend and the amount if any, proposed to be carried to a reserve fund shall be mentioned in the said report.

44. The profit and loss account shall inter alia show, arranged under the most convenient heads, the amount of gross income, distinguishing the several sources from which it has been derived and the amount of gross expenditure distinguishing the expenses of the establishment, salaries and other like matters. Every item of expenditure fairly chargeable against the year's income shall be brought into account so that a just balance of profit and loss may be laid before the meeting and in cases where any item of expenditure which may in fairness be distributed over several years has been incurred in any one year, the whole amount of such shall be stated, with the addition of the reasons why only a portion of such expenditure is charged against the income of the year.

45. Once at least in every year, the accounts of the Company shall be audited and the correctness of the balance sheet and the profit and loss accounts ascertained and certified by an auditor to be nominated by the Minister of Tripura State, who shall regulate the appointment, rights and duties of the auditor as well as his remuneration which shall be paid out of the funds of the Company. The auditor thus appointed by the Minister shall be deemed to have been vested with powers and duties as mentioned in section 145 of the Indian Companies Act 1913, as amended by Act XXII of 1936 A. D.

46. A notice may be given by the Company to any member either personally or by sending it by post to him to his registered address.

47. Where a notice is sent by post, service of the notice shall be deemed to be effected by properly addressing, prepaying and posting a letter containing the notice and unless the contrary is proved, to have been effected at the time at which the letter would be delivered in the ordinary course of post.

48. A notice may be given by the Company to the joint-holders of a share by giving the notice to the joint-holder named first in the register in respect of the share.

49. A notice may be given by the Company to the persons entitled to a share in consequence of the death or insolvency of a member by sending it through the post in a prepaid letter addressed to them by name or by title of the representatives of the deceased, or assignee of the insolvent or by any like description at the address (if any) in India supplied for the purpose by the persons claiming to be so entitled or by giving the notice in any manner in which the same might have been given if the death or insolvency had not occurred.

50. Notice of every general meeting shall be given in the manner hereinbefore mentioned to every member of the Company except those

members who have not supplied to the Company an address within India for the giving of notices to them and also to every person entitled to a share in consequence of the death or insolvency of a member, who but for his death or insolvency would be entitled to receive notice of the meeting. Notice of all meetings shall be given in due time to the Directors nominated by the State of Tripura, and His Highness' Nijtahabil, who shall have the right and power of giving votes and shall be deemed members of the Company so far as the proceedings of the meeting are concerned. No other persons shall be entitled to receive notices of general meetings.

51. Any person whom His Highness the Maharaja Manikya Bahadur of Tripura may have the pleasure to nominate to represent Nijtahabil Office shall be entitled to vote according to the provision contained in this Charter in relation to the shares held by the said Office and shall be eligible to be elected a Director and shall exercise all the powers and rights of a share-holder as mentioned in this Charter. The nomination shall be in writing and kept at the registered office of the Company. The nomination may be revoked at any time or from time to time and any other person nominated in the place of the former shall be taken as his substitute with all the powers and rights as stated above, from the date of such nomination.

52. The business of the Company shall be managed by the Directors, who may pay all expenses incurred in getting up and incorporating the Company and may exercise all such powers of the Company as are not, by the Indian Companies Act or any statutory modifications thereof for the time being in force, or by the provisions contained in this Charter, required to be exercised by the Company in general meeting, subject nevertheless to any regulation of this Charter, to the provisions of the said Act and to such regulation being not inconsistent with the aforesaid regulation and provision as may be prescribed by the Company in general meeting ; but no regulation made by the Company in general meeting shall invalidate any prior act of the Directors which would have been valid if that regulation had not been made.

53. Without prejudice to the general powers conferred by section 52 supra and the other powers conferred by this Charter elsewhere, the Directors shall have power to borrow from time to time and secure payment of any sum or sums of money as may be required for the purpose of the Company.

54. The Directors may secure the repayment of such moneys, upon such terms and conditions, as they think fit, in particular by mortgaging, charging, hypothecating, or pledging any lands, buildings, machinery, goods, securities, investments or other property of the Company or by such means as the Directors deem expedient, subject only to this that in so doing with regard to the buildings and the lands on which they stand the previous sanction of the State of Tripura shall be necessary.

55. The amount for the time being remaining undischarged of moneys borrowed or raised by the Directors for the purposes of the

Company (otherwise than by the issue of share capital) shall not at any time exceed the issued share capital of the Company without the sanction of the Company in general meeting.

56. The Directors shall submit a true copy of the bond of all sorts of mortgages and charges affecting the property of the Company within 21 days from the date of execution or registration thereof, whichever date is later, to the Minister, Tripura State, or to any other officer specially empowered by the Minister or by law for the time being in force.

57. The Directors shall keep a Register of the Directors and shall submit an annual list of members and a summary of particulars relating thereto and notice of any alteration of share-capital or conversion of shares into stock and copies of special resolution and a copy of the Register of Directors and notifications of any changes therein, to the Minister, Tripura State, or to any other officer specially empowered by the Minister or by any law for the time being in force.

58. The Directors shall cause minutes to be kept in books provided for the purpose :—

(a) of all appointments of officers made by the Directors.

(b) of the name of the Directors present at each meeting of the Directors and of any committee of the Directors.

(c) of all resolutions and proceedings of all meetings of the Company and of the Directors and of committees of Directors ; every Director present at any meeting of Directors or committee of Directors shall sign his name in a book to be kept for the purpose.

59. The Company may from time to time in general meeting increase or reduce the number of Directors and may also determine in what rotation the increased or reduced number is to go out of office.

60. Any casual vacancy occurring in the Board of Directors, may be filled up by the Directors, but the person so chosen shall be subject to retirement at the same time as if he had become a Director on the day on which the Director in whose place he is appointed was last elected a Director.

61. The Company may by an extraordinary resolution remove any Director before the expiration of his period of office, except the Directors nominated by the State of Tripura and His Highness' Nijtahabil Office and may, by an ordinary resolution, appoint another person in his stead ; the person so appointed shall be subject to retirement at the same time as if he had become a Director on the day on which the Director in whose place he is appointed was last elected a Director.

62. The Directors may meet together for the despatch of business, adjourn and otherwise regulate their meetings, as they think fit. Questions arising at any meeting shall be decided by a majority of votes. In case of an equality of votes, the Chairman shall have a second or casting vote. A Director may, and the Secretary or the

Officer-in-charge of the office shall, on the requisition of a Director, at any time, summon a meeting of Directors.

63. The quorum necessary for the transaction of the business of the Directors may be fixed by the Directors and unless so fixed shall be three including the Director nominated by the State of Tripura, provided that no business can be done in any meeting at which either the Director nominated by the State or the Director nominated from Nijtahabil office is not present ; but this provision will not apply to any adjourned meeting.

64. The continuing Directors may act notwithstanding any vacancy in their body, but if and so long as their number is reduced below the number fixed by or pursuant to the regulations of this Charter as the necessary quorum of Directors, the continuing Directors may act for the purpose of increasing the number of Directors to that number or of summoning a general meeting of the Company, but for no other purpose.

65. The Directors may delegate any of their powers to committees consisting of such member or members of their body as they think fit.

66. All acts done by any meeting of the Directors or of a committee of Directors or by any person acting as a Director shall notwithstanding that it be afterwards discovered that there was some defect in the appointment of any such Directors or persons acting as aforesaid, or that they or any of them were disqualified, be as valid as if every such person had been duly appointed and was qualified to be a Director.

67. A resolution in writing signed by all the Directors shall be as valid and effectual as if it had been passed at a meeting of the Directors duly called and constituted.

68. The books of account shall be kept at the registered office of the Company or at such other place as the Directors shall think fit and shall be open to inspection by the Directors during business hours.

69. The Directors shall from time to time determine whether and to what extent and at what times and places and under what conditions or regulations the accounts and books of the Company or any of them shall be open to the inspection of members not being Directors ; no member (not being a Director) shall have any right of inspecting any account or books or document of the Company except as conferred by law or authorised by the Directors or by the Company in general meeting.

70. Preliminary expenses are estimated to be Rs. 1000/— only.

71. The financial year of the Company shall be counted from 1st Baishakh to the end of Chaitra according to Tripura Era.

72. The Company shall take settlement of land from the State of Tripura for the purpose of erecting buildings, houses, sheds,

godowns, stalls, out-houses, and making gardens, parks, paths, lanes, bye-lanes, drains, tanks, appurtenant to the hotel, on terms and conditions to be settled between the Company and the State of Tripura. If the requisite land is in the possession and ownership of any person other than the State of Tripura, then the Company shall make a declaration in writing to the Minister, specifying the land which it desires to acquire and the purposes to which such land will be put and if it shall appear to the Minister that such land is necessary for the purpose of its business, he shall make necessary arrangements for the acquisition of such land and shall settle the land with the Company on such terms and conditions as deemed fit.

73. The State of Tripura shall have the option to purchase fully paid up shares of the Company of the value equal or approximate to the amount of ***Nazar*** payable to the State by the Company for the settlement of land as hereinbefore mentioned in lieu of the amount of ***Nazar*** to be paid in cash.

74. Any infringement, violation or contravention of the mandates, rules, regulations, and provisions contained in this Charter, in the shape of act or omission thereof shall be deemed as an offence triable by a first class Magistrate and every person found responsible for the said infringement, violation or contravention shall, without prejudice to any other liability, be liable to a fine not exceeding one thousand rupees, or a fine not exceeding Rs. 50/— for every day during which the said infringement, violation or contravention continues, and in default, to imprisonment of either description as the Court thinks fit for a period of three months.

75. The Company shall furnish every member with copies of the profit and loss account or the income and expenditure account, balance sheet and the auditors' report on payment of a charge to be determined by the Directors.

76. The affairs of the Company may be wound up either (a) compulsorily or (b) voluntarily or (c) voluntarily under the supervision of the High Court of Tripura.

77. In the case of winding up the provisions similar to those in the Indian Companies Act VII of 1913 as amended by Act XXII of 1936, or any subsequent statutory modification thereof on the part of the Government of India or rules as near thereto as there can be, shall apply subject to this modification that the High Court referred to therein will mean the High Court of the State of Tripura in its original special jurisdiction and the Registrar of Joint Stock Company shall mean the Minister of State of Tripura or any other officer of the State specially empowered in this behalf.

78. If the affairs of the Company be wound up compulsorily a liquidator shall be appointed for the purpose and the liquidator so appointed shall be known by the name of State Liquidator. The person appointed under clause (b) and (c) section 75 supra as liquidator for

winding up of the affairs of the Company shall be known by the name of "Voluntary Liquidator" or "Voluntary Liquidator under supervision" respectively. The powers of the Liquidators as above will be the same as that of the Liquidators respectively under the provisions of the Indian Companies Act and the said modification thereof.

79. If the affairs of the Company be wound up and the assets available for distribution among the members as such be insufficient to repay the whole of the paid up capital, such assets shall be distributed so that as nearly as may be the losses shall be borne by the members in proportion to the capital paid up, or which ought to have been paid up at the commencement of the winding up, on the shares held by them respectively, and if in the winding up the assets available for distribution among the members shall be more than sufficient to repay the whole of the capital paid up at the commencement of the winding up, the excess shall be distributed among the members in proportion to the capital at the commencement of the winding up, or which ought to have been paid up on shares held by them respectively.

80. In case of disposal of assets at the time of the winding up His Highness the Maharaja Manikya Bahadur of Tripura will have the first option of refusal, and in case the State of Tripura chooses to purchase, the same will be purchased at a fair valuation to be determined by a representative duly appointed on behalf of the Company, and by the then Minister of the State of Tripura, and upon there arising any difference of opinion between them, by a special umpire nominated by His Highness the Maharaja Manikya Bahadur of Tripura, whose valuation shall be accepted as final, and upon such exercise of the option to purchase as aforesaid by the State of Tripura the purchase price paid by the said State of Tripura as well as the Reserve fund, if any, of the Company shall be distributed amongst the share-holders at that time registered in the books of the Company in the manner hereinbefore mentioned.

81. Every Director, Managing Director, Manager, Secretary, Auditor and other officers or servant of the Company shall be idemnified by the Company against all losses and damages incurred by them, and it shall be the duty of the liquidator out of the funds of the Company to pay all costs, losses, and expenses which any such Director, Managing Director, Manager, Secretary, Auditor and officer or servant of the Company may incur and become liable to by reason of any contract entered into or act or deed done by him as such Director, Managing Director, Manager, Secretary, Auditor, officer or servant or in any way in the discharge of his duties, including travelling expenses, and the amount for which such idemnity is provided shall immediately attach as a lien on the property of the Company, and have priority as between the members over all other claims.

82. No Director, Managing Director, Secretary, Auditor or other officer or servant of the Company shall be liable for the acts, receipts, neglects or defaults of any other Director or officer or for joining in any

receipt or other act for conformity or for any loss or expense happening to the Company through the insufficiency or deficiency of title to any property acquired by order of the Directors for or on behalf of the Company, or for the insufficiency or deficiency of any security in or upon which any of the moneys of the Company shall be invested, or for any loss or damage arising from the bankruptcy, insolvency or tortious act of any person with whom any money, securities or effects shall be deposited, or for any loss occasioned by any error of judgement or oversight on his part, or for any other loss, damage or misfortune whatever which shall happen in execution of the duties of his office or in relation thereto unless the same happen through his own dishonesty.

83. No member shall be entitled to visit or inspect the Company's properties, stores or belongings without the previous permission of the Board of Directors or the Managing Director or require discovery of any information respecting any detail of the Company's trading, or any matter which is or may be in the nature of trade secret process which may relate to the conduct of business of the Company and which in the opinion of the Board or Managing Director, will be inexpedient in the interest of the members of the Company to communicate to the public.

84. In all other matters relating to the business of the Company for which any provisions similar to those contained in the Indian Companies Act 1913 as amended by Act XXII of 1936 have not been made all the provisions similar to those contained in the said Act and applicable to a Private Company, which are not inconsistent with the provisions of this Charter will apply.

85. In case of an interpellation in any General Meetings as to any subjects at least three days' notice will be given for preparation.

86. In this Charter the word "Minister" or the words "Minister, Tripura State" shall denote the "Minister of Commerce and Industry" for the time being, and the words "Tripura State" or "State of Tripura" shall mean the "Council of Ministers" known as "*Mantri Parishad.*"

Letter from His Highness Maharaja Manikya Sir Bir Bikram Kishore Deb Barman Bahadur, K. C. S. I., Maharaja of Tripura, to the Agent to the Governor-General, Eastern States, Ranchi, dated the 29th March 1937, on the subject of accession of Tripura State to the Federation of India.

TRIPURA STATE.

FROM

HIS HIGHNESS MAHARAJA MANIKYA
SIR BIR BIKRAM KISHORE DEB BARMAN
BAHADUR, K. C. S. I.,
MAHARAJA OF TRIPURA.

To

THE AGENT TO THE GOVERNOR-GENERAL,
EASTERN STATES,
RANCHI.

No. 4637–P/XVII–1

Dated, Agartala, the 29th March, 1937

SUBJECT :—Accession of Tripura State to the Federation of India.

MY ESTEEMED FRIEND,

With reference to Political Agent Mr. Ray's letter No. 1244 P/111–48 dated the 18th/19th August, 1936, to my Minister, on the subject of accession to the Federation, I have the honour to state that on a consideration of all the facts and circumstances relating to the new constitution for India as embodied in the Government of India Act, 1935, I have come to the conclusion that Tripura State may accede to the proposed Federation of India subject, however, to the safeguards and limitations indicated in this letter and its annexures.

2. I desire to express my grateful appreciation of the sympathetic assistance and advice which I received from His Excellency the Viceroy's Special Representative in the examination of the problems connected with the question of accession of my State to the Federation. Difficulty was, however, experienced in regard to the interpretation of points upon which admittedly no authoritative views of the Government of India could be given. Moreover, as a matter of normal procedure, no Court of law is likely to admit evidence of any common understanding between a State and the Government of India in regard to any point,

though the accession of the State to the Federation may be founded upon such understanding. It is therefore desirable that a serious effort should be made to explore the possibility of adopting some legal expedient for putting on record, and making available for the assistance of the Courts, the intentions of the parties and the agreed understandings between them.

3. It will be observed that the draft standard form of the Instrument of Accession which was forwarded under cover of the letter referred to above, has been modified by me in certain particulars to represent the amended form in which I should prefer to execute the Instrument. Perhaps it is not necessary for me to explain the points of difference between the draft Instrument forwarded by the Political Agent and the amended form in which I am enclosing it herewith, as these points have already formed the subject of discussion between representatives of the Government and those of different Indian States.

4. As regards the Schedules to the Instrument, the most important is the one dealing with the Federal Legislative List. After giving my best consideration to the matter, I have suggested necessary limitations upon the scope of certain items of that list which I am prepared to accept as Federal Legislative subjects. Those items of the Federal Legislative List that do not find mention in the Schedule annexed to the revised draft Instrument, are not acceptable to me, until at least I am convinced of the necessity of accepting them after due consideration of any suggestions that may be forthcoming hereafter in the course of further negotiations in this matter.

5. In this connection, I would particularly refer to item No. 36 of the Federal Legislative List which I am unable to accept. I am advised that acceptance of this item would enable the Federation to regulate and control the whole subject of mining and oilfields in the State. Laws might be passed laying down how mines and oilfields should be exploited and by whom, and such matters as prospecting licenses could also be brought under Federal control. I am, therefore, not prepared to hand over such wide and undefined powers to the Federation. Tripura State has considerable mineral resources not yet developed, and I feel sure you will appreciate my inability to accept this item which may prove a serious handicap in the way of economic exploitation of our mineral resources. I am definitely of opinion that a restrictive policy which may at any time be justified on the conditions prevailing in British India, where mineral development has perhaps

reached its maximum capacity in certain respects, may prove altogether unsuitable and harmful to this State. It is true that restrictive legislation under item 36 will be passed only when Federal control is declared by the Legislature to be expedient in the public interest ; but if a line of action is found to be justified in the case of British India, a declaration like this may be made by the Federal Legislature in spite of the opposition of the States' representatives who will, after all, form a minority.

6. Besides indicating my views in connection with the draft Instrument of Accession and the Federal Legislative List in the annexures to this letter, I desire to make a few observations for consideration in connection with the question of accession of my State to the Federation.

7. Having regard to the complicated character of the problems involved in the Federal scheme, it is not possible for any individual Ruler to deal exhaustively with all the points of importance that present themselves. I would, therefore, request that any further amendments of the draft Instrument or limitations in connection with the Federal Legislative List as may be found acceptable to the Government in the case of the Indian States generally, should be made applicable to my State as well. Moreover, should action be taken as a result of representations made by any other State in regard to the general financial aspects of the Federal scheme, the benefit of such action should be extended to my State. I trust that there will be no discrimination against Tripura as regards the general terms on which accession of the States to Federation may be permitted.

8. Opinion is not unanimous as to whether the reference to 'extradition' in item No. 3 of the Federal Legislative List will include extradition between a British Indian unit of the Federation and a Federated State, as also interstatal extradition. It is held by some that inter-unit extradition is included within the scope of item No. 3 of the Concurrent Legislative List, which forms part of the Seventh Schedule to the Government of India Act. If this view prevails with the authorities, I shall have to consider whether or not I shall accept this item of the Concurrent Legislative List as a Federal subject, later on. For the present I accept item 3 of the Federal Legislative List No. I without any limitation, on the assumption that it does not include extradition to or from the State from or to other parts of India.

9. The State will not be acceding for income-tax under item 54 of the Federal Legislative List, but will be subject to the power given by Section 138 (3) of the Government of India Act, 1935, to the Federal Government to levy a contribution corresponding to a surcharge, upon the State. Sub-section (3) of Section 138 will, therefore, have to be accepted in the Instrument of Accession, and a provision may be inserted in the First Schedule to the Instrument, somewhat on the following lines :—

"I accept the following matter, namely :—

Provision for the payment by the State of a contribution to the revenues of the Federation in the circumstances and assessed on the basis mentioned in sub-section (3) of Section 138 of the said Act :

subject to the following limitations :

1. The Federal Legislature shall not have power to make laws for the payment by the State of any such contribution unless the rate of the corresponding surcharge for Federal purposes imposed by the Federal Legislature under Section 138 of the Act exceeds......*annas in the rupee.

2. For the purpose of assessing the contribution of the State the net proceeds which would result from the levying of the said surcharge in the State (to which net proceeds the said contribution is to be equivalent) shall be determined on the footing that—

(a) All income of the Ruler of this State and members of his family and property occupied by them, shall be deemed to be exempt from the said surcharge ;

(b) The rate at which the said surcharge is deemed to be levied in the State shall be less, by......*annas in the rupee than the rate at which such surcharge is actually levied in British India :

and accordingly the Federal Legislature shall not have power to make laws for the State providing for the payment of a contribution by the State unless such contribution is assessed in the aforesaid manner."

10. Although legislative jurisdiction of the Federation will be operative within my State to the extent that I accept the items in the Federal Legislative List, I am anxious that there should be the least direct interposition of the executive authority of the Federation for the purpose of carrying on, in my territory, the administration of the subjects covered by those items. I need hardly emphasise the

* NOTE—The rate to be inserted will be the rate of the 1931 surcharges in force at the latest convenient date before Federation commences.

importance that I attach to this condition. It is to my mind essential that accession of my State to Federation should not lessen or curtail the authority of the State administration in the eyes of the people, even in respect of the matters which are accepted by me as Federal subjects. There are two alternative methods that have been laid down in the Government of India Act for entrusting the executive administration of Federal Legislative measures to the authorities of a Federated State. The draft standard form of the Instrument of Accession as forwarded by the Political Agent contemplates the insertion of certain additional clauses in suitable cases for the execution of an agreement for the purpose of entrusting administration of the accepted subjects to a State as a condition of its accession to Federation. This procedure is based upon Section 125 of the Government of India Act ; whereas the other alternative provision is contained in Section 124 under which it will be optional for the Federal authorities to entrust the administration of any particular subject to the agency of a State. I have had the advantage of knowing from His Excellency the Viceroy's Representative, the Government point of view in this matter. While fully appreciating the arguments for discrimination as to whether particular subjects should be entrusted to the agency of a State administration under either of these two Sections of the Act, I would strongly urge that if such discrimination is inevitable it should be made only in consideration of the character of the different subjects for administration, and not as a matter of differential treatment of individual States. It is understood that whenever Federal functions may have to be entrusted to a Provincial Government for purposes of administration, action will be taken under Section 124. In so far as functions in respect of any such subject may not be entrusted to Tripura by virtue of an agreement under Section 125, it is essential that this State should be placed precisely in the same position as any Provincial unit for purposes of carrying out agency functions on behalf of the Federal Government. The standard of efficiency which we aim at in the administration of this State will, I venture to think, fully justify the same measures of power and authority being entrusted to us as in the case of any Provincial Government in our neighbourhood, in respect of Federal functions to be delegated under Section 124. I should like to add that I consider it imperative that local administration of the laws of the Federal Legislature under the following items of the Federal Legislative List should be entrusted to my State, namely :—

Items 3, 15, 16, 17, 24, 26, 27, 29, 30, 32, 33, 34, 35, 42, 43, 45, 46 and 59.

11. As to recognition by His Majesty of a Court in an Indian State as a High Court under Section 217 of the Government of India Act, I venture to hope that the High Court of this State will receive such recognition for purposes of all the provisions of the Act, in which reference is made to a High Court in a Federated State.

12. As regards the rights and privileges of a State and its Ruler, a difference of opinion exists as to the procedure for safeguarding them. These rights and privileges may be classified under two different heads : (1) rights and privileges relating to the items in the Federal Legislative List which are accepted by the State as Federal subjects ; and (2) rights and privileges relating to matters outside that category. As regards the first class of these rights, it is felt that they should be included in the Instrument of Accession, in such a manner as to bring them within the purview of the jurisdiction of the Federal Court. In this view of the matter, a proposal has been made that this class of rights should be enumerated in a Schedule to the Instrument of Accession itself and referred to in a specific clause of the Instrument. As regards the rights belonging to the second class mentioned above, the protection afforded by Sections 12 (1) (g) and 52 (f) of the Government of India Act may be sufficient, and they may therefore be enumerated in a list which may be referred to by the Governor-General or the Governor of a Province, as the case may be, for the purpose of taking action under those sections. I am enclosing an illustrative list of both these classes of rights leaving it to the authorities to decide how best to safeguard them in the light of representations made by the different States. The lists cannot claim to be exhaustive ; and it is earnestly hoped that a further opportunity will be available for revising and, if necessary, enlarging them.

13. While on this subject, I should like to point out that there are certain rights and privileges which may not have been enjoyed by all the States and Rulers alike, though there does not appear to be any valid justification for any invidious distinction being made between State and State in those matters. It may be that in certain instances a State has not sufficiently pressed its claims but the door is not definitely closed against a reconsideration of such matters under present circumstances. It is to be hoped that Federation will not stereotype inequalities of this kind, but that before accession of the States takes place, the Government will review the whole situation in the light of present day circumstances and the implications of future constitutional changes. Should such a course be followed by the authorities some of the

discriminatory privileges may possibly be extended to a State like Tripura. Apart from cases of deliberate differentiation, there may be instances in which certain rights were not extended to this State merely as a result of oversight on the part of the authorities, or omission on the part of the State itself to bring to the notice of the authorities the necessity of the extension of the privileges conceded to others. I desire to add that I may have occasion to make a further representation on this point.

YOUR SINCERE FRIEND,

(Sd.) B. B. K. Manikya,

MAHARAJA OF TRIPURA.

Annexures

1. Revised draft of the standard form of the Instrument of Accession.
2. First Schedule to the Instrument of Accession.
3. Illustrative List of Rights and Privileges.

Instrument of Accession of His Highness Maharaja Manikya Sir Bir Bikram Kishore Deb Barman Bahadur, K. C. S. I., Maharaja of Tripura.

WHEREAS proposals for the establishment of a Federation of India comprising such Indian States as may accede thereto and the Provinces of British India constituted as autonomous Provinces have been discussed between representatives of His Majesty's Government, of the Parliament of the United Kingdom, of the Rulers of the Indian States, and of British India ;

AND WHEREAS those proposals contemplated that the Federation of India should be constituted by an Act of the Parliament of the United Kingdom and by the accession of Indian States ;

AND WHEREAS provision for the constitution of a Federation of India under the Crown consisting of the Indian States, the Provinces called Governors' Provinces, and the Provinces called Chief Commissioners' Provinces, has now been made in the Government of India Act, 1935, but it is by that Act provided that the Federation shall not be established until such date as His Majesty may by Proclamation declare and such declaration cannot be made until the requisite number of Indian States have acceded to the Federation ;

AND WHEREAS the said Act cannot apply to any of my territories save by virtue of my consent and concurrence signified by my accession to the Federation ;

NOW THEREFORE,

I, Maharaja Manikya Sir Bir Bikram Kishore Deb Barman Bahadur, Maharaja of Tripura,

In the exercise of my sovereignty in and over my said State,

DO hereby execute this my INSTRUMENT OF ACCESSION

and

1. I HEREBY DECLARE that subject to His Majesty's acceptance of this Instrument, I accede to the Federation of India as established under the Government of India Act, 1935, (hereinafter referred to as "the Act") with the intent that His Majesty the King, the Governor-General of India, the Federal Legislature, the Federal Court and any other Federal Authority established for the purposes of the Federation shall, by virtue of this my Instrument of Accession, but subject always

to the terms thereof, and for the purposes only of the Federation, exercise in relation to the State of Tripura (hereinafter referred to as "this State") such functions as may be vested in them by or under the Act.

2. **I HEREBY ASSUME** the obligation of ensuring that due effect is given to the provisions of the Act within this State so far as they are applicable therein by virtue of this my Instrument of Accession.

3. **NOTHING IN THIS INSTRUMENT** shall affect the rights and obligations of the Ruler of this State in relation to the Crown with respect to any matters not within the functions exercisable by, or on behalf of the Federation by virtue of this Instrument and no Federal Authority shall have jurisdiction with respect to such rights and obligations.

4. **NO FUNCTION** in respect of any matters specified in the First Schedule hereto or under any provision ofthe Act which applies to this State by virtue of this Instrument of Accession shall be exercised in relation to this State by any authority other than a Federal Authority and save in accordance with the terms of this Instrument.

5. **I ACCEPT** the matters specified in the First Schedule hereto as the matters with respect to which the Federal Legislature may make laws for this State, and in this Instrument and in the said First Schedule I specify the limitations to which the power of the Federal Legislature to make laws for this State, and the exercise of the executive authority of the Federation in this State, are respectively to be subject.

Where under the First Schedule hereto the power of the Federal Legislature to make laws for this State with respect to any matter specified in that Schedule is subject to a limitation, the executive authority of the Federation shall not be exercisable in this State with respect to that matter otherwise than in accordance with and subject to that limitation.

The Federal Legislature shall not have power to make laws for this State save with respect to matters so specified and subject to such limitations.

6. **THE** particulars to enable due effect to be given to the provisions of Sections 147 and 149 of the Act are set forth in the second Schedule hereto.

7. **REFERENCES** in this Instrument to laws of the Federal Legislature include references to Ordinances promulgated, Acts enacted and laws made by the Governor-General of India under Sections 42 to 45 of the Act inclusive.

8. **NOTHING IN THIS INSTRUMENT** affects the continuance of my sovereignty in and over this State or, save as provided by the Instrument or by any law of the Federal Legislature made in accordance

therewith, the continuance of any of my powers, authority and rights, and the exercise of any of such powers, authority and rights in and over this State is, save as above, reserved to me.

9. NOTHING in this Instrument shall be construed as authorising Parliament to legislate for or exercise jurisdiction over this State or its Ruler in any respect.

Provided that the accession of this State to the Federation shall not be affected by any amendment of the provision of the Act mentioned in the Second Schedule thereto, and the references in this Instrument to the Act shall be construed as references to the Act as amended by any such amendment; but no such amendment shall, unless it is accepted by the Ruler of this State in an Instrument supplementary to this Instrument, extend the functions which by virtue of this Instrument are exercisable by His Majesty or any Federal Authority in relation to this State.

10. WHEREAS I am desirous that functions in relation to the administration in this State of laws of the Federal Legislature which apply therein shall be exercised by the Ruler of this State and his officers, and the terms of an agreement in that behalf have been mutually agreed between me and the Governor General of India and are set out in the Schedule hereto.

NOW THEREFORE I hereby declare that I accede to the Federation with the assurance that the said agreement will be executed and the said agreement when executed shall be deemed to form part of this Instrument and shall be construed and have effect accordingly.

11. THE Schedules hereto annexed shall form an integral part of this Instrument.

12. THE provisions contained in Part VI of the Act with respect to interference with water supplies, being Sections 130 to 133 thereof inclusive, are not to apply in relation to this State.

13. THIS INSTRUMENT shall be binding on me as from the date on which His Majesty signifies his acceptance thereof, provided that if the Federation of India is not established before the day of Nineteen Hundred and , this Instrument shall, on that day, become null and void for all purposes whatsoever.

14. I HEREBY DECLARE that I execute this Instrument for myself, my heirs and successors, and that accordingly any reference in this Instrument to me or to the Ruler of this State is to be construed as including a reference to my heirs and successors.

THIS INSTRUMENT OF ACCESSION (then follows the attestation to be drawn with all due formality appropriate to the declaration of a Ruler).

FIRST SCHEDULE TO THE INSTRUMENT OF ACCESSION.

Items of the Federal Legislative list which His Highness The Maharaja Manikya Bahadur of Tripura is prepared to accept, and the limitations subject to which he is prepared to accept them.

The power of the Federal Legislature shall be subject to the following general limitations as well as to the specific limitations in respect of the items hereinbelow specified.

GENERAL LIMITATIONS.

(a) The Federal Legislature shall not levy or impose any tax or duty in or upon this State or provide for the payment of any contribution by the State which discriminates against the State.

(b) No land or other property shall be acquired in this State on behalf of His Majesty for any Federal purposes, or on behalf of the Federal Railway Authority or any other authority of the Federation, except with the consent of the Ruler and upon such terms as may be mutually agreed upon.

(c) The Federal agents, officers and representatives, while engaged in the exercise of their functions in this State, shall be subject to, and observe the laws and Regulations of, the State, not inconsistent with the due exercise of their Federal functions.

(d) The legislative power of the Federal Legislature to make laws for this State shall not, except in items 44, 45, 46 and 47, imply the power to impose any duty or tax.

Items as contained in the Act.	Proposed limitations.
ITEM NO. 1. His Majesty's naval, military and air forces borne on the Indian establishment and any other armed force raised in India by the Crown, not being forces for employment in Indian States or military or armed police maintained by Provincial Governments ; any armed forces which are not forces of His Majesty, but are attached to or operating with any of His Majesty's naval, military or air forces borne on the Indian establishment ; central intelligence bureau ; preventive detention in British India for reasons of State connected with	1. The Federal Legislature shall not have power to make laws affecting the right of this State that the officers of all units of any armed forces of the State which may be attached to or operating with any of His Majesty's naval, military or air forces borne on the Indian establishment, shall be officers of this State. 2. Any law of the Federal Legislature with respect to the discipline of or promotion in any armed forces of this State which may be attached to or operating with any of His Majesty's naval

Items as contained in the Act.	Proposed limitations.
ITEM No. 1 (*Contd.*) defence, external affairs or the discharge of the functions of the Crown in its relations with Indian States.	military or air forces borne on the Indian establishment, shall be in accordance with and give effect to any agreement between this State and the Governor-General of India with respect to such discipline or promotion. 3. No forces coming under this item shall enter this State, except at the request of His Majesty's Representative and in the exercise of the functions of the Crown in its relations with Indian States. 4. The employment of State troops outside the State shall be subject to existing agreements and shall depend on the ability of the State to spare them without jeopardising internal security. 5. The Federal Government shall not have the right to introduce or enforce conscription or any other form of compulsory military service in the State.
ITEM No. 2. Naval, military and air force works; local self-government in cantonment areas (not being cantonment areas of Indian State troops); the regulation of house accommodation in such areas, and, within British India, the delimitation of such areas.	1. The Federal Legislature shall not have power to make such laws in respect of military and air force works belonging to this State. 2. The Federal Legislature shall not have power to make laws for this State establishing such naval, military and air force works without the consent of the Ruler of this State, provided that such consent shall not be unreasonably withheld.
ITEM No. 3. External affairs; the implementing of treaties and agreements with other countries; extradition, including the surrender of criminals and accused persons to parts of His Majesty's dominions outside India.	*No limitation.*

Items as contained in the Act.	Proposed limitations.
ITEM No. 4.	
Ecclesiastical affairs, including European cemeteries,	The power of the Federal Legislature to make laws for this State with respect to ecclesiastical affairs shall be limited to the provision of Christian ministrations for members of His Majesty's forces or persons in the service of the Crown in India.
ITEM No. 5.	
Currency, coinage and legal tender.	Federal Legislation regarding coinage should not prejudicially affect the rights of the State to strike coins in commemoration of the accession of a Ruler or special occasions of similar nature.
ITEM No. 6.	
Public debt of the Federation.	*No limitation.*
ITEM No. 7.	
Posts and telegraphs, including telephones, wireless, broadcasting, and other like forms of communication ; Post Office Savings Bank.	1. Federal Legislation under this item shall not apply to telegraphs and telephones wholly within and owned or controlled by the State, nor prohibit the establishment by the Ruler in this State of wireless and broadcasting stations subject to Federal rules and Regulations, and the manufacture of apparatus therefor. 2. No wireless or broadcasting station or other like forms of communication shall be established in this State without the consent of the Ruler of this State, provided that such consent shall not be unreasonably withheld. 3. No banking operations shall be carried on by the Post Offices in this State without the consent of the Ruler.
ITEM No. 8.	
Federal Public Services and Federal Public Service Commission.	The Federal Legislature shall not have power to pass legislation exempting the Federal Officers from any tax leviable by this State.

Items as contained in the Act.	Proposed limitations.
ITEM NO. 9. Federal pensions, that is to say, pensions payable by the Federation or out of Federal revenues.	*No limitation.*
ITEM NO. 10. Works, lands and buildings vested in, or in the possession of, His Majesty for the purposes of the Federation (not being naval, military or air force works), but as regards property situate in a Province, subject always to Provincial legislation, save in so far as Federal law otherwise provides and, as regards property in a Federated State held by virtue of any lease or agreement with that State, subject to the terms of that lease or agreement.	*No limitation.*
ITEM NO. 11. The Imperial Library, the Indian Museum, the Imperial War Museum, the Victoria Memorial, and any similar institution controlled or financed by the Federation.	The Federal Legislature shall not have power to make laws providing for the establishment in this State without the consent of the Ruler, of any institution falling within the item, provided that such consent shall not be unreasonably withheld.
ITEM NO. 12. Federal agencies and institutes for the following purposes, that is to say, for research, for professional or technical training or for the promotion of special studies.	The Federal Legislature shall not have power to make laws providing for the establishment in this State without the consent of the Ruler, of any institution falling within this item, provided that such consent shall not be unreasonably withheld.
ITEM NO. 13. The Benares Hindu University and the Aligarh Muslim University.	*No limitation.*
ITEM NO. 14. The Survey of India, the Geological, Botanical and Zoological Surveys of India; Federal meteorological organisations.	1. If the Ruler of this State gives notice to the Governor-General of India that he objects to the entry into the State

Items as contained in the Act.	Proposed limitations.
ITEM No. 14 *(Contd).*	of any named officer or agent of the Federation, charged with the performance of functions in relation to any of the matters mentioned in this item, such officer or agent shall not have authority to enter the State or perform such functions therein. 2. The information acquired or the materials collected in such surveys shall be placed unreservedly at the disposal of this State, and in regard to the Geological Survey shall be kept confidential if so required by the State. 3. Federal Legislation under this item shall not affect the right of this State to conduct surveys of any description mentioned therein, independently of the Federal authorities.
ITEM No. 15. Ancient and historical monuments; archæological sites and remains.	1. Federal Legislation under this item shall apply only to such monuments, sites and remains in this State as the Ruler may designate. 2. The Federal Legislature shall not have power to make any law depriving this State of its proprietory right in archæological antiquities discovered within its territories, or to remove them out of the State without the consent of the Ruler. 3. The functions of the Federation with respect to this item shall be exercised within this State only with the consent of the Ruler, provided that such consent shall not be unreasonably withheld.
ITEM No. 16. Census.	The Federal Legistature shall not have power to make laws for this State affecting the authority of the Ruler to

Items as contained in the Act.	Proposed limitations.
ITEM NO. 16 (*Contd.*)	determine the classification and designation of the people of the State in regard to their religion, caste, creed or social status, for purposes of Census operations.
ITEM NO. 17. Admission into, and emigration and expulsion from India, including in relation thereto, the regulation of the movements in India of persons who are not British subjects domiciled in India, subjects of any Federated State, or British subjects, domiciled in the United Kingdom ; pilgrimages to places beyond India.	No law made by the Federal Legislature in respect of any one of the subjects in this item shall affect the right and power of the Ruler to refuse to admit into his territories, or to expel therefrom, any person or persons whose admission into or presence in the said territories may, in his opinion, be undesirable.
ITEM NO. 18. Port quarantine ; seamen's and marine hospitals, and hospitals connected with port quarantine.	*No limitation.*
ITEM NO. 19. Import and export across customs frontiers as defined by the Federal Government.	1. The Federal Legislature shall not have power to make laws defining as a customs frontier one that passes through any part of the territory of this State. 2. Nothing in this item shall affect the right of this State to levy import and export duties on goods coming to and going from its territories.
ITEM NO. 20. Federal railways ; the regulation of all railways other than minor railways in respect of safety, maximum and minimum rates and fares, station and service terminal charges ; interchange of traffic and the responsibility of the railway administration as carriers of goods and passengers ; the regulation of minor railways in respect	1. The Federal Legislature shall not have power to authorise the carrying on by the railways, within the territory of this State, of ancillary undertakings referred to in Section 181 (2) of the Act, without the consent of the Ruler. 2. The Federal Legislature shall not have power to make laws affecting the

Items as contained in the Act.	Proposed limitation
ITEM No. 24 (*Contd*).	customs aerodromes or the enactment or execution by the State of laws requiring air-craft importing goods into the State to alight, be examined or pay duties at such aerodromes. 5. The Federal Legislature shall not have power to make laws for this State with respect to, or prohibiting the manufacture of, air-craft or parts of air-craft in the State. 6. The civil, criminal and fiscal jurisdiction of this State shall remain unaffected by any laws that may be made by the Federal Legislature in respect of air-navigation.
ITEM No. 25. Light-houses, including lightships, beacons and other provision for the safety of shipping and aircraft.	1. The Federal Legislature shall not have power to make laws for this State providing for the establishment in the State of lighthouses, beacons, or other provision for the safety of air-craft without the consent of the Ruler of the State, provided that such consent shall not be unreasonably withheld. 2. The Federal Legislature shall not have power to make laws for this State with respect to, or prohibiting the manufacture in the State, of lighthouses, beacons or other provision for the safety of air-craft, or parts of lighthouses, beacons, or such other provision in the State. 3. Federal Legislation under this item shall not prevent this State from erecting its own lighthouses subject to conformity with the provisions of law on the subject.
ITEM No. 26. Carriage of passengers and goods by sea or by air.	1. The Federal Legislature shall not have power to restrict the right of this State to permit the operation of intra-State services.

Items as contained in the Act.	Proposed limitations.
ITEM No. 26 (*Contd*).	2. The Federal Legislature shall not have power to make laws for this State affecting the prohibition or restriction by the State of air-craft taking up or setting down passengers or goods in the State without its consent. 3. The Federal Legislature shall not have power to make laws for this State affecting the prohibition or restriction by the State of air navigation over areas that may from time to time be declared by the State to be prohibited or restricted areas. 4. The Federal Legislature shall not have power to make laws for this State affecting the maintenance by the State of customs aerodromes or the enactment or execution by the State of laws requiring air-craft importing goods into the State to alight, be examined or pay duties at such aerodromes. 5. The Federal Legislature shall not have power to make laws for this State with respect to, or prohibiting the manufacture of, air-crafts or parts of air-craft in the State.
ITEM No. 27. Copyright, inventions, designs, trade-marks and merchandise marks.	*No limitation.*
ITEM No. 28. Cheques, bills of exchange, promissory notes and other like instruments.	*No limitation.*
ITEM No. 29. Arms ; firearms : ammunition.	1. By virtue of this entry, the authority of the Federation with respect to this State shall be confined only to export and import of firearms and ammunition across the borders of the State.

Items as contained in the Act.	Proposed limitations.
ITEM No. 29 (*Contd*).	2. In any Federal Legislation and Rules on the subject— (a) the existing right of the Ruler to control the manufacture, licensing, possession and carrying of arms and firearms as well as other functions of local administration within the State territory, and (b) the *status quo* as regards facilities at present enjoyed by the people of the State in respect of possession of arms and ammunition within the State, including the exemption of certain classes thereof from payment of fees for licenses valid in the State, shall be recognized and maintained.
ITEM No. 30. Explosives.	The power of the Federal Legislature to make laws for this State under this item shall be limited to the making of laws with respect to the possession, storage and transport of explosives by persons other than the Military or Police Forces of the State or other Departments of the State.
ITEM No. 31. Opium, so far as regards cultivation and manufacture, or sale for export.	*No limitation.*
ITEM No. 32. Petroleum and other liquids and substances declared by Federal law to be dangerously inflammable, so far as regards possession, storage and transport.	The Federal Legislature shall not have power to make laws for this State with respect to the possession, storage or transport of petroleum or other motor spirit by the Military or Police Forces of the State or other Departments of the State.

Items as contained in the Act.	Proposed limitations.
ITEM No. 33. Corporations, that is to say, the incorporation, regulation and winding-up of trading corporations, including banking, insurance and financial corporations, but not including corporations owned or controlled by a Federated State and carrying on business only within that State or co-operative societies, and of corporations whether trading or not, with objects not confined to one unit.	The Federal Legislature shall not have power to make laws for this State affecting :— (a) The exclusion by the State of any corporation (other than a corporation owned or controlled by the Federation) from carrying on business within the State or the imposition by the State of conditions subject to which a corporation (other than as aforesaid) may so carry on business ; or (b) Provision by the State that the assets situate within the State of any corporation which carries on or has carried on business within the State shall be wound up in the Courts of the State, and provision by the State for giving priority in such winding-up proceedings to debts due to the State or the Ruler, Provided that (except as regards such priority) such winding-up shall be conducted in accordance with any Federal Law applicable thereto ; or (c) The incorporation, regulation and winding-up by the State of trading corporations, including banking, insurance and financial corporations, having objects confined to the State.
ITEM No. 34. Development of industries, where development under Federal control is declared by Federal law to be expedient in the public interest.	1. The power of the Federal Legislature to make laws for this State with respect to development of industries shall be limited to providing for subsidies, and national institutions for furthering the development of industries by research, education or propaganda, not being institutions empowered to carry on or control any industry. 2. The Federal Legislature shall not have power to make laws for this State affecting the provision by the State of subsidies for industries carried on within the State.

Items as contained in the Act,	Proposed limitations.
ITEM No. 35. Regulation of labour and safety in mines and oilfields.	The Federal Legislature shall not have power to make laws for this State in respect of regulation of labour in mines and oil-fields except for the purpose of securing safety of such labour.
ITEM No. 37. The law of insurance except as regards insurance undertaken by a Federated State, and the regulation of the conduct of insurance business, except as respects business undertaken by a Federated State ; Government insurance, except so far as undertaken by a Federated State, or, by virtue of any entry in the Provincial Legislative List or the Concurrent Legislative List, by a Province.	*No limitation.*
ITEM No. 38. Banking, that is to say, the conduct of banking business by corporations other than corporations owned or controlled by a Federated State and carrying on business only within that State.	*No limitation.*
ITEM No. 39. Extension of the powers and jurisdiction of members of a police force belonging to any part of British India to any area in another Governor's Province or Chief Commissioner's Province, but not so as to enable the police of one part to exercise powers and jurisdiction elsewhere without the consent of the Government of the Province or the Chief Commissioner, as the case may be ; extension of the powers and jurisdiction of members of a police force belonging to any unit to railway areas outside that unit.	Members of the police force belonging to another unit shall exercise powers or jurisdiction in this State only where an agreement has been made between the State and such other unit in that behalf.

Items as contained in the Act.	Proposed limitations.
ITEM NO. 41. The salaries of the Federal Ministers, of the President and Vice-President of the Council of State and of the Speaker of the Federal Assembly ; the salaries and allowances and privileges of the members of the Federal Legislature and to such extent as is expressly authorised by Part II of this Act, the punishment of persons who refuse to give evidence or produce documents before Committees of the Legislature.	The Federal Legislature shall not have power to make laws for this State— (a) Making compulsory the attendance before a Chamber of the Federal Legislature or a Committee thereof of any person who is in the service of the Ruler of the State or the giving of evidence by any such person unless the Ruler shall have consented to the attendance of or the giving of evidence by, such person ; or (b) Making compulsory the production before a Chamber of the Federal Legislature or a Committee thereof, of any document which an officer designated by the Ruler of the State for that purpose shall certify to be a confidential document relating to the affairs of the State or to the personal affairs of the Ruler or his family ; or (c) Imposing any punishment on any such person as aforesaid who refused to attend or give evidence or on any person who refused to produce any such document as aforesaid.
ITEM NO. 42. Offences against laws with respect to any of the matters in this list.	The Federal Legislature shall not have power to make laws for this State with respect to offences against laws which under this Instrument of Accession the Federal Legislature has not the power to make for the State.
ITEM NO. 43. Inquiries and statistics for the purpose of any of the matters in this list.	1. The Federal Legislature shall not have power to make laws for this State with respect to inquiries or statistics for the purpose of any matter with respect to which the Federal Legislature has not, under this Instrument of Accession, the power to make laws for the State. 2. The Federal Legislature shall not have power to make laws for this State

Items as contained in the Act.	Proposed limitations.
ITEM No. 43 (*Contd*).	affecting the making or holding of inquiries or the collection or publication of statistics by the State, or in pursuance of any laws of the State as regards any matter.
ITEM No. 44. Duties of customs, including export duties.	1. The Federal Legislature shall not have power to make laws defining as a customs frontier one that passes through any part of the territory of this State. 2. Nothing in this item shall affect the right of this State to levy import and export duties on goods coming to and going from its territories.
ITEM No. 45. Duties of excise on tobacco and other goods manufactured or produced in India, except— (a) alcoholic liquors for human consumption ; (b) opium, Indian hemp and other narcotic drugs and narcotics ; non-narcotic drugs ; (c) medicinal and toilet preparations containing alcohol, or any substances included in sub-paragraph (b) of this entry.	1. The Federal Legislature shall not have power to prohibit or restrict the right of this State to levy and retain excise duties upon any goods in addition to the excise duties, if any, imposed upon such goods by the Federation. 2. The Federal Legislature shall not have power to make laws for this State affecting the right of the State to continue to share with the Government of India the revenue derived from the existing excise on matches and mechanical lighters, as also to obtain an allotment from the duty on petroleum for purposes of road development in the State. 3. The Federal Legislature shall not have power to make laws for this State authorising the levy of duties of excise on agricultural (except tobacco and dairy products. *N. B.—The above limitations on this item are not to be deemed as final. A further communication may be made on the subject.*

Items as contained in the Act.	Proposed limitations.
ITEM No. 46. Corporation Tax.	The Federal Legislature shall not have power to make laws providing for the levying of Corporation Tax on any corporation owned or controlled by, and working within, this State, or for the inclusion in any contribution made by this State in lieu of Corporation Tax of any sum in respect of the income of any such corporation, provided that in the case of corporations controlled by the State this exemption shall apply only to the extent of this control.
ITEM No. 47. Salt.	*No limitation.*
ITEM No. 59. Fees in respect of any of the matters in this list, but not including fees taken in any Court.	The power of the Federal Legislature to make laws for this State with respect to fees shall be limited to the matters with respect to which, under the Instrument of Accession of this State, the Federal Legislature has power to make laws for this State.

Illustrative List of Rights and Privileges.

I. RIGHTS AND PRIVILEGES RELATING TO ITEMS IN THE FEDERAL LEGISLATIVE LIST WHICH ARE ACCEPTED AS FEDERAL SUBJECT.

1. The right of the State to continue to receive an apportionment of the proceeds of any customs or excise duty levied by the Federation on Motor Spirits and Matches.

2. The right of the Ruler to import free from customs or from any other duty, goods intended for his personal use and for the use of the members of his family (Government Resolution).

3. The right or privilege of exemption from customs duty on the personal luggage of the Ruler as well as reasonable quantities of alcoholic liquors, tobacco, motor cars and motor cycles while returning from abroad. (Government Resolution).

4. The right or privilege of the Ruler to import free from customs duties, arms and ammunition for his personal use, and the exemption from licenses in respect of fire-arms and ammunition. (Arms Act).

5. The right or privilege to carry firearms and ammunition enjoyed by the Ruler and members of his family and by their retainers in other units without a license. (Arms Act).

6. The exemption enjoyed by the Ruler in respect of 30 retainers while accompanying him to British India from operation of the Arms Act.

7. The privileges enjoyed by noblemen and high officials of the State designated by Government to import arms and ammunition from British India for their personal use.

8. Existing rights enjoyed by the Ruler regarding telegraphic communication.

9. Maintenance of rights or privileges accruing under the following Resolutions of the Government of India:

   i. Resolution No 524-I, dated 18th October, 1933, as amended by Resolution No. F 25-R/30 dated 19th June, 1931, regarding Telephones in Indian States.

   ii. Resolution No. 242-I, dated 5th December, 1933, regarding Telegraphs.

   iii. Resolution on Wireless communications—British India and Indian States Memoranda on the development of Wireless communications in British India and Indian States, dated 25th January, 1922, by the Director of Wireless.

iv. Resolution No. 496-I, dated 27th May, 1926, and the Summary of the Chamber of Princes, 1926, regarding Wireless Telegraphy and Telephones in Indian States.

v Resolution No. 159 R/31 dated 8th August, 1932, regarding Air Navigation.

vi. Resolution No. F. 178 R/30 dated 22nd February, 1932, regarding Radio Broadcasting.

vii. Resolution No. 202-I of 6th December, 1923, as subsequently amended regarding construction and maintenance of Indian State Railways.

II. Rights and Privileges relating to Non-Federal Matters.

These arise from different sources :

(A) The obligations of the Crown of the United Kingdom for the defence and protection of the Ruler, the Ruling dynasty of the State, and the territories of the Ruler

(B) Agreements with the Government of India, *e. g.*—

1. The right of the State to continue to procure without restriction, supplies of alcoholic liquor, Indian hemp (bhang) and narcotic drugs, such as, charas and ganja, from British Indian Provinces, without payment of any tax or duty levied by Governments of such Provinces.

2. Similar right to obtain supplies of opium, necessary for consumption within the State, from the Government of India, without payment of any tax or duty levied by the Government of India or any Provincial Government.

3. The right to obtain from British India necessary supplies of (1) absolute alcohol and rectified spirit, (2) spirituous medicinal preparations, and (3) medicinal opium, cocaine, morphine and similar drugs, for use in the charitable dispensaries and hospitals in the State territory, free from any duty in British India.

(C) Rights and privileges arising from existing laws and regulations in British India, and notifications and resolutions of the Government of India. The following may be mentioned by way of illustration :—

1. Complete immunity of the Ruler from every kind of jurisdiction of all Courts in British India. This is founded on the basic principles of conflict of laws. A specific authority for this immunity is to be found in the judgment of Bargrave Deana, J., in Statham V. Statham (1912 P. C., p. 92). So far as civil liberties are concerned,

Sections 85 and 86 of the Civil Procedure Code of British India recognise this immunity. Immunity is also enjoyed under Section 133 of the Code of Civil Procedure.

2. Immunity from Municipal taxation, such as octroi, of the personal property, whether moveable or immoveable, of the Ruler. This immunity is also founded on the principles of conflict of laws. A reference to this immunity is to be found in Macartney V. Garbutt (24 Q. B. D., 368).

3. Exemption of the Ruler from the operation of the Indian Motor Vehicles Act, and the Rules made thereunder. (Vide the Motor Vehicles Native States' Rules, 1916, Government of India notification No. 627, dated the 6th July, 1916.)

4. Reciprocity in matters of licensing and registration in respect of Motor Vehicles licensed in the State (Vide the Motor Vehicles Native States' Rules, 1916 ; Government of India notification No. 627 dated the 6th July, 1916 ; Government of India, Foreign and Political Department letter No. 1697-I. A., dated the 14th August, 1916).

5. The right of a Ruler to be governed by his personal laws as in force in his State, with reference to immoveable property held by him in British India. (Vide CWN vol. XXIX, p 287).

6. The protection of the Ruler and his Government from acts or attempts to excite disaffection by people outside his State and protection of the Ruler and his family from slander. (Vide the Indian States Protection against Disaffection Act, 1922 ; the Indian States Protection Act, 1934 ; and the Foreign Relations Act, 1932).

7. Resolution of the Foreign and Political Department, No. 2563-1161–Internal, dated 19th December, 1922, regarding the acquisition of residential property in British India.

8. Resolution of the Foreign and Political Department, No. 248-R/32 dated 22nd September, 1933, regarding acquisition of non-residential property in British India.

Tripura State Press.

TRIPURA STATE

Letter from Capt. His Highness Maharaja Manikya Sir Bir Bikram Kishore Deb Barman Bahadur, K.C.S.I., Maharaja of Tripura, to His Excellency The Most Honourable the Marquess of Linlithgow, P C., Kt., G.M.S.I., G.M.I.E., O.B.E., D.L., T.D., Viceroy of India, Simla, dated the 10th July, 1939, on the subject of accession of Tripura State to the Federation of India.

TRIPURA STATE

CAMP.

SAVOY HOTEL.

London, the 10th July, 1939,

MY ESTEEMED FRIEND,

I address Your Excellency with reference to Your Excellency's letter of the 27th January, 1939, on the subject of accession of my State to the All-India Federation as contemplated in the Government of India Act of 1935.

2. Your Excellency has been pleased to enquire whether I am prepared to execute an Instrument of Accession on behalf of the Tripura State within the terms indicated in documents (1) and (2) annexed to the letter under reply, and I may say that I am grateful for the time that Your Excellency has graciously allowed and for the discretion that Your Excellency has very kindly left to me in arriving at a decision in a matter of such vital importance.

3. I can assure Your Excellency that I have given the question my most serious and earnest consideration in view of the grave responsibility that lies on me as the mouthpiece of my State, my Dynasty, and my people and of the solemn obligations that I owe to the Crown as well as to India as a whole, and I may be permitted to state frankly that my anxiety has been all the greater as the terms offered now are desired to be regarded in all essentials incapable of further relaxation.

4. For some time past the political atmosphere in India has been changing and there is now a tendency on the part of dominant political parties in British India to regard the Ruling Princes as unwelcome partners in the Federation, and even to have recourse to coercive steps to interfere with the status, sovereignty and integrity of the States. Your Excellency will kindly pardon me if I say that this changed aspect of things cannot but affect the ardour and enthusiasm with which the idea of an All-India Federation was originally received by the Princely Order.

5. I hope Your Excellency will understand the anxious concern of the Ruling Dynasties in formulating a decision under the changed circumstances. Alive as every Ruler has to be to the dangers that stare his State in the face, he naturally turns to Your Excellency for protection and if he evinces a desire to have his position adequately safeguarded I can assure Your Excellency that it is purely from the instinct of self-preservation.

6. I have, in common perhaps with my brother Princes, tried to get all available advice to come to a proper decision and to have the position of my State carefully scrutinised in the light of the terms offered. I may assure Your Excellency that my intention has been not only to secure the integrity of my State but to be of every assistance in the realisation of the ideal of an All-India Federation. Two important conferences of Ruling Princes and Ministers, recently held, have carefully examined the

documents received with Your Excellency's letter and have come to the conclusion that some of the terms are detrimental to the interests of Indian States. I refer to the reports of the Hydari Committee and the Gwalior Conference of Ministers which I have had the advantage of examining and which, I believe, are already before Your Excellency. I may be permitted to state that I find myself in general agreement with the views expressed in these reports and while willing to urge these views on my own behalf, I do not think I need repeat them here. Eager as I am, however, to join the Federation I would crave Your Excellency's indulgence to enumerate below certain features in particular in the scheme now proposed which call for modification to make it fully acceptable.

7 (*a*). The provisions proposed for the protection of the rights of my State and the rights and dignity of the Ruler thereof, in the federal sphere as well as outside it, are not adequate and satisfactory. It has always been assumed that the internal autonomy of the units within the Federation would be respected. The legal structure of Federation is directed to this end and exists as much to protect the units within their fields as to give authority to the Centre in its own field. Thus, for example, in answer to Query No. 7000, the then Secretary of State the Right Hon'ble Sir Samuel Hoare, stated : " The whole basis of our Federal Scheme is that we do not interfere in the internal management of the States except to the extent that they have surrendered powers to the Federal Government." When in the Joint Select Committee, the then Secretary of State was asked what was meant by the phrase "Protection of the rights of any Indian States," he replied "there is a point here that does directly concern the Provinces. The kind of case we had in mind was the need for intervention : supposing within a Province, a movement was growing up, such as the kind of movement of which we have had examples, in which large bodies of a particular community or a particular mode of thought march in from the Province into a neighbouring State and stir up trouble in the State. In cases of that kind we felt there ought to be power to prevent such movement of that kind, endangering the stability of an Indian State." It has been an unfortunate experience that in certain recent instances, the protection which the Indian States were encouraged to expect at the hands of the neighbouring units, under the assurances quoted above, was not forthcoming in spite of the special responsibilities laid upon the Provincial Governors in that behalf under section 52(1) (f) of the Government of India Act, corresponding to the special responsibilities of the Governor-General under section 12 (1) (g). It is not, therefore, considered safe to rely upon the special responsibilities of the Governor-General under section 12 (1) (g) of the Act as the sole means of protection of the rights of an Indian State and of the rights and dignity of its Ruler.

(*b*). As regards the question of administration of Federal laws and the proposed agreement under section 125 of the Act, I may be permitted to say that this section was specifically incorporated at the instance of the States to enable them to reserve executive authority and thus to differentiate between the States and the Provinces. The arrangements for the administration of Federal laws proposed under the Revised Draft Instrument were not previously discussed with the States and are unsatisfactory in so far as they are not in consonance with the terms of that section. The principle of parity with the Provinces now urged, though not unreasonable at first sight, may not be altogether helpful as there is no knowing what powers of administration will be allowed to the Provinces by the Centre from time to time. I would, therefore, urge that the entries in the Federal list in respect of which executive administration is to be entrusted to my State be specifically mentioned in the proposed agreement.

(*c*). The provisions of the scheme affecting the economic and financial position of my State appeared to me unsatisfactory even in the original Draft Instrument of Accession as was indicated in the limitations suggested by me thereto. Many of these limitations—general and specific—have now been disallowed. Changes of a fundamental character have, moreover, been introduced by the proposed amendment of entries 19 and 44 of the Federal Legislative List and section 297 of the Act which may prejudicially affect the financial position of my State.

The proposal for the stabilisation of the conditions and amounts of the income derived from customs duties by the State on the basis of the conditions and figures for the year 1936-37 is likely to have a far reaching adverse effect on its revenues.

A substantial portion of the income of my State is derived from land customs duties. In an undeveloped and growing State restrictions have often to be put upon export and import and rates of duty altered for special reasons. The stabilisation of the standard of 1936-37 therefore cannot but prove to be highly injurious to the interests of my State.

I may be permitted to refer, by way of illustration, to an export duty on paddy and rice imposed in my State for a special purpose with effect from 1937-38. The cultivated area in the State generally fringes its frontiers and there is at present a lack of suitable communications with the interior which stands in the way of proper distribution of agricultural produce throughout the State. These circumstances operate to provide an artificial stimulus to export to the detriment of the interests of the people, including the producers themselves who are very often at the mercy of outside traders. For the purpose of preventing uneconomic exploitation and of financing the opening out of the country by road development, my Durbar imposed this duty on rice and paddy exported for trade purposes only, and earmarked the total amount thereof, which is fairly substantial, for road making. Road development work must considerably suffer if this income is lost to the State.

(*d*). In regard to development of mines and oilfields, the acceptance of entry 36 specially in respect of oil and coal, has been insisted on. Both these minerals exist in the State and it is expected that steps for working out oil at least will be fully initiated in the near future. Your Excellency will, I trust, realise that to accept entry 36 would be to subordinate the development of my State, so far as these commodities are concerned, to any general policy of the Federal Government. I should not wonder if this leads to restriction of development which cannot but materially injure my State. A restrictive policy which may be justifiable under conditions prevailing in British India, where development of certain mineral resources has perhaps reached its peak, may prove altogether unsuitable and harmful to this State. I, therefore, hope that my State will be allowed not to federate on entry 36 so as to be free to develop its mineral resources on its own lines.

(*e*). In this connection I would also urge that acceptance of entry 35 regarding regulation of labour and safety in mines and oilfields should be subject to the limitation previously suggested by me. My principal reason is that in the present backward condition of the State any labour legislation, other than that regarding safety, which may be desirable in the circumstances of British India may prove unsuitable in our case. Such legislation may also produce undesirable repercussions on other forms of labour not covered by entry 35.

(*f*). I may also mention that I attach much importance to the following limitation in respect of entry 14 regarding geological survey—"Federal Legislation under this item shall not affect the right of the State to conduct geological survey independently of Federal authorities."

(*g*). As regards entry 29 about arms and ammunition, the circumstances in my State are somewhat peculiar, as possession of firearms is often a necessity for protection of crops and lives from wild animals. Easy conditions of possession are therefore called for and I trust Your Excellency will agree that in this matter the State is the proper judge. It cannot at the same time be said that the State Arms Act proved inadequate as regards control even in trying circumstances. It was for this reason that I urged the maintenance of the *status quo* in my first letter. The extent of limitation now suggested is altogether insufficient and must occasion great difficulty if not reconsidered.

8. I fervently hope that Your Excellency will appreciate the reasons that have stood in the way of my accepting unconditionally the terms now offered. It is needless for me to repeat that my attitude is due solely to my anxiety to safeguard the interests of my State and the welfare of my people and I trust that ways and means may yet be found to remove, by suitable modification of the scheme, the doubts, as indicated above, that I still entertain in signifying my readiness to accede to the proposed Federation.

I remain,
with much consideration,
Your Excellency's sincere friend,

B. B. K. MANIKYA,

Maharaja Manikya of Tripura.

His Excellency the most Honourable

The Marquess of Linlithgow

P.C., KT., G.M.S.I., G.M.I.E., D.L., T.D.,

Viceroy of India, Simla.